The Nature of Art

The Nature of Art

Edited

by

John Gassner

and

Sidney Thomas

CROWN PUBLISHERS, INC., NEW YORK

This book is offered as a tribute to Eugène Delacroix
Great painter and great writer on art
on the centennial of his death

"What is beautiful is beautiful, I don't care in what period it was done or for whom: as soon as there are two of us to admire Charlet and Géricault, you have the proof, in the first place, that they are admirable, and in the second, that they can find admirers. I shall admire what deserves it to the day of my death, and if I am the last of my race, I shall tell myself that after the night which is to follow me on the hemisphere that I inhabit, there will be daybreak again somewhere, and that man, still having a heart and a mind, will get his enjoyment from those two things."

Journal, September 1, 1854

© *1964 by John Gassner and Sidney Thomas*
Library of Congress Catalog Card Number: 63-21126
Printed in the United States of America

PREFACE

On June 29, 1856, Delacroix noted in his Journal: "Dinner today with Villot and his wife. We talked painting all evening; that puts me into a good frame of mind."

This is a book of people talking about painting—some wisely, some amusingly, some outrageously. It is intended for the general reader who is interested in art and delights in good writing, though there is much here that should be new and useful even to the specialist. This is not another documentary history of art, a task which has already been superbly accomplished by Elizabeth Holt; nor, despite the fact that many artists are included, is it another book of statements by artists on art, such as the fascinating collection by Robert Goldwater and Marco Treves. The two tests that have been applied to every selection in this book are: Is it noteworthy or, at the very least, intriguing writing; and does it say something worth listening to about art? If students and their instructors should come to consider this volume a useful reference or supplementary text, it will be because it introduces art as a living experience.

The range of art is so enormous, and so much has been written on it, that in order to make a book of manageable proportions we have restricted ourselves to Western art, and within that art, mainly to painting and sculpture. Architecture has been deliberately slighted, not because we thought it unimportant—quite the contrary—but because it would take another book almost the size of this one to do justice to it.

We have not attempted to represent either, except in isolated statements, the whole field of aesthetic theory. To try to do anything like justice to the great thinkers from Plato on who have dealt with the philosophy of art, and especially to try to cover the complex and technical developments of recent writing in this field, would demand an entirely different kind of book from the one we envisioned.

The richness and variety of the literature of art are so great that our chief problem has been one of selection and exclusion. What has gone into the book has, of course, to a certain extent been determined by our own personal preferences. No anthology would be worth reading that did not reflect an individuality, even sometimes an eccentricity, of taste. However, there are certain things that no one could exclude from a collection of this sort, especially a first collection, without laying himself open to justified charges of obstinate neglect of the reader's interests. The literature of art has its classics as well as any other literature, and it has been our responsibility to present these classics to the reader.

In order to do so, we have violated what has become almost an unwritten law of the anthology: keep it short, keep it light. A major writer can be adequately represented only by a major selection, substantial enough to convey an adequate sense of his contribution. Such writers as Vasari, Reynolds, Ruskin, Fry, and many others have therefore been given at length, wherever possible by complete essays or by self-contained sections from a basic work. As a result, the reader of this collection can trace in detail the great critical problems, traditions, and controversies that have enlivened the history of art.

Not that the brief, the pungent, and the entertaining have been avoided. This is a book meant for browsing as well as for sustained reading. Writers like Haydon, Butler, Fuseli, Blake, and Delacroix can be enjoyed in snatches: but this does not make them any the less profound or stimulating than many of the writers represented at greater length. These are writers who are intensely alive, and bring to the discussion of art a gift for pungent phrasing, for vivid anecdote, and often for nobility of style that makes them delightful companions.

Art and the artist have formed the subjects of many works of fiction, but most of this kind of writing has been unusable for this collection for one reason or another. Proust's Elstir is a magnificent creation, a great portrait of an impressionist painter; he cannot, however, be isolated from the infinitely complex and interwoven fabric of the novel in which he appears. Similarly, though for somewhat different reasons, Maugham's *The Moon and Sixpence* must be read in its entirety. A few fictional works that we remembered as interesting or provocative in their treatment of art turned out on rereading to be rather disappointing.

Works of fiction, however, obviously belong in this book. The chapter from Zola's *L'œuvre* is, we believe, a most valuable selection: a striking recreation, by a man who knew most of the painters of the time intimately, of the impact of the new impressionist and realist art on an astounded public.

We have also limited the poetic excerpts. We could easily have given Browning's "Fra Lippo Lippi" or his "Andrea del Sarto"; both are brilliant recreations of great Renaissance artists. But we have selected Keats's "Ode on a Grecian Urn," which is, of course, one of the great literary statements about art—no piece in this entire collection was a more inevitable choice.

A word about the organization of the book: The simplest way to present this material would have been in chronological order of the writers represented. Such an arrangement, however, although a natural one, would have obscured the importance and meaning of many of the selections. The arrangement we have chosen, first by issues and then by historical periods, allows the reader to see differences of approach to the same problem, sometimes fascinating similarities between widely separated writers, sometimes (as with Leonardo) amazing anticipations of artistic problems not yet defined or grappled with by the writer's contemporaries. That this method of organization is completely satisfactory and without occasional awkwardness we would not contend. It is simply, in our opinion, the best that is possible for writing as varied and wide-ranging as that contained in this book.

A few writers who unquestionably belong in this book are missing for reasons beyond our control. In general, however, we have received enthusiastic cooperation from those whose help we solicited for this project. We are only too conscious of the errors of omission that we must have committed, but we can say without hesitation that what is here is all worth reading, much of it worth savoring and rereading. It will, we expect, produce in the reader that good frame of mind that Delacroix enjoyed after his dinner with the Villots.

TABLE OF CONTENTS

THE BAROQUE

NEOCLASSICISM AND THE GRAND STYLE

ROMANTICISM AND REALISM

THE MODERN ART MOVEMENT

LIST OF ILLUSTRATIONS

THE MONA LISA—LEONARDO DA VINCI   (*Louvre, Paris*)

THE ARTIST AND HIS PUBLIC

The interplay between art and its public, which results in different responses to the same work of art in different periods, is perhaps best exemplified by the history of so celebrated a painting as Leonardo da Vinci's masterpiece. This becomes in effect a history of taste and is treated as such by the distinguished philosopher and specialist in aesthetics, Professor George Boas. Although the vagaries of taste have often been commented on, they have rarely been treated with the fascinating completeness of historical detail given in this essay.

George Boas

The Mona Lisa in the History of Taste[1]

The search for aesthetic standards by means of which any work of art can be finally judged would seem to presuppose either that every such work is an unchanging entity, or that, regardless of whether it changes or not, it should always be judged in the same way. Neither of these presuppositions appears tenable to the writer of this paper, who holds, on the contrary, that works of art are not the locus of one value, known as "beauty" or something similar, but are rather multivalent, that certain of their values are experienced by some persons, others by others, and that there is no *a priori* method—except that of fiat—of determining which of the many values are properly "aesthetic." One objection usually raised against this position is that there happen to be some works of art which "the judgment of posterity" has always held to be admirable or "great," and

[1] Reprinted from *Journal of the History of Ideas*, April, 1940, Vol. I, No. 2.

that one has only to examine their characteristics to discover what the distinguishing marks of great works of art are. The Parthenon, the *Aeneid, Hamlet,* and so on, it is maintained, have always enjoyed a high reputation. They are great by almost universal consent; or, if there have been periods when they were not highly esteemed, that is because the people of those periods had poor taste.

It cannot be denied that there are works of art which have almost always been greatly admired. (For the sake of the argument one may neglect those times when they were not discussed at all, having been overlooked for some reason or other.) But having admitted that, one faces the question whether the name, *Hamlet,* or the Parthenon, or the *Aeneid,* has always meant the same thing. Physically, the words or the shapes of stone in which they are embodied have changed little, though the little is not without some importance; but the physical basis of these and other works of art is only a small part of them. More important is what people have looked for in them and either found or not found. Thus the *Aeneid* as a Roman epic differs from the *Aeneid* as an instrument of magic, and *Hamlet* as a chivalric tragedy of revenge differs from *Hamlet* as a Freudian drama. It may be argued that the work of art as the artist intended it is the real work of art, and that we should suspend judgment until we have recaptured it in its primitive state. In most cases such a quest is probably futile, for we often have no way of knowing what an artist intended, and in any event we can, for the most part, only reconstruct what he intended from what we ourselves find. And that is to no small extent dependent upon our education and our original nature. Moreover, to recapture through study an artist's intention is different from reacting directly to a work of art; and the professor of English literature who, having studied Elizabethan language and customs and theatrical practice and the biography of Shakespeare, reads *Hamlet,* is not psychologically identical with the Elizabethan spectator who went to the theater and saw *Hamlet* during which might be called its lifetime. Whatever else Shakespeare may have been up to, he was certainly not producing plays for professors of English to study three hundred years after his death. We may reasonably conclude that to define the work of art as the work intended by the artist gives us only the slenderest clues to appropriate standards for judging it.

The purpose of this paper is to take one of the works of art which have been most admired until recent times, and to examine briefly what critics or commentators of different periods have said about it.

From what they said we hope to be able to infer what they were looking for. We are not so much interested in knowing why they admired the work of art as in knowing what they saw in it. It will be found that in at least this one case the work of art was identical with itself throughout history in name only. We have chosen as our example Leonardo's "Mona Lisa."

I

The "Mona Lisa," it should be recalled, is usually considered to be a portrait of the wife of Francesco del Giocondo, painted between 1503 and 1506. There is no conclusive evidence that it was intended as an allegory, though the background does not put that beyond the bounds of possibility.[2] No mention is made of it in the artist's literary remains, so that we do not know at what the artist himself was aiming. We do, however, know what he thought the proper fashion of representing women was, and that will be pointed out later.

Leonardo's contemporaries apparently did not consider the "Mona Lisa" his most important work. Several accounts of Italian painting, written during Leonardo's life or a little later, fail even to mention it. This is true of *Il Libro di Antonio Billi*[3] and of an anonymous work written during the forties of the sixteenth century.[4] Paolo Giovio, writing after Leonardo's death, says simply that he painted the portrait of Mona Lisa, "wife of Francesco del Giocondo, which was bought by King Francis I, it is said, for 4000 *scudi*."[5] In the short *Vita* he mentions the "Last Supper" and tells the story of Louis XII's desire to cut it out of the wall on which it was painted, and the "Virgin and Saint Anne," but does not mention the "Mona Lisa." There is nothing here, except the unusually high price, which is of interest. The same may be said of the comment of Raffaelo Borghini, made in 1584, that the portrait was such *che non puo l'arte far davantaggio*.[6] More to the point is the criticism of Lomazzo, who praises it along with portraits by Raphael and Andrea del Sarto as peculiarly adapted to its subject.[7]

2 Everything about this famous picture has been disputed. We have accepted the traditional name of the sitter, but A. Venturi in the *Enciclopedia Italiana* maintains that she was Costanza d'Avalos and that the misty background did have allegorical significance. See his section in the article on Leonardo. L. Roger-Milès, in his *Léonard de Vinci et les Jocondes*, 1923, pp. 68 ff., maintains that it is not even a portrait.

3 See de Fabriczy, *Arch. Stor. Ital.*, ser. V, tom. 7.

4 *Ibid.*

5 See Tiraboschi, *Stor. della lett. Ital.*, T. VI, p. iv, lib. iii, c. 7, xxxii (Venice, 1823, VI, 4-5, p. 1602).

6 See *Il Riposo*, Florence, 1584, p. 370 f.

7 G. P. Lomazzo, *Trattato dell' arte della pittura*, etc., Milan, 1584-85, p. 434.

The most influential of the earlier comments on the "Mona Lisa" is that of Vasari, which established a tradition. This paragraph is the best known of the classical statements, and it was apparently the source of most of the anecdotes repeated in later times about the picture. It was first published in 1550, some forty-odd years after the portrait was painted. The passage runs as follows:

> Whoever shall desire to see how far art can imitate nature, may do so to perfection in this head, wherein every peculiarity that could be depicted by the utmost subtlety of the pencil has been faithfully reproduced. The eyes have the lustrous brightness and moisture which is seen in life, and around them are those pale, red, and slightly livid circles, also proper to nature, with the lashes, which can only be copied as they are with the greatest difficulty; the eyebrows also are represented with the closest exactitude, where fuller and where more thinly set, with the separate hairs delineated as they issue from the skin, every turn being followed, and all the pores exhibited in a manner that could not be more natural than it is: the nose, with its beautiful and delicately roseate nostrils, might be easily believed to be alive; the mouth, admirable in its outline, has the lips uniting the rose-tints of their colour with that of the face, in the utmost perfection, and the carnation of the cheek does not appear to be painted, but truly of flesh and blood: he who looks earnestly at the pit of the throat cannot but believe that he sees the beating of the pulses, and it may be truly said that this work is painted in a manner well calculated to make the boldest master tremble, and astonishes all who behold it, however well accustomed to the marvels of art. Mona Lisa was exceedingly beautiful, and while Leonardo was painting her portrait, he took the precaution of keeping some one constantly near her, to sing or play on instruments, or to jest and otherwise amuse her, to the end that she might continue cheerful, and so that her face might not exhibit the melancholy expression often imparted by painters to the likenesses they take. In this portrait of Leonardo's on the contrary there is so pleasing an expression, and a smile so sweet, that while looking at it one thinks it rather divine than human, and it has ever been esteemed a wonderful work, since life itself could exhibit no other appearance.[8]

There are two important features in this criticism: first, it is Leonardo's skill that is the subject of admiration, rather than the effect of the picture upon the observer, or the "self-expression" of the artist, or a symbol of something called "the times"; second, the painter's skill

[8] Giorgio Vasari, *Lives of the Most Eminent Painters, Sculptors, and Architects,* tr. by Mrs. Jonathan Foster, London, 1876, II, p. 384 f. It is perhaps worth noting that in the eighteenth century Leonardo was to be blamed by at least one writer for too great fidelity to nature, uncorrected by a study of the antique. See [Dezallier d'Argenville,] *Abrégé de la Vie des plus Fameux Peintres,* 1745, p. 74.

is supposed to be directed towards reproducing a natural object as faithfully as possible.

To think of the artist as a craftsman who learns and applies a technique is, of course, not unusual in the history of criticism. Even the most fervent admirer of Croce would admit that some artists are more skillful technicians than others. But to focus one's appreciation upon this has been by no means a universal practice among critics. Forgetting, for the purposes of this paper, the past history of such an attitude, as seen, for instance, in the elder Pliny, it is not improbable that technical skill became particularly interesting in the Renaissance, when *homo faber* began experimenting and inventing as he had not done since Alexandrian days.

But one may praise an artist's skill and yet not believe that it was oriented towards a reproduction of "nature." One may admire the exquisite technique of an Odilon Redon, for instance, or a Braque, and say nothing whatsoever about the likeness of its result to anything natural. One may admire the technique of a Byzantine fresco in which the "natural" is almost completely recreated and transformed. The idea that "nature" was of interest and importance in her own right belongs to a period in which men seek to observe facts and record them, and think that observation and record are good in themselves. Vasari, who was himself a painter, is perhaps more sensitive to technical excellence than a critic who has no experience in producing works of art. His own paintings are, like those of most of his contemporaries, admirably skillful in perspective and other tricks of illusion. It is therefore possible, though not probable, that he was simply erecting his own type of skill into a standard for all artists.

It would, however, be sheer pedantry to attempt to prove what everyone knows, namely, that the Renaissance in Italy was marked by an almost religious regard for what later became natural science, and by a delight in the arts which helped man understand the things of nature.[9] The whole matter has been clearly and succinctly told by Burckhardt

---

[9] As early as 1493 Bellincioni had written a sonnet on another portrait by Leonardo, that of Cecilia Gallerani, the mistress of Ludovico Sforza. The sonnet plays upon the rivalry between art and nature and begins,

> Di chi ti adiri? A chi invidia Natura?
> Al vince che ha ritratto una tua stella . . .

(For the whole sonnet, see *Le Rime di Bernardo Bellincioni*, ed. by Pietro Fanfani, Bologna, 1878.) The idea is, of course, a literary commonplace and for that very reason of peculiar interest. The portrait, it may be added, seems to have disappeared. A similar idea is found in the Latin verses on a portrait of Lucrezia Crivelli in *The Notebooks of Leonardo da Vinci*, 1938, II, 394.

in his *The Civilization of the Renaissance in Italy,* and requires no retelling. But it may be said that the Italians of this period were the first men to rediscover natural beauty, to write biographies again, as the Alexandrians did, to describe in detail the human face and form, to collect strange animals and even strange people. It is in keeping with this taste that the sketch-books of Jacopo Bellini, of Leonardo, of Pisanello, and of their contemporaries are filled with drawings of animals, flowers, clouds, mountains, and other natural things.

But "fidelity to nature" is a notoriously equivocal formula. The multiple meanings of "nature" and its derivatives have been discriminated by A. O. Lovejoy and we shall not attempt to expand upon his treatment of the subject.[10] But we must notice what the phrase meant to Vasari and earlier to Leonardo. In the passage quoted from the biographer and critic, one observes that the artist is praised for reproducing the likeness of his sitter as Apelles is said to have reproduced the likeness of his grapes. Just as the birds in the classical instance pecked at the painted grapes, so the observer of the "Mona Lisa" believes the original to be before him, with beating pulses and living eyes. But before the passage is over one finds that Leonardo is praised also for painting the woman with a pleasant and smiling expression, as she appeared when listening to cheerful music or jesting talk; so that "while looking at it one thinks it rather divine than human."

How much literary exaggeration is expressed in these last words and how much they echo a Neoplatonic strain is hard to tell. Even in Leonardo, whose interest in reproducing natural objects led to these amazing anatomical and botanical and geological drawings, there are Neoplatonic elements. If he says, on the one hand, "Wisdom is the daughter of experience," and backs it up with minutely detailed studies of what he observes, he says on the other, "Nature is full of infinite causes which were never set forth in experience."[11] If he says, "O marvellous Necessity, thou with supreme reason constrainest all effects to be the direct result of their causes, and by a supreme and irrevocable law every natural action obeys thee by the shortest possible process," he also says, "Nature being capricious and taking pleasure in creating and producing a continuous succession of lives and forms. . . ."[12] Which of these Natures he saw as he drew his sketches, there is now no saying.

10 See *Primitivism in Antiquity,* pp. 447 ff., and "Nature as Aesthetic Norm," *Mod. Lang. Notes,* XLII (1927), pp. 444 ff.

11 *Notebooks,* I, 85 and 77, respectively.

12 *Ibid.,* I, 253 and 80 respectively. For a denial of the presence of Neoplatonism in Leonardo, see E. Panofsky, *Studies in Iconology,* 1939, p. 182.

But the probability is that most of his contemporaries saw in the sketches after they were drawn the capriciously creative and fertile Nature rather than the mechanistic and purely geometrical.

For a hundred or more years after Vasari there is little or no mention of the "Mona Lisa." According to the French historian, Lemonnier,[13] Leonardo and his Italian *confrères* who were called to France by Francis I "furent traités avec toutes sortes d'égards et reçurent des appointements en rapport avec leur réputation." There was even circulated the old story that Leonardo died in the King's arms, a story now discredited.[14] But although more of his authentic pictures belonged to the crown—and now to the French Republic—than to any other single collector, most French writings of the sixteenth, seventeenth, and even eighteenth centuries are silent about him.[15] He is not mentioned in the letters of Marguerite d'Angoulême,[16] in the works of Rabelais, Montaigne—not even in his *Journal de Voyage*—nor the Pleiade; the courtiers, who might have seen at least the *Mona Lisa,* say nothing that we have been able to discover of either the picture or its author; even Louis Leroy, whose *De la Vicissitude ou variété des choses de l'univers* (1579) lists the painters whose works have raised his times to eminence, omits Leonardo's name. One possible reason for this is that the "Mona Lisa" belonged to the King and therefore not many people had the chance to see it. But the most famous pictures and sculptures of the time were made familiar to the interested public by engravings, and if Leonardo had captured the imagination of Frenchmen, his works would doubtless have been both known and spoken of, as those of Raphael were.[17]

In the middle of the seventeenth century, Leonardo's name and the "Mona Lisa" emerge once more. Père Dan, who made a catalogue of

[13] In Lavisse's *Histoire de France*, V, i, 316.

[14] See L. Roger-Milès, *op. cit.*, pp. 15 f. The story, as is well known, dates from the time of Vasari.

[15] Though Poussin drew the illustrations for the edition of the *Trattato* which appeared in the middle of the seventeenth century, Leonardo was not so highly esteemed as Raphael, for instance, or even some of the lesser painters. *Cf.* A. Fontaine, *Les doctrines d'art en France*, 1909, p. 3.

[16] The sister of his great French patron, who, according to Roger-Milès, *op. cit.*, p. 65, is portrayed in Leonardo's (?) *Marriage of Saint Catherine.*

[17] The portrait could only have been seen by persons admitted to the "gilt cabinet" at Fontainebleau, which would have required special permission. It was removed to Versailles by Louis XIV, probably after 1694, the late date on which it appears in the inventories of Fontainebleau (See *La Grande Encyclopédie*, XVIII, p. 950). It was not exhibited in the Louvre until after the Revolution. It does not appear to have been engraved until the nineteenth century. For its history in France, see the catalogue of the Louvre by Georges Lafenestre and Eugène Richtenberger, tr. by B. H. Dausseron, p. 56.

the works of art at Fontainebleau, calls it the *premier en estime, comme une merveille de la peinture.*[18] In whose estimation it ranked first and why it was considered a marvel are not revealed. Félibien, somewhat later, continues the Vasari tradition.

> This is one of the most finished of his works. It is said that he took so much pleasure in working on it that he spent four months on it, and that while he was painting this lady there was always someone near her who sang or played some musical instrument, so as to keep her joyful and prevent her from assuming that melancholy air which comes over one easily when one is inactive and motionless.
>
> Truly, said Pymandre, if I may give my opinion, the time which he put into it was well spent, for I have never seen anything more finished or more expressive. There is so much grace and so much sweetness in the eyes and features of this face, that it appears to be alive. When one looks at this portrait, one would say it was a real woman who takes pleasure in being seen.
>
> It is true, I replied, that Leonardo appears to have taken particular care to finish it well. And Francis I considered this picture to be one of the most finished products of this painter, wished to own it, and paid four thousand *écus* for it.[19]

The excellence of Leonardo's artistry is judged in this passage by its "finish" in the representation of a gentle and sweet woman's face. The time given to the work, four months, becomes a matter of the greatest interest to subsequent critics, who vary it as they will. Vasari had said that Leonardo "loitered" over it for four years—not months— and then had left it unfinished. Lanzi, pointing out the unfinished state of most of Leonardo's pictures, continues by saying that the impression of lack of finish is attributable to the artist's having left certain portions of his pictures less precisely finished than others. This deficiency, he says, cannot be detected always by the best judges. "The portrait, for instance, of Mona Lisa Gioconda, . . . was minutely examined by Mariette in the collection of the king of France, and it was declared to be carried to so high a degree of finish that it was impossible to surpass it."[20] Stendhal passes on the story, saying that the artist "never con-

[18] *Trésor des Merveilles de Fontainbleau* (1624), quoted by Rigollot, *Cat. de l'oeuvre de Léonard de Vinci*, 1849, pp. 652 ff. Cassiano del Pozzo in 1625 saw the painting and commented on its bad condition. See Müntz, *Léonard de Vinci*, 1899, p. 421.

[19] André Félibien, *Entretiens sur les vies et sur les òuvrages des plus excellents Peintres anciens et modernes*, 2d ed., 1685-1688, I, 193 f.

[20] Luigi Lanzi, *The History of Painting in Italy*, tr. by Thomas Roscoe, new ed. rev., 1853. The history was first published in 1789 and was considered for many years authoritative. It was translated and revised by the Reverend G. W. D. Evans in 1848. In translation the passage appears, "the labor of four years, and, after all, left unfinished." Mariette was the author of the *Abecedario de Pierre Jean Mariette*, which I have not seen.

sidered it finished."[21] Delecluze reduces the time to three years.[22] The story continues to our own day through Houssaye, the American Moses F. Sweetser, his contemporary, Mrs. Charles W. Heaton, Gabriel Séailles, Mantz, Edward McCurdy, E. V. Lucas, and even Elbert Hubbard.[23]

II

For some three hundred years no one appears to have seen anything mysterious about this painting. It was the portrait of a certain merchant's wife in a cheerful mood, and what was found extraordinary in it was its fidelity to nature. But a merchant's wife is still a woman, and women began to occupy a curious position in many early nineteenth-century minds. They had previously been cruel, coquettish, vain, deceitful, gentle, fickle, tender, weak, but they had rarely been enigmatic. On the contrary, men knew them only too well. But the early nineteenth century introduced a new woman into the history of ideas— *la femme fatale.*[24]

The *femme fatale* emerged with Romanticism. She was all sensation and feeling, as against masculine rationality. She captured men by her apparent passivity, lying in wait like a fascinating serpent for the flitting bird who was the male. Whether the Romanticists knew it or not, she could trace her ancestry back to the Eve of Philo Judaeus. The Romantic critics, whether they were engaged in interpreting paintings or poetry, treated their works of art as if they were hieroglyphs. Each had a hidden "meaning" which only the initiated could uncover. To be one of the initiated, one must have a peculiar kind of sensitivity, an eye that not merely saw the perceptual screen of things but penetrated to something called the reality behind it. Such metaphors in practice meant that the critic was not to record what he saw, but to let his imagination freely play about the work of art and to report what it constructed.

What Vasari was for the pre-nineteenth-century critic, Théophile

21 *Hist. de la Peinture en Italie,* 1817, I, 223 f.

22 *Léonard de Vinci,* 1841, p. 29.

23 See respectively, *Hist. de Léonard de Vinci,* pp. 439 ff.; *Leonardo da Vinci,* Boston, 1879, p. 59; *Leonardo da Vinci and his Works,* 1874, p. 51 f.; *Léonard de Vinci,* 1892, p. 140; *Leonardo da Vinci,* 1898, II, 158; *Leonardo da Vinci,* 1904, p. 113; *Leonardo da Vinci,* 1926, p. 9; *Little Journeys to the Homes of Eminent Artists,* 1902, X, ii, p. 46. Elbert Hubbard translated the sum of 4000 *scudi* into eighty thousand dollars. Stendhal had been content with forty five thousand francs.

24 This is, of course, a commonplace, but see Mario Praz, *The Romantic Agony,* 1933, ch. IV, esp. pp. 243 ff. The reader also would do well to complete what follows in our text by pursuing Mr. Berenson's suggestion of the influence of Lavater and the other physiognomists. See his *The Study and Criticism of Italian Art,* 1916, p. 24.

Gautier and Walter Pater became for their contemporaries and successors. Both started a tradition—in apparent independence of each other
—which has not died even today. Gautier's paragraph was the earlier
published.

> Leonardo da Vinci retained the finesse of the Gothic period while
> animating it with a spirit entirely modern. . . . The faces of Vinci seem
> to come from the upper spheres to be reflected in a glass or rather in
> a mirror of tarnished steel, where their image remains eternally fixed
> by a secret similar to that of the daguerreotype. We have seen these
> faces before, but not upon this earth: in some previous existence per-
> haps, which they recall to us vaguely. How explain otherwise the
> strange, almost magic charm which the portrait of Mona Lisa has for
> even the least enthusiastic natures? Is it her beauty? Many faces by
> Raphael and other painters are more correct. She is no longer even
> young; her age must be that loved by Balzac, thirty years; through the
> subtle modelling we divine the beginnings of fatigue, and life's finger
> has left its imprint on this peachlike cheek. Her costume, because
> of the darkening of the pigments, has become almost that of a widow;
> a crêpe veil falls with the hair along her face; but the expression, wise,
> deep, velvety, full of promise, attracts you irresistibly and intoxicates
> you, while the sinuous, serpentine mouth, turned up at the corners,
> in the violet shadows, mocks you with so much gentleness, grace, and
> superiority, that you feel suddenly intimidated, like a schoolboy before
> a duchess. The head with its violet shadows, seen as through black
> gauze, arrests one's dreams as one leans on the museum railing before
> her, haunts one's memory like a symphonic theme. Beneath the form
> *expressed,* one feels a thought which is vague, infinite, *inexpressible,*
> like a musical idea. One is moved, troubled, images *already seen* pass
> before one's eyes, voices whose note seems familiar whisper languorous
> secrets in one's ears; repressed desires, hopes which drive one to despair
> stir painfully in the shadow shot with sunbeams; and you discover that
> your melancholy arises from the fact that la Joconde three hundred
> years ago greeted your avowal of love with this same mocking smile
> which she retains even to-day on her lips.[25]

Here simple fidelity to nature has completely disappeared; the eternal feminine has taken its place. The "Mona Lisa" is not the portrait
of a young woman; she has ripened through experience. She recalls past
lives, stirs up repressed desires, mocks you with her smile. At once a
new strain enters into French criticism. Whereas the earlier critics
had seen sweetness and gentleness, the later began to see something
more troubling. Even Taine, who was scarcely a victim of "the Romantic agony," found the famous smile "doubting, licentious, Epicurean,

25 Théophile Gautier *et al., Les Dieux et les demi-dieux de la peinture,* [1863], p. 24 f.
The article on Leonardo first appeared in 1858. For further information about it, see
Spoelberch de Lovenjoul, *Hist. des oeuvres de Théophile Gautier,* pp. 160, 262 ff.

deliciously tender, ardent, sad," and united it to the smiles of the Saint John, the Saint Anne, and other Vincian smiles.[26] Houssaye, one of the co-authors of Gautier's book, who was interested enough in facts to write a Life of Leonardo, also is captivated by the new mystery. He feels it his duty to bring in her "charm, provocative and ineffable, cruel and divine, sybilline and voluptuous."[27] This diabolical charm appears also, somewhat intensified, in Charles Blanc and Paul Mantz.

> Before a painting so wonderful and so admired, the time which was consumed in painting it is explained either by the fact that the artist experienced the fascination which he has so well expressed, and prolonged as far as possible the sweets of conversation with this charming woman, or that he had difficulty in expressing the proud serenity and restrained provocation of this face whose smile, at certain moments, seems satanic and still magnetises us by its long and voluptuous glances. It seems that after having carried the modelling to the point of the most delicate shading, to imperceptible accents, and thus brought it close to us by palpitating truth, the artist may have desired then to withdraw it into the mystery of half-light, to hold it remote from our gaze by shrouding it in a gauze and to make it appear as a dream amid a wild landscape, against an unbelievable background of little mountains, blue, rocky, pointed, cut from crystal, and like stalactites turned upwards towards the skies.[28]

All that was lacking now was an explanation of the mysterious charm of this face. The explanation must lie, according to romantic procedure, in the life of the painter, and it was not hard to find reasons for believing that the original Lisa was the mistress of the painter.[29] Charles Clément told the extraordinary story in full. He noticed, he says, that whereas the men's heads by Leonardo were all individualized, those of the women were all identical. On a panel belonging to the Orleans family was discovered a reclining female whose features were those of La Gioconda. In the Fesch Collection and in the Hermitage are two half-length nudes with the same face. The original Lisa was the third wife of Giocondo—so that her husband must have been much older than she. Leonardo was young, witty and handsome when he painted her. The portrait at which "he worked or pretended to work" for four years never became the property of her husband. Finally, it is from the

26 H. Taine, *Voyage en Italie*, 1902 (1st ed. 1865), II, 409.

27 Arsène Houssaye, *op. cit.*, p. 125.

28 *Hist. des peintres de toutes les écoles. École Florentine*, 1879. See p. 27 f. for the full account. It is typical of writers of this school that they will say, "stalactites turned upwards towards the skies" rather than "stalagmites."

29 *Michelangelo, Leonardo da Vinci and Raphael*, tr. by Louisa Corhan, (n. d.), pp. 201 ff.; French ed. 1861. A poem on the same theme was produced by M. A. Dollfus and may be found in Houssaye, *op. cit.*, pp. 335 f.

time when he painted the "Mona Lisa" that the other female heads begin to resemble hers.

As a matter of cold fact it requires no deep observation of Leonardo's portrait to see how little it resembles the Saint Anne and the Saint John and the various Madonnas. The one common character is the smile, but the series of thirty or more archaic maidens in the Acropolis museum in Athens have an identical smile, which they share with many other archaic statues of both men and women. Are we to conclude from this anything except that such smiles were the fashion of the times? Leonardo's saints and other supernatural beings do resemble one another; he gave them a certain "ideal" head. But the portraits attributed to him are individualized. The face of the "Mona Lisa" cannot be said to resemble the face of "La Belle Ferronière," if that portrait be indeed by him. And neither of them closely resembles his saints.

Pater's famous passage on our painting is of course better known to English readers than Gautier's, and was perhaps the source of most later American and English interpretations of it. Pater suggests more than he states, whether from timidity, ignorance, or critical principle, but one may vaguely discern through his poetic prose that, like Clément, he finds a disconcerting similarity running through all the female heads and, like Gautier, a symbol of metempsychosis. The symbolism, he maintains, is not "crude," but the picture has "a subdued and graceful mystery." He believes that the "unfathomable smile, always with a touch of something sinister in it," plays over all of Leonardo's work. "From childhood we see this image defining itself on the fabric of his dreams; and but for express historical testimony, we might fancy that this was but his ideal lady, embodied and beheld at last." He suggests a fusion of his dream and the real Mona Lisa. And then follows the purple passage which has been reprinted even in anthologies of poetry. In that face "strange thoughts and fantastic reveries and exquisite passions" are "deposited cell by cell" upon the flesh. "All the thoughts and experiences of the world have been etched and moulded there, in that they have of power to refine and make expressive the outward form, the animalism of Greece, the lust of Rome, the reverie of the middle age with its spiritual ambition and imaginative loves, the return of the Pagan world, the sins of the Borgias." Mona Lisa becomes the "fancy of perpetual life," a reincarnation of Leda, Helen, Saint Anne.[30]

30 Walter Pater, *The Renaissance,* 1st ed., 1873. The essay itself was first published in the *Fortnightly Review,* Nov. 1869, pp. 494 ff. Donald A. Stauffer, in an interesting article,

Few art critics of the nineteenth century, capable of reading Pater, resisted his musical style, and we find dozens of imitators of him in the years that followed the publication of *The Renaissance*. Mrs. Charles W. Heaton, for instance, saw in the portrait, "a sweet but perplexing poem," and a visible embodiment of "the words of the preacher, 'vanitas vanitatum.' "[31] Mr. Frank Preston Stearns, after a passage on the "meaning" of the smile, dwells upon the sense of mystery in Leonardo's character, which is "expressed without reservation" in this picture.[32] Elbert Hubbard, in one of his *Little Journeys*, brought in the words of the Preacher, as well as those of Walter Pater, added Cleopatra to Leda, Helen, and Saint Anne, and filled three pages with an eloquent description of a smile which he called "ineffable."[33] Mr. George B. Rose expressed the usual thoughts about the "inscrutability" of the smile, "a smile that is only on the lips, while in the eyes there are unsounded depths. Vainly we question her; like the Sphinx her riddle eludes us still."[34] Mr. Edward McCurdy, after an analysis of the details of the portrait, concludes, "Thus, on the very confines of fantasy, and girt about with suggestions of strange lights and furtive shadows, he has created in this portrait of Madonna Lisa, third wife of a Florentine official, a myth of the embodiment of which men dream as of the eternal enigma of womanhood."[35]

III

From Gautier and Pater, as is clear, runs a tradition which is the very opposite of that started by Vasari. Whereas the Italian biographer

Monna Melancholia (*Sewanee Review*, XL, 89 ff.) gives reasons for believing that Pater had never seen the original of the *Mona Lisa* and had superimposed Dürer's *Melancholy I* upon it in his memory. For intimations of an influence of Gautier on Pater through Swinburne, called to my attention by Professor Meyer Schapiro, see Louise Rosenblatt, *L'Idée de l'art pour l'art etc.*, 1931, p. 105.

31 *Leonardo da Vinci and his Works*, 1874, p. 52.

32 *The Midsummer of Italian Art*, 1895, p. 60. Though the Notebooks had not as yet been published when Mr. Stearns's book appeared, the *Treatise on Painting* alone might have shown him that Leonardo was enamored more of precision and clarity than of mystery.

33 *Little Journeys to the Homes of Eminent Artists*, X, no. 2, pp. 46-50, (Feb. 1902). Hubbard's opinion of the picture may not seem important; but he was considered a great authority on "culture" by the general public of his day. The circulation of his *Little Journeys* was always large and his writings must have been the source of the aesthetics of many unschooled Americans.

34 *The World's Leading Painters*, 1912, p. 50. In a similar vein Laura Spencer Porter conveyed to the ladies of America the "meaning" of the *Mona Lisa* in the *Woman's Home Companion*, April, 1914, (XLI, p. 54).

35 *Leonardo da Vinci*, 1904, pp. 115 f. It is interesting to observe that James Jackson Jarves, the American collector and critic, who alone of the writers cited—and many others not cited—knew the Italian painters of the Renaissance intimately, was almost unique in his time in continuing the Vasari tradition rather than what we have called the Romantic. See his *Art Studies of the Old Masters of Italy*, 1861, I, p. 400.

and critic chiefly saw in the "Mona Lisa" a wonderful technical feat, the reproduction of a natural object, the French and English "aesthetes" saw it as a hieroglyph which required not simply contemplation but deciphering. It would appear to have become second nature to think of a picture—at least of this picture—as something of a rebus, a symbol whose meaning could be discovered only by a critic's intuition. That this school of writers attributed their theory of artistry to the artists whose works interested them need surprise no one. Critics are in the habit of reading an artist's mind.

This habit became strengthened when the psychology of Sigmund Freud achieved popularity. The nineteenth and twentieth centuries have been noteworthy, among other things, for a peculiar paradox: a combination of great scientific accomplishment with anti-intellectualism. Early in the former century, Schopenhauer began to argue that the understanding was created by the will to serve its own ends, an argument which he sought to deduce from Kantian principles. These ends, however, were not those of Kant's Practical Reason; they were, on the contrary, purely biological; and it was easy for Schopenhauer's successors to identify them with sexual ends. An artist, according to Freud, is a man whose sexual frustrations are released symbolically in pictures or statues or other works of art. Appetites which would never pass the Censor if expressed in their true nature, are permitted to appear in disguise.

As is well known, according to this theory the fundamental appetite of the human male is his love for his mother, known as the Oedipus Complex. Since incest in most Occidental society is not encouraged, the Oedipus Complex can only be released through art, and hence a Freudian critic will be likely to see in a picture a symbol of the artist's passion for his mother. Here, it will be observed, the critic assumes that the artist is not communicating something to the observer—he is really concealing something from the observer—but unconsciously expressing something of himself. When this something is revealed, it does not mean that the picture will be liked any the more; no standard of aesthetic judgment is implied in the psychoanalysis of a work of art. But it is clear that what mainly interests a Freudian, in any such work, will be the discovery of the unconscious motive. Freud's interpretation follows.

> It was quite possible that Leonardo was fascinated by the smile of Mona Lisa because it had awakened something in him which had slumbered in his soul for a long time, in all probability an old mem-

ory.[36] This memory was of sufficient importance to stick to him once it had been aroused; he was forced continually to provide it with new expression. The assurance of Pater that we can see an image like that of Mona Lisa defining itself from Leonardo's childhood on the fabric of his dreams, seems worthy of belief and deserves to be taken literally.

Vasari mentions as Leonardo's first artistic endeavors, "heads of women who laugh." The passage, which is beyond suspicion, as it was not meant to prove anything, reads more precisely as follows: "He formed in his youth some laughing feminine heads out of lime, which have been reproduced in plaster, and some heads of children, which were as beautiful as if modeled by the hands of a master. . . ."

Thus we discover that his practice of art begin with the representation of two kinds of objects, which would perforce remind us of the two kinds of sexual objects which we have inferred from the analysis of his vulture phantasy. If the beautiful children's heads were reproductions of his own childish persons, then the laughing women were nothing else but reproductions of Caterina, his mother, and we are beginning to have an inkling of the possibility that his mother possessed that mysterious smile which he lost, and which fascinated him so much when he found it again in the Florentine lady. . . .[37]

Not only is Freud able to construct a part of the hidden life of Leonardo from the "Mona Lisa," he is also able to build up the life of the artist's mother. Since she was not married to Piero da Vinci, she was forced to "compensate herself for not having a husband."

In the manner of all ungratified mothers she thus took her little son in place of her husband, and robbed him of a part of his virility by the too early maturing of his eroticism. . . . When in the prime of his life Leonardo re-encountered that blissful and ecstatic smile as it had once encircled his mother's mouth in caressing, he had long been under the ban of an inhibition forbidding him ever again to desire such tenderness from women's lips. But as he had become a painter he endeavored to reproduce this smile with his brush and burnish all his pictures with it, whether he executed them himself or whether they were done by his pupils under his direction, as in Leda, John, and Bacchus.[38]

The way was now open for further embroidering on this psychological background, and critics were not slow to follow it. Pictures became clues to the subconscious labyrinths of an artist's mind. Regardless of the fact that this particular picture seemed to have been painted as a portrait, which might lead one to suppose that its appearance was

---

36 According to Vasari, the smile had to be artificially produced and preserved.

37 Sigmund Freud, *Leonardo da Vinci*, 1916, pp. 85 ff. There is no objective evidence that Caterina resembled Lisa, in smile or otherwise.

38 *Ibid.*, p. 91 ff.

to a large extent determined by the attributes of the woman who sat for it, its main interest was now held to lie in what it could tell us about the man who made it. This shift in critical attention was the kind of reversal of opinion best illustrated in the Hegelian dialectic. Whereas in Vasari the picture was considered with reference to its closeness to the objective world of nature, in Freud it is considered as a disclosure of the most intimately subjective world, the so-called Unconscious. But since the world which it reveals can be known only by means of a theory which is applied to the particular object, rather than one which has been deduced from it, the critic has only to make up his mind what was in the artist's Unconscious and then discover it spread out before him in the picture.

One finds a still more remarkable example of this in the volume written on our artist by Rachel Annand Taylor, *Leonardo the Florentine*. For her the "Mona Lisa" is a phase in Leonardo's transition from concealment to avowal of his homosexuality. It is, she says,[39] "as if he were afraid to see his Narcissus except in a disguise." Presumably when he painted his Saint John, he was no longer ashamed to see his Narcissus. But even if he were not, it is hardly likely that he painted the picture in order to inform the world that he had conquered his shame. This becomes doubly true if one accepts the Freudian theory that art is always a symbolical rather than a literal satisfaction of repressions.

Happily, we are not engaged in an examination of Freudianism. Our purpose is simply to indicate how it reoriented aesthetic comment on this picture in the twentieth century. A writer now feels it possible to assume that a painter is painting for himself rather than for an observer, and that, if an observer should present himself before a picture, he should find in it what the artist himself concealed in it. But since only initiated Freudians know what is concealed in pictures, the uninitiated observer fails to see what the picture really is, or "means." He is in the position of a European ignorant of Chinese looking at Chinese characters and thinking they are merely patterns.

If the "Mona Lisa" at the present time is considered old-fashioned, that is probably to be attributed more to the writings of the Gautier-Pater school than to those of the psychoanalysts. Leonardo himself is far from old-fashioned; but it is now the scientific and philosophical Leonardo rather than the artistic. This paper is not concerned with the decline of interest in the painting, but we may be permitted to

[39] Rachel Annand Taylor, *Leonardo the Florentine*, 1927, esp. pp. 350-354. Only one who has gone through the whole of this book can get its full flavor.

suggest that M. Paul Valéry is probably right in saying that the association of "mystery" with the picture has had more influence than any
other one thing in disgusting people with it.[40]

The tendency in the criticism of painting from about 1910 to the
beginning of surrealism has been technical. It has consisted largely in
studies of form, color, drawing. Only since Marxian criticism became
fashionable has there been much attention paid to subject matter. But
in such criticism little is said of adequacy of representation—fidelity
to "nature"; the critic is concerned only with the "social significance"
of the work of art. Hence to such critics, the "Mona Lisa" would have
no great interest, unless, perhaps, as an illustration of the rise of the
middle class, for the lady so carefully portrayed was probably a
bourgeoise.

It may not be inappropriate to terminate with a celebrated passage
from the artist's note-books about the portraiture of women. "Women,"
Leonardo says, "should be represented in modest attitudes with legs
close together, arms folded, and their heads low and bending sideways."[41] The head of La Gioconda is not bending sideways, but otherwise the precept appears to be carried out in the painting. Add to it
the memorandum on the importance of painting faces in a nebulous
light, and you begin to have a clue to his method of portraiture. This
will throw no light on what is "expressed" by the picture, nor is that,
fortunately, our affair. We know that Leonardo was attracted by
chiaroscuro and busy with the means of utilizing it. We may fittingly
leave to psychiatrists the problem why such things interested him.

Our purpose in this paper has been merely to show how a given
work of art may in different periods have essentially different content—
and therefore be admired for different, if not for contradictory, reasons.
If this instance is typical, it would appear that works of art which
"withstand the test of time" change their natures as the times change.
The work of art becomes thus the locus of a new set of values determined by the preconceptions or the predominant interest of the
new critic or observer.

40 See his *Leonardo da Vinci*, 1929, p. 58. For other hostile criticisms of this celebrated
picture, see Berenson's *The Study and Criticism of Italian Art*, pp. 3 f.; A. C. Barnes, *The
Art in Painting*, 1925, p. 368; P. Dearmer, "Leonardo da Vinci, a Criticism," *Contemporary
Review*, Vol. 135 (1929), p. 217. The Italian Futurists, in their campaign to liberate Italian
art from the museum pieces, quite naturally attacked it. A good example may be found in
Soffici's *Giornale di Bordo*, 1915, p. 147: "In tram.—Vedo scritto su un muro a grandi
lettere bianche su fondo blu: GIOCONDA: ACQUA PURGATIVA ITALIANA. E piu giù la faccia
melensa di Monna Lisa. Finalmente. Ecco che si comincia anche da noi a far della buona
critica artistica."
41 *The Notebooks of Leonardo da Vinci*, p. 240.

*This, like many of Fry's best pieces, was written originally as a book
review. Though now almost forty years old, it is still an amazingly
relevant and up-to-date discussion of one of the central problems of
"art appreciation."*

Roger Fry
Culture and Snobbism[1]

It is a nice point, and one on which
I have never yet been able to make up my mind, whether culture is
more inimical to art than barbarism, or *vice versâ*. Culture, no doubt,
tends to keep a tradition in existence, but just when the tradition
thus carefully tended through some winter of neglect begins to show
signs of life by putting out new shoots and blossoms, culture must
needs do its best to destroy them. As the guardian and worshipper of
the dead trunk, it tries to wipe off such impertinent excrescences, unable as it is to recognise in them the signs of life.

The late Sir Claude Phillips, for instance, pays tribute throughout
his book, *Emotion in Art*,[2] to the greatest achievements of the art of
the past; he exalted and kept alive the memory of Titian and Giorgione, but when he comes to talk of his contemporaries he makes us
wonder what he found to admire in the old masters by speaking in
almost the same glowing terms of Böcklin and Fritz von Uhde; he
alludes to Monet, but he is silent about Seurat and Sisley and Cézanne,
not to mention those more modern artists whom also he had every
opportunity to appraise.

For this book of reprinted articles makes it quite clear that Sir
Claude was a very distinguished High Priest of Culture. The unction
of his style was as oil to feed the undying flame in the Temple, and the
savour of his epithets rose like incense before its altars. Like many
great ecclesiastics, he was also an accomplished man of the world,
neither an ascetic nor a prude; like them he enjoyed polished society,
good wine, good food, and good stories. He was a charming and witty
companion, whose good things were drawn from the vast store of learning and experience which his wonderful memory retained. But like
other ecclesiastics, when he entered the Temple indued with his
priestly garments, his whole manner changed. His language took on

1 From *Transformations* by Roger E. Fry. New York: Brentano's, *n.d.*
2 *Emotion in Art*, by Sir Claude Phillips. London: Heinemann, 1925.

the peculiar unction of almost all devotional writing, and he bowed perpetually before the great gods of his Temple and rarely alluded to one of them without some time-honoured and sanctifying epithet. The very quality of his phrases changed; they took on the liturgical resonance which relegates sense to a subsidiary position. Perhaps Ruskin had showed the way, but it was Phillips more than any one else who framed and consolidated the ritual and liturgical use of the great Temple of Culture. He borrowed, no doubt, from other religions, but he adapted with extraordinary tact and skill. Thus it was that he came week after week to intone in the columns of the *Daily Telegraph* those reverential, decorous, and richly adorned services, some of which are reprinted here. Throughout these pages we hear "the blessed mutter of the Mass"—a Mass in which the names of all the deities and saints and all their great works are brought up in succession. It hardly matters whether Sir Claude Phillips says anything about their works or not; the main purpose is served if one after another their glorious names are brought to the worshipper's mind, in order to arouse his reverent awe and conduce to his edification. As we read these pages we are conscious of the presence of the Thrones, Dominations, Principalities, and Powers of the realm of art; we share humbly and at a distance in that new communion of the Saints. Almost infallibly Sir Claude strikes the right devotional attitude and finds the edifying epithet.

One of the well-known signs of this attitude is the reference to holy beings by some allusive translocution. A well-trained ecclesiastic having once named Elijah could hardly fail afterwards to refer to him as the "indomitable Tishbite." The effect of this is admirable, it assumes that reverent familiarity on the worshipper's part which is so desirable. Thus, Sir Claude has his repertory of allusions, "the gentle Urbinate," "the bee of Urbino," "the divine Sanzio," "the faultless Andrea," "the Frate," "the poet-painter of Valenciennes," "the great Cadorine," by which we are, as it were, made free of the mysteries. Still more significant is the fact that not even the objects that have to do with the cult may be left without their appropriate adjective. I quote a passage in which he speaks of dancing in art: "Akin to these, but perhaps more vigorous still, and with less of cosmic suavity, are the child-angels who in joyous procession pass dancing along the front and sides of Donatello's "Cantoria," once in the Cathedral of Santa Maria del Fiore at Florence, but now in the little museum at the back of that mighty church." Here the information given in the last phrase is, of course, quite irrelevant to the argument, but it seems to bring up vague memories of holy things, and, what reveals the attitude, even this little scrap of topography helps to elevate us by reason of the insertion of the word "mighty." The true emotional touch is shown by this almost unconscious gesture. But let me quote another passage where the fervour of Sir Claude's Apostolate has more scope:

"And Mantegna, harsh and tender, severe with a more than Roman severity, and yet of a mysticism in devotion as intense as that of any contemporary master, maintains the beholder in realms where the spirit droops and can hardly follow. The sublimity of Michelangelo himself is equalled in a 'Sybil and Prophet' of very moderate dimensions, formerly in the collection of the Duke of Buccleugh; the 'Infant Christ, as Ruler of the World,' of the Mond collection, stands apart in the quiet intensity with which it expresses worship on the one hand, and, on the other, the irradiation of the Universe by Divine Love. The 'Madonnas' of the Poldi-Pezzoli at Milan and the Gallery at Bergamo, express, as by hardly any other master they have been expressed, the sublime devotion, the tragic apprehension, of maternal love that is all human and yet in its immensity Divine. Face to face with his 'Adoration of the Magi' (formerly in the Ashburton collection), we experience the feeling of religious awe, almost of terror, that possessed the Wise Men of the East when, though royal still in splendour and in gravity, they knelt subdued and prostrate in worship at the feet of the Divine Babe."

There surely is the full organ roll of the Anglican liturgy at its best; see how the very names of Italian towns and of ducal collectors help to swell the diapason, and urge the worshipper to fresh ecstasies of acquiescence.

Decidedly Sir Claude Phillips was a great High Priest in that religion of culture which is so well adapted to the emotional needs of polite societies, and let me add that he had to the full the sense of his sacerdoce. He was the first to denounce any act of vandalism, he was the most scrupulous in avoiding any hint of simony, the most punctilious in the assertion of the claims of his religion, and the most conscientious in their observance.

There remains, of course, the question with which I started, what relation, if any, has this religion of culture to art? Some connection it surely has. It would be impossible for any one to have written these glowing pages unless he had looked long and with some genuine emotion at the innumerable masterpieces whose images he recalls and whose glories he recounts. But so far as I can find, there is no single piece of strictly aesthetic appreciation in the whole of this book. Not once does Sir Claude come into contact with the actual vision of the artist. So far, indeed, does his habit of day-dreaming about pictures instead of looking at them go, that in an essay on "What the Brush cannot Paint," he actually says that, "The word-painting of the poet gives as definite a vision as that which arises from the brush-work of the painters." The word "definite" here is, of course, the exact opposite of the truth—the essence, and to a great extent the value, of the poet's image lying precisely in its indefiniteness.

But Sir Claude did not accept definite images from pictures. He allowed the vision to set up in his mind an emotional state in which the vision itself was lost in the vague overtones of associated ideas and feelings. He shows his method when he says: "Not Millais in his 'Chill October,' not even Theodore Rousseau or Diaz, painting the festering herbage on some dark pool of the forest, walled in by the trees from which the last sere leaves drop in the silence, one by one." It matters little how poor the quality of the painting is (and how poor are these he cites!), when this agreeable daydream with its soothing verbal accompaniment replaces so rapidly the painter's vision.

It is to this that we must look for the explanation of the strange paradox of this fervent hierodule of Raphael, Titian, and Poussin giving his priestly blessing to Böcklin and Fritz von Uhde, and turning aside from the more sincere efforts of modern art to write long rhapsodies over sentimental war-pictures which have already passed into Time's rubbish heap.

No doubt, then, Sir Claude derived a very genuine enjoyment from works of art, but I think that enjoyment was obtained without any direct communion with the artists' sensibility; what he saw and felt was the dramatic interpretation of the scene and its decorative setting, but most of all he felt the status of the work in question in the hierarchy of art, its cultural value, the exact degree of reverence which it might rightly claim from the devout. Reverence is, indeed, the key to all such religious attitudes, and reverence is, of course, as inimical to true aesthetic experience as it is to the apprehension of truth. Reverence, and that goodwill which belongs to edification, may be, perhaps, of use to help the beginner to overcome the first difficulties of approach to what is finest in art, but if he is to get any real aesthetic experience, he must learn to eschew reverence and to distrust his goodwill.

This is, indeed, the greatest difficulty of criticism, for past esthetic experiences always tend to stereotype themselves in our minds and set

up within us the religious attitude. Sir Claude Phillips not only did
not understand this, but would have looked upon such an attempt to
react purely and freely in each case as a blasphemy against the whole
religion of culture.

I still find I must leave the question open. Picture galleries and
museums are Temples of Culture, not of Art. The artist and the esthete
use them, no doubt: indeed, they depend on them; they would, none
the less, never have had the social prestige, nor, perhaps, the energy, to
have created them. The artist's debt to culture in that respect is immense, but he pays it in full when he discovers that the same social
prestige of culture will turn upon him the moment he tries to create
along the lines of the tradition which culture has preserved. To the
cultured man the unpardonable sin is the creation of just those works
which will become the ark of the covenant to some succeeding generation of cultured men.

This question of the part played by culture in a civilisation prompts
the similar question of the *rôle* of snobbism. This useful word, the
interest which we have received on lending the word "snob" to the
French, describes a well-known class of experiences. Snobbery, from
which it comes, describes the uncritical and enthusiastic acceptance
of certain social values or pretensions, and snobbism should, I think,
be kept for the distinct phenomenon of the equally blind acceptance
of certain spiritual values or pretensions, whether intellectual or
aesthetic.

Can we distinguish between culture and snobbism? In both a certain
religious attitude of worship is evident, and they are concerned largely
with the same values. In both, too, communion with fellow worshippers is a matter of supreme importance, so that it is not always an
easy matter to say of a particular act of devotion or article of faith
to which Church it belongs. It may, indeed, partake of both, since these
are not mutually exclusive doctrines.

There is, however, I think, a difference of mental attitude which
the words enable us to distinguish. The snobbist, by his pilgrimage
to the "right" picture gallery at the "right" moment, and his display
there of the "right" enthusiasm before the "right" works of art is really
upheld by the consciousness that those acts bring him into close communion with a certain group of people, and it is not altogether remote
from his consciousness, although, perhaps, kept below its surface, that
those people are socially influential. His acts tend to make certain that
he will be "in the swim." It is this subtle connection between a certain

aesthetic creed and its social adherents that is, perhaps, too frankly revealed by the word "snobbism." The man of culture, on the other hand, lives in a world more detached from these considerations. His communion is not only with the living. By his acts of devotion he unites himself to a long line of historical precedents. He upholds the tradition which sensitive and contemplative spirits have handed on from generation to generation. And, since the verdicts of aesthetic sensibility have a tendency to violent fluctuations, this traditional esthetic doctrine has called to its aid the steadying influence of learning and scholarship. So that the devotees of culture often acquire more merit by what they know about the history of a work of art than by what they feel in front of it. To them an artist does not become a serious artist until a learned monograph has been consecrated to his life work. Thus the cultured, linked to the past by a long line of predecessors and filled with a sense of responsibility for the future, tend to adopt a conservative attitude to contemporary art. Their imprimatur must not be lightly given. They yield in the end, and become the guardians of what they resisted, judging, perhaps rightly, that only its irresistibility justifies this consecration. The snobbist, on the other hand, whilst always respectful of learning, is too anxious to know the latest word to await its judgment. He tends, therefore, to march in step with the vanguard of any aesthetic movement as soon as its victory is no longer in doubt. Until victory is fairly in view the movements of the true snobbist afford a fascinating spectacle, he—or perhaps she, for, thanks to the quicker social sense of women, they form the greatest and most devout part of the communion—shows the greatest anxiety and trepidation. A too overt adherence to the new doctrine at such a moment would precipitate him along a social blind alley and leave him in a position from which recovery is difficult and sometimes slightly ridiculous. On the other hand, to be left behind on the right track, though a fault more easily repaired, is to miss a supreme opportunity.

In thus describing some of the familiar experiences of modern life which affect the production of works of art, I have, I confess, a little oversimplified for the sake of clearness. The situation is never so definite as I have suggested. To represent the true facts we must allow for the admixture in infinitely varying doses according to temperament and character of genuine aesthetic feeling. Since social facts are of supreme importance to people's lives the social sense is likely to be more alert and potent than the aesthetic, but it not unfrequently happens, especially with the young, that, impelled at first merely by a vague, and in itself respectable, instinct to share in the most vivid life of the day, not to be too much "out of it," they do acquire a genuine appreciation of works of art and pass through snobbism into the ranks of that small group of amateurs—in the proper sense of the word— whose influence is most profound in the creation and survival of works of art.

What is most to be admired in culture is its love of the contemplative attitude and its passion for exact scholarship. Its besetting sin is an overcautious timidity, its desire for security above everything, its fear of life. Snobbism, at least, has the merit of trusting to the life of the moment with a certain recklessness. The roads of culture have been long laid down and are well patrolled, the snobbist follows into newly opened territory, and however anxiously he watches events, is bound to miss a genius or back a dud now and again.

Primarily, however, we are not concerned here with the psychology of the cultured or snobbist, but with the effect on art of their varying influence. And this can hardly be exaggerated, since the emergence and survival of any particular work of art are, I believe, as strictly conditioned by its ambience as is the emergence and survival of a type of animal or plant.

The artist, in whose breast the divine flame is kindled, finds himself confronted, then, with these two religions of culture and snobbism. But he is also aware of the presence of a vast inert mass, the great body of Philistines. These are the aesthetic atheists who own no obedience to any doctrine, whose only allegiance is to their untutored and wayward satisfaction. These he regards from the first as enemies; but they are his frank and loyal enemies. Mr. Podsnap's view of the arts he knows. It is clear, concise and perfectly intelligible. Dickens has explained it once for all in the following terms:

"Mr. Podsnap's notions of the Arts in their integrity might have been stated thus. Literature; large print, respectively descriptive of getting up at eight, shaving close at a quarter-past, breakfasting at nine, going to the City at ten, coming home at half-past four, and dining at seven. Painting and sculpture; models and portraits representing Professors of getting up at eight, etc. Music; a respectable performance (without variations) on stringed and wind instruments, sedately expressive of getting up at 8, etc. Nothing else to be permitted to those same vagrants the Arts, on pain of excommunication. Nothing else To Be—anywhere!"—("Our Mutual Friend.")

The artist knows, then, exactly where he stands with the Philistine.

With culture, too, his position is ascertainable. He finds himself, indeed, inspired and consoled by the great tradition which culture guards and proclaims. Through culture he is made free of the great art of the past and is encouraged to emulate its glories. It is only when he proceeds to do so that culture turns on him a sterner aspect. In imitating the attitude of the great masters he cannot possibly repeat their results, and thereupon the Grand Inquisitors of Culture scent heresy and make ready the *Auto da Fé*.

In this quandary snobbism alone appears to hold out a succouring hand. To express anything at all is a crime with the Philistine, to express anything vital is a crime with culture, among the snobbists alone novelty may, under certain circumstances, be a positive virtue. It must be a novelty that is not altogether unprepared for, it must go further along a track to which snobbism has recently become habituated. Then, and then only, the snobbist will help with unstinting generosity.

The artist, then, is likely to find in snobbism his most potent ally, but, as happens in other alliances, he is likely at times to feel more kindly towards his open antagonist the Philistine than he does towards an ally whose activities are capricious and uncertain. He will find snobbism always pressing forward to catch the last word, far too eager to see any point in subtle or unobtrusive work. He will find it continually the victim of charlatanism and advertisement, or even where, as may well happen, it has accepted genuine talent, doing so with so undiscriminating an enthusiasm that only the strongest and purest natures can resist its dangerous seduction. His indignation will be the greater in that in its light-hearted way snobbism distorts the values and confuses the issues in just those things that he most cherishes, until he may come to regard it as the abomination of desolation desecrating his holiest places.

What I have elsewhere defined as the "Opificer"[3] is backed by considerable funds, both from the patronage of the State and other public bodies, and from the private patronage of the Philistine. But the pure artist finds that, apart from the support of those few individuals who not only have cultivated by careful study a natural love of art but possess the means to gratify their passion, almost the only fund on which he can rely depends on the favour of snobbism. At rather rare intervals in modern life this favour has been actively exercised, and when such a situation arises, as it has notoriously of late years in Paris,

[3] *Art and Commerce*. London: Hogarth Press, 1926.

the enthusiasm of the snobbist has stirred to activity a crowd of speculative buyers who hope by spotting the winner in the field of aspiring talent to reap fabulous profits.

The artist, too, in so complex a world must be upheld by a religious conviction, an unwavering faith by which to steer his course among the devious currents of modern civilisation. Since he is in a small minority his creed will always tend to have a protestant tinge. He is a protestant against the materialism of Mr. Podsnap, against the pontifical authority of the high priests of Culture, and against the capricious interferences of Snobbism. His religion, too, is a very intimate personal affair, it compels him to the assertion, often with fanatical vehemence, of his private values. He is a member of no wide communion—may, indeed, shun all communion whatever, though more probably he links himself in a close alliance with the few who share his convictions.

It is to Paris of the mid-nineteenth century, from 1830 to 1870, that we must turn to study the heroic period of this religion, the epoch of its great saints and martyrs. There we see to what a pitch of ecstasy and devotion this faith could raise its votaries. It was the age when Daumier produced almost day by day, for some infinitesimal sum, masterpieces of tragic irony which made ministers tremble with rage and hate, and landed him in prison: it was the age when the Odéon was run by a director madly in love with poetry, who, backed by a troupe of famished but heroic actors, produced romantic plays one after another in the face of the outraged bourgeoisie and the frenzied enthusiasm of the Bohemians: it was the age when the fervour touched even the cafetiers and restaurant keepers, and a Mère Cadet would extend credit year after year, without a hint or a frown, to her penniless clients: it was the age when through the thousand accidents of open-air life in the streets and gardens of Paris the faithful, whether poets, actors, painters or musicians, discovered one another by almost invisible signs, and cemented life-long friendships on the strength of a chance word.[4]

It was an age when snobbism scarcely existed or had not as yet tendered its munificence to the genuine artist. He, indeed, had to rely entirely on the far slenderer aid which disinterested but passionate amateurs could afford him—and these, it must be remembered, are always the decisive factor in the highest kinds of artistic creation—and on the unstinting generosity with which the faithful helped one another out of their own poverty.

[4] *Vide* the story of Emile Deray in Theodore de Banville's "Mes Souvenirs."

And here we touch on a curious economic accident the importance of which as a determining condition of art production has never been properly emphasised. In modern life great works of art have generally been, and, I suspect, almost must be, produced in defiance of the tastes and predilections of society at large. The artist, therefore, except in those cases where he possesses inherited means, must be able to live and function on an extremely small sum. He must exist almost as sparrows do, by picking up the crumbs that fall from the rich man's table. That is to say, that Bohemian life, a life deprived of all superfluous and unnecessary elements, must not be too degrading, and must leave those who follow it some amenities, especially the possibility of meeting and exchanging their impressions and convictions. These conditions are fulfilled only where the standard of life in general is not too exacting. At first sight it may appear to make no difference whether the rule of life is, as in the United States, that salaries are high and prices and profits are also high, or, as in France, that salaries and prices are both low. But, in point of fact, one condition, the American, is fatal to the existence of a true Bohemia, and the other is propitious. In the case of America the sum necessary to support life is a large one, and though it can be earned with proportionate ease, it can only be earned by some work the value of which society can recognise at once. In the case of France it is, or certainly was in the nineteenth century, so small that it might be picked up by part-time work at any one of the smaller crafts of industrial design for which France is conspicuous.

The highly organised production on a grand scale of America, with its large wages and high profits, leaves far fewer of those interstices in the social system into which the artist can insert himself, than does a society based on a multiplicity of small and individual producers. Here, indeed, we touch on one of those small accidental factors in social life which may exercise a decisive influence on artistic production. What wonder, then, that periods of artistic creation, and importance are as hard to predict or account for as the weather itself! Hitherto we have not made anything like as strenuous an effort at estimating and calculating these forces and conditions, doubtless because societies always tend to regard their spiritual products as superfluities. And yet there is a certain irony in the fact that every civilisation is ultimately judged by what of spiritual value it has contributed to the human patrimony. It is only at each present moment that this appears to be of so little consequence as to be negligible by the governing class.

*No one has ever more incisively characterized the academic mentality,
or better dealt with the insipidities and hypocrisies of the Philistine
approach to art, then Haydon in the following passages.*

Benjamin Robert Haydon
Artists, Be Humble and Discreet

I find the artists most favoured by
the great are those of no education, or those who conceal what they
have. The love of power and superiority is not trod on if a man of
genius is ignorant when a gentleman is informed. "Great folks," said
Johnson, "don't like to have their mouths stopped." I believe it, and
how often have I had occasion to curse my better information when
my love of truth induced me to prove I knew more than a man of rank.

A man of rank came up to me and said, "Do you know, Mr. Haydon,
I think Titian's grounds were so and so." As long as I listened he
appeared placid; but this was putting a poker into a powder-barrel. I
exploded, and poured forth all I had obtained from experience and
reading. He looked grave—hummed—talked of the weather, and took
up his hat with a "Good morning." I can't think how Reynolds managed these things. Northcote says he always appeared ignorant. . . .

Genius is dependent on title for development—at least for employment. Because rank, at any rate, is entitled to civility, on the principle
of rank being a reward to the possessor or his ancestor for some personal qualification or heroic deed—of course centuries of possession
say something for conduct—and because whatever tends to obstruct
genius and deprive it of employment is pernicious to its display.
Painters should, therefore, not be talkers except with their brushes, or
writers except on their art; because the display of too much power
when others know something, is apt to excite envy and injure a
painter's development of his art. Men are content that you should
know more of painting than they do, but they don't like that you
should know as much of any other thing; because they feel if this man
can paint and yet be informed as well as we are in other matters, we
are nobody and we won't patronise him. But if this man knows nothing
out of his art, why we are somebody in something. We can spell and
he can't; we know French, and he does not; we read Homer, and he
knows nothing of him. In a word, we can talk at dinner and he must

be silent, except when we want to know a matter where it is no disgrace that he should know more than ourselves, on the same principle as we tolerate a tailor, a shoemaker, a carpenter, a butcher or a surgeon.

Therefore, oh ye artists who can spell, speak French and read Homer, never show your patrons they speak bad French, or read bad Greek, and spell carelessly; but listen to their French as if it was Racine's, to their Greek as if old Homer himself were spouting, and read their epistles as if they had orthography, grammar and common sense. Do this and you will drink their claret, adorn their rooms, ride their horses, visit their châteaux and eat their venison. But if, on the contrary, you answer the French not meant for you to understand, rectify their quotations which you are not supposed ever to have heard of, and discuss opinions only put forth for you to bow to, you will not eat their venison, you will not adorn their apartments, you will not ride their horses, you will not drink their claret, or visit their châteaux, at any rate more than once. And so, artists, be humble and discreet.

(Autobiography and Memoirs)

Art by Committee

The reason of these perpetual failures in matters of decoration in England, whether in architecture, sculpture, or painting, is, that the management is left to commissioners and committees, which is all very well when the subjects to be settled are commercial or political and every member knows something of what he is to discuss, but is perfectly ludicrous where Art is concerned and nobody but the professional man knows one iota about the matter.

Committees are composed generally of men of rank and station, who have little to do, while each has a crotchet of his own. Crotchet after crotchet is proposed, till some day, after endless discussion, on a slack attendance, with hardly a quorum, up gets a persevering member, proposes his own crotchet, which is carried by a majority of one out of five, and this is called the prevailing sense of the committee.

(Autobiography and Memoirs)

Westward the Course of Empire

Portraiture is always independent of art and has little or nothing to do with it. It is one of the staple manufactures of the Empire.

Wherever the British settle, wherever they colonise, they carry, and
will ever carry, trial by jury, horse-racing and portrait painting.

(Autobiography and Memoirs)

It Will Never Do in This Country![1]

How many follies, vices, and imbecilities are plausibly excused by
this plausible expression. You will find this expression on the tongue
of all those who from idleness, incompetency, or irresolution have
failed in literature, politics, morals, or Art. If an author has failed in
a Tragedy, "it will never do in this country," is the excuse. If a Military
Man has lost a battle instead of gaining it—"the English are not a
Military Nation." If an Artist knows nothing of the figure & is afraid
to expose his ignorance by venturing an attempt, the poor country
has the blame. If a painter prefers the immediate profits of portrait
painting to the more distant rewards of higher walks, if a patron likes
small pictures instead of large, because the meanness of his soul is
greater than the expansion of his mind, if a painter has turned picture
dealer, or sunk into a connoisseur,—in short whatever has been unsuccessfully attempted or not attempted at all, because of failure or of
cowardice, is attributed to the country and never to the follies and
weaknesses of those who have tried. You will find hundreds of historical
students affirm [with] the utmost enthusiasm that if the English went
as naked as the Greeks, if every face had a Grecian nose, if their colour
was brown instead of rosey, their eyes black instead of blue, if the
weather was not so cloudy or the winter not so cold, if we were all
catholics and the churches not so dark, they would have succeeded as
historical painters like other men—bless them! And do they suppose
that the minds who could be stopped by such difficulties are the minds
to be great in Art?—Weakness!—He that does not make the most of
his actual situation whatever the difficulties be, will make nothing of
any situation whatever be the facilities. Dictated to Bewick while my
eyes are ill.

(Diary, July 18, 1818)

The Royal Academy

The Royal Academy is the great head of the Corruption of the Art.
All the honors of the Art & State are showered on the Portrait painters,

[1] *Diary* excerpts here and elsewhere are from *The Diary of Benjamin Robert Haydon,*
Vols. I and II, ed. by Willard Bissell Pope. Cambridge: Harvard University Press, 1960.

and the Historical Painter is considered as a poor deluded enthusiast, who the Portrait Painters in their infinite condescension will not forget to admit as associate perhaps when their rival Parties cannot agree about an Election, and so pitch on him as a man of no consequence. This feeling of course is spread among their dependents, and every mushroom portrait painter in embryo, who has just power enough to disfigure the Apollo, or smudge away hands in shadow he cannot execute, walks about the Academy with his frog[ged] greatcoat, cuts his chalk with an air of importance, is often abstracted with visionary prospect of knighthood, that gleams afar [to] his inward eye, warms himself at the stove with the confidential ease of assured success, eats the bread he brought to rub out his defects, & lounges down the Strand, as spruce as a Bond Street hero. And shall these creatures, these gilded with Academical honors, like nauseous pills that the Public who are the Patients may not perceive their concealed filth, and shall these have the leading powers of the state and honors of the Art?

It is not against the Academy against which the press has lifted its powerful arm, but against these poor Creatures who like Caterpillars have crept into it. The Academy is an excellent Institution. But it is an Institution instead of serving the great cause for which it was founded, is perverted from its original intentions by Mr. Macgylp the Painter, Mr. Nigle the Portrait, & Mr. Tint the Drawing Master. Of course Mr. Macgylp is a member, of course he paints Mrs. Gull. Of course Mrs. Gull will be ill if the [picture] be not in view in the Roy. Academy. Of course Mr. Gull, Master Gull, and the three Miss Gulls & Mrs. Robert Todd & Mr. George Todd, Mr. Dawson, Master Wildman, and the four Miss Blackmans must go & see Mrs. Gull's portrait. Mr. Macgylp is then recommended to large city connections, paints the Lord Mayor, the Speaker of the House of Commons, the Lord Chancellor, and the King, gets a Knighthood, is President of the Royal Academy, sits between the Ministers & Royal family at the Dinner, gives the toasts with great loyalty, speaks bad French to the Foreign Ambassadors and worse English to the Nobility, takes a large house & keeps up a large establishment, dies & is buried in St. Paul's, and everybody talks of the great painter who perhaps never put two eyes in good drawing, or who when put in comparison with the lowest Italian of the Lombard School dwindles to annihilation. Mrs. Gull & Mr. Macgylp are now to be judged by those who have now no interest in telling untruths and neither Mrs. Robert Todd or the Miss Blackmans can now have any effect.

(*Diary*, May 21, 1817)

AN OUTRAGED PUBLIC CONFRONTS
MODERN ART

This uncomprehending explosion of rage is typical of the reaction which the first large show of post-impressionist art in England produced, not simply from the general public but from intellectuals as well.

Wilfred Scawen Blunt[1]

15th Nov. (1910)—To the Grafton Gallery to look at what are called the Post-Impressionist pictures sent over from Paris. The exhibition is either an extremely bad joke or a swindle. I am inclined to think the latter, for there is no trace of humour in it. Still less is there a trace of sense or skill or taste, good or bad, or art or cleverness. Nothing but that gross puerility which scrawls indecencies on the walls of a privy. The drawing is on the level of that of an untaught child of seven or eight years old, the sense of colour that of a tea-tray painter, the method that of a schoolboy who wipes his fingers on a slate after spitting on them . . .

from *My Diaries*

The famous Armory Show of 1913 was not America's first introduction to modern art; but what gave it an overwhelming impact was its bringing together for the first time in America of a large body of works that in their variety and richness of artistic achievement made it clear that the

1 W. S. Blunt (1840-1922), English traveler, diplomat, anti-imperialist, and liberal defender of minorities.

*modern movement in art was a mainstream and not an eddy. The fury
and incomprehension of the academic painters and critics are perfectly
expressed in the review by Kenyon Cox. The effect of the show on the
general public, shocked, bewildered, suspicious of a hoax, but at the
same time respectful, impressed, aware of freshness and force, is captured in the review by Theodore Roosevelt.*

Kenyon Cox

The "Modern" Spirit in Art: Some Reflections Inspired by the Recent International Exhibition[1]

It is proper to begin an account of
the extraordinary exhibition of modern art recently held in New York
with an acknowledgment that it is well such an exhibition should be
held and that, therefore, the thanks of the public are due to the gentlemen who got it together. We have heard a great deal about the Post-
Impressionists and the Cubists; we have read expositions of their ideas
and methods which have had a plausible sound in the absence of the
works to be explained; we have had some denunciation and ridicule,
some enthusiastic praise, and a great deal of half-frightened and wholly
puzzled effort to understand what, it was taken for granted, must have
some real significance; but we have not heretofore had an opportunity
of seeing the things themselves—the paintings and sculpture actually
produced by these men. Now the things are quite indescribable and
unbelievable. Neither the praises of their admirers, the ridicule of their
opponents, nor the soberest attempt at impartial description can give
any idea of them. No reproduction can approach them. They must
be seen to be believed possible, and therefore it is well that they should
have been seen. From this point of view my only regret is that the
Association of American Painters and Sculptors did not see fit to
include some representation of the Futurists in their exhibition, that
the whole thing might be done once for all. In a case of necessity one
may be willing to take a drastic emetic and may even humbly thank
the medical man for the efficacy of the dose. The more thorough it is the
less chance is there that it may have to be repeated.

Of course I cannot pretend to have approached the exhibition
entirely without prejudice. One cannot have studied and practised art

---

[1] From *Harper's Weekly,* March 15, 1913. Kenyon Cox (1856-1919) was a leading academic painter and critic of the pre-World War I period.

for forty years without the formation of some opinions—even of some convictions. But I remembered the condemnation of Corot and Millet by Gérôme and Cabanel; I remembered the natural conservatism of middle age; I took to heart the admonition of the preface to the catalogue, that "to be afraid of what is different or unfamiliar is to be afraid of life." I meant to make a genuine effort to sort out these people, to distinguish their different aims and doctrines, to take notes and to analyze, to treat them seriously if disapprovingly. I cannot do it. Nor can I laugh. This thing is not amusing; it is heartrending and sickening. I was quoted the other day as having said that the human race is rapidly approaching insanity. I never said it, but if I were convinced that this is really "modern Art" and that these men are representative of our time, I should be constrained to believe it.

In recollecting the appalling morning I spent in this place certain personalities do, however, define themselves and certain tendencies make themselves clear. It is no time for squeamishness or for standing upon "professional courtesy," and such persons as I may mention I shall treat quite frankly—in this respect, at least, I may follow their own example. Fortunately there is little necessity of dwelling upon the American part of the show. It contains some good work by artists who must wonder at the galley aboard which they find themselves, some work with real merit by men who have aided in the launching of the galley, and a great deal of bad work which, however, seldom reaches the depths of badness attainable by Frenchmen and Germans. But this work, good, bad, and indifferent, is either perfectly well known or is so paled by comparison that it needs no mention. Some of it is silly, but little of it is dangerous. There is one American, however, who must be spoken of because he has pushed the new doctrines to a conclusion in some respects more logical and complete than have any of the foreigners. In the wildest productions of Picabia or Picasso there is usually discernible, upon sufficiently painstaking investigation, some faint trace of the natural objects which are supposed to have inspired them; and even when this disappears the title remains to show that such objects have existed. It has remained for Mr. Marsden Hartley to take the final step and to arrange his lines and spots purely for their own sake, abandoning all pretense of representation or even of suggestions. He exhibits certain rectangles of paper covered with a maze of charcoal lines which are catalogued simply as Drawing No. 1, Drawing No. 2, etc.

This, I say, is the logical end, for the real meaning of this Cubist

movement is nothing else than the total destruction of the art of painting—that art of which the dictionary definition is "the art of representing, by means of figures and colors applied on a surface, objects
presented to the eye or to the imagination." Two years ago I wrote:
"We have reached the edge of the cliff and must turn back or fall
into the abyss." Deliberately and determinedly these men have stepped
over the edge. Now the total destruction of painting as a representative
art is a thing which a lover of painting could hardly envisage with
entire equanimity, yet one may admit that such a thing might take
place and yet an art remain that should have its own value. A Turkish
rug or a tile from the Alhambra is nearly without representative
purpose, but it has intrinsic beauty and some conceivable human use.
The important question is what it is proposed to substitute for this
art of painting which the world has cherished since there were men
definitely differentiated from beasts. They have abolished the representation of nature and all forms of recognized and traditional decoration; what will they give us instead? And here is the difference between
Mr. Hartley and his Parisian brothers. His "drawings" are purely
nugatory. If one finds it impossible to imagine the kind of human being
that could take any pleasure in them one is free to admit that there is
nothing especially disgusting about them. But one cannot say as much
for the works of the Frenchmen. In some strange way they have made
their work revolting and defiling. To have looked at it is to have
passed through a pathological museum where the layman has no right
to go. One feels that one has seen not an exhibition, but an exposure.

Of course the work of these artistic anarchists formed only a part
of the exhibition. A serious attempt was made to get together a representative showing of the artists whom they consider their forerunners,
and a number of the smaller galleries contained what might be considered a series of illustrations of Meier-Graefe. A good many critics
who find the latest manifestations of the "modern" spirit quite intolerable are yet able to maintain a complacent satisfaction in these earlier
exemplifications of it and even, by contrast, to increase their pleasure
in work which seems relatively sane and wholesome. I wish I could
feel, as they do, that there is a sudden dislocation with the appearance
of Matisse and that everything before him falls naturally into its place
as a continuation of the great tradition. I wish I were not forced to see
that the easy slope to Avernus began as far back as the sixties of the
last century. The lack of discipline and the exaltation of the individual
have been the destructive forces of modern art, and they began their

work long ago. For a time the persistence of earlier ideals and the possession by the revolutionaries of the very training which they attacked as unnecessary saved the art from entire dissolution. Now all discipline has disappeared, all training is proclaimed useless, and individualism has reached the pitch of sheer insanity or triumphant charlatanism.

The decadence did not begin with Ingres and Delacroix and Corot, though the ultras would fain utilize the glory of these masters as a covering for their own nakedness. It seems to me clear that it did begin with Manet and Whistler. It is impossible not to sympathize with the revolt against an unintelligent literalism which these men began. It is equally impossible not to see that they suffered from the lack of training and from the lack of a normal relation to their public, and that, in spite of great beauties, their work is ineffectual and fragmentary. There was little of it here, and that not of the best, but there was enough of it, as there was of the more purely Impressionist work of Monet and Renoir and the rest, to show its relation to the *degringolade* which followed. The Impressionists denied the necessity of any knowledge of form or structure and decried the acquisition of such knowledge. They preached "the innocence of the eye." It was not the business of an artist to know what anything is like or how it is made—his affair was only how it looks. Neither had he any right to compose or select, though, as a matter of fact, they could not help composing and selecting. The colored spot and the vibration of light—these were the sole objects of study. Quite at the end of the Impressionist movement came Seurat, the inventor of a new theory and a new technique which was to revolutionize painting. Two little pictures here, quite dingy and colorless and faded into unimportance, marked the failure of Pointillism. Then came Henri Rousseau, Maurice Denis, Odillon Redon, Mathew Maris, and the more interesting group especially known as Post-Impressionists, Cézanne, Van Gogh, and Gauguin. With these men it is not knowledge of form alone that is unnecessary, but knowledge of any kind. The artist is no longer to occupy himself with the problem of how things look—he is interested only in how he feels about things. Impressionism is too scientific and its discipline too rigid. Even the study of light hampers the effort of self-expression, and is to be thrown away, as impressionism had thrown away the study of form.

One of the oddest of them all is Rousseau, a revolutionist *sans le savoir.* He seems to have been one of those harmless amateurs who continue sending perfectly hopeless pictures before the juries of exhibitions without ever getting them exhibited. He lived a long and obscure life, and died, and then some one discovered that because he had obviously no training and no knowledge he must have had personality. For a generation which demands naïveté and spontaneity above all other qualities he is a valuable acquisition, for his naïveté is the real thing. His work is perfectly innocent and entirely inept and his pictures resemble the productions, on a larger scale than usual, of a child of seven. There is no one else like him. Maurice Denis is an amiable caricature of Puvis de Chavannes, not without a certain charm, but exaggerating the weaknesses of his model and reducing the method to the verge of absurdity. Odillon Redon is a dreamer in lines as Maris is a dreamer in colors. Both are poets if you will, but neither is a draughtsman or a painter. Their absorption in the subjective vision has prevented their acquiring a sound and definite method of expression.

Cézanne is by far the most interesting as he is the most extravagantly praised of the modernists. I believe him to have been a perfectly sincere searcher, and I admit in him some of the elements of genius. He seems to have had a sense of essential character in portraiture, just as he had a sense of the essential squareness of houses and the essential roundness of apples. He seems always to have aimed at the great things. But he seems to me absolutely without talent and absolutely cut off from tradition. He could not learn to paint as others did, and he spent his life in the hopeless attempt to create a new art of painting for himself. Fumblingly and partially he can express himself to the few—he will never have anything for the many. If Cézanne is a builder, Gauguin is a decorator, but a decorator tainted with insanity. His arrangements of line are sometimes noble and graceful, but the things he represents are often hideous. His color is sometimes beautiful, but it is always unnecessarily false and often unpleasantly morbid. "The Spirit of Evil" haunts more of his pictures than the one so named. In the work of Van Gogh which was shown at the armory I can find little either of the great qualities he is said to have possessed or of the madness that finally overcame him. All I can be sure of is an experiment in impressionistic technique by a painter too unskilled to give quality to an evenly laid coat of pigment.

All these men were, I think, honest enough; unbalanced, undisciplined, and self-absorbed, but not self-glorifiers. I cannot think the same of the two I have next to name. How far mental disease mingles with inordinate self-esteem and immoderate self-exploitation in the later work of Rodin it is difficult to say. Some of his later sculpture and almost all of his drawings are the more lamentable in that they mark the ruin of a great talent. As to Matisse I am no longer in doubt; it is not madness that stares at you from his canvases, but leering effrontery.

Believing as I do, that there are still commandments in art as in morals, and still laws in art as in physics, I have no fear that this kind of art will prevail, or even that it can long endure. But it may do a good deal of harm while it lasts. It may dazzle the young students of art with the prospect of an easily attained notoriety which they cannot distinguish from fame, and prevent their acquiring any serious training during the years when, if ever, such training must be acquired; it may so debauch criticism that it shall lose what little authority or usefulness it still retains; it may corrupt public taste and stimulate an appetite for excitement that is as dangerous as the appetite for any other poisonous drug; finally, it may juggle out of the pockets of the gullible a few dollars that will be far more wasted than if they were thrown into the sea. To the critics it is useless to speak. How shall we instruct our self-appointed instructors? The students and the public may possibly listen, and for them I have a few words of earnest advice.

To the student I would say: Distrust all short cuts to art or to glory. No work worth doing was ever done without long preparation and continuous endeavor. The success that is attained in a month will be forgotten in a year. To the public I would say: Do not allow yourselves to be blinded by the sophistries of the foolish dupes or the self-interested exploiters of all this charlatanry. Remember that it is for you that art is created, and judge honestly for yourselves whether this which calls itself art is useful to you or to the world. You are not infallible, but your instincts are right in the main, and you are, after all, the final judges. If your stomach revolts against this rubbish it is because it is not fit for human food. Let no man persuade you to stuff yourselves with it.

Theodore Roosevelt

A Layman's Views of an Art Exhibition[1]

The recent "International Exhibition of Modern Art" in New York was really noteworthy. Messrs. Davies, Kuhn, Gregg, and their fellow-members of the Association of

[1] From *The Outlook*, March 22, 1913. Theodore Roosevelt (1858-1919), twenty-sixth President of the United States, was throughout his life intensely interested in the arts. At this period, he was a regular writer for *The Outlook*.

American Painters and Sculptors have done a work of very real value in securing such an exhibition of the works of both foreign and native painters and sculptors. Primarily their purpose was to give the public a chance to see what has recently been going on abroad. No similar collection of the works of European "Moderns" has ever been exhibited in this country. The exhibitors are quite right as to the need of showing to our people in this manner the art forces which of late have been at work in Europe, forces which cannot be ignored.

This does not mean that I in the least accept the view that these men take of the European extremists whose pictures are here exhibited. It is true, as the champions of these extremists say, that there can be no life without change, no development without change, and that to be afraid of what is different or unfamiliar is to be afraid of life. It is no less true, however, that change may mean death and not life, and retrogression instead of development. Probably we err in treating most of these pictures seriously. It is likely that many of them represent in the painters the astute appreciation of the power to make folly lucrative which the late P. T. Barnum showed with his faked mermaid; and now and then one of this kind with enough money will buy a Cubist picture, or a picture of a misshapen nude woman, repellant from every standpoint.

In some ways it is the work of the American painters and sculptors which is of most interest in this collection, and a glance at this work must convince anyone of the real good that is coming out of the new movements, fantastic though many of the developments of these new movements are. There was one note entirely absent from the exhibition, and that was the note of the commonplace. There was not a touch of simpering, self-satisfied conventionality anywhere in the exhibition. Any sculptor or painter who had in him something to express and the power of expressing it found the field open to him. He did not have to be afraid because his work was not along ordinary lines. There was no stunting or dwarfing, no requirement that a man whose gift lay in new directions should measure up or down to stereotyped and fossilized standards.

For all this there can be only hearty praise. But this does not in the least mean that the extremists whose paintings and pictures were represented are entitled to any praise, save, perhaps, that they have helped to break fetters. Probably in any reform movement, any progressive movement, in any field of life, the penalty for avoiding the commonplace is a liability to extravagance. It is vitally necessary to move forward and to shake off the dead hand, often the fossilized dead hand, of the reactionaries; and yet we have to face the fact that there is apt to be a lunatic fringe among the votaries of any forward movement. In this recent art exhibition the lunatic fringe was fully in evidence, especially in the rooms devoted to the Cubists and the Futurists, or Near-Impressionists. I am not entirely certain which of the two latter terms should be used in connection with some of the various pictures and representations of plastic art—and, frankly, it is not of the least consequence. The Cubists are entitled to the serious attention of all who find enjoyment in the colored puzzle pictures of the Sunday newspapers. Of course there is no reason for choosing the cube as a symbol, except that it is probably less fitted than any other mathematical expression for any but the most formal decorative art. There is no reason why people should not call themselves Cubists, or Octagonists, Parallelopipedonists, or Knights of the Isosceles Triangle, or Brothers of the Cosine, if they so desire; as expressing anything serious and permanent, one term is as fatuous as another. Take the picture which for some reason is called *A naked man going down stairs*. There is in my bathroom a really good Navajo rug which, on any proper interpretation of the Cubist theory, is a far more satisfactory and decorative picture. Now if, for some inscrutable reason, it suited somebody to call this rug a picture of, say, *A well-dressed man going up a ladder,* the name would fit the facts just about as well as in the case of the Cubist picture of the *Naked man going down stairs.* From the standpoint of terminology each name would have whatever merit inheres in a rather cheap straining after effect; and from the standpoint of decorative value, of sincerity, and of artistic merit, the Navajo rug is infinitely ahead of the picture.

As for many of the human figures in the pictures of the Futurists, they show that the school would be better entitled to the name of the "Past-ists." I was interested to find that a man of scientific attainments who had likewise looked at the pictures had been struck, as I was, by their resemblance to the later work of the paleolithic artists of the French and Spanish caves. There are interesting samples of the strivings for the representation of the human form among artists of many different countries and times, all in the same stage of paleolithic culture, to be found in a recent number of the "Revue d'Ethnographie." The paleolithic artist was able to portray the bison, the mammoth, the reindeer, and the horse with spirit and success, while he still stumbled painfully in the effort to portray man. This stumbling effort in his case

NUDE DESCENDING A STAIRCASE—MARCEL DUCHAMP (*Philadelphia Museum of Art,*
Arensberg Collection)

represented progress, and he was entitled to great credit for it. Forty thousand years later, when entered into artificially and deliberately, it represents only a smirking pose of retrogression, and is not praise-worthy. So with much of the sculpture. A family group of precisely the merit that inheres in a structure made of the wooden blocks in a nursery is not entitled to be reproduced in marble. Admirers speak of the kneeling female figure by Lehmbruck—I use "female" advisedly, for although obviously mammalian it is not especially human—as "full of lyric grace," as "tremendously sincere," and "of a jewel-like precious-ness." I am not competent to say whether these words themselves represent sincerity or merely a conventional jargon; it is just as easy to be conventional about the fantastic as about the commonplace. In any event one might as well speak of the "lyric grace" of a praying mantis, which adopts much the same attitude; and why a deformed pelvis should be called "sincere," or a tibia of giraffe-like length "pre-cious," is a question of pathological rather than artistic significance. This figure and the absurd portrait head of some young lady have the merit that inheres in extravagant caricature. It is a merit, but it is not a high merit. It entitles these pieces to stand in sculpture where nonsense rhymes stand in literature and the sketches of Aubrey Beards-ley in pictorial art. These modern sculptured caricatures in no way approach the gargoyles of Gothic cathedrals, probably because the modern artists are too self-conscious and make themselves ridiculous by pretentiousness. The makers of the gargoyles knew very well that the gargoyles did not represent what was most important in the Gothic cathedrals. They stood for just a little point of grotesque reaction against, and relief from, the tremendous elemental vastness and gran-deur of the Houses of God. They were imps, sinister and comic, grim and yet futile, and they fitted admirably into the framework of the theology that found its expression in the towering and wonderful piles which they ornamented.

Very little of the work of the extremists among the European "mod-erns" seems to be good in and for itself; nevertheless it has certainly helped any number of American artists to do work that is original and serious; and this not only in painting but in sculpture. I wish the exhibition had contained some of the work of the late Marcius Symonds; very few people knew or cared for it while he lived; but not since Turner has there been another man on whose canvas glowed so much of that unearthly "light that never was on land or sea." But the exhibition contained so much of extraordinary merit that it is ungrateful even to mention an omission. To name the pictures one would like to possess—and the bronzes and tanagras and plasters—would mean to make a catalogue of indefinite length. One of the most striking pictures was the "Terminal Yards"—the seeing eye was there, and the cunning hand. I should like to mention all the pictures of the President of the Association, Arthur B. Davies. As first-class decorative work of an entirely new type, the very unexpected pictures of Sheriff Bob Chanler have a merit all their own. The "Arizona Desert," the "Canadian Night," the group of girls on the roof of a New York tenement house, the studies in the Bronx Zoo, the "Heracles," the studies for the Utah monument, the little group called "Gossip" which has something of the quality of the famous Fifteenth Idyl of Theocritus, the "Pelf," with its grim suggestiveness—these, and a hundred others, are worthy of study, each of them; I am naming at random those which at the moment I happen to recall. I am not speaking of the acknowledged masters, of Whistler, Puvis de Chavannes, Monet; nor of John's children; nor of Cézanne's old woman with a rosary; nor of Redon's marvelous color pieces—a worthy critic should speak of these. All I am trying to do is to point out why a layman is grateful to those who arranged this exhibition.

I believe that the man who painted this picture is not an imbecile, but the man who paid such a price for it is surely one.

> Edgar Degas—*said at a time late in his life when one of his pictures was resold for a fantastic price.*

They [the jury of the Salon] have rejected my picture on whose sale I was legitimately counting, the picture which had already been recommended to likely buyers who had promised to acquire it at the exhibition, if it appeared to them to merit the high praise which had been made of it to them . . . A series of articles was all ready, by influential critics, to brew for me a success at the Salon, and here these ruffians, these daubers with pontifical positions, of which the jury has been composed, make me lose the fruits of that campaign!

> Marcellin Desboutin, April 17, 1874
> (quoted in John Rewald, *History of Impressionism,* p. 68)

[Van Gogh] was essentially a popular painter, who missed popularity because the populace of his time was not ready to see as pictures what was not finished.

> Leo Stein, *Appreciation*

ART AND SOCIETY

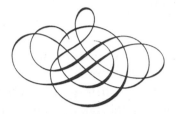

The excerpts from Delacroix's Journal[1] *printed in this collection show a personality of great dignity and rectitude, increasingly withdrawn from the world and increasingly finding solace only in his own work and the love of art; and a mind, subtle, curious, committed, returning again and again to the basic concerns of art.*

Eugène Delacroix
The Aging Artist[1]

Saw Mlle. Rachel in *Cinna* [Corneille's tragedy]. Beauvallet is certainly not bad as Augustus, especially at the end. There is a man who is making progress; and so he is getting wrinkled, and probably white-haired, something that the wig of Augustus prevented my judging.

Consider this: the actor who, according to common report, has been bad or mediocre all his life, or at least throughout his youth—the age of strength and feeling—now becomes passable or excellent when he no longer has teeth or breath; and shall the same not be true in the other art? Do I not write better and with more facility than in the past? Scarcely do I take up my pen, when ideas crowd in and fill my brain as in the past, and not only that, but what I formerly found very difficult—close relationship and measure—come to me naturally, and at the very time that I conceive what I have to say.

And in painting, does not the same thing occur? Whence does it

---

1 From *The Journal of Eugène Delacroix*, transl. from the French by Walter Pach. New York: Crown Publishers, Inc., 1948.

44

come that nowadays I do not know a single instant of boredom when I have the brush in my hand, and that I feel that, if only my strength were sufficient, I should not stop painting save to eat and sleep? I remember that in the past, in that so-called age of verve and of the strength of the imagination, with my lack of experience in all those fine qualities, I was halted at every step, and frequently disgusted. It is a pitiful derision of nature that she should place us in the situation that age prepares for us. One's maturity is complete, and the imagination as fresh, as active as ever, especially because of the silence of mad and impetuous passion, which age carries away; but strength is lacking, the senses are worn down and demand repose more than movement. And yet with all these drawbacks what a consolation it is that comes from work! How glad I am no longer to be forced to find my happiness where I had to search for it in the past! From what savage tyranny have I not been snatched by this weakening of the body? What used to preoccupy me the least was my painting. And so one must do what one can; if nature rejects work for more than a certain number of moments, one must not do her violence, but count oneself happy over the things which she still has for us; we must not be so attached to the quest for praise—which is nothing but wind: we must get our enjoyment from the work itself and from the delightful hours that follow it, feeling to the full that this repose has been paid for with that salutary fatigue which maintains the health of the soul. And that reacts on the health of the body; it prevents the rust of the years from clogging the sentiments which are noble.

Journal, October 12, 1852

This Enchanting Work

I have begun this year by pursuing my work at the church just as usual; I am paying my visits only by card, for that does not disturb me at all, and I have been at work all day; what a happy life! What a celestial compensation for my isolated state, as they call it! Brothers, parents, relatives of every kind and friends living together quarrel and detest each other more or less, without saying a word that is free from deceit. Painting harasses me and torments me, indeed in a thousand ways, like the most exacting mistress; for the last four months, I have been fleeing at daybreak and I hasten to this enchanting work as to the feet of the most cherished mistress; what had appeared easy, from a distance, now offers to me horrible and incessant difficulties. But how does it happen that this eternal combat, instead of breaking me down, lifts me up, and instead of discouraging me, consoles me and fills up my time so well, what I have left of it? A happy compensation for the things that the good years of youth have carried away with them: a noble use for the moments of my old age which is besieging me from a thousand directions, but which still leaves me the strength to surmount bodily suffering and the ills of the soul!

Journal, January 1, 1861

Three Reflections on Genius

1.

At Leblond's. Interesting discussion about genius and unusual men. Dimier thought that great passions were the source of genius. I think that it is imagination alone, or better still, what amounts to the same thing, that delicacy of the organs that makes one see what others do not see, and which makes one see in a different way. I was saying that even great passions joined to imagination lead most often to disorder in the mind, etc. Dufresne said a very true thing: what made a man unusual was, fundamentally, a way utterly peculiar to himself of seeing things. He applied it to the great captains, etc., and finally to the great minds of all sorts. So, there are no rules for great souls: rules are only for people who have merely the talent that can be acquired. The proof is that they do not transmit this faculty. He was saying: "How much reflection is needed to create a beautiful, expressive head, a hundred times more than for a problem, and yet at bottom, the matter is merely one of instinct, for it cannot explain what brings it about." I note now that my mind is never more excited to create than when it sees a mediocre version of a subject that is suitable to me.

Journal, April 27, 1824

2.

What makes men of genius, or rather, what they make, is not new ideas, it is that idea—possessing them—that what has been said has still not been said enough.
Journal, May 15, 1824

3.

The gift of inventing powerfully, which is genius.

Journal, October 22, 1860

*This essay is not only the most important statement of Morris' aesthetic
philosophy. It is also the best expression in English writing of the doctrine that art and society are inextricably connected, and that the health
of the one involves the health of the other.*

William Morris
The Aims of Art[1]

In considering the Aims of Art, that
is, why men toilsomely cherish and practise Art, I find myself compelled
to generalize from the only specimen of humanity of which I know
anything; to wit, myself. Now, when I think of what it is that I desire,
I find that I can give it no other name than happiness. I want to be
happy while I live; for as for death, I find that, never having experienced it, I have no conception of what it means, and so cannot even
bring my mind to bear upon it. I know what it is to live; I cannot
even guess what it is to be dead. Well, then, I want to be happy, and
even sometimes, say generally, to be merry; and I find it difficult to
believe that that is not the universal desire: so that, whatever tends
towards that end I cherish with all my best endeavour. Now, when I
consider my life further, I find out, or seem to, that it is under the
influence of two dominating moods, which for lack of better words
I must call the mood of energy and the mood of idleness: these two
moods are now one, now the other, always crying out in me to be
satisfied. When the mood of energy is upon me, I must be doing
something, or I become mopish and unhappy; when the mood of idleness is on me, I find it hard indeed if I cannot rest and let my mind
wander over the various pictures, pleasant or terrible, which my own
experience or my communing with the thoughts of other men, dead or
alive, have fashioned in it; and if circumstances will not allow me to
cultivate this mood of idleness, I find I must at the best pass through
a period of pain till I can manage to stimulate my mood of energy
to take its place and make me happy again. And if I have no means
wherewith to rouse up that mood of energy to do its duty in making me
happy, and I have to toil while the idle mood is upon me, then am I
unhappy indeed, and almost wish myself dead, though I do not know
what that means.

Furthermore, I find that while in the mood of idleness memory

[1] From *Signs of Change,* by William Morris. London: Longmans, Green and Co., 1903.

amuses me, in the mood of energy hope cheers me; which hope is sometimes big and serious, and sometimes trivial, but that without it there is no happy energy. Again, I find that while I can sometimes satisfy this mood by merely exercising it in work that has no result beyond the passing hour—in play, in short—yet that it presently wearies of that and gets languid, the hope therein being too trivial, and sometimes even scarcely real; and that on the whole, to satisfy my master the mood, I must either be making something or making believe to make it.

Well, I believe that all men's lives are compounded of these two moods in various proportions, and that this explains why they have always, with more or less of toil, cherished and practised art.

Why should they have touched it else, and so added to the labour which they could not choose but do in order to live? It must have been done for their pleasure, since it has only been in very elaborate civilizations that a man could get other men to keep him alive merely to produce works of art, whereas all men that have left any signs of their existence behind them have practised art.

I suppose, indeed, that nobody will be inclined to deny that the end proposed by a work of art is always to please the person whose senses are to be made conscious of it. It was done *for* some one who was to be made happier by it; his idle or restful mood was to be amused by it, so that the vacancy which is the besetting evil of that mood might give place to pleased contemplation, dreaming, or what you will; and by this means he would not so soon be driven into his workful or energetic mood: he would have more enjoyment, and better.

The restraining of restlessness, therefore, is clearly one of the essential aims of art, and few things could add to the pleasure of life more than this. There are, to my knowledge, gifted people now alive who have no other vice than this of restlessness, and seemingly no other curse in their lives to make them unhappy: but that is enough; it is "the little rift within the lute." Restlessness makes them hapless men and bad citizens.

But granting, as I suppose you all will do, that this is a most important function for art to fulfil, the question next comes, at what price do we obtain it? I have admitted that the practice of art has added to the labour of mankind, though I believe in the long run it will not do so; but in adding to the labour of man has it added, so far, to his pain? There always have been people who would at once say yes to that question; so that there have been and are two sets of people who dislike and contemn art as an embarrassing folly. Besides the pious ascetics, who look upon it as a worldly entanglement which prevents men from keeping their minds fixed on the chances of their individual happiness or misery in the next world; who, in short, hate art, because they think that it adds to man's earthly happiness—besides these, there are also people who, looking on the struggle of life from the most reasonable point that they know of, contemn the arts because they think that they add to man's slavery by increasing the sum of his painful labour: if this were the case, it would still, to my mind, be a question whether it might not be worth the while to endure the extra pain of labour for the sake of the extra pleasure added to rest; assuming, for the present, equality of condition among men. But it seems to me that it is not the case that the practice of art adds to painful labour; nay more, I believe that, if it did, art would never have arisen at all, would certainly not be discernible, as it is, among peoples in whom only the germs of civilization exist. In other words, I believe that art cannot be the result of external compulsion; the labour which goes to produce it is voluntary, and partly undertaken for the sake of the labour itself, partly for the sake of the hope of producing something which, when done, shall give pleasure to the user of it. Or, again, this extra labour, when it *is* extra, is undertaken with the aim of satisfying that mood of energy by employing it to produce something worth doing, and which, therefore, will keep before the worker a lively hope while he is working; and also by giving it work to do in which there is absolute immediate pleasure. Perhaps it is difficult to explain to the non-artistic capacity that this definite sensuous pleasure is always present in the handiwork of the deft workman when he is working successfully, and that it increases in proportion to the freedom and individuality of the work. Also you must understand that this production of art, and consequent pleasure in work, is not confined to the production of matters which are works of art only, like pictures, statues, and so forth, but has been and should be a part of all labour in some form or other: so only will the claims of the mood of energy be satisfied.

Therefore the Aim of Art is to increase the happiness of men, by giving them beauty and interest of incident to amuse their leisure, and prevent them wearying even of rest, and by giving them hope and bodily pleasure in their work; or, shortly, to make man's work happy and his rest fruitful. Consequently, genuine art is an unmixed blessing to the race of man.

But as the word "genuine" is a large qualification, I must ask leave to attempt to draw some practical conclusions from this assertion of the

Aims of Art, which will, I suppose, or indeed hope, lead us into some controversy on the subject; because it is futile indeed to expect anyone to speak about art, except in the most superficial way, without encountering those social problems which all serious men are thinking of; since art is and must be, either in its abundance or its barrenness, in its sincerity or its hollowness, the expression of the society amongst which it exists.

First, then, it is clear to me that, at the present time, those who look widest at things and deepest into them are quite dissatisfied with the present state of the arts, as they are also with the present condition of society. This I say in the teeth of the supposed revivification of art which has taken place of late years: in fact, that very excitement about the arts amongst a part of the cultivated people of to-day does but show on how firm a basis the dissatisfaction above mentioned rests. Forty years ago there was much less talk about art, much less practice of it, than there is now; and that is specially true of the architectural arts, which I shall mostly have to speak about now. People have consciously striven to raise the dead in art since that time, and with some superficial success. Nevertheless, in spite of this conscious effort, I must tell you that England, to a person who can feel and understand beauty, was a less grievous place to live in then than it is now; and we who feel what art means know well, though we do not often dare to say so, that forty years hence it will be a more grievous place to us than it is now if we still follow up the road we are on. Less than forty years ago—about thirty—I first saw the city of Rouen, then still in its outward aspect a piece of the Middle Ages: no words can tell you how its mingled beauty, history, and romance took hold on me; I can only say that, looking back on my past life, I find it was the greatest pleasure I have ever had: and now it is a pleasure which no one can ever have again: it is lost to the world for ever. At that time I was an undergraduate of Oxford. Though not so astounding, so romantic, or at first sight so mediæval as the Norman city, Oxford in those days still kept a great deal of its earlier loveliness: and the memory of its grey streets as they then were has been an abiding influence and pleasure in my life, and would be greater still if I could only forget what they are now—a matter of far more importance than the so-called learning of the place could have been to me in any case, but which, as it was, no one tried to teach me, and I did not try to learn. Since then the guardians of this beauty and romance so fertile of education, though professedly engaged in "the higher education" (as the futile system of compromises which they follow is nicknamed), have ignored it utterly, have made its preservation give way to the pressure of commercial exigencies, and are determined apparently to destroy it altogether. There is another pleasure for the world gone down the wind; here, again, the beauty and romance have been uselessly, causelessly, most foolishly thrown away.

These two cases are given simply because they have been fixed in my mind; they are but types of what is going on everywhere throughout civilization: the world is everywhere growing uglier and more commonplace, in spite of the conscious and very strenuous efforts of a small group of people towards the revival of art, which are so obviously out of joint with the tendency of the age that, while the uncultivated have not even heard of them, the mass of the cultivated look upon them as a joke, and even that they are now beginning to get tired of.

Now, if it be true, as I have asserted, that genuine art is an unmixed blessing to the world, this is a serious matter; for at first sight it seems to show that there will soon be no art at all in the world, which will thus lose an unmixed blessing; it can ill afford to do that, I think.

For art, if it has to die, has worn itself out, and its aim will be a thing forgotten; and its aim was to make work happy and rest fruitful. Is all work to be unhappy, all rest unfruitful, then? Indeed, if art is to perish, that will be the case, unless something is to take its place—something at present unnamed, undreamed of.

I do not think that anything will take the place of art; not that I doubt the ingenuity of man, which seems to be boundless in the direction of making himself unhappy, but because I believe the springs of art in the human mind to be deathless, and also because it seems to me easy to see the causes of the present obliteration of the arts.

For we civilized people have not given them up consciously, or of our free will; we have been *forced* to give them up. Perhaps I can illustrate that by the detail of the application of machinery to the production of things in which artistic form of some sort is possible. Why does a reasonable man use a machine? Surely to save his labour. There are some things which a machine can do as well as a man's hand, *plus* a tool, can do them. He need not, for instance, grind his corn in a hand-quern; a little trickle of water, a wheel, and a few simple contrivances will do it all perfectly well, and leave him free to smoke his pipe and think, or to carve the handle of his knife. That, so far, is unmixed gain in the use of a machine—always, mind you, supposing equality of condition among men; no art is lost, leisure or time for more pleasurable work is gained. Perhaps a perfectly reasonable and free man would stop there in his dealings with machinery; but such reason and freedom are too much to expect, so let us follow our machine-inventor a step farther. He has to weave plain cloth, and finds doing so dullish on the one hand, and on the other that a power-loom will weave the cloth nearly as well as a hand-loom: so, in order to gain more leisure or time for more pleasurable work, he uses a power-loom, and foregoes the small advantage of the little extra art in the cloth. But so doing, as far as the art is concerned, he has not got a pure gain; he has made a bargain between art and labour, and got a makeshift as a consequence. I do not say that he may not be right in so doing, but that he has lost as well as gained. Now, this is as far as a man who values art and is reasonable would go in the matter of machinery *as long as he was free*—that is, was not *forced* to work for another man's profit; so long as he was living in a society *that had accepted equality of condition.* Carry the machine used for art a step farther, and he becomes an unreasonable man, if he values art and is free. To avoid misunderstanding, I must say that I am thinking of the modern machine, which is as it were alive, and to which the man is auxiliary, and not of the old machine, the improved tool, which is auxiliary to the man, and only works as long as his hand is thinking; though I will remark, that even this elementary form of machine has to be dropped when we come to the higher and more intricate forms of art. Well, as to the machine proper used for art, when it gets to the stage above dealing with a necessary production that has accidentally some beauty about it, a reasonable man with a feeling for art will only use it when he is *forced* to. If he thinks he would like ornament, for instance, and knows that the machine cannot do it properly, and does not care to spend the time to do it properly, why should he do it at all? He will not diminish his leisure for the sake of making something he does not want unless some man or band of men force him to it; so he will either go without the ornament, or sacrifice some of his leisure to have it genuine. There will be a sign that he wants it very much, and that it will be worth his trouble: in which case, again, his labour on it will not be mere trouble, but will interest and please him by satisfying the needs of his mood of energy.

This, I say, is how a reasonable man would act if he were free from man's compulsion; not being free, he acts very differently. He has long passed the stage at which machines are only used for doing work repulsive to an average man, or for doing what could be as well done by a machine as a man, and he instinctively expects a machine to be invented whenever any product of industry becomes sought after. He is the slave to machinery; the new machine *must* be invented, and when invented he *must*—I will not say use it, but be used by it, whether he likes it or not.

But why is he the slave to machinery? Because he is the slave to the system for whose existence the invention of machinery was necessary.

And now I must drop, or rather have dropped, the assumption of the equality of condition, and remind you that, though in a sense we are all the slaves of machinery, yet that some men are so directly without any metaphor at all, and that these are just those on whom the great body of the arts depends—the workmen. It is necessary for the system which keeps them in their position as an inferior class that they should either be themselves machines or be the servants to machines, in no case having any interest in the work which they turn out. To their employers they are, so far as they are workmen, a part of the machinery of the workshop or the factory; to themselves they are proletarians, human beings working to live that they may live to work: their part of craftsmen, of makers of things by their own free will, is played out.

At the risk of being accused of sentimentality, I will say that since this is so, since the work which produces the things that should be matters of art is but a burden and a slavery, I exult in this at least, that it cannot produce art; that all it can do lies between stark utilitarianism and idiotic sham.

Or indeed is that merely sentimental? Rather, I think, we who have learned to see the connection between industrial slavery and the degradation of the arts have learned also to hope for a future for those arts; since the day will certainly come when men will shake off the yoke, and refuse to accept the mere artificial compulsion of the gambling market to waste their lives in ceaseless and hopeless toil; and when it does come, their instincts for beauty and imagination set free along with them, will produce such art as they need; and who can say that it will not as far surpass the art of past ages as that does the poor relics of it left us by the age of commerce?

A word or two on an objection which has often been made to me when I have been talking on this subject. It may be said, and is often, You regret the art of the Middle Ages (as indeed I do), but those who produced it were not free; they were serfs, or gild-craftsmen surrounded by brazen walls of trade restrictions; they had no political rights, and were exploited by their masters, the noble caste, most grievously. Well, I quite admit that the oppression and violence of the Middle Ages had its effect on the art of those days, its shortcomings are traceable to them; they repressed art in certain directions, I do not doubt that; and for that reason I say, that when we shake off the present oppression as we shook off the old, we may expect the art of the days of real freedom to rise above that of those old violent days. But I do say that it was possible then to have social, organic, hopeful progressive art; whereas now such poor scraps of it as are left are the result of individual and wasteful struggle, are retrospective and pessimistic. And this hopeful art was possible amidst all the oppression of those days, because the instruments of that oppression were grossly obvious, and were external to the work of the craftsman. They were laws and customs obviously intended to rob him, and open violence of the highway-robbery kind. In short, industrial production was not the instrument used for robbing the "lower classes;" it is now the main instrument used in that honourable profession. The mediæval craftsman was free in his work, therefore he made it as amusing to himself as he could; and it was his pleasure and not his pain that made all things beautiful that were made, and lavished treasures of human hope and thought on everything that man made, from a cathedral to a porridge-pot. Come, let us put it in the way least respectful to the mediæval craftsman, most polite to the modern "hand:" the poor devil of the fourteenth century, his work was of so little value that he was allowed to waste it by the hour in pleasing himself—and others; but our highly-strung mechanic, his minutes are too rich with the burden of perpetual profit for him to be allowed to waste one of them on art; the present system will not allow him—cannot allow him—to produce works of art.

So that there has arisen this strange phenomenon, that there is now a class of ladies and gentlemen, very refined indeed, though not perhaps as well informed as is generally supposed, and of this refined class there are many who do really love beauty and incident—*i.e.*, art, and would make sacrifices to get it; and these are led by artists of great manual skill and high intellect, forming altogether a large body of demand for the article. And yet the supply does not come. Yes, and moreover, this great body of enthusiastic demanders are no mere poor and helpless people, ignorant fisher-peasants, half-mad monks, scatter-brained sansculottes—none of those, in short, the expression of whose needs has shaken the world so often before, and will do yet again. No, they are of the ruling classes, the masters of men, who can live without labour, and have abundant leisure to scheme out the fulfilment of their desires; and yet I say they cannot have the art which they so much long for, though they hunt it about the world so hard, sentimentalizing the sordid lives of the miserable peasants of Italy and the starving proletarians of her towns, now that all the picturesqueness has departed from the poor devils of our own country-side, and of our own slums. Indeed, there is little of reality left them anywhere, and that little is fast fading away before the needs of the manufacturer and his ragged regiment of workers, and before the enthusiasm of the archæological restorer of the dead past. Soon there will be nothing left except the lying dreams of history, the miserable wreckage of our museums and picture-galleries, and the carefully guarded interiors of our æsthetic drawing-rooms, unreal and foolish, fitting witnesses of the life of corruption that goes on there, so pinched and meagre and cowardly, with its concealment and ignoring, rather than restraint of, natural longings; which does not forbid the greedy indulgence in them if it can but be decently hidden.

The art then is gone, and can no more be "restored" on its old lines than a mediæval building can be. The rich and refined cannot have it though they would, and though we will believe many of them would. And why? Because those who could give it to the rich are not allowed by the rich to do so. In one word, slavery lies between us and art.

I have said as much as that the aim of art was to destroy the curse of labour by making work the pleasurable satisfaction of our impulse towards energy, and giving to that energy hope of producing something worth its exercise.

Now, therefore, I say, that since we cannot have art by striving after its mere superficial manifestation, since we can have nothing but its sham by so doing, there yet remains for us to see how it would be if we let the shadow take care of itself and try, if we can, to lay hold of the substance. For my part I believe, that if we try to realize the aims of art without much troubling ourselves what the aspect of the art itself shall be, we shall find we shall have what we want at last: whether it is to be called art or not, it will at least be *life;* and, after all, that is what we want. It may lead us into new splendours and beauties of visible art; to architecture with manifolded magnificence free from the curious incompleteness and failings of that which the older times have produced—to painting, uniting to the beauty which mediæval art attained the realism which modern art aims at; to sculpture, uniting the beauty of the Greek and the expression of the Renaissance with some third quality yet undiscovered, so as to give us the images of men and women splendidly alive, yet not disqualified from making, as all true sculpture should, architectural ornament. All this it may do; or, on the other hand, it may lead us into the desert, and art may seem to be dead amidst us; or feebly and uncertainly to be struggling in a world which has utterly forgotten its old glories.

For my part, with art as it now is, I cannot bring myself to think that it much matters which of these dooms awaits it, so long as each bears with it some hope of what is to come; since here, as in other matters, there is no hope save in Revolution. The old art is no longer fertile, no longer yields us anything save elegantly poetical regrets; being barren, it has but to die, and the matter of moment now is, as to how it shall die, whether *with* hope or *without* it.

What is it, for instance, that has destroyed the Rouen, the Oxford of *my* elegant poetic regret? Has it perished for the benefit of the people, either slowly yielding to the growth of intelligent change and new happiness? or has it been, as it were, thunderstricken by the tragedy which mostly accompanies some great new birth? Not so. Neither phalangstere nor dynamite has swept its beauty away, its destroyers have not been either the philanthropist or the Socialist, the co-operator or the anarchist. It has been sold, and at a cheap price indeed: muddled away by the greed and incompetence of fools who do not know what life and pleasure mean, who will neither take them themselves nor let others have them. That is why the death of that beauty wounds us so: no man of sense or feeling would dare to regret such losses if they had been paid for by new life and happiness for the people. But there is the people still as it was before, still facing for its part the monster who destroyed all that beauty, and whose name is Commercial Profit.

I repeat, that every scrap of genuine art will fall by the same hands if the matter only goes on long enough, although a sham art may be left in its place, which may very well be carried on by *dilettanti* fine gentlemen and ladies without any help from below; and, to speak plainly, I fear that this gibbering ghost of the real thing would satisfy a great many of those who now think themselves lovers of art; though it is not difficult to see a long vista of its degradation till it shall become at last a mere laughing-stock; that is to say, if the thing were to go on: I mean, if art were to be for ever the amusement of those whom we now call ladies and gentlemen.

But for my part I do not think it will go on long enough to reach such depths as that; and yet I should be hypocritical if I were to say that I thought that the change in the basis of society, which would enfranchise labour and make men practically equal in condition, would lead us by a short road to the splendid new birth of art which I have mentioned, though I feel quite certain that it would not leave what we now call art untouched, since the aims of that revolution do include the aims of art—viz., abolishing the curse of labour.

I suppose that this is what is likely to happen; that machinery will go on developing, with the purpose of saving men labour, till the mass of the people attain real leisure enough to be able to appreciate the pleasure of life; till, in fact, they have attained such mastery over Nature that they no longer fear starvation as a penalty for not working more than enough. When they get to that point they will doubtless turn themselves and begin to find out what it is that they really want to do. They would soon find out that the less work they did (the less work unaccompanied by art, I mean), the more desirable a dwelling-place the earth would be; they would accordingly do less and less work, till the mood of energy, of which I began by speaking, urged them on afresh: but by that time Nature relieved by the relaxation of man's work, would be recovering her ancient beauty, and be teaching men the old story of art. And as the Artificial Famine, caused by men working for the profit of a master, and which we now look upon as a matter of course, would have long disappeared, they would be free to do as they chose, and they would set aside their machines in all cases where the work seemed pleasant or desirable for handiwork; till in all crafts where production of beauty was required, the most direct communication between a man's hand and his brain would be sought for. And there would be many occupations also, as the processes of agriculture, in which the voluntary exercise of energy would be thought so delightful, that people would not dream of handing over its pleasure to the jaws of a machine.

In short, men will find out that the men of our days were wrong in first multiplying their needs, and then trying, each man of them, to evade all participation in the means and processes whereby those needs are satisfied; that this kind of division of labour is really only a new and wilful form of arrogant and slothful ignorance, far more injurious to the happiness and contentment of life than the ignorance of the processes of Nature, of what we sometimes call *science*, which men of the earlier days unwittingly lived in.

They will discover, or rediscover rather, that the true secret of
happiness *lies in the taking a genuine interest in all the details of daily
life,* in elevating them by art instead of handing the performance of
them over to unregarded drudges, and ignoring them; and that in cases
where it was impossible either so to elevate them and make them
interesting, or to lighten them by the use of machinery, so as to make
the labour of them trifling, that should be taken as a token that the
supposed advantages gained by them were not worth the trouble and
had better be given up. All this to my mind would be the outcome of
men throwing off the burden of Artificial Famine, supposing, as I
cannot help supposing, that the impulses which have from the first
glimmerings of history urged men on to the practice of Art were still
at work in them.

Thus and thus only *can* come about the new birth of Art, and I think
it *will* come about thus. You may say it is a long process, and so it is;
but I can conceive of a longer. I have given you the Socialist or Opti-
mist view of the matter. Now for the Pessimist view.

I can conceive that the revolt against Artificial Famine or Capitalism,
which is now on foot, may be vanquished. The result will be that the
working class—the slaves of society—will become more and more
degraded; that they will not strive against overwhelming force, but,
stimulated by that love of life which Nature, always anxious about
the perpetuation of the race, has implanted in us, will learn to bear
everything—starvation, overwork, dirt, ignorance, brutality. All these
things they will bear, as, alas! they bear them too well even now; all
this rather than risk sweet life and bitter livelihood, and all sparks of
hope and manliness will die out of them.

Nor will their masters be much better off: the earth's surface will
be hideous everywhere, save in the uninhabitable desert; Art will
utterly perish, as in the manual arts so in literature, which will become,
as it is indeed speedily becoming, a mere string of orderly and calculated ineptitudes and passionless ingenuities; Science will grow more
and more one-sided, more incomplete, more wordy and useless, till at
last she will pile herself up into such a mass of superstition, that beside
it the theologies of old time will seem mere reason and enlightenment.
All will get lower and lower, till the heroic struggles of the past to
realize hope from year to year, from century to century, will be utterly
forgotten, and man will be an indescribable being—hopeless, desire-
less, lifeless.

And will there be deliverance from this even? Maybe: man may, after some terrible cataclysm, learn to strive towards a healthy animalism, may grow from a tolerable animal into a savage, from a savage into a barbarian, and so on; and some thousands of years hence he may be beginning once more those arts which we have now lost, and be carving interlacements like the New Zealanders, or scratching forms of animals on their cleaned blade-bones, like the pre-historic men of the drift.

But in any case, according to the pessimist view, which looks upon revolt against Artificial Famine as impossible to succeed, we shall wearily trudge the circle again, until some accident, some unforeseen consequence of arrangement, makes an end of us altogether.

That pessimism I do not believe in, nor, on the other hand, do I suppose that it is altogether a matter of our wills as to whether we shall further human progress or human degradation; yet, since there are those who are impelled towards the Socialist or Optimistic side of things, I must conclude that there is some hope of its prevailing, that the strenuous efforts of many individuals imply a force which is thrusting them on. So that I believe that the "Aims of Art" will be realized, though I know that they cannot be, so long as we groan under the tyranny of Artificial Famine. Once again I warn you against supposing, you who may specially love art, that you will do any good by attempting to revivify art by dealing with its dead exterior. I say it is the *aims of art* that you must seek rather than the *art itself;* and in that search we may find ourselves in a world blank and bare, as the result of our caring at least this much for art, that we will not endure the shams of it.

Anyhow, I ask you to think with me that the worst which can happen to us is to endure tamely the evils that we see; that no trouble or turmoil is so bad as that; that the necessary destruction which reconstruction bears with it must be taken calmly; that everywhere—in State, in Church, in the household—we must be resolute to endure no tyranny, accept no lie, quail before no fear, although they may come before us disguised as piety, duty, or affection, as useful opportunity and good-nature, as prudence or kindness. The world's roughness, falseness, and injustice will bring about their natural consequences, and we and our lives are part of those consequences; but since we inherit also the consequences of old resistance to those curses, let us each look to it to have our fair share of that inheritance also, which, if nothing else come of it, will at least bring to us courage and hope; that is, eager life while we live, which is above all things the Aim of Art.

Kenneth Clark
Art and Society[1]

Art is an extensive word. In this essay I limit it to the branch of art that I know best, the visual arts: and I take this term to cover everything made in response to the feeling that certain events or objects of contemplation, seen or imagined, are so important that they must be recorded; and that certain objects of use are so important that they must be enriched. These two aspects of visual art I refer to as image and ornament. They used to be called "fine art" and "applied art," and in the nineteenth century were severely distinguished from one another. Today we tend to minimize this distinction. We believe that the form-creating instinct can express itself in both ornament and image; all ornament, however abstract, suggests some visual experience; all images, however factual, reveal some sense of design. Both are forms of order. And both are sacramental. "What is this sacrament?" as the catechism says. "The outward and visible sign of an inward and spiritual grace." Both image and ornament are revelations of a state of mind and social temper.

Having accepted this basic unity, however, these two branches of visual art show very great differences, especially in their relationship to society, and I shall consider them separately. I think it true to say that all image art of any value has been made by, or on behalf of, a small minority: not necessarily a governing class in a political sense, but a governing class in an intellectual and spiritual sense. Since I shall often refer to this minority, I must decide what to call it. Plato's "governors" is too narrow a term, Rousseau's *volanté générale* is too wide and too mysterious. For the sake of brevity I have referred to it as an *élite:* although in fact it is not elected, and may be drawn from any class of society.

Images are not made for fun. In fact it is almost true to say that all image art of value illustrates or confirms a system of belief held by an elite, and very often is employed consciously as a means of maintaining that system. Obvious examples are the theocratic art of Egypt, the Parthenon with its Olympian embodiment of Greek philosophy, the stained glass of Chartres and Bourges illustrating not only Christian legend but the whole superstructure of patriotic theology, the temples of Angkor and Borobudur, the Basilica of Assisi and its Buddhist

[1] *Harper's Magazine*, August, 1961.

equivalent Ajanta, the Stanze of Raphael, and so forth, down to David's picture of the "Oath of the Horatii." The list could be expanded till in the end it would include most of the greatest visible feats of human imagination and all of those which are in any way related to society and do not depend solely on the genius of an individual artist. It seems that an image achieves the concentration, clarity, and rhythmic energy which make it memorable only when it illustrates or confirms what a minority believes to be an important truth.

The images provided for the majority by the elite may be more, or less, popular. Franciscan art in the thirteenth century and Baroque art in the seventeenth century were two attempts to create a new repertoire of images which should be more popular than that which preceded it. Both consciously exploited emotionalism. But the artists who gave the finest expression of those styles—let us say Cimabue and Bernini—were working for a small group of patrons, and were deeply receptive of their ideas. Bernini's "Saint Theresa" became a popular image; it revealed to the majority a hidden need. But it was Bernini's own invention and in its origin it owed nothing to popular demands. Even the images which we first believe to have a popular origin—for example those charming woodcuts known as *images d'Epinal*—are for the most part naïve and imperfect memories of images already invented for the elite by such an artist as Philippe de Champagne. The only exceptions I can think of are those anecdotal strips which simply tell a story, often with the help of balloons of text. Such were the illustrations of late antique manuscripts, the painting of popular artists like Pacino di Bonaguida, the *Biblia Pauperum* and its derivatives, and a number of Japanese scrolls, like the comic animals attributed to Toba Sojo. These, I believe, are the only forms of autochthonous popular image art before the nineteenth century, and I mention them now because they reveal a fundamental characteristic of all popular art: that it is concerned with narration.

At first sight ornament would seem to be a more popular form of expression than image. Ornament has the character of a language— nineteenth-century writers used, quite properly, to speak of the grammar of ornament—and in so far as it is a living language it is accepted almost unconsciously by the majority. However, there is this difference, that whereas language seems to have evolved unconsciously from mass needs, a system of ornament has seldom been invented by "the people." In fact I can think of only one exception: the pottery of the Mexican Indians, which is outstandingly beautiful and does seem to be a genuine popular creation. In Europe good folk ornament turns out almost always to be a cruder rendering of a minority style: and I think the same is true of China, India, Persia, and the whole Moslem culture. I would even extend this to the most vital and expressive of all ornament styles—that produced by the so-called folk-wandering peoples. I believe that the finest Scythian ornaments were by a great artist working for a chief, and that most of what has been discovered in Scandinavia or Scotland is a half-understood imitation of these aristocratic adornments.

In ornament the ulterior motive is less strong than in the image. It does not openly recommend a system. But no one maintains that it exists solely to please the eye, and lacks ulterior motive altogether. It is an assertion of status—whether in a cope or crown or crosier or *portrait royal* or precious reliquary. This fact, which has been worked out in detail by Marxist historians, is taken by them as a condemnation of art; and, as everyone knows, Veblen coined for it the expression "conspicuous waste." This expression is apt, but I do not find it at all damaging. All art is waste in a material sense; and the idea that things should be made more precious-looking in accordance with the status of the user seems to me entirely fitting. I think that a bishop should have finer vestments than a deacon and that the portal of a cathedral should be more richly ornamented than the door of a warehouse. I would go further, and say that ornament is inseparable from hierarchy. It is not only the result, but the cause of status. The carving on the corner capitals of the Doge's Palace and the central window of the Palazzo Farnese confer a kind of kingship on those points of the buildings. In a democratic building, where all windows are equal, no ornament is permissible; although I understand that the higher executives may have more windows.

So I would deduce from history this first law (in the Ruskinian sense) of the relationship of art and society: that visual art, whether it takes the form of images or ornament, is made by a minority for a minority, and would add this rider, that the image-making part is usually controlled in the interests of a system, and that the ornamental part is usually the index of status.

Created by a minority: yes, but accepted by the majority unquestionably, eagerly, and with a sense of participation. The degree of physical participation in the great popular works of art is hard to assess. We know that in the building of the Gothic cathedrals—Chartres is the most familiar example—whole villages moved to be nearer the work, and men were prepared to learn subsidiary crafts in order to help the professional masons. We can assume that the same was true of Boro-budur or Ellora, although the economic status of the workers may have been different. A parallel in modern life would be the building of a great liner in Clydebank, where the whole life of the town depends on the work. But apart from this active participation, one has only to read the accounts of how in the great ages of artistic creation works of art were brought into existence—the long and serious thought which preceded the commission, the public anxiety about its progress, the joy when it was at last accomplished, and the procession in which it was carried to its destination, to the sound of bells and singing of a Te Deum—one has only to come upon such documents, common enough in the Middle Ages and Renaissance, and applicable, surely, to Olympia and the Acropolis of Athens, to recognize that the society of those times needed art, believed without question in the value of art, and participated imaginatively in its making. So this would be my second law: that a healthy and vital relationship between art and society exists when the majority feel that art is absolutely necessary to them, to confirm their beliefs, to inform them about matters of lasting importance, and to make the invisible visible.

Now in saying that this is the *healthiest* relationship between art and society, I must not be understood as saying that these are the *only* circumstances under which good works of art can be produced. Even before 1870 great pictures were painted by individuals who had no relationship with society at all and whose work was distasteful or incom-prehensible to the majority. Rembrandt and Turner, in their later phases, are obvious examples. In the history of art, as in all history, nothing poses a more delicate problem of interpretation than the rela-tionship between individual genius and the general will. But even if we believe, as I am inclined to do, that inspiration is more likely to illuminate an individual than a mass and that all the memorable forms of art were originally invented by individuals of genius, we must agree that at certain periods these individuals are isolated, at others they enlist behind them a whole army of assent and participation.

Nor is this direct relationship of need and unquestioning belief certain to produce good art. Artistic faculties are somewhat unequally —we may think unfairly—distributed among the peoples of the globe; and although the relationship may be sound, not all needs have the same validity. However, I am sufficiently a Ruskinian to believe that when a society, over a long period, produces an art which is lacking in vitality and imaginative power, but which nevertheless seems to be accepted by the majority, there is something wrong with that society.

This brings me back to the part of my opening definition, where I said that art was a sacrament; and I must now consider how an inward and spiritual grace can be given outward and visible form. The answer is, through symbols. A symbol is a sort of analogy in the physical sphere for some spiritual or intellectual experience. Usually it is the concentration of several related experiences so complex that they cannot be expressed in any rational form, and so intense that a physical symbol suggests itself unconsciously. We know from the saints of every religion that the most poignant spiritual experiences demand expression by physical analogies, and, in spite of Pascal and Spinoza, we may infer that spiritual experiences which remain abstract are not usually very intense. Symbols may start as a result of private revelations, but their value in art depends on the degree to which they can be felt and accepted by others. In fact nearly all intensely felt symbols have some universal quality, which makes them comprehensible even when their maker believes them to be peculiar to himself. But it is also true that the sacramental character of art is far more easily achieved when the principal objects of belief have already been given a symbolic form which is generally recognized and accepted: in other words, when there is an established mythology and iconography.

In this question of art and society the importance of an accepted iconography cannot be overstated. Without it the network of beliefs and customs which holds a society together may never take shape as art. If an iconography contains a number of sufficiently powerful symbols, it can positively alter a philosophic system. The points of dogma for which no satisfactory image can be created tend to be dropped from popular religious exposition, and episodes which have scarcely occupied the attention of theologians tend to grow in importance if they produce a compelling image. I would go so far as to say that the failure to discover a satisfactory symbol for the Holy Ghost has seriously impaired our concept of the Trinity.

Let me give an example of iconographic triumph and disaster from one painter in one place: Titian in Venice. In the Frari his sublime image of the "Assumption of the Virgin" is so corporeally convincing that it provided a point of departure for Baroque painting, and this image was to float in the background of Catholic imagination down to our own day. In the "Salute" is Titian's painting of Pentecost, a work over which he took great pains, but without success. It was the

final blow to a subject which had never found an impressive icono-
graphical form, and which in spite of its theological importance, gradually faded from the consciousness of popular Catholicism. Let me take
another example from Buddhism. It had been categorically laid down
that the Buddha must not be portrayed, and in the earliest scenes of
his life, such as those on the stupa at Sanchi, the central point of each
episode is left a blank—an empty chair or a deserted boat. This insult
to the image-making faculty was not to be borne, and a representation
of the Buddha was finally accepted. But where did it come from? From
the imitation, in the fringes of the Buddhist world, of some Praxitelian
"Apollo." Thus the most extreme example of spirituality was embodied
by the most concrete expression of physical beauty. Conversely, dogma
may triumph over the popular love of imagery in a theocratic society,
and produce an iconography, like that of later Buddhism, with its
10,000 Buddhas, which deprives images of all artistic quality.

Lest it should be thought that this question of iconography does not
apply to modern life, let me add that it is not confined to dogmatic
religion. For example, the iconography of the Romantic Movement
from 1790 to 1830 was almost as compulsive as if it had been laid down
by the Council of Trent. The tiger—in Blake, Stubbs, Géricault,
Delacroix, Barye, and a dozen lesser artists; the cloud—in Wordsworth
and Byron, Shelley, Turner, and Constable; the shipwreck—in Byron,
Turner, Goya, Géricault, Delacroix, and Victor Hugo: these are symbols of Romanticism, used and accepted unconsciously because they
expressed the new worship of nature and power, and a new sense of
destiny. I think it would be a mistake to call this state of mind a
religion. That word should be reserved for beliefs which are based on
a book of holy writ and involve certain formal observances. But at
least we can say that the belief in nature, which expressed itself in the
landscape painting of the nineteenth century and has remained the
most productive source of popular art to this day, is a nonmaterial
belief. It is something which cannot be justified by reason alone and
seems to lift the life of the senses onto a higher plane.

This suggests another "law" in the relationship of art and society:
that it is valuable only when the spiritual life is strong enough to
insist on some sort of expression through symbols. No great social arts
can be based on material values or physical sensations alone.

This "law" leads me to consider the problem of luxury art. Now, it
would be dishonest for me to take a puritanical or Veblenist view of
luxury art. Moreover there is a point—Watteau's "Enseigne de Ger-

saint" is an example—at which the sensuous quality of luxury art is so fine that it offers a spiritual experience. We are playing with words and concepts which, as we breathe on them, become alive and flutter from our hands. Still, the fact remains that, in the long run, luxury art implies the reverse of what I have called a healthy relationship between art and society and so has a deadening effect. The most obvious example is the art of eighteenth-century France, where, however, the arrogant elaboration demanded by powerful patrons is sometimes sweetened, and given lasting value, by a reasonable belief in the *douceur de vivre*. But the predominance of luxury art in the eighteenth century is a short and harmless episode compared to that long slumber of the creative imagination which lasted from the end of the second century B.C. to the third century A.D. For almost five hundred years not a single new form of any value was invented except, perhaps, in architecture. Works from the preceding centuries were reproduced interminably— made smoother and sweeter for private collectors, bigger and coarser for the public.

What can we say of the relations of this art to the society which produced and accepted it? That no one believed in its symbols; that no one looked to it for confirmation or enlightenment. In short that no one wanted it, except as a conventional form of display. The Romans did not want art and they did not make it; but they collected it.

The problem of luxury art is complicated by the fact that the periods in which it predominates are usually periods when the art of the past is collected and esteemed. This was obviously the case in Hellenized Rome and in eighteenth-century England; conversely the idea of collecting and displaying works of an earlier period was hardly known in those cultures where the need for art was strong and widely diffused. One must distinguish, of course, between the fruitful use by artists of earlier works, which took place in thirteenth-century Rheims no less than in fifteenth-century Florence, and the competitive accumulation of collectors. The feeling for the art of the past in Donatello or Ghiberti is entirely different from that of the eighteenth-century connoisseurs— at once more passionate and more practical. "How can I use these admirable inventions to give my own message?" "How can I surpass them in truth or expressive power?" These are the questions aroused by the work of the past in the great ages of art. In periods of luxury art, on the other hand, works of the past are collected at worst for reasons of prestige and at best in order to establish a standard of taste. The concept of good taste is the virtuous profession of luxury art. But one cannot imagine it existing in the twelfth century, or even in the

Renaissance; and without going into the complex question of what the words can mean, I am inclined to doubt if a completely healthy relationship between art and society is possible while the concept of good taste exists.

Such, then, are the deductions that I would make from studying the history of art; and I have ventured, in the nineteenth-century manner, to call them laws. It is arguable that this word should never be applied to the historical process: we see too little. But at least we can say that these are strong probabilities which should be our first criteria when we come to examine the relations of art to society at the present day. In doing so I may be allowed one assumption: that fundamentally human beings have not changed. The picture of human nature which we derive from the Book of Kings or the Fourth Dynasty Egyptian portrait heads in Cairo and Boston is much the same as what we know today, and I think we may safely assume that it will take more than television and the internal combustion engine to change us. In fact, I would suppose that we have more in common with the Middle Ages than our fathers had, because to us universal destruction is an actual possibility, whereas to our fathers it was only a pious fiction. However, if human nature has not changed, human society has; and changed as the result of a basic shift of mental outlook.

This change can be described in one word: materialism. The word has taken on a pejorative sense, but materialism has been the source of achievements which have added immeasurably to the well-being and happiness of mankind. Whether as the dialectical materialism of the East or the liberal materialism of the West, it has given to masses of men a new standard of living, a new sense of status, and a new hope. These benefits have been achieved because materialism has been the philosophical basis of two outstanding human activities, one in the moral and one in the intellectual sphere: humanitarianism and science. These are the integrating forces of our culture, and they are as powerful, and as all-pervasive, as was Christianity in the Middle Ages.

Now, how does this underlying philosophy of materialism relate to art? One cannot help being aware of one very serious obstacle. Materialism and all its children are dedicated to measurement. Bentham's philosophy was based on the greatest good for the greatest *number*. Democracy depends on counting the *number* of votes. All social studies are based on statistics. Science, although it claims to have outgrown that phase, reached its present position by an unprecedented accuracy of measurement.

In its century of triumph, measurement has even become an article of faith. The potential of faith in the human mind is probably fairly constant, but it attaches itself to different ideas or manifestations at different periods. The bones of the Saints, the Rights of Man, psychoanalysis—all these have been the means of precipitating a quantity of faith which is always in solution. People probably believe as much nonsense today as they did in the Middle Ages; but we demand of our precipitant that it *look* as if it could be proved—that it appear to be measurable. People might have believed in art during the last fifty years if its effects could have been stated in an immense table of figures or a very complicated graph; of course they would not have checked the figures or understood the graph, but the existence of these symbols of measurement would have sustained their faith.

But we cannot measure the amount of satisfaction which we derive from a song. We cannot even measure the relative greatness of artists, and attempts to do so by giving marks, popular in the eighteenth century, produced ridiculous results; Giulio Romano always came out top of the poll, which as we all know, by some unanalyzable form of knowledge, is incorrect. The more honest philosophers of materialism have recognized that art cannot be measured in material terms. Bentham invented the unforgettable comparison between pushpin and poetry, coming down on the side of pushpin because more people wanted it. Poetry he defined as "misrepresentation," which is the liberal counterpart to Veblen's "conspicuous waste." The philosophers of dialectical materialism have accepted art only in so far as its magical properties have conceded the right to enjoy and even to produce art among the rights of minorities. Art is the opiate of the few.

How are the philosophic assumptions of materialism reflected in the actual status of art in modern society? It is incontrovertible that fine art, as the word is usually understood, is the preserve of a very small minority. We must not be bamboozled by the claim that more people listen to "good" music or visit picture galleries; nor even by the fact that a few of us have tricked the unsuspecting viewer into looking at old pictures on television. Similar claims could be made for the nineteenth century—for example, during the Manchester Art Treasures Exhibition in 1857, special trains ran from all over England, and whole factories closed down in order that the workers could enjoy the experience of art; and yet the next fifty years saw the consolidation of a Philistinism unequaled since the Roman Republic.

Anyone who has been concerned with those "arts" which really depend on the support of a majority—the cinema, television, or whole-

sale furnishing—knows that the minority which is interested in art is
so small as to be irrelevant in any serious calculation. In England,
the majority is not merely apathetic, but hostile to art. A recent
example was the film of *The Horse's Mouth,* which the exhibitors
would not show (in spite of brilliant acting and hilarious comedy)
simply because the leading character was an artist. If only, they said, he
had been a schoolmaster or a doctor! This is perfectly understandable.
The existence of these freakish members of society whose usefulness
cannot be demonstrated, but who often seem to be enjoying themselves
and sometimes even to be making money, is an affront to the ordinary
hard-working man. It is fair to say that in spite of this feeling, artists
are treated tolerantly in democratic countries.

We should be grateful for this tolerance, but does it not fall far short
of my second condition for a healthy relationship between art and
society: that the majority feel art to be absolutely necessary to them;
that they are not merely consumers, but participants; and that they
receive works of art as the expression of their own deepest feelings?

Before answering this question, I must look back at my original
definition of the word "art." Do the majority still feel that material
things must be made more precious? Do they still feel that certain
images are so important that they must be preserved? In a sense the
answer is "yes." The majority still want ornament on their clothes,
their furnishing fabrics, their wallpapers, and many objects of daily use.
More than this, they still mind very much how things look, independent of their utility. Whether it be dress or automobile design,
they are still in the grip of style. They and the designers are swept
along by a blind destiny, a mysterious force which they cannot analyze,
but of which they are acutely conscious when they look back at the
fashions of twenty years ago.

But no one pretends that, in the last fifty years, the use of ornament
has revealed a satisfactory relationship between art and society. Ruskin
and William Morris supposed that this was due to the intervention of
the machine. But this theory turns out to be applicable only to the
Gothic style. In almost every other style the machine is an extended
tool that can be used with confidence; and for that matter a great deal
of the ornament of the past, from the Viking goldsmith work of Sutton
Hoo to the inlaid panels of the Taj Mahal, is entirely devoid of manual
sensibility and might just as well have been made by a machine.

From a technical point of view, the premises on which ornamental
art is produced have not greatly changed. When we examine it in the

light of my other laws, however, the change is considerable. With a single exception, the ornament favored by the majority is no longer made for an elite; and it no longer has any underlying sense of symbolic meaning. In one branch of art—in architecture—it has almost ceased to exist; and although we have now grown used to buildings without ornament, the historian must record that this is a unique event in the history of art, and one which would certainly have shocked those famous architects of the past who gave so much thought to the character of their ornament, and counted upon it at all points of focus and transition. The great refusal of modern architecture was perhaps a necessary purge and had certain health-giving consequences. But often it is simply an impoverishment, an excuse for meanness and a triumph for the spirit that denies. That it is not the expression of a popular will we learn when we look down the blank face of a modern building into the shop windows at its base; and this leads me to the exception I mentioned just now: it is women's dress. There, it seems to me, the compulsion is so strong that a healthy relationship between art and society is never lost. I am not suggesting that all fashions are equally good— of course there are moments of failing invention and false direction. But they always right themselves because there is an indestructible *volonté générale*—an interaction between the elite and the masses, a sense of status and an unconscious feeling for symbolism.

If the position of ornament in modern society is uneasy and incomplete, the position of image art has suffered a far more drastic change, owing to the invention of the camera. The public hunger for memorable and credible images has in no way declined, but it is satisfied every day by illustrated papers; and the love of landscape which, as I said, was one of the chief spiritual conquests of the nineteenth century, is fed by colored postcards. I am not denying that there is an element of art in press photography; I will also admit that I derive a pleasure from colored postcards which must, I suppose, be called aesthetic. I prefer a good colored postcard to a bad landscape painting. But in both these projections of the image, much of what we believe gives art its value is necessarily omitted. There is selection, but no order, and no extension of the imaginative faculty.

To realize how destructive has been the effect of the camera on image art, consider the art of portraiture. The desire to hand down one's likeness to posterity produced one of the chief social arts of the postmedieval world. It did so because the portrait painters of the time had behind them an immense weight of *volonté générale*. The sitters participated because they knew that their desire to perpetuate their likenesses could not be achieved in any other way. Now, no one supposes that a photograph, however skillful, is comparable with a Goya as a work of art, or even as a likeness. But the fact that photography exists, and can tell us far more accurately than a mediocre painting what people looked like, has knocked away the foundation upon which portraiture rested. There is no longer a feeling of participation in the sitters. The portrait painter no longer feels that he is really needed, any more than ornament is needed on a building; and so he, too, has become an anachronism.

The portrait is typical of the decline of confidence in art which is felt unconsciously by the mass of people as a result of the camera. There is however one form of popular imagery which is not entirely dependent on photography, and that is the poster. Here, a number of my conditions for a healthy relationship between art and society obtain. Posters are made on behalf of a minority and aim at supporting some belief; they appeal to a majority, and millions of people derive from them what they take to be information about matters which they believe to be important. Moreover, posters achieve their effects through the use of symbols, and it is a curious fact that the ordinary man will accept in posters a symbolic treatment, a freedom from realism, which he would not accept in a picture framed in a gallery, simply because a poster does not exist for its own sake, but is concerned with something he needs. All this is true, and yet we know that in spite of many effective and memorable posters, advertising has not produced an art comparable to the windows of Chartres Cathedral; and never can. The reason is, of course, that it lacks what I have called the sacramental element in art. I said earlier that the nearest equivalent in modern life to the building of a medieval cathedral was the construction of a giant liner. But the liner is built for the convenience of passengers and the benefit of shareholders. The cathedral was built to the glory of God. One might add that advertising art is concerned with lies, of a relatively harmless and acceptable kind; but one must remember that the great art of the past was also concerned with lies, often of a much more dangerous kind. The difference is not one of truth, but of the different realms to which these two forms of art belong—the realm of matter and the realm of spirit.

I need not press any further the point that the philosophy of materialism is hostile to art. But what about its two noble kinsmen, humanitarianism and science? Although they are to a great extent committed to measurement, they are not wholly materialistic. They recognize values which we may call moral, intellectual, and even aesthetic. They are the integrating beliefs of the last 150 years. How are they connected with art?

The more enlightened supporters of humanitarianism have often bewailed the fact that art seems to have flourished in societies which were quite the reverse of humane. Yet we feel instinctively that this is natural; that kindness, mildness, decency, are not as likely to produce art as violence, passion, and ruthlessness. One of the most ancient and persistent images in art is the lion devouring a horse or deer; and it must puzzle the humanitarian mind that this bloodthirsty episode came to be accepted as a suitable decoration for pagan sarcophagi; then entered Christian iconography as a symbol of the spiritual life; and finally became the dominating motif of the only great religious painter of the nineteenth century, Delacroix. The answer is given in Blake's *Marriage of Heaven and Hell,* and I will not be so foolish as to elaborate it. But I may quote the words of a great living painter: "It isn't enough to have the eyes of a gazelle; you also need the claws of a cat in order to capture your bird alive and play with it before you eat it and so join its life to yours." To put it less picturesquely, art depends on a condition of spiritual energy, which must devour and transform all that is passive and phlegmatic in life, and no amount of good will can take the place of this creative hunger.

I am not saying that violence and brutality *beget* art, or that there is not still far too much violence and brutality left in the world. The bright new towns in our welfare state are an achievement of which humanity may be proud. But do not let us suppose that this peaceful, humdrum, hell-free, de-Christianized life has been achieved without loss. And apart from the unlikeliness of art being forged at such a low temperature, the doctrine of equality and the drift toward equality, on which such a society depends, run counter to one of my first laws. We have many reliable indications of what Mr. and Mrs. Honest Everyman really want. We don't need surveys and questionnaires— only a glance at suburban or provincial furniture stores and television advertisements. There we see the art of a prosperous democracy—the art that is easily unwrapped—the art of least resistance. This would not matter much, were it not that Gresham's law—that bad money drives out good—is equally true of spiritual currency; and we are all surrounded by far more bad art than we are aware of. I observed during the war, when the amount of conspicuous waste was cut down in the interest of economy, and objects of daily use, like teacups, were made without even a curve, let alone a pattern, that the appetite for real works of art was much keener and more discriminating than it was before.

With science the position is rather different. It is not so much a soil in which art will not grow as it is a rival crop. The development of physical science in the last hundred years has been one of the most colossal efforts the human intellect has ever made. Now, I think it is arguable that human beings can produce, in a given epoch, only a certain amount of creative power, and that this is directed to different ends at different times; and I believe that the dazzling achievements of science during the last seventy years have deflected many of these skills and endowments which go to the making of a work of art. To begin with, there is the sheer energy. In every molding of a Florentine palace we are conscious of an immense intellectual energy, and it is the absence of this energy in the nineteenth-century copies of Renaissance buildings which makes them seem so dead. To find a form with the same vitality as the window moldings of the Palazzo Strozzi, I must wait till I get back into an airplane, and look at the relation of the engine to the wing. That form is alive, not (as used to be said) because it is functional—many functional shapes are entirely uninteresting—but because it is animated by the breath of modern science.

The deflections from art to science are the more serious because these are not, as used to be supposed, two contrary activities, but draw on many of the same capacities of the human mind. In the last resort each depends on the imagination. Artist and scientist alike are trying to give concrete form to dimly apprehended ideas. Both, in the words of Aristotle's famous definition of poetry, are hoping "to see similars in dissimilars." "All science," says Dr. Bronowski, "is the search for unity in hidden likenesses, and the starting point is an image, because then the unity is before our mind's eye." He gives the example of how Copernicus' notion of the solar system was inspired by the old astrological image of man with the signs of the Zodiac distributed about his body, and notices how Copernicus uses warm-blooded expressions to describe the chilly operations of outer space. "The earth conceives from the sun" or "The sun rules a family of stars." Our scientists are no longer as anthropomorphic as that; but they still depend on humanly comprehensible images, and the valid symbols of our time, invented to embody some scientific truth, have taken root in the popular imagination. Do those red and blue balls connected by rods really resemble a type of atomic structure? I am too ignorant to say, but I accept the symbol just as an early Christian accepted the Fish or the Lamb, and I find it echoed or even (it would seem) anticipated in the work of modern artists like Kandinsky and Miró.

Finally there is the question of popular interest and approval. The position of science in the modern world illustrates clearly what I meant by a vital relationship with society. Science is front-page news; every child has a scientific toy; small boys dream of space ships; big boys know how to make a radio set. What does a compulsory visit to an art museum mean compared to this? An opportunity to fool about and hide behind the showcases? And, at the other end of the scale, the research scientist has universities competing for his favors with millions of dollars worth of plant and equipment, while principalities and powers wait breathless for his conclusions. So he goes to work, as Titian once did, confident that he will succeed, because he knows that everybody needs him.

Such are the conclusions which force themselves upon me when I examine, in the light of history, the present relations of art and society. Those who care for art and feel a sense of loyalty to their own times may feel it their duty to refute these conclusions, but I think they will find it difficult to do so without straining the evidence. Does this mean that a broadly based social art is unlikely to appear for a long time? I am inclined to think so. This is not as catastrophic as it sounds. At least 90 per cent of our fellow countrymen get on very well without art, and I don't quite know why we should bother about them or try to persuade them to take an interest. No one tries to persuade me to take an interest in racing. And yet some instinct I can neither define nor defend makes me believe that people without art are incomplete and that posterity will have a poor opinion of them; and so I peer anxiously into the dark scene I have described. This is what I find.

The fact that art is not only tolerated, but actually supported by government and municipal funds, although it is hardly worth a single vote and practically no politician has the faintest belief or interest in it, shows that it has retained some of its magic power. The unbelieving majority still recognize that the believing minority, in picture galleries and concert halls, achieve a state of mind of peculiar value. There are very few people who have never had an aesthetic experience, either from the sound of a band or the sight of a sunset or the action of a horse. The words "beauty" and "beautiful" often pass the lips of those who have never looked at a work of art—oftener, perhaps, than they pass the lips of museum curators—and some meaning must be attached to them.

I believe that the majority of people really long to experience that moment of pure, disinterested, nonmaterial satisfaction which causes them to ejaculate the word "beautiful"; and since this experience can be obtained more reliably through works of art than through any other means, I believe that those of us who try to make works of art more accessible are not wasting our time. But how little we know of what we are doing. I am not even sure that museum art and its modern derivatives, however extended and skillfully contrived, will ever bring about a healthy relationship between art and society. It is too deeply rooted in cultural values which only a small minority can acquire.

Here we reach the crux of the problem: the nature of the elite. It was my first conclusion that art cannot exist without one, my second that the elite must inspire confidence in the majority. During the last hundred years values in art have been established by a minority so small and so cut off from the sources of life, that it cannot be called an elite in my sense of the word. Let us call it a priesthood, and add that in preserving its mysteries from the profanation of all-conquering materialism, it has made them rather too mysterious. There is something admirable in all forms of bigotry, but I do not believe that we can return to a healthy relationship between art and society over so narrow a bridge. On the contrary, I believe that our hope lies in an expanding elite, an elite drawn from every class, and with varying degrees of education, but united in a belief that nonmaterial values can be discovered in visible things.

Is it fatuous to interpret the large scale of books on art and the relative success of certain television programs as a sign that such an elite is forming? But even if these are genuine snowdrops, and not paper flowers stuck in the woods by hopeful highbrows, many obstacles will remain. There is a lack of an iconography. There is the glut of false art which blunts our appetites. There is even the danger that true art may be degraded through the media of mass communications. But I believe that all these obstacles can be overcome if only the *need* for art, which lies dormant and unperceived in the spirit of every man, yet is manifested by him unconsciously every day, can be united with the *will* to art which must remain the endowment, and the responsibility, of the happy few.

The mode of production in material life determines the social, political, and intellectual life processes in general. It is not the consciousness of men that determines their being, but, on the contrary, their social being that determines their consciousness. . . .

It is well known that certain periods of highest development of art stand in no direct connection with the general development of society, nor with the material basis and the skeleton structure of its organization.

Karl Marx, *Critique of Political Economy*

Like other artists, Delacroix had to come to terms with the strong tendency of painters to imitate other painters. That so enormously talented an artist as Delacroix should have accepted imitation while stressing originality and boldness provides an insight into the nature of artistic creativity.

Eugène Delacroix
On Originality in Art

Art is so long that, to arrive at the systematizing of certain principles which really govern every department of art the whole of a lifetime is needed. Men of born talent instinctively find the means for expressing their ideas; with them there is a mixture of spontaneous impulses and of groupings, across which the idea comes to the light with a charm that is perhaps more particular than the one offered by the production of a consummate master.

At the dawn of a talent there is something naive and bold at the same time, recalling the graces of childhood and also its happy freedom from care as to the conventions which govern grown men. That is what renders all the more surprising that boldness to be seen in the work of illustrious masters at a late period of their career. To be bold, when one may compromise one's past, is the greatest sign of strength.

If I remember rightly, Napoleon places Turenne above all other captains, because he notices that his plans became more audacious the more he advanced in age. Napoleon himself has given the example of that extraordinary quality.

In the arts, particularly, very deep feeling is necessary if the originality of thought is to be maintained despite the habits to which even talent is fatally inclined to abandon itself. After having spent a great part of his life in accustoming the public to his genius, it is very difficult for the artist to keep from repeating himself, and to renew his talent, so to speak, in order not to fall, in his turn, into that very fault of banality and the commonplace which is characteristic of men and of schools as they grow old.

Gluck has given a most remarkable example of that power of the will, which was no other than the power of his genius. Rossini went on renewing himself down to his last masterpiece, which prematurely closed his illustrious career of masterpieces. Raphael, Mozart, etc.

Boldness. One should not, however, attribute this boldness, which is the seal of the great artists, solely to that gift for renewal, for the rejuvenation of talent by means of new effects. There are men who give their measure from the very start, and in whom a sublime monotony is the principal quality. Michelangelo never varied the physiognomy of that terrible talent, which in itself has renewed all the modern schools and given them the irresistible urge by which they are characterized.

Rubens was Rubens at once. It is remarkable that he never even varied his execution, that he modified it very little, even after receiving it from his master. If he copies Leonardo da Vinci, Michelangelo, Titian—and he copied unceasingly—it seems that he showed himself to be more Rubens than in his original works.

Imitation. One always begins by imitating.

It is well agreed that what is called *creation* in the great artists is nothing but a special manner possessed by each one in his seeing, coordinating and rendering of nature. But not only have these great men created nothing in the proper sense of the word, which means of *nothing* to make *something,* but, even more, in order to form their talent or to keep it healthy, they have had to imitate their predecessors, and imitate them almost unceasingly, whether voluntarily or unwittingly.

Raphael, the greatest of painters, was most sedulous in imitating: imitation of his master, a thing that left in his style traces that were never effaced; imitation of the antique and of the masters who had preceded him, but freeing himself by degrees from the swaddling clothes in which he found them wrapped, and finally imitation of his contemporaries such as Albrecht Dürer the German, Titian, Michelangelo, etc.

Journal, March 1, 1859

There was never an artistic period.
There never was an art-loving nation.

James McNeill Whistler, *Ten O'Clock Lecture,* 1885

When a work of art appears to be in advance of its period, it is really the period that has lagged behind the work of art.

Jean Cocteau, *A Call to Order*

ART AND MORALITY

Benjamin West
The Virtuous Artist

(Virtue, always indispensable, is of the first consequence in the life of the elegant artist; whose contemplations are, or should be, always sedate, and whose mind should be always tranquil and at home.) But that is impossible on the supposition that his life is not the regular life of virtue.(History will constantly show us in all the brightest characters of the world the most conspicuous virtues.)

> —From West's Presidential Discourse
> to the Royal Academy, December 1792

John Ruskin
The Moral Content of Art

Take, for instance, one of the most perfect poems or pictures (I use the words as synonymous) which modern times have seen: [Sir Edwin Landseer's] the "Old Shepherd's Chief-mourner." Here the exquisite execution of the glossy and crisp hair of the dog, the bright, sharp touching of the green bough beside it, the clear painting of the wood of the coffin and the folds of the blanket, are language—language clear and expressive in the highest degree. But the close pressure of the dog's breast against the wood, the convulsive clinging of the paws, which has dragged the blanket off the

COLONEL GUY JOHNSON—BENJAMIN
WEST (*National Gallery, Mellon
Collection, Washington, D.C.*)

trestle, the total powerlessness of the head laid, close and motionless, upon its folds, the fixed and tearful fall of the eye in its utter hopelessness, the rigidity of repose which marks that there has been no motion nor change in the trance of agony since the last blow was struck on the coffin-lid, the quietness and gloom of the chamber, the spectacles marking the place where the Bible was last closed, indicating how lonely has been the life—how unwatched the departure of him who is now laid solitary in his sleep; these are all thoughts—thoughts by which the picture is separated at once from hundreds of equal merit, as far as mere painting goes, by which it ranks as a work of high art.

From *Modern Painters,* Part I, Sec. i, Chap. 2

People have a very mistaken notion that their conventions are something more than conventions.

Leo Stein, *Appreciation*

R. A. M. Stevenson

Some Remarks on Morality in Art[1]

Those persons who are disquieted about the bearing of art upon morals turn round Rubens like a sanitary inspector sniffing about the apertures of a suspicious system of drainage. Immediately after the painter's death the moral character of his work was impugned, not by those princes of the church and the world who had been his patrons, but by the plump female burgess who had been his wife. Helen Fourment shuddered at the voluptuousness of his nymphs and goddesses; she would have destroyed several pictures, and one in particular, save for the amount of money offered for it by the Duke of Richelieu. Money avails much in a question of morals, as much with this kind of lady as fashion with one of a higher or gayer position. That aspect of the morals which looks askance at the nude is too trivial and too temporary a manifestation of human activity to occupy people who keep their eye on art from Assyria and Egypt onwards. A second view of the question has been held by Ruskin and by those who get all their views of painting from the study and practice of literature. According to them, the moral tone of the painter must be considered the main cause of his work, and painting should be a method of preaching which should be prefaced with prayer. A third set of people when they talk of the influence of morals on the painter mean temperament, which certainly counts for much both in morals and in art. This is only to say that all human activities, artistic or non-artistic, interested or disinterested, have their roots in the same life.

I distinguish between the effect of temperament and the effect of moral considerations upon a man. One is aesthetic; the other is not. Most men, I think, in no way conceive of moral judgments as feelings of aesthetic disgust or delight in actions, but rather regard them as restraints imposed by reason on these very feelings in the interests of the community. In real life, the man who has no interest in problems of conduct is stupidly dense to his surroundings. In the world of fiction, conduct affects the drama of life, affects its language, and so affects all the subjects of a poet or playwright. Even the most artificial and transient of these social regulations of conduct interest the writer: they

[1] From *Peter Paul Rubens* (*The Portfolio*, No. 35), by R. A. M. Stevenson. London: Seeley and Co., 1898.

form the bulk of the motifs of light reading. But they cannot easily supply direct motifs for the figure painter, still less for the landscape artist. On the other hand, if they offer no subjects to the painter, I cannot see that rules of self-mortification greatly influence the artistic temperament one way or the other. Restraint balks the temperament that leads to direct and passionate acts in life, but it very little affects the feelings to which one gives expression in art. In fact, people should not closely consult men's lives for the reasons of their artistic perform-ances; the man of genius speaks of feelings that, whatever they may be, have been always suppressed by the world.

But it is through his temperament that the artist works; and since temperament is an influence in moral decisions, there may be a sort of second cousinship twice removed between paint and morals. Tempera-ment works upon the landscape painter as effectively as upon the figure man; it can turn him to large forms, to savage colour, or to peddling minuteness of pattern, and glassy smoothness of pigment; just as it turns a figure painter to broad fleshy types, or to sharp bony models that show their anatomical structure.

Temperament directed Rubens in the choice of his types, and it is in reality colder temperaments, not stricter moralists, that have turned against his work. Patronised by princes and churchmen in his day, a favorite of fashion in our own country till the end of the first half of this century, Rubens has proved a stumbling block to the modern Purists and Aesthetes, who can scarcely hear his name without agita-tion. Twenty years ago, when I confessed my admiration at Rubens's Medicis pictures I was looked upon by a circle of Purists as a person who had just committed an act of public indecency. "Oh those horrible fat women," say all who confuse art and nature, who cannot separate the contemplation of beauty from the animal distaste or desire of possession. When asked to look at Rubens's pictures one is not asked to fall on the necks of his models any more than one is required to feel bloodthirsty when looking at a battle-piece. Anything strong and consistent in character may be fit for a scheme of formal art; for the working out of a pattern. And when we deal with impressionistic art, who shall say what is an unfit motif? Light may break into delicious radiance upon corruption or ordure. In your real life you may refuse the society of people who are not thin, tall, willowy, virginal and built in clean, flat planes of bone and hard flesh; yet in the imagined world of art you may allow Rubens to open the door upon a bevy of rich beauties that offer to the flood of warm light succulent forms, ample

shapes, curved, coloured and creamy surfaces. So you may hate to wet
your feet in dew and yet delight in the long grass of a "Morning"
by Corot.

Neither in his art nor in his life is there any real ground to reproach
Rubens with conventional immorality; but against the refinement of
his taste and the force of his imagination it is argued that he married
two baggy women and could not forget them in his painting. These
critics should remember that his tastes and his art, if not his culture,
were all of a piece and natural to his temperament. In this century
people condemn a man because his art is indifferent to his taste as a
man; because, in a word, he loves art for art's sake; yet with the same
breath almost they condemn the man whose art was the expression of
his life. How would meager forms have suited that broad flowing brush?
To Rubens, the husband of Helen Fourment, flesh was enticing in its
largeness, its soft luminosity, its creamy evenness of tint, and he painted
it with more sense of joy, and, as far as colour is concerned, with more
insight than any other man.

The most immoral and disgraceful and dangerous thing that anybody
can do in the arts is knowingly to feed back to the public its own
ignorance and cheap tastes.

> Edmund Wilson, *Memoirs of Hecate County*

We know that the tail must wag the dog, for the horse is drawn by the
cart;
But the Devil whoops, as he whooped of old: "It's clever, but is it Art?"

> Rudyard Kipling, *The Conundrum of the Workshops*

Art imitates art more than it imitates nature. (*L'art imite l'art bien
plus que la nature.*)

> Jean Charbonneaux

"Without art, the crudeness of reality would make the world unbearable."

> Ecrasia in Bernard Shaw's *Back to Methuselah*

Like Ruskin before him, Lawrence approaches art through morality: the separation of art from life preached by so many modern critics is anathema to him. But Lawrence's morality is, of course, quite different from Ruskin's. For Lawrence, and this is the point of view developed throughout this important statement of his artistic convictions, true morality consists in a healthy and profound instinctualism, a free and uninhibited emotional life; and only this kind of morality, he maintains, can produce great art.

D. H. Lawrence
Art and the Dread of the Instincts[1]

The reason the English produce so few painters is not that they are, as a nation, devoid of a genuine feeling for visual art: though to look at their productions, and to look at the mess which has been made of actual English landscape, one might really conclude that they were, and leave it at that. But it is not the fault of the God that made them. They are made with aesthetic sensibilities the same as anybody else. The fault lies in the English attitude to life. . . .

All alike, cultured and uncultured, they are still dominated by that unnamed, yet overmastering dread and hate of the instincts deep in the body, dread of the strange intuitional awareness of the body, dread of anything but ideas. . . .

The dread of the instincts included the dread of intuitional awareness. 'Beauty is a snare'—'Beauty is but skin-deep'—'Handsome is as handsome does'—'Looks don't count'—'Don't judge by appearances'—if we only realized it, there are thousands of these vile proverbs which have been dinned into us for over two hundred years. They are all of them false. Beauty is not a snare, nor is it skin-deep, since it always involves a certain loveliness of modelling, and handsome doers are often ugly and objectionable people, and if you ignore the look of the thing you plaster England with slums and produce at last a state of spiritual depression that is suicidal, and if you don't judge by appearances, that is, if you can't trust the impression which things make on you, you are a fool. But all these base-born proverbs born in the cash-box, hit direct against the intuitional consciousness. Naturally, man gets a great deal of his life's satisfaction from beauty, from a certain

[1] Abstracted from "Introduction to His Paintings," published in *Phoenix* by D. H. Lawrence. New York: The Viking Press, 1936.

sensuous pleasure in the look of the thing. The old Englishman built his hut of a cottage with a childish joy in its appearance, purely intuitional and direct. The modern Englishman has a few borrowed ideas, simply doesn't know *what* to feel, and makes a silly mess of it: though perhaps he is improving, hopefully, in this field of architecture and house-building. The intuitional faculty, which alone relates us in direct awareness to physical things and substantial presences, is atrophied and dead, and we don't know *what* to feel. We know we ought to feel something, but what?—Oh, tell us what! And this is true of all nations, the French and Italians as much as the English. Look at new French suburbs! Go through the crockery and furniture departments in the *Dames de France* or any big shop. The blood in the body stands still, before such *crétin* ugliness. One has to decide that the modern bourgeois is a *crétin*.

This movement against the instincts and the intuition took a moral tone in all countries. It started in hatred. Let us never forget that modern morality has its roots in hatred, a deep, evil hate of the instinctive, intuitional, procreative body. This hatred is made more virulent by fear, and an extra poison is added to the fear by unconscious horror of syphilis. And so we come to modern bourgeois consciousness, which turns upon the secret poles of fear and hate. That is the real pivot of all bourgeois consciousness in all countries: fear and hate of the instinctive intuitional, procreative body in man or woman. But of course this fear and hate had to take on a righteous appearance, so it became moral, said that the instincts, intuitions and all the activities of the procreative body were evil, and promised a *reward* for their suppression. That is the great clue to bourgeois psychology: the reward business. It is screamingly obvious in Maria Edgeworth's tales, which must have done unspeakable damage to ordinary people. Be good, and you'll have money. Be wicked, and you'll be penniless at last, and the good ones will have to offer you a little charity. This is sound working morality in the world. And it makes one realize that, even to Milton, the true hero of *Paradise Lost* must be Satan. But by this baited morality the masses were caught and enslaved to industrialism before ever they knew it; the good got hold of the goods, and our modern 'civilization' of money, machines, and wage-slaves was inaugurated. The very pivot of it, let us never forget, being fear and hate, the most intimate fear and hate, fear and hate of one's own instinctive, intuitive body, and fear and hate of every other man's and every other woman's warm, procreative body and imagination.

Now it is obvious what result this will have on the plastic arts, which depend entirely on the representation of substantial bodies, and on the intuitional perception of the *reality* of substantial bodies. The reality of substantial bodies can only be perceived by the imagination, and the imagination is a kindled state of consciousness in which intuitive awareness predominates. The plastic arts are all imagery, and imagery is the body of our imaginative life, and our imaginative life is a great joy and fulfilment to us, for the imagination is a more powerful and more comprehensive flow of consciousness than our ordinary flow. In the flow of true imagination we know in full, mentally and physically at once, in a greater, enkindled awareness. At the maximum of our imagination we are religious. And if we deny our imagination, and have no imaginative life, we are poor worms who have never lived.

In the seventeenth and eighteenth centuries we have the deliberate denial of intuitive awareness, and we see the results on the arts. Vision became more optical, less intuitive and painting began to flourish. But what painting! Watteau, Ingres, Poussin, Chardin have some real imaginative glow still. They are still somewhat free. The puritan and the intellectual has not yet struck them down with his fear and hate obsession. But look at England! Hogarth, Reynolds, Gainsborough, they are all already bourgeois. The coat is really more important than the man. It is amazing how important clothes suddenly become, how they *cover* the subject. An old Reynolds colonel in a red uniform is much more a uniform than an individual, and as for Gainsborough, all one can say is: What a lovely dress and hat! What really expensive Italian silk! This painting of garments continued in vogue, till pictures like Sargent's seem to be nothing but yards and yards of satin from the most expensive shops, having some pretty head popped on the top. The imagination is quite dead. The optical vision, a sort of flashy coloured photography of the eye, is rampant.

In Titian, in Velasquez, in Rembrandt the people are there inside their clothes all right, and the clothes are imbued with the life of the individual, the gleam of the warm procreative body comes through all the time, even if it be an old, half-blind woman or a weird, ironic little Spanish princess. But modern people are nothing inside their garments, and a head sticks out at the top and hands stick out of the sleeves, and it is a bore. Or, as in Lawrence or Raeburn, you have something very pretty but almost a mere cliché, with very little instinctive or intuitional perception to it.

After this, and apart from landscape and water-colour, there is strictly no English painting that exists. As far as I am concerned, the pre-Raphaelites don't exist; Watts doesn't, Sargent doesn't, and none of the moderns.

There is the exception of Blake. Blake is the only painter of imaginative pictures, apart from landscape, that England has produced. And unfortunately there is so little Blake, and even in that little the symbolism is often artificially imposed. Nevertheless, Blake paints with real intuitional awareness and solid instinctive feeling. He dares handle the human body, even if he sometimes makes it a mere ideograph. And no other Englishman has even dared handle it with alive imagination. Painters of composition-pictures in England, of whom perhaps the best is Watts, never quite get beyond the level of cliché, sentimentalism, and *funk*. Even Watts is a failure, though he made some sort of try: even Etty's nudes in York fail imaginatively, though they have some feeling for flesh. And the rest, the Leightons, even the moderns don't really do anything. They never get beyond studio models and clichés of the nude. The image never gets across to us, to seize intuitively. It remains merely optical.

Landscape, however, is different. Here the English exist and hold their own. But, for me, personally, landscape is always waiting for something to occupy it. Landscape seems to be *meant* as a background to an intenser vision of life, so to my feeling painted landscape is background with the real subject left out.

Nevertheless, it can be very lovely, especially in water-colour, which is a more bodiless medium, and doesn't aspire to very substantial existence, and is so small that it doesn't try to make a very deep seizure on the consciousness. Water-colour will always be more of a statement than an experience.

And landscape, on the whole, is the same. It doesn't call up the more powerful responses of the human imagination, the sensual passional responses. Hence it is the favourite modern form of expression in painting. There is no deep conflict. The instinctive and intuitional consciousness is called into play, but lightly, superficially. It is not confronted with any living, procreative body.

Hence the English have delighted in landscape, and have succeeded in it well. It is a form of escape for them, from the actual human body they so hate and fear, and it is an outlet for their perishing aesthetic desires. For more than a century we have produced delicious water-colours, and Wilson, Crome, Constable, Turner are all great landscape-painters. Some of Turner's landscape compositions are, to my feelings, among the finest that exist. They still satisfy me more even than van Gogh's or Cézanne's landscapes, which make a more violent assault on the emotions, and repel a little for that reason. Somehow I don't want landscape to make a violent assault on my feelings. Landscape is background with the figures left out or reduced to minimum, so let it stay back. Van Gogh's surging earth and Cézanne's explosive or rattling planes worry me. Not being profoundly interested in landscape, I prefer it to be rather quiet and unexplosive.

But, of course, the English delight in landscape is a delight in escape. It is always the same. The northern races are so innerly afraid of their own bodily existence, which they believe fantastically to be an evil thing—you could never find them feel anything but uneasy shame, or an equally shameful gloating, over the fact that a man was having intercourse with his wife, in his house next door—that all they cry for is an escape. And, especially, art must provide that escape. . . .

And in France? In France it was more or less the same, but with a difference. The French, being more rational, decided that the body had its place, but that it should be rationalized. The Frenchman of today has the most reasonable and rationalized body possible. His conception of sex is basically hygienic. A certain amount of copulation is good for you. *Ça fait du bien au corps!* sums up the physical side of a Frenchman's ideas of love, marriage, food, sport and all the rest. Well, it is more sane, anyhow, than the Anglo-Saxon terrors. The Frenchman is afraid of syphilis and afraid of the procreative body, but not quite so deeply. He has known for a long time that you can take precautions. And he is not profoundly imaginative. . . .

Courbet, Daumier, Degas, they all painted the human body. But Daumier satirized it, Courbet saw it as a toiling thing, Degas saw it as a wonderful instrument. They all of them deny it its finest qualities, its deepest instincts, its purest intuitions. They prefer, as it were, to industrialize it. They deny it the best imaginative existence.

And the real grand glamour of modern French art, the real outburst of delight came when the body was at last dissolved of its substance, and made part and parcel of the sunlight-and-shadow scheme. Let us say what we will, but the real grand thrill of modern French art was the discovery of light, the discovery of light, and all the subsequent discoveries of the impressionists, and of the post-impressionists, even Cézanne. No matter how Cézanne may have reacted from the impressionists, it was they, with their deliriously joyful discovery of light and 'free' colour, who really opened his eyes. Probably the most joyous moment in the whole history of painting was the moment when the incipient impressionists discovered light, and with it, colour. Ah, then they made the grand, grand escape into freedom, into infinity, into light and delight. They escaped from the tyranny of solidity and the menace of mass-form. They escaped, they escaped from the dark procreative body which so haunts a man, they escaped into the open air, *plein air* and *plein soleil:* light and almost ecstasy.

Like every other human escape, it meant being hauled back later with the tail between the legs. Back comes the truant, back to the old doom of matter, of corporate existence, of the body sullen and stubborn and obstinately refusing to be transmuted into pure light, pure colour, or pure anything. It is not concerned with purity. Life isn't. Chemistry and mathematics and ideal religion are, but these are only small bits of life, which is itself bodily, and hence neither pure nor impure.

After the grand escape into impressionism and pure light, pure colour, pure bodilessness—for what is the body but a shimmer of lights and colours!—poor art came home truant and sulky, with its tail between its legs. And it is this return which now interests us. We know the escape was illusion, illusion, illusion. The cat had to come back. So now we despise the 'light' blighters too much. We haven't a good word for them. Which is nonsense, for they too are wonderful, even if their escape was into *le grand néant,* the great nowhere.

But the cat came back. And it is the home-coming tom that now has our sympathy: Renoir, to a certain extent, but mostly Cézanne, the sublime little grimalkin, who is followed by Matisse and Gauguin and Derain and Vlaminck and Braque and all the host of other defiant and howling cats that have come back, perforce, to form and substance and *thereness,* instead of delicious nowhereness.

Without wishing to labour the point, one cannot help being amused at the dodge by which the impressionists made the grand escape from the body. They metamorphosed it into a pure assembly of shifting lights and shadows, all coloured. A web of woven, luminous colour was a man, or a woman—and so they painted her, or him: a web of woven shadows and gleams. Delicious! and quite true as far as it goes. A purely optical, truth: which paint is supposed to be. And they painted delicious pictures: a little too delicious. They bore us, at the moment. They bore people like the very modern critics intensely. But very modern critics need not be so intensely bored. There is something very lovely about the good impressionist pictures. And ten years hence critics will be bored by the present run of post-impressionists, though not so passionately bored, for these post-impressionists don't move us as the impressionists moved our fathers. We have to persuade ourselves, and we have to persuade one another to be impressed by the post-impressionists, on the whole. On the whole, they rather depress us. Which is perhaps good for us.

But modern art criticism is in a curious hole. Art has suddenly gone into rebellion, against all the canons of accepted religion, accepted good form, accepted everything. When the cat came back from the delicious impressionist excursion, it came back rather tattered, but bristling and with its claws out. The glorious escape was all an illusion. There was substance in the world, a thousand times be damned to it! There *was* the body, the great lumpy body. There it was. You had it shoved down your throat. What really existed was lumps, lumps. Then paint 'em. Or else paint the thin 'spirit' with gaps in it and looking merely dishevelled and 'found out'. Paint had found the spirit out.

This is the sulky and rebellious mood of the post-impressionists. They still hate the body—hate it. But, in a rage, they admit its existence, and paint it as huge lumps, tubes, cubes, planes, volumes, spheres, cones, cylinders, all the 'pure' or mathematical forms of substance. As for landscape, it comes in for some of the same rage. It has also suddenly gone lumpy. Instead of being nice and ethereal and non-sensual, it was discovered by Van Gogh to be heavily, overwhelmingly substantial and sensual. Van Gogh took up landscape in heavy spadefuls. And Cézanne had to admit it. Landscape, too, after being, since Claude Lorrain, a thing of pure luminosity and floating shadows, suddenly exploded, and came tumbling back on to canvases of artists in lumps. With Cézanne, landscape 'crystallized', to use one of the favourite terms of the critics, and it has gone on crystallizing into cubes, cones, pyramids, and so forth ever since.

The impressionists brought the world at length, after centuries of effort, into the delicious oneness of light. At last, at last! Hail, holy Light! the great natural One, the universal, the universalizer! We are not divided, all one body we—one in Light, lovely light! No sooner had this paean gone up than the post-impressionists, like Judas, gave the show away. They exploded the illusion, which fell back to the canvas of art in a chaos of lumps.

This new chaos, of course, needed new apologists who therefore rose up in hordes to apologize, almost, for the new chaos. They felt a little guilty about it, so they took on new notes of effrontery, defiant as any Primitive Methodists, which, indeed, they are: the Primitive Methodists of art criticism. These evangelical gentlemen at once ran up their chapels, in a Romanesque or Byzantine shape, as was natural for a primitive and a methodist, and started to cry forth their doctrines in the decadent wilderness. They discovered once more that the aesthetic experience was an ecstasy, an ecstasy granted only to the chosen few, the elect, among whom said critics were, of course, the arch-elect. This was outdoing Ruskin. It was almost Calvin come to art. But let scoffers scoff, the aesthetic ecstasy was vouchsafed only to the few, the elect, and even then only when they had freed their minds of false doctrines. They had renounced the mammon of 'subject' in pictures, they went whoring no more after the Babylon of painted 'interest', nor did they hanker after the flesh-pots of artistic 'representation'. Oh, purify yourselves, ye who would know the aesthetic ecstasy, and be lifted up to the 'white peaks of artistic inspiration'. Purify yourselves of all base hankering for a tale that is told, and of all low lust for likenesses. Purify yourselves, and know the one supreme way, the way of Significant Form. I am the revelation and the way! I am Significant Form, and my unutterable name is Reality. Lo, I am Form and I am Pure, behold, I am Pure Form. I am the revelation of Spiritual Life, moving behind the veil. I come forth and make myself known, and I am Pure Form, behold, I am Significant Form. . . .

No, I am afraid modern criticism has done altogether too much for modern art. If painting survives this outburst of ecstatic evangelism, which it will, it is because people do come to their senses, even after the silliest vogue.

And so we can return to modern French painting, without having to quake before the bogy, or the Holy Ghost of Significant Form: a bogy which doesn't exist if we don't mind leaving aside our self-importance when we look at a picture.

The actual fact is that in Cézanne modern French art made its first step back to real substance, to objective substance, if we may call it so. Van Gogh's earth was still subjective earth, himself projected into the earth. But Cézanne's apples are a real attempt to let the apple exist in its own separate entity, without transfusing it with personal emotion. Cézanne's great effort was, as it were, to shove the apple away from him, and let it live of itself. It seems a small thing to do: yet it is the first real sign that man has made for several thousands of years that he is willing to admit that matter *actually* exists. Strange as it may seem, for thousands of years, in short, ever since the mythological Fall', man has been preoccupied with the constant preoccupation of the denial of the existence of matter, and the proof that matter is only a form of spirit. And then, the moment it is done, and we realize finally that matter is only a form of energy, whatever that may be, in the same instant matter rises up and hits us over the head and makes us realize that it exists absolutely, since it is compact energy itself.

Cézanne felt it in paint, when he felt for the apple. Suddenly he felt the tyranny of mind, the white, worn-out arrogance of the spirit, the mental consciousness, the enclosed ego in its sky-blue heaven self-painted. He felt the sky-blue prison. And a great conflict started inside him. He was dominated by his old mental consciousness, but he wanted terribly to escape the domination. He wanted to *express* what he suddenly, convulsedly knew! the existence of matter. He terribly wanted to paint the real existence of the body, to make it artistically palpable. But he couldn't. He hadn't got there yet. And it was the torture of his life. He wanted to be himself in his own procreative body—and he couldn't. He was, like all the rest of us, so intensely and exclusively a mental creature, or a spiritual creature, or an egoist, that he could no longer identify himself with his intuitive body. He wanted to, terribly. At first he determined to do it by sheer bravado and braggadocio. But no good; it couldn't be done that way. He had, as one critic says, to become humble. But it wasn't a question of becoming humble. It was a question of abandoning his cerebral conceit and his 'willed ambition' and coming down to brass tacks. Poor Cézanne, there he is in his self-portraits, even the early showy ones, peeping out like a mouse and saying: I *am* a man of flesh, am I not? For he was not quite, as none of us are. The man of flesh has been slowly destroyed through centuries, to give place to the man of spirit, the mental man, the ego, the self-conscious I. And in his artistic soul Cézanne knew it, and wanted to rise in the flesh. He couldn't do it, and it embittered him. Yet, with his apple, he did shove the stone from the door of the tomb.

He wanted to be a man of flesh, a real man: to get out of the sky-blue prison into real air. He wanted to live, really live in the body, to know the world through his instincts and his intuitions, and to be himself in his procreative blood, not in his mere mind and spirit. He wanted it, he wanted it terribly. And whenever he tried, his mental consciousness, like a cheap fiend, interfered. If he wanted to paint a woman, his mental consciousness simply overpowered him and wouldn't let him paint the woman of flesh, the first Eve who lived before any of the fig-leaf nonsense. He couldn't do it. If he wanted to paint people intuitively and instinctively, he couldn't do it. His mental concepts shoved in front, and these he *wouldn't* paint—mere representations of what the *mind* accepts, not what the intuitions gather—and they, his mental concepts, wouldn't let him paint from intuition; they shoved in between all the time, so he painted his conflict and his failure, and the result is almost ridiculous.

Woman he was not allowed to know by intuition; his mental self, his ego, that bloodless fiend, forbade him. Man, other men, he was likewise not allowed to know—except by a few, few touches. The earth likewise he was not allowed to know: his landscapes are mostly acts of rebellion against the mental concept of landscape. After a fight tooth-and-nail for forty years, he did succeed in knowing an apple, fully; and, not quite as fully, a jug or two. That was all he achieved.

It seems little, and he died embittered. But it is the first step that counts, and Cézanne's apple is a great deal, more than Plato's Idea. Cézanne's apple rolled the stone from the mouth of the tomb, and if poor Cézanne couldn't unwind himself from his cerements and mental winding-sheet, but had to lie still in the tomb, till he died, still he gave us a chance. . . .

The most interesting figure in modern art, and the only really interesting figure, is Cézanne: and that, not so much because of his achievement as because of his struggle. Cézanne was born in Aix in Provence in 1839: small, timorous, yet sometimes bantam defiant, sensitive, full of grand ambition, yet ruled still deeper by a naïve, Mediterranean sense of truth or reality, imagination, call it what you will. He is not a big figure. Yet his struggle is truly heroic. He was a bourgeois, and one must never forget it. He had a moderate bourgeois income. But a bourgeois in Provence is much more real and human than a bourgeois in Normandy. He is much nearer the actual people, and the actual people are much less subdued by awe of his respectable bourgeois money.

Cézanne was naïve to a degree, but not a fool. He was rather insignificant, and grandeur impressed him terribly. Yet still stronger in him was the little flame of life where he *felt* things to be true. He didn't betray himself in order to get success, because he couldn't: to his nature it was impossible: he was too pure to be able to betray his own small real flame for immediate rewards. Perhaps that is the best one can say of a man, and it puts Cézanne, small and insignificant as he is, among the heroes. He would *not* abandon his own vital imagination.

He was terribly impressed by physical splendour and flamboyancy,

as people usually are in the lands of the sun. He admired terribly the
splendid virtuosity of Paul Veronese and Tintoretto, and even of later
and less good baroque painters. He wanted to be like that—terribly he
wanted it. And he tried very, very hard, with bitter effort. And he
always failed. It is a cant phrase with the critics to say 'he couldn't
draw'. Mr Fry says. 'With all his rare endowments, he happened to
lack the comparatively common gift of illustration, the gift that any
draughtsman for the illustrated papers learns in a school of commercial art.'

Now this sentence gives away at once the hollowness of modern
criticism. In the first place, can one learn a 'gift' in a school of commercial art, or anywhere else? A gift surely is given, we tacitly assume,
by God or Nature or whatever higher power we hold responsible for
the things we have no choice in.

Was, then, Cézanne devoid of this gift? Was he simply incapable
of drawing a cat so that it would look like a cat? Nonsense! Cézanne's
work is full of accurate drawing. His more trivial pictures, suggesting
copies from other masters, are perfectly well drawn—that is, conventionally: so are some of the landscapes, so even is that portrait of M.
Geffroy and his books, which is, or was, so famous. Why all these cant
phrases about not being able to draw? Of course Cézanne could draw,
as well as anybody else. And he had learned everything that was necessary in the art-schools.

He *could* draw. And yet, in his terrifically earnest compositions in
the late Renaissance or baroque manner, he drew so badly. Why? Not
because he couldn't. And not because he was sacrificing 'significant
form' to 'insignificant form', or mere slick representation, which is
apparently what artists themselves mean when they talk about drawing.
Cézanne knew all about drawing: and he surely knew as much as his
critics do about significant form. Yet he succeeded neither in drawing
so that things looked right, nor combining his shapes so that he achieved
real form. He just failed.

He failed, where one of his little slick successors would have succeeded with one eye shut. And why? Why did Cézanne fail in his early
pictures? Answer that, and you'll know a little better what art is. He
didn't fail because he understood nothing about drawing or significant
form or aesthetic ecstasy. He knew about them all, and didn't give a
spit for them.

Cézanne failed in his earlier pictures because he was trying with
his mental consciousness to do something which his living Provençal

body didn't want to do, or couldn't do. He terribly wanted to do something grand and voluptuous and sensuously satisfying, in the Tintoretto manner. Mr Fry calls that his 'willed ambition', which is a good phrase, and says he had to learn humility, which is a bad phrase.

The 'willed ambition' was more than a mere willed ambition—it was a genuine desire. But it was a desire that thought it would be satisfied by ready-made baroque expressions, whereas it needed to achieve a whole new marriage of mind and matter. If we believed in reincarnation, then we should have to believe that after a certain number of new incarnations into the body of an artist, the soul of Cézanne *would* produce grand and voluptuous and sensually rich pictures—but not at all in the baroque manner. Because the pictures he actually did produce with undeniable success are the first steps in that direction, sensual and rich, with not the slightest hint of baroque, but new, the man's new grasp of substantial reality.

There was, then, a certain discrepancy between Cézanne's *notion* of what he wanted to produce, and his other, intuitive knowledge of what he *could* produce. For whereas the mind works in possibilities, the intuitions work in actualities, and what you *intuitively* desire, that is possible to you. Whereas what you mentally or 'consciously' desire is nine times out of ten impossible: hitch your wagon to a star, and you'll just stay where you are.

So the conflict, as usual, was not between the artist and his medium, but between the artist's *mind* and the artist's *intuition* and *instinct*. And what Cézanne had to learn was not humility—cant word!—but honesty, honesty with himself. It was not a question of any gift or significant form or aesthetic ecstasy: it was a question of Cézanne being himself, just Cézanne. And when Cézanne is himself he is not Tintoretto, nor Veronese, nor anything baroque at all. Yet he is something *physical,* and even sensual: qualities which he had identified with the masters of virtuosity. . . .

What we have to thank Cézanne for is not his humility, but for his proud high spirit that refused to accept the glib utterances of his facile mental self. He wasn't poor-spirited enough to be facile—nor humble enough to be satisfied with visual and emotional clichés. Thrilling as the baroque masters were to him in themselves, he realized that as soon as he reproduced them he produced nothing but cliché. The mind is full of all sorts of memory, visual, tactile, emotional memory, memories, groups of memories, systems of memories. A cliché is just a worn-out memory that has no more emotional or intuitional root, and has become a habit. Whereas a novelty is just a new grouping of clichés, a new arrangement of accustomed memories. That is why a novelty is so easily accepted: it gives the little shock or thrill of surprise, but it does not *disturb* the emotional and intuitive self. It forces you to see nothing new. It is only a novel compound of clichés. The work of most of Cézanne's successors is just novel, just a new arrangement of clichés, soon growing stale. And the clichés are Cézanne's clichés, just as in Cézanne's own earlier pictures the clichés were all, or mostly, baroque clichés.

Cézanne's early history as a painter is a history of his fight with his own cliché. His consciousness wanted a new realization. And his ready-made mind offered him all the time a ready-made expression. And Cézanne, far too inwardly proud and haughty to accept the ready-made clichés that came from his mental consciousness, stocked with mem-ories, and which appeared mocking at him on his canvas, spent most of his time smashing his own forms to bits. To be a true artist, and to the living imagination, the cliché is the deadly enemy. Cézanne had a bitter fight with it. He hammered it to pieces a thousand times. And still it reappeared.

Now again we can see why Cézanne's drawing was so bad. It was bad because it represented a smashed, mauled cliché, terribly knocked about. If Cézanne had been willing to accept his own baroque cliché, his drawing would have been perfectly conventionally 'all right', and not a critic would have had a word to say about it. But when his drawing was conventionally all right, to Cézanne himself it was mock-ingly all wrong, it was cliché. So he flew at it and knocked all the shape and stuffing out of it, and when it was so mauled that it was all wrong, and he was exhausted with it, he let it go; bitterly, because it still was not what he wanted. And here comes in the comic element in Cézanne's pictures. His rage with the cliché made him distort the cliché sometimes into parody, as we see in pictures like "The Pasha" and "La Femme." 'You *will* be cliché, will you?' he gnashes. 'Then *be* it!' And he shoves it in a frenzy of exasperation over into parody. And the sheer exasperation makes the parody still funny; but the laugh is a little on the wrong side of the face.

This smashing of the cliché lasted a long way into Cézanne's life; indeed, it went with him to the end. The way he worked over and over his forms was his nervous manner of laying the ghost of his cliché, burying it. Then when it disappeared perhaps from his forms them-selves, it lingered in his composition, and he had to fight with the *edges* of his forms and contours, to bury the ghost there. Only his colour he knew was not cliché. He left it to his disciples to make it so.

In his very best pictures, the best of the still-life compositions, which seem to me Cézanne's greatest achievement, the fight with the cliché is still going on. But it was in the still-life pictures he learned his final method of *avoiding* the cliché; just leaving gaps through which it fell into nothingness. So he makes his landscape succeed.

In his art, all his life long, Cézanne was tangled in a twofold activity. He wanted to express something, and before he could do it he had to fight the hydra-headed cliché, whose last head he could never lop off. The fight with the cliché, is the most obvious thing in his pictures. The dust of battle rises thick and the splinters fly wildly. And it is this dust of battle and flying of splinters which his imitators still so fervently imitate. If you give a Chinese dressmaker a dress to copy, and the dress happens to have a darned rent in it, the dressmaker carefully tears a rent in the new dress, and darns it in exact replica. And this seems to be the chief occupation of Cézanne's disciples, in every land. They absorb themselves reproducing imitation mistakes. He let off various explosions in order to blow up the stronghold of the cliché, and his followers make grand firework imitations of the explosions, without the faintest inkling of the true attack. They do, indeed make an onslaught on representation, true-to-life representation: because the explosion in Cézanne's pictures blew them up. But I am convinced that what Cézanne himself wanted *was* representation. He *wanted* true-to-life representation. Only he wanted it *more* true to life. And once you have got photography, it is a very, very difficult thing to get representation *more* true-to-life: which it has to be.

Cézanne was a realist, and he wanted to be true to life. But he would not be content with the optical cliché. With the impressionists, purely optical vision perfected itself and fell *at once* into clichés, with a startling rapidity. Cézanne saw this. Artists like Courbet and Daumier were not purely optical, but the other element in these two painters, the intellectual element, was cliché. To the optical vision they added the concept of force-pressure, almost like an hydraulic brake, and this force-pressure concept is mechanical, a cliché, though still popular. And Daumier added mental satire, and Coubet added a touch of a sort of socialism: both cliché and unimaginative.

Cézanne wanted something that was neither optical nor mechanical nor intellectual. And to introduce into our world of vision something which is neither optical nor mechanical nor intellectual-psychological requires a real revolution. It was a revolution Cézanne began, but which nobody, apparently, has been able to carry on.

He wanted to touch the world of substance once more with the intuitive touch, to be aware of it with the intuitive awareness, and to express it in intuitive terms. That is, he wished to displace our present mode of mental visual consciousness, the consciousness of mental concepts, and substitute a mode of consciousness that was predominantly intuitive, the awareness of touch. In the past the primitive painted intuitively, but *in the direction* of our present mental-visual, conceptual form of consciousness. They were working away from their own intuition. Mankind has never been able to trust the intuitive consciousness, and the decision to accept the trust marks a very great revolution in the course of human development.

Without knowing it, Cézanne, the timid little conventional man sheltering behind his wife and sister and the Jesuit father, was a pure revolutionary. When he said to his models: 'Be an apple! Be an apple!' he was uttering the foreword to the fall not only of Jesuits and the Christian idealists together, but to the collapse of our whole way of consciousness, and the substitution of another way. If the human being is going to be primarily an apple, as for Cézanne it was, then you are going to have a new world of men: a world which has very little to say, men that can sit still and just be physically there, and be truly nonmoral. That was what Cézanne meant with his: 'Be an apple!' He knew perfectly well that the moment the model began to intrude her personality and her 'mind', it would be cliché and moral, and he would have to paint cliché. The only part of her that was not banal, known *ad nauseam,* living cliché, the only part of her that was not living cliché was her appleyness. Her body, even her very sex, was known, nauseously: *connu! connu!* the endless chance of known cause-and-effect, the infinite web of the hated cliché which nets us all down in utter boredom. He knew it all, he hated it all, he refused it all, this timid and 'humble' little man. He knew, as an artist, that the only bit of a woman which nowadays escapes being ready-made and ready-known cliché is the appley part of her. Oh, be an apple, and leave out all your thoughts, all your feelings, all your mind and all your personality, which we know all about and find boring beyond endurance. Leave it all out—and be an apple! It is the appleyness of the portrait of Cézanne's wife that makes it so permanently interesting: the appleyness, which carries with it also the feeling of knowing the other side as well, the side you don't see, the hidden side of the moon. For the intuitive apperception of the apple is so *tangibly* aware of the apple that it is aware of it *all round,* not only just of the front. The eye sees only fronts, and the mind, on the whole, is satisfied with fronts. But intuition needs all-roundedness, and instinct needs insideness. The true imagination is forever curving round to the other side, to the back of presented appearance.

So to my feeling the portraits of Madame Cézanne, particularly the portrait in the red dress, are more interesting than the portrait of M. Geffroy, or the portraits of the housekeeper or the gardener. In the same way the "Card-Players" with two figures please me more than those with four.

But we have to remember, in his figure-paintings, that while he was painting the appleyness he was also deliberately painting *out* the so-called humanness, the personality, the 'likeness', the physical cliché. He had deliberately to paint it out, deliberately to make the hands and face rudimentary, and so on, because if he had painted them in fully they would have been cliché. He *never* got over the cliché denominator, the intrusion and interference of the ready-made concept, when it came to people, to men and women. Especially to women he could only give a cliché response—and that maddened him. Try as he might, women remained a known, ready-made cliché object to him, and he *could not* break through the concept obsession to get at the intuitive awareness of her. Except with his wife—and in his wife he did at least know the appleyness. But with his housekeeper he failed somewhat. She was a bit cliché, especially the face. So really is M. Geffroy.

With men Cézanne often dodged it by insisting on the clothes, those stiff cloth jackets bent into thick folds, those hats, those blouses, those curtains. Some of the "Card-Players," the big ones with four figures, seem just a trifle banal, so much occupied with painted stuff, painted clothing, and the humanness a bit cliché. Not good colour, nor clever composition, nor 'planes' of colour, nor anything else will save an emotional cliché from being an emotional cliché, though they may, of course, garnish it and make it more interesting.

Where Cézanne did sometimes escape the cliché altogether and really give a complete intuitive interpretation of actual objects is in some of the still-life compositions. To me these good still-life scenes are purely representative and quite true to life. Here Cézanne did what he wanted to do: he made the thing quite real, he didn't deliberately leave anything out, and yet he gave us a triumphant and rich intuitive vision of a few apples and kitchen pots. For once his intuitive consciousness triumphed, and broke into utterance. And here he is inimitable. His imitators imitate his accessories of tablecloths folded like tins, etc. —the unreal parts of his pictures—but they don't imitate the pots and apples, because they can't. It's the real appleyness, and you can't imitate it. Every man must create it new and different out of himself: new and different. The moment it looks 'like' Cézanne, it is nothing.

But at the same time Cézanne was triumphing with the apple and appleyness he was still fighting with the cliché. When he makes Madame Cézanne most *still*, most appley, he starts making the universe slip uneasily about her. It was part of his desire: to make the human form, the *life* form, come to rest. Not static—on the contrary. Mobile but come to rest. And at the same time he set the unmoving material world into motion. Walls twitch and slide, chairs bend or rear up a little, cloths curl like burning paper. Cézanne did this partly to satisfy his intuitive feeling that nothing is really *statically* at rest—a feeling he seems to have had strongly—as when he watched the lemons shrivel or go mildewed, in his still-life group, which he left lying there so long so that he *could* see that gradual flux of change: and partly to fight the cliché, which says that the inanimate world *is* static, and that walls *are* still. In his fight with the cliché he denied that walls are still and chairs are static. In his intuitive self he *felt* for their changes.

And these two activities of his consciousness occupy his later landscapes. In the best landscapes we are fascinated by the mysterious *shiftiness* of the scene under our eyes; it shifts about as we watch it. And we realize, with a sort of transport, how intuitively *true* this is of landscape. It is *not* still. It has its own weird anima, and to our wide-eyed perception it changes like a living animal under our gaze. This is a quality that Cézanne got marvellously.

Then again, in other pictures he seems to be saying; Landscape is not like this and not like this and not like this and not . . . etc.—and every *not* is a little blank space in the canvas, defined by the remains of an assertion. Sometimes Cézanne builds up a landscape essentially out of omissions. He puts fringes on the complicated vacuum of the cliché, so to speak, and offers us that. It is interesting in a *repudiative* fashion, but it is not the new thing. The appleyness, the intuition has gone. We have only a mental repudiation. This occupies many of the later pictures: and ecstasizes the critics.

And Cézanne was bitter. He had never, as far as his *life* went, broken through the horrible glass screen of the mental concepts, to the actual *touch* of life. In his art he had touched the apple, and that was a great deal. He had intuitively known the apple and intuitively brought it forth on the tree of his life, in paint. But when it came to anything beyond the apple, to landscape, to people, and above all to nude woman, the cliché had triumphed over him. The cliché had triumphed over him, and he was bitter, misanthropic. How not to be misanthropic when men and women are just clichés to you, and you hate the cliché? Most people, of course, love the cliché—because most people *are* the cliché. Still, for all that, there is perhaps more appleyness in man, and even in nude woman, than Cézanne was able to get at. The cliché obtruded, so he just abstracted away from it. Those last water-colour landscapes are just coloured sort of edges. The blank is vacuum, which was Cézanne's last word against the cliché. It is a vacuum and the edges are there to assert the vacuity.

And the very fact that we can reconstruct almost instantly a whole landscape from the few indications Cézanne gives, shows what a cliché the landscape is, how it exists already ready-made, in our minds, how it exists in a pigeon-hole of the consciousness, so to speak, and you need only be given its number to be able to get it out, complete. Cézanne's last water-colour landscapes, made up of a few touches on blank paper, are a satire on landscape altogether. *They leave so much to the imagination!*—that immortal cant phrase, which means they give you the clue to a cliché and the cliché comes. That's what the cliché exists for. And that sort of imagination is just a rag-bag memory stored with thousands and thousands of old and really worthless sketches, images, etc., clichés.

We can see what a fight it means, the escape from the domination of the ready-made mental concept, the mental consciousness stuffed full of clichés that intervene like a complete screen between us and life. It means a long, long fight, that will probably last for ever. But Cézanne did get as far as the apple. I can think of nobody else who has done anything.

When we put it in personal terms, it is a fight in a man between his own ego, which is his ready-made mental self which inhabits either a sky-blue, self-tinted heaven or a black, self-tinted hell, and his other free intuitive self. Cézanne never freed himself from his ego, in his life. He haunted the fringes of experience. 'I who am so feeble in life'— but at least he knew it. At least he had the greatness to feel bitter about it. Not like the complacent bourgeois who now 'appreciate' him! . . .

All great Art and Literature is propaganda.

Preface by Bernard Shaw to *On the Rocks*

Benjamin Robert Haydon
The False Delicacy of the English Public

The Taste of the English Nobility shrinks from contemplating the naked breast of a lovely Woman, their daughters must be corrupted and their wives debauched, but they see nothing distasteful [in] the drunken beastliness of Teniers, and no lady is ashamed to put her eye to a Dutch Boor[1] pissing in a corner, or disgorging the contents of a drunken stomach in his wife's lap. No doubt they're shocking to write, but is it not more shocking to paint? and still more shocking to dwell upon, & more shocking yet to hang in one's drawing room, to shew on one's rout days! to point out the fascinating loveliness of our exquisite Women. This is the truth & I'll tell them so one day.

(*Diary*, January 30, 1816)

The most entertaining thing in this World at present is to go into Hyde Park, stroll quietly amongst the groups of all classes, and listen to the remarks on the bronze figure now erected in honor of Wellington—the Dear Papa.

The sensation created by the erection of the Bronze figure in the Park is just such a one as might have been anticipated the first time a naked, colossal figure was placed in public view in England. With the best disposition to the Arts, the Nobility & the people have yet to learn that nakedness is not indecency, and there are some in the world who can contemplate it unaccompanied with disgust, appetite, or shame.

(*Diary*, July 20, 1822)

Wordsworth Confronts Cupid and Psyche

Once as I was walking with Wordsworth in Pall Mall we ran into Christie's . . . In the corner stood the group of Cupid and Psyche kissing. After looking some time he turned round to me with an expression I shall never forget, and said, "The Dev-ils!"

(*Autobiography and Memoirs*)

[1] Peasant.

ART AND REALITY

Here is a chapter, complete in itself, from one of the most profound and challenging books on art published in recent years, one which should be read and studied in its entirety by anyone seriously interested in art.

E. H. Gombrich
Truth and the Stereotype[1]

The schematism by which our understanding deals with the phenomenal world . . . is a skill so deeply hidden in the human soul that we shall hardly guess the secret trick that Nature here employs.

Immanuel Kant, *Kritik der reinen Vernunft*

I

In his charming autobiography, the German illustrator Ludwig Richter relates how he and his friends, all young art students in Rome in the 1820's, visited the famous beauty spot of Tivoli and sat down to draw. They looked with surprise, but hardly with approval, at a group of French artists who approached the place with enormous baggage, carrying large quantities of paint which they applied to the canvas with big, coarse brushes. The Germans, perhaps roused by this self-confident artiness, were determined on the opposite approach. They selected the hardest, best-pointed pencils,

---

[1] *Art and Illusion* by E. H. Gombrich. New York: Pantheon Books, 1960.

CARL A. RUDISILL LIBRARY
LENOIR RHYNE COLLEGE

which could render the motif firmly and minutely to its finest detail, and each bent down over his small piece of paper, trying to transcribe what he saw with the utmost fidelity. "We fell in love with every blade of grass, every tiny twig, and refused to let anything escape us. Everyone tried to render the motif as objectively as possible."

Nevertheless, when they then compared the fruits of their efforts in the evening, their transcripts differed to a surprising extent. The mood, the color, even the outline of the motif had undergone a subtle transformation in each of them. Richter goes on to describe how these different versions reflected the different dispositions of the four friends, for instance, how the melancholy painter had straightened the exuberant contours and emphasized the blue tinges. We might say he gives an illustration of the famous definition by Emile Zola, who called a work of art "a corner of nature seen through a temperament."

It is precisely because we are interested in this definition that we must probe it a little further. The "temperament" or "personality" of the artist, his selective preferences, may be one of the reasons for the transformation which the motif undergoes under the artist's hands, but there must be others—everything, in fact, which we bundle together into the word "style," the style of the period and the style of the artist. When this transformation is very noticeable we say the motif has been greatly "stylized," and the corollary to this observation is that those who happen to be interested in the motif, for one reason or another, must learn to discount the style. This is part of that natural adjustment, the change in what I call "mental set," which we all perform quite automatically when looking at old illustrations. We can "read" the Bayeux tapestry without reflecting on its countless "deviations from reality." We are not tempted for a moment to think the trees at Hastings in 1066 looked like palmettes and the ground at that time consisted of scrolls. It is extreme example, but it brings out the all-important fact that the word "stylized" somehow tends to beg the question. It implies there was a special activity by which the artist transformed the trees, much as the Victorian designer was taught to study the forms of flowers before he turned them into patterns. It was a practice which chimed in well with ideas of Victorian architecture, when railways and factories were built first and then adorned with the marks of a style. It was not the practice of earlier times.

The very point of Richter's story, after all, is that style rules even where the artist wishes to reproduce nature faithfully, and trying to analyze these limits to objectivity may help us get nearer to the riddle of style. One of these limits . . . is indicated in Richter's story by the contrast between coarse brush and fine pencil. The artist, clearly, can render only what his tool and his medium are capable of rendering. His technique restricts his freedom of choice. The features and relationships the pencil picks out will differ from those the brush can indicate. Sitting in front of his motif, pencil in hand, the artist will, therefore, look out for those aspects which can be rendered in lines—as we say in a pardonable abbreviation, he will tend to see his motif in terms of lines, while, brush in hand, he sees it in terms of masses.

The question of why style should impose similar limitations is less easily answered, least of all when we do not know whether the artist's intentions were the same as those of Richter and his friends.

Historians of art have explored the regions where Cézanne and van Gogh set up their easels and have photographed their motifs. Such comparisons will always retain their fascination since they almost allow us to look over the artist's shoulder—and who does not wish he had this privilege? But however instructive such confrontations may be when handled with care, we must clearly beware of the fallacy of "stylization." Should we believe the photograph represents the "objective truth" while the painting records the artist's subjective vision—the way he transformed "what he saw"? Can we here compare "the image on the retina" with the "image in the mind"? Such speculations easily lead into a morass of unprovables. Take the image on the artist's retina. It sounds scientific enough, but actually there never was *one* such image which we could single out for comparison with either photograph or painting. What there was was an endless succession of innumerable images as the painter scanned the landscape in front of him, and these images sent a complex pattern of impulses through the optic nerves to his brain. Even the artist knew nothing of these events, and we know even less. How far the picture that formed in his mind corresponded to or deviated from the photograph it is even less profitable to ask. What we do know is that these artists went out into nature to look for material for a picture and their artistic wisdom led them to organize the elements of the landscape into works of art of marvelous complexity that bear as much relationship to a surveyor's record as a poem bears to a police report.

Does this mean, then, that we are altogether on a useless quest? That artistic truth differs so much from prosaic truth that the question of objectivity must never be asked? I do not think so. We must only be a little more circumspect in our formulation of the question.

II

The National Gallery in Washington possesses a landscape painting by a nineteenth-century artist which almost seems made to clarify this issue.

It is an attractive picture by George Inness of "The Lackawanna Valley," which we know from the master's son was commissioned in 1855 as an advertisement for a railroad. At the time there was only one track running into the roundhouse, "but the president insisted on having four or five painted in, easing his conscience by explaining that the road would eventually have them." Inness protested, and we can see that when he finally gave in for the sake of his family, he shame-facedly hid the patch with the nonexistent tracks behind puffs of smoke. To him this patch was a lie, and no aesthetic explanation about mental images or higher truth could have disputed this away.

But, strictly speaking, the lie was not in the painting. It was in the advertisement, if it claimed by caption or implication that the painting gave accurate information about the facilities of the railway's round-houses. In a different context the same picture might have illustrated a true statement—for instance, if the president had taken it to a share-holders' meeting to demonstrate improvements he was anxious to make. Indeed in that case, Inness' rendering of the nonexistent tracks might conceivably have given the engineer some hints about where to lay them. It would have served as a sketch or blueprint.

Logicians tell us—and they are not people to be easily gainsaid—that the terms "true" and "false" can only be applied to statements, propositions. And whatever may be the usage of critical parlance, a picture is never a statement in that sense of the term. It can no more be true or false than a statement can be blue or green. Much confusion has been caused in aesthetics by disregarding this simple fact. It is an understandable confusion because in our culture pictures are usually labeled, and labels, or captions, can be understood as abbreviated statements. When it is said "the camera cannot lie," this confusion is apparent. Propaganda in wartime often made use of photographs falsely labeled to accuse or exculpate one of the warring parties. Even in scientific illustrations it is the caption which determines the truth of the picture. In a *cause célèbre* of the last century, the embryo of a pig, labeled as a human embryo to prove a theory of evolution, brought about the downfall of a great reputation. Without much reflection, we can all expand into statements the laconic captions we find in museums

and books. When we read the name "Ludwig Richter" under a landscape painting, we know we are thus informed that he painted it and
can begin arguing whether this information is true or false. When we
read "Tivoli," we infer the picture is to be taken as a view of that
spot, and we can again agree or disagree with the label. How and
when we agree, in such a case, will largely depend on what we want to
know about the object represented. The Bayeux tapestry, for instance,
tells us there was a battle at Hastings. It does not tell us what Hastings
"looked like."

Now the historian knows that the information pictures were expected
to provide differed widely in different periods. Not only were images
scarce in the past, but so were the public's opportunities to check their
captions. How many people ever saw their ruler in the flesh at sufficiently close quarters to recognize his likeness? How many traveled
widely enough to tell one city from another? It is hardly surprising,
therefore, that pictures of people and places changed their captions
with sovereign disregard for truth. The print sold on the market as a
portrait of a king would be altered to represent his successor or enemy.

There is a famous example of this indifference to truthful captions
in one of the most ambitious publishing projects of the early printing
press, Hartmann Schedel's so-called "Nuremberg Chronicle" with
woodcuts by Dürer's teacher Wolgemut. What an opportunity such a
volume should give the historian to see what the world was like at
the time of Columbus! But as we turn the pages of this big folio, we
find the same woodcut of a medieval city recurring with different captions as Damascus, Ferrara, Milan, and Mantua. Unless we are prepared
to believe these cities were as indistinguishable from one another as
their suburbs may be today, we must conclude that neither the pub-
lisher nor the public minded whether the captions told the truth. All
they were expected to do was to bring home to the reader that these
names stood for cities.

These varying standards of illustration and documentation are of
interest to the historian of representation precisely because he can
soberly test the information supplied by picture and caption without
becoming entangled too soon in problems of aesthetics. Where it is a
question of information imparted by the image, the comparison with
the correctly labeled photograph should be of obvious value. Three
topographical prints representing various approaches to the perfect
picture post card should suffice to exemplify the results of such an
analysis.

The first shows a view of Rome from a German sixteenth-century newssheet reporting a catastrophic flood when the Tiber burst its banks. Where in Rome could the artist have seen such a timber structure, a castle with black-and-white walls, and a steep roof such as might be found in Nuremberg? Is this also a view of a German town with a misleading caption? Strangely enough, it is not. The artist, whoever he was, must have made some effort to portray the scene, for this curious building turns out to be the Castel Sant' Angelo in Rome, which guards the bridge across the Tiber. A comparison with a photograph shows that it does embody quite a number of features which belong or belonged to the castle: the angel on the roof that gives it its name, the main round bulk, founded on Hadrian's mausoleum, and the outworks with the bastions that we know were there.

I am fond of this coarse woodcut because its very crudeness allows us to study the mechanism of portrayal as in a slow-motion picture. There is no question here of the artist's having deviated from the motif in order to express his mood or his aesthetic preferences. It is doubtful, in fact, whether the designer of the woodcut ever saw Rome. He probably adapted a view of the city in order to illustrate the sensational news. He knew the Castel Sant' Angelo to be a castle, and so he selected from the drawer of his mental stereotypes the appropriate cliché for a castle—a German *Burg* with its timber structure and high-pitched roof. But he did not simply repeat his stereotype—he adapted it to its particular function by embodying certain distinctive features which he knew belonged to that particular building in Rome. He supplies some information over and above the fact that there is a castle by a bridge.

Once we pay attention to this principle of the adapted stereotype, we also find it where we would be less likely to expect it: that is, within the idiom of illustrations, which look much more flexible and therefore plausible.

The example from the seventeenth century, from the views of Paris by that well-known and skillful topographical artist Matthäus Merian, represents Notre Dame and gives, at first, quite a convincing rendering of that famous church. Comparison with the real building, however, demonstrates that Merian has proceeded in exactly the same way as the anonymous German woodcutter. As a child of the seventeenth century, his notion of a church is that of a lofty symmetrical building with large, rounded windows, and that is how he designs Notre Dame. He places the transept in the center with four large, rounded windows on either side, while the actual view shows seven narrow, pointed Gothic windows to the west and six in the choir. Once more portrayal means for Merian the adaptation or adjustment of his formula or scheme for churches to a particular building through the addition of a number of distinctive features—enough to make it recognizable and even acceptable to those who are not in search of architectural information. If this happened to be the only document extant to tell us about the Cathedral of Paris, we would be very much misled.

One last example in this series: a nineteenth-century lithograph of Chartres Cathedral, done in the heyday of English topographical art. Here, surely, we might expect a faithful visual record. By comparison with the previous instances, the artist really gives a good deal of accurate information about that famous building. But he, too, it turns out, cannot escape the limitations which his time and interests impose on him. He is a romantic to whom the French cathedrals are the greatest flowers of the Gothic centuries, the true age of faith. And so he conceives of Chartres as a Gothic structure with pointed arches and fails to record the Romanesque rounded windows of the west façade, which have no place in his universe of form.

I do not want to be misunderstood here. I do not want to prove by these examples that all representation must be inaccurate or that all visual documents before the advent of photography must be misleading. Clearly, if we had pointed out to the artist his mistake, he could have further modified his scheme and rounded the windows. My point is rather that such matching will always be a step-by-step process—how long it takes and how hard it is will depend on the choice of the initial schema to be adapted to the task of serving as a portrait. I believe that in this respect these humble documents do indeed tell us a lot about the procedure of any artist who wants to make a truthful record of an individual form. He begins not with his visual impression but with his idea or concept: the German artist with his concept of a castle that he applies as well as he can to that individual castle, Merian with his idea of a church, and the lithographer with his stereotype of a cathedral. The individual visual information, those distinctive features I have mentioned, are entered, as it were, upon a pre-existing blank or formulary. And, as often happens with blanks, if they have no provisions for certain kinds of information we consider essential, it is just too bad for the information.

The comparison, by the way, between the formularies of administration and the artist's stereotypes is not my invention. In medieval parlance there was one word for both, a *simile*, or pattern, that is applied to individual incidents in law no less than in pictorial art.

And just as the lawyer or the statistician could plead that he could never get hold of the individual case without some sort of framework provided by his forms or blanks, so the artist could argue that it makes no sense to look at a motif unless one has learned how to classify and catch it within the network of a schematic form. This, at least, is the conclusion to which psychologists have come who knew nothing of our historical series but who set out to investigate the procedure anyone adopts when copying what is called a "nonsense figure," an inkblot, let us say, or an irregular patch. By and large, it appears, the procedure is always the same. The draftsman tries first to classify the blot and fit it into some sort of familiar schema—he will say, for instance, that it is triangular or that it looks like a fish. Having selected such a schema to fit the form approximately, he will proceed to adjust it, noticing for instance that the triangle is rounded at the top, or that the fish ends in a pigtail. Copying, we learn from these experiments, proceeds through the rhythms of schema and correction. The schema is not the product of a process of "abstraction," of a tendency to "simplify"; it represents the first approximate, loose category which is gradually tightened to fit the form it is to reproduce.

III

One more important point emerges from these psychological discussions of copying: it is dangerous to confuse the way a figure is drawn with the way it is seen. "Reproducing the simplest figures," writes Professor Zangwill, "constitutes a process itself by no means psychologically simple. This process typically displays an essentially constructive or reconstructive character, and with the subjects employed, reproduction was mediated pre-eminently through the agency of verbal and geometrical formulae. . . ."

If a figure is flashed on a screen for a short moment, we cannot retain it without some appropriate classification. The label given it will influence the choice of a schema. If we happen to hit on a good description we will succeed best in the task of reconstruction. In a famous investigation by F. C. Bartlett, students had to draw such a "nonsense figure" from memory. Some called it a pickax and consequently drew it with pointed prongs. Others accepted it as an anchor and subsequently exaggerated the size of the ring. There was only one person who reproduced the shape correctly. He was a student who had labeled the shape for himself "a pre-historic battle axe." Maybe he was trained in classifying such objects and was therefore able to portray the figure that happened to correspond to a schema with which he was familiar.

Where such a pre-existing category is lacking, distortion sets in. Its effects become particularly amusing when the psychologist imitates the parlor game of "drawing consequences." Thus F. C. Bartlett had an Egyptian hieroglyph copied and recopied till it gradually assumed the familiar shape and formula of a pussycat.

To the art historian these experiments are of interest because they help to clarify certain fundamentals. The student of medieval art, for instance, is constantly brought up against the problem of tradition through copy. Thus the copies of classical coins by Celtic and Teutonic tribes have become fashionable of late as witnesses to the barbaric "will-to-form." These tribes, it is implied, rejected classical beauty in favor of the abstract ornament. Maybe they really disapproved of naturalistic shapes, but if they did we would need other evidence. The fact that in being copied and recopied the image became assimilated into the schemata of their own craftsmen demonstrates the same tendency which made the German woodcut transform the Castel Sant' Angelo into a timbered *Burg*. The "will-to-form" is rather a "will-to-make-conform," the assimilation of any new shape to the schemata and patterns an artist has learned to handle.

The Northumbrian scribes were marvelously skilled in the weaving of patterns and the shaping of letters. Confronted with the task of copying the image of a man, the symbol of St. Matthew, from a very different tradition, they were quite satisfied to build it up from those units they could handle so well. The solution in the famous Echternach Gospels is so ingenious as to arouse our admiration. It is creative, not because it differs from the presumed prototype—Bartlett's pussycat also differs from the owl—but because it copes with the challenge of the unfamiliar in a surprising and successful way. The artist handles the letter forms as he handles his medium, with complete assurance in creating from it the symbolic image of a man.

But did the designer of the Bayeux tapestry act very differently? He was obviously trained in the intricate interlace work of eleventh-century ornament and adjusted these forms as far as he thought necessary to signify trees. Within his universe of form this procedure was both ingenious and consistent.

Could he have done otherwise? Could he have inserted naturalistic renderings of beeches or firs if only he had wanted to? The student of art is generally discouraged from asking this question. He is supposed to look for explanations of style in the artist's will rather than in his skill. Moreover, the historian has little use for questions of might-have-been. But is not this reluctance to ask about the degree of freedom that exists for artists to change and modify their idiom one of the reasons why we have made so little progress in the explanation of style?

In the study of art no less than in the study of man, the mysteries of success are frequently best revealed through an investigation of failures. Only a pathology of representation will give us some insight into the mechanisms which enabled the masters to handle this instrument with such assurance.

Not only must we surprise the artist when he is confronted with an unfamiliar task that he cannot easily adjust to his means; we must also know that his aim was in fact portrayal. Given these conditions, we may do without the actual comparison between photograph and representation that was our starting point. For, after all, nature is sufficiently uniform to allow us to judge the information value of a picture even when we have never seen the specimen portrayed. The beginnings of illustrated reportage, therefore, provide another test case where we need have no doubt about the will and can, consequently, concentrate on the skill.

IV

Perhaps the earliest instance of this kind dates back more than three thousand years, to the beginnings of the New Kingdom in Egypt, when the Pharaoh Thutmose included in his picture chronicle of the Syrian campaign a record of plants he had brought back to Egypt. The inscription, though somewhat mutilated, tells us that Pharaoh pronounces these pictures to be "the truth." Yet botanists have found it hard to agree on what plants may have been meant by these renderings. The schematic shapes are not sufficiently differentiated to allow secure identification.

An even more famous example comes from the period when medieval art was at its height, from the volume of plans and drawings by the Gothic master builder, Villard de Honnecourt, which tells us so much about the practice and outlook of the men who created the French cathedrals. Among the many architectural, religious, and symbolic drawings of striking skill and beauty to be found in this volume, there is a curiously stiff picture of a lion, seen *en face*. To us, it looks like an ornamental or heraldic image, but Villard's caption tells us that he regarded it in a different light: *"Et sacies bien,"* he says, *"qu'il fu contrefais al vif."* "Know well that it is drawn from life." These words obviously had a very different meaning for Villard than they have for us. He can have meant only that he had drawn his schema in the presence of a real lion. How much of his visual observation he allowed to enter into the formula is a different matter.

Once more the broadsheets of popular art show us to what extent this attitude survived the Renaissance. The letterpress of a German woodcut from the sixteenth century informs us that we here see "the exact counterfeit" of a kind of locust that invaded Europe in menacing swarms. But the zoologist would be rash to infer from this inscription that there existed an entirely different species of creatures that has never been recorded since. The artist had again used a familiar schema, compounded of animals he had learned to portray, and the traditional formula for locusts that he knew from an Apocalypse where the locust plague was illustrated. Perhaps the fact that the German word for a locust is *Heupferd* (hay horse) tempted him to adopt a schema of a horse for the rendering of the insect's prance.

The creation of such a name and the creation of the image have, in fact, much in common. Both proceed by classifying the unfamiliar with the familiar, or more exactly, to remain in the zoological sphere, by creating a subspecies. Since the locust is called a kind of horse it must therefore share some of its distinctive features.

The caption of a Roman print of 1601 is as explicit as that of the German woodcut. It claims the engraving represents a giant whale that had been washed ashore near Ancona the same year and "was drawn accurately from nature." (*"Ritratto qui dal naturale appunto."*) The claim would be more trustworthy if there did not exist an earlier print recording a similar "scoop" from the Dutch coast in 1598. But surely the Dutch artists of the late sixteenth century, those masters of realism, would be able to portray a whale? Not quite, it seems, for the creature looks suspiciously as if it had ears, and whales with ears, I am assured on higher authority, do not exist. The draftsman probably mistook one of the whale's flippers for an ear and therefore placed it far too close to the eye. He, too, was misled by a familiar schema, the schema of the typical head. To draw an unfamiliar sight presents greater difficulties than is usually realized. And this, I suppose, was also the reason why the Italian preferred to copy the whale from another print. We need not doubt the part of the caption that tells the news from Ancona, but to portray it again "from the life" was not worth the trouble.

In this respect, the fate of exotic creatures in the illustrated books of the last few centuries before the advent of photography is as instructive as it is amusing. When Dürer published his famous woodcut of a rhinoceros, he had to rely on secondhand evidence which he filled in from his own imagination, colored, no doubt, by what he had learned of the most famous of exotic beasts, the dragon with its armored body. Yet it has been shown that this half-invented creature served as a model for all renderings of the rhinoceros, even in natural-history books, up to the eighteenth century. When, in 1790, James Bruce published a drawing of the beast in his *Travels to Discover the Source of the Nile,* he proudly showed that he was aware of this fact:

"The animal represented in this drawing is a native of Tcherkin, near Ras el Feel . . . and this is the first drawing of the rhinoceros with a double horn that has ever yet been presented to the public. The first figure of the Asiatic rhinoceros, the species having but one horn, was painted by Albert Dürer, from the life. . . . It was wonderfully ill-executed in all its parts, and was the origin of all the monstrous forms under which that animal has been painted, ever since. . . . Several modern philosophers have made amends for this in our days; Mr. Parsons, Mr. Edwards, and the Count de Buffon, have given good figures of it from life; they have indeed some faults, owing chiefly to preconceived prejudices and inattention. . . . This . . . is the first that has been published with two horns, it is designed from the life, and is an African."

If proof were needed that the difference between the medieval draftsman and his eighteenth-century descendant is only one of degree, it could be found here. For the illustration, presented with such flourishes of trumpets, is surely not free from "preconceived prejudices" and the all-pervading memory of Dürer's woodcut. We do not know exactly what species of rhinoceros the artist saw at Ras el Feel, and the comparison of his picture with a photograph taken in Africa may not, therefore, be quite fair. But I am told that none of the species known to zoologists corresponds to the engraving claimed to be drawn *al vif!*

The story repeats itself whenever a rare specimen is introduced into Europe. Even the elephants that populate the paintings of the sixteenth and seventeenth centuries have been shown to stem from a very few archetypes and to embody all their curious features, despite the fact that information about elephants was not particularly hard to come by.

These examples demonstrate, in somewhat grotesque magnification, a tendency which the student of art has learned to reckon with. The familiar will always remain the likely starting point for the rendering of the unfamiliar; an existing representation will always exert its spell over the artist even while he strives to record the truth. Thus it was remarked by ancient critics that several famous artists of antiquity had made a strange mistake in the portrayal of horses: they had represented them with eyelashes on the lower lid, a feature which belongs to the human eye but not to that of the horse. A German ophthalmologist who studied the eyes of Dürer's portraits, which to the layman appear to be such triumphs of painstaking accuracy, reports somewhat similar mistakes. Apparently not even Dürer knew what eyes "really look like."

This should not give us cause for surprise, for the greatest of all the visual explorers, Leonardo himself, has been shown to have made mistakes in his anatomical drawings. Apparently he drew features of the human heart which Galen made him expect but which he cannot have seen.

The study of pathology is meant to increase our understanding of health. The sway of schemata did not prevent the emergence of an art of scientific illustration that sometimes succeeds in packing more correct visual information into the image than even a photograph contains. But the diagrammatic maps of muscles in our illustrated anatomies are not "transcripts" of things seen but the work of trained observers who build up the picture of a specimen that has been revealed to them in years of patient study.

Now in this sphere of scientific illustration it obviously makes sense to say that Thutmose's artists or Villard himself could not have done what the modern illustrator can do. They lacked the relevant schemata, their starting point was too far removed from their motif, and their style was too rigid to allow a sufficiently supple adjustment. For so much certainly emerges from a study of portrayal in art: you cannot create a faithful image out of nothing. You must have learned the trick if only from other pictures you have seen.

V

In our culture, where pictures exist in such profusion, it is difficult to demonstrate this basic fact. There are freshmen in art schools who have facility in the objective rendering of motifs that would appear to belie this assumption. But those who have given art classes in other cultural settings tell a different story. James Cheng, who taught painting to a group of Chinese trained in different conventions, once told me of a sketching expedition he made with his students to a famous beauty spot, one of Peking's old city gates. The task baffled them. In the end, one of the students asked to be given at least a picture post card of the building so that they would have something to copy. It is stories such as these, stories of breakdowns, that explain why art has a history and artists need a style adapted to a task.

I cannot illustrate this revealing incident. But luck allows us to study the next stage, as it were—the adjustment of the traditional vocabulary of Chinese art to the unfamiliar task of topographical portrayal in the Western sense. For some decades Chiang Yee, a Chinese writer and painter of great gifts and charm, has delighted us with contemplative records of the Silent Traveller, books in which he tells of his encounters with scenes and people of the English and Irish countryside and elsewhere. I take an illustration from the volume on the English Lakeland.

It is a view of Derwentwater. Here we have crossed the line that separates documentation from art. Mr. Chiang Yee certainly enjoys the adaptation of the Chinese idiom to a new purpose; he wants us to see the English scenery for once "through Chinese eyes." But it is precisely for this reason that it is so instructive to compare his view with a typical "picturesque" rendering from the Romantic period. We see how the relatively rigid vocabulary of the Chinese tradition acts as a selective screen which admits only the features for which schemata exist. The artist will be attracted by motifs which can be rendered in his idiom. As he scans the landscape, the sights which can be matched successfully with the schemata he has learned to handle will leap forward as centers of attention. The style, like the medium, creates a mental set which makes the artist look for certain aspects in the scene around him that he can render. Painting is an activity, and the artist will therefore tend to see what he paints rather than to paint what he sees.

It is this interaction between style and preference which Nietzsche summed up in his mordant comment on the claims of realism:

> "All Nature faithfully"—But by what feint
> Can Nature be subdued to art's constraint?
> Her smallest fragment is still infinite!
> And so he paints but what he likes in it.
> What does he like? He likes, what he can paint!

There is more in this observation than just a cool reminder of the limitations of artistic means. We catch a glimpse of the reasons why these limitations will never obtrude themselves within the domain of art itself. Art presupposes mastery, and the greater the artist the more surely will he instinctively avoid a task where his mastery would fail to serve him. The layman may wonder whether Giotto could have painted a view of Fiesole in sunshine, but the historian will suspect that, lacking the means, he would not have wanted to, or rather that he could not have wanted to. We like to assume, somehow, that where there is a will there is also a way, but in matters of art the maxim should read that only where there is a way is there also a will. The individual can enrich the ways and means that his culture offers him; he can hardly wish for something that he has never known is possible.

The fact that artists tend to look for motifs for which their style and training equip them explains why the problem of representational skill looks different to the historian of art and to the historian of visual information. The one is concerned with success, the other must also observe the failures. But these failures suggest that we sometimes assume a little rashly that the ability of art to portray the visible world developed, as it were, along a uniform front. We know of specialists in art—of Claude Lorrain, the master of landscape whose figure paintings were poor, of Frans Hals who concentrated almost exclusively on portraits. May not skill as much as will have dictated this type of preference? Is not all naturalism in the art of the past selective?

A somewhat Philistine experiment would suggest that it is. Take the next magazine containing snapshots of crowds and street scenes and walk with it through any art gallery to see how many gestures and types that occur in life can be matched from old paintings. Even Dutch genre paintings that appear to mirror life in all its bustle and variety will turn out to be created from a limited number of types and gestures, much as the apparent realism of the picaresque novel or of Restoration comedy still applies and modifies stock figures which can be traced back for centuries. There is no neutral naturalism. The artist, no less than the writer, needs a vocabulary before he can embark on a "copy" of reality.

VI

Everything points to the conclusion that the phrase the "language of art" is more than a loose metaphor, that even to describe the visible world in images we need a developed system of schemata. This conclusion rather clashes with the traditional distinction, often discussed in the eighteenth century, between spoken words which are conventional signs and painting which uses "natural" signs to "imitate" reality. It is a plausible distinction, but it has led to certain difficulties. If we assume, with this tradition, that natural signs can simply be copied from nature, the history of art represents a complete puzzle. It has become increasingly clear since the late ninteenth century that primitive art and child art use a language of symbols rather than "natural signs." To account for this fact it was postulated that there must be a special kind of art grounded not on seeing but rather on knowledge, an art which operates with "conceptual images." The child—it is argued—does not look at trees; he is satisfied with the "conceptual" schema of a tree that fails to correspond to any reality since it does not embody the characteristics of, say, birch or beech, let alone those of individual trees. This reliance on construction rather than on imitation was attributed to the peculiar mentality of children and primitives who live in a world of their own.

But we have come to realize that this distinction is unreal. Gustaf Britsch and Rudolf Arnheim have stressed that there is no opposition between the crude map of the world made by a child and the richer map presented in naturalistic images. All art originates in the human mind, in our reactions to the world rather than in the visible world itself, and it is precisely because all art is "conceptual" that all representations are recognizable by their style.

Without some starting point, some initial schema, we could never get hold of the flux of experience. Without categories, we could not sort our impressions. Paradoxically, it has turned out that it matters relatively little what these first categories are. We can always adjust them according to need. Indeed, if the schema remains loose and flexible, such initial vagueness may prove not a hindrance but a help. An entirely fluid system would no longer serve its purpose; it could not register facts because it would lack pigeonholes. But how we arrange the first filing system is not very relevant.

The progress of learning, of adjustment through trial and error, can be compared to the game of "Twenty Questions," where we identify an object through inclusion or exclusion along any network of classes. The traditional initial scheme of "animal, vegetable, or mineral" is certainly neither scientific nor very suitable, but it usually serves us well enough to narrow down our concepts by submitting them to the corrective test of "yes" or "no." The example of this parlor game has become popular of late as an illustration of that process of articulation through which we learn to adjust ourselves to the infinite complexity of this world. It indicates, however crudely, the way in which not only organisms but even machines may be said to "learn" by trial and error. Engineers at their thrilling work on what they call "servo mechanisms," that is, self-adjusting machines, have recognized the importance of some kind of "initiative" on the part of the machine. The first move such a machine may make will be, and indeed must be, a random movement, a shot in the dark. Provided a report of success or failure, hit or miss, can be fed back into the machine, it will increasingly avoid the wrong moves and repeat the correct ones. One of the pioneers in this field has recently described this machine rhythm of schema and correction in a striking verbal formula: he calls all learning "an arboriform stratification of guesses about the world." Arboriform, we may take it, here describes the progressive creation of classes and subclasses such as might be described in a diagrammatic account of "Twenty Questions."

We seem to have drifted far from the discussion of portrayal. But it is certainly possible to look at a portrait as a schema of a head modified by the distinctive features about which we wish to convey information. The American police sometimes employ draftsmen to aid witnesses in the identification of criminals. They may draw any vague face, a random schema, and let witnesses guide their modifications of selected features simply by saying "yes" or "no" to various suggested standard alterations until the face is sufficiently individualized for a search in the files to be profitable. This account of portrait drawing by remote control may well be over-tidy, but as a parable it may serve its purpose. It reminds us that the starting point of a visual record is not knowledge but a guess conditioned by habit and tradition.

Need we infer from this fact that there is no such thing as an objective likeness? That it makes no sense to ask, for instance, whether Chiang Yee's view of Derwentwater is more or less correct than the nineteenth-century lithograph in which the formulas of classical landscapes were applied to the same task? It is a tempting conclusion and one which recommends itself to the teacher of art appreciation because it brings home to the layman how much of what we call "seeing" is conditioned by habits and expectations. It is all the more important to clarify how far this relativism will take us. I believe it rests on the confusion between pictures, words, and statements which we saw arising the moment truth was ascribed to paintings rather than to captions.

If all art is conceptual, the issue is rather simple. For concepts, like pictures, cannot be true or false. They can only be more or less useful for the formation of descriptions. The words of a language, like pictorial formulas, pick out from the flux of events a few signposts which allow us to give direction to our fellow speakers in that game of "Twenty Questions" in which we are engaged. Where the needs of users are similar, the signposts will tend to correspond. We can mostly find equivalent terms in English, French, German, and Latin, and hence the idea has taken root that concepts exist independently of language as the constituents of "reality." But the English language erects a signpost on the roadfork between "clock" and "watch" where the German has only *"Uhr."* The sentence from the German primer, *"Meine Tante hat eine Uhr,"* leaves us in doubt whether the aunt has a clock or a watch. Either of the two translations may be wrong as a description of a fact. In Swedish, by the way, there is an additional roadfork to distinguish between aunts who are "father's sisters," those who are "mother's sisters," and those who are just ordinary aunts. If we were to play our game in Swedish we would need additional questions to get at the truth about the timepiece.

This simple example brings out the fact, recently emphasized by Benjamin Lee Whorf, that language does not give name to pre-existing things or concepts so much as it articulates the world of our experience. The images of art, we suspect, do the same. But this difference in styles or languages need not stand in the way of correct answers and descriptions. The world may be approached from a different angle and the information given may yet be the same.

From the point of view of information there is surely no difficulty in discussing portrayal. To say of a drawing that it is a correct view of Tivoli does not mean, of course, that Tivoli is bounded by wiry lines. It means that those who understand the notation will derive *no false information* from the drawing—whether it gives the contour in a few lines or picks out "every blade of grass" as Richter's friends wanted to do. The complete portrayal might be the one which gives as much correct information about the spot as we would obtain if we looked at it from the very spot where the artist stood.

Styles, like languages, differ in the sequence of articulation and in the number of questions they allow the artist to ask; and so complex is the information that reaches us from the visible world that no picture will ever embody it all. This is not due to the subjectivity of vision but to its richness. Where the artist has to copy a human product he can, of course, produce a facsimile which is indistinguishable from the original. The forger of banknotes succeeds only too well in effacing his personality and the limitations of a period style.

But what matters to us is that the correct portrait, like the useful map, is an end product on a long road through schema and correction. It is not a faithful record of a visual experience but the fruitful construction of a relational model.

Neither the subjectivity of vision nor the sway of conventions need lead us to deny that such a model can be constructed to any required degree of accuracy. What is decisive here is clearly the word "required." The form of representation cannot be divorced from its purpose and the requirements of the society in which the given visual language gains currency.

This is one of the most interesting of recent attempts to deal with the age-old question of art as imitation of reality. Maritain brings to the discussion of this question firm philosophic convictions and a trained sensibility which make his criticism of modern painting worth the attention even of those who do not share his basic assumption.

Jacques Maritain
Beauty and Modern Painting[1]

New Thresholds, New Anatomies

1. Painters as well as writers are exposed to suffer the inner division whose symptoms were a particular feature of the nineteenth century, and to be deceived by the myth of the artist as a hero; but less so, I think, than poets and writers: because they can less easily shift toward the spiritual glorification of the ego, being bound, willy-nilly, to the world of visible matter and corporeal existence, to *Nature*. Yet this very fact is for modern painting a source of unheard of difficulties in the very line of its own creative development. The obligation to recast the visible fabric of things in order to make them an expression of creative subjectivity entails now inevitable drawbacks, now accidental failures, and causes many victims.

The first victim was the human figure. The impotency of modern art to engender in beauty except at the expense of the beauty of the human figure is a disquieting symptom.[2] If it is true that the human body is the most beautiful work in natural creation; and that the human face is naturally sacred, because it is the visible sign and the natural sacrament of human personality, and because in it an immortal soul shows through —then the impotency I just mentioned, and which can be found, to one degree or another, in all great contemporary painters, cannot be

---

[1] *Creative Intuition in Art and Poetry*, by Jacques Maritain. New York: Pantheon Books, 1953.

[2] "L'aboutissement de l'art, c'est la figure," Cézanne said. (Ambroise Vollard, *Paul Cézanne*, Paris: Crès, 1924, p. 135.)

"We must believe that it was impossible at once to preserve the beauty of forms, poetry and renewal. Was it not at the point where academicism had been the most insistent that the break would take place? 'Deformation' especially attacked the human shape, both of face and of body. As landscapes had not been subject to such strict canons, they escaped this doubtless temporary necessity, which would signalize an epoch. In any case, there are today no more beautiful landscapes than those of Rouault. . . ." Raïssa Maritain, *We Have Been Friends Together* (New York: Longmans, Green, 1942), p. 162.

"The figures I do," van Gogh wrote, "almost always seem to me horrid, not to mention how they seem to others. . . ." From a letter to Emile Bernard, last week of June. 1888. In *Letters to Emile Bernard* (New York: Museum of Modern Art, 1938), p. 47.

GIRL BEFORE A MIRROR—PABLO PICASSO   *(Museum of Modern Art, New York)*

considered a slight defect. The fact was, no doubt, inevitable: precisely because the human figure carries the intrinsic exigencies of natural beauty to a supreme degree of integration, it is particularly difficult to recast its visible fabric except in deforming it. Will this difficulty be overcome some day? As long as it is not, that is, as long as the recasting in question has not become, as it was in El Greco, a change into something more human than the human appearance, modern painting will be in possession of every means to express spirituality, save the most normal one.

I just spoke of the great contemporary painters. In them the impotency not to impoverish or damage the form of man, either by blotting out its richness in significance, or by brutalizing or distorting it, is only a lack as a rule.

In the later manner of Picasso, it has become the expression of a positive aggressiveness, but always subordinate to the liberty of the creative line, and to that other kind of poetic freedom which is *black humor,* and to an inherent sense of beauty (not as to these disfigured human bodies, but as to the work as a whole). Yet we have also to do today with a particularly unfortunate, and illegitimate, progeny of great contemporary painters—the School of Degradation, I would say— and with the avid followers who mistook Picasso's cruel hieroglyphs for animal frenzy. They have found in his lesson a means of releasing the resentments of a boorish soul and of getting at little cost the admiration of an idiotic public. They cling furiously to the human figure, but to make it into a putrid foetus or a disintegrated lizard or kangaroo armed with pincers and topped by a stupid eye or a fiendish set of teeth. Where Heraclitus had said, "The most beautiful of the apes is hideous in comparison with the human race,"[3] they offer us a human race hideous in comparison with the ugliest of the apes. These painters, without being Surrealists, enforce in practice, not only with regard to man's face and body, but with regard to the very work, the surrealist dismissal of beauty, and they probably believe they convey a prophetic message to mankind. They are of interest mainly to anthropologists, who may compare their mental processes with that through which, in Tantrist or in Aztec sculpture, the human countenance became a magical instrument for fright and terror, and contempt for man. (But then, at least, the work itself had sometimes its own beauty.)

2. What matters to us is that there are other painters, who really

3 Plato, *Hipp. M.* 289 A. (Diels, Fragment 82).

count in the movement of creative research, and who keep on being intent on doing a work, and being intent on beauty. These painters have been confronted with a growing difficulty inseparable from the advance of modern painting: namely the fact that, in proportion as the creativity of the spirit strives for greater and greater liberation in order for the Self to be revealed in the work, Nature discloses greater obstacles, or rather demands from poetic intuition a ceaselessly growing power, in order for things to be grasped, and expressed in the work, without hampering or thwarting the simultaneous expression of subjectivity and the freedom of the creative spirit. What was twenty years ago an invaluable conquest over naturalism will seem now still tainted with naturalism. Any representation whatever of natural appearances is seen as an obstacle to the free creativity of the spirit. And it is, in actual fact, as long as it has not yet been purified and transfigured in the pungent night of creative intuition. The road of creative intuition, however, is exacting and solitary, it is the road to the unknown, it passes through the sufferings of the spirit. Artists are always tempted to prefer the road of technical discoveries.

Cubism set out to transpose natural appearances by decomposing and reshaping them in reference to the free expansion of forms and volumes in a newly organized space, which depends on the construction requirements of painting-as-painting, and makes our vision less bound to the limitations and opacity of matter (may it be possible to have all the sides of an object simultaneously present to the eye!). It provided us in this way with a number of admirable paintings.

Futurism, less fortunate as a rule in its achievements, except for some remarkable pictures of Severini's,[4] attempted a similar transposition in

4 Since this time Severini has come a long way, and learned a great deal in the course of a constantly progressing effort. He has become one of the most powerful renovators of sacred art, and our greatest master in mosaic and fresco. In an essay written on him in 1930 ("Gino Severini," in *Peintres Nouveaux*, No. 40, Paris: Gallimard, 1930; reprinted in *Art and Poetry*, New York: Philosophical Library, 1943), I observed, with respect to his decoration of the churches of Semsales and La Roche, in Switzerland, that "art is brought remarkably close to religious use by the most daring modern researches, requiring as they do much formal purification. It is not the newness of their means, but rather the spirit from which they seek inspiration that often keeps them apart from such usage. It would need an essential purification, an interior renovation of this spirit—which does not happen without a sort of agony, and which the majority refuses. Semsales and La Roche show us the victory of a painter who has lived out the modern anxieties and discoveries, and has never renounced them, and who has been rendered master of his soul at the same time by a great inner deepening." During long years of tenacious labor the authority of Severini did not cease growing. By his meditation on the laws of number and the logic of abstract proportions, and by his passionate attachment to all the concrete details of honest work, straightforward and rigorous, he affirmed more and more the natural kinship which relates him to the seekers of the early Italian Renaissance. While pursuing his re-

reference to the lively shiftings and mutual interpenetration of visual impressions produced by motion.

While dislocating natural appearances, neither Cubism nor Futurism did actually break with them. They tried to bring out from them a new visual significance—but by making this effort only with respect to external sensibility, and by relying finally on the discovery of a new technique, new tricks and means. It was possible for a Chagall or a Malevich to denounce Cubism's obdurate naturalism.

Then there was, for a few years, another school—a one-man school, to tell the truth—which I should like to call the School of Transmutation. I am alluding to Marcel Duchamp's[5] radical experiment. I take it here as an instance of a possible theory which it is of philosophical interest to disengage in its generality. I imagine that, from this point of view, we might express this attempt at integral transmutation in the following way.

The painter looks at Things, at the universe of visible Being—intent to grasp in it some reality beyond appearances and some hidden meaning. He receives the poetic spark (even though charged perhaps with a somewhat sadistic electricity). Then he sets out to express what he has grasped, not by simply transposing the natural appearances of the objects involved, but by using the totally different appearances of other objects belonging in a totally separate sphere—without any flash of intuitive similarity springing forth between these distant objects: so that the secret reality grasped in Being will be expressed, enigmatically, through a totally new creation totally contrived by his own spirit. A bride will become an insidious machine whose anatomy displays an ironical and icy complication of cylinders, pipes, and bevel gears.

Natural appearances will be totally transmuted into forms which pertain to another world of objects. The painter is an alchemist. He transmutes lead into gold, or gold into lead, kings, queens, and nudes into the volumes and surfaces of imaginary engines in motion, through

---

search in pure painting, he decorated a number of churches in French-speaking Switzerland, and recently composed the great mosaic of St. Peter's Church in Fribourg, a masterwork of modern religious art, which was solemnly inaugurated on September 16, 1951.

Speaking of religious art, I would like to say how much we are indebted to Maurice Denis, who was an excellent artist and critic both, and to Alexandre Cingria. I would like also to point out the particular importance, in contemporary research, of André Girard's work, which unites to an exceptional degree science and inspiration, together with admirable imaginative richness and pictorial generosity.

[5] Marcel Duchamp is the youngest of the three Villon brothers. The most recent notice on him was written by Katherine Kuh for the Catalog of the Exhibition of the Arensberg Collection at the Art Institute of Chicago, in 1949.

which the ambiguous reality intended by him and the successive moments of its manifestation in time and movement are spread out in space.

Such an attempt was logically conceivable. It had an exceptional theoretical interest. It was indeed an attempt at the impossible. For the entire process runs against the nature of our spiritual faculties.

Creative intuition and imagination do not proceed in an angelic or demonic manner. They are human, bound to the alertness of sense perception. They grasp a certain transapparent reality through the instrumentality of the eye and of certain natural appearances—they cannot express or manifest it except through the instrumentality of these same natural appearances, recreated, recast, transposed of course, not cast aside and totally replaced by other appearances proper to another realm of Things in the world of visible Being. It's as good as having the soul of a flower in an elephant. In genuine metaphor the illuminating image arrives from another world, as a bird through the window of your room, to quicken the transposition of natural appearances and their power of significance: it supersedes them only for an instant, it does not suppress them. Here, on the contrary, there is no illumination, nor illuminating image. The Thing within which creative intuition has caught its diamond is not illuminated, it is killed. The other Thing which has been conjured up does not suggest it, it absorbs it, and expresses it only in secret cipher. The process cuts off in human art the intellect from its inescapable connection with sense perception. It is unnatural in itself.

As a matter of fact, notwithstanding the homage paid by Neoromantic and Surrealist critics to Marcel Duchamp, we must observe that in his own work poetic intuition, strong as it may have been at the start, is in reality quickly superseded by pure intellectuality. Even at the initial moment, in the germinal grasping, there is more of an intellectual scheme or an idea (the craftsman idea) than of poetic knowledge. The spiritual spark was less revealing than contriving—contriving the ironical or cynical concept of a formula of transmutation. And what appears striking in the execution of the work is not attentiveness to the impalpable spirituality of creative emotion, but rather—together with a half sarcastic obsession with machinery and the devices of engineering —an extremely careful elaboration, a patient preparation of sketches and well-calculated essays, winding up in the production of some shady sophisticated myth, like that myth of the "celibate machine," doubtless highly typical of our time, which has captured the imagination of highbrowed gapers fond of hermetic marvels.

Be that as it may, an attempt at the impossible is apt to win admirers, not followers. Only Marcel Duchamp, with the enigmatic gifts of a searching mind, was able to instruct us about the significance of transmutation as a solution to the difficulties of modern painting. His experiment was bound to remain solitary. Even he himself stopped painting. After the few works which for some years impassioned Paris's esoteric circles, he gave up creative art[6] for another art of calculation, in which he had always been interested. He is now playing chess in New York.

Nonrepresentative Beauty

3. It is still a prolongation of Cubism that painting has continued to seek the seemingly unattainable way out of its present predicament. Is some other solution possible? Is there not a short cut? It is no longer a question of attempting the impossible, but rather of rejecting part of too heavy a burden. Let us turn away from Things, and from any concern for grasping in them any transapparent reality and hidden meaning. Let us by the same token give up completely, or as completely as possible, natural appearances as transposed and transfigured as they may be, and any representation of Things. Let us renounce the existential world of Nature completely, or as completely as possible. Will not art be revealed at last in its true essence, be freed at last from any trace of naturalism, express at last freely the free creativity of the spirit and the release of creative subjectivity?

It is in this way, I think, that the notion of nonrepresentative art imposed itself on the initiators of the School of Abstraction. And here we have what I would call the genuine concept of abstract art. Modern abstract art is subjective in intention, quite contrary to the objective abstract art of Islam. But modern abstract art, in so far as it is true to its original concept, implies in no way a repudiation of beauty. On the contrary, if it divorces itself from the Things of Nature, it is with a view to being more fully true to the free creativity of the spirit, that is, to poetry, and therefore to tend toward beauty, the end beyond the end of poetry, in a manner more faithful to the infinite amplitude of beauty. That's why I would say in this connection nonrepresentative or nonfigurative beauty as well as nonrepresentative or nonfigurative art.

"Suprematism"—another word for abstract art—"Suprematism," wrote Malevich, "is the rediscovery of that pure art which in the course of time, and by an accretion of 'things,' had been lost to sight. . . . The

---

[6] Except as regards his occasional collaboration with Hans Richter for some motion pictures.

happy liberating touch of nonobjectivity drew me out into the 'desert' where only feeling is real. . . . From the suprematist point of view, the appearances of natural objects are in themselves meaningless; the essential thing is feeling—in itself and completely independent of the context in which it has been evoked."[7]

At least nonfigurative art delivers us radically from the ugliness and stupidity in the image of man which have invaded contemporary painting. It does so by getting clear of the human figure. And at least it has —I mean in its most genuine representatives—a sense of the beauty of rhythm and harmony, and of the pleasure of the intelligence-permeated eye. I know that abstract art presents itself in a multiplicity of contrast-

[7]Kazimir Malevich, *Die gegenstandlose Welt* (Munich: Bauhausbuecher, 1927); in *Artists on Art* (New York: Pantheon Books, 1945), pp. 452-53. In 1913, Malevich had exhibited in Moscow a picture of a black square on a white field.

Cf. Mondrian: "The new art has continued and culminated the art of the past in such a way that the new painting, by employing 'neutral' or universal forms, expresses itself only through the relationships of line and color. While in the art of the past these relationships are veiled by the particular form, in the new art they are made clear through the use of neutral or universal forms. Because these forms become more and more neutral as they approach a state of universality, neoplasticism uses only a single neutral form: the rectangular area in varying dimensions. Since this form, when composed, completely annihilates itself for lack of contrasting forms, line and color are completely freed." Ibid., p. 427.

In his essay "Introduction to Abstract," in *Art News, November,* 1950, Thomas B. Hess remarks that today some American painters, Rothko for instance, who "like Mondrian refuse to invite recollections of nature," are trying to attain "the 'experience of objectlessness' which the pioneer abstractionist Malevich considered the supreme sensation in art" by doing "for color what the Cubists did for form" and endeavoring in this way to "project their deepest emotions into the canvas" (p. 158).

In the views that Kandinsky, the greatest representative, I think, of nonobjective art, offered (and which related to some sort of Platonic idealism blended with Mrs. Blavatsky's peculiar spiritualism), abstract painting appears as starting a kind of angelistic attempt to act directly on human souls through forms that are to be produced in accordance only with the "principle of inner necessity." (That is why he "enviously" looked at "the nonmaterial art of music," hoping to "reciprocate it with his own medium.") "[The] choice of object (one of the elements in the harmony of form) must be decided only by the corresponding vibration of the human soul." "The freer the abstract form, the purer and more primitive is its appeal. In a composition, therefore, where the material side may be more or less superfluous, it can be accordingly more or less omitted and replaced by the nonobjective forms or through abstractions of dematerialized objects. In any case of translation into the abstract or the employment of nonobjective forms, the artist's sole judge, guide, and principal consideration should be his feeling." For Kandinsky feeling— though merely subjective in the sense that it was neither dependent on the visible world, nor made intentional so as to disclose the transapparent meanings of this visible world— had nevertheless an ideal objective value, as a way to penetrate into the spiritual world of "the eternal truth embraced by art." Consequently, though "the artist may employ any form to express himself," and though the "expression of personality" is one of the "three mystical elements" of art, the expression of personality is destined progressively to lose importance, and to fade away before the final aim, the attainment of "pure and eternal artistry," "the main element of art, irrespective of time and space." "The process of development in art consists, so to speak, of the separation of the pure and eternal art from the element of personality as well as from the element of an epoch." Vasili Kandinsky, *On the Spiritual in Art* (New York: Hilla Rebay, 1946), pp. 20, 25, 35, 51-52, 55-56.

ing forms, and that it is sometimes infected by the animal frenzy and
the aggressive resentment of which I spoke a moment ago. Be that as
it may, I remain grateful for the thoughtful effort of Mondrian and
Kandinsky toward perfect and restful balance. Abstract art is able to
provide us with an element of contemplation, and repose of the soul—
only, it is true, by quitting the realm of the human, even of the living,
even of the existential reality of being, and by offering to our eyes,
along the lines of some Platonic ideal, the peace of geometrical surfaces,
wire constructions, or wooden artifacts.

4. Yet in actual fact the theory rests on false premises, and this attempt at a new solution—so disinterested and earnest in its beginnings
—involves a basic illusion. The short cut was a blind alley.

Abstract painters are right in telling us that they are not "opposed
to nature"[8] and do not break away from nature in the sense that they
use and combine prime elements and various kinds of pure units or sensory determinants which they have extracted and singled out from
nature, and that they are essentially concerned with laws of dynamic
equilibrium, laws of proportional correspondences, optical laws, psychophysical laws which are grounded on nature; and even that the spontaneous gushing forth of arbitrary forms on their paper or their canvas
depends on a nature which is their own subjective nature.[9] But all that
is beside the point. The point is that nonrepresentative painting breaks
away from Nature as an existential whole, turns away from Things and
the grasping of Things, and renounces seeing into the inner depths of
the world of Nature, of visible and corporeal Being.

Now if it is true that creative subjectivity awakens to itself only by
simultaneously awakening to Things, in a single process which is poetic
knowledge; and that the way by which the free creativity of the spirit
enters into act is essentially poetic intuition, and that poetic intuition
is nothing but the grasping of Things and the Self together through
connaturality and intentional emotion—then it must be said that in
breaking away from the existential world of Nature, from Things and
the grasping of Things, nonrepresentative art, by this very fact, con-
demns itself to fall short of its own dearest purposes and the very ends
for the sake of which it came to life. Cut off from the mystery of integral
reality to be obscurely attained in some of its transapparent aspects—

8 Mondrian, 1937; in *Artists on Art*, p. 428.

9 Ozenfant likes to stress in this connection the presence, in the unconscious tendencies
of our human nature, of "preforms" which are the preexisting "form of a need" (and
which are only, I think, another name for the connaturality with logos or proportion
inherent in our mind and senses).

in other words, cut off from poetic intuition—any effort to express freely the free creativity of the spirit, and to reveal the depths of creative subjectivity is bound to slow extinction. In actual fact, instead of tending more faithfully to the infinite amplitude of beauty, all lunges and efforts of poetry cannot prevent nonrepresentative art from tending of itself to the most limited form of beauty, the mute beauty, with almost no echoing power, of the best balanced objects produced by mechanical arts. There is no exercise of the free creativity of the spirit without poetic intuition. Painting and sculpture cannot do without poetic intuition. The crucial mistake of abstract art has been to reject —unwittingly—poetic intuition, while rejecting systematically the existential world of Things.

There is a curious sentence in the passage from Malevich I quoted a moment ago. "The appearances of natural objects," he said, "are in themselves meaningless; the essential thing is feeling"—feeling "completely independent of the context in which it has been evoked." He did not perceive that through feeling the intellect obscurely grasps the meanings in which Things abound, and which are conveyed to an attentive eye through the appearances of natural objects. Feeling for him remained merely subjective feeling, was not raised to spiritual intentionality. He remained secluded from the infinite meaningfulness of the existential world of Nature.

I would hate to be too systematic myself. Poetry is capable of worming its way in anywhere. I do not deny that in the most strictly nonrepresentative painting there are still possibilities for poetry. Even when an artist closes his eyes to things, he has still seen them, his soul is unconsciously inhabited by the forms of the universe. And thus it is possible that, while turning away from the existential world of things, the unconscious presence of this very world in the secret recesses of the painter may be enough to load some subjective feeling, unrelated to any given thing, with the spiritual élan of poetic intuition. It is possible for a painter who obeys only his merely subjective feeling (merely subjective at least in appearance), or else a free impulse of the unconscious (both the automatic and the spiritual unconscious intermingled), to trace, in total freedom from any representation whatever, lines and forms which are instinct with beauty and poetry—melodic as it were, and apt to move the heart, just as music can. My point is that such possibilities remain exceptional—and, in the last analysis, very limited; and that one cannot try to develop therefrom a specific form of art without pushing painting farther and farther away from the very sources of poetic intuition and creative emotion.

All in all, abstract art, taken as a system, is in the same predicament as idealist philosophy. Both are walled in. Even all the psychophysical laws with which nonrepresentative painting is so much concerned, and which deals with the most complex and subtle and fluent effects produced on sensations by elementary sense stimuli in relation to one another and to the environment, cannot be known in a separate manner and applied in the aprioristic way for which abstract art is looking. Painters know them only in their concrete and factual results, and in the very Things to be manifested in the work, and through creative experience intent on the existential world of Nature.

Turning away from the difficult task of grasping more and more profoundly and expressing more and more revealingly the transapparent aspects of Things, it is not surprising that, in the course of time, abstract art should appear to the growing flock of its adepts a mere way to escape poetic intuition. As a matter of fact it was to wind up in a new sort of academicism. At last it becomes again possible to take painting easily. A new eagerness for recipe and formula spares people the self-abnegation and the ordeals imposed by poetic creativity. Thus it is that we are now offered in exhibitions, art magazines, and modern art museums —together with infrequent works whose genuine poetry recalls that of the originators, and with valuable achievements and inventions in the field of merely decorative painting—a gaudy multitude of convolutions, angles, or cobwebs and amoeboid or filiform mucosities, all of them meant to express the originality of the creative self, in pictures which lack personality to such a point that they can scarcely be distinguished one from another. Everyone joins in willy-nilly, spurred by the noble iron rod of imitation, fashion, and the art dealers.

5. *Practicing scales is not giving a concert.* As an exercise or an experiment, nonrepresentative painting has, I think, unquestionable value. It unbinds the imagination, discloses to the eye of the painter a world of unforeseen possibilities, relationships, correspondences, rhythms, and equilibria, enables him more perfectly to master the prime elements of his means of expression; and over and above all it teaches him himself, in complete freedom, through the release of his own singular inventive resources as a sensitive instrument. All that, nevertheless, has to do with technique, not with poetry, or at best with making technique more supple and tractable to poetry. In this particular order, practice in abstract art has perhaps been made by the very development of modern painting a necessary moment in the individual painter's self-education. And with regard to the general evolu-

tion of painting, it was also, perhaps, and for the same reasons, an unavoidable moment. Yet in relation to art's real life, and to the progress in creativity and self-awareness achieved in the last hundred years, the irruption of nonrepresentative art can hardly be considered an advance in the process. Of itself it points rather at a period of stagnation or regression.

It must be noticed, furthermore, that in what is commonly labeled abstract art today, there are trends which already step in reality out of abstract art. When a painter happens—contrary to the theory—to be actually intent on the existential world of Nature and put in motion by poetic intuition, but uses abstract or nonrepresentative forms as means of expression, these forms are not in reality purely abstract or nonrepresentative. They make present on the canvas, they *represent*—be it in the most bare and dematerialized manner—some vital element, a rhythm, a contrast, a contour which has been seen in Nature and which is just enough to suggest some natural appearance with the significance it is laden with, even if this meaningful appearance moves you without your being able to recognize or identify the Thing to which it belongs. Condensed and simplified as they may be, natural appearances are there. Through them the existential world of Nature is there. It is there with that particular inner depth and those particular meanings which knowledge through connaturality and intentional emotion have disclosed to the painter together with his own subjectivity. By way of forms still impoverished and half-mute, but derived from Nature in actual fact, the work expresses, not a merely subjective feeling symbolized according to the requirements of psychophysical laws, but, together with an intuitive feeling, some diffident aspect of the reality of the visible world. Such painting, which is, it seems to me, characteristic of the effort of some contemporary painters still designated as abstract painters,[10] is in reality no more purely abstract art than cubism was.

[10] I might mention at this point Theodore Brenson, Clyfford Still, or Arthur Osver. But the production of contemporary American painting is so abundant and variegated that one hesitates to pick a few names among so many. While the strictly nonrepresentational current is still very strong, some artists are seeking their way in half abstraction. Many others—and this is of greater interest for our present considerations—have set themselves free from the nonrepresentative system but remain close to modern abstractionism and owe to it either a firm geometrical substructure (e.g., Randall Thompson or Lamar Dodd), or a particularly refined and airy poetry (e.g., William Palmer, Lyonel Feininger, or Howard Cook). In sharp contrast with abstract painting, the effort that Edwin Dickinson has pursued for many years along the lines of the American Romantic tradition points to a personal reinterpretation of nature which corresponds, it seems to me, to a significant trend of our times. This Romantic tradition is being revived, prodded somewhat by Surrealist influences, in a number of young painters whose work deserves particular attention.

May we believe that in this way a new development will come about, and finally set free contemporary painting from the academicism of the nonrepresentative system? No doubt a spontaneous process progressively reintegrating Nature in the inner movement of abstract research would be of greater interest than that kind of compromise, extrinsically mixing pieces of dull natural forms with nonfigurative formulas, which can also be observed today here and there.

Natural Appearances and Creative Intuition

6. In any case the truth of the matter is that creative intuition is today, and has always been, and will ever be, the primary power of authentic renewal. Salvation in art comes only through creative intuition.

The great mistake has been to put the instrumental and secondary before the principal and primary, and to search for an escape through the discovery of a new external approach and new technical revolutions, instead of passing first through the creative source, and thus taking a risk, but having a chance to find a real solution. Another mistake, connected with the first, has been to conceive of forward movement only in terms of a flight from Naturalism, as if it were enough to run farther and farther away from an error to get at the truth. The mistake has been to look for freedom *from* something—first from an error: servile imitation or copy of natural appearances, but then from the existential world of Nature itself, and from any kind of representation whatever of natural appearances—instead of looking for freedom *to* achieve in one's work a more and more genuine revelation both of Things and the Self, and *to* obey creative forces in a manner truer and truer to a deeper and deeper poetic intuition.

Everyone must in the end consent to be led into the desert. But we should not mistake the desert of emotion and feeling cut off from Nature for the desert of man's spirit in its struggle with the Angel.

To tell the truth, there is a need for a restatement of the old question of imitation (though the word itself is hopelessly wrong). It is perfectly clear that imitation in the sense of a sheer copy of natural appearances achieved in such a way that the image deceives the eye and is taken for the thing is a wrong notion, directly opposed to the nature of art.[11] But

---

11 And yet Leonardo was not ashamed to vindicate painting with such arguments: "A painting representing a father of a family happened to be caressed by his grandchildren, although they were still in long clothes: the dog and the cat of the household did likewise, and it was a wondrous sight to see. . . . I once saw a painting deceive a dog by its likeness to his master and the animal was overjoyed to see it. I have also seen dogs bark

Aristotle never had such a notion in mind. He meant that delight in seeing (or beauty) is all the greater as the object seen conveys a greater amount of intuitive knowledge: thus in art and poetry the object is also a sign—through which some transapparent reality is made intuitively known. Does not dance "imitate mores"?[12] What is "imitated"—or made visibly known—is not natural appearances but secret or transapparent reality through natural appearances. Furthermore St. Thomas insisted that art imitates nature *in her operation*—not in respect to natural appearances, but in respect to the ways in which nature herself operates. To create his work of lines and colors the painter imitates nature as he would imitate another painter. He does not copy nature as an object, he steals from nature, he extracts from his observation of, and connivance with her, the operative ways through which nature manages her own raw materials of form, color, and light to impress on our eye and mind an emotion of beauty. This is quite a peculiar type of imitation indeed, which consists in the act of making oneself instructed by a reluctant and jealous master: pilfering rather than imitation. Here we have such secrets as that of the flamelike form detected by Michelangelo, or that of inherent irregularity detected by Renoir, or that of the cylinder, sphere, and cone structure detected by Cézanne. One day, after a walk in the wintertime, Rouault told me he had just discovered, by looking at snow-clad fields in the sunshine, how to paint the white trees of spring. Such a genuine concept of "imitation" affords a ground and a justification for the boldest kinds of transposition, transfiguration, deformation, or recasting of natural appearances, in so far as they are a means to make the work manifest intuitively the transapparent reality which has been grasped by the artist.

Yet the fact remains that this genuine concept of imitation, correctly understood, expresses a necessity to which human art is bound: first, with regard to the transapparent reality to be "imitated" or intuitively manifested; second, with regard to natural appearances themselves as to be used *instrumentally* (or as means mastered by art, and thus as transposed and recast with a view to the end): for without the instrumentality of natural appearances made present or "represented" in such a way, the intended manifestation cannot be *intuitive*, that is, the

and try to bite other dogs in a picture; and a monkey frolic like anything before the painting of a monkey, and swallows flying about and alighting upon the painted railings, depicted on the windows of buildings." In Péladan, *Textes choisis de Léonard de Vinci* (Paris: Mercure de France, 1907), pp. 175, 180.

12 Aristotle, *Poetics*, ch. 1, 1447 a 28: "By the rhythms of his attitudes," the dancer represents "the characters of men, their actions and passions together."

work falls short of the essence of art. As I have previously noticed, it is through the instrumentality of natural appearances that things reveal some of their secret meanings to the artist's intuition: it is also through the instrumentality of natural appearances—necessarily recast, and perhaps drastically so—that the same secret meaning can be intuitively revealed in and by the work. Taken in this correct philosophical sense, the law of "imitation" (misleading as this unhappy word may be), the law of transference or re-production is inescapable.

7. Modern art obeys an essential necessity of growth made more exacting by self-awareness, when it claims greater and greater freedom with respect to natural appearances: not, I say, freedom *from* any representation whatsoever of natural appearances, but freedom *in* this very representation, and freedom *to* transpose and recast natural appearances at its own pleasure, on the condition that the recasting in question causes the work to manifest intuitively, or reveal, a transapparent reality grasped in the existential world of Things. In abstract painting this condition is lacking, to one degree or another.

Contemporary painting will get out of its predicament when it understands that the only way to effective transposition, deformation, recasting, or transfiguration of natural appearances passes through poetic intuition. Poetic intuition does as it pleases with natural appearances. It catches them in its own inner music. In its expansion toward the work it takes them away from their material existence in nature, and makes them attuned to itself. Then it is not by any technical trick of decomposition of forms, it is by virtue of the inner pressure, in the natural forms thus quickened by creative emotion, toward going beyond themselves, and telling more than what they are, and becoming parts of a total song laden with meaning and significance, that natural forms are deformed and transposed, transfigured and recast.[13]

It is also by virtue of poetic intuition, embracing the total organization of the work and imposing on it its requirements for unitary objective expression, that each form is sensed and determined in relation

[13] An observation made on Marin by Jerome Mellquist in his book, *The Emergence of an American Art* (New York: Scribner, 1942), seems to me particularly relevant here. "Once more," he says, "as certain of the critics have noted, Marin exhibited that strange gift of his for drawing from the atmosphere the signs and symbols by which, through his own graphic shorthand, he can somehow summarize the essence of a place. He had learned this first, perhaps, from his etchings. But here and throughout the works which have followed his first contact with the Cubists, it became a kind of calligraphic notation which put nature into the most compact and 'transportable' of forms. These are equivalents for its shapes and figures, with each hieroglyphic reminding us of the unchanging and ineluctable realities of nature." (pp. 400-401.)

to all others, and that the picture expands with harmonic plenitude in the total inner space which is proper to it as a self-sufficient unit.

This internal *number* of the work answers a basic necessity which ancient masters were perfectly aware of—Cubism and abstract painting only put a new emphasis on it. I think that there is more real novelty in a particular element which contemporary research is bringing out, and which refers directly to the poetic sense. Modern art, it seems to me, has become exceptionally aware of the importance of the *metaphorical interference* that poetic intuition naturally releases, in other words of the impact of that "illuminating image"—a form, an object, a glimmer, a bit of a world, emerging from elsewhere into the center of the stage—by which the intuitive significance of the work is increased, as it were, boundlessly. I note the fact in passing—it is in relation to poetry that I shall try to analyze further the nature of the illuminating image. To have laid hands on this proper asset of poets is one of the authentic conquests of modern painting.

Painting, in reality, is not trapped today in a blind alley. Roads are open, there are signposts, precisely in relation to the points I just discussed. If I were asked to mention some names, I would say the Romanesque primitive, Hieronymus Bosch, Tintoretto, El Greco, Piranesi, Georges de Latour, Claude, Goya in the past; and, in our age, Cézanne, Rouault, Braque, Chagall, what is best and most durable in Picasso, and certain findings of the Surrealist painters.

In doing so I do not mean at all, of course, to point to any particular way out, but to point to a certain inspiration to find a way out—an inspiration to which, I believe, significant and liberating testimonies have been given. Every great painter blocks the way he himself has opened, and exhausts, as it were, the possibilities which this way might offer. The question, to be sure, has never been to walk in the footsteps of such masters; the question is to scrutinize them with such love as to become free from them, and to feed on their experiences and inner flame humbly and stubbornly enough to discover new directions without even thinking of it.

Despite the conditions of our present state of civilization, so hostile to creative freedom, there will always be artists who have fortitude enough to turn toward the inner sources, and trust in the power of the small translucid cloud of poetic intuition. They will be able to get out —by walking, rather than by reasoning—of the various entanglements I have tried to analyze in this chapter, and to be unselfish in the very awakening of creative subjectivity. For the painter as for the poet there is no other way to regain interior unity, being entirely turned toward the end beyond the end, and thus being perhaps also given, in addition, a new possibility of communion with his fellow men in this modern world of ours which is sick with a repressed, brutally frustrated longing for unity, beauty, and poetry.

A nation's art products and its scientific activities are not mere national property; they are international possessions, for the joy and service of the whole world. The nations hold them in trust for humanity.

> Havelock Ellis, *The Task of Social Hygiene*

They could not give me the least pleasure, and contained a mixture of Paganism and Papacy wholly inconsistent with the [puritanical] religious instruction I received at Walworth.

> John Ruskin (on Raphael's great frescoes in the Vatican)

The nude, when painted by vulgar men, is inevitably indecent.

> Philip G. Hamerton (quoted by John Rewald, *History of Impressionism*, p. 74) said this specifically of Manet's "Déjeuner sur l'Herbe"

He is the greatest artist who has embodied, in the sum of his works, the greatest number of the greatest ideas.

> John Ruskin, *Modern Painters*, I

Emotion resulting from a work of art is only of value when it has not been obtained by sentimental blackmail.

> Jean Cocteau, *A Call to Order*

Art ranks with amusements; fine arts, fine amusements.

> Homer Saint-Gaudens

Blondes come high; Old Masters last longer.

> William Randolph Hearst

The sinews of art, like those of war, are money.

> Samuel Butler

Freud himself, in his famous essay on Leonardo, was the first to apply the psychoanalytical method to the study of the creative artist. Many trained and amateur psychoanalysts have since followed in his steps, with results that have sometimes been stimulating, and sometimes appalling in their ignorance and misdirection. The following essay is one of the sanest and most useful of psychoanalytical writings on art.

Franz Alexander
The Psychoanalyst Looks at Contemporary Art[1]

Products of art can be looked upon from two different points of view: the aesthetic and the psychologic. The aesthetician and the art critic try to evaluate their artistic merit. The psychologist is not primarily concerned with what is a good or a bad painting; he considers the works of artists as valuable personal documents which throw light upon the personality of their originator. Like dreams or daydreams, works of literature, painting, and sculpture are products of the creative fantasy which reflect the psychology of the artist. The psychological study of art products may serve not only for the study of the artist as a person, but also for the study of the emotional climate of a historical period. Because the work of an artist is a reflection of his personality as well as a reflection of the spirit of its times, the literature and art of a given period are most important documents for the historian of culture. I am primarily concerned here with the question: in what way does contemporary art express the spirit of our era, as Byzantine art expressed the mentality of the Middle Ages, or impressionism the outlook of the second half of the nineteenth century?

In order to answer this question, one must first of all establish the characteristic features of contemporary painting. As in every past historical period as well as at present, there is a great divergence in subject matter and technique used by the different artists. In spite of these individual differences, there are fundamental similarities. It is not difficult, even for a nonexpert, to recognize Byzantine painting or to distinguish a Renaissance product from a nineteenth-century impressionist picture. Obviously, there are certain common features which are characteristic of a period, although it is not always easy to define them precisely.

Earlier art historians tried to explain these common features pri-

---

[1] *Explorations in Psychoanalysis*, ed. by Robert Lindner. New York: Julian Press, 1953.

marily from the point of view of the techniques used by the artists. It is only recently that some cultural historians have attempted to understand the prevailing style in art characteristic of a historical period from the cultural climate to which all persons living in a given time and place are equally exposed. Naturally, there are always exceptions—artists who do not represent the current trend. In trying to define the characteristic features of contemporary painting, we shall disregard those works which are not representative of our times. An artist of today may try to paint in the style of Rembrandt or Titian, but such exceptional cases must be explained on a highly individual basis. They may offer most interesting opportunities to study the psychology of such atypical artists, but they are not suitable for reconstructing the prevailing ideological trends and spirit of our times.

What, then, are the most basic common features in contemporary paintings? One basic similarity consists either in the complete absence of real objects or in their radical distortion. In modern painting this trend is referred to as nonobjective art, or abstract art. There may be a lack of any reference to real objects, as for example in some paintings of Mondrian or Klee. In other works the objects are fragmented into their constituent parts and reassembled in different perspective, as in cubist paintings. In these it is sometimes well-nigh impossible to recognize the fragmented object, the product often resembling a piece of a picture puzzle. Again, in other paintings, the object is simply distorted but is still recognizable, or is reduced to its most elementary, often geometrically simplified, formal and basic color components.

Another feature consists in the distortion of the spatial configuration without fragmentation of the objects—in placing disconnected objects side by side. Another type of distortion consists in emphasizing certain aspects of the object which are commonly considered to be unpleasant. This may result in grotesque, ugly, or fear-inspiring effects, as for example in many of Grosz's drawings. In using such an expression as "ugly," I do not refer to the artistic merits of a painting. To represent ugliness is just as legitimate a function of art as to represent something which may be called pretty. Othello's deed was certainly ugly, yet is the subject of a great piece of literature.

Another frequent feature in both modern and psychotic products is the tendency toward the fantastic, the eerie, the mystical, and toward dreamlike symbolism. Examples are certain paintings of Chagall, Miró, Dali, Tanguy, and many others. Another feature is the tendency to use primitive perspective or to mix different perspectives, presenting an object from all sides at the same time. This is not to be confused with the primitive way in which different perspectives were used by some early Renaissance painters.

All these characteristics, from the point of view of psychology, can be interpreted as the manifestation of a central trend: withdrawal from the world as perceived through the sense organs, and substituting for it a newly created, different kind of world. Of course, almost every artist, unlike a photographer, substitutes for the mere reproduction of the world of senses his own interpretation of his object. The mildest forms of this tendency are simplification, omission, and emphasis, utilized to a greater or lesser degree by artists of all periods. This reinterpretation, however, goes much farther in contemporary painting than in the works of most great masters of the past. The great freedom of reinterpretation of the environment as perceived by our senses is characteristic of the contemporary painter. Everything which appears ephemeral and nonessential is omitted and certain fundamentals are emphasized, as in the postimpressionist paintings of Van Gogh or Cézanne.

The next step in this direction is abstraction, which may go as far as reducing the object to its simplest geometric outlines. Or the negation of a real world of senses may manifest itself in distortion. This is usually not a simple negation of the world as it is; it often has a hostile component; it expresses an angry denial of the world as it is commonly perceived. For the psychologist this emphasis on the grotesque, or what one ordinarily would call unpleasant, is a clear confession of resentful rejection. Even stronger rejection is expressed in the completely object-less paintings. Only the very basic components of the visual universe are retained—color and line, light and dark. From these basic elements the artist creates a new view of a spatial world which contains no real objects. The cubist revolution contained both trends: the denial of the world as it is along with an even stronger motivational force to rearrange the fragmented parts of objects in a new, seemingly wanton but really highly consistent manner. It is as if the artist would challenge the creator and prove that he too can create a world according to his own system.

As I said before, every artist creates his own world. The question is how much he retains of these actual elements as they are perceived by the senses. Most contemporary artists go much farther than their predecessors, with the exception of the primitives, in utilizing for the reconstruction of the world only the most basic elements, such as lines and colors, and disregarding what might be called the incidental combination of lines, forms, and colors as they appear in the environment.

It is like transposing a melody from one key to another. The great contemporary painters, such as Braque and Picasso, use the same artistic skill with which the old masters represented the real world we live in, to transform this world according to a consistent formula of their own. In the work of one of the forerunners of the era, Modigliani, the re-creative urge is the strongest. He is really not so much a revolutionary as a reformer. Modigliani gives expression to his reforming urge in a consistent, longitudinal distortion of proportions and bilateral symmetry. This has sometimes been misinterpreted as a mannerism. In reality it is but inner consistency in distortion. Otherwise Modigliani retains much of the technique of the old masters and even has a flavor of the Renaissance in his work.

Denial and radical re-creation of the world of the senses is one of the all-pervasive keynotes in contemporary art. The "re-creator" of the world sometimes uses technological motifs, as does, for example, Léger. It appears as if the artist would envy the engineer who has actually succeeded in reshaping the surface of the globe and in superimposing upon the work of nature a new, technologically created, man-made world. Another way of creating a completely new world populated with dreamlike symbols is prevalent in the work of Miró and Tanguy.

We see, then, that the denial of the real world of objects is a well-nigh universal characteristic of contemporary art. It is not merely a reinterpretation of the world—this is universal in every art—but a fundamental transformation combined with an aggressive denial of the objects in the form they are commonly perceived. The ways and means of this re-creation are widely different, according to the inclination and personality of the painter. The emphasis may be more on either denial, rejection and ridicule, or on magic re-creation. In some nonobjective painters, for example, Mondrian, the nihilistic rejection of everything which even reminds one of the real world, is the main issue. Ridicule of any order or reason is outstanding in Dadaism, as if the more unexpected and the more random the juxtaposition of the elments, the better the collage. Since everybody retains in himself a residue of childish revolt against the obligation to be orderly and sensible, this type of repudiation of order and reason has a secret appeal similar to Freud's explanation of the so-called nonsense jokes.

The question arises: is this trend in contemporary art—to reject and to remodel the surrounding world—unique? Some students of aesthetics will have a ready answer! These features are not at all characteristic of contemporary art alone—they are present in every form of art and literature. No *real* artist ever tries to give merely a faithful reproduction of reality. The specific creative act consists precisely in the artist's attempt to re-create in his own manner the surrounding world. This re-creative urge may manifest itself in many different ways and is present even in the realist painter and writer. It has often been emphasized that the great artist reproduces the essence of the subject. A Rembrandt portrait of an old man, while it represents one specific person, at the same time condenses into the work the universal features of all the old men who ever lived and will live in the future. The presentation of the universal, the timeless, the essential, has long been considered one of the main accomplishments of the artist. The conventional formulation of aesthetics, that the writer and the artist express the universal through the specific, the abstract through the concrete, applies also to impressionist art. The meadow in an impressionist painting is not a meadow in general, but a meadow at 3:30 on an afternoon in June.

Another creative accomplishment of the artist is the condensation into one concrete example of the significant interrelationships among the objects depicted. A street of Paris by Pissarro is more than the representation of one special geographical location in the metropolis; it reflects the spirit of contemporary Paris through the fleeting impression made upon the onlooker. The ensemble, the tree-lined sidewalks, the advertisements, the color and attire of the milling crowd, all together have a common denominator expressing something essentially characteristic of the city. The artist's creation is to condense all this in one composition, not merely photographic, yet a faithful reproduction of one fleeting impression. In a sense it is much more realistic than a photograph because the visual impression is a highly selective act which emphasizes, distorts, and omits various details. The camera can never show how reality actually reflects itself in the onlooker.

When technical terms enter into common usage, they have a tendency to lose their original meaning. After they are in use for a while, the terms begin to live their own lives, gradually developing new connotations and thus becoming a source of confusion. This is precisely what happened to the words "impressionism" and "expressionism." Nothing is further from the truth than "the saying" that the impressionist represents the outer world, the expressionist the inner world. The impressionist expresses something extremely subjective just as does the expressionist painter. Both represent, although in very different ways, the manner in which the world affects them. Both express their relation to the world. Negation of the world is as much an expression of a relation as is acceptance. The real difference between the two schools lies in their acceptance or rejection of the world. The impressionist painters of the nineteenth century had a warm attachment to the world. Their pictures express more than acceptance—they express both curiosity and adoration. And this adoring love extends not only to sunshine, but to the rain, the fog, the meadow, the city street, the *boite,* the stage, the delicate ankles of the ballerina, and the robust petty bourgeois in the garden restaurant. What the impressionist represents is not the real world of objects but his warm acceptance of this world to which he trustingly exposes himself and which he takes in faithfully and lovingly. To be sure, the primary interest of the impressionist era is in the man-made world: the street, the park, the sidewalk café, the dance hall, the beach with umbrellas; and not so much the forest, the wild mountain peak, or the stormy sea—not unadulterated nature, which was the preferred topic of the romantics. The confident, urbane Western European looked with love and pride upon his own creation. Paris became a principal theme as the pinnacle of this individualistic, enterprising world—of a world which believed in unlimited progress, in reason and science, and in whose hierarchy of values art, literature, and music, the basic sciences and philosophy, as in Plato's *Republic,* occupied the highest rank. This intellectual élite had its own exclusive society, which it exposed to the masses in the café and the literary cabaret. The public, particularly the well-to-do middle class, participated vicariously in this life, looking through the peepholes of literature, painting, and the stage. Their own preoccupation with industry and commerce, which supplied the material foundation of this progressing world, appeared to them a humdrum existence the main purpose of which, at least in theory, was to make this exalted aesthetic hedonism of the spiritual élite possible. In practice, of course, this existence was mostly meager indeed, but in theory material wealth was there to serve the spiritual progress of knowledge, art, literature, and the art of living; money was not an end in itself.

Then suddenly in the summer of 1914, in a Balkan slum district, the fatal explosion took place and the bubble of this aesthetic culture burst. The European's crude awakening was a sudden and overwhelming one. The real forces of the world—industry, the military machine, and diplomacy—which until now had modestly and tacitly remained in the background and ceded the arena of public life to art, science, the stage, and literature, took over the scene of history overnight. "Blood and gold" are ruling the world, lamented the poet Andreas Ady, the Hungarian Verlaine, who sipped his absinthe in the sidewalk cafés of Paris and Budapest, and was one of the most sensitive exponents of decadence. With one stroke the painters and poets showed themselves to be nothing but the luxuries of a wealthy, carefree, and peaceful era; the industrial producer, the soldier, and the diplomat regained the leading role from which they were removed for a short and happy period of history. And the exponents of the aesthetic ideology, thus deprived of their *raison d'être,* turned around and revolted against a world which showed up the futility of their esoteric existence. Their answer was at first angry indignation and scorn, and then total rejection of the world which now so convincingly disclosed its sordid realities. "The real world is ugly, not worth-while—why give it the consideration to depict it as it is!" Not the pleasing superstructure but the ugly skeleton became the popular subject. "We, the painters and writers, shall show you how repugnant and ridiculous the world is and we shall rebuild it according to our own magic formula." It was not said in these words, but this is what the Blue Riders in Munich, the futurists in Italy, the Dadaists in Switzerland, the Bohème of the Café du Dôme, professed. The futurist Marinetti, who also invented the symbol of fascism, announced at a demonstration in Paris: "Destroy syntax! Sabotage the adjective!" And in Berlin, at the opening of a fall exhibition of paintings: "Destroy the museums! Burn down the libraries!"[2] Now the aesthetic vibrations of the moment, so removed from the actual brutal facts of life, were no longer a worthy subject of art. Now the desperate efforts of Schnitzler's Anatole to endow his love affairs with suburban ingénues with the esoteric illusions by which this anemic Vienna playboy tried to enrich his bland, uneventful life, suddenly belonged to the era of yesterday, which had lost all its meaning in the dynamic present. To continue to indulge in the sentimental contemplation of the boulevard, extracting from it all shades of subjective variations of mood, was no longer appropriate in a Paris which had just recently been saved by its taxi drivers from military invasion. Impressionism, the hedonistic exploitation of the leisurely moment, became just as incompatible with the spirit of the day as a jazz band at a funeral. And thus almost overnight, in the second decade of the twentieth century, this loving acceptance of the world changed into its opposite, into an angry rejection.

All this, of course, did not come so suddenly as it would appear at

2 Walter Mehring, *The Lost Library,* pp. 129-130.

first sight. About the turn of the century the suspicion of having been double-crossed began to grow in the European mind. At first only the artists and writers, the forerunners of their time, gave expression to a change of attitude. What the artist anticipated by presentiment, the rest of us realized a few years later. For us it was in August of 1914 that this period of Western history came to an end. For the insensitive it appeared as a sudden collapse; in reality, it was a gradual disintegration. Indeed, the collapse of nineteenth-century ideology, its confidence in steady progress, its aesthetic, hedonistic value system in which the arts, music, literature, and pure science occupied a supreme position, and above all, the unquestioned loving acceptance of the world as man made it, was not as sudden as it appeared to the average man. The signs of decline, presaging the apocalypse, were numerous and steadily growing. The truth that every development contains the germs of its own destruction, and that these latent destructive forces increase as the trend approaches its pinnacle can be demonstrated in the literature and arts at the close of the century. In literature it appeared as the decadent movement. In the poetry of Verlaine, Hofmannsthal, and Rilke, the enjoyment of the moment was mixed with a bittersweet melancholy, a wistful preoccupation with yesterday, an undertone of futility. Hauser characterizes this decadent component in impressionistic literature which was prominent in Vienna:

> The Viennese represent the purest form of the impressionism which forgoes all resistance to the stream of experience. Perhaps it is the ancient and tired culture of this city, the lack of all active national politics, and the great part played in literary life by foreigners, especially Jews, which gives Viennese impressionism its peculiarly subtle and passive character. This is the art of the sons of rich bourgeois, the expression of the joyless hedonism of that "second generation" which lives on the fruits of its fathers' work. They are nervous and melancholy, tired and aimless, skeptical and ironical about themselves, these poets of exquisite moods which evaporate in a trice and leave nothing behind but the feeling of evanescence, of having missed one's opportunities, and the consciousness of being unfit for life.[3]

In England the literary witticism, the provocative aphorism which challenged both reason and victorian complacency, are more virile portents of the same ideological revolt. In Sweden Strindberg, and in Germany Wedekind, were exposing the less savory features of man.

The detachment from the world of reality and the turning toward

[3] *The Social History of Art*, Vol. II, p. 908.

the mystical symbolism of the unconscious is seen also in the symbolic poetry of Mallarmé and the symbolic paintings of Redon. The first signs of the urge to replace the world with another more consistent than the old, but still retaining the semblance of reality, appear in the postimpressionistic paintings of Van Gogh and Cézanne. The new Rousseauism of Gauguin, his return to primitive culture and unimproved nature, is another form of repudiation of the Western world. The most evolutionary event in these ideological developments, however, came just about the turn of the century, when Freud proposed his theory of the unconscious mind.

In both art and literature, the estrangement from the world as it appears was progressing relentlessly. With his emphasis on essentials, the skeletal structure of the body which is the same in everyone, the contemporary painter tacitly expresses his scorn for the credulity of the impressionist, who was so easily taken in by the pleasing surface, by clothing, by facial expression, by the skin and the muscles. These only hide the basic realities of the body, the viscera and the bony structure which can best be reproduced by simple geometric configurations. All the surface manifestations of the world, all the aesthetic bric-a-brac by which the ferocious animal, man, tries to hide his real nature were to be disregarded. Blood and gold, and we may add, the blast furnace, are ruling the world. The hypocritical and anemic aestheticism of the last century was a self-deception in which the decadent bourgeois could for a little while indulge himself, so long as he was not challenged by the underground forces of society. As soon as the great masses of humanity became mobilized and clamored for a place in the sun, this decadent aesthetic bubble disappeared like the foam on a wave in a stormy ocean. Writes Ortega y Gasset, the visionary Spanish philosopher:

> The mass crushes beneath it everything that is different, everything that is excellent, individual, qualified, and select. Anybody who is not like everybody, who does not think like everybody, runs the risk of being eliminated.[4]

In the dynamic world of Hitler, Mussolini, and Stalin, and in the era of industrial mass production, the impressionistic and individualistic cultivation of the moment has no place. This is a century of action and not of idle contemplation. From illusions, from the ever-changing, evanescent impressions of the moment, we must return to the basic essentials, not only in social life but also in art and literature, no

4 *The Revolt of the Masses.*

matter whether they are pleasing or not.

This is what the artists and writers of the early twentieth century express not in so many words, not in theory, but in their own medium of communication. And yet it was difficult, if not impossible, for the artists and writers to change their outlook at a moment's notice. They came into conflict with themselves, having to repudiate everything they professed yesterday and to reject a world in which they grew up. This was, after all, the only world they knew, the world in which they themselves were rooted. The most significant features of contemporary art and literature can be understood only when one realizes that the proponents of expressionism, abstractionism, and surrealism belong to this generation of transition. Their deep-seated conflict, their division of soul, accounts for those features with which the psychiatrist is so well acquainted, and which are reminiscent of psychopathology. They could not merely reject the external world because this world had already made a deep imprint upon their own personality; they had to repudiate a part of the self, that part which psychoanalysis calls the rational conscious ego, which is nothing but the imprint of the external world upon the original unorganized mass of impulses and desires which Freud called the id. The conscious ego is the internal representative of the world of reality as against the original basic instinctual forces. It is the ego which demands the adjustment of the subjective impulses to the world. Since the rational ego of this generation was the heritage of the nineteenth century, their rebellion forced them to disavow this part of their own self. "The ego must be extirpated from literature," demanded Marinetti in Milan.[5] The result was an elemental breakthrough, from the unconscious, of the primitive disorganized impulses of the id. And this is why the unconscious mind as it manifests itself in dreams, in psychopathological symptoms, and in the uncontrolled train of thoughts during free association, became the dominant note of contemporary art and literature. The unconscious broke through most clearly in the symbolism and dreamlike products of surrealistic paintings. The unconscious reveals itself directly in dreams, and dreams are primarily products of visual fantasy. Therefore surrealistic painting is a most appropriate representation of unconscious mental activity.

Rejection of reality and rebellion against it, however, do not constitute a static mental condition; they represent no final solution. Not even a psychotic can remain in a state of unrelieved revolt. He rejects the world but he must rebuild it according to his own imagery in the

5 Mehring, *op. cit.*

form of illusions and hallucinations. Every person does the same in his dreams and daydreams. In fantasy we can correct those aspects of the world which we are not ready to accept and which interfere with our subjective desires that are not adapted to reality. The similarity between the mental processes of the psychotics and the dreams of normal persons has long been recognized. Psychotics in a sense live continuously in a dream world; a healthy person indulges in such wishful distortions of reality only for a brief moment when the organism withdraws from the environment and is relieved from the strenuous task of conforming to the unalterable and sometimes very disturbing facts of reality. Every dream is a rejection of the undesirable aspects of the world, but it is also an attempt to make the world more acceptable. In order to accomplish this, the dreamer regresses to more primitive forms of mental activity. Rational thinking is expressed in words and is a highly advanced form of mental activity which is adjusted to reality. Everyone has to acquire the ability to think rationally during the process of intellectual maturation. In order to return to wishful thinking, the shackles of conscious verbal thinking must be discarded. In the dream one resumes the more infantile forms of mental activity which are characterized by magic and wish fulfillment. In dreams the ordinary rules of logic are abandoned, the unconscious does not know the limitations of time and space. The unorthodoxy of space relations in contemporary drawings and paintings most appropriately expresses not the empirical space which is conveyed to us by our senses, but the type of space which appears in our dreams. The role of symbols is similar. Pictorial symbols are often based on vague similarities and are therefore in sharp contrast with the precise distinction of meaning conveyed by words.

This affinity of contemporary art to the unconscious mind, particularly dream life, explains certain similarities between paintings of schizophrenics and those of contemporary artists. This similarity has been noted by various psychiatrists and also by artists. Some of them, like Dubuffet, derived great stimulation from studying the drawings of schizophrenic patients. The schizophrenic also withdraws his interest from a world which has become unpalatable and replaces his realistic perceptions with the wishful creation of his own fantasy, his delusions, illusions, and hallucinations. In dreams, as in the fantasy products of schizophrenics, the unconscious mind reveals itself in its full nakedness.

This comparison of contemporary paintings with the products of schizophrenics should not be interpreted as an evaluation of their artistic merits. There are gifted psychotics just as there are gifted neurotics. If Lombroso was right in maintaining that between genius and insanity there is only a narrow dividing line, insanity certainly does not exclude artistic talent. There are several examples of great artists suffering from major psychiatric conditions. Neither does this comparison mean that modern artists are mentally disturbed. To my knowledge, the mental health of modern painters is no different from that of older masters. We find among them mentally healthy persons and neurotics as well as borderline psychotics. Their mental health or illness certainly cannot account for those features in their work which I am considering here. The similarity is based on the close affinity of contemporary art to the deep unconscious layers of the personality which both contemporary artists and schizophrenics reveal directly. In addition to these similarities there are also great and significant differences. The good contemporary artists attempt to communicate their unconscious processes in an organized fashion. The psychotic's paintings, on the other hand, show disorganization, mostly a flight from the world, with much less constructive effort to recapture the lost contact with the world. The attempt to negotiate a new kind of relation to the world is the main striving of the modern artist.

The withdrawal from the realistic world of objects and the return to the nonrational magic world of symbols and wishful distortions is unavoidably accompanied by confusion and anxiety. Disturbed by confusion and anxiety, the individual tries to recapture the world by reshaping it in fantasy. As we have seen, contemporary art attempts this in a radical way by magic and symbolism and by return to the basic elements of line and color. Some of these paintings express little more than utter confusion, but mostly there is an attempt to bring order into chaos. In cubistic paintings both trends are there: the first impression is that of complete disorder but, on further contemplation, gradually a fascinating and novel principle of organization can be discovered. In other contemporary paintings, as in Mondrian's work, the confusion is completely avoided by offering a simple geometric configuration and the harmony of pure colors and lines. But the artist can achieve this perfect order and harmony only by ignoring the rich variety of the world that surrounds him. This is an orderly but badly impoverished world. The artist tries to recapture mastery over the very little which remains after he repudiates reality. A white square on a black background exhibited by Malevitch in 1913 was the ultimate logical consequence of this defeatist trend to ignore the surrounding universe, which had become so unpalatable. What a contrast between this geometric art, essentially a defeatist attempt to master the nothing, and the magnificent attempts of a Cézanne or a Van Gogh to introduce into the real world new principles of visual organization!

As mentioned before, in every art the world is re-created to some degree, but the artist mostly attempts a more or less realistic re-creation. In contemporary art the re-creation is more radical than in any previous cultural era. It is the diametric opposite of impressionism, the last and most advanced phase of a cultural development which started with the Renaissance, when European man became liberated from the medieval restrictions upon free inquiry and began to discover the world around him. The uniformity and rigidity of Byzantine paintings gradually gave place to a hitherto unknown freedom to see the world as it is. The background became more and more realistic as well as the facial expression and the body. In all fields of mental activity the trend was the same. Man began to explore the earth, then the celestial bodies, the animal and human organism, and finally the self and the society in which he lives. In art this same trend toward exploration and mastery of the world remained consistent until the end of the nineteenth century. The realistic representation of distinct objects was followed by the impressionist discovery of how to reproduce the medium between the objects. Light and air and the representation of the world in its totality, in the interaction of all its constituent parts, became the aim of painting.

Hauser, in his *Social History of Art,* maintains that the first real ideological revolution since the Renaissance occurred in the twentieth century. The consistent trend toward the exploration and acceptance of the world was not interrupted until our present era, in spite of the fact that many of the innovations in science, art, and literature were accepted only after a period of repudiation. Yet Kepler's astronomical theory was only a step further in the direction initially taken by Galileo and Copernicus, and Einstein's physics was a step beyond Newton. In art, impressionism was at first violently rejected, and yet it was but the last step in the same consistent trend toward the pictorial discovery of the world which started with Giotto.

The first actual reversal of trend against this steadily progressing realism and rationalism is what we are witnessing today. It appeared in literature as a revolt against reason in the use of words according to their acoustic qualities instead of their meaning, in irrational and symbolic stage productions, and finally in the direct representation of the unconscious in free association. In painting it appeared as the withdrawal from representing the world of reality, in the distortion of spatial relations and the objects themselves. The real revolution consists, however, in the repudiation of the loving acceptance of the world of reality and in the revolt against reason. In politics the same trend manifests itself in the totalitarian emphasis on irrational motivations, on violence, vengeance, and greed, on the praise of a dangerous life. It appears in the form of political adventure and the abolition of freedom of thought and inquiry.

Indeed, looking upon current ideological trends from this perspective offers a gloomy picture. Is this, however, a precise interpretation of the prevailing cultural trend? It is unquestionably true that this century began with a revolt against the nineteenth-century value system, which had remained essentially the same since the Renaissance. That this revolt in literature and art manifested itself in a repudiation of the world of the senses and of reason—which is man's weapon to master the world—is also true. That this revolt was followed in art by an attempt to re-create the external reality by archaic unrealistic and magic mental activities is equally valid. And there can be little doubt that the concurrent fascist and communist developments in Eastern and Central Europe are the manifestations of unbridled instincts in politics. They also have a regressive character and are basically irrational and reactionary movements. The question is how to evaluate all these disturbing facts from the larger perspective of history. Are we at the beginning of a new period of medieval obscurantism in which the individual will lose all his spiritual and political freedom and, in order to have himself as an individual, will have to be content with withdrawal into the archaic wishful imagery of his unconscious mind? In his fear and confusion will he yield to some kind of tyranny and give up all further attempts to master realistically his environment and his fate by increasing his own knowledge, understanding, and reason? Will he be satisfied with powerless protest, flaunting his contempt of reason, ridiculing the world, and retreating into a dream world of surrealistic magic?

One can also look upon these cultural developments in a different manner. The present trend in art and literature may reflect a new step in the exploration of the world: the exploration of the unconscious. For almost four centuries man turned his interest outward, learning more about the nature of the universe than in any other period of history; he gradually translated his theoretical knowledge into a technological mastery over the forces of nature. During all these impressive accomplishments of extroverted activities, he completely forgot the exploration of his own self. He knew of himself only as much as he wanted to. He built up the illusion of himself as a progressive, rational, basically benign, and socially minded personality, striving for truth, for the cultivation of beauty, and for the realization of social justice. This was taught in the humanistic gymnasiums of the European continent and in the public schools of England. Those writers, artists, and philosophers who challenged this rosy picture of man's personality were disregarded or ridiculed by the official academies of culture. And the parents and teachers, the intellectual leaders, were alerted and on guard against the repeated onslaughts against their own repressions.

Their chief enemy was the Viennese neurologist, Freud, ostracized by the medical society because of his revolutionary teachings concerning the role of sex and the unconscious mind in the causation of neurosis. With the outbreak of the First World War the self-deceptive, complacent ideology began to crumble. And after the war, with the collapse of the political and economic structure of Europe, everything which hitherto was considered safe and stable was swept away. The controlling forces of the personality, in order to keep in check the asocial and irrational forces of the unconscious, need reinforcement from the outside in the form of parental example, law and police, the authority of the state, the teachings of the church and the school. But the disintegrating political and economic structure of Europe could no longer supply these external reinforcements. The older generation had failed in the eyes of the young. They were held responsible for the fiasco of the old system, whether it was the constitutional monarchy, the four-per-cent rate of interest, the gold standard, which appeared to be assured forever, or the conventional standards of the professors, upheld by the academies of the sciences and arts. The external authorities, the living representatives of our internal standards, became discredited, and the unconscious forces swept through the barriers of the conventional code. The unconscious—with all its elemental forces, mysticism, and irrationality—arose to the surface. It became the principal object of psychology and the social sciences, of art and literature, and it dominated the internal political life of nations as well as world politics. Are we witnessing at this very moment a brief lull before the storm? Will man be able to bring those unleashed, destructive forces under his control again?

The same question on a smaller scale confronts the psychoanalyst every day in his practice. With his therapeutic technique, he tries to bring the unconscious impulses of the patient to the surface. The traditional apprehension with which psychoanalysis was received, the fear that this procedure might unleash all the asocial propensities of the patient, and turn a hitherto harmless neurotic into a selfish, ruthless person, has proven unfounded. We have learned just the opposite. Repression, denial, hypocritical self-deception, have been inadequate defenses against the instinctive forces of man. The only remedy is to make the patient conscious of his deeper impulses. At first the barriers of repression must be overcome before a new and more extended control over the self can be obtained. Not even in a well-conducted treatment does this process of self-revelation always take place without occasional dramatic episodes. When this happens we say that the patient is "acting out." From the point of view of history, the last forty years of Western civilization may be considered as a brief episode of acting out. Who can tell, however, whether or not we are at the end of this dynamic but chaotic phase of cultural and political history? One thing is certain, that if and when we have been able to develop new internal standards and a new relation to a world which has changed faster than our adaptive capacity, a wiser and more conscious humanity will arise. The chaotic eruption of the unconscious has already contributed new dynamic forces which gradually can be brought under the control of reason and utilized constructively. It has already opened up new avenues of artistic expression. From his acquaintance with the unconscious archaic layers of the mind, the artist, in the same way as the scientist, has gained new materials and techniques for expressing a new relationship to the world.

Freud was not only the discoverer of the unconscious but also the inventor of a technique by which the unconscious forces, after being mobilized, can be brought under the control of the rational mind. After the scientific mastery of the unconscious, its artistic mastery will follow.

In American contemporary art the trend toward reconstruction is more pronounced than the rebellious denial of the world which was so characteristic in the early European developments. In Europe the movement started as an open rebellion against the orderly and optimistic approach of the nineteenth century. Soon after the movement reached the shores of the United States[6] it lost much of its bitter and revolutionary connotation and became influenced by the mechanical

[6] The Armory Show in New York in 1913.

and reconstructive spirit of an advanced industrial civilization. The effort to bring the unconscious under rational control is conspicuous in the works of many American painters.

There is no room at this time, however, for complacency. We have arrived at a crossroads of cultural development. The complete collapse of Western civilization or a new positive acceptance of the world and the rule of reason are the alternatives. Should the outcome be favorable, we shall have to come to terms with the world around us. Revolt and rejection of reality are destructive reactions and cannot represent a permanent solution. There is no choice—the road must eventually lead back to reality and reason. Life is dependent upon the environment. It is two-way traffic: we express ourselves but we also receive from the environment. Art expresses the relationship of the self to the surrounding world. Negation and re-creation of the world with the help of magic must eventually yield to a more realistic solution. This of necessity will modify artistic style and expression. The naked unconscious, as it often appears in contemporary art, is not a suitable way of communication. It must go through the prism of the organizing portion of the personality, the conscious ego, in order to become meaningful. The artist eventually will emerge from the surrealistic detour through the depths of the unconscious mind with a fresh point of view, richer, and with a new constructive message which he cannot express in this era of negation and confusion.

All passes. Art alone
   Enduring stays to us.
The Bust outlasts the throne,—
   The Coin, Tiberius.

                Austin Dobson, *Ars Victrix*

All art is but imitation of nature. (*Omnis ars
   naturae imitatio est.*)

               Seneca, *Epistle to Lucilius*

   Art is a delayed echo.

             George Santayana

I have seen, and heard, much of cockney impudence before now; but never expected to hear a coxcomb ask two hundred guineas for flinging a pot of paint in the public's face.

            John Ruskin concerning Whistler's "Nocturne
            in Black and Gold," *Fors Clavigera*, Letter 79

Horatio Greenough
False Sculpture and False Architecture

1

The work [the tympanum of the capitol in Washington] has another defect as sculpture. It is the translation of rhetoric into stone—a feat often fatal to the rhetoric, always fatal to the stone.

2

I am not going to criticize [the Smithsonian]. I have not quite recovered from my alarm. There is still a certain mystery about those towers and steep belfreys that makes me uneasy. This is a practical land. They must be for something. Is no *coup d'état* lurking there? Can they be merely ornaments, like the tassels to a University cap?

Aesthetics at Washington, pp. 10, 18

Nothing is so poor and melancholy as an art that is interested in itself and not in its subject.

George Santayana

Remember that the most beautiful things in the world are the most useless; peacocks and lilies for instance.

John Ruskin, *The Stones of Venice,* I.

Not only is there but one way of *doing* things rightly, but there is only one way of *seeing* them, and that is seeing the whole of them.

ibid.

The real fines down to a single sharp impression, a relic more or less flitting of moments gone by, a tremulous wisp constantly reforming.

Walter Pater

Art is but nature to advantage dressed
What oft was thought but ne'er so well expressed.

Alexander Pope, *Essay on Criticism*

L'art est une harmonie parallèle à la nature.

Cézanne

THE CLASSICAL IDEAL

Here, in the following chapter, in the course of a detailed examination of a specific artistic problem, is one of the finest commentaries yet written on the classical ideal and the Greek achievement in art.

Kenneth Clark
The Naked and the Nude[1]

The English language, with its elaborate generosity, distinguishes between the naked and the nude. To be naked is to be deprived of our clothes, and the word implies some of the embarrassment most of us feel in that condition. The word "nude," on the other hand, carries, in educated usage, no uncomfortable overtone. The vague image it projects into the mind is not of a huddled and defenseless body, but of a balanced, prosperous, and confident body: the body re-formed. In fact, the word was forced into our vocabulary by critics of the early eighteenth century to persuade the artless islanders that, in countries where painting and sculpture were practiced and valued as they should be, the naked human body was the central subject of art.

For this belief there is a quantity of evidence. In the greatest age of painting, the nude inspired the greatest works; and even when it ceased to be a compulsive subject it held its position as an academic exercise and a demonstration of mastery. Velásquez, living in the prudish and corseted court of Philip IV and admirably incapable of idealization, yet felt bound to paint the "Rokeby Venus." Sir Joshua Reynolds, wholly without the gift of formal draftsmanship, set great store by his

---

1 *The Nude: A Study in Ideal Form* by Kenneth Clark. New York: Pantheon Books, 1956.

"Cymon and Iphigenia." And in our own century, when we have shaken off one by one those inheritances of Greece which were revived at the Renaissance, discarded the antique armor, forgotten the subjects of mythology, and disputed the doctrine of imitation, the nude alone has survived. It may have suffered some curious transformations, but it remains our chief link with the classic disciplines. When we wish to prove to the Philistine that our great revolutionaries are really respectable artists in the tradition of European painting, we point to their drawings of the nude. Picasso has often exempted it from that savage metamorphosis which he has inflicted on the visible world and has produced a series of nudes that might have walked unaltered off the back of a Greek mirror; and Henry Moore, searching in stone for the ancient laws of its material and seeming to find there some of those elementary creatures of whose fossilized bones it is composed, yet gives to his constructions the same fundamental character that was invented by the sculptors of the Parthenon in the fifth century before Christ.

These comparisons suggest a short answer to the question, "What is the nude?" It is an art form invented by the Greeks in the fifth century, just as opera is an art form invented in seventeenth-century Italy. The conclusion is certainly too abrupt, but it has the merit of emphasizing that the nude is not the subject of art, but a form of art.

It is widely supposed that the naked human body is in itself an object upon which the eye dwells with pleasure and which we are glad to see depicted. But anyone who has frequented art schools and seen the shapeless, pitiful model that the students are industriously drawing will know this is an illusion. The body is not one of those subjects which can be made into art by direct transcription—like a tiger or a snowy landscape. Often in looking at the natural and animal world we joyfully identify ourselves with what we see and from this happy union create a work of art. This is the process students of aesthetics call empathy, and it is at the opposite pole of creative activity to the state of mind that has produced the nude. A mass of naked figures does not move us to empathy, but to disillusion and dismay. We do not wish to imitate; we wish to perfect. We become, in the physical sphere, like Diogenes with his lantern looking for an honest man; and, like him, we may never be rewarded. Photographers of the nude are presumably engaged in this search, with every advantage; and having found a model who pleases them, they are free to pose and light her in conformity with their notions of beauty; finally, they can tone down and accentuate by retouching. But in spite of all their taste and skill, the result is hardly ever satisfactory to those whose eyes have grown accustomed to the harmonious simplifications of antiquity. We are immediately disturbed by wrinkles, pouches, and other small imperfections, which, in the classical scheme, are eliminated. By long habit we do not judge it as a living organism, but as a design; and we discover that the transitions are inconclusive, the outline is faltering. We are bothered because the various parts of the body cannot be perceived as simple units and have no clear relationship to one another. In almost every detail the body is not the shape that art had led us to believe it should be. Yet we can look with pleasure at photographs of trees and animals, where the canon of perfection is less strict. Consciously or unconsciously, photographers have usually recognized that in a photograph of the nude their real object is not to reproduce the naked body, but to imitate some artist's view of what the naked body should be. Rejlander was the most Philistine of the early photographers, but, perhaps without knowing it, he was a contemporary of Courbet, and with this splendid archetype somewhere in the background he produced one of the finest (as well as one of the first) photographs of the nude. He succeeded partly because his unconscious archetype was a realist. The more nearly ideal the model, the more unfortunate the photographs that try to imitate it—as those in the style of Ingres or Whistler prove.

So that although the naked body is no more than the point of departure for a work of art, it is a pretext of great importance. In the history of art, the subjects that men have chosen as nuclei, so to say, of their sense of order have often been in themselves unimportant. For hundreds of years, and over an area stretching from Ireland to China, the most vital expression of order was an imaginary animal biting its own tail. In the Middle Ages drapery took on a life of its own, the same life that had inhabited the twisting animal, and became the vital pattern of Romanesque art. In neither case had the subject any independent existence. But the human body, as a nucleus, is rich in associations, and when it is turned into art these associations are not entirely lost. For this reason it seldom achieves the concentrated aesthetic shock of animal ornament, but it can be made expressive of a far wider and more civilizing experience. It is ourselves and arouses memories of all the things we wish to do with ourselves; and first of all we wish to perpetuate ourselves.

This is an aspect of the subject so obvious that I need hardly dwell on it; and yet some wise men have tried to close their eyes to it. "If the nude," says Professor Alexander, "is so treated that it raises in the spectator ideas or desires appropriate to the material subject, it is false art, and bad morals." This high-minded theory is contrary to experience.

In the mixture of memories and sensations aroused by Rubens' "Andromeda" or Renoir's "Bather" are many that are "appropriate to the material subject." And since these words of a famous philosopher are often quoted, it is necessary to labor the obvious and say that no nude, however abstract, should fail to arouse in the spectator some vestige of erotic feeling, even though it be only the faintest shadow—and if it does not do so, it is bad art and false morals. The desire to grasp and be united with another human body is so fundamental a part of our nature that our judgment of what is known as "pure form" is inevitably influenced by it; and one of the difficulties of the nude as a subject for art is that these instincts cannot lie hidden, as they do, for example, in our enjoyment of a piece of pottery, thereby gaining the force of sublimation, but are dragged into the foreground, where they risk upsetting the unity of responses from which a work of art derives its independent life. Even so, the amount of erotic content a work of art can hold in solution is very high. The temple sculptures of tenth-century India are an undisguised exaltation of physical desire; yet they are great works of art because their eroticism is part of their whole philosophy.

Apart from biological needs, there are other branches of human experience of which the naked body provides a vivid reminder—harmony, energy, ecstasy, humility, pathos; and when we see the beautiful results of such embodiments, it must seem as if the nude as a means of expression is of universal and eternal value. But this we know historically to be untrue. It has been limited both in place and in time. There are naked figures in the paintings of the Far East; but only by an extension of the term can they be called nudes. In Japanese prints they are part of *ukioye,* the passing show of life, which includes, without comment, certain intimate scenes usually allowed to pass unrecorded. The idea of offering the body for its own sake, as a serious subject of contemplation, simply did not occur to the Chinese or Japanese mind, and to this day raises a slight barrier of misunderstanding. In the Gothic North the position was fundamentally very similar. It is true that German painters in the Renaissance, finding that the naked body was a respected subject in Italy, adapted it to their needs, and evolved a remarkable convention of their own. But Dürer's struggles show how artificial this creation was. His instinctive responses were curiosity and horror, and he had to draw a great many circles and other diagrams before he could brace himself to turn the unfortunate body into the nude.

Only in countries touching on the Mediterranean has the nude been at home; and even there its meaning was often forgotten. The Etruscans, owing three quarters of their art to Greece, never abandoned a type of tomb figure in which the defunct man displays his stomach with a complacency that would have shocked a Greek profoundly. Hellenistic and Roman art produced statues and mosaics of professional athletes who seem satisfied with their monstrous proportions. More remarkable still, of course, is the way in which the nude, even in Italy and Greece, is limited by time. It is the fashion to speak of Byzantine art as if it were a continuation of Greek; the nude reminds us that this is one of the refined excesses of specialization. Between the Nereids of late Roman silver and the golden doors of Ghiberti the nudes in Mediterranean art are few and insignificant—a piece of modest craftsmanship like the Ravenna ivory "Apollo and Daphne," a few *objets de luxe,* like the Veroli Casket, with its cartoon-strip Olympus, and a number of Adams and Eves whose nakedness seldom shows any memory of antique form. Yet, during a great part of that millennium, the masterpieces of Greek art had not yet been destroyed, and men were surrounded by representations of the nude more numerous and, alas, infinitely more splendid than any that have come down to us. As late as the tenth century the "Knidian Aphrodite" of Praxiteles, which had been carried to Constantinople, it is said, by Theodosius, was praised by the Emperor Constantine Porphyrogenitus; and a famous bronze copy of it is mentioned by Robert de Clari in his account of the taking of Constantinople by the Crusaders. Moreover, the body itself did not cease to be an object of interest in Byzantium: this we may deduce from the continuation of the race. Athletes performed in the circus; workmen, stripped to the waist, toiled at the building of St. Sophia. There was no want of opportunity for artists. That their patrons did not demand representations of the nude during this period may be explained by a number of reasonable-looking causes—fear of idolatry, the fashion for asceticism, or the influence of Eastern art. But in fact such answers are incomplete. The nude had ceased to be the subject of art almost a century before the official establishment of Christianity. And during the Middle Ages there would have been ample opportunity to introduce it both into profane decoration and into such sacred subjects as show the begining and the end of our existence.

Why, then, does it never appear? An illuminating answer is to be found in the notebook of the thirteenth-century architect, Villard de Honnecourt. This contains many beautiful drawings of draped figures, some of them showing a high degree of skill. But when Villard draws two nude figures in what he believes to be the antique style the result is painfully ugly. It was impossible for him to adapt the stylistic conventions of Gothic art to a subject that depended on an entirely different system of forms. There can be few more hopeless misunderstandings in art than his attempt to render that refined abstraction, the antique torso, in terms of Gothic loops and pothooks. Moreover, Villard has constructed his figures according to the pointed geometrical scheme of which he himself gives us the key on another page. He evidently felt that the divine element in the human body must be expressed through geometry. Cennino Cennini, the last chronicler of medieval practice, says, "I will not tell you about irrational animals, because I have never learned any of their measurements. Draw them from nature, and in this respect you will achieve a good style." The Gothic artists could draw animals because this involved no intervening abstraction. But they could not draw the nude because it was an idea: an idea that their philosophy of form could not assimilate.

As I have said, in our Diogenes search for physical beauty our instinctive desire is not to imitate but to perfect. This is part of our Greek inheritance, and it was formulated by Aristotle with his usual deceptive simplicity. "Art," he says, "completes what nature cannot bring to a finish. The artist gives us knowledge of nature's unrealized ends." A great many assumptions underlie this statement, the chief of which is that everything has an ideal form of which the phenomena of experience are more or less corrupted replicas. This beautiful fancy has teased the minds of philosophers and writers on aesthetics for over two thousand years, and although we need not plunge into a sea of speculation, we cannot discuss the nude without considering its practical application, because every time we criticize a figure, saying that a neck is too long, hips are too wide or breasts too small; we are admitting, in quite concrete terms, the existence of ideal beauty. Critical opinion has varied between two interpretations of the ideal, one unsatisfactory because it is too prosaic, the other because it is too mystical. The former begins with the belief that although no individual body is satisfactory as a whole, the artist can choose the perfect parts from a number of figures and then combine them into a perfect whole. Such, we are told by Pliny, was the procedure of Zeuxis when he constructed his "Aphrodite" out of the five beautiful maidens of Kroton, and the advice reappears in the earliest treatise on painting of the postantique world, Alberti's *Della Pittura*. Dürer went so far as to say that he had "searched through two or three hundred." The argument is repeated again and again for four centuries, never more charmingly than by the French seventeenth-century theorist, Du Fresnoy, whom I shall quote in Mason's translation:

> For tho' our casual glance may sometimes meet
> With charms that strike the soul and seem complete,
> Yet if those charms too closely we define,
> Content to copy nature line for line,
> Our end is lost. Not such the master's care,
> Curious he culls the perfect from the fair;
> Judge of his art, thro' beauty's realm he flies,
> Selects, combines, improves, diversifies;
> With nimble step pursues the fleeting throng,
> And clasps each Venus as she glides along.

Naturally, the theory was a popular one with artists: but it satisfies neither logic nor experience. Logically, it simply transfers the problem from the whole to the parts, and we are left asking by what ideal pattern Zeuxis accepted or rejected the arms, necks, bosoms, and so forth of his five maidens. And even admitting that we do find certain individual limbs or features that, for some mysterious reason, seem to us perfectly beautiful, experience shows us that we cannot often recombine them. They are right in their setting, organically, and to abstract them is to deprive them of that rhythmic vitality on which their beauty depends.

To meet this difficulty the classic theorists of art invented what they called "the middle form." They based this notion on Aristotle's definition of nature, and in the stately language of Sir Joshua Reynolds' *Discourses* it seems to carry some conviction. But what does it amount to, translated into plain speech? Simply that the ideal is composed of the average and the habitual. It is an uninspiring proposition, and we are not surprised that Blake was provoked into replying, "All Forms are Perfect in the Poet's Mind but these are not Abstracted or compounded from Nature, but are from the Imagination." Of course he is right. Beauty is precious and rare, and if it were like a mechanical toy, made up of parts of average size that could be put together at will, we should not value it as we do. But we must admit that Blake's interjection is more a believer's cry of triumph than an argument, and we must ask what meaning can be attached to it. Perhaps the question is best answered in Crocean terms. The ideal is like a myth, in which the finished form can be understood only as the end of a long process of accretion. In the beginning, no doubt, there is the coincidence of widely diffused desires and the personal tastes of a few individuals endowed with the gift of simplifying their visual experiences into easily comprehensible shapes. Once this fusion has taken place, the resulting image, while still in a plastic state, may be enriched or refined upon by succeeding generations. Or, to change the metaphor, it is like a receptacle into which more and more experience can be poured. Then, at a certain point, it is full. It sets. And, partly because it seems to be completely satisfying, partly because the mythopoeic faculty has declined, it is accepted as true. What both Reynolds and Blake meant by ideal beauty was really the diffused memory of that peculiar physical type developed in Greece between the years 480 and 440 B.C., which in varying degrees of intensity and consciousness furnished the mind of Western man with a pattern of perfection from the Renaissance until the present century.

Once more we have returned to Greece, and it is now time to consider some peculiarities of the Greek mind that may have contributed to the formation of this indestructible image.

The most distinctive is the Greek passion for mathematics. In every branch of Hellenic thought we encounter a belief in measurable proportion that, in the last analysis, amounts to a mystical religion; and as early as Pythagoras it had been given the visible form of geometry. All art is founded on faith, and inevitably the Greek faith in harmonious numbers found expression in their painting and sculpture; but precisely how we do not know. The so-called canon of Polykleitos is not recorded, and the rules of proportion that have come down to us through Pliny and other ancient writers are of the most elementary kind. Probably the Greek sculptors were familiar with a system as subtle and elaborate as that of their architects, but we have scarcely any indication as to what it was. There is, however, one short and obscure statement in Vitruvius that, whatever it meant in antiquity, had a decisive influence on the Renaissance. At the beginning of the third book, in which he sets out to give the rules for sacred edifices, he suddenly announces that these buildings should have the proportions of a man. He gives some indication of correct human proportions and then throws in a statement that man's body is a model of proportion because with arms or legs extended it fits into those "perfect" geometrical forms, the square and the circle. It is impossible to exaggerate what this simple-looking proposition meant to the men of the Renaissance. To them it was far more than a convenient rule: it was the foundation of a whole philosophy. Taken together with the musical scale of Pythagoras, it seemed to offer exactly that link between sensation and order, between an organic and a geometric basis of beauty, which was (and perhaps remains) the philosopher's stone of aesthetics. Hence the many diagrams of figures standing in squares or circles that illustrate the treatises on architecture or aesthetics from the fifteenth to the seventeenth century.

Vitruvian man, as this figure has come to be called, appears earlier than Leonardo da Vinci, but it is in Leonardo's famous drawing in Venice that he receives his most masterly exposition; also, on the whole the most correct, for Leonardo makes only two slight deviations from Vitruvius, whereas most of the other illustrations follow him very sketchily. This is not one of Leonardo's most attractive drawings, and it must be admitted that the Vitruvian formula does not provide any guarantee of a pleasant-looking body. The most carefully worked-out

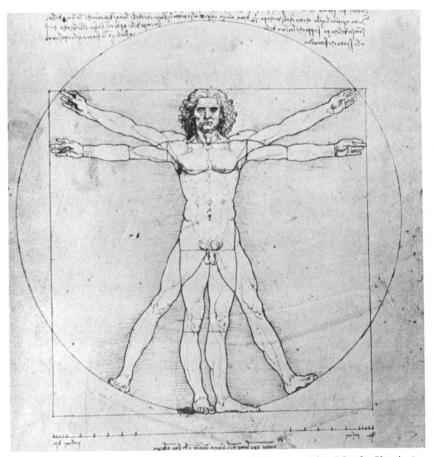

VITRUVIAN MAN—LEONARDO DA VINCI (*Library of St. Mark, Venice*)

illustration of all, in the Como Vitruvius of 1521, shows an ungraceful figure with head too small and legs and feet too big. Especially troublesome was the question of how the square and the circle, which were to establish the perfect form, should be related to one another. Leonardo, on no authority that I can discover, said that in order to fit into a circle the figure should stretch apart his legs so that he was a fourteenth shorter than if they were together. But this arbitrary solution did not please Cesariano, the editor of the Como Vitruvius, who inscribed the square in the circle, with unfortunate results. We see that from the point of view of strict geometry a gorilla might prove to be more satisfactory than a man.

How little systematic proportion alone can be relied on to produce physical beauty is shown by Dürer's engraving known as the "Nemesis" or "Large Fortune." It was executed in 1501, and we know that in the preceding year Dürer had been reading Vitruvius. In this figure he has applied Vitruvian principles of measurement down to the last detail: according to Professor Panofsky, even the big toe is operative. He has also taken his subject from a work by Poliziano, the same humanist poet who inspired Botticelli's "Birth of Venus" and Raphael's "Galatea." But in spite of these precautions he has not achieved the classical ideal. That he did so later was owing to the practice of relating his system to antique figures. It was not his squares and circles that enabled him to master classical proportions, but the fact that he applied them to memories of the "Apollo Belvedere" and the "Medici Venus"— forms "perfected in the poet's mind." And it was from these, in the end, that he derived the beautiful nude figure of Adam in his famous engraving of the "Fall."

Francis Bacon, as we all know, said, "There is no excellent beauty that hath not some strangeness in the proportion. A man cannot tell whether Apelles or Albert Dürer were the more trifler; where of the one would make a personage by geometrical proportions: the other by taking the best part out of divers faces to make one excellent." This very intelligent observation is unfair to Dürer, and suggests that Bacon, like the rest of us, had not read his book on human proportions, only looked at the plates. For, after 1507, Dürer abandoned the idea of imposing a geometrical scheme on the body, and set about deducing ideal measurements from nature, with a result, as may be imagined, somewhat different from his analyses of the antique; and in his introduction he forcefully denies the claim that he is providing a standard of absolute perfection. "There lives no man upon earth," he says, "who can give a final judgment upon what the most beautiful shape of a man may be; God only knows that .... 'Good' and 'better' in respect of beauty are not easy to discern, for it would be quite possible to make two different figures, neither conforming with the other, one stouter, the other thinner, and yet we might scarce be able to judge which of the two excelled in beauty."

So the most indefatigable and masterly constructor of ideal proportions abandoned them halfway through his career, and his work, from the "Nemesis" onward, is a proof that the idea of the nude does not depend on analyzable proportions alone. And yet when we look at the splendidly schematized bodies of Greek sculpture, we cannot resist the conviction that some system did exist. Almost every artist or writer on art who has thought seriously about the nude has concluded that it must have some basis of construction that can be stated in terms of measurement; and I myself, when trying to explain why a photograph did not satisfy me, said that I missed the sense of simple units clearly related to one another. Although the artist cannot construct a beautiful nude by mathematical rules, any more than the musician can compose a beautiful fugue, he cannot ignore them. They must be lodged somewhere at the back of his mind or in the movements of his fingers. Ultimately he is as dependent on them as an architect.

Dipendenza: that is the word used by Michelangelo, supreme as a draftsman of the nude and as an architect, to express his sense of the relationship between these two forms of order. And in the pages that follow I often made use of architectural analogies. Like a building, the nude represents a balance between an ideal scheme and functional necessities. The figure artist cannot forget the components of the human body, any more than the architect can fail to support his roof or forget his doors and windows. But the variations of shape and disposition are surprisingly wide. The most striking instance is, of course, the change in proportion between the Greek and the Gothic idea of the female body. One of the few classical canons of proportion of which we can be certain is that which, in a female nude, took the same unit of measurement for the distance between the breasts, the distance from the lower breast to the navel, and again from the navel to the division of the legs. This scheme we shall find carefully maintained in all figures of the classical epoch and in most of those which imitated them down to the first century. Contrast a typical Gothic nude of the fifteenth century, the "Eve" in the Vienna gallery attributed to Memlinc. The components are—naturally—the same. The basic pattern of the female body is still an oval, surmounted by two spheres; but the oval has grown incredibly long, the spheres have grown distressingly small. If we apply our unit of measurement, the distance between the breasts, we find that the navel is exactly twice as far down the body as it is in the classic scheme. This increased length of body is made more noticeable because it is unbroken by any suggestion of ribs or muscles. The forms are not conceived as individual blocks, but seem to have been drawn out of one another as if they were made of some viscous material. It is usual to speak of this kind of Gothic nude as "natural-istic," but is Memlinc's "Eve" really closer to the average (for this is what the word means) than the antique nude? Such, at all events, was certainly not the painter's intention. He aimed at producing a figure that would conform to the ideals of his time, that would be the kind of shape men liked to see; and by some strange interaction of flesh and spirit this long curve of the stomach has become the means by which the body has achieved the ogival rhythm of late Gothic architecture.

A rather less obvious example is provided by Sansovino's "Apollo" on the Loggetta in Venice. It is inspired by the "Apollo Belvedere," but although Sansovino, like all his contemporaries, thought that the antique figure was of unsurpassable beauty, he has allowed himself a fundamental difference in his construction of the body. We may describe this by saying that the antique male nude is like a Greek temple, the flat frame of the chest being carried on the columns of the legs; whereas the Renaissance nude is related to the architectural system that produced the central-domed church; so that instead of the sculptural interest depending on a simple, frontal plane, a number of axes radiate from one center. Not only the elevations but, so to say, the ground plans of these figures would have an obvious relationship to their respective architectures. What we may call the multiple-axis nude continued until the classicistic revival of the eighteenth century. Then, when architects were reviving the Greek-temple form, sculptors once more gave to the male body the flatness and frontality of a frame building. Ultimately the *dipendenza* of architecture and the nude expresses the relationship we all so earnestly desire between that which is perfected by the mind and that which we love. Poussin, writing to his friend Chantelou in 1642, said, "The beautiful girls whom you will have seen in Nîmes will not, I am sure, have delighted your spirit any less than the beautiful columns of Maison Carrée; for the one is no more than an old copy of the other." And the hero of Claudel's *Partage de midi*, when at last he puts his arms round his beloved, utters, as the first pure expression of his bliss, the words "O Colonne!"

So our surmise that the discovery of the nude as a form of art is connected with idealism and faith in measurable proportions seems to be true, but it is only half the truth. What other peculiarities of the Greek mind are involved? One obvious answer is their belief that the body was something to be proud of, and should be kept in perfect trim.

We need not suppose that many Greeks looked like the "Hermes" of Praxiteles, but we can be sure that in fifth-century Attica a majority of the young men had the nimble, well-balanced bodies depicted on the early red-figure vases. On a vase in the British Museum is a scene that will arouse sympathy in most of us, but to the Athenians was ridiculous and shameful—a fat youth in the gymnasium embarrassed by his ungraceful figure, and apparently protesting to a thin one, while two young men of more fortunate development throw the javelin and the discus. Greek literature from Homer and Pindar downward contains many expressions of this physical pride, some of which strike unpleasantly on the Anglo-Saxon ear and trouble the minds of schoolmasters when they are recommending the Greek ideal of fitness. "What do I care for any man?" says the young man Kritobolos in the *Symposium* of Xenophon; "I am beautiful." And no doubt this arrogance was increased by the tradition that in the gymnasium and the sportsground such young men displayed themselves totally naked.

The Greeks attached great importance to their nakedness. Thucydides, in recording the stages by which they distinguished themselves from the barbarians, gives prominence to the date at which it became the rule in the Olympic games, and we know from vase paintings that the competitors at the Panathenaic festival had been naked ever since the early sixth century. Although the presence or absence of a loincloth does not greatly affect questions of form, and in this study I shall include figures that are lightly draped, psychologically the Greek cult of absolute nakedness is of great importance. It implies the conquest of an inhibition that oppresses all but the most backward people; it is like a denial of original sin. This is not, as is sometimes supposed, simply a kind of paganism: for the Romans were shocked by the nakedness of Greek athletes, and Ennius attacked it as a sign of decadence. Needless to say, he was wide of the mark, for the most determined nudists of all were the Spartans, who scandalized even the Athenians by allowing women to compete, lightly clad, in their games. He and subsequent moralists considered the matter in purely physical terms; but, in fact, Greek confidence in the body can be understood only in relation to their philosophy. It expresses above all their sense of human wholeness. Nothing that related to the whole man could be isolated or evaded; and this serious awareness of how much was implied in physical beauty saved them from the two evils of sensuality and aestheticism.

At the same party where Kritobalos brags about his beauty Xenophon describes the youth Autolykos, victor of the Pankration, in whose honor the feast was being given. "Noting the scene," he says, "the first idea to strike the mind is that beauty has about it something regal; and the more so if it chance to be combined (as now in the person of Autolykos) with modesty and self-respect. Even as when a splendid object blazes forth at night, the eyes of men are riveted, so now the beauty of Autolykos drew on him the gaze of all; nor was there one of those onlookers but was stirred to his soul's depth by him who sat there. Some fell into unwonted silence, while the gestures of the rest were equally significant."

This feeling, that the spirit and body are one, which is the most familiar of all Greek characteristics, manifests itself in their gift of giving to abstract ideas a sensuous, tangible, and, for the most part, human form. Their logic is conducted in the form of dialogues between real men. Their gods take visible shape, and on their appearance are usually mistaken for half-familiar human beings—a maidservant, a shepherd, or a distant cousin. Woods, rivers, even echoes are shown in painting as bodily presences, solid as the living protagonists, and often more prominent. Here we reach what I take to be the central point of our subject: "Greek statues," said Blake, in his *Descriptive Catalogue,* "are all of them representations of spiritual existences, of gods immortal, to the mortal, perishing organ of sight; and yet they are embodied and organised in solid marble." The bodies were there, the belief in the gods was there, the love of rational proportion was there. It was the unifying grasp of the Greek imagination that brought them together. And the nude gains its enduring value from the fact that it reconciles several contrary states. It takes the most sensual and immediately interesting object, the human body, and puts it out of reach of time and desire; it takes the most purely rational concept of which mankind is capable, mathematical order, and makes it a delight to the senses; and it takes the vague fears of the unknown and sweetens them by showing that the gods are like men and may be worshiped for their life-giving beauty rather than their death-dealing powers.

To recognize how completely the value of these spiritual existences depends on their nudity, we have only to think of them as they appear, fully clothed, in the Middle Ages or early Renaissance. They have lost all their meaning. When the Graces are represented by three nervous ladies hiding behind a blanket, they no longer convey to us the civilizing influence of beauty. When Herakles is a lumbering *Lundsknecht* weighed down by fashionable armor, he cannot increase our sense of well-being by his own superabundant strength. Conversely, when nude figures, which had been evolved to express an idea, ceased to do so, and were represented for their physical perfection alone, they soon lost their value. This was the fatal legacy of neoclassicism, and Coleridge, who lived through the period, summed up the situation in some lines he added to the translation of Schiller's *Piccolomini:*

> *The intelligible powers of ancient poets,*
> *The fair humanities of old religion,*
> *The Power, the Beauty and the Majesty,*
> *That had their haunts in dale or piney mountain,*
> *. . . all these have vanished.*
> *They live no longer in the faith of reason.*

The academic nudes of the nineteenth century are lifeless because they no longer embodied real human needs and experiences. They were among the hundreds of devalued symbols that encumbered the art and architecture of the utilitarian century.

The nude had flourished most exuberantly during the first hundred years of the classical Renaissance, when the new appetite for antique imagery overlapped the medieval habits of symbolism and personification. It seemed then that there was no concept, however sublime, that could not be expressed by the naked body, and no object of use, however trivial, that would not be the better for having been given human shape. At one end of the scale was Michelangelo's "Last Judgment"; at the other the door knockers, candelabra, or even handles of knives and forks. To the first it might be objected—and frequently was—that nakedness was unbecoming in a representation of Christ and His saints. This was the point put forward by Paolo Veronese when he was tried by the Inquisition for including drunkards and Germans in his picture of the marriage of Cana: to which the chief inquisitor gave his immortal reply, "Do you not know that in these figures by Michelangelo there is nothing that is not spiritual—*non vi è cosa se non de spirito?*" And to the second it might be objected—and frequently is—that the similitude of the naked Venus is not what we need in our hand when we are cutting up our food or knocking at a door, to which Benvenuto Cellini would have replied that since the human body is the most perfect of all forms we cannot see it too often. In between these two extremes was that forest of nude figures, painted or carved, in stucco, bronze, or stone, which filled every vacant space in the architecture of the sixteenth century.

Such an insatiable appetite for the nude is unlikely to recur. It arose from a fusion of beliefs, traditions, and impulses very remote from our age of essence and specialization. Yet even in the new self-governing kingdom of the aesthetic sensation the nude is enthroned. The intensive application of great artists has made it into a sort of pattern for all formal constructions, and it is still a means of affirming the belief in ultimate perfection. "For soule is forme, and doth the bodie make," wrote Spenser in his *Hymne in Honour of Beautie,* echoing the words of the Florentine Neoplatonists, and although in life the evidence for the doctrine is inconclusive, it is perfectly applicable to art. The nude remains the most complete example of the transmutation of matter into form.

Nor are we likely once more to cut ourselves off from the body, as in the ascetic experiment of medieval Christianity. We may no longer worship it, but we have come to terms with it. We are reconciled to the fact that it is our lifelong companion, and since art is concerned with sensory images the scale and rhythm of the body is not easily ignored. Our continuous effort, made in defiance of the pull of gravity, to keep ourselves balanced upright on our legs affects every judgment on design, even our conception of which angle shall be called "right." The rhythm of our breathing and the beat of our hearts are part of the experience by which we measure a work of art. The relation of head to body determines the standard by which we assess all other proportions in nature. The disposition of areas in the torso is related to our most vivid experiences, so that, abstract shapes, the square and the circle, seem to us male and female; and the old endeavor of magical mathematics to square the circle is like the symbol of physical union. The starfish diagrams of Renaissance theorists may be ridiculous, but the Vitruvian principle rules our spirits, and it is no accident that the formalized body of the "perfect man" became the supreme symbol of European belief. Before the "Crucifixion" of Michelangelo we remember that the nude is, after all, the most serious of all subjects in art; and that it was not an advocate of paganism who wrote, "The Word was made flesh, and dwelt among us . . . full of grace and truth."

As a storyteller, Haydon is superb. The classic example of his narrative gifts is, of course, his famous account of "the immortal dinner" he gave for Lamb, Wordsworth, Keats, and others. Equally good, however, are the following passages dealing with the history of the Elgin marbles and Fuseli's confrontation of them.

Benjamin Robert Haydon
The History of the Elgin Marbles

It was also about this time that whispers and rumours began to spread in the art against the Elgin Marbles, and very quickly reached my ears. I was up in a moment, and ready to fight to the last gasp in their defence, for having studied them night and day it was natural that I should feel astonished at hearing from various quarters that their beauty, truth, and originality were questioned by a great authority in matters of art. As this difference of opinion eventually led to a great battle, I may as well in this place give a slight memoir of these divine fragments.

Lord Elgin, who was a man of fine taste, on receiving his appointment as Ambassador to the Porte [Turkey], in 1800, consulted with Harrison of Chester how he could render his influence at Constantinople available for the improvement of art, with reference to the glorious remains of Athens.

Harrison told me (in 1821) that he immediately advised his Lordship to procure, if possible, casts from the Ionic columns at the angle of the pediment, to show how the Greeks turned the volute round at

THREE GODDESSES FROM THE ELGIN MARBLES   (*The British Museum, London*)

that point, and also suggested that sculpture would be greatly benefited by casts from any fine works remaining. Lord Elgin, thus advised, having first failed in obtaining the support of the Government (who with all their love for the arts did not feel themselves at all justified in advancing the public money for such objects), and being unable to meet the enormous demands of English artists and moulders, proceeded to obtain on his road the assistance of foreign artists, who were more moderate in their terms. After much trouble he at last established at Athens six moulders and artists to draw, cast, and mould everything valuable in art, whether sculpture, architecture, or inscription.

So far Lord Elgin entertained no further notions, but when his artists informed him of the daily ravages of the Turks, and added that, during their stay, several works of sculpture had been injured, fired at, and even pounded into lime to build houses with;—when he found that of a whole temple existing in Stuart's day, near the Ilissus, not a stone was then to be seen;—when he learnt that all the English travellers who came to Athens, with their natural love of little bits, broke off arms or noses to bring home as relics;—he naturally concluded that in fifty years' time, at such a rate of devastation, scarce a fragment of architecture or sculpture would remain.

His position was a delicate one. Suspended between the desire of saving from ruin and enriching his country with works which he felt were unequalled in beauty, and his dread of that which he knew would be immediately imputed to him, viz. having taken advantage of his public power and position to further private and pecuniary objects, he was tormented, as all men are tormented who, contemplating a service to their fellow-creatures, feel the sad certainty that, for a time, they will stir up their hatred and provoke persecution instead of receiving legitimate gratitude and reward.

With the energy of a daring will he resolved that the bold step was the only rational one, and having made up his mind he directly applied to the Porte for leave to mould and remove, and for a special licence to dig and excavate. Who will censure his resolution and decision? No one will now; but everyone did then. A hue and cry was raised. It was swelled by Byron. Lord Elgin was lampooned, abused, and every motive imputed to him but the one by which alone he was impelled.

But Lord Elgin was a man not easily daunted; he put up his scaffoldings in spite of epigrams, and commenced removing what remained of the sculptures and architecture. After nearly five years of constant anxieties and disappointment those remains of matchless beauty, the

glorious Elgin Marbles, were at least got down to the Pirœus,[1]—at last
they were embarked,—at last the ship set sail, and while, with a fair
wind and shining sun, she was scudding away for old England, the pilot
ran her on a rock, and down went marbles and ship in many fathoms
water! Here was a misery; but Hamilton, Lord Elgin's secretary, who
was with them, did not despair. He hired a set of divers from the opposite coast of Asia Minor, and after immense perseverance recovered
every case. Not a fragment was missing; again they started; again the
winds blew, and the sun shone, and after many weeks they were at last
safely landed and lodged in Richmond Gardens, to set the whole art
world in an uproar.

Lord Elgin, who little knew the political state of art, was not prepared for any opposition. Innocent noble! he believed that the marbles
had only to be seen to be appreciated! He little knew that there was a
Royal Academy which never risked injury to its preponderance for
the sake of art. He little knew that there were societies of dilettanti,
who frowned at any man who presumed to form a collection unless
under their sanction, so that they should share any repute which might
accrue. He little knew that an eminent scholar, who was forming a
collection of bronzes, which he meant to leave to the nation, and who
having, like most eminent scholars, an intense admiration of what was
ancient, believed that nobody but himself knew anything of art or
nature, would become jealous at this sudden irruption into what he
considered his exclusive domain.

However little poor Lord Elgin knew of these matters, he soon discovered that we *had* a Royal Academy, that we *had* societies of dilettanti, and that we *had* an eminent scholar collecting bronzes, whose
ipse dixit no one dared dispute, be he what he might in rank, station
or talent; and Lord Elgin soon discovered also that this eminent
scholar, with the natural jealousy of a collector, meant to take the field
against the originality, beauty, nature and skill of his Lordship's marbles. At the first dinner-party at which Lord Elgin met him, he cried
out in a loud voice, "You have lost your labour, my Lord Elgin; your
marbles are overrated; they are not Greek, they are Roman of the time
of Hadrian." Lord Elgin, totally unprepared for such an assault, did
not reply, for he did not know what to say.

If Payne Knight had no foundation but historical evidence for such
an opinion, his evidence was shallow indeed, and if it proceeded from

---

[1] Piraeus, the harbor city of Athens.

his knowledge as a connoisseur, the perfection of the works he wished to traduce at once proved that his judgement, taste, and feeling, were utterly beneath notice. But such was the effect of Payne Knight's opinion, that the marbles went down in fashionable estimation from that hour. Government cooled, and artists became frightened because an eminent scholar, jealous of their possessor, denied the superiority of these glorious remains. Lord Elgin, feeling this, in utter despair removed them to Park Lane, built a shed over them and left them, as he feared, to an unmerited fate. Many melancholy, many poetical moments did I enjoy there, musing on these mighty fragments piled on each other, covered with dirt, dripping with damp, and utterly neglected for seasons together. But I gained from these sublime relics the leading principles of my practice, and I saw that the union of nature and idea was here so perfect, that the great artist in his works, seemed more like an agent of the Creator to express vitality by marble than a mere human genius.

Yet notwithstanding the excellence of these divine works, notwithstanding that their faithfulness to nature was distinctly proved by comparison with the forms of the finest boxers of the day, notwithstanding that their beauty was proclaimed by the mighty voice of public approbation, the learned despot of dinner-parties would not be beaten, and eight years passed over in apathy on the part of the British Government.

(Autobiography and Memoirs)

In the championship of the Elgin marbles, Haydon found the perfect cause. Nothing in Haydon's career was more admirable, or in the end more serviceable to art, than his leadership in the fight to have the British government accept the authenticity of these sculptures, and to provide adequate care and display room for them.

The Greeks Were Gods

To Park Lane then we went, and after passing through the hall and thence into an open yard, entered a damp, dirty penthouse where lay the marbles ranged within sight and reach. The first thing I fixed my eyes on was the wrist of a figure in one of the female groups, in which were visible, though in a feminine form, the radius and ulna. I was astonished, for I had never seen them hinted at in any female wrist in the antique. I darted my eye to the elbow, and saw the outer condyle visibly affecting the shape as in nature. I saw that the arm was in repose and the soft parts in relaxation. That combination of nature and idea which I had felt was so much wanting for high art was here displayed to midday conviction. My heart beat! If I had seen nothing else I had beheld sufficient to keep me to nature for the rest of my life. But when I turned to the Theseus and saw that every form was altered by action or repose,—when I saw that the two sides of his back varied, one side stretched from the shoulder blade being pulled forward, and the other side compressed from the shoulder-blade being pushed close to the spine as he rested on his elbow, with the belly flat because the bowels fell into the pelvis as he sat,—and when, turning to the Ilissus, I saw the belly protruded, from the figure lying on its side,—and again, when in the figure of the fighting metope I saw the muscle shown under the one arm-pit in that instantaneous action of darting out, and left out in the other arm-pits because not wanted—when I saw, in fact, the most heroic style of art combined with all the essential detail of actual life, the thing was done at once and for ever.

Here were principles which the common sense of the English people would understand; here were principles which I had struggled for in my first picture with timidity and apprehension; here were the principles which the great Greeks in their finest time established, and here was I, the most prominent historical student, perfectly qualified to appreciate all this by my own determined mode of study under the influence of my old friend the watchmaker—perfectly comprehending the hint at the skin by knowing well what was underneath it!

Oh, how I inwardly thanked God that I was prepared to understand all this! Now I was rewarded for all the petty harassings I had suffered. Now was I mad for buying Albinus without a penny to pay for it? Now was I mad for lying on the floor hours together, copying its figures? I felt the future, I foretold that they would prove themselves the finest things on earth, that they would overturn the false beau-ideal, where nature was nothing, and would establish the true beau-ideal, of which nature alone is the basis.

I shall never forget the horses' heads—the feet in the metopes! I felt as if a divine truth had blazed inwardly upon my mind and I knew that they would at last rouse the art of Europe from its slumber in the darkness.

I do not say this *now*, when all the world acknowledges it, but I said it then, *when no one would believe me.* I went home in perfect excitement . . . I passed the evening in a mixture of torture and hope; all night I dozed and dreamed of the marbles. I rose at five in a fever of excitement, tried to sketch the Theseus from memory, did so, and saw that I comprehended it. I worked that day and another and another, fearing that I was deluded. At last I got an order for myself; I rushed away to Park Lane; the impression was more vivid than before. I drove off to Fuseli, and fired him to such a degree that he ran upstairs, put on his coat and away we sallied. I remember that first a coal-cart with eight horses stopped us as it struggled up one of the lanes of the Strand; then a flock of sheep blocked us up; Fuseli, in a fury of haste and rage, burst into the middle of them, and they got between his little legs and jostled him so much that I screamed with laughter in spite of my excitement. He swore all along the Strand like a little fury. At last we came to Park Lane. Never shall I forget his uncompromising enthusiasm. He strode about saying, "De Greeks were godes! de Greeks were godes!"

(Autobiography and Memoirs)

Compare this with the celebrated sonnet "On Seeing the Elgin Marbles for the First Time" written by Haydon's young friend, John Keats.

> My spirit is too weak; mortality
> Weighs heavily on me like unwilling sleep,
> And each imagined pinnacle and steep
> Of godlike hardship tells me I must die
> Like a sick eagle looking at the sky.
> Yet 'tis a gentle luxury to weep,
> That I have not the cloudy winds to keep
> Fresh for the opening of the morning's eye.
> Such dim-conceived glories of the brain
> Bring round the heart an indescribable feud;
> So do these wonders a most dizzy pain,
> That mingles Grecian grandeur with the rude
> Wasting of old Time—with a billowy main,
> A sun, a shadow of a magnitude.

The Greeks were not a people specially devoted to art, but to politics.

Leo Stein, *Appreciation*

This poem is a magnificent statement of the classical ideal as seen and transformed by the romantics—a far different thing from the neoclassicism of the eighteenth century.

John Keats
Ode on a Grecian Urn

1

Thou still unravished bride of quietness,
    Thou foster-child of Silence and slow Time,
Sylvan historian, who canst thus express
    A flowery tale more sweetly than our rhyme:
What leaf-fringed legend haunts about thy shape
    Of deities or mortals, or of both,
        In Tempe or the dales of Arcady?
    What men or gods are these? What maidens loth?
What mad pursuit? What struggle to escape?
    What pipes and timbrels? What wild ecstasy?

2

Heard melodies are sweet, but those unheard
    Are sweeter; therefore, ye soft pipes, play on;
Not to the sensual ear, but, more endeared
    Pipe to the spirit ditties of no tone:
Fair youth, beneath the trees, thou canst not leave
    Thy song, nor ever can those trees be bare;
        Bold Lover, never, never canst thou kiss,
Though winning near the goal—yet, do not grieve;
        She cannot fade, though thou hast not thy bliss,
    For ever wilt thou love, and she be fair!

3

Ah, happy, happy boughs! that cannot shed
    Your leaves, nor ever bid the Spring adieu;
And, happy melodist, unwearied,
    For ever piping songs for ever new.
More happy love! more happy, happy love!

For ever warm and still to be enjoyed,
　　For ever panting, and for ever young;
All breathing human passion far above,
　　That leaves a heart high-sorrowful and cloyed,
　　A burning forehead, and a parching tongue.

4

Who are these coming to the sacrifice?
　　To what green altar, O mysterious priest,
Lead'st thou that heifer lowing at the skies,
　　And all her silken flanks with garlands drest?
What little town by river or sea shore,
　　Or mountain-built with peaceful citadel,
　　Is emptied of this folk, this pious morn?
And, little town, thy streets for evermore
　　Will silent be; and not a soul to tell
　　Why thou art desolate, can e'er return.

5

O Attic shape! Fair attitude! with brede
　　Of marble men and maidens overwrought,
With forest branches and the trodden weed;
　　Thou, silent form! dost tease us out of thought
As doth eternity: Cold Pastoral!
　　When old age shall this generation waste,
　　Thou shalt remain, in midst of other woe
Than ours, a friend to man, to whom thou say'st,
　　"Beauty is truth, truth beauty,"—that is all
　　Ye know on earth, and all ye need to know.

Horatio Greenough
True Classicism

　　　　The men who have reduced loco-
motion to its simplest elements, in the trotting wagon and the yacht
America, are nearer to Athens at this moment than they who would
bend the Greek temple to every use. I contend for Greek principles,
not Greek things.

Aesthetics at Washington, p. 12

THE MEDIEVAL SYNTHESIS

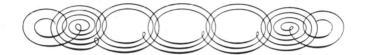

Adams saw in the worship of the Virgin a centralizing force that gave meaning and unity to medieval life and art: a celebrated chapter of his posthumously published autobiography, The Education of Henry Adams, *draws a contrast between medieval and modern civilization in terms of the two symbols of the Virgin and the dynamo.*

Adams' great work on twelfth- and thirteenth-century France, Mont-Saint-Michel and Chartres, *was first privately printed in 1905. It was one of the first, and is still one of the most successful, attempts at a cultural synthesis weaving together art, history, literature, religion, and philosophy. From it, we extract three sections, each dealing with a different aspect of the supreme artistic achievement of Chartres Cathedral, but all paying eloquent tribute to the cult of the Virgin as the* vis genetrix *of Chartres.*

Henry Brooks Adams
I. Towers and Portals[1]

. . . The towers have taken much time, though they are the least religious and least complicated part of church architecture, and in no way essential to the church; indeed, Saint Bernard thought them an excrescence due to pride and worldliness, and this is merely Saint Bernard's way of saying that they were an ornament created to gratify the artistic sense of beauty. Beautiful as they are, one's eyes must drop at last down to the church itself. If the spire symbolizes aspiration, the door symbolizes the way; and the portal

[1] Excerpts from three chapters of *Mont-Saint-Michel and Chartres* by Henry Brooks Adams. Boston: Houghton, Mifflin Company, 1905.

of Chartres is the type of French doors; it stands first in the history of Gothic art; and, in the opinion of most Gothic artists, first in the interest of all art, though this is no concern of ours. Here is the Way to Eternal Life as it was seen by the Church and the Art of the first crusade!

The fortune of this monument has been the best attested Miracle de la Vierge in the long list of the Virgin's miracles, for it comes down, practically unharmed, through what may with literal accuracy be called the jaws of destruction and the flames of hell. Built some time in the first half of the twelfth century, it passed, apparently unscathed, through the great fire of 1194 which burnt out the church behind, and even the timber interior of the towers in front of it. Owing to the enormous mass of timber employed in the structure of the great churches, these recurrent fires were as destructive as fire can be made, yet not only the portals with their statuary and carving, but also the lancet windows with their glass, escaped the flames; and, what is almost equally strange, escaped also the hand of the builder afterwards, who, if he had resembled other architects, would have made a new front of his own, but who, with piety unexampled, tenderly took the old stones down, one by one, and replaced them forty feet in advance of their old position. The English wars and the wars of religion brought new dangers, sieges, and miseries; the revolution of 1792 brought actual rapine and waste; boys have flung stones at the saints; architects have wreaked their taste within and without; fire after fire has calcined the church vaults; the worst wrecker of all, the restorer of the nineteenth century, has prowled about it; yet the porch still stands, mutilated but not restored, burned but not consumed, as eloquent a witness to the power and perfections of Our Lady as it was seven hundred years ago, and perhaps more impressive.

You will see portals and porches more or less of the same period elsewhere in many different places,—at Paris, Le Mans, Sens, Autun, Vézelay, Clermont-Ferrand, Moissac, Arles,—a score of them; for the same piety has protected them more than once; but you will see no other so complete or so instructive, and you may search far before you will find another equally good in workmanship. Study of the Chartres portal covers all the rest. The feeling and motive of all are nearly the same, or vary only to suit the character of the patron saint; and the point of all is that this feeling is the architectural child of the first crusade. At Chartres one can read the first crusade in the portal, as at Mont-Saint-Michel in the Aquilon and the promenoir.

MONT-SAINT-MICHEL, VIEW FROM THE SOUTH

The Abbé Bulteau gives reason for assuming the year 1117 as the approximate date of the sculpture about the west portal, and you saw at Mont-Saint-Michel, in the promenoir of Abbot Roger II, an accurately dated work of the same decade; but whatever the date of the plan, the actual work and its spirit belong to 1145 or thereabouts. Some fifty years had passed since the crusaders streamed through Constantinople to Antioch and Jerusalem, and they were daily going and returning. You can see the ideas they brought back with the relics and missals and enamels they bought in Byzantium. Over the central door is the Christ, which might be sculptured after a Byzantine enamel, with its long nimbus or aureole or glory enclosing the whole figure. Over the left door is an Ascension, bearing the same stamp; and over the right door, the seated Virgin, with her crown and her two attendant archangels, is an empress. Here is the Church, the Way, and the Life of the twelfth century that we have undertaken to feel, if not to understand!

First comes the central doorway, and above it is the glory of Christ, as the church of Chartres understood Christ in the year 1150; for the glories of Christ were many, and the Chartres Christ is one. Whatever Christ may have been in other churches, here, on this portal, he offers himself to his flock as the herald of salvation alone. Among all the imagery of these three doorways, there is no hint of fear, punishment, or damnation, and this is the note of the whole time. Before 1200, the Church seems not to have felt the need of appealing habitually to terror; the promise of hope and happiness was enough; even the portal at Autun, which displays a Last Judgment, belonged to Saint Lazarus the proof and symbol of resurrection. A hundred years later, every church portal showed Christ not as Saviour but as Judge, and He presided over a Last Judgment at Bourges and Amiens, and here on the south portal, where the despair of the damned is the evident joy of the artist, if it is not even sometimes a little his jest, which is worse. At Chartres Christ is identified with His Mother, the spirit of love and grace, and His Church is the Church Triumphant.

Not only is fear absent; there is not even a suggestion of pain; there is not a martyr with the symbol of his martyrdom; and what is still more striking, in the sculptured life of Christ, from the Nativity to the Ascension, which adorns the capitals of the columns, the single scene that has been omitted is the Crucifixion. There, as everywhere in this portal, the artists seem actually to have gone out of their way in order to avoid a suggestion of suffering. They have pictured Christ and His Mother in all the other events of their lives; they have represented evangelists; apostles; the twenty-four old men of the Apocalypse; saints, prophets, kings, queens, and princes, by the score; the signs of the zodiac, and even the seven liberal arts: grammar, rhetoric, dialectics, arithmetic, geometry, astronomy, and music; everything is there except misery.

Perhaps Our Lady of Chartres was known to be peculiarly gracious and gentle, and this may partially account also for the extreme popularity of her shrine; but whatever the reason, her church was clearly intended to show only this side of her nature, and to impress it on her Son. You can see it in the grave and gracious face and attitude of the Christ, raising His hand to bless you as you enter His kingdom; in the array of long figures which line the entrance to greet you as you pass; in the expression of majesty and mercy of the Virgin herself on her throne above the southern doorway; never once are you regarded as a possible rebel, or traitor, or a stranger to be treated with suspicion, or as a child to be impressed by fear.

Equally distinct, perhaps even more emphatic, is the sculptor's earnestness to make you feel, without direct insistence, that you are entering the Court of the Queen of Heaven who is one with her Son and His Church. The central door always bore the name of the "Royal

WEST FAÇADE, CHARTRES CATHEDRAL

Door," because it belonged to the celestial majesty of Christ, and naturally bears the stamp of royalty; but the south door belongs to the Virgin and to us. Stop a moment to see how she receives us, remembering, or trying to remember, that to the priests and artists who designed the portal, and to the generations that went on the first and second crusades, the Virgin in her shrine was at least as living, as real, as personal an empress as the Basilissa at Constantinople!

On the lintel immediately above the doorway is a succession of small groups: first, the Annunciation; Mary stands to receive the Archangel Gabriel, who comes to announce to her that she is chosen to be the Mother of God. The second is the Visitation, and in this scene also Mary stands, but she already wears a crown; at least, the Abbé Bulteau says so, although time has dealt harshly with it. Then, in the centre, follows the Nativity; Mary lies on a low bed, beneath, or before, a sort of table or cradle on which lies the Infant, while Saint Joseph stands at the bed's head. Then the angel appears, directing three shepherds to the spot, filling the rest of the space.

In correct theology, the Virgin ought not to be represented in bed, for she could not suffer like ordinary women, but her palace at Chartres is not much troubled by theology, and to her, as empress-mother, the pain of child-birth was a pleasure which she wanted her people to share. The Virgin of Chartres was the greatest of all queens, but the most womanly of women, as we shall see; and her double character is sustained throughout her palace. She was also intellectually gifted in the highest degree. In the upper zone you see her again, at the Presentation in the Temple, supporting the Child Jesus on the altar, while Simeon aids. Other figures bring offerings. The voussures of the arch above contain six archangels, with curious wings, offering worship to the Infant and His Imperial Mother. Below are the signs of the zodiac; the Fishes and the Twins. The rest of the arch is filled by the seven liberal arts, with Pythagoras, Aristotle, Cicero, Euclid, Nicomachus, Ptolemy, and Priscian as their representatives, testifying to the Queen's intellectual superiority.

In the centre sits Mary, with her crown on her head and her Son in her lap, enthroned, receiving the homage of heaven and earth; of all time, ancient and modern; of all thought, Christian and Pagan; of all men, and all women; including, if you please, your homage and mine, which she receives without question, as her due; which she cannot be said to claim, because she is above making claims; she is empress. Her left hand bore a sceptre; her right supported the Child, Who looks directly forward, repeating the Mother's attitude, and raises His right hand to bless, while His left rests on the orb of empire. She and her Child are one.

All this was noble beyond the nobility of man, but its earthly form was inspired by the Empire rather than by the petty royalty of Louis-le-Gros or his pious queen Alix of Savoy. One mark of the period is the long, oval nimbus; another is the imperial character of the Virgin; a third is her unity with the Christ which is the Church. To us, the mark that will distinguish the Virgin of Chartres, or, if you prefer, the Virgin of the Crusades, is her crown and robes and throne. According to M. Rohault de Fleury's "Iconographie de la Sainte Vierge" (ii, 62), the Virgin's headdress and ornaments had been for long ages borrowed from the costume of the Empresses of the East in honour of the Queen of Heaven. No doubt the Virgin of Chartres was the Virgin recognized by the Empress Helena, mother of Constantine, and was at least as old as Helena's pilgrimage to Jerusalem in 326. She was not a Western, feudal queen, nor was her Son a feudal king; she typified an authority which the people wanted, and the fiefs feared; the Pax Romana; the omnipotence of God in government. In all Europe, at that time, there was no power able to enforce justice or to maintain order, and no symbol of such a power except Christ and His Mother and the Imperial Crown.

This idea is very different from that which was the object of our pilgrimage to Mont-Saint-Michel; but since all Chartres is to be one long comment upon it, you can lay the history of the matter on the shelf for study at your leisure, if you ever care to study into the weary details of human illusions and disappointments, while here we pray to the Virgin and absorb ourselves in the art, which is your pleasure and which shall not teach either a moral or a useful lesson. The Empress Mary is receiving you at her portal, and whether you are an impertinent child, or a foolish old peasant-woman, or an insolent prince, or a more insolent tourist, she receives you with the same dignity; in fact, she probably sees very little difference between you. An empress of Russia to-day would probably feel little difference in the relative rank of her subjects, and the Virgin was empress over emperors, patriarchs, and popes. Any one, however ignorant, can feel the sustained dignity of the sculptor's work, which is asserted with all the emphasis he could put into it. Not one of these long figures which line the three doorways but is an officer or official in attendance on the Empress or her Son, and bears the stamp of the Imperial Court. They are mutilated, but, if they have been treated with indigity, so were often their temporal rivals, torn to pieces, trampled on, to say nothing of being merely beheaded or poisoned, in the Sacred Palace and the Hippodrome, without losing that peculiar Oriental dignity of style which seems to drape the least dignified attitudes. The grand air of the twelfth century is something like that of a Greek temple; you can, if you like, hammer every separate stone to pieces, but you cannot hammer out the Greek style. . . .

II. The Virgin of Chartres

We must take ten minutes to accustom our eyes to the light, and we had better use them to seek the reason why we come to Chartres rather than to Rheims or Amiens or Bourges, for the cathedral that fills our ideal. The truth is, there are several reasons; there generally are, for doing the things we like; and after you have studied Chartres to the ground, and got your reasons settled, you will never find an antiquarian to agree with you; the architects will probably listen to you with contempt; and even these excellent priests, whose kindness is great, whose patience is heavenly, and whose good opinion you would so gladly gain, will turn from you with pain, if not with horror. The Gothic is singular in this; one seems easily at home in the Renaissance; one is not too strange in the Byzantine; as for the Roman, it is ourselves; and we could walk blindfolded through every chink and cranny of the Greek mind; all these styles seem modern, when we come close to them; but the Gothic gets away. No two men think alike about it, and no woman agrees with either man. The Church itself never agreed about it, and the architects agree even less than the priests. To most minds it casts too many shadows; it wraps itself in mystery; and when people talk of mystery, they commonly mean fear. To others, the Gothic seems hoary with age and decrepitude, and its shadows mean death. What is curious to watch is the fanatical conviction of the Gothic enthusiast, to whom the twelfth century means exuberant youth, the eternal child of Wordsworth, over whom its immortality broods like the day; it is so simple and yet so complicated; it sees so much and so little; it loves so many toys and cares for so few necessities; its youth is so young, its age so old, and its youthful yearning for old thought is so disconcerting, like the mysterious senility of the baby that—

> Deaf and silent, reads the eternal deep,
> Haunted forever by the eternal mind.

One need not take it more seriously than one takes the baby itself. Our amusement is to play with it, and to catch its meaning in its smile; and whatever Chartres may be now, when young it was a smile. To the Church, no doubt, its cathedral here has a fixed and administrative meaning, which is the same as that of every other bishop's seat and with which we have nothing whatever to do. To us, it is a child's fancy; a toy-house to please the Queen of Heaven,—to please her so much that she would be happy in it,—to charm her till she smiled.

The Queen Mother was as majestic as you like; she was absolute; she could be stern; she was not above being angry; but she was still a woman, who loved grace, beauty, ornament,—her toilette, robes, jewels;—who considered the arrangements of her palace with attention, and liked both light and colour; who kept a keen eye on her Court, and exacted prompt and willing obedience from king and archbishops as well as from beggars and drunken priests. She protected her friends and punished her enemies. She required space, beyond what was known in the Courts of kings, because she was liable at all times to have ten thousand people begging her for favours—mostly inconsistent with law —and deaf to refusal. She was extremely sensitive to neglect, to disagreeable impressions, to want of intelligence in her surroundings. She was the greatest artist, as she was the greatest philosopher and musician and theologist, that ever lived on earth, except her Son, Who, at Chartres, is still an Infant under her guardianship. Her taste was infalliable; her sentence eternally final This church was built for her in this spirit of simple-minded, practical, utilitarian faith,—in this singleness of thought, exactly as a little girl sets up a doll-house for her favourite blonde doll. Unless you can go back to your dolls, you are out of place here. If you can go back to them, and get rid for one small hour of the weight of custom, you shall see Chartres in glory.

The palaces of earthly queens were hovels compared with these palaces of the Queen of Heaven at Chartres, Paris, Laon, Noyon, Rheims, Amiens, Rouen, Bayeux, Coutances,—a list that might be stretched into a volume. The nearest approach we have made to a palace was the Merveille at Mont-Saint-Michel, but no Queen had a palace equal to that. The Merveille was built, or designed, about the year 1200; toward the year 1500, Louis XI built a great castle at Loches in Touraine, and there Queen Anne de Bretagne had apartments which still exist, and which we will visit. At Blois you shall see the residence which served for Catherine de Medicis till her death in 1589. Anne de Bretagne was trebly queen, and Catherine de Medicis took her standard of comfort from the luxury of Florence. At Versailles you can see the apartments which the queens of the Bourbon line occupied through their century of magnificence. All put together, and then trebled in importance, could not rival the splendour of any single cathedral dedicated to Queen Mary in the thirteenth century; and of them all, Chartres was built to be peculiarly and exceptionally her delight.

One has grown so used to this sort of loose comparison, this reckless waste of words, that one no longer adopts an idea unless it is driven in with hammers of statistics and columns of figures. With the irritating demand for literal exactness and perfectly straight lines which lights up every truly American eye, you will certainly ask when this exaltation of Mary began, and unless you get the dates, you will doubt the facts. It is your own fault if they are tiresome; you might easily read them all in the "Iconographie de la Sainte Vierge," by M. Rohault de Fleury, published in 1878. You can start at Byzantium with the Empress Helena in 326, or with the Council of Ephesus in 431. You will find the Virgin acting as the patron saint of Constantinople and of the Imperial residence, under as many names as Artemis or Aphrodite had borne. As Godmother (Θεομητηρ), Deipara (Θεοτοκος),

Pathfinder ('Οδηγήτρια), she was the chief favourite of the Eastern Empire, and her picture was carried at the head of every procession and hung on the wall of every hut and hovel, as it is still wherever the Greek Church goes. In the year 610, when Heraclius sailed from Carthage to dethrone Phocas at Constantinople, his ships carried the image of the Virgin at their mastheads. In 1143, just before the flèche on the Chartres clocher was begun, the Basileus John Comnenus died, and so devoted was he to·the Virgin that, on a triumphal entry into Constantinople, he put the image of the Mother of God in his chariot, while he himself walked. In the Western Church the Virgin had always been highly honoured, but it was not until the crusades that she began to overshadow the Trinity itself. Then her miracles became more frequent and her shrines more frequented, so that Chartres, soon after 1100, was rich enough to build its western portal with Byzantine splendour. A proof of the new outburst can be read in the story of Citeaux. For us, Citeaux means Saint Bernard, who joined the Order in 1112, and in 1115 founded his Abbey of Clairvaux in the territory of Troyes. In him, the religious emotion of the half-century between the first and second crusades (1095–1145) centred as in no one else. He was a French precursor of Saint Francis of Assisi who lived a century later. If we were to plunge into the story of Citeaux and Saint Bernard we should never escape, for Saint Bernard incarnates what we are trying to understand, and his mind is further from us than the architecture. You would lose hold of everything actual, if you could comprehend in its contradictions the strange mixture of passion and caution, the austerity, the self-abandonment, the vehemence, the restraint, the love, the hate, the miracles, and the scepticism of Saint Bernard. The Cistercian Order, which was founded in 1098, from the first put all its churches under the special protection of the Virgin, and Saint Bernard in his time was regarded as the apple of the Virgin's eye. Tradition as old as the twelfth century, which long afterwards gave to Murillo the subject of a famous painting, told that once, when he was reciting before her statue the "Ave Maris Stella," and came to the words, "Monstra te esse Matrem," the image, pressing its breast, dropped on the lips of her servant three drops of the milk which had nourished the Saviour. The same miracle, in various forms, was told of many other persons, both saints and sinners; but it made so much impression on the mind of the age that, in the fourteenth century, Dante, seeking in Paradise for some official introduction of the foot of the Throne, found no intercessor with the Queen of Heaven more potent than Saint Bernard. You can still read Bernard's hymns to the Virgin, and even his sermons, if you like. To him she was the great mediator. In the eyes of a culpable humanity, Christ was too sublime, too terrible, too just, but not even the weakest human frailty could fear to approach his Mother. Her attribute was humility; her love and pity was infinite. "Let him deny your mercy who can say that he has ever asked it in vain."

Saint Bernard was emotional and to a certain degree mystical, like Adam de Saint-Victor, whose hymns were equally famous, but the emotional saints and mystical poets were not by any means allowed to establish exclusive rights to the Virgin's favour. Abélard was as devoted as they were, and wrote hymns as well. Philosophy claimed her, and Albert the Great, the head of scholasticism, the teacher of Thomas Aquinas, decided in her favour the question: "Whether the Blessed Virgin possessed perfectly the seven liberal arts." The Church at Chartres had decided it a hundred years before by putting the seven liberal arts next her throne, with Aristotle himself to witness; but Albertus gave the reason: "I hold that she did, for it is written, 'Wisdom has built herself a house, and has sculptured seven columns.' That house is the blessed Virgin; the seven columns are the seven liberal arts. Mary, therefore, had perfect mastery of science." Naturally she had also perfect mastery of economics, and most of her great churches were built in economic centres. The guilds were, if possible, more devoted to her than the monks; the bourgeoisie of Paris, Rouen, Amiens, Laon, spend money by millions to gain her favour. Most surprising of all, the great military class was perhaps the most vociferous. Of all inappropriate haunts for the gentle, courteous, pitying Mary, a field of battle seems to be the worst, if not distinctly blasphemous; yet the greatest French warriors insisted on her leading them into battle, and in the actual mêlée when men were killing each other, on every battle-field in Europe, for at least five hundred years, Mary was present, leading both sides. The battle-cry of the famous Constable du Guesclin was "Notre-Dame-Guesclin"; "Notre-Dame-Coucy" was the cry of the great Sires de Coucy; "Notre-Dame-Auxerre"; "Notre-Dame-Sancerre"; "Notre-Dame-Hainault"; "Notre-Dame-Gueldres"; "Notre-Dame-Bourbon"; "Notre-Dame-Bearn";—all well-known battle-cries. The King's own battle at one time cried, "Notre-Dame-Saint-Denis-Montjoie"; the Dukes of Burgundy cried, "Notre-Dame-Bourgogne"; and even the soldiers of the Pope were said to cry, "Notre-Dame-Saint-Pierre."

The measure of this devotion, which proves to any religious American mind, beyond possible cavil, its serious and practical reality, is the money it cost. According to statistics, in the single century between 1170 and 1270, the French built eighty cathedrals and nearly five hundred churches of the cathedral class, which would have cost, according to an estimate made in 1840, more than five thousand millions to replace. Five thousand million francs is a thousand million dollars, and this covered only the great churches of a single century. The same scale of expenditure had been going on since the year 1000, and almost every parish in France had rebuilt its church in stone; to this day France is strewn with the ruins of this architecture, and yet the still preserved churches of the eleventh and twelfth centuries, among the churches that belong to the Romanesque and Transition period, are numbered by hundreds until they reach well into the thousands. The share of this capital which was—if one may use a commercial figure—invested in the Virgin cannot be fixed, any more than the total sum given to religious objects between 1000 and 1300; but in a spiritual and artistic sense, it was almost the whole, and expressed an intensity of conviction never again reached by any passion, whether of religion, of loyalty, of patriotism, or of wealth; perhaps never even parallelled by any single economic effort, except in war. Nearly every great church of the twelfth and thirteenth centuries belonged to Mary, until in France one asks for the church of Notre Dame as though it meant cathedral; but, not satisfied with this, she contracted the habit of requiring in all churches a chapel of her own, called in English the "Lady Chapel," which was apt to be as large as the church but was always meant to be handsomer; and there, behind the high altar, in her own private apartment, Mary sat, receiving her innumerable suppliants, and ready at any moment to step up upon the high altar itself to support the tottering authority of the local saint.

Expenditure like this rests invariably on an economic idea. Just as the French of the nineteenth century invested their surplus capital in a railway system in the belief that they would make money by it in this life, in the thirteenth they trusted their money to the Queen of Heaven because of their belief in her power to repay it with interest in the life to come. The investment was based on the power of Mary as Queen rather than on any orthodox Church conception of the Virgin's legitimate station. Papal Rome never greatly loved Byzantine empresses or French queens. The Virgin of Chartres was never wholly sympathetic to the Roman Curia. To this day the Church writers—

like the Abbé Bulteau or M. Rohault de Fleury—are singularly shy of the true Virgin of majesty, whether at Chartres or at Byzantium or wherever she is seen. The fathers Martin and Cahier at Bourges alone felt her true value. Had the Church controlled her, the Virgin would perhaps have remained prostrate at the foot of the Cross. Dragged by a Byzantine Court, backed by popular insistence and impelled by overpowering self-interest, the Church accepted the Virgin throned and crowned, seated by Christ, the Judge throned and crowned; but even this did not wholly satisfy the French of the thirteenth century who seemed bent on absorbing Christ in His Mother, and making the Mother the Church, and Christ the Symbol.

The Church had crowned and enthroned her almost from the beginning, and could not have dethroned her if it would. In all Christian art—sculpture or mosaic, painting or poetry—the Virgin's rank was expressly asserted. Saint Bernard, like John Comnenus, and probably at the same time (1120–40), chanted hymns to the Virgin as Queen:—

O salutaris Virgo Stella Maris
Generans prolem, Æquitatis solem,
Lucis auctorem, Retinens pudorem,
   Suscipe laudem!

Celi Regina Per quam medicina
Datur ægrotis, Gratia devotis,
Gaudium mœstis, Mundo lux cœlestis,
   Spesque salutis;

Aula regalis, Virgo specialis,
Posce medelam Nobis et tutelam,
Suscipe vota, Precibusque cuncta
   Pelle molesta!

O saviour Virgin, Star of Sea,
Who bore for child the Son of Justice,
The source of Light, Virgin always
   Hear our praise!

Queen of Heaven who have given
Medicine to the sick, Grace to the devout,
Joy to the sad, Heaven's light to the world
   And hope of salvation;

Court royal, Virgin typical,
Grant us cure and guard,
Accept our vows, and by prayers
   Drive all griefs away!

As the lyrical poet of the twelfth century, Adam de Saint-Victor seems to have held rank higher if possible than that of Saint Bernard, and his hymns on the Virgin are certainly quite as emphatic an assertion of her majesty:—

Imperatrix supernorum!
Superatrix infernorum!
Eligenda via cœli,
Retinenda spe fideli,
Separatos a te longe
Revocatos ad te junge
   Tuorum collegio!

Empress of the highest,
Mistress over the lowest,
Chosen path of Heaven,
Held fast by faithful hope,
Those separated from you far,
Recalled to you, unite
   In your fold!

To delight in the childish jingle of the mediæval Latin is a sign of a futile mind, no doubt, and I beg pardon of you and of the Church for wasting your precious summer day on poetry which was regarded

as mystical in its age and which now sounds like a nursery rhyme; but
a verse or two of Adam's hymn on the Assumption of the Virgin completes the record of her rank, and goes to complete also the documentary proof of her majesty at Chartres:—

Salve, Mater Salvatoris!	Mother of our Saviour, hail!
Vas electum! Vas honoris!	Chosen vessel! Sacred Grail!
Vas cœlestis Gratiæ!	Font of celestial grace!
Ab æterno Vas provisum!	From eternity forethought!
Vas insigne! Vas excisum	By the hand of Wisdom wrought!
Manu sapientiæ!	Precious, faultless Vase!
Salve, Mater pietatis,	Hail, Mother of Divinity!
Et totius Trinitatis	Hail, Temple of the Trinity!
Nobile Triclinium!	Home of the Triune God!
Verbi tamen incarnati	In whom the Incarnate Word had birth,
Speciale majestati	The King! to whom you gave on earth
Præparans hospitium!	Imperial abode.
O Maria! Stella maris!	Oh, Maria! Constellation!
Dignitate singularis,	Inspiration! Elevation!
Super omnes ordinaris	Rule and Law and Ordination
Ordines cœlestium!	Of the angels' host!
In supremo sita poli	Highest height of God's Creation,
Nos commenda tuæ proli,	Pray your Son's commiseration,
Ne terrores sive doli	Lest, by fear or fraud, salvation
Nos supplantent hostium!	For our souls be lost!

Constantly—one might better say at once, officially, she was addressed
in these terms of supreme majesty: "Imperatrix supernorum!" "Cœli
Regina!" "Aula regalis!" but the twelfth century seemed determined
to carry the idea out to its logical conclusion in defiance of dogma.
Not only was the Son absorbed in the Mother, or represented as under
her guardianship, but the Father fared no better, and the Holy Ghost
followed. The poets regarded the Virgin as the "Templum Trinitatis"; totius Trinitatis nobile Triclinium." She was the refectory of
the Trinity—the "Triclinium"—because the refectory was the largest
room and contained the whole of the members, and was divided in
three parts by two rows of columns. She was the "Templum Trinitatis,"
the Church itself, with its triple aisle. The Trinity was absorbed in her.

This is a delicate subject in the Church, and you must feel it with
delicacy, without brutally insisting on its necessary contradictions. All
theology and all philosophy are full of contradictions quite as flagrant
and far less sympathetic. This particular variety of religious faith is
simply human, and has made its appearance in one form or another
in nearly all religions; but though the twelfth century carried it to an
extreme, and at Chartres you see it in its most charming expression,
we have got always to make allowances for what was going on beneath

the surface in men's minds, consciously or unconsciously, and for the latent scepticism which lurks behind all faith. The Church itself never quite accepted the full claims of what was called Mariolatry. One may be sure, too, that the bourgeois capitalist and the student of the schools, each from his own point of view, watched the Virgin with anxious interest. The bourgeois had put an enormous share of his capital into what was in fact an economical speculation, not unlike the South Sea Scheme, or the railway system of our own time; except that in one case the energy was devoted to shortening the road to Heaven; in the other, to shortening the road to Paris; but no serious schoolman could have felt entirely convinced that God would enter into a business partnership with man, to establish a sort of joint-stock society for altering the operation of divine and universal laws. The bourgeois cared little for the philosophical doubt if the economical result proved to be good, but he watched this result with his usual practical sagacity, and required an experience of only about three generations (1200–1300) to satisfy himself that relics were not certain in their effects; that the Saints were not always able or willing to help; that Mary herself could not certainly be bought or bribed; that prayer without money seemed to be quite as efficacious as prayer with money; and that neither the road to Heaven nor Heaven itself had been made surer or brought nearer by an investment of capital which amounted to the best part of the wealth of France. Economically speaking, he became satisfied that his enormous money-investment had proved to be an almost total loss, and the reaction on his mind was as violent as the emotion. For three hundred years it prostrated France. The efforts of the bourgeoisie and the peasantry to recover their property, so far as it was recoverable, have lasted to the present day and we had best take care not to get mixed in those passions.

If you are to get the full enjoyment of Chartres, you must, for the time, believe in Mary as Bernard and Adam did, and feel her presence as the architects did, in every stone they placed, and every touch they chiselled. You must try first to rid your mind of the traditional idea that the Gothic is an intentional expression of religious gloom. The necessity for light was the motive of the Gothic architects. They needed light and always more light, until they sacrificed safety and common sense in trying to get it. They converted their walls into windows, raised their vaults, diminished their piers, until their churches could no longer stand. You will see the limits at Beauvais; at Chartres we have not got so far, but even here, in places where the Virgin wanted it,—

as above the high altar,—the architect has taken all the light there was to take. For the same reason, fenestration became the most important part of the Gothic architect's work, and at Chartres was uncommonly interesting because the architect was obliged to design a new system, which should at the same time satisfy the laws of construction and the taste and imagination of Mary. No doubt the first command of the Queen of Heaven was for light, but the second, at least equally imperative, was for colour. Any earthly queen, even though she were not Byzantine in taste, loved colour; and the truest of queens—the only true Queen of Queens—had richer and finer taste in colour than the queens of fifty earthly kingdoms, as you will see when we come to the immense effort to gratify her in the glass of her windows. Illusion for illusion,—granting for the moment that Mary was an illusion,—the Virgin Mother in this instance repaid to her worshippers a larger return for their money than the capitalist has ever been able to get, at least in this world, from any other illusion of wealth which he has tried to make a source of pleasure and profit.

The next point on which Mary evidently insisted was the arrangement for her private apartments, the apse, as distinguished from her throne-room, the choir; both being quite distinct from the hall, or reception-room of the public, which was the nave with its enlargements in the transepts. This arrangement marks the distinction between churches built as shrines for the deity and churches built as halls of worship for the public. The difference is chiefly in the apse, and the apse of Chartres is the most interesting of all apses from this point of view.

The Virgin required chiefly these three things, or, if you like, these four: space, light, convenience; and colour decoration to unite and harmonize the whole. This concerns the interior; on the exterior she required statuary, and the only complete system of decorative sculpture that existed seems to belong to her churches:—Paris, Rheims, Amiens, and Chartres. Mary required all this magnificence at Chartres for herself alone, not for the public. As far as one can see into the spirit of the builders, Chartres was exclusively intended for the Virgin, as the Temple of Abydos was intended for Osiris. The wants of man, beyond a mere roof-cover, and perhaps space to some degree, enter to no very great extent into the problem of Chartres. Man came to render homage or to ask favours. The Queen received him in her palace, where she alone was at home, and alone gave commands.

The artist's second thought was to exclude from his work everything that could displease Mary; and since Mary differed from living queens only in infinitely greater majesty and refinement, the artist could admit only what pleased the actual taste of the great ladies who dictated taste at the Courts of France and England, which surrounded the little Court of the Counts of Chartres What they were—these women of the twelfth and thirteen centuries—we shall have to see or seek in other directions; but Chartres is perhaps the most magnificent and permanent monument they left of their taste, and we can begin here with learning certain things which they were not.

In the first place, they were not in the least vague, dreamy, or mystical in a modern sense;—far from it! They seemed anxious only to throw the mysteries into a blaze of light; not so much physical, perhaps,—since they, like all women, liked moderate shadow for their toilettes,—but luminous in the sense of faith. There is nothing about Chartres that you would think mystical, who know your Lohengrin, Siegfried, and Parsifal. If you care to make a study of the whole literature of the subject, read M. Mâle's *Art Religieux du XIIIe Siècle en France,* and use it for a guide-book. Here you need only note how symbolic and how simple the sculpture is, on the portals and porches. Even what seems a grotesque or an abstract idea is no more than the simplest child's personification. On the walls you may have noticed the *Ane qui vielle,*—the ass playing the lyre; and on all the old churches you can see "bestiaries," as they were called, of fabulous animals, symbolic or not; but the symbolism is as simple as the realism of the oxen at Laon. It gave play to the artist in his effort for variety of decoration, and it amused the people,—probably the Virgin also was not above being amused;—now and then it seems about to suggest what you would call an esoteric meaning, that is to say, a meaning which each one of us can consider private property reserved for our own amusement, and from which the public is excluded; yet, in truth, in the Virgin's churches the public is never excluded, but invited. The Virgin even had the additional charm to the public that she was popularly supposed to have no very marked fancy for priests as such; she was a queen, a woman, and a mother, functions, all, which priests could not perform. Accordingly, she seems to have had little taste for mysteries of any sort, and even the symbols that seem most mysterious were clear to every old peasant-woman in her church. The most pleasing and promising of them all is the woman's figure you saw on the front of the cathedral in Paris; her eyes bandaged; her head bent down; her crown falling; without cloak or royal robe; holding in her hand a guidon or banner with its staff broken in more than one place. On the opposite pier stands another woman, with royal mantle, erect and commanding. The symbol is so graceful that one is quite eager to know its meaning; but every child in the Middle Ages would have instantly told you that the woman with the falling crown meant only the Jewish Synagogue, as the one with the royal robe meant the Church of Christ.

Another matter for which the female taste seemed not much to care was theology in the metaphysical sense. Mary troubled herself little about theology except when she retired into the south transept with Pierre de Dreux. Even there one finds little said about the Trinity, always the most metaphysical subtlety of the Church. Indeed, you might find much amusement here in searching the cathedral for any distinct expression at all of the Trinity as a dogma recognized by Mary. One cannot take seriously the idea that the three doors, the three portals, and the three aisles express the Trinity, because, in the first place, there was no rule about it; churches might have what portals and aisles they pleased; both Paris and Bourges have five; the doors themselves are not allotted to the three members of the Trinity, nor are the portals; while another more serious objection is that the side doors and aisles are not of equal importance with the central, but mere adjuncts and dependencies, so that the architect who had misled the ignorant public into accepting so black a heresy would have deserved the stake, and would probably have gone to it. Even this suggestion of trinity is wanting in the transepts, which have only one aisle, and in the choir, which has five, as well as five or seven chapels, and, as far as an ignorant mind can penetrate, no triplets whatever. Occasionally, no doubt, you will discover in some sculpture or window, a symbol of the Trinity, but this discovery itself amounts to an admission of its absence as a controlling idea, for the ordinary worshipper must have been at least as blind as we are, and to him, as to us, it would have seemed a wholly subordinate detail. Even if the Trinity, too, is anywhere expressed, you will hardly find here an attempt to explain its metaphysical meaning—not even a mystic triangle.

The church is wholly given up to the Mother and the Son. The Father seldom appears; the Holy Ghost still more rarely. At least, this is the impression made on an ordinary visitor who has no motive to be orthodox; and it must have been the same with the thirteenth-century worshipper who came here with his mind absorbed in the perfections of Mary. Chartres represents, not the Trinity, but the identity of the Mother and Son. The Son represents the Trinity, which is thus absorbed in the Mother. The idea is not orthodox, but this is no affair of ours. The Church watches over its own.

The Virgin's wants and tastes, positive and negative, ought now to be clear enough to enable you to feel the artist's sincerity in trying to satisfy them; but first you have still to convince yourselves of the people's sincerity in employing the artists. This point is the easiest of all, for the evidence is express. In the year 1145 when the old flèche was begun,—the year before Saint Bernard preached the second crusade at Vézelay,—Abbot Haimon, of Saint-Pierre-sur-Dives in Normandy, wrote to the monks of Tutbury Abbey in England a famous letter to tell of the great work which the Virgin was doing in France and which began at the Church of Chartres. "Hujus sacræ institutionis ritus apud Carnotensem ecclesiam est inchoatus." From Chartres it had spread through Normandy, where it produced among other things the beautiful spire which we saw at Saint-Pierre-sur-Dives. "Postremo per totam fere Normanniam longe lateque convaluit ac loca per singula Matri misericordiæ dicata præcipue occupavit." The movement affected especially the places devoted to Mary, but ran through all Normandy, far and wide. Of all Mary's miracles, the best attested, next to the preservation of her church, is the building of it; not so much because it surprises us as because it surprised even more the people of the time and the men who were its instruments. Such deep popular movements are always surprising, and at Chartres the miracle seems to have occurred three times, coinciding more or less with the dates of the crusades, and taking the organization of a crusade, as Archbishop Hugo of Rouen described it in a letter to Bishop Thierry of Amiens. The most interesting part of this letter is the evident astonishment of the writer, who might be talking to us to-day, so modern is he:—

> The inhabitants of Chartres have combined to aid in the construction of their church by transporting the materials; our Lord has rewarded their humble zeal by miracles which have roused the Normans to imitate the piety of their neighbours. . . . Since then the faithful of our diocese and of other neighbouring regions have formed associations for the same object; they admit no one into their company unless he has been to confession, has renounced enmities and revenges, and has reconciled himself with his enemies. That done, they elect a chief, under whose direction they conduct their waggons in silence and with humility.

The quarries at Berchères-l'Evêque are about five miles from Chartres. The stone is excessively hard, and was cut in blocks of considerable size, as you can see for yourselves; blocks which required great effort to transport and lay in place. The work was done with feverish rapidity, as it still shows, but it is the solidest building of the age, and without a sign of weakness yet. The Abbot told, with more surprise than pride, of the spirit which was built into the cathedral with the stone:—

Who has ever seen!—Who has ever heard tell, in times past, that powerful princes of the world, that men brought up in honour and in wealth, that nobles, men and women, have bent their proud and haughty necks to the harness of carts, and that, like beasts of burden, they have dragged to the abode of Christ these waggons, loaded with wines, grains, oil, stone, wood, and all that is necessary for the wants of life, or for the construction of the church? But while they draw these burdens, there is one thing admirable to observe; it is that often when a thousand persons and more are attached to the chariots,—so great is the difficulty,—yet they march in such silence that not a murmur is heard, and truly if one did not see the thing with one's eyes, one might believe that among such a multitude there was hardly a person present. When they halt on the road, nothing is heard but the confession of sins, and pure and suppliant prayer to God to obtain pardon. At the voice of the priests who exhort their hearts to peace, they forget all hatred, discord is thrown far aside, debts are remitted, the unity of hearts is established. But if any one is so far advanced in evil as to be unwilling to pardon an offender, or if he rejects the counsel of the priest who has piously advised him, his offering is instantly thrown from the wagon as impure, and he himself ignominiously and shame-fully excluded from the society of the holy. There one sees the priests who preside over each chariot exhort every one to penitence, to con-fession of faults, to the resolution of better life! There one sees old people, young people, little children, calling on the Lord with a sup-pliant voice, and uttering to Him, from the depth of the heart, sobs and sighs with words of glory and praise! After the people, warned by the sound of trumpets and the sight of banners, have resumed their road, the march is made with such ease that no obstacle can retard it. . . . When they have reached the church they arrange the wagons about it like a spiritual camp, and during the whole night they celebrate the watch by hymns and canticles. On each waggon they light tapers and lamps; they place there the infirm and sick, and bring them the precious relics of the Saints for their relief. Afterwards the priests and clerics close the ceremony by processions which the people follow with devout heart, imploring the clemency of the Lord and of his Blessed Mother for the recovery of the sick.

Of course, the Virgin was actually and constantly present during all this labour, and gave her assistance to it, but you would get no light on the architecture from listening to an account of her miracles, nor do they heighten the effect of popular faith. Without the conviction of her personal presence, men would not have been inspired; but, to us, it is rather the inspiration of the art which proves the Virgin's presence, and we can better see the conviction of it in the work than in the words. Every day, as the work went on, the Virgin was present, directing the architects, and it is this direction that we are going to study, if you have now got a realizing sense of what it meant. Without this sense, the church is dead. Most persons of a deeply religious nature would tell you emphatically that nine churches out of ten actually were dead-born, after the thirteenth century, and that church architecture became a pure matter of mechanism and mathematics; but that is a question for you to decide when you come to it; and the pleasure consists not in seeing the death, but in feeling the life.

Now let us look about!

III. The Twelfth-Century Glass

. . . In all France there exists barely a dozen good specimens of twelfth-century glass. Besides these [three lancet] windows at Chartres and the fragments at Saint-Denis, there are windows at Le Mans and Angers and bits at Vendôme, Chalons, Poitiers, Rheims, and Bourges; here and there one happens on other pieces, but the earliest is the best, because the glass-makers were new at the work and spent on it an infinite amount of trouble and money which they found to be unnecessary as they gained experience. Even in 1200 the value of these windows was so well understood, relatively to new ones, that they were preserved with the greatest care. The effort to make such windows was never repeated. Their jewelled perfection did not suit the scale of the vast churches of the thirteenth century. By turning your head toward the windows of the side aisles, you can see the criticism which the later artists passed on the old work. They found it too refined, too brilliant, too jewel-like for the size of the new cathedral; the play of light and colour allowed the eye too little repose; indeed, the eye could not see their whole beauty, and half their value was thrown away in this huge stone setting. At best they must have seemed astray on the bleak, cold, windy plain of Beauce,—homesick for Palestine or Cairo,—yearning for Monreale or Venice,—but this is not our affair, and, under the protection of the Empress Virgin, Saint Bernard himself could have afforded to sin even to drunkenness of colour. With trifling expense of

imagination one can still catch a glimpse of the crusades in the glory
of the glass. The longer one looks into it, the more overpowering it
becomes, until one begins almost to feel an echo of what our two hundred and fifty million arithmetical ancestors, drunk with the passion
of youth and the splendour of the Virgin, have been calling to us from
Mont-Saint-Michel and Chartres. No words and no wine could revive
their emotions so vividly as they glow in the purity of the colours; the
limpidity of the blues; the depth of the red; the intensity of the green;
the complicated harmonies; the sparkle and splendour of the light; and
the quiet and certain strength of the mass.

With too strong direct sun the windows are said to suffer, and become a cluster of jewels—a delirium of coloured light. The lines, too,
have different degrees of merit. These criticisms seldom strike a chance
traveller, but he invariably makes the discovery that the designs within
the medallions are childish. He may easily correct them, if he likes, and
see what would happen to the window; but although this is the alpha-
bet of art, and we are past spelling words of one syllable, the criticism
teaches at least one lesson. Primitive man seems to have had a natural
colour-sense, instinctive like the scent of a dog. Society has no right to
feel it as a moral reproach to be told that it has reached an age when
it can no longer depend, as in childhood, on its taste, or smell, or sight,
or hearing, or memory; the fact seems likely enough, and in no way
sinful; yet society always denies it, and is invariably angry about it;
and, therefore, one had better not say it. On the other hand, we can
leave Delacroix and his school to fight out the battle they began against
Ingres and his school, in French art, nearly a hundred years ago, which
turned in substance on the same point. Ingres held that the first motive
in colour-decoration was line, and that a picture which was well drawn
was well enough coloured. Society seemed, on the whole, to agree with
him. Society in the twelfth century agreed with Delacroix. The French
held then that the first point in colour-decoration was colour, and they
never hesitated to put their colour where they wanted it, or cared
whether a green camel or a pink lion looked like a dog or a donkey
provided they got their harmony or value. Everything except colour
was sacrificed to line in the large sense, but details of drawing were
conventional and subordinate. So we laugh to see a knight with a blue
face, on a green horse, that looks as though drawn by a four-year-old
child, and probably the artist laughed, too; but he was a colourist, and
never sacrificed his colour for a laugh.

We tourists assume commonly that he knew no better. In our sim-

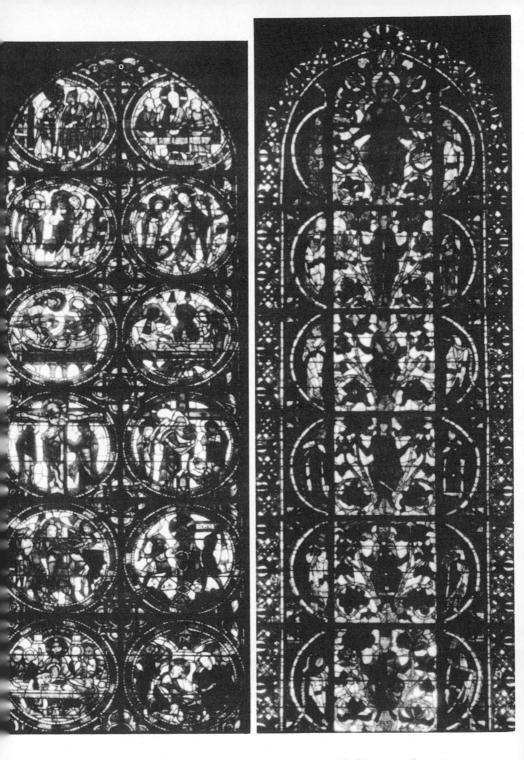

STAINED GLASS AT CHARTRES, THE TREE OF JESSE—*Cl. Houvet, Rep. Int.*

ple faith in ourselves, great hope abides, for it shows an earnestness hardly less than that of the crusaders; but in the matter of colour one is perhaps less convinced, or more open to curiosity. No school of colour exists in our world to-day, while the Middle Ages had a dozen; but it is certainly true that these twelfth-century windows break the French tradition. They had no antecedent, and no fit succession. All the authorities dwell on their exceptional character. One is sorely tempted to suspect that they were in some way an accident; that such an art could not have sprung, in such perfection, out of nothing, had it been really French; that it must have had its home elsewhere—on the Rhine—in Italy—in Byzantium—or in Bagdad.

The same controversy has raged for near two hundred years over the Gothic arch, and everything else mediæval, down to the philosophy of the schools. The generation that lived during the first and second crusades tried a number of original experiments, besides capturing Jerusalem. Among other things, it produced the western portal of Chartres, with its statuary, its glass, and its flèche, as a by-play; as it produced Abélard, Saint Bernard, and Christian of Troyes, whose acquaintance we have still to make. It took ideas wherever it found them;—from Germany, Italy, Spain, Constantinople, Palestine, or from the source which has always attracted the French mind like a magnet —from ancient Greece. That it actually did take the ideas, no one disputes, except perhaps patriots who hold that even the ideas were original; but to most students the ideas need to be accounted for less than the taste with which they were handled, and the quickness with which they were developed. That the taste was French, you can see in the architecture, or you will see if ever you meet the Gothic elsewhere; that it seized and developed an idea quickly, you have seen in the arch, the flèche, the porch, and the windows, as well as in the glass; but what we do not comprehend, and never shall, is the appetite behind all this; the greed for novelty: the fun of life. Every one who has lived since the sixteenth century has felt deep distrust of every one who lived before it, and of every one who believed in the Middle Ages. True it is that the last thirteenth-century artist died a long time before our planet began its present rate of revolution; it had to come to rest, and begin again; but this does not prevent astonishment that the twelfth-century planet revolved so fast. The pointed arch not only came as an idea into France, but it was developed into a system of architecture and covered the country with buildings on a scale of height never before attempted except by the dome, with an expenditure of wealth that would make a railway system look cheap, all in a space of about fifty years; the glass came with it, and went with it, at least as far as concerns us; but, if you need other evidence, you can consult Renan, who is the highest authority: "One of the most singular phenomena of the literary history of the Middle Ages," says Renan of Averroës, "is the activity of the intellectual commerce, and the rapidity with which books were spread from one end of Europe to the other. The philosophy of Abélard during his lifetime (1100–42) had penetrated to the ends of Italy. The French poetry of the trouvères counted within less than a century translations into German, Swedish, Norwegian, Icelandic, Flemish, Dutch, Bohemian, Italian, Spanish"; and he might have added that England needed no translation, but helped to compose the poetry, not being at that time so insular as she afterwards became. "Such or such a work, composed in Morocco or in Cairo, was known at Paris and at Cologne in less time than it would need in our days for a German book of capital importance to pass the Rhine"; and Renan wrote this in 1852 when German books of capital importance were revolutionizing the literary world.

One is apt to forget the smallness of Europe, and how quickly it could always be crossed. In summer weather, with fair winds, one can sail from Alexandria or from Syria, to Sicily, or even to Spain and France, in perfect safety and with ample room for freight, as easily now as one could it then, without the aid of steam; but one does not now carry freight of philosophy, poetry, or art. The world still struggles for unity, but by different methods, weapons, and thought. The mercantile exchanges which surprised Renan, and which have puzzled historians, were in ideas. The twelfth century was as greedy for them in one shape as the nineteenth century in another. France paid for them dearly, and repented for centuries; but what creates surprise to the point of incredulity is her hunger for them, the youthful gluttony with which she devoured them, the infallible taste with which she dressed them out. The restless appetite that snatched at the pointed arch, the stone flèche, the coloured glass, the illuminated missal, the chanson and roman and pastorelle, the fragments of Aristotle, the glosses of Avicenne, was nothing compared with the genius which instantly gave form and flower to them all.

This episode merely means that the French twelfth-century artist may be supposed to have known his business, and if he produced a grotesque, or a green-faced Saint, or a blue castle, or a syllogism, or a song, that he did it with a notion of the effect he had in mind. The glass window was to him a whole,—a mass,—and its details were his amusement; for the twelfth-century Frenchman enjoyed his fun, though it was sometimes rather heavy for modern French taste, and less refined than the Church liked. These three twelfth-century windows, like their contemporary portal outside, and the flèche that goes with them, are the ideals of enthusiasts of mediæval art; they are above the level of all known art, in religious form; they are inspired; they are divine! This is the claim of Chartres and its Virgin. Actually, the French artist, whether architect, sculptor, or painter in glass, did rise here above his usual level. He knew it when he did it, and probably he attributed it, as we do, to the Virgin; for these works of his were hardly fifty years old when the rest of the old church was burned; and already the artist felt the virtue gone out of him. He could not do so well in 1200 as he did in 1150; and the Virgin was not so near.

The proof of it—or, if you prefer to think so, the proof against it— is before our eyes on the wall above the lancet windows. When Villard de Honnecourt came to Chartres, he seized at once on the western rose as his study, although the two other roses were probably there, in all their beauty and lightness. He saw in the western rose some quality of construction which interested him; and, in fact, the western rose is one of the flowers of architecture which reveals its beauties slowly without end; but its chief beauty is the feeling which unites it with the portal, the lancets, and the flèche. The glassworker here in the interior had the same task to perform. The glass of the lancets was fifty years old when the glass for the rose was planned; perhaps it was seventy, for the exact dates are unknown, but it does not matter, for the greater the interval, the more interesting is the treatment. Whatever the date, the glass of the western rose cannot be much earlier or much later than that of the other roses, or that of the choir, and yet you see at a glance that it is quite differently treated. On such matters one must, of course, submit to the opinion of artists, which one does the more readily because they always disagree; but until the artists tell us better, we may please ourselves by fancying that the glass of the rose was intended to harmonize with that of the lancets, and unite it with the thirteenth-century glass of the nave and transepts. Among all the thirteenth-century windows the western rose alone seems to affect a rivalry in brilliancy with the lancets, and carries it so far that the separate medallions and pictures are quite lost,—especially in direct sunshine,—blending in a confused effect of opals, in a delirium of colour and light, with a result like a cluster of stones in jewelry. Assuming as one must, in want of the artist's instruction, that he knew what he wanted to do, and did it, one must take for granted that he treated the rose as a whole, and aimed at giving it harmony with the three precious windows beneath. The effect is that of a single large ornament; a round breastpin, or what is now called a sunburst, of jewels, with three large pendants beneath.

We are ignorant tourists, liable to much error in trying to seek motives in artists who worked seven hundred years ago for a society which thought and felt in forms quite unlike ours, but the mediæval pilgrim was more ignorant than we, and much simpler in mind; if the idea of an ornament occurs to us, it certainly occurred to him, and still more to the glassworker whose business was to excite his illusions. An artist, if good for anything, foresees what his public will see; and what his public will see is what he ought to have intended—the measure of his genius. If the public sees more than he himself did, this is his credit; if less, this is his fault. No matter how simple or ignorant we are, we ought to feel a discord or a harmony where the artist meant us to feel it, and when we see a motive, we conclude that other people have seen it before us, and that it must, therefore, have been intended. Neither of the transept roses is treated like this one; neither has the effect of a personal ornament; neither is treated as a jewel. No one knew so well as the artist that such treatment must give the effect of a jewel. The Roses of France and of Dreux bear indelibly and flagrantly the character of France and Dreux; on the western rose is stamped with greater refinement but equal decision the character of a much greater power than either of them.

No artist would have ventured to put up, before the eyes of Mary in Majesty, above the windows so dear to her, any object that she had not herself commanded. Whether a miracle was necessary, or whether genius was enough, is a point of casuistry which you can settle with Albertus Magnus or Saint Bernard, and which you will understand as little when settled as before; but for us, beyond the futilities of unnecessary doubt, the Virgin designed this rose; not perhaps in quite the same perfect spirit in which she designed the lancets, but still wholly for her own pleasure and as her own idea. She placed upon the breast of her Church—which symbolized herself—a jewel so gorgeous that no earthly majesty could bear comparison with it, and which no other heavenly majesty has rivalled. As one watches the light play on it, one is still overcome by the glories of the jewelled rose and its three gemmed pendants; one feels a little of the effect she meant it to produce even on infidels, Moors, and heretics, but infinitely more on the men who feared and the women who adored her;—not to dwell too long upon it, one admits that hers is the only Church. One would admit anything that she should require. If you had only the soul of a shrimp, you would crawl, like the Abbé Suger, to kiss her feet.

Unfortunately she is gone, or comes here now so very rarely that we never shall see her; but her genius remains as individual here as the genius of Blanche of Castile and Pierre de Dreux in the transepts. That the three lancets were her own taste, as distinctly as the Trianon was the taste of Louis XIV, is self-evident. They represent all that was dearest to her; her Son's glory on her right; her own beautiful life in the middle; her royal ancestry on her left: the story of her divine right, thrice-told. The pictures are all personal, like family portraits. Above them the man who worked in 1200 to carry out the harmony, and to satisfy the Virgin's wishes, has filled his rose with a dozen or two little compositions in glass, which reveal their subjects only to the best powers of a binocle. Looking carefully, one discovers at last that this gorgeous combination of all the hues of Paradise contains or hides a Last Judgment—the one subject carefully excluded from the old work, and probably not existing on the south portal for another twenty years. If the scheme of the western rose dates from 1200, as is reasonable to suppose, this Last Judgment is the oldest in the church, and makes a link between the theology of the first crusade, beneath, and the theology of Pierre Mauclerc in the south porch. The churchman is the only true and final judge on his own doctrine, and we neither know nor care to know the facts; but we are as good judges as he of the feeling, and we are at full liberty to feel that such a Last Judgment as this was never seen before or since by churchman or heretic, unless by virtue of the heresy which held that the true Christian must be happy in being damned since such is the will of God. That this blaze of heavenly light was intended, either by the Virgin or by her workmen, to convey ideas of terror or pain, is a notion which the Church might possibly preach, but which we sinners knew to be false in the thirteenth century as well as we know it now. Never in all these seven hundred years has one of us looked up at this rose without feeling it to be Our Lady's promise of Paradise.

Here as everywhere else throughout the church, one feels the Virgin's presence, with no other thought than her majesty and grace. To the Virgin and to her suppliants, as to us, who though outcasts in other churches can still hope in hers, the Last Judgment was not a symbol of God's justice or man's corruption, but of her own infinite mercy.

The Trinity judged, through Christ;—Christ loved and pardoned, through her. She wielded the last and highest power on earth and in hell. In the glow and beauty of her nature, the light of her Son's infinite love shone as the sunlight through the glass, turning the Last Judgment itself into the highest proof of her divine and supreme authority. The rudest ruffian of the Middle Ages, when he looked at this Last Judgment, laughed; for what was the Last Judgment to her! An ornament, a plaything, a pleasure! a jewelled decoration which she wore on her breast! Her chief joy was to pardon; her eternal instinct was to love; her deepest passion was pity! On her imperial heart the flames of hell showed only the opaline colours of heaven. Christ the Trinity might judge as much as He pleased, but Christ the Mother would rescue; and her servants could look boldly into the flames. . . .

The close relationship between art and social life has often been noted, but Huizinga's account of the application of art to society in France and the Netherlands is intellectual history at its best: immense learning combined with a sense of the color and texture of a vanished way of life. This succinct summary of relationships forms a chapter in his celebrated historical study The Waning of the Middle Ages. *The connection between art and life was particularly evident during the Middle Ages and during the dawn of the Renaissance.*

Johan Huizinga
Art and Life[1]

If a man of culture of 1840 had been asked to characterize French civilization in the fifteenth century in a few words, his answer would probably have been largely inspired by impressions from Barante's *Histoire des Ducs de Bourgogne* and Hugo's *Notre Dame de Paris*. The picture called up by these would have been grim and dark, scarcely illuminated by any ray of serenity and beauty.

[1] From *The Waning of the Middle Ages*, by Johan Huizinga. New York: St. Martin's Press, Inc., 1949.

The experiment repeated to-day would yield a very different result. People would now refer to Joan of Arc, to Villon's poetry, but above all to the works of art. The so-called primitive Flemish and French masters—Van Eyck, Rogier van der Weyden, Foucquet, Memling, with Claus Sluter, the sculptor, and the great musicians—would dominate their general idea of the epoch. The picture would altogether have changed its colour and tone. The aspect of mere cruelty and misery as conceived by romanticism, which derived its information chiefly from the chronicles, would have made room for a vision of pure and naïve beauty, of religious fervour and profound mystic peace.

It is a general phenomenon that the idea which works of art give us of an epoch is far more serene and happy than that which we glean in reading its chronicles, documents, or even literature. Plastic art does not lament. Even when giving expression to sorrow or pain it transports them to an elegiac sphere, where the bitter taste of suffering has passed away, whereas the poets and historians, voicing the endless griefs of life, always keep their immediate pungency and revive the harsh realities of bygone misery.

Now, our perception of former times, our historical organ, so to say, is more and more becoming visual. Most educated people of to-day owe their conception of Egypt, Greece, or the Middle Ages, much more to the sight of their monuments, either in the original or by reproductions, than to reading. The change of our ideas about the Middle Ages is due less to a weakening of the romantic sense than to the substitution of artistic for intellectual appreciation.

Still, this vision of an epoch resulting from the contemplation of works of art is always incomplete, always too favourable, and therefore fallacious. It has to be corrected in more than one sense. Confining ourselves to the period in question, we first have to take into consideration the fact that, proportionately, far more of the written documents than of the monuments of art have been preserved. The literature of the declining Middle Ages, with some few exceptions, is known to us fairly completely. We have products of all genres: the most elevated and the most vulgar, the serious and the comic, the pious and the profane. Our literary tradition reflects the whole life of the epoch. Written tradition, moreover, is not confined to literature: official records, in infinite number, enable us to augment almost indefinitely the accuracy of our picture.

Art, on the contrary, is by its very nature limited to a less complete and less direct expression of life. Moreover, we only possess a very special fraction of it. Outside ecclesiastical art very little remains. Profane art and applied art have only been preserved in rare specimens. This is a serious want, because these are just the forms of art which would have most clearly revealed to us the relation of artistic production to social life. The modest number of altar-pieces and tombs teaches us too little in this respect; the art of the epoch remains to us as a thing apart from the history of the time. Now, really to understand art, it is of great importance to form a notion of the function of art in life; and for that it does not suffice to admire surviving masterpieces, all that has been lost asks our attention too.

Art in those times was still wrapped up in life. Its function was to fill with beauty the forms assumed by life. These forms were marked and potent. Life was encompassed and measured by the rich efflorescence of the liturgy: the sacraments, the canonical hours of the day and the festivals of the ecclesiastical year. All the works and all the joy of life, whether dependent on religion, chivalry, trade or love, had their marked form. The task of art was to adorn all these concepts with charm and colour; it is not desired for its own sake, but to decorate life with the splendour which it could bestow. Art was not yet a means, as it is now, to step out of the routine of everyday life to pass some moments in contemplation; it had to be enjoyed as an element of life itself, as the expression of life's significance. Whether it served to sustain the flight of piety or to be an accompaniment to the delights of the world, it was not yet conceived as mere beauty.

Consequently, we might venture the paradox that the Middle Ages knew only applied art. They wanted works of art only to make them subservient to some practical use. Their purpose and their meaning always preponderated over their purely æsthetic value. We should add that the love of art for its own sake did not originate in an awakening of the craving for beauty, but developed as a result of superabundant artistic production. In the treasuries of princes and nobles, objects of art accumulated so as to form collections. No longer serving for practical use, they were admired as articles of luxury and of curiosity; thus the taste for art was born which the Renaissance was to develop consciously.

In the great works of art of the fifteenth century, notably in the altar-pieces and tombs, the nature of the subject was far more important than the question of beauty. Beauty was required because the subject was sacred or because the work was destined for some august purpose. This purpose is always of a more or less practical sort. The triptych served to intensify worship at the great festivals and to preserve the memory of the pious donors. The altar-piece of the Lamb by the brothers Van Eyck was opened at high festivals only. Religious pictures were not the only ones which served a practical purpose. The magistrates of the towns ordered representations of famous judgments to decorate the law courts, in order to solemnly exhort the judges to do their duty. Such are the judgment of Cambyses, by Gerard David, at Bruges; that of the Emperor Otto, by Dirk Bouts, at Louvain; and the lost pictures by Rogier van der Weyden, once at Brussels.

The following example may serve to illustrate the importance attached to the subjects represented. In 1384 an interview took place at Lelinghem for the purpose of bringing about an armistice between France and England. The duke of Berry had the naked walls of the old chapel, where the negotiating princes were to meet, covered with tapestry representing battles of antiquity. But John of Gaunt, duke of Lancaster, as soon as he saw them on entering, demanded that these pictures of war should be removed, because those who aspire to peace ought not to have scenes of combat and of destruction before their eyes. The tapestries were replaced by others representing the instruments of the Passion.

The importance of the subject is closely connected with the artistic value in the case of portraits, which even now preserve some moral significance, as souvenirs or heirlooms, because the sentiments determining their use are as vital as ever. In the Middle Ages portraits were ordered for all sorts of purposes, but rarely, we may be certain, to obtain a masterpiece of art. Besides gratifying family affection and pride, the portrait served to enable betrothed persons to make acquaintance. The embassy sent to Portugal by Philip the Good in 1428, to ask for the hand of a princess, was accompanied by Jan van Eyck, with orders to paint her portrait. Court chroniclers liked to keep up the fiction that the royal fiancé had fallen in love with the unknown princess on seeing her portrait—for instance, Richard II of England when courting the little Isabelle of France, aged six. Sometimes it is even said that a selection was made by comparing portraits of different parties. When a wife had to be found for the young Charles VI, according to the *Religieux de Saint Denis,* the choice lay between a Bavarian, an Austrian and a Lorraine duchess. A painter of talent was sent to the three courts; three portraits were submitted to the king, who chose the young Isabella of Bavaria, judging her by far the most beautiful.

Nowhere was the practical use of works of art weightier than in connection with tombs, by far the most important domain of the sculpture of the epoch. The wish to have an effigy of the deceased was so strong that it claimed satisfaction even before the construction of the tomb. At the burial of a man of rank, he is represented either by a living man or by an effigy. At the funeral service of Bertrand du Guesclin, at Saint Denis, "four men-at-arms, armed cap-à-pie, mounted on four chargers, well appointed and caparisoned, representing the dead man as he was alive," entered the church. An account of the Polignacs of 1375 relating to a funeral ceremony shows the item: "Six shillings to Blaise for representing the dead knight at the funeral." At royal interments a figure of leather, in state dress, represented the deceased. Great pains were taken to obtain a good likeness. Sometimes there is more than one of these effigies in the cortège. Visitors to Westminster Abbey know these figures. Perhaps the origin of making funeral masks, which began in France in the fifteenth century, is to be found here.

As all art was more or less applied art, the distinction between artists and craftsmen did not arise. The great masters in the service of the courts of Flanders, of Berry, or of Burgundy, each of them an artist of a very marked personality, did not confine themselves to painting pictures and to illuminating manuscripts; they were not above colouring statues, painting shields and staining banners, or designing costumes for tournaments and ceremonies. Thus Melchior Broederlam, court painter to the first duke of Burgundy, after holding the same position in the household of his father-in-law, the count of Flanders, puts the finishing touches to five sculptured chairs for the palace of the counts. He repairs and paints some mechanical apparatus at the castle of Hesdin, used for wetting the guests with water by way of a surprise. He does work on a carriage for the duchess. He directs the sumptuous decoration of the fleet which the duke had assembled at Sluys in 1387 for an expedition against the English, which, however, did not take place. So, too, at wedding festivities and funeral ceremonies court painters were laid under contribution. Statues were painted in Jan van Eyck's workshop. He himself made a sort of map of the world for Duke Philip, on which the towns and the countries were painted with marvellous delicacy. Hugo van der Goes designed posters advertising a papal indulgence at Ghent. When the Archduke Maximilian was a prisoner at Bruges in 1488, the painter Gerard David was sent for, to decorate with pictures the wickets and shutters of his prison.

Of all the handiwork of the masters of the fifteenth century, only a portion of a very special nature has survived: some tombs, some altar-pieces and portraits, numerous miniatures, also a certain number of objects of industrial art, comprising vessels used in religious worship, sacerdotal dress and church furniture, but of secular work, except woodwork and chimneys, scarcely anything is left. How much more should we know of the art of the fifteenth century if we could compare the bathing and hunting pieces of Jan van Eyck and Rogier van der Weyden with their *pietàs* and madonnas. It is not only profane pictures we lack. There are whole departments of applied art of which we can hardly even form a conception. For this we lack the power to compare with the priestly vestments that have been preserved, the court costumes with their precious stones and tiny bells, that have perished: we lack the actual sight of the brilliantly decorated war-ships of which miniatures give us but a conventional and clumsy representation. Froissart, who, as a rule, is little susceptible to impressions of beauty, fairly exults in his descriptions of the splendours of a decked-out fleet, with its streamers, gay with blazonry, floating from the mast-heads, and some reaching to the water. The ship of Philippe le Hardi, decorated by Broederlam, was painted azure and gold; large heraldic shields surrounded the pavilion of the castle; the sails were studded with daisies and the initials of the duke and the duchess, and bore the motto *Il me tarde*. The nobles vied with each other in lavishing money on the decoration of their vessels. Painters had a good time of it, says Froissart; there were not enough of them to go around, and they got whatever prices they asked. According to him, many nobles had their ship-masts entirely covered with gold leaf. Guy de la Trémoïlle spent £2,000 on decorations. "And all this was paid by the poor people of France. . . ."

These lost products of decorative art would have revealed to us, above all, extravagant sumptuousness. This trait is characteristic of the epoch; it is to be found equally in the works which we do possess, but as we study these only for the sake of their beauty, we pay little attention to this element of splendour and of pomp, which no longer interests us, but which was just what people of that time prized most.

Burgundo-French culture of the expiring Middle Ages tends to oust beauty by magnificence. The art of this period exactly reflects this spirit. All that we cited above as characteristic of the mental processes of the epoch: the craving to give a definite form to every idea, and the overcrowding of the mind with figures and forms systematically arranged—all this reappears in art. There, too, we find the tendency to leave nothing without form, without figure, without ornament. The flamboyant style of architecture is like the postlude of an organist who cannot conclude. It decomposes all the formal elements endlessly; it interlaces all the details; there is not a line which has not its counter-line. The form develops at the expense of the idea, the ornament grows rank, hiding all the lines and all the surfaces. A *horror vacui* reigns, always a symptom of artistic decline.

All this means that the border-line between pomp and beauty is being obliterated. Decoration and ornament no longer serve to heighten the natural beauty of a thing; they are overgrowing it and threaten to stifle it. The further we get away from pure plastic art, the more this rank-ness of formal decorative motifs is accentuated. This may be very clearly observed in sculpture. In the creation of isolated figures this overgrowth of forms does not occur: the statues of Moses' well and the "plourants" of the tombs are as sober as the figures of Donatello. But where sculpture is performing a decorative function we at once find the overgrowth. In looking at the tabernacle of Dijon, every one will be struck by a lack of harmony between the sculpture of Jacques de Baerze and the paint-ing of Broederlam. The picture, painted for its own sake, is simple and sober; the reliefs, on the contrary, in which the purpose is decorative, are complicated and overloaded. We notice the same contrast between painting and tapestry. Textile art, even when representing scenes and figures, remains limited by its technique to decorative conception and expression; hence we find the same craving for excessive ornamentation.

In the art of costume, the essential qualities of pure art, that is to say, measure and harmony, vanish altogether, because splendour and adornment are the sole objects aimed at. Pride and vanity introduce a sensual element incompatible with pure art. No epoch ever witnessed such extravagance of fashion as that extending from 1350 to 1480. Here we can observe the unhampered expansion of the æsthetic sense of the time. All the forms and dimensions of dress are ridiculously exag-gerated. The female head-dress assumes the conical shape of the "hen-nin," a form evolved from the little coif, keeping the hair under the kerchief. High and bombed foreheads are in fashion, with the temples shaved. Low-necked dresses make their appearance. The male dress had features still more bizarre—the immoderate length of the points of the shoes, called "poulaines," which the knights at Nicopolis had to cut off, to enable them to flee; the laced waists; the baloon-shaped sleeves stand-ing up at the shoulders; the too long "houppelandes" and the too short doublets; the cylindrical or pointed bonnets; the hoods draped about the head in the form of a cock's comb or a flaming fire. A state costume was ornamented by hundreds of precious stones.

The taste for unbridled luxury culminated in the court fêtes. Every
one has read the descriptions of the Burgundian festivities at Lille in
1454, at which the guests took the oath to undertake the crusade, and
at Bruges in 1468, on the occasion of the marriage of Charles the Bold
with Margaret of York. It is hard to imagine a more absolute contrast
than that of these barbarous manifestations of arrogant pomp and the
pictures of the brothers Van Eyck, Dirk Bouts and Rogier van der Weyden, with their sweet and tranquil serenity. Nothing could be more
insipid and ugly than the "entremets," consisting of gigantic pies enclosing complete orchestras, full-rigged vessels, castles, monkeys and whales,
giants and dwarfs, and all the boring absurdities of allegory. We find it
difficult to regard these entertainments as something more than exhibitions of almost incredible bad taste.

Yet we must not exaggerate the distance separating the two extreme
forms of the art of the fifteenth century. In the first place, it is important to realize the function of festivals in the society of that time. They
still preserved something of the meaning they have in primitive societies, that of the supreme expression of their culture, the highest mode
of a collective enjoyment and an assertion of solidarity. At epochs of
great renovations of society, like that of the French Revolution, we see
that festivals resume this social and æsthetic function.

Modern man is free, when he pleases, to seek his favourite distrac-
tions individually, in books, music, art or nature. On the other hand,
at a time when the higher pleasures were neither numerous nor accessible to all, people felt the need of such collective rejoicings as festivals. The more crushing the misery of daily life, the stronger the
stimulants that will be needed to produce that intoxication with beauty
and delight without which life would be unbearable. The fifteenth century, profoundly pessimistic, a prey to continual depression, could not
forgo the emphatic affirmation of the beauty of life, afforded by these
splendid and solemn collective rejoicings. Books were expensive, the
country was unsafe, art was rare, the individual lacked the means of
distraction. All literary, musical and artistic enjoyment was more or less
closely connected with festivals.

Now festivals, in so far as they are an element of culture, require
other things than mere gaiety. Neither the elementary pleasures of
gaming, drinking and love, nor luxury and pomp as such, are able to
give them a framework. The festival requires style. If those of modern
times have lost their cultural value, it is because they have lost style. In
the Middle Ages the religious festival, because of its high qualities of

style founded on the liturgy itself, for a long time dominated all the forms of collective cheerfulness. The popular festival, which had its own elements of beauty in song and dance, was linked up with those of the Church. It is towards the fifteenth century that an independent form of civil festival with a style of its own disengages itself from the ecclesiastical one. The "rhetoricians" of Northern France and the Netherlands are the representatives of this evolution. Till then only princely courts had been able to equip secular festivals with form and style, thanks to the resources of their wealth and the social conception of courtesy.

Nevertheless, the style of the courtly festival could not but remain greatly inferior to that of religious festivals. In the latter worship and rejoicing in common were always the expression of a sublime thought, which lent them a grace and dignity that even the excesses of their frequently burlesque details could not affect. On the other hand, the ideas glorified by the secular feast were nothing more than those of chivalry and of courtly love. The ritual of chivalry, no doubt, was rich enough to give these festivities a venerable and solemn style. There were the accolade, the vows, the chapters of the orders, the rules of the tournaments, the formalities of homage, service and precedence, all the dignified proceedings of kings-at-arms and heralds, all the brightness of blazonry and armour. But this did not suffice to satisfy all aspirations. The court fêtes were expected to visualize in its entirety the dream of the heroic life. And here style failed. For in the fifteenth century the apparatus of chivalrous fancy was no longer anything but vain conventions and mere literature.

The staging of the amazing festivities of Lille or of Bruges is, so to say, applied literature. The ponderousness of material representation destroyed the last remainder of charm which literature with the lightness of its airy reveries had hitherto preserved. The unfaltering seriousness with which these monstrous pageants were organized is truly Burgundian. The ducal court seems to have lost, by its contact with the North, some qualities of the French spirit. For the preparation of the banquet of Lille, which was to crown and conclude a series of banquets which the nobles provided, each in his turn, vying with each other in magnificence, Philip the Good appointed a committee, presided over by a knight of the Golden Fleece, Jean de Lannoy. The most trusted counsellors of the duke—Antoine de Croy, the chancellor Nicolas Rolin himself—were frequently present at the sessions of the committee, of which Olivier de la Marche was a member. When the latter in his memoirs comes to this chapter, a feeling of awe still comes over him.

"Because great and honourable achievements deserve a lasting renown and perpetual remembrance . . . ," thus he begins the narrative of these memorable things. It is needless to reprint it here, as it belongs to the *loci communes* of historical literature.

Even from across the sea people came to view the gorgeous spectacle. Besides the guests, a great number of noble spectators were present at the feast, disguised for the most part. First every one walked about to admire the fixed show-pieces; later came the "entremets," that is to say, representations of "personnages" and tableaux vivants. Olivier himself played the important part of Holy Church, making his appearance in a tower on the back of an elephant, led by a gigantic Turk. The tables were loaded with the most extravagant decorations. There were a rigged and ornamented carack, a meadow surrounded by trees with a fountain, rocks, and a statue of Saint Andrew, the castle of Lusignan with the fairy Mélusine, a bird-shooting scene near a windmill, a wood in which wild beasts walked about, and, lastly, a church with an organ and singers, whose songs alternated with the music of the orchestra of twenty-eight persons, which was placed in a pie.

The problem for us is to determine the quality of taste or bad taste to which all this bears witness. It goes without saying that the mythological and allegorical tenor of these "entremets" cannot interest us. But what was the artistic execution worth? What people looked for most was extravagance and huge dimensions. The tower of Gorcum represented on the table of the banquet of Bruges in 1468 was 46 feet high. La Marche says of a whale, which also figured there: "And certainly this was a very fine entremets, *for* there were more than forty persons in it." People were also much attracted by mechanical marvels: living birds flying from the mouth of a dragon conquered by Hercules, and suchlike curiosities, in which, to us, any idea of art is altogether lacking. The comic element was of a very low class: boars blow the trumpet in the tower of Gorcum; elsewhere goats sing a motet, wolves play the flute, four large donkeys appear as singers—and all this in honour of Charles the Bold, who was a good musician.

I would not, however, suggest that there may not have been many an artistic masterpiece among the pretentious and ridiculous curiosities. Let us not forget that the men who enjoyed these Gargantuan decorations were the patrons of the brothers Van Eyck and of Rogier van der Weyden—the duke himself, Rolin, the donor of the altars of Beaune and of Autun, Jean Chevrot, who commissioned Rogier to paint "The Seven Sacraments," now at Antwerp. What is more, it was the painters themselves who designed these show-pieces. If the records do not mention Jan van Eyck or Rogier as having contributed to similar festivities, they do give the names of the two Marmions and Jacques Daret. For the fête of 1468 the services of the whole corporation of painters were requisitioned; they were summoned in haste from Ghent, Brussels, Louvain, Tirlemont, Mons, Quesnoy, Valenciennes, Douai, Cambray, Arras, Lille, Ypres, Courtray, Oudenarde, to work at Bruges. It is impossible to believe that their handiwork was ugly. The thirty vessels decorated with the arms of the duke's domains the sixty images of women dressed in the costumes of their country, "carrying fruit in baskets and birds in cages. . . ." I should be ready to give more than one mediocre church-picture to see them.

We may go further, at the risk of being thought paradoxical, and affirm that we have to take this art of showpieces, which has disappeared without leaving a trace, into account, if we would thoroughly understand the art of Claus Sluter.

Of all the forms of art, sepulchral sculpture is most fettered by the exigencies of its purpose. The sculptors charged with making the ducal tombs were not left free to create beautiful things; they had to exalt the glory of the deceased prince. The painter can always give free rein to his imagination; he is never obliged to limit himself strictly to commissioned work. It is probable, on the other hand, that the sculptor of this epoch rarely worked except on specified tasks. The motifs of his art, moreover, are limited in number and fixed by a rigorous tradition. It is true that painters and sculptors are equally servants of the ducal household; Jan van Eyck, as well as Sluter and his nephew, Claus de Werve, bore the title of "varlet de chambre," but for the two latter, the service is far more real than for the painters. The two great Dutchmen whom the irresistible attraction of French art life drew for good from their native country were completely monopolized by the duke of Burgundy. Claus Sluter inhabited a house at Dijon which the duke placed at his disposal; there he lived as a gentleman, but at the same time as a servant of the court. His nephew and successor, Claus de Werve, is the tragic type of an artist in the service of princes: kept back at Dijon year after year, to finish the tomb of Jean sans Peur, for which the financial means were never forthcoming, he saw his artistic career, so brilliantly begun, ruined by fruitless waiting.

Thus the art of the sculptor at this epoch is a servile art. On the other hand, sculpture is generally little influenced by the taste of an epoch, because its means, its material and its subjects are limited and little subject to change. When a great sculptor appears, he creates everywhere and always that *optimum* of purity and simplicity which we call classic. The human form and its drapery are susceptible of few variations. The masterpieces of carving of the different ages are very much alike, and, for us, Sluter's work shares this eternal identity of sculpture.

Nevertheless, on examining it more closely, we notice that especially the art of Sluter bears the marks of being influenced by the taste of the time (not to call it Burgundian taste) as far as the nature of sculpture permits. Sluter's works have not been preserved as they were, and as the master intended them to be. We must picture the well of Moses as it was in 1418, when the papal legate granted an indulgence to whosoever should come to visit it in a pious spirit. It must be remembered that the well is but a fragment, a part of a calvary with which the first duke of Burgundy of the house of Valois intended to crown the well of of his Carthusian monastery of Champmol. The principal part, that is to say, the crucified Christ with the Virgin, Saint John and Mary Magdalen, had almost completely disappeared before the French Revolution. There remains only the pedestal, surrounded by the statues of the six prophets who predicted the death of the Saviour, with a cornice supported by angels. The whole composition is in the highest degree a representation, "une œuvre parlante," a show, closely related as such to the tableaux vivants or the "personnages" of the princely entries and of the banquets. There, too, the subjects were borrowed, for choice, from the prophecies relating to the coming of Christ. Like these "personnages," the figures surrounding the well hold scrolls containing the text of their predictions. It rarely happens in sculpture that the written word is of such importance. We can only fully realize the marvellous art here displayed in *hearing* these sacred and solemn words. *Immolabit eum universa multitudo filiorum Israel ad vesperum;* this is Moses' sentence. *Foderunt manus meas et pedes meos, dinumeraverunt omnia ossa mea;* this is David's. Jeremiah says: *O vos omnes qui transitis per viam, attendite et videte si est dolor sicut dolor meus.*[2] Isaiah, Daniel, Zachariah, all announce the death of the Lord. It is like a threnody of six voices rising up to the cross. Now in this feature lies the essence of the work. The gestures of the hands by which the attention is directed to the texts are so emphatic, and there is an expression of such poignant grief on the faces, that the whole is in some danger of losing the *ataraxia*

---

[2] Exodus xii. 6: "And the whole assembly of the congregation of Israel shall kill it in the evening." Psalm xxii. 16, 17: "They pierced My hands and My Feet. They told all My bones." Lamentations of Jeremiah i. 12: "All ye that pass by, behold, and see if there be any sorrow like unto My sorrow."

which marks great sculpture. It appeals too directly to the spectator. Compared with the figures of Michelangelo, those of Sluter are too expressive, too personal. If more had come down to us of the calvary supported by the prophets than the head and the torso of Christ, of a stark majesty, this expressive character would be still more evident.

The spectacular character of the calvary of Champmol also came into prominence in the luxurious decorations of the work. We must picture it in all its polychrome splendour, for Jean Malouel, the artist, and Herman of Cologne, the gilder, were not sparing of vivid colours and brilliant effects. The pedestals were green, the mantles of the prophets were gilt, their tunics red and azure with golden stars. Isaiah, the gloomiest of all, wore a dress of gold-cloth. The open spaces were filled with golden suns and initials. The pride of blazonry displayed itself not only round the columns below the figures, but on the cross itself, which was entirely gilt. The extremities of the arms of the cross, shaped like capitals, bore the coats of arms of Burgundy and Flanders. Can one ask for better proof of the spirit in which the duke conceived this great monument of his piety? As a crowning "bizarrerie," a pair of spectacles of gilded brass, the work of Hannequin de Hacht, were placed on Jeremiah's nose.

This serfdom of a great art controlled by the will of a princely patron is tragic, but it is at the same time exalted by the heroic efforts of the great sculptor to shake off his shackles. The figures of the "plourants" around the sarcophagus had for a long time been an obligatory motif in Burgundian sepulchral art. These weeping figures were not meant to express grief in general; the sculptor was bound to give a faithful representation of the funeral cortège with the dignitaries present at the burial. But the genius of Sluter and his pupils succeeded in transforming this motif into the most profound expression of mourning known in art, a funeral march in stone.

Is it so certain, after all, that we are right in thinking of the artist as struggling with the lack of taste and refinement of his patron? It is quite possible that Sluter himself considered Jeremiah's spectacles a very happy find. In the men of that epoch artistic taste was still blended with the passion for what is rare or brilliant. In their simplicity they could enjoy the bizarre as if it were beauty. Objects of pure art and articles of luxury and curiosity were equally admired. Long after the Middle Ages the collections of princes contained works of art mixed up indiscriminately with knick-knacks made of shells and of hair, wax statues of celebrated dwarfs and such-like articles. At the castle of Hesdin, where side by side with art treasures the "engins d'esbatement" (contrivances for amusement) usual in princely pleasure-grounds were found in abundance, Caxton saw a room ornamented with pictures representing the history of Jason, the hero of the Golden Fleece. The artist is unknown, but was probably a distinguished master. To heighten the effect, a "machinerie" was annexed which could imitate lightning, thunder, snow and rain, in memory of the magic arts of Medea.

In the shows at the entries of princes inventive fancy stuck at nothing. When Isabella of Bavaria made her entry into Paris in 1389, there was a white deer with gilt antlers, and a wreath round its neck, stretched out on a "lit de justice," moving its eyes, antlers, feet, and at last raising a sword. At the moment when the queen crossed the bridge to the left of Notre Dame, an angel descended "by means of well-constructed engines" from one of the towers, passed through an opening of the hangings of blue taffeta with golden fleurs-de-lis which covered the bridge, and put a crown on her head. Then the angel "was pulled up again as if he had returned to heaven of his own accord." Philip the Good and Charles VIII were treated to similar descents. Lefèvre de Saint Remy greatly admired the spectacle of four trumpeters and twelve nobles on artificial horses, "sallying forth and caracoling in such a way that it was a fine thing to see."

Time the destroyer has made it easy for us to separate pure art from all these gewgaws and bizarre trappings, which have completely disappeared. This separation which our æsthetic sense insists upon, did not exist for the men of that time. Their artistic life was still enclosed within the forms of social life. Art was subservient to life. Its social function was to enhance the importance of a chapel, a donor, a patron, or a festival, but never that of the artist. Fully to realize its position and scope in this respect is now hardly possible. Too little of the material surroundings in which art was placed, and too few of the works of art themselves, have come down to us. Hence the priceless value of the few works by which private life, outside courts and outside the Church, is revealed to us. In this respect no painting can compare with the portrait of Jean Arnolfini and of his wife, by Jan van Eyck, in the National Gallery. The master, who, for once, need not portray the majesty of divine beings nor minister to aristocratic pride, here freely followed his own inspiration: it was his friends whom he was painting on the occasion of their marriage. Is it really the merchant of Lucca, Jean Arnoulphin, as he was called in Flanders, who is represented? Jan van Eyck painted this face twice (the other portrait is at Berlin); we can hardly imagine a less Italian-looking physiognomy, but the description of the picture in the inventory of Margaret of Austria, "Hernoul le fin with his wife in a chamber," leaves little room for doubt. However this may be, the persons represented were friends of Van Eyck; he himself witnesses to it by the ingenious and delicate way in which he signs his work, by an inscription over the mirror: *Johannes de Eyck fuit hic,* 1434.

THE ANNUNCIATION—JAN VAN EYCK

"Jan van Eyck was here." Only a moment ago, one might think. The sound of his voice still seems to linger in the silence of this room. All that tenderness and profound peace, which only Rembrandt was to recapture, emanate from this picture. That serene twilight hour of an age, which we seemed to know and yet sought in vain in so many of the manifestations of its spirit, suddenly reveals itself here. And here at last this spirit proves itself happy, simple, noble and pure, in tune with the lofty church music and the touching folk-songs of the time.

So perhaps we imagine a Jan van Eyck escaping from the noisy gaiety and brutal passions of court life, a Jan van Eyck of the simple heart, a dreamer. It does not require a great effort of fancy to call up the "varlet de chambre" of the duke, serving the great lords against his will, suffering all the disgust of a great artist obliged to belie his sublime ideal of art by contributing to the mechanical devices of a festival.

Nothing, however, justifies us in forming such a conception of his personality. This art, which we admire, bloomed in the atmosphere of that aristocratic life, which repels us. The little we know of the lives of fifteenth-century painters shows them to us as men of the world and courtiers. The duke of Berry was on good terms with his artists. Froissart saw him in familiar conversation with André Beauneveu in his marvellous castle of Mehun sur Yevre. The three brothers of Limburg, the great illuminators, come to offer the duke, as a New Year's present, a surprise in the shape of a new illuminated manuscript, which turned out to be "a dummy book, made of a block of white wood painted to look like a book, in which there were no leaves and nothing was written." Jan van Eyck, without doubt, moved constantly in court circles. The secret diplomatic missions entrusted to him by the duke required a man of the world. He passed, moreover, for a man of letters, reading classic authors and studying geometry. Did he not, by an innocent whim, disguise in Greek letters his modest device, *Als ik kan* (As I can)?

The intellectual and moral life of the fifteenth century seems to us to be divided into two clearly separated spheres. On the one hand, the civilization of the court, the nobility and the rich middle classes: ambitious, proud and grasping, passionate and luxurious. On the other hand, the tranquil sphere of the "devotio moderna," of the *Imitation of Christ*, of Ruysbroeck and of Saint Colette. One would like to place the peaceful and mystic art of the brothers Van Eyck in the second of these spheres, but it belongs rather to the other. Devout circles were hardly in touch with the great art that flourished at this time. In music they disapproved of counterpoint, and even of organs. The rule of Windesheim forbade the embellishment of the singing by modulations,

Très Riches Heures du duc de Berry "Le Mois d'Octobre"—POL DE LIMBOURG
(*Photographie Giraudon*)

and Thomas à Kempis said: "If you cannot sing like the nightingale and the lark, then sing like the crows and the frogs, which sing as God meant them to." The music of Dufay, Busnois, Okeghem, developed in the chapels of the courts. As to painting, the writers of the "devotio moderna" do not speak of it; it was outside their range of thought. They wanted their books in a simple form and without illuminations. They would probably have regarded the altar-piece of the Lamb as a mere work of pride, and actually did so regard the tower of Utrecht Cathedral.

The great artists generally worked for other circles than those of the devout townspeople. The art of the brothers Van Eyck and of their followers, though it sprang up in municipal surroundings and was fostered by town circles, cannot be called a bourgeois art. The court and the nobility exercised too powerful an attraction. Only the patronage of princes permitted the art of miniature to raise itself to the degree of artistic refinement which characterizes the work of the brothers of Limburg and the artists of the Hours of Turin. The employers of the great painters were, besides the princes themselves, the great lords, temporal or spiritual, and the great upstarts with whom the Burgundian epoch abounds, all gravitating towards the court. The ground for the difference between Franco-Flemish and Dutch art in this period lies in the fact that the latter still preserves some traits of simple soberness recalling the little out-of-the-way towns, such as Haarlem, where it was born. And even Dirk Bouts went south and painted at Louvain and Brussels.

Among the patrons of fifteenth-century art may be named Jean Chevrot, bishop of Tournay, whom a scutcheon designates as the donor of that work of touching and fervent piety, now at Antwerp, "The Seven Sacraments." Chevrot is the type of the court prelate; as a trusted counsellor of the duke, he was full of zeal for the affairs of the Golden Fleece and for the crusade. Another type of donor is represented by Pierre Bladelin, whose austere face is seen on the Middelburg altar-piece, now at Berlin. He was the great capitalist of those times; from the post of receiver of Bruges, his native town, he rose to be paymaster-general of the duke. He introduced control and economy into the ducal finances. He was appointed treasurer of the Golden Fleece and knighted. He was sent to England to ransom Charles of Orléans. The duke wished to charge him with the administration of the finances of the expedition against the Turks. He employed his wealth, which was the wonder of his contemporaries, on works of embankment and the founding of a new town in Flanders, to which he gave the name of Middelburg, after the town in Zeeland of that name.

Other notable donors—Judocus Vydt, the canon Van de Paele, the Croys, the Lannoys—belonged to the very rich, noble or burgher, ancient or new, of their time. Most famous of all is Nicolas Rolin, the chancellor, "sprung from little people," jurist, financier, diplomat. The great treaties of the dukes, from 1419 to 1435, are his work. "He used to govern everything quite alone and manage and bear the burden of all business by himself, be it of war, be it of peace, be it of matters of finance." By methods which were not above suspicion he amassed enormous wealth, which he spent on all sorts of pious and charitable foundations. Nevertheless, people spoke with hatred of his avarice and pride, and had no faith in the devotional feelings which inspired his pious works. This man whom we see in the Louvre kneeling so devoutly in the picture painted for him by Jan van Eyck for Autun, his native town, and again in that by Rogier van der Weyden, destined for his hospital of Beaune, passed for a mind only set on earthly things. "He always harvested on earth," says Chastellain, "as though the earth was to be his abode for ever, in which his understanding erred and his prudence abased him, when he would not set bounds to that, of which his great age showed him the near end." This is corroborated by Jacques du Clercq in these terms: "The aforesaid chancellor was reputed one of the wise men of the kingdom, to speak temporally; for as to spiritual matters, I shall be silent."

Are we, then, to look for a hypocritical expression in the face of the donor of La Vierge au Chancelier Rolin? Let us remember, before condemning him, the riddle presented by the religious personality of so many other men of his time, who also combined rigid piety with excesses of pride, of avarice and of lust. The depths of these natures of a past age are not easily sounded.

In the piety interpreted by the art of the fifteenth century, the extremes of mysticism and of gross materialism meet. The faith pictured here is so direct that no earthly figure is too sensual or too heavy to express it. Van Eyck may drape his angels and divine personages with ponderous and stiff brocades, glittering with gold and precious stones; to call up the celestial sphere he has no need of the flowing garments and sprawling limbs of the baroque style.

Yet neither this art nor this faith is primitive. By using the term primitive to designate the masters of the fifteenth century we run the risk of a misunderstanding. They are primitive in a purely chronological sense, in so far as, for us, they are the first to come, and no older painting is known to us. But if to this designation we attach the meaning of a primitive spirit, we are egregiously mistaken. For the spirit which this art denotes is the same which we pointed out in religious life: a spirit rather decadent than primitive, a spirit involving the utmost elaboration, and even decomposition, of religious thought through the imagination.

In very early times the sacred figures had been seen as endlessly remote: awful and rigid. Then, from the twelfth century downward, the mysticism of Saint Bernard introduced a pathetic element into religion, which contained immense possibilities of growth. In the rapture of a new and overflowing piety people tried to share the sufferings of Christ by the aid of his imagination. They were no longer satisfied with the stark and motionless figures, infinitely distant, which romanesque art had given to Christ and His Mother. All the forms and colours which imagination drew from mundane reality were now lavished by it upon the celestial beings. Once let loose, pious fancy invaded the whole domain of faith and gave a minutely elaborate shape to every holy thing.

At first verbal expression had been in advance of pictorial and plastic art. Sculpture was still adhering to the formal rigidity of preceding ages, when literature undertook to describe all the details, both physical and mental, of the drama of the cross. A sort of pathetic naturalism arose, for which the *Meditationes vitae Christi,* early attributed to Saint Bonaventura, supplied the model. The nativity, the childhood, the descent from the cross, each received a fixed form, a vivid colouring. How Joseph of Arimathea mounted the ladder, how he had to press the hand of the Lord in order to draw out the nail, was all described in minute detail.

In the meantime, towards the end of the fourteenth century, pictorial technique had made so much progress that it more than overtook literature in the art of rendering these details. The naïve, and at the same time refined, naturalism of the brothers Van Eyck was a new form of pictorial expression; but viewed from the standpoint of culture in general, it was but another manifestation of the crystallizing tendency of thought which we noticed in all the aspects of the mentality of the declining Middle Ages. Instead of heralding the advent of the Renaissance, as is generally assumed, this naturalism is rather one of the ultimate forms of development of the medieval mind. The craving to turn every sacred idea into precise images, to give it a distinct and clearly outlined form, such as we observed in Gerson, in the *Roman de la Rose,* in Denis the Carthusian, controlled art, as it controlled popular beliefs and theology. The art of the brothers Van Eyck closes a period.

It is unfortunate that Ruskin should be remembered today mainly as the narrow-minded dogmatist who attacked Whistler and could not understand what impressionism was all about. As a young man, he had the courage and insight to praise the work of J. M. W. Turner and to exalt Gothic architecture. The first half of the chapter on "The Nature of Gothic" from The Stones of Venice, *most of which is given in the following selection, has been called by Sir Kenneth Clark "one of the noblest things written in the nineteenth century." It is the great statement of Ruskin's view of the social basis of art.*

John Ruskin
The Nature of Gothic[1]

§ II. . . . Every building of the Gothic period differs in some important respect from every other; and many include features which, if they occurred in other buildings, would not be considered Gothic at all; so that all we have to reason upon is merely, if I may be allowed so to express it, a greater or less degree of *Gothicness* in each building we examine. And it is this Gothicness,— the character which, according as it is found more or less in a building, makes it more or less Gothic,—of which I want to define the nature; and I feel the same kind of difficulty in doing so which would be encountered by any one who undertook to explain, for instance, the nature of Redness, without any actual red thing to point to, but only orange and purple things. Suppose he had only a piece of heather and a dead oak-leaf to do it with. He might say, the color which is mixed with the yellow in this oak-leaf, and with the blue in this heather, would be red, if you had it separate; but it would be difficult, nevertheless, to make the abstraction perfectly intelligible: and it is so in a far greater degree to make the abstraction of the Gothic character intelligible, because that character itself is made up of many mingled ideas, and can consist only in their union. That is to say, pointed arches do not constitute Gothic, nor vaulted roofs, nor flying buttresses, nor grotesque sculptures; but all or some of these things, and many other things with them, when they come together so as to have life.

§ III. Observe also, that in the definition proposed, I shall only endeavor to analyze the idea which I suppose already to exist in the reader's mind. We all have some notion, most of us a very determined

[1] From *The Stones of Venice* by John Ruskin. London: 1851.

one, of the meaning of the term Gothic; but I know that many persons have this idea in their minds without being able to define it; that is to say, understanding generally that Westminster Abbey is Gothic, and St. Paul's is not, that Strasburg Cathedral is Gothic, and St. Peter's is not, they have, nevertheless, no clear notion of what it is that they recognize in the one or miss in the other, such as would enable them to say how far the work at Westminster or Strasburg is good and pure of its kind; still less to say of any nondescript building, like St. James's Palace or Windsor Castle, how much right Gothic element there is in it, and how much wanting. And I believe this inquiry to be a pleasant and profitable one; and that there will be found something more than usually interesting in tracing out this grey, shadowy, many-pinnacled image of the Gothic spirit within us; and discerning what fellowship there is between it and our Northern hearts. And if, at any point of the inquiry, I should interfere with any of the reader's previously formed conceptions, and use the term Gothic in any sense which he would not willingly attach to it, I do not ask him to accept, but only to examine and understand, my interpretation, as necessary to the intelligibility of what follows in the rest of the work.

§ IV. We have, then, the Gothic character submitted to our analysis, just as the rough mineral is submitted to that of the chemist, entangled with many other foreign substances, itself perhaps in no place pure, or ever to be obtained or seen in purity for more than an instant; but nevertheless a thing of definite and separate nature, however inextricable or confused in appearance. Now observe: the chemist defines his mineral by two separate kinds of character; one external, its crystalline form, hardness, lustre, &c.; the other internal, the proportions and nature of its constituent atoms. Exactly in the same manner, we shall find that Gothic architecture has external forms, and internal elements. Its elements are certain mental tendencies of the builders, legibly expressed in it; as fancifulness, love of variety, love of richness, and such others. Its external forms are pointed arches, vaulted roofs, &c. And unless both the elements and the forms are there, we have no right to call the style Gothic. It is not enough that it has the Form, if it have not also the power and life. It is not enough that it has the Power, if it have not the form. We must therefore inquire into each of these characters successively; and determine first, what is the Mental Expression, and secondly, what the Material Form, of Gothic architecture, properly so called.

1st. Mental Power or Expression. What characters, we have to discover, did the Gothic builders love, or instinctively express in their work, as distinguished from all other builders?

§ v. Let us go back for a moment to our chemistry, and note that, in defining a mineral by its constituent parts, it is not one nor another of them, that can make up the mineral, but the union of all: for instance, it is neither in charcoal, nor in oxygen, nor in lime, that there is the making of chalk, but in the combination of all three in certain measures, they are all found in very different things from chalk, and there is nothing like chalk either in charcoal or in oxygen, but they are nevertheless necessary to its existence.

So in the various mental characters which make up the soul of Gothic. It is not one nor another that produces it; but their union in certain measures. Each one of them is found in many other architectures besides Gothic; but Gothic cannot exist where they are not found, or, at least, where their place is not in some way supplied. Only there is this great difference between the composition of the mineral, and of the architectural style, that if we withdraw one of its elements from the stone, its form is utterly changed, and its existence as such and such a mineral is destroyed; but if we withdraw one of its mental elements from the Gothic style, it is only a little less Gothic than it was before, and the union of two or three of its elements is enough already to bestow a certain Gothicness of character, which gains in intensity as we add the others, and loses as we again withdraw them.

§ vi. I believe, then, that the characteristic or moral elements of Gothic are the following, placed in the order of their importance:

1. Savageness.   4. Grotesqueness.
2. Changefulness.   5. Rigidity.
3. Naturalism.   6. Redundance.

These characters are here expressed as belonging to the building; as belonging to the builder, they would be expressed thus: 1. Savageness, or Rudeness. 2. Love of Change. 3. Love of Nature. 4. Disturbed Imagination. 5. Obstinacy. 6. Generosity. And I repeat, that the withdrawal of any one, or any two, will not at once destroy the Gothic character of a building, but the removal of a majority of them will. I shall proceed to examine them in their order.

§ vii. 1. SAVAGENESS. I am not sure when the word "Gothic" was first generically applied to the architecture of the North; but I presume that, whatever the date of its original usage, it was intended to imply reproach, and express the barbaric character of the nations among whom that architecture arose. It never implied that they were literally of Gothic lineage, far less that their architecture had been originally invented by the Goths themselves; but it did imply that they and their buildings together exhibited a degree of sternness and rudeness, which, in contradistinction to the character of Southern and Eastern nations, appeared like a perpetual reflection of the contrast between the Goth and the Roman in their first encounter. And when that fallen Roman, in the utmost impotence of his luxury, and insolence of his guilt, became the model for the imitation of civilized Europe, at the close of the so-called Dark ages, the word Gothic became a term of unmitigated contempt, not unmixed with aversion. From that contempt, by the exertion of the antiquaries and architects of this century, Gothic architecture has been sufficiently vindicated; and perhaps some among us, in our admiration of the magnificent science of its structure, and sacredness of its expression, might desire that the term of ancient reproach should be withdrawn, and some other, of more apparent honorableness, adopted in its place. There is no chance, as there is no need, of such a substitution. As far as the epithet was used scornfully, it was used falsely; but there is no reproach in the word, rightly understood; on the contrary, there is a profound truth, which the instinct of mankind almost unconsciously recognizes. It is true, greatly and deeply true, that the architecture of the North is rude and wild; but it is not true, that, for this reason, we are to condemn it, or despise. Far otherwise: I believe it is in this very character that it deserves our profoundest reverence.

§ VIII. The charts of the world which have been drawn up by modern science have thrown into a narrow space the expression of a vast amount of knowledge, but I have never yet seen any one pictorial enough to enable the spectator to imagine the kind of contrast in physical character which exists between Northern and Southern countries. We know the differences in detail, but we have not that broad glance and grasp which would enable us to feel them in their fulness. We know that gentians grow on the Alps, and olives on the Apennines; but we do not enough conceive for ourselves that variegated mosaic of the world's surface which a bird sees in its migration, that difference between the district of the gentian and of the olive which the stork and the swallow see far off, as they lean upon the sirocco wind. Let us, for a moment, try to raise ourselves even above the level of their flight, and imagine the Mediterranean lying beneath us like an irregular lake, and all its

ancient promontories sleeping in the sun: here and there an angry spot
of thunder, a grey stain of storm, moving upon the burning field; and
here and there a fixed wreath of white volcano smoke, surrounded by
its circle of ashes; but for the most part a great peacefulness of light,
Syria and Greece, Italy and Spain, laid like pieces of a golden pavement
into the sea-blue, chased, as we stoop nearer to them, with bossy beaten
work of mountain chains, and glowing softly with terraced gardens,
and flowers heavy with frankincense, mixed among masses of laurel,
and orange and plumy palm, that abate with their grey-green shadows
of the burning of the marble rocks, and of the ledges of porphyry slop-
ing under lucent sand. Then let us pass farther towards the north, until
we see the orient colors change gradually into a vast belt of rainy green,
where the pastures of Switzerland, and poplar valleys of France, and
dark forests of the Danube and Carpathians stretch from the mouths
of the Loire to those of the Volga, seen through clefts in grey swirls of
rain-cloud and flaky veils of the mist of the brooks, spreading low along
the pasture lands: and then, farther north still, to see the earth heave
into mighty masses of leaden rock and heathy moor, bordering with a
broad waste of gloomy purple that belt of field and wood, and splinter-
ing into irregular and grisly islands amidst the northern seas, beaten
by storm and chilled by ice-drift, and tormented by furious pulses of
contending tide, until the roots of the last forests fail from among the
hill ravines, and the hunger of the north wind bites their peaks into
barrenness; and, at last, the wall of ice, durable like iron, sets, death-
like, its white teeth against us out of the polar twilight. And, having
once traversed in thought its gradation of the zoned iris of the earth in
all its material vastness, let us go down nearer to it, and watch the
parallel change in the belt of animal life: the multitudes of swift and
brilliant creatures that glance in the air and sea, or tread the sands of
the southern zone; striped zebras and spotted leopards, glistening ser-
pents, and birds arrayed in purple and scarlet. Let us contrast their
delicacy and brilliancy of color, and swiftness of motion, with the frost-
cramped strength, and shaggy covering, and dusky plumage of the
northern tribes; contrast the Arabian horse with the Shetland, the tiger
and leopard with the wolf and bear, the antelope with the elk, the bird
of paradise with the osprey: and then, submissively acknowledging the
great laws by which the earth and all that it bears are ruled throughout
their being, let us not condemn, but rejoice at the expression by man
of his own rest in the statutes of the lands that gave him birth. Let us
watch him with reverence as he sets side by side the burning gems, and

smoothes with soft sculpture the jasper pillars, that are to reflect a ceaseless sunshine, and rise into a cloudless sky: but not with less reverence let us stand by him, when, with rough strength and hurried stroke, he smites an uncouth animation out of the rocks which he has torn from among the moss of the moorland, and heaves into the darkened air the pile of iron buttress and rugged wall, instinct with work of an imagination as wild and wayward as the northern sea; creations of ungainly shape and rigid limb, but full of wolfish life; fierce as the winds that beat, and changeful as the clouds that shade them.

There is, I repeat, no degradation, no reproach in this, but all dignity and honorableness; and we should err grievously in refusing either to recognise as an essential character of the existing architecture of the North, or to admit as a desirable character in that which it yet may be, this wildness of thought, and roughness of work; this look of mountain brotherhood between the cathedral and the Alp; this magnificence of sturdy power, put forth only the more energetically because the fine finger-touch was chilled away by the frosty wind, and the eye dimmed by the moor-mist, or blinded by the hail; this outspeaking of the strong spirit of men who may not gather redundant fruitage from the earth, nor bask in dreamy benignity of sunshine, but must break the rock for bread, and cleave the forest for fire, and show, even in what they did for their delight, some of the hard habits of the arm and heart that grew on them as they swung the axe or pressed the plough.

§ IX. If, however, the savageness of Gothic architecture, merely as an expression of its origin among Northern nations, may be considered, in some sort, a noble character, it possesses a higher nobility still, when considered as an index, not of climate, but of religious principle.

In the 13th and 14th paragraphs of Chapter XXI of the first volume of this work, it was noticed that the systems of architectural ornament, properly so called, might be divided into three:—1. Servile ornament, in which the execution or power of the inferior workman is entirely subjected to the intellect of the higher:—2. Constitutional ornament, in which the executive inferior power is, to a certain point, emancipated and independent, having a will of its own, yet confessing its inferiority and rendering obedience to higher powers;—and 3. Revolutionary ornament, in which no executive inferiority is admitted at all. I must here explain the nature of these divisions at somewhat greater length.

Of Servile ornament, the principal schools are the Greek, Ninevite, and Egyptian; but their servility is of different kinds. The Greek master-workman was far advanced in knowledge and power above the Assyrian or Egyptian. Neither he nor those for whom he worked could endure the appearance of imperfection in anything; and, therefore, what ornament he appointed to be done by those beneath him was composed of mere geometrical forms,—balls, ridges, and perfectly symmetrical foliage,—which could be executed with absolute precision by line and rule, and were as perfect in their way when completed, as his own figure sculpture. The Assyrian and Egyptian, on the contrary, less cognizant of accurate form in anything, were content to allow their figure sculpture to be executed by inferior workmen, but lowered the method of its treatment to a standard which every workman could reach, and then trained him by discipline so rigid, that there was no chance of his falling beneath the standard appointed. The Greek gave to the lower workman no subject which he could not perfectly execute. The Assyrian gave him subjects which he could only execute imperfectly, but fixed a legal standard for his imperfection. The workman was, in both systems, a slave.[2]

§ x. But in the mediæval, or especially Christian, system of ornament, this slavery is done away with altogether; Christianity having recognized, in small things as well as great, the individual value of every soul. But it not only recognizes its value; it confesses its imperfection, in only bestowing dignity upon the acknowledgment of unworthiness. That admission of lost power and fallen nature, which the Greek or Ninevite felt to be intensely painful, and, as far as might be, altogether refused, the Christian makes daily and hourly, contemplating the fact of it without fear, as tending, in the end, to God's greater glory. Therefore, to every spirit which Christianity summons to her service, her exhortation is: Do what you can, and confess frankly what you are unable to do; neither let your effort be shortened for fear of failure, nor your confession silenced for fear of shame. And it is, perhaps, the principal admirableness of the Gothic schools of architecture, that they thus receive the results of the labor of inferior minds; and out of fragments full of imperfection, and betraying that imperfection in every touch, indulgently raise up a stately and unaccusable whole.

2 The third kind of ornament, the Renaissance, is that in which the inferior detail becomes principal, the executor of every minor portion being required to exhibit skill and possess knowledge as great as that which is possessed by the master of the design; and in the endeavor to endow him with this skill and knowledge, his own original power is overwhelmed, and the whole building becomes a wearisome exhibition of well-educated imbecility. We must fully inquire into the nature of this form of error, when we arrive at the examination of the Renaissance schools.

§ xi. But the modern English mind has this much in common with that of the Greek, that it intensely desires, in all things, the utmost completion or perfection compatible with their nature. This is a noble character in the abstract, but becomes ignoble when it causes us to forget the relative dignities of the nature itself, and to prefer the perfectness of the lower nature to the imperfection of the higher; not considering that as, judged by such a rule, all the brute animals would be preferable to man, because more perfect in their functions and kind, and yet are always held inferior to him, so also in the works of man, those which are more perfect in their kind are always inferior to those which are, in their nature, liable to more faults and shortcomings. For the finer the nature, the more flaws it will show through the clearness of it; and it is a law of this universe, that the best things shall be seldomest seen in their best form. The wild grass grows well and strongly, one year with another; but the wheat is, according to the greater nobleness of its nature, liable to the bitter blight. And therefore, while in all things that we see, or do, we are to desire perfection, and strive for it, we are nevertheless not to set the meaner thing, in its narrow accomplishment, above the nobler thing, in its mighty progress; not to esteem smooth minuteness above shattered majesty; not to prefer mean victory to honorable defeat; not to lower the level of our aim, that we may the more surely enjoy the complacency of success. But, above all, in our dealings with the souls of other men, we are to take care how we check, by severe requirements or narrow caution, efforts which might otherwise lead to a noble issue; and, still more, how we withhold our admiration from great excellences, because they are mingled with rough faults. Now, in the make and nature of every man, however rude or simple, whom we employ in manual labor, there are some powers for better things: some tardy imagination, torpid capacity of emotion, tottering steps of thought, there are, even at the worst; and in most cases it is all our own fault that they *are* tardy or torpid. But they cannot be strengthened, unless we are content to take them in their feebleness, and unless we prize and honor them in their imperfection above the best and most perfect manual skill. And this is what we have to do with all our laborers; to look for the *thoughtful* part of them, and get that out of them, whatever we lose for it, whatever faults and errors we are obliged to take with it. For the best that is in them cannot manifest itself, but in company with much error. Understand this clearly: You can teach a man to draw a straight line, and to cut one; to strike a curved line, and to carve it; and to copy and carve any number of given lines or forms, with admirable speed and perfect precision; and you find his work perfect of its kind: but if you ask him to think about any of those forms, to consider if he cannot find any better in his own head, he stops; his execution becomes hesitating; he thinks, and ten to one he thinks wrong; ten to one he makes a mistake in the first touch he gives to his work as a thinking being. But you have made a man of him for all that. He was only a machine before, an animated tool.

§ xii. And observe, you are put to stern choice in this matter. You must either make a tool of the creature, or a man of him. You cannot make both. Men were not intended to work with the accuracy of tools, to be precise and perfect in all their actions. If you will have that precision out of them, and make their fingers measure degrees like cogwheels, and their arms strike curves like compasses, you must unhumanize them. All the energy of their spirits must be given to make cogs and compasses of themselves. All their attention and strength must go to the accomplishment of the mean act. The eye of the soul must be bent upon the finger-point, and the soul's force must fill all the invisible nerves that guide it, ten hours a day, that it may not err from its steely precision, and so soul and sight be worn away, and the whole human being be lost at last—a heap of sawdust, so far as its intellectual work in this world is concerned; saved only by its Heart, which cannot go into the form of cogs and compasses, but expands, after the ten hours are over, into fireside humanity. On the other hand, if you will make a man of the working creature, you cannot make a tool. Let him but begin to imagine, to think, to try to do anything worth doing; and the engine-turned precision is lost at once. Out come all his roughness, all his dulness, all his incapability; shame upon shame, failure upon failure, pause after pause: but out comes the whole majesty of him also; and we know the height of it only, when we see the clouds settling upon him. And, whether the clouds be bright or dark, there will be transfiguration behind and within them.

§ xiii. And now, reader, look round this English room of yours, about which you have been proud so often, because the work of it was so good and strong, and the ornaments of it so finished. Examine again all those accurate mouldings, and perfect polishings, and unerring adjustments of the seasoned wood and tempered steel. Many a time you have exulted over them, and thought how great England was, because her slightest work was done so thoroughly. Alas! if read rightly, these perfectnesses are signs of a slavery in our England a thousand times more bitter and more degrading than that of the scourged Africans, or helot Greek. Men may be beaten, chained, tormented, yoked like cattle, slaughtered like summer flies, and yet remain in one sense, and the best sense, free. But to smother their souls within them, to blight and hew into rotting pollards the suckling branches of their human intelligence, to make the flesh and skin which, after the worm's work on it, is to see God, into leathern thongs to yoke machinery with,—this it is to be slave-masters indeed; and there might be more freedom in England, though her feudal lords' lightest words were worth men's lives, and though the blood of the vexed husbandman dropped in the furrows of her fields, than there is while the animation of her multitudes is sent like fuel to feed the factory smoke, and the strength of them is given daily to be wasted into the fineness of a web, or racked into the exactness of a line.

§ XIV. And, on the other hand, go forth again to gaze upon the old cathedral front, where you have smiled so often at the fantastic ignorance of the old sculptors: examine once more those ugly goblins, and formless monsters, and stern statues, anatomiless and rigid; but do not mock at them, for they are signs of the life and liberty of every workman who struck the stone; a freedom of thought, and rank in scale of being, such as no laws, no charters, no charities can secure; but which it must be the first aim of all Europe at this day to regain for her children.

§ XV. Let me not be thought to speak wildly or extravagantly. It is verily this degradation of the operative into a machine, which, more than any other evil of the times, is leading the mass of the nations everywhere into vain, incoherent, destructive struggling for a freedom of which they cannot explain the nature to themselves. Their universal outcry against wealth, and against nobility, is not forced from them either by the pressure of famine, or the sting of mortified pride. These do much, and have done much in all ages; but the foundations of society were never yet shaken as they are at this day. It is not that men are ill fed, but that they have no pleasure in the work by which they make their bread and therefore look to wealth as the only means of pleasure. It is not that men are pained by the scorn of the upper classes, but they cannot endure their own; for they feel that the kind of labor to which they are condemned is verily a degrading one, and makes them less than men. Never had the upper classes so much sympathy with the lower, or charity for them, as they have at this day, and yet never were they so much hated by them: for, of old, the separation between the noble and the poor was merely a wall built by law; now it is a veritable difference in level of standing, a precipice between upper and lower grounds in the field of humanity, and there is pestilential air at the bottom of it. I know not if a day is ever to come when the nature of right freedom will be understood, and when men will see that to obey another man, to labor for him, yield reverence to him or to his place, is not slavery. It is often the best kind of liberty,— liberty from care. The man who says to one, Go, and he goeth, and to another, Come, and he cometh, has, in most cases, more sense of restraint and difficulty than the man who obeys him. The movements of the one are hindered by the burden on his shoulder; of the other, by the bridle on his lips: there is no way by which the burden may be lightened; but we need not suffer from the bridle if we do not champ at it. To yield reverence to another, to hold ourselves and our lives at his disposal, is not slavery; often, it is the noblest state in which a man can live in this world. There is, indeed, a reverence which is servile, that is to say, irrational or selfish: but there is also noble reverence, that is to say, reasonable and loving; and a man is never so noble as when he is reverent in this kind; nay, even if the feeling pass the bounds of mere reason, so that it be loving, a man is raised by it. Which had, in reality, most of the serf nature in him,—the Irish peasant who was lying in wait yesterday for his landlord, with his musket muzzle thrust through the ragged hedge; or that old mountain servant, who, 200 years ago, at Inverkeithing, gave up his own life and the lives of his seven sons for his chief?[3]—and as each fell, calling forth his brother to the death, "Another for Hector!" And therefore, in all ages and all countries, reverence has been paid and sacrifice made by men to each other, not only without complaint, but rejoicingly; and famine, and peril, and sword, and all evil, and all shame, have been borne willingly in the causes of masters and kings; for all these gifts of the heart ennobled the men who gave, not less than the men who received them, and nature prompted, and God rewarded the sacrifice. But to feel their souls withering within them, unthanked, to find their whole being sunk into an unrecognized abyss, to be counted off into a heap of mechanism, numbered with its wheels, and weighed with its hammer strokes;—this nature bade note,—this God blesses not,—this humanity for no long time is able to endure.

§ xvi. We have much studied and much perfected, of late, the great civilized invention of the division of labor; only we give it a false

[3] Vide Preface to "Fair Maid of Perth."

name. It is not, truly speaking, the labor that is divided; but the men:
—Divided into mere segments of men—broken into small fragments
and crumbs of life; so that all the little piece of intelligence that is left
in a man is not enough to make a pin, or a nail, but exhausts itself in
making the point of a pin, or the head of a nail. Now it is a good and
desirable thing, truly, to make many pins in a day; but if we could only
see with what crystal sand their points were polished,—sand of human
soul, much to be magnified before it can be discerned for what it is,—
we should think there might be some loss in it also. And the great cry
that rises from all our manufacturing cities, louder than their furnace
blast, is all in very deed for this,—that we manufacture everything
there except men; we blanch cotton, and strengthen steel, and refine
sugar, and shape pottery; but to brighten, to strengthen, to refine, or
to form a single living spirit, never enters into our estimate of advantages. And all the evil to which that cry is urging our myriads can be
met only in one way: not by teaching nor preaching, for to teach them
is but to show them their misery, and to preach to them, if we do
nothing more than preach, is to mock at it. It can be met only by a
right understanding, on the part of all classes, of what kinds of labor
are good for men, raising them, and making them happy; by a determined sacrifice of such convenience, or beauty, or cheapness as is to
be got only by the degradation of the workman; and by equally determined demand for the products and results of healthy and ennobling
labor.

§ xvii. And how, it will be asked, are these products to be recognized, and this demand to be regulated? Easily: by the observance of
three broad and simple rules:

1. Never encourage the manufacture of any article not absolutely
necessary, in the production of which *Invention* has no share.

2. Never demand an exact finish for its own sake, but only for some
practical or noble end.

3. Never encourage imitation or copying of any kind, except for the
sake of preserving record of great works.

The second of these principles is the only one which directly rises
out of the consideration of our immediate subject; but I shall briefly
explain the meaning and extent of the first also, reserving the enforce-
ment of the third for another place.

1. Never encourage the manufacture of anything not necessary, in
the production of which invention has no share.

For instance. Glass beads are utterly unnecessary, and there is no design or thought employed in their manufacture. They are formed by first drawing out the glass into rods; these rods are chopped up into fragments of the size of beads by the human hand, and the fragments are then rounded in the furnace. The men who chop up the rods sit at their work all day, their hands vibrating with a perpetual and exquisitely timed palsy, and the beads dropping beneath their vibration like hail. Neither they, nor the men who draw out the rods, or fuse the fragments, have the smallest occasion for the use of any single human faculty; and every young lady, therefore, who buys glass beads is engaged in the slave-trade, and in a much more cruel one than that which we have so long been endeavoring to put down.

But glass cups and vessels may become the subjects of exquisite invention; and if in buying these we pay for the invention, that is to say for the beautiful form, or color, or engraving, and not for mere finish of execution, we are doing good to humanity.

§ xviii. So, again, the cutting of precious stones, in all ordinary cases, requires little exertion of any mental faculty; some tact and judgment in avoiding flaws, and so on, but nothing to bring out the whole mind. Every person who wears cut jewels merely for the sake of their value is, therefore, a slave-driver.

But the working of the goldsmith, and the various designing of grouped jewellery and enamel-work, may become the subject of the most noble human intelligence. Therefore, money spent in the purchase of well-designed plate, of precious engraved vases, cameos, or enamels, does good to humanity; and, in work of this kind, jewels may be employed to heighten its splendor; and their cutting is then a price paid for the attainment of a noble end, and thus perfectly allowable.

§ xix. I shall perhaps press this law farther elsewhere, but our immediate concern is chiefly with the second, namely, never to demand an exact finish, when it does not lead to a noble end. For observe, I have only dwelt upon the rudeness of Gothic, or any other kind of imperfectness, as admirable, where it was impossible to get design or thought without it. If you are to have the thought of a rough and untaught man, you must have it in a rough and untaught way; but from an educated man, who can without effort express his thoughts in an educated way, take the graceful expression, and be thankful. Only *get* the thought, and do not silence the peasant because he cannot speak good grammar, or until you have taught him his grammar. Grammar and refinement are good things, both, only be sure of the better thing first. And thus in art, delicate finish is desirable from the greatest

masters, and is always given by them. In some places Michael Angelo,
Leonardo, Phidias, Perugino, Turner, all finished with the most exquisite care; and the finish they give always leads to the fuller accomplishment of their noble purposes. But lower men than these cannot
finish, for it requires consummate knowledge to finish consummately,
and then we must take their thoughts as they are able to give them. So
the rule is simple: Always look for invention first, and after that, for
such execution as will help the invention, and as the inventor is capable
of without painful effort, and *no more.* Above all, demand no refinement of execution where there is no thought, for that is slaves' work,
unredeemed. Rather choose rough work than smooth work, so only that
the practical purpose be answered, and never imagine there is reason
to be proud of anything that may be accomplished by patience and
sandpaper.

§ xx. I shall only give one example, which however will show the
reader what I mean, from the manufacture already alluded to, that of
glass. Our modern glass is exquisitely clear in its substance, true in its
form, accurate in its cutting. We are proud of this. We ought to be
ashamed of it. The old Venice glass was muddy, inaccurate in all its
forms, and clumsily cut, if at all. And the old Venetian was justly
proud of it. For there is this difference between the English and Venetian workman, that the former thinks only of accurately matching his
patterns, and getting his curves perfectly true and his edges perfectly
sharp, and becomes a mere machine for rounding curves and sharpen-
ing edges, while the old Venetian cared not a whit whether his edges
were sharp or not, but he invented a new design for every glass that he
made, and never moulded a handle or a lip without a new fancy in it.
And therefore, though some Venetian glass is ugly and clumsy enough,
when made by clumsy and uninventive workmen, other Venetian glass
is so lovely in its forms that no price is too great for it; and we never
see the same form in it twice. Now you cannot have the finish and the
varied form too. If the workman is thinking about his edges, he cannot
be thinking of his design; if of his design, he cannot think of his
edges. Choose whether you will pay for the lovely form or the perfect
finish, and choose at the same moment whether you will make the
worker a man or a grindstone.

§ xxi. Nay, but the reader interrupts me,—"If the workman can
design beautifully, I would not have him kept at the furnace. Let him
be taken away and made a gentleman, and have a studio, and design
his glass there, and I will have it blown and cut for him by common
workmen, and so I will have my design and my finish too."

All ideas of this kind are founded upon two mistaken suppositions: the first, that one man's thoughts can be, or ought to be, executed by another man's hands; the second, that manual labor is a degradation, when it is governed by intellect.

On a large scale, and in work determinable by line and rule, it is indeed both possible and necessary that the thoughts of one man should be carried out by the labor of others; in this sense I have already defined the best architecture to be the expression of the mind of manhood by the hands of childhood. But on a smaller scale, and in a design which cannot be mathematically defined, one man's thoughts can never be expressed by another: and the difference between the spirit of touch of the man who is inventing, and of the man who is obeying directions, is often all the difference between a great and a common work of art. How wide the separation is between original and second-hand execution, I shall endeavor to show elsewhere; it is not so much to our purpose here as to mark the other and more fatal error of despising manual labor when governed by intellect; for it is no less fatal an error to despise it when thus regulated by intellect, than to value it for its own sake. We are always in these days endeavoring to separate the two; we want one man to be always thinking, and another to be always working, and we call one a gentleman, and the other an operative; whereas the workman ought often to be thinking, and the thinker often to be working, and both should be gentlemen, in the best sense. As it is, we make both ungentle, the one envying, the other despising, his brother; and the mass of society is made up of morbid thinkers, and miserable workers. Now it is only by labor that thought can be made healthy, and only by thought that labor can be made happy, and the two cannot be separated with impunity. It would be well if all of us were good handicraftsmen in some kind, and the dishonor of manual labor done away with altogether; so that though there should still be a trenchant distinction of race between nobles and commoners, there should not, among the latter, be a trenchant distinction of employment, as between idle and working men, or between men of liberal and illiberal professions. All professions should be liberal, and there should be less pride felt in peculiarity of employment, and more in excellence of achievement. And yet more, in each several profession, no master should be too proud to do its hardest work. The painter should grind his own colors; the architect work in the mason's yard with his men; the master-manufacturer be himself a more skilful operative than any man in his mills; and the distinction between one man and another be only in experience and skill, and the authority and wealth which these must naturally and justly obtain.

§ XXII. I should be led far from the matter in hand, if I were to pursue this interesting subject. Enough, I trust, has been said to show the reader that the rudeness or imperfection which at first rendered the term "Gothic" one of reproach is indeed, when rightly understood, one of the most noble characters of Christian architecture, and not only a noble but an *essential* one. It seems a fantastic paradox, but it is nevertheless a most important truth, that no architecture can be truly noble which is *not* imperfect. And this is easily demonstrable. For since the architect, whom we will suppose capable of doing all in perfection, cannot execute the whole with his own hands, he must either make slaves of his workmen in the old Greek, and present English fashion, and level his work to a slave's capacities, which is to degrade it; or else he must take his workmen as he finds them, and let them show their weaknesses together with their strength, which will involve the Gothic imperfection, but render the whole work as noble as the intellect of the age can make it.

§ XXIII. But the principle may be stated more broadly still. I have confined the illustration of it to architecture, but I must not leave it as if true of architecture only. Hitherto I have used the words imperfect and perfect merely to distinguish between work grossly unskilful, and work executed with average precision and science; and I have been pleading that any degree of unskilfulness should be admitted, so only that the laborer's mind had room for expression. But, accurately speaking, no good work whatever can be perfect, and *the demand for perfection is always a sign of a misunderstanding of the ends of art.*

§ XXIV. This for two reasons, both based on everlasting laws. The first, that no great man ever stops working till he has reached his point of failure; that is to say, his mind is always far in advance of his powers of execution, and the latter will now and then give way in trying to follow it; besides that he will always give to the inferior portions of his work only such inferior attention as they require; and according to his greatness he becomes so accustomed to the feeling of dissatisfaction with the best he can do, that in moments of lassitude or anger with himself he will not care though the beholder be dissatisfied also. I believe there has only been one man who would not acknowledge this necessity, and strove always to reach perfection, Leonardo; the end of his vain effort being merely that he would take ten years to a picture, and leave it unfinished. And therefore, if we are to have great men working at all, or less men doing their best, the work will be imperfect, however beautiful. Of human work none but what is bad can be perfect, in its own bad way.[4]

§ xxv. The second reason is, that imperfection is in some sort essential to all that we know of life. It is the sign of life in a mortal body, that is to say, of a state of progress and change. Nothing that lives is, or can be, rigidly perfect; part of it is decaying, part nascent. The foxglove blossom,—a third part bud, a third part past, a third part in full bloom,—is a type of the life of the world. And in all things that live there are certain irregularities and deficiencies which are not only signs of life, but sources of beauty. No human face is exactly the same in its lines on each side, no leaf perfect in its lobes, no branch in its symmetry. All admit irregularity as they imply change; and to banish imperfection is to destroy expression, to check exertion, to paralyse vitality. All things are literally better, lovelier, and more beloved for the imperfections which have been divinely appointed, that the law of human life may be Effort, and the law of human judgment, Mercy.

Accept this then for a universal law, that neither architecture nor any other noble work of man can be good unless it be imperfect; and let us be prepared for the otherwise strange fact, which we shall discern clearly as we approach the period of the Renaissance, that the first cause of the fall of the arts of Europe was a relentless requirement of perfection, incapable alike either of being silenced by veneration for greatness, or softened into forgiveness of simplicity.

Thus far then of the Rudeness or Savageness, which is the first mental element of Gothic architecture. It is an element in many other healthy architectures also, as in Byzantine and Romanesque; but true Gothic cannot exist without it.

§ xxvi. The second mental element above named was CHANGEFULNESS, or Variety.

I have already enforced the allowing independent operation to the inferior workman, simply as a duty *to him,* and as ennobling the architecture by rendering it more Christian. We have now to consider what reward we obtain for the performance of this duty, namely, the perpetual variety of every feature of the building.

Wherever the workman is utterly enslaved, the parts of the building

[4] The Elgin marbles are supposed by many persons to be "perfect." In the most important portions they indeed approach perfection, but only there. The draperies are unfinished, the hair and wool of the animals are unfinished, and the entire bas-reliefs of the frieze are roughly cut.

must of course be absolutely like each other; for the perfection of his execution can only be reached by exercising him in doing one thing, and giving him nothing else to do. The degree in which the workman is degraded may be thus known at a glance, by observing whether the several parts of the building are similar or not; and if, as in Greek work, all the capitals are alike, and all the mouldings unvaried, then the degradation is complete; if, as in Egyptian or Ninevite work, though the manner of executing certain figures is always the same, the order of design is perpetually varied, the degradation is less total; if, as in Gothic work, there is perpetual change both in design and execution, the workman must have been altogether set free.

§ xxvii. How much the beholder gains from the liberty of the laborer may perhaps be questioned in England, where one of the strongest instincts in nearly every mind is that Love of Order which makes us desire that our house windows should pair like our carriage horses, and allows us to yield our faith unhesitatingly to architectural theories which fix a form for everything and forbid variation from it. I would not impeach love of order: it is one of the most useful elements of the English mind; it helps us in our commerce and in all purely practical matters; and it is in many cases one of the foundation stones of morality. Only do not let us suppose that love of order is love of art. It is true that order, in its highest sense, is one of the necessities of art, just as time is a necessity of music; but love of order has no more to do with our right enjoyment of architecture or painting, than love of punctuality with the appreciation of an opera. Experience, I fear, teaches us that accurate and methodical habits in daily life are seldom characteristic of those who either quickly perceive, or richly possess, the creative powers of art; there is, however, nothing inconsistent between the two instincts, and nothing to hinder us from retaining our business habits, and yet fully allowing and enjoying the noblest gifts of Invention. We already do so, in every other branch of art except architecture, and we only do *not* so there because we have been taught that it would be wrong. Our architects gravely inform us that, as there are four rules of arithmetic, there are five orders of architecture, we, in our simplicity, think that this sounds consistent, and believe them. They inform us also that there is one proper form for Corinthian capitals, another for Doric, and another for Ionic. We, considering that there is also a proper form for the letters A, B, and C, think that this also sounds consistent, and accept the proposition. Understanding, therefore, that one form of the said capitals is proper, and no other, and having a conscientious horror of all impropriety, we allow the architect to provide us with the said capitals, of the proper form, in such and such a quantity, and in all other points to take care that the legal forms are observed; which having done, we rest in forced confidence that we are well housed.

§ xxviii. But our higher instincts are not deceived. We take no pleasure in the building provided for us, resembling that which we take in a new book or a new picture. We may be proud of its size, complacent in its correctness, and happy in its convenience. We may take the same pleasure in its symmetry and workmanship as in a well-ordered room, or a skilful piece of manufacture. And this we suppose to be all the pleasure that architecture was ever intended to give us. The idea of reading a building as we would read Milton or Dante, and getting the same kind of delight out of the stones as out of the stanzas, never enters our minds for a moment. And for good reason:—There is indeed rhythm in the verses, quite as strict as the symmetries or rhythm of the architecture, and a thousand times more beautiful, but there is something else than rhythm. The verses were neither made to order, nor to match, as the capitals were; and we have therefore a kind of pleasure in them other than a sense of propriety. But it requires a strong effort of comon sense to shake ourselves quit of all that we have been taught for the last two centuries, and wake to the perception of a truth just as simple and certain as it is new: that great art, whether expressing itself in words, colors, or stones, does *not* say the same thing over and over again; that the merit of architectural, as of every other art, consists in its saying new and different things; that to repeat itself is no more a characteristic of genius in marble than it is of genius in print; and that we may, without offending any laws of good taste, require of an architect, as we do of a novelist, that he should be not only correct, but entertaining.

Yet all this is true, and self-evident; only hidden from us, as many other self-evident things are, by false teaching. Nothing is a great work of art, for the production of which either rules or models can be given. Exactly so far as architecture works on known rules, and from given models, it is not an art, but a manufacture; and it is, of the two procedures, rather less rational (because more easy) to copy capitals or mouldings from Phidias, and call ourselves architects, than to copy heads and hands from Titian, and call ourselves painters.

§ xxix. Let us then understand at once, that change or variety is as much a necessity to the human heart and brain in buildings as in books; that there is no merit, though there is some occasional use, in monotony; and that we must no more expect to derive either pleasure or profit from an architecture whose ornaments are of one pattern, and whose pillars are of one proportion, than we should out of a universe in which the clouds were all of one shape, and the trees all of one size.

§ xxx. And this we confess in deeds, though not in words. All the pleasure which the people of the nineteenth century take in art, is in pictures, sculpture, minor objects of virtù, or mediæval architecture, which we enjoy under the term picturesque: no pleasure is taken anywhere in modern buildings, and we find all men of true feeling delighting to escape out of modern cities into natural scenery: hence, as I shall hereafter show, that peculiar love of landscape which is characteristic of the age. It would be well, if, in all other matters, we were as ready to put up with what we dislike, for the sake of compliance with established law, as we are in architecture.

§ xxxi. How so debased a law ever came to be established, we shall see when we come to describe the Renaissance schools: here we have only to note, as the second most essential element of the Gothic spirit, that it broke through that law wherever it found it in existence; it not only dared, but delighted in, the infringement of every servile principle; and invented a series of forms of which the merit was, not merely that they were new, but that they were *capable of perpetual novelty*. The pointed arch was not merely a bold variation from the round, but it admitted of millions of variations in itself; for the proportions of a pointed arch are changeable to infinity, while a circular arch is always the same. The grouped shaft was not merely a bold variation from the single one, but it admitted of millions of variations in its grouping, and in the proportions resultant from its grouping. The introduction of tracery was not only a startling change in the treatment of window lights, but admitted endless changes in the interlacement of the tracery bars themselves. So that while in all living Christian architecture the love of variety exists, the Gothic schools exhibited that love in culminating energy; and their influence, wherever it extended itself, may be sooner and farther traced by this character than by any other; the tendency to the adoption of Gothic types being always first shown by greater irregularity and richer variation in the forms of the architecture it is about to supersede, long before the appearance of the pointed arch or of any other recognizable *outward* sign of the Gothic mind.

§ xxxii. We must, however, herein note carefully what distinction there is between a healthy and a diseased love of change; for as it was in healthy love of change that the Gothic architecture rose, it was partly in consequence of diseased love of change that it was destroyed. In order to understand this clearly, it will be necessary to consider the different ways in which change and monotony are presented to us in nature; both having their use, like darkness and light, and the one incapable of being enjoyed without the other: change being most delightful after some prolongation of monotony, as light appears most brilliant after the eyes have been for some time closed.

§ xxxiii. I believe that the true relations of monotony and change may be most simply understood by observing them in music. We may therein notice, first, that there is a sublimity and majesty in monotony which there is not in rapid or frequent variation. This is true throughout all nature. The greater part of the sublimity of the sea depends on its monotony; so also that of desolate moor and mountain scenery; and especially the sublimity of motion, as in the quiet, unchanged fall and rise of an engine beam. So also there is sublimity in darkness which there is not in light.

§ xxxiv. Again, monotony after a certain time, or beyond a certain degree, becomes either uninteresting or intolerable, and the musician is obliged to break it in one or two ways: either while the air or passage is perpetually repeated, its notes are variously enriched and harmonized; or else, after a certain number of repeated passages, an entirely new passage is introduced, which is more or less delightful according to the length of the previous monotony. Nature, of course, uses both these kinds of variation perpetually. The sea-waves, resembling each other in general mass, but none like its brother in minor divisions and curves, are a monotony of the first kind; the great plain, broken by an emergent rock or clump of trees, is a monotony of the second.

§ xxxv. Farther: in order to the enjoyment of the change in either case, a certain degree of patience is required from the hearer or observer. In the first case, he must be satisfied to endure with patience the recurrence of the great masses of sound or form, and to seek for entertainment in a careful watchfulness of the minor details. In the second case, he must bear patiently the infliction of the monotony for some moments, in order to feel the full refreshment of the change. This is true even of the shortest musical passage in which the element of monotony is employed. In cases of more majestic monotony, the patience required is so considerable that it becomes a kind of pain,— a price paid for the future pleasure.

§ xxxvi. Again: the talent of the composer is not in the monotony, but in the changes: he may show feeling and taste by his use of monotony in certain places or degrees; that is to say, by his *various* employment of it; but it is always in the new arrangement or invention that his intellect is shown, and not in the monotony which relieves it.

Lastly: if the pleasure of change be too often repeated, it ceases to be delightful, for then change itself becomes monotonous, and we are driven to seek delight in extreme and fantastic degrees of it. This is the diseased love of change of which we have above spoken.

§ xxxvii. From these facts we may gather generally that monotony is, and ought to be, in itself painful to us, just as darkness is; that an architecture which is altogether monotonous is a dark or dead architecture; and, of those who love it, it may be truly said, "they love darkness rather than light." But monotony in certain measure, used in order to give value to change, and, above all, that *transparent* monotony which, like the shadows of a great painter, suffers all manner of dimly suggested form to be seen through the body of it, is an essential in architectural as in all other composition; and the endurance of monotony has about the same place in a healthy mind that the endurance of darkness has: that is to say, as a strong intellect will have pleasure in the solemnities of storm and twilight, and in the broken and mysterious lights that gleam among them, rather than in mere brilliancy and glare, while a frivolous mind will dread the shadow and the storm; and as a great man will be ready to endure much darkness of fortune in order to reach greater eminence of power or felicity, while an inferior man will not pay the price; exactly in like manner a great mind will accept, or even delight in, monotony which would be wearisome to an inferior intellect, because it has more patience and power of expectation, and is ready to pay the full price for the great future pleasure of change. But in all cases it is not that the noble nature loves monotony, any more than it loves darkness or pain. But it can bear with it, and receives a high pleasure in the endurance or patience, a pleasure necessary to the well-being of this world; while those who will not submit to the temporary sameness, but rush from one change to another, gradually dull the edge of change itself, and bring a shadow and weariness over the whole world from which there is no more escape.

§ xxxviii. From these general uses of variety in the economy of the world, we may at once understand its use and abuse in architecture. The variety of the Gothic schools is the more healthy and beautiful, because in many cases it is entirely unstudied, and results, not from the mere love of change, but from practical necessities. For in one point of view Gothic is not only the best, but the *only rational* architecture, as being that which can fit itself most easily to all services, vulgar or noble. Undefined in its slope of roof, height of shaft, breadth of arch, or disposition of ground plan, it can shrink into a turret, expand into a hall, coil into a staircase, or spring into a spire, with undegraded grace and unexhausted energy; and whenever it finds occasion for change in its form or purpose, it submits to it without the slightest sense of loss either to its unity or majesty,—subtle and flexible like a fiery serpent, but ever attentive to the voice of the charmer. And it is one of the chief virtues of the Gothic builders, that they never suffered ideas of outside symmetries and consistencies to interfere with the real use and value of what they did. If they wanted a window, they opened one; a room, they added one; a buttress, they built one; utterly regardless of any established conventionalities of external appearance, knowing (as indeed it always happened) that such daring interruptions of the formal plan would rather give additional interest to its symmetry than injure it. So that, in the best times of Gothic, a useless window would rather have been opened in an unexpected place for the sake of the surprise, than a useful one forbidden for the sake of symmetry. Every successive architect, employed upon a great work, built the pieces he added in his own way, utterly regardless of the style adopted by his predecessors; and if two towers were raised in nominal correspondence at the sides of a cathedral front, one was nearly sure to be different from the other, and in each the style at the top to be different from the style at the bottom.

§ xxxix. These marked variations were, however, only permitted as part of the great system of perpetual change which ran through every member of Gothic design, and rendered it as endless a field for the beholder's inquiry, as for the builder's imagination: change, which in the best schools is subtle and delicate, and rendered more delightful by intermingling of a noble monotony; in the more barbaric schools is somewhat fantastic and redundant; but, in all, a necessary and constant condition of the life of the school. Sometimes the variety is in one feature, sometimes in another; it may be in the capitals or crockets, in the niches or the traceries, or in all together, but in some one or other of the features it will be found always. If the mouldings are constant, the surface sculpture will change; if the capitals are of a fixed design, the traceries will change; if the traceries are monotonous, the capitals will change; and if even, as in some fine schools, the early English for example, there is the slightest approximation to an unvarying type of mouldings, capitals, and floral decoration, the variety is found in the disposition of the masses, and in the figure sculpture.

§ XL. . . . A picture or poem is often little more than a feeble utterance of man's admiration of something out of himself; but architecture approaches more to a creation of his own, born of his necessities, and expressive of his nature. It is also, in some sort, the work of the whole race, while the picture or statue are the work of one only, in most cases more highly gifted than his fellows. And therefore we may expect that the first two elements of good architecture should be expressive of some great truths commonly belonging to the whole race, and necessary to be understood or felt by them in all their work that they do under the sun. And observe what they are: the confession of Imperfection and the confession of Desire of Change. The building of the bird and the bee needs not express anything like this. It is perfect and unchanging. But just because we are something better than birds or bees, our building must confess that we have not reached the perfection we can imagine, and cannot rest in the condition we have attained. If we pretend to have reached either perfection or satisfaction, we have degraded ourselves and our work. God's work only may express that; but ours may never have that sentence written upon it,—"And behold, it was very good." And, observe again, it is not merely as it renders the edifice a book of various knowledge, or a mine of precious thought, that variety is essential to its nobleness. The vital principle is not the love of *Knowledge,* but the love of *Change.* It is that strange *disquietude* of the Gothic spirit that is its greatness; that restlessness of the dreaming mind, that wanders hither and thither among the niches, and flickers feverishly around the pinnacles, and frets and fades in labyrinthine knots and shadows along wall and roof, and yet is not satisfied, nor shall be satisfied. The Greek could stay in his triglyph furrow, and be at peace; but the work of the Gothic heart is fretwork still, and it can neither rest in, nor from, its labor, but must pass on, sleeplessly, until its love of change shall be pacified for ever in the change that must come alike on them that wake and them that sleep.

§ XLI. The third constituent element of the Gothic mind was stated to be NATURALISM; that is to say, the love of natural objects for their own sake, and the effort to represent them frankly, unconstrained by artistical laws.

This characteristic of the style partly follows in necessary connexion with those named above. For, so soon as the workman is left free to represent what subjects he chooses, he must look to the nature that is round him for material, and will endeavor to represent it as he sees it, with more or less accuracy according to the skill he possesses, and with much play of fancy, but with small respect for law. There is, however, a marked distinction between the imaginations of the Western and Eastern races, even when both are left free, the Western, or Gothic, delighting most in the representation of facts, and the Eastern (Arabian, Persian, and Chinese) in the harmony of colors and forms. Each of these intellectual dispositions has its particular forms of error and abuse, which, though I have often before stated, I must here again briefly explain; and this the rather, because the word Naturalism is, in one of its senses, justly used as a term of reproach, and the questions respecting the real relations of art and nature are so many and so confused throughout all the schools of Europe at this day, that I cannot clearly enunciate any single truth without appearing to admit, in fellowship with it, some kind of error, unless the reader will bear with me in entering into such an analysis of the subject as will serve us for general guidance.

§ XLII. We are to remember, in the first place, that the arrangement of colors and lines is an art analogous to the composition[5] of music, and entirely independent of the representation of facts. Good coloring does not necessarily convey the image of anything but itself. It consists in certain proportions and arrangements of rays of light, but not in likenesses to anything. A few touches of certain greys and purples laid by a master's hand on white paper, will be good coloring; as more touches are added beside them, we may find out that they were intended to represent a dove's neck, and we may praise, as the drawing advances, the perfect imitation of the dove's neck. But the good coloring does not consist in that imitation, but in the abstract qualities and relations of the grey and purple.

In like manner, as soon as a great sculptor begins to shape his work out of the block, we shall see that its lines are nobly arranged, and of noble character. We may not have the slightest idea for what the forms are intended, whether they are of man or beast, of vegetation or drapery. Their likeness to anything does not affect their nobleness. They are magnificent forms, and that is all we need care to know of them, in order to say whether the workman is a good or bad sculptor.

§ XLIII. Now the noblest art is an exact unison of the abstract value,

5 I am always afraid to use this word "Composition;" it is so utterly misused in the general parlance respecting art. Nothing is more common than to hear divisions of art into "form, composition, and color," or "light and shade and composition," or "sentiment and composition," or it matters not what else and composition; the speakers in each case attaching a perfectly different meaning to the word, generally an indistinct one, and always a wrong one. Composition is, in plain English, "putting together," and it means the putting together of lines, of forms, of colors, of shades, or of ideas. Painters compose in color, compose in thought, compose in form, and compose in effect: the word being of use merely in order to express a scientific, disciplined, and inventive arrangement of any of these, instead of a merely natural or accidental one.

with the imitative power, of forms and colors. It is the noblest composition, used to express the noblest facts. But the human mind cannot in general unite the two perfections: it either pursues the fact to the neglect of the composition, or pursues the composition to the neglect of the fact.

§ XLIV. And it is intended by the Deity that it *should* do this; the best art is not always wanted. Facts are often wanted without art, as in a geological diagram; and art often without facts, as in a Turkey carpet. And most men have been made capable of giving either one or the other, but not both; only one or two, the very highest, can give both.

Observe then. Men are universally divided, as respects their artistical qualifications, into three great classes; a right, a left, and a centre. On the right side are the men of facts, on the left the men of design,[6] in the centre the men of both.

The three classes of course pass into each other by imperceptible gradations. The men of facts are hardly ever altogether without powers of design; the men of design are always in some measure cognizant of facts; and as each class possesses more or less of the powers of the opposite one, it approaches to the character of the central class. Few men, even in that central rank, are so exactly throned on the summit of the crest that they cannot be perceived to incline in the least one way or the other, embracing both horizons with their glance. Now each of these classes has, as I above said, a healthy function in the world, and correlative diseases or unhealthy functions; and, when the work of either of them is seen in its morbid condition, we are apt to find fault with the class of workmen, instead of finding fault only with the particular abuse which has perverted their action. . . .

What, then, are the diseased operations to which the three classes of workmen are liable?

§ XLVI. Primarily, two; affecting the two inferior classes:

1st, When either of those two classes Despises the other;

2nd, When either of the two classes Envies the other; producing, therefore, four forms of dangerous error.

First, when the men of facts despise design. This is the error of the common Dutch painters, of merely imitative painters of still life, flowers, &c., and other men who, having either the gift of accurate imitation or strong sympathies with nature, suppose that all is done when the imitation is perfected or sympathy expressed. A large body of English

---

[6] Design is used in this place as expressive of the power to arrange lines and colors nobly. By facts, I mean facts perceived by the eye and mind, not facts accumulated by knowledge.

landscapists come into this class, including most clever sketchers from nature, who fancy that to get a sky of true tone, and a gleam of sunshine or sweep of shower faithfully expressed, is all that can be required of art. These men are generally themselves answerable for much of their deadness of feeling to the higher qualities of composition. They probably have not originally the high gifts of design, but they lose such powers as they originally possessed by despising, and refusing to study, the results of great power of design in others. Their knowledge, as far as it goes, being accurate, they are usually presumptuous and self-conceited, and gradually become incapable of admiring anything but what is like their own works. They see nothing in the works of great designers but the faults, and do harm almost incalculable in the European society of the present day by sneering at the compositions of the greatest men of the earlier ages,[7] because they do not absolutely tally with their own ideas of "Nature."

§ XLVII. The second form of error is when the men of design despise facts. All noble design must deal with facts to a certain extent, for there is no food for it but in nature. The best colorist invents best by taking hints from natural colors; from birds, skies, or groups of figures. And if, in the delight of inventing fantastic color and form the truths of nature are wilfully neglected, the intellect becomes comparatively decrepit, and that state of art results which we find among the Chinese. The Greek designers delighted in the facts of the human form, and became great in consequence; but the facts of lower nature were disregarded by them, and their inferior ornament became, therefore, dead and valueless.

§ XLVIII. The third form of error is when the men of facts envy design: that is to say, when, having only imitative powers, they refuse to employ those powers upon the visible world around them; but, having been taught that composition is the end of art, strive to obtain the inventive powers which nature has denied them, study nothing but the works of reputed designers, and perish in a fungous growth of plagiarism and laws of art.

Here was the great error of the beginning of this century; it is the error of the meanest kind of men that employ themselves in painting, and it is the most fatal of all, rendering those who fall into it utterly useless, incapable of helping the world with either truth or fancy, while,

---

[7] "Earlier," that is to say, pre-Raphaelite ages. Men of this stamp will praise Claude, and such other comparatively debased artists; but they cannot taste the work of the thirteenth century.

in all probability, they deceive it by base resemblances of both, until it hardly recognizes truth or fancy when they really exist.

§ XLIX. The fourth form of error is when the men of design envy facts; that is to say, when the temptation of closely imitating nature leads them to forget their own proper ornamental function, and when they lose the power of the composition for the sake of graphic truth; as, for instance, in the hawthorn moulding so often spoken of round the porch of Bourges Cathedral, which, though very lovely, might perhaps, as we saw above, have been better, if the old builder, in his excessive desire to make it look like hawthorn, had not painted it green.

§ L. It is, however, carefully to be noted, that the two morbid conditions to which the men of facts are liable are much more dangerous and harmful than those to which the men of design are liable. The morbid state of men of design injures themselves only; that of the men of facts injures the whole world. The Chinese porcelain-painter is, indeed, not so great a man as he might be, but he does not want to break everything that is not porcelain; but the modern English fact-hunter, despising design, wants to destroy everything that does not agree with his own notions of truth, and becomes the most dangerous and despicable of iconoclasts, excited by egotism instead of religion. Again: the Bourges sculptor, painting his hawthorns green, did indeed somewhat hurt the effect of his own beautiful design, but did not prevent any one from loving hawthorn: but Sir George Beaumont, trying to make Constable paint grass brown *instead* of green, was setting himself between Constable and nature, blinding the painter, and blaspheming the work of God. . . .

§ LXIV. . . . The Gothic builders were of that central class which unites fact with design; but . . . the part of the work which was more especially their own was the truthfulness. Their power of artistical invention or arrangement was not greater than that of Romanesque and Byzantine workmen: by those workmen they were taught the principles, and from them received their models, of design; but to the ornamental feeling and rich fancy of the Byzantine the Gothic builder added a love of *fact* which is never found in the South. Both Greek and Roman used conventional foliage in their ornament, passing into something that was not foliage at all, knotting itself into strange cup-like buds or clusters, and growing out of lifeless rods instead of stems; the Gothic sculptor received these types, at first, as things that ought to be, just as we have a second time received them; but he could not rest in them. He saw there was no veracity in them, no knowledge, no vitality. Do what he would, he could not help liking the true leaves better; and cautiously, a little at a time, he put more of nature in his work, until at last it was all true, retaining, nevertheless, every valuable character of the original well-disciplined and designed arrangement.

§ LXV. Nor is it only in external and visible subject that the Gothic workman wrought for truth: he is as firm in his rendering of imaginative as of actual truth; that is to say, when an idea would have been by a Roman, or Byzantine, symbolically represented, the Gothic mind realizes it to the utmost. For instance, the purgatorial fire is represented in the mosaic of Torcello (Romanesque) as a red stream, longitudinally striped like a riband, descending out of the throne of Christ, and gradually extending itself to envelope the wicked. When we are once informed what this means, it is enough for its purpose; but the Gothic inventor does not leave the sign in need of interpretation. He makes the fire as like real fire as he can; and in the porch of St. Maclou at Rouen the sculptured flames burst out of the Hades gate, and flicker up, in writhing tongues of stone, through the interstices of the niches, as if the church itself were on fire. This is an extreme instance, but it is all the more illustrative of the entire difference in temper and thought between the two schools of art, and of the intense love of veracity which influenced the Gothic design.

§ LXVI. I do not say that this love of veracity is always healthy in its operation. I have above noticed the errors into which it falls from despising design; and there is another kind of error noticeable in the instance just given, in which the love of truth is too hasty, and seizes on a surface truth instead of an inner one. For in representing the Hades fire, it is not the mere *form* of the flame which needs most to be told, but its unquenchableness, its Divine ordainment and limitation, and its inner fierceness, not physical and material, but in being the expression of the wrath of God. And these things are not to be told by imitating the fire that flashes out of a bundle of sticks. If we think over his symbol a little, we shall perhaps find that the Romanesque builder told more truth in that likeness of a blood-red stream, flowing between definite shores and out of God's throne, and expanding, as if fed by a perpetual current, into the lake wherein the wicked are cast, than the Gothic builder in those torch-flickerings about his niches. But this is not to our immediate purpose; I am not at present to insist upon the faults into which the love of truth was led in the later Gothic times, but on the feeling itself, as a glorious and peculiar characteristic of the Northern builders. For, observe, it is not, even in the above instance, love of truth, but want of thought, which *causes* the fault. The love of truth, as such, is good, but when it is misdirected by thoughtlessness or over-excited by vanity, and either seizes on facts of small value, or gathers them chiefly that it may boast of its grasp and apprehension, its work may well become dull or offensive. Yet let us not, therefore, blame the inherent love of facts, but the incautiousness of their selection, and impertinence of their statement. . . .

§ LXXII. The fourth essential element of the Gothic mind was above stated to be the sense of the GROTESQUE . . . It is the less necessary to insist upon it here, because every reader familiar with Gothic architecture must understand what I mean, and will, I believe, have no hesitation in admitting that the tendency to delight in fantastic and ludicrous, as well as in sublime, images, is a universal instinct of the Gothic imagination.

§ LXXIII. The fifth element above named was RIGIDITY; and this character I must endeavor carefully to define, for neither the word I have used, nor any other that I can think of, will express it accurately. For I mean, not merely stable, but *active* rigidity; the peculiar energy which gives tension to movement, and stiffness to resistance, which makes the fiercest lightning forked rather than curved, and the stoutest oak-branch angular rather than bending, and is as much seen in the quivering of the lance as in the glittering of the icicle.

§ LXXIV. . . . Egyptian and Greek buildings stand, for the most part, by their own weight and mass, one stone passively incumbent on another: but in the Gothic vaults and traceries there is a stiffness analogous to that of the bones of a limb, or fibres of a tree; an elastic tension and communication of force from part to part, and also a studious expression of this throughout every visible line of the building. And, in like manner, the Greek and Egyptian ornament is either mere surface engraving, as if the face of the wall had been stamped with a seal, or its lines are flowing, lithe, and luxuriant; in either case, there is no expression of energy in framework of the ornament itself. But the Gothic ornament stands out in prickly independence, and frosty fortitude, jutting into crockets, and freezing into pinnacles; here starting up into a monster, there germinating into a blossom; anon knitting itself into a branch, alternately thorny, bossy, and bristly, or writhed into every form of nervous entanglement; but, even when most graceful, never for an instant languid, always quickset; erring, if at all, ever on the side of brusquerie.

§ LXXV. The feelings or habits in the workman which give rise to this character in the work, are more complicated and various than those indicated by any other sculptured expression hitherto named. There is, first, the habit of hard and rapid working; the industry of the tribes of the North, quickened by the coldness of the climate, and giving an expression of sharp energy to all they do, as opposed to the languor of the Southern tribes, however much of fire there may be in the heart of that languor, for lava itself may flow languidly. There is also the habit of finding enjoyment in the signs of cold, which is never found, I believe, in the inhabitants of countries south of the Alps. Cold is to them an unredeemed evil, to be suffered, and forgotten as soon as may be; but the long winter of the North forces the Goth (I mean the Englishman, Frenchman, Dane, or German), if he would lead a happy life at all, to find sources of happiness in foul weather as well as fair, and to rejoice in the leafless as well as in the shady forest. And this we do with all our hearts; finding perhaps nearly as much contentment by the Christmas fire as in the summer sunshine, and gaining health and strength on the ice-fields of winter, as well as among the meadows of spring. So that there is nothing adverse or painful to our feelings in the cramped and stiffened structure of vegetation checked by cold; and instead of seeking, like the Southern sculptor, to express only the softness of leafage nourished in all tenderness, and tempted into all luxuriance by warm winds and glowing rays, we find pleasure in dwelling upon the crabbed, perverse, and morose animation of plants that have known little kindness from earth or heaven, but, season after season, have had their best efforts palsied by frost, their brightest buds buried under snow, and their goodliest limbs lopped by tempest.

§ LXXVI. There are many subtle sympathies and affections which join to confirm the Gothic mind in this peculiar choice of subject; and when we add to the influence of these, the necessities consequent upon the employment of a rougher material, compelling the workman to seek for vigor of effect, rather than refinement of texture or accuracy of form, we have direct and manifest causes for much of the difference between the northern and southern cast of conception: but there are indirect causes holding a far more important place in the Gothic heart, though less immediate in their influence on design. Strength of will, independence of character, resoluteness of purpose, impatience of undue control, and that general tendency to set the individual reason against authority, and the individual deed against destiny, which, in the Northern tribes, has opposed itself throughout all ages to the languid submission, in the Southern, of thought to tradition, and purpose to fatality, are all more or less traceable in the rigid lines, vigorous and various masses, and daringly projecting and independent structure of the Northern Gothic ornament: while the opposite feelings are in like manner legible in the graceful and softly guided waves and wreathed bands,

in which Southern decoration is constantly disposed; in its tendency to
lose its independence, and fuse itself into the surface of the masses upon
which it is traced; and in the expression seen so often, in the arrangement of those masses themselves, of an abandonment of their strength
to an inevitable necessity, or a listless repose.

§ LXXVII. There is virtue in the measure, and error in the excess, of
both these characters of mind, and in both of the styles which they have
created; the best architecture, and the best temper, are those which
unite them both; and this fifth impulse of the Gothic heart is therefore
that which needs most caution in its indulgence. It is more definitely
Gothic than any other, but the best Gothic building is not that which
is *most* Gothic: it can hardly be too frank in its confession of rudeness,
hardly too rich in its changefulness, hardly too faithful in its naturalism; but it may go too far in its rigidity, and, like the great Puritan
spirit in its extreme, lose itself either in frivolity of division, or perversity of purpose. It actually did so in its later times; but it is gladdening to
remember that in its utmost nobleness, the very temper which has been
thought most adverse to it, the Protestant spirit of self-dependence and
inquiry, was expressed in its every line. Faith and aspiration there were,
in every Christian ecclesiastical building, from the first century to the
fifteenth; but the moral habits to which England in this age owes the
kind of greatness that she has,—the habits of philosophical investigation, of accurate thought, of domestic seclusion and independence, of
stern self-reliance, and sincere upright searching into religious truth,—
were only traceable in the features which were the distinctive creation
of the Gothic schools, in the veined foliage, and thorny fret-work, and
shadowy niche, and buttressed pier, and fearless height of subtle pinnacle and crested tower, sent like an "unperplexed question up to
Heaven."

§ LXXVIII. Last, because the least essential, of the constituent elements
of this noble school, was placed that of REDUNDANCE,—the uncalculat-
ing bestowal of the wealth of its labor. There is, indeed, much Gothic,
and that of the best period, in which this element is hardly traceable,
and which depends for its effect almost exclusively on loveliness of
simple design and grace of uninvolved proportion: still, in the most
characteristic buildings, a certain portion of their effect depends upon
accumulation of ornament; and many of those which have most influence on the minds of men, have attained it by means of this attribute
alone. And although, by careful study of the school, it is possible to
arrive at a condition of taste which shall be better contented by a few
perfect lines than by a whole façade covered with fretwork, the build-

ing which only satisfies such a taste is not to be considered the best. For the very first requirement of Gothic architecture being, as we saw above, that it shall both admit the aid, and appeal to the admiration, of the rudest as well as the most refined minds, the richness of the work is, paradoxical as the statement may appear, a part of its humility. No architecture is so haughty as that which is simple; which refuses to address the eye, except in a few clear and forceful lines; which implies, in offering so little to our regards, that all it has offered is perfect; and disdains, either by the complexity or the attractiveness of its features, to embarrass our investigation, or betray us into delight. That humility, which is the very life of the Gothic school, is shown not only in the imperfection, but in the accumulation, of ornament. The inferior rank of the workman is often shown as much in the richness, as the roughness, of his work; and if the co-operation of every hand, and the sympathy of every heart, are to be received, we must be content to allow the redundance which disguises the failure of the feeble, and wins the regard of the inattentive. There are, however, far nobler interests mingling, in the Gothic heart, with the rude love of decorative accumulation: a magnificent enthusiasm, which feels as if it never could do enough to reach the fulness of its ideal; an unselfishness of sacrifice, which would rather cast fruitless labor before the altar than stand idle in the market; and, finally, a profound sympathy with the fulness and wealth of the material universe, rising out of that Naturalism whose operation we have already endeavored to define. The sculptor who sought for his models among the forest leaves, could not but quickly and deeply feel that complexity need not involve the loss of grace, nor richness that of repose; and every hour which he spent in the study of the minute and various work of Nature, made him feel more forcibly the barrenness of what was best in that of man: nor is it to be wondered at, that, seeing her perfect and exquisite creations poured forth in a profusion which conception could not grasp nor calculation sum, he should think that it ill became him to be niggardly of his own rude craftsmanship; and where he saw throughout the universe a faultless beauty lavished on measureless spaces of broidered field and blooming mountain, to grudge his poor and imperfect labor to the few stones that he had raised one upon another, for habitation or memorial. The years of his life passed away before his task was accomplished; but generation succeeded generation with unwearied enthusiasm, and the cathedral front was at last lost in the tapestry of its traceries, like a rock among the thickets and herbage of spring.

THE RENAISSANCE

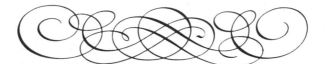

Though only a second-rate artist, Vasari was a first-rate writer and he survives, not primarily as a painter, but as the author of Lives of the Most Eminent Italian Painters, Sculptors, and Architects *(first published in 1550, and then in a greatly expanded second edition in 1568), certainly the best-known and probably the most influential of all books on art. The product of years of indefatigable research during the course of which Vasari traveled throughout Italy, it contains a great deal of authentic information on the lives of Italian artists from Giotto to Vasari himself. It is also the chief source of many legends—some of them palpably false—about these same artists that have become as firmly fixed in the popular mind as Washington's cherry tree exploit or Shakespeare's deer stealing.*

But Vasari's Lives *is important not simply as a collection of biographical fact and fiction. It also developed the idea that was to remain dominant until challenged by Ruskin in the 1850's: that the Middle Ages had been a period of barbarism and cultural decay, and that art had been revived in a new golden age ushered in by Giotto, which reached its peak in Vasari's own day, two centuries later, with Michelangelo. Above all, Vasari was mainly responsible for the concept of the "great artist," no longer as great craftsman only, but as divinely gifted genius, as superman and seer.*

Giorgio Vasari
Giotto and the Circle

[The pope's messenger] repaired one morning to the workshop where Giotto was occupied with his labours. He declared the purpose of the pope, and the manner in which that pontiff desired to avail himself of his assistance, and finally, requested to have a drawing, that he might send it to his holiness. Giotto, who was very courteous, took a sheet of paper, and a pencil dipped in red colour; then, resting his elbow on his side, to form a sort of compass, with one turn of the hand he drew a circle, so perfect and exact that it was a marvel to behold. This done, he turned, smiling to the courtier, saying, "Here is your drawing." "Am I to have nothing more than this?" inquired the latter, conceiving himself to be jested with. "That is enough and to spare," returned Giotto: "Send it with the rest, and you will see if it will be recognized." The messenger, unable to obtain anything more, went away very ill-satisfied, and fearing that he had been fooled. Nevertheless, having dispatched the other drawings to the pope, with the names of those who had done them, he sent that of Giotto also, relating the mode in which he had made his circle, without moving his arm and without compasses; from which the pope, and such of the courtiers as were well versed in the subject, perceived how far Giotto surpassed all the other painters of his time.

This, like many of the things in Vasari's life of Giotto, who had been dead for more than 200 years when Vasari began to write, is pure legend; but it is instructive legend. To Vasari, the miracle of Giotto, the great founder of "modern" Florentine painting, was to a large extent a technical miracle: Giotto was able to bring a new expressive quality into painting because he had made himself master of a new technique.

Giotto and the Fly

It is said that Giotto, when he was still a boy, and studying with Cimabue, once painted a fly on the nose of a figure on which Cimabue himself was employed, and this so naturally, that when the master returned to continue his work, he believed it to be real, and lifted his hand more than once to drive it away before he should go on with the painting.

The love of illusionism, of optical trickery, is a characteristic feature of Renaissance painting. This is the first of Vasari's admiring tributes to the artist's power to fool the spectator; he tells similar stories about others, including Leonardo.

The Gates of Paradise: Ghiberti's Baptistry Doors

The justice of the praises bestowed on Lorenzo for this work may be inferred from the words of Michael Angelo Buonarotti, who, standing to look at these doors, and being asked what he thought of them, and whether they were beautiful, replied in these words:—*"They are so beautiful, that they might fittingly stand at the gates of Paradise,"* a truly appropriate tribute, and offered by him who could well judge of the work.

Uccello's Mistress Perspective

Paolo Uccello left . . . a wife, who was wont to relate that Paolo would stand the whole night through, beside his writing-table, seeking new terms for the expression of his rules in perspective; and when entreated by herself to take rest and sleep, he would reply, "Oh, what a delightful thing is this perspective!" And it is doubtless true, that as this study was delightful to him, no less valuable and useful has it been rendered, by his means, to those who have occupied themselves with similar studies in after times.

ROUT AT SAN ROMANO—PAOLO UCCELLO   (*National Gallery, London*)

Brunelleschi and the Egg

The other architects desired that Filippo should explain his purpose minutely, and show his model as they had shown theirs. This he would not do, but proposed to all the masters, foreigners and compatriots, that he who could make an egg stand upright on a piece of smooth marble, should be appointed to build the Cupola, since in doing that, his genius would be made manifest. They took an egg accordingly, and all those masters did their best to make it stand upright, but none discovered the method of doing so. Wherefore, Filippo, being told that he might make it stand himself, took it daintily into his hands, gave the end of it a blow on the plane of the marble, and made it stand upright. Beholding this, the artists loudly protested, exclaiming, that they could all have done the same; but Filippo replied, laughing, that they might also know how to construct the Cupola, if they had seen the model and design.

> *This, of course, is a story better known to most people in connection with Columbus (and was first told about him in a book that appeared in 1565). The question of priority is meaningless: what we have here is a popular folk story attached now to one, now to another, individual.*

Donatello's Lo Zuccone

[This] is considered the most extraordinary and most beautiful work ever produced by Donatello, who, when he intended to affirm a thing in a manner that should preclude all doubt, would say, "By the faith that I place in my Zuccone." And while he was working on this statue he would frequently exclaim, while looking at it, "Speak then! why wilt thou not speak?"

The Character of Fra Angelico

Fra Giovanni was kindly to all, and moderate in all his habits, living temperately, and holding himself entirely apart from the snares of the world. He used frequently to say, that he who practised the art of painting had need of quiet, and should live without cares or anxious thoughts; adding, that he who would do the work of Christ should perpetually remain with Christ. He was never seen to display anger among the brethren of his order; a thing which appears to me most extraordinary, nay, almost incredible; if he admonished his friends, it was with gentleness and a quiet smile; and to those who sought his works, he would reply with the utmost cordiality, that they had but to obtain the assent of the prior, when he would assuredly not fail to do what they desired. In fine, this never sufficiently to be lauded father was most humble, modest, and excellent in all his words and works; in his painting he gave evidences of piety and devotion, as well as of ability, and the saints that he painted have more of the air and expression of sanctity than have those of any other master.

It was the custom of Fra Giovanni to abstain from retouching or improving any painting once finished. He altered nothing, but left all as it was done the first time, believing, as he said, that such was the will of God. It is also affirmed that he would never take the pencil in hand until he had first offered a prayer. He is said never to have painted a Crucifix without tears streaming from his eyes, and in the countenances and attitudes of his figures it is easy to perceive proof of his sincerity, his goodness, and the depth of his devotion to the religion of Christ.

The Exploits of Fra Filippo Lippi

I

It is said that Fra Filippo was much addicted to the pleasures of sense, insomuch that he would give all he possessed to secure the gratification of whatever inclination might at the moment be predominant; but if he could by no means accomplish his wishes, he would then depict the object which had attracted his attention, in his paintings, and endeavour by discoursing and reasoning with himself to diminish the violence of his inclination. It was known that, while occupied in the pursuit of his pleasures, the works undertaken by him received little or none of his attention; for which reason Cosimo de' Medici, wishing him to execute a work in his own palace, shut him up, that he might not waste his time in running about; but having endured this confinement for two days, he then made ropes with the sheets of his bed, which he cut to pieces for that purpose, and so having let himself down from a window, escaped, and for several days gave himself up to his amusements. When Cosimo found that the painter had disappeared, he caused him to be sought, and Fra Filippo at last returned to his work, but from that time forward Cosimo gave him liberty to go in and out at his pleasure, repenting greatly of having previously shut him up when he considered the danger that Fra Filippo had incurred by his folly in descending from the window; and ever afterwards, labouring to keep him to his work by kindness only, he was by this means much more promptly and effectually served by the painter, and was wont to say that the excellencies of rare genius were as forms of light and not beasts of burden.

II

Having then received a commission from the nuns of Santa Margherita, to paint a picture for the high altar of their church, he one day chanced to see the daughter of Francesco Buti, a citizen of Florence, who had been sent to the Convent, either as a novice or boarder. Fra Filippo, having given a glance at Lucrezia, for such was the name of the girl, who was exceedingly beautiful and graceful, so persuaded the nuns, that he prevailed on them to permit him to make a likeness of her, for the figure of the Virgin in the work he was executing for them. The result of this was, that the painter fell violently in love with Lucrezia, and at length found means to influence her in such a manner, that he led her away from the nuns, and on a certain day, when she had gone forth to do honour to the Cintola of our Lady, a venerated relic preserved at Prato and exhibited on that occasion, he bore her from their keeping. By this event the nuns were deeply disgraced, and the father of Lucrezia was so grievously afflicted thereat, that he never more recovered his cheerfulness, and made every possible effort to regain his child. But Lucrezia, whether retained by fear or by some other cause, would not return, but remained with Filippo, to whom she bore a son, who was also called Filippo, and who eventually became a most excellent and very famous painter like his father.

Andrea del Castagno and the "Murder" of Domenico Veneziano

Andrea, blinded by envy at the praises which he heard given to the abilities of Domenico, determined to rid himself of his presence, and after having reflected on various methods of accomplishing this evil design, he at length fixed on one, which he put in execution in the following manner:—

One evening, in the summer time, Domenico, taking his lute, as was his custom, went forth from Santa Maria Nuova, leaving Andrea in his room drawing, the latter having refused his invitation to accompany him to their amusements as usual, under the pretext that he had to prepare certain drawings of importance. Domenico, having thus gone forth alone to his recreations, Andrea, disguising his person, set himself to wait for his companion's return at the corner of a street; and when Domenico, on his way home, arrived at the place, he fell upon him with a certain leaden weight, and therewith crushed the lute and chest of his victim with repeated blows. But even this did not appear to him sufficient for his purpose, and with the same weapon he struck his victim heavily on the head; then, leaving him lying on the ground, he returned to his room in Santa Maria Nuova, where, having locked the door, he sat down to his drawing as he had been left by Domenico.

Meanwhile the noise had been heard, and the servants hastening out, and, finding what had happened, went first to call Andrea, and to relate the bad news to the traitor and murderer himself; who, running to where the others all stood around Domenico, was not to be consoled, nor did he cease from crying, "Alas my brother! alas my brother!" Finally, the murdered man expired in his arms, and in spite of all the efforts made to discover who had committed that homicide, it was never known, nor would the truth ever have been made manifest, if Andrea himself, finding his death approaching, had not divulged it in confession.

This famous story is a classic example of the unreliability of much of Vasari's biographical detail. Andrea del Castagno, the "murderer," died in 1457; Domenico Veneziano, the "victim," died in 1461.

Andrea of the Hanged Men

In the year 1478, when Giuliano de' Medici was killed, and Lorenzo his brother wounded in the church of Santa Maria del Fiore, by the Pazzi and others, their adherents and fellow conspirators; it was resolved by the Signoria, that all who had taken part in the plot should be painted as traitors on the façade of the palace of the Podesta: whereupon, the work being offered to Andrea del Castagno, he, as the servant of, and much beholden to the house of Medici, accepted the office very willingly; and having set himself to the work, he executed it in such a manner that it was a perfect wonder. It would indeed not be possible adequately to describe the art and judgement displayed in these figures, for the most part copied from the life, and hung up by the feet in the strangest attitudes, which were infinitely varied and exceedingly fine. The approbation which this work obtained from the whole city, but more especially from those who were well versed in the art of painting, caused the artist to be no longer named Andrea del Castagno, but he was ever afterwards called Andrea degl' Impiccati.

Vasari has here transposed an incident of 1434 to the Pazzi con-spiracy of 1478, twenty-one years after Andrea's death.

The Ghirlandaio Brothers Uphold the Dignity of Painting

For the abbey of Passignano, which belongs to the monks of Vallombrosa, Domenico executed certain works in company with his brother David and Bastiano of Gemignano. The two latter, finding themselves ill-treated and poorly fed by the monks before the arrival of Domenico, had recourse to the abbot, requesting him to give orders that they should have better food, since it was not decent that they should be treated like bricklayers' hod-men. This the abbot promised them to do, and excused himself by saying, that what they complained of had happened more from the ignorance of the monk who had the charge of strangers, than from evil intention. But when Domenico arrived, the same mismanagement still continued; whereupon David, seeking the abbot once more, apologized for pressing him, with the assurance that he did it not on his own account but for his brother's sake, whose merits and abilities deserved consideration. The abbot, however, like an ignorant man as he was, made no other reply. In the evening, there-fore, when they sat down to supper, the monk entrusted with the care of strangers, came as usual with a board, whereupon were porringers in the usual fashion, and coarse meats fit only for common labourers. Whereupon David rose in a rage, threw the soup over the friar, and seizing the great loaf from the board, he fell upon him therewith, and belaboured him in such a fashion that he was carried to his cell more dead than alive. The abbot, who had already gone to bed, arose on hearing the clamour, believing the monastery to be falling down, and finding the monk in a bad condition, began to reproach David. But the latter replied in a fury, bidding him begone from his sight, and declaring the talents of Domenico to be worth more than all the hogs of abbots of his sort that had ever inhabited the monastery. The abbot being thus brought to his senses, did his best from that moment to treat them like honourable men as they were.

Domenico Ghirlandaio: the Insatiable Painter

This artist found so much pleasure in his labours, and was so willing to satisfy all who desired to possess his works, that he commanded his scholars to accept whatever commission was brought to the *Bottega,* even though it were hoops for women's baskets, declaring that if they would not paint them he would do it himself, to the end that none might depart from his workshops dissatisfied. But when household cares were laid upon him, he complained bitterly, and committed the charge of all expenditure to his brother David, saying to him, "Leave me to work and do thou provide, for now that I have begun to get into the spirit and comprehend the method of this art, I grudge that they do not commission me to paint the whole circuit of all the walls of Florence with stories"; thus proving the resolved and invincible character of his mind in whatever he undertook.

Raphael's Genius Astounds and Kills

Having packed up his work . . . Raphael addressed it to the care of Francia, who, as being his friend, was to see it placed on the altar of the chapel for which the picture was destined: with the proper framework and ornaments, which had been already prepared for it. This was an office which pleased Francia greatly, since he would thus have the long-desired opportunity of seeing the works of Raphael. Wherefore, having opened the letter written to him by the latter, wherein that master begged him to repair any scratch that might be found on the painting, and further requested, that, if he perceived any defect, he would, as a friend, correct it for him, Francia caused the picture, with the greatest joy, to be taken into a good light, and had it removed from its case. But such was the astonishment it caused him, and so great was his admiration for it, that, perceiving his own error and the foolish presumption with which he had weakly believed in his own superiority, he took it deeply to heart, and, falling ill with his grief, in a very short time he died of its effects.

The Painter's Grief Dominated by his Art

It is related of Luca Signorelli that he had a son killed in Cortona, a youth of singular beauty in face and person, whom he had tenderly loved. In his deep grief, the father caused the child to be despoiled of his clothing, and, with extraordinary constancy of soul, uttering no complaint and shedding no tear, he painted the portrait of his dead child, to the end that he might still have the power of contemplating, by means of the work of his own hands, that which nature had given him, but which an adverse fortune had taken away.

The story has a nineteenth-century parallel in Claude Monet's account of how, watching distraught beside the deathbed of his young wife, he became aware to his horror that he was observing with a painter's eye the changing colors of her face.

The Burning of the Vanities

Now it happened at the time of which we now speak that Fra Girolamo Savonarola, of Ferrara, a renowned theologian of the order of Preachers, was in the convent of San Marco, where Baccio [Fra Bartolommeo] attended his preaching with infinite devotion and with all the respect which he felt for the person of the preacher: he thus became closely intimate with Fra Girolamo, and spent almost all his time in the convent, having contracted a friendship with the other monks also. Girolamo meanwhile continued to preach daily; and his zeal increasing, he daily declaimed from the pulpit against licentious pictures, among other things; showing how these, with music and books of similar character, were calculated to lead the mind to evil; he also asserted his conviction, that in houses where young maidens dwelt, it was dangerous and improper to retain pictures wherein there were undraped figures. Now it was the custom in that city to erect cabins of firewood and other combustibles on the public piazza during the time of Carnival, and on the night of Shrove Tuesday, these huts being set a-blaze, the people were wont to dance around them while thus burning, men and women that is to say, joining hands, according to ancient custom, encircled these fires, with songs and dances. On the return of the Carnival following the period of which we now speak, however, Fra Girolamo's exhortations had so powerfully affected the people, that instead of these accustomed dances, they brought pictures and works in sculpture, many by the most excellent masters—all which they cast into the fire, with books and musical instruments, which were burnt in like manner—a most lamentable destruction; and more particularly as to the paintings. To this pile brought Baccio della Porta all his studies and drawings which he had made from the nude figure, when they were consumed in the flames. His example was followed by Lorenzo di Credi, and by many others, who received the appellation of the *Piagnoni* [the weepers].

> *This notorious bonfire of art took place in 1496, when Savonarola was at the height of his prestige and power in Florence. He had begun his public preaching in 1491, and the death of Lorenzo the Magnificent in 1492 and the expulsion of the Medici in 1494 had made him master of Florence. In 1498 he fell from power and was hanged and burned. The words of Savonarola had a powerful effect on the aging Botticelli and the youthful Michelangelo, lying dormant in Michelangelo for many years, only to take strong hold of him in the latter part of his career.*

Andrea del Sarto as Embezzler

The promptitude of Andrea in his works, and the easy character of the man, who was satisfied with everything around him, were both agreeable to King Francis [I]; he gave very great satisfaction to the whole court also, painting numerous pictures and executing various works of different kinds for the nobles.

And now, had Andrea del Sarto only reflected on all that he had escaped from, and duly weighed the advantageous character of that position to which fate had conducted him, I make no doubt but that, to say nothing of riches, he might have attained to great honours. But one day being employed on the figure of a St. Jerome doing penance, which he was painting for the mother of the king, there came to him certain letters from Florence; these were written to him by his wife, and from that time (whatever may have been the cause) he began to think of leaving France; he asked permission to that effect from the French king accordingly, saying that he desired to return to Florence, but that when he had arranged his affairs in that city, he would return without fail to his majesty: he added, that when he came back his wife should accompany him, to the end that he might remain in France the more quietly; and that he would bring with him pictures and sculptures of great value. The king, confiding in these promises, gave him money for the purchase of those pictures and sculptures, Andrea taking an oath on the gospels to return within the space of a few months, and that done he departed to his native city.

He arrived safely in Florence, enjoying the society of his beautiful wife and that of his friends, with the sight of his native city during several months; but when the period specified by the king, and that at which he ought to have returned, had come and passed, he found himself at the end, not only of his own money, but what with building, indulging himself in various pleasures and doing no work, of that belonging to the French monarch also, the whole of which he had consumed. He was nevertheless determined to return to France, but the prayers and tears of his wife had more power than his own necessities, or the faith which he had pledged to the king: he remained therefore in Florence, and the French monarch was so greatly angered thereby, that for a long time after he would not look at the paintings of Florentine masters, and declared that if Andrea ever fell into his hands he would have no regard whatever to the distinction of his endowments, but would do him more harm than he had before done him good. Andrea del Sarto remained in Florence therefore, as we have said, and from a highly eminent position he sank to the very lowest, procuring a livelihood and passing his time as he best might.

This is one of the best known of all Vasari's anecdotes, and forms a central feature of Browning's great poem. While not so demonstrably false as the account of Andrea del Castagno's murderous wrath, it is still highly dubious. What does seem fairly certain, however, is that Francis I was angered by Andrea del Sarto's precipitate return to Florence.

The Divine Leonardo

The richest gifts are occasionally seen to be showered, as by celestial influence, on certain human beings, nay, they sometimes supernaturally and marvellously congregate in one sole person; beauty, grace, and talent being united in such a manner, that to whatever the man thus favoured may turn himself, his every action is so divine as to leave all other men far behind him, and manifestly to prove that he has been specially endowed by the hand of God himself, and has not obtained his pre-eminence by human teaching, or the power of man. This was seen and acknowledged by all men in the case of Leonardo da Vinci, in whom, to say nothing of his beauty of person, which yet was such that it has never been sufficiently extolled, there was a grace beyond expression which was rendered manifest without thought or effort in every act and deed, and who had besides so rare a gift of talent and ability, that to whatever subject he turned his attention, however difficult, he presently made himself absolute master of it. Extraordinary power was in his case conjoined with remarkable facility, a mind of regal boldness and magnanimous daring; his gifts were such that the celebrity of his name extended most widely, and he was held in the highest estimation, not in his own time only, but also, and even to a greater extent, after his death, nay, this he has continued, and will continue to be by all succeeding ages.

Truly admirable, indeed, and divinely endowed was Leonardo da Vinci.

This is remarkable testimony to the impact of Leonardo's creative personality on his own time, coming as it does from a partisan of Michelangelo. Nowhere is Vasari more a man of the Renaissance than in his treatment of Leonardo, with its vision of the perfect man, supreme in beauty, grace, and strength, as well as in intellect and talent.

Verrocchio and Leonardo's Angel

Andrea Verrocchio . . . painted . . . the Baptism of Christ by St. John, and being assisted in it by Leonardo da Vinci, then a youth and Andrea's disciple, the former painted therein the figure of an angel, which was much superior to the other parts of the picture. Perceiving this, Andrea resolved never again to take pencil in hand, since Leonardo, though still so young, had acquitted himself in that art better than he had done.

Looking at this picture, one can easily understand how Verrocchio could have despaired, for the angel at the left—now universally accepted as Leonardo's—makes everything else in the picture seem wooden and lifeless.

Leonardo and the Birds

In conversation Leonardo was indeed so pleasing that he won the hearts of all hearers, and though possessing so small a patrimony only that it might almost be called nothing, while he yet worked very little, he still constantly kept many servants and horses, taking extraordinary delight in the latter: he was indeed fond of all animals, ever treating them with infinite kindness and consideration; as a proof of this it is related, that when he passed places where birds were sold, he would frequently take them from their cages, and having paid the price demanded for them by the sellers, would then let them fly into the air, thus restoring to them the liberty they had lost.

This charming anecdote would seem to indicate a tenderheartedness in Leonardo not otherwise manifested in his writings or life. It may also, as many writers have speculated, simply show his passionate interest in the observation of flight.

The Painting of the Last Supper

It is related that the Prior of the Monastery was excessively importunate in pressing Leonardo to complete the picture; he could in no way comprehend wherefore the artist should sometimes remain half a day together absorbed in thought before his work, without making any progress that he could see; this seemed to him a strange waste of time, and he would fain have had him work away as he could make the men do who were digging in his garden, never laying the pencil out of his hand. Not content with seeking to hasten Leonardo, the Prior even complained to the Duke, and tormented him to such a degree that the latter was at length compelled to send for Leonardo, whom he courteously entreated to let the work be finished, assuring him nevertheless that he did so because compelled by the importunities of the Prior. Leonardo, knowing the Prince to be intelligent and judicious, determined to explain himself fully on the subject with him, although he had never chosen to do so with the Prior. He therefore discoursed with him at some length respecting art, and made it perfectly manifest to his comprehension, that men of genius are sometimes producing most when they seem to be labouring least, their minds being occupied in the eludication of their ideas, and in the completion of those conceptions to which they afterwards give form and expression with the hand. He further informed the Duke that there were still wanting to him two heads, one of which, that of the Saviour, he could not hope to find on earth, and had not yet attained the power of presenting it to himself in imagination, with all that perfection of beauty and celestial grace which appeared to him to be demanded for the due representation of the Divinity incarnate. The second head still wanting was that of Judas, which also caused him some anxiety, since he did not think it possible to imagine a form of feature that should properly render the countenance of a man who, after so many benefits received from his master, had possessed a heart so depraved as to be capable of betraying his Lord and the Creator of the world; with regard to that second, however, he would make search, and, after all—if he could find no better, he need never be at any great loss, for there would always be the head of that troublesome and impertinent Prior. This made the Duke laugh with all his heart, he declared Leonardo to be completely in the right, and the poor Prior, utterly confounded, went away to drive on the digging in his garden, and left Leonardo in peace.

> *It is instructive to compare this, with its emphasis on the hidden workings of the creative imagination, with Vasari's anecdote of Giotto and the Circle, where technical facility is regarded as the signature of genius.*

The *"Mona Lisa"*

For Francesco del Giocondo, Leonardo undertook to paint the portrait of Mona Lisa, his wife, but, after loitering over it for four years, he finally left it unfinished. This work is now in the possession of King

Francis of France, and is at Fontainebleau. Whoever shall desire to see how far art can imitate nature, may do so to perfection in this head, wherein every peculiarity that could be depicted by the utmost subtlety of the pencil has been faithfully reproduced. The eyes have the lustrous brightness and moisture which is seen in life, and around them are those pale, red, and slightly livid circles, also proper to nature, with the lashes, which can only be copied, as these are, with the greatest difficulty; the eyebrows also are represented with the closest exactitude, where fuller and where more thinly set, with the separate hairs delineated as they issue from the skin, every turn being followed and all the pores exhibited in a manner that could not be more natural than it is: the nose, with its beautiful and delicately roseate nostrils, might be easily believed to be alive; the mouth, admirable in its outline, has the lips uniting the rose-tints of their colour with that of the face, in the utmost perfection, and the carnation of the cheek does not appear to be painted, but truly of flesh and blood: he who looks earnestly at the pit of the throat cannot but believe that he sees the beating of the pulses, and it may be truly said that this work is painted in a manner well calculated to make the boldest master tremble, and astonishes all who behold it, however well accustomed to the marvels of art. Mona Lisa was exceedingly beautiful, and while Leonardo was painting her portrait, he took the precaution of keeping some one constantly near her, to sing or play on instruments, or to jest and otherwise amuse her, to the end that she might continue cheerful, and so that her face might not exhibit the melancholy expression often imparted by painters to the likenesses they take. In this portrait of Leonardo's, on the contrary, there is so pleasing an expression, and a smile so sweet, that while looking at it one thinks it rather divine than human, and it has ever been esteemed a wonderful work, since life itself could exhibit no other appearance.

This gives us the "Mona Lisa" as it must have been before the combined actions of time, dirt, and varnish had virtually destroyed its original coloring. Vasari's description of the eyebrows, however, raises something of a mystery. The "Mona Lisa" today has, and seems always to have had, the plucked eyebrows of a Florentine lady of her time.

The Pride of Leonardo

Leonardo da Vinci was a man of very high spirit, and was very generous in all his actions: it is related of him that, having once gone to the bank to receive the salary which Piero Soderini caused to be paid to him every month, the cashier was about to give him certain paper packets of pence, but Leonardo refused to receive them, remarking, at the same time, "I am no penny-painter."

This story, whether true or not, is a vivid illustration of the new conception of the artist's status that both Leonardo and Michelangelo shared and for which they were mainly instrumental in securing acceptance: the "fine artist" rather than the "penny-painter."

The Follies of Leonardo

Leonardo . . . having composed a kind of paste from wax, made of this, while it was still in its half-liquid state, certain figures of animals, entirely hollow and exceedingly slight in texture, which he then filled with air. When he blew into these figures he could make them fly through the air, but when the air within had escaped from them they fell to the earth. One day the vine-dresser of the Belvedere found a very curious lizard, and for this creature Leonardo constructed wings, made from the skins of other lizards, flayed for the purpose; into these wings he put quicksilver, so that when the animal walked, the wings moved also, with a tremulous motion: he then made eyes, horns, and a beard for the creature, which he tamed and kept in a case: he would then show it to the friends who came to visit him, and all who saw it ran away terrified. He more than once, likewise, caused the intestines of a sheep to be cleansed and scraped until they were brought into such a state of tenuity that they could be held within the hollow of the hand, having then placed in a neighboring chamber a pair of blacksmith's bellows, to which he had made fast one end of the intestines, he would blow into them until he caused them to fill the whole room, which was a very large one, insomuch that whoever might be therein was compelled to take refuge in a corner: he thus showed them transparent and full of wind, remarking that, whereas they had previously been contained within a small compass, they were now filling all space, and this, he would say, was a fit emblem of talent or genius. He made numbers of these follies in various kinds, occupied himself much with mirrors and optical instruments, and made the most singular experiments in seeking oils for painting, and varnishes to preserve the work when executed.

A number of these "follies" obviously served an experimental purpose for Leonardo. Some of them, on the other hand, sprang from the Renaissance passion for curious inventions, toys, and allegorical devices. It is useless to regret the time Leonardo wasted on such amusements: they were a necessary part of his life.

Michelangelo: the God-Given Genius

While the best and most industrious artists were labouring, by the light of Giotto and his followers, to give the world examples of such power as the benignity of their stars and the varied character of their fantasies enabled them to command, and while desirous of imitating the perfection of Nature by the excellence of Art, they were struggling to attain that high comprehension which many call intelligence, and were universally toiling, but for the most part in vain, the Ruler in Heaven was pleased to turn the eyes of his clemency towards earth, and perceiving the fruitlessness of so many labours, the ardent studies pursued without any result, and the presumptuous self-sufficiency of men, which is farther from truth than is darkness from light, he resolved, by way of delivering us from such great errors, to send to the world a spirit endowed with universality of power in each art, and in every profession, one capable of showing by himself alone what is the perfection of art in the sketch, the outline, the shadows, or the lights, one who could give relief to Paintings, and with an upright judgement could operate as perfectly in Sculpture; nay, who was so highly accomplished in Architecture also, that he was able to render our habitations secure and commodious, healthy and cheerful, well-proportioned, and enriched with the varied ornaments of art.

The Almighty Creator was also pleased to accompany the above with the comprehension of the true Philosophy and the adornment of graceful Poesy, to the end that the world might select and admire in him an extraordinary example of blamelessness in life and every action, as well as of perfection in all his works: insomuch that he might be considered by us to be of a nature rather divine than human. And as the Supreme Ruler perceived that in the execution of all these sublime arts, Painting, Sculpture, and Architecture, the Tuscan genius has ever been raised high above all others, the men of that country displaying more zeal in study, and more constantly in labour, than any other people of Italy, so did he resolve to confer the privilege of his birth on Florence, as worthy above all other cities to be his country, and as justly meriting that the perfections of every art should be exhibited to the world by means of one who should be her citizen.

This extraordinary statement forms the opening paragraphs of Vasari's life of Michelangelo, by far the longest and most valuable of the Lives *in the Second Edition. It is, of course, the work of an idolator; but so firmly does Vasari believe in the divine origin of great artistic genius that he uses very similar terms in the characterization of Leonardo da Vinci given above.*

Michelangelo and Lorenzo the Magnificent

Lorenzo the Magnificent retained at that time the Sculptor Bertoldo at his garden on the Piazza, not so much as Curator and Guardian of the many fine antiquities collected there at great cost, as because Lorenzo desired to form a good School of Painters and Sculptors; wherefore he wished that the students should have for their chief and guide the above-named Bertoldo, who had been a disciple of Donat[ell]o. . . To this end he requested Domenico Ghirlandaio to send to the garden any youth whom he might find disposed to the study of sculpture, when Lorenzo promised to provide for his progress, hoping thus to create, so to speak, such artists as should do honour to his city.

By Domenico, therefore, were presented to him among others, Michelagnolo and Francesco Granacci, as excellent for this purpose. They went to the garden accordingly, and found there Torrigiano, a youth of the Torrigiani family, who was executing in terra certain figures in full relief which Bertoldo had given him. Seeing this, and aroused to emulation, Michelagnolo began to attempt the same; when Lorenzo, perceiving his fine abilities, conceived great hope of his future success, and he, much encouraged, took a piece of marble, after having been there but a few days, and set himself to copy the head of an old Faun from the antique. The nose of the original was much injured, the mouth was represented laughing, and this Michelagnolo, who had never before touched the chisel or marble, did in fact copy in such a manner, that the Magnifico was utterly amazed. Lorenzo, furthermore, perceived that the youth had departed to a certain extent from the original, having opened the mouth according to his own fancy, so that the tongue and all the teeth were in view; he then remarked in a jesting manner to the boy, "Thou shouldst have remembered that old folks never retain all their teeth, some of them are always wanting." Michelagnolo, who loved that Signor, as much as he respected him, believed in his simplicity that Lorenzo had spoken in earnest, and no sooner saw his back turned than he broke out a tooth, filling the gum in such sort as to make it seem that the tooth had dropped out, he then waited impatiently the return of the Signor. When the latter saw what was done he was much amazed, and often laughed at the circumstance with his friends, to whom he related it as a marvel, resolving meanwhile to assist Michelagnolo and put him forward.

He sent for Lodovico, therefore, requesting the latter to entrust the youth to his care, and saying that he would treat him as a son of his own, to which Lodovico consented gladly; when Lorenzo gave orders that a room in his own house should be prepared for Michelagnolo, and caused him to eat at his own table with his sons and other persons of worth and quality.

Michelangelo and the Statute of Snow

It is said that Piero de' Medici, the heir of Lorenzo, who had been long intimate with Michelagnolo, often sent for him when about to purchase cameos or other antiques; and that, one winter, when much snow fell in Florence, he caused Michelagnolo to make in his court a Statue of Snow, which was exceedingly beautiful. His father, seeing him thus honoured for his abilities, and beginning to perceive that he was esteemed by the great, now began to clothe him in a more stately manner than he had before done.

> *Fictioneers have made a great to-do about the deliberate humiliation visited on Michelangelo by this commission. But as Vasari's tone shows, there was no humiliation intended or felt. Leonardo,*

*we may remind ourselves, made mechanical toys for the Duke of
Milan, and Shakespeare, at the end of his career as playwright in
1613, designed an impresa[1] to be carried at a tilt by Lord Rutland.*

Michelangelo as Manufacturer of a Fake Antique

He commenced a Sleeping Cupid, also in marble and the size of
life. This being finished was shown as a fine work, by means of Baldassare del Milanese to Pier-Francesco, who having declared it beautiful,
Baldassare then said to Michelagnolo, "I am certain that, if you bury
this Statue for a time, and then send it to Rome so treated, that it may
look old, you may get much more for it than could be obtained here;"
and this Michelagnolo is said to have done, as indeed he very easily
could, that or more, but others declare that it was Milanese who, having
taken this Cupid to Rome, there buried it, and afterwards sold it as an
antique to the Cardinal San Giorgio for two hundred crowns . . . Cardinal San Giorgio had, meanwhile, discovered that the Cupid had been
made in Florence, and having ascertained the whole truth, he compelled Milanese to return the money and take back the Statue . . . San
Giorgio, meanwhile, incurred no small ridicule and even censure in
the matter, he not having been able to appreciate the merit of the
work; for this consisted in its absolute perfection, wherein, if a modern
work be equal to the ancient, wherefore not value it as highly? for is
it not a mere vanity to think more of the name than the fact? But men
who regard the appearance more than the reality, are to be found in all
times.

*Vasari's comment is undoubtedly true, but somewhat beside the
point. Michelangelo was guilty of sharp practice, and the Cardinal
had been cheated.*

Michelangelo's First Pietà

The love and care which Michelagnolo had given to this group
were such that he there left his name—a thing which he never did again
for any work—on the cincture while girdles the robe of Our Lady; for
it happened one day that Michelagnolo, entering the place where it

---

[1] A device or emblem or motto.

was erected, found a large assemblage of strangers from Lombardy there, who were praising it highly; one of these asking who had done it, was told "Our Hunchback of Milan;" hearing which, Michelagnolo remained silent, although surprised that his work should be attributed to another. But one night he repaired to Saint Peter's with a light and his chisels, to engrave his name as we have said on the figure.

The Battle of Cascina

When the renowned painter, Leonardo da Vinci, was painting in the Great Hall of the Council, as we have related in his Life, Piero Soderini, who was then Gonfaloniere, moved by the extraordinary ability which he perceived in Michelagnolo, caused him to be entrusted with one portion of that Hall, when our artist finished a façade (whereon he represented the War of Pisa), in competition with Leonardo. For this work Michelagnolo secured a room in the Hospital of the Dyers at Sant' Onofrio; and here he commenced a very large Cartoon, but would never permit any one to see it in progress. The work exhibited a vast number of nude figures bathing in the River Arno, as men do in hot days, and at this moment the enemy is heard to be attacking the Camp. The soldiers who were bathing, spring forth in haste to seize their arms, which many are portrayed by the divine hand of Michelagnolo as hurriedly doing. Some are affixing their cuirasses or other portions of their armour, while others are already mounted and commencing the battle on horseback.

Among the figures in this work was that of an old man who, to shelter himself from the heat, has wreathed a garland of ivy round his head, and, seated on the earth, is labouring to draw on his stockings, but is impeded by the humidity of his limbs. Hearing the sound of the drums and the cries of the soldiers, he is struggling violently to get one of the stockings on, the action of the muscles and distortion of the mouth evince the zeal of his efforts, and prove him to be toiling all over, even to the points of his feet. There were drummers, and other figures also, hastening to the Camp with their clothes in their arms, all displaying the most singular attitudes; some were standing, others kneeling or stooping forward, or half-suspended between all these positions; some were falling down, others springing high in the air and exhibiting the most difficult foreshortenings. There were innumerable groups besides, all sketched in different manners, some of the figures

being merely outlined in charcoal, others shaded off, some with the
features clearly defined, and lights thrown in, Michelagnolo desiring
to show the extent of his knowledge in that vocation; and of a truth
the artists were struck with amazement, perceiving, as they did, that
the master had in that Cartoon laid open to them the very highest
resources of art: nay, there are some who still declare that they have
never seen anything equal to that work, either from his own hand or
that of any other, and they do not believe that the genius of any other
man will ever more attain to such perfection. Nor does this appear to
be exaggerated, since all who have designed from and copied that Cartoon (as it was the habit for both natives and strangers to do), have
finally become excellent in Art.

*This is worth giving at length; for the "Battle of Cascina," which
Michelangelo never brought beyond the cartoon or preparatory
drawing stage (even the cartoon was soon destroyed), was an
epochal event in the history of art and served, as Vasari indicates,
as a school for a whole generation of artists. It survives only in
descriptions and copies.*

Michelangelo and Pope Julius II

He sometimes complained of the manner in which the Pope hastened
forward the work [of the Sistine Chapel ceiling], seeing that he was
thereby prevented from giving it the finish which he would have desired to bestow; His Holiness constantly inquiring when it would be
completed. On one occasion, therefore, Michelagnolo replied, "It will
be finished when I shall have done all that I believed required to satisfy
Art." "And we command," rejoined the Pontiff, "that you satisfy our
wish to have it done quickly;" adding finally, that if it were not at once
completed, he would have him Michelagnolo, thrown headlong from
the scaffolding.

The Sistine Chapel Ceiling Frescoes

Bramante, who was the friend and kinsman of Raffaello, and but
little disposed to befriend Michelagnolo, availed himself of his absence
to influence the mind of Julius, whom he saw to be much inclined to

CREATION OF MAN—MICHELANGELO   (*Sistine Chapel, Rome*)

works of Sculpture, and hoping so to contrive that, on the return of Michelagnolo, His Holiness should no longer think of completing the Sepulchre, Bramante suggested that for a man to prepare his tomb during life was an evil augury and a kind of invitation to death. At a word, the Pontiff was persuaded to employ Michelagnolo on his return in the painting of that Chapel, which had been constructed in the Palace and at the Vatican, in memory of his uncle Pope Sixtus. Bramante and the other rivals of Michelagnolo, thinking they should thus detach him from his Sculpture, in which they saw that he was perfect, and throw him into despair, they being convinced that by compelling him to paint in fresco they should also bring him to exhibit works of less perfection, (he having but little experience in that branch of art), and thus prove himself inferior to Raphael. Or even supposing him to succeed in the work, it was almost certain that he would be so much enraged against the Pope as to secure the success of their purpose, which was to rid themselves of his presence.

> *Bramante was, for Vasari, the villain constantly conspiring against his hero; in this case, satisfyingly, the villain ultimately was hoist with his own petard.*

Some Sayings of Michelangelo

I *On Popular Judgment*

Going to see a work in sculpture which was about to be fixed in its place, the sculptor took great pains to arrange the lights, that the work might be seen well, when Michelagnolo said:—"Do not trouble yourself; the principal question is, how it will bear the light of the Piazza,"—meaning to imply that when a work is given to public view, the people judge it, whether good or bad.

II *On Originality in Art*

A painter had executed a story, for which he had taken so many parts from drawings and other pictures, that there was nothing in it which was not copied: this being shown to Michelagnolo, and his opinion requested, he made answer, "It is very well; but at the day of Judgement, when every body shall retake its own limbs, what will this Story do, for then it will have nothing remaining?"—a warning to those who would practise art that they should do something for themselves.

III *On Marriage for the Artist*

A priest, who was his friend, said to him, " 'Tis a pity that you have not married, that you might have left children to inherit the fruit of these honourable toils;" when Michelagnolo replied, "I have only too much of a wife in my art, and she has given me trouble enough; as to my children, they are the works that I shall leave; and if they are not worth much, they will at least live for some time. Woe to Lorenzo Ghiberti, if he had not made the gates of San Giovanni; for his children and grandchildren have sold or squandered all that he left; but the gates are still in their place."

IV *On His Old Age*

Vasari was sent one night by Pope Julius III. to the house of Michelagnolo for a design, and the master was then working at the Pietà in marble which he afterwards broke, knowing by the knock, who stood at the door, he descended with a lamp in his hand, and having ascertained what Vasari wanted, he sent Urbino for the drawing, and fell into conversation on other matters. Vasari meanwhile turned his eyes on a Leg of the Christ on which Michelagnolo was working and endeavouring to alter it; but to prevent Vasari from seeing this, he suffered the lamp to fall from his hand, and they remained in darkness. He then called to Urbino to bring a light, and stepping beyond the enclosure in which was the work, he remarked: "I am so old that death often pulls me by the cape, and bids me go with him; some day I shall fall myself, like this lamp, and the light of life will be extinguished."

Vasari as Critic

I *Painting and Poetry*

He who knows how closely, not only painting, but all the arts of design resemble poetry, knows also that verse proceeding from the poetic *furor* is the only good and true poesy: in like manner the works of men excellent in the arts of design, are much better when produced by the force of a sudden inspiration, than when they are the result of long beating about, and gradually spinning forth with pains and labour. Whoever has the clear idea of what he desires to produce in his mind, as all ought to have from the first instant, will ever march confidently and with readiness towards the perfection of the work which he proposes to execute.

> *This linkage of painting and poetry is a favorite theme of Renaissance criticism, and derives ultimately from the Latin poet Horace's "ut pictura poesis." One of the reasons for this emphasis, and particularly for the stress on inspiration in painting, was undoubtedly the desire to raise the painter to the dignity and intellectual status of the poet.*

II *The Overuse of Perspective*

Paolo Uccello would have proved himself the most original and inventive genius ever devoted to the art of painting, from the time of Giotto downwards, had he bestowed but half the labour on the delineation of men and animals that he lost and threw away over the minutiæ of perspective. For, although these studies are meritorious and good in their way, yet he who is addicted to them beyond measure, wastes his time, exhausts his intellect, and weakens the force of his conceptions, insomuch that he frequently diminishes the fertility and readiness of his resources, which he renders ineffectual and sterile. Nay, whoever bestows his attention on these points, rather than on the delineation of the living figure, will frequently derive from his efforts a dry and angular hardness of manner, which is a very common result of too close a consideration of minute points . . . It is only when the spirit of inspiration is roused, when the intellect demands to be in action, that effectual labour is secured; then only are thoughts worthy of expression conceived, and things great, excellent, and sublime accomplished.

III   *The Realism of Masaccio*

In the picture [in the Brancacci Chapel] which represents St. Peter administering the rite of Baptism, there is a figure which has always been most highly celebrated; it is that of a naked youth, among those who are baptized, and who is shivering with the cold. This is in all respects so admirable and in so fine a manner, that it has ever since been held in reverence and admiration by all artists, whether of those times or of a later period. This chapel has indeed been continually frequented by an infinite number of students and masters, for the sake of the benefit to be derived from these works, in which there are still some heads so beautiful and lifelike, that we may safely affirm no artist of that period to have approached so nearly to the manner of the moderns as did Masaccio. His works do indeed merit all the praise they have received, and the rather as it was by him that the path was opened to the excellent manner prevalent in our own times; to the truth of which we have testimony in the fact that all the most celebrated sculptors and painters since Masaccio's day have become excellent and illustrious by studying their art in this chapel.

IV   *The St. George of Donatello*

For the Guild of Armourers, Donatello executed a most animated figure of St. George, in his armour. The brightness of youthful beauty, generosity, and bravery shine forth in his face; his attitude gives evidence of a proud and terrible impetuosity; the character of the saint is indeed expressed most wonderfully, and life seems to move within that stone. It is certain that in no modern figure has there yet been seen so much animation, nor so life-like a spirit in marble, as nature and art have combined to produce by the hand of Donato in this statue.

V   *Piero della Francesca's "Dream of Constantine"*

Superior to all besides [in the Arezzo frescoes], whether for conception or execution, is the representation of Night, as given by this master: in this picture is an angel; the figure, admirably foreshortened, is descending with the head downwards, bearing the insignia of Victory to Constantine, who is sleeping in his pavilion, watched by a chamberlain, and guarded by armed men, whose forms are obscurely seen in the darkness. These figures, with the tent, and all within a certain distance, are illumined by the light which proceeds from the angel himself, and which is managed with the utmost care and judgement. In this work, Piero della Francesca has shown the importance of copying things as they really are, and of taking nature and reality for the models; this he has done excellently well, and has thereby given later artists the opportunity of profiting by his example, and in doing so to arrive at the high position which they have attained in our day.

VI   *Fra Angelico's "Coronation of the Virgin"*

The subject is the Coronation of the Virgin by Jesus Christ: the principal figures are surrounded by a choir of angels, among whom are vast numbers of saints and holy personages, male and female. These figures are so numerous, so well executed, in attitudes so varied, and with expressions of the head so richly diversified, that one feels infinite pleasure and delight in regarding them. Nay, one is convinced that those blessed spirits can look no otherwise in heaven itself, or, to speak under correction, could not, if they had forms, appear otherwise; for all the saints, male and female, assembled here, have not only life and expression, most delicately and truly rendered, but the colouring also of the whole work would seem to have been given by the hand of a saint, or of an angel like themselves.

VII   *Theory and Practice*

Be the natural qualities of a man what they may, his judgement can never be brought to perfection if he be deprived of the advantages resulting from the accompaniment of learning . . . Theory, when separated from practice, is, for the most part, found to avail very little; but when theory and practice chance to be happily united in the same person, nothing can be more suitable to the life and vocation of artists, as well because art is rendered much richer and more perfect by the aid of science, as because the councils and writings of learned artists have, in themselves, a greater efficacy, and obtain a higher degree of credit, than can be accorded to the words or works of those who know nothing beyond the simple process they use, and which they put in practice, well or ill, as it may chance.

VIII *Art as Imitation of Nature*

When artists seek no more, in the works they produce, than to imitate their masters, or some other eminent person, whose manner may please them, in the attitudes of their figures, the air of their heads, or the folds of their draperies, and confine themselves to the studying of these particulars; although with time and labour, they may execute works similar to those they admire, yet they never attain, by these means alone, to the perfection of their art, since it is obvious that he rarely presses forward who is content to follow behind. And the imitation of Nature herself is at an end for that artist whom long practice has confirmed in the manner he has adopted: for as imitation is the fixed art of representing exactly what you desire to copy, so it is a very fine thing, provided that you take pure Nature only for your guide, without the intervention of your master's manner, or that of others, who have also reduced to a manner what they first took from Nature: seeing that, however truthful and natural the works of any master may appear, it is not possible that with all his diligence, he can make it such as that it shall be equal to Nature herself, nay, even though he select the best parts, he can never set them together into a body of such perfection as to make Art outstrip Nature. Then, if this be so, it follows, that objects taken directly from Nature are alone calculated to make painting and sculpture perfect, and that he who studies artists only, and not bodies and things natural, must of necessity have his works inferior to the reality, nay, less excellent than those of the master from whom he takes his manner. Accordingly, it has happened to many of our artists, that not having studied anything but the manner of their masters, and having thus left Nature out of view, they have failed to acquire any knowledge of her, neither have they got beyond the master they have imitated, but have done great wrong to their own genius. Whereas, if they had studied the manner of their masters and natural objects at the same time, they would have produced more effectual fruits than they have now done.

> *Art as imitation, mimesis, is one of the great commonplaces of Renaissance criticism; but what gives this statement of Vasari's penetration and force is his insistence on the need for a fresh vision and a direct confrontation of nature. In his own time, the imitation*

of the manner of the great masters, especially Michelangelo, domi-
nated Italian painting; and, ironically, Vasari himself was one of
the most slavish and mannered of Michelangelo's followers. The
concept of imitation that Vasari is here warning against was to
harden into the doctrine of Neoclassicism expressed by Pope:

"Learn hence for ancient rules a just esteem;
To copy nature is to copy them."

IX   *Raphael's "Transfiguration"*

Raphael also painted a picture for the Cardinal and Vice-chancellor
Giulio de' Medici, a Transfiguration namely, which was destined to be
sent into France. This he executed with his own hand, and labouring at
it continually, he brought it to the highest perfection, depicting the
Saviour transfigured on Mount Tabor, with eleven of the disciples
awaiting him at the foot of the Mount. To these is meanwhile brought
a youth possessed of a spirit, who is also awaiting the descent of Christ,
by whom he is to be liberated from the demon. The possessed youth is
shown in a distorted attitude stretching forth his limbs, crying, rolling
his eyes, and exhibiting in every movement the suffering he endures;
the flesh, the veins, the pulses, are all seen to be contaminated by the
malignity of the spirit, the terror and pain of the possessed being rendered further manifest by his pallid colour and writhing gestures. This
figure is supported by an old man in whose widely open eyes the light
is reflected, he is embracing and seeking to comfort the afflicted boy, his
knitted brow and the expression of his face show at once the apprehension he feels, and the force with which he is labouring to combat his
fears; he looks fixedly at the Apostles as if hoping to derive courage and
consolation from their aspect. There is one woman among others in
this picture who is the principal figure therein, and who, kneeling
before the two just described, turns her head towards the apostles, and
seems by the movement of her arms in the direction of the possessed
youth, to be pointing out his misery to their attention. The Apostles
also, some of whom are standing, some seated, and others kneeling, give
evidence of the deep compassion they feel for that great misfortune.

In this work the master has of a truth, produced figures and heads of
such extraordinary beauty, so new, so varied, and at all points so admirable, that among the many works executed by his hand, this, by the
common consent of all artists, is declared to be the most worthily renowned, the most excellent, the most divine. Whoever shall desire to see

in what manner Christ transformed into the Godhead should be represented, let him come and behold it in this picture. The Saviour is shown floating over the mount in the clear air; the figure, foreshortened, is between those of Moses and Elias, who, illumined by his radiance, awaken into life beneath the splendour of the light. Prostrate on the earth are Peter, James, and John, in attitudes of great and varied beauty, one has his head bent entirely to the ground, another defends himself with his hands from the brightness of that immense light, which proceeds from the splendour of Christ, who is clothed in vestments of snowy whiteness, his arms thrown open and the head raised towards heaven, while the essence and Godhead of all the three persons united in himself, are made apparent in their utmost perfection by the divine art of Raphael.

But as if that sublime genius had gathered all the force of his powers into one effort, whereby the glory and the majesty of art should be made manifest in the countenance of Christ; having completed that, as one who had finished the great work which he had to accomplish, he touched the pencils no more, being shortly afterwards overtaken by death.

For over three centuries, until the latter half of the nineteenth century, Raphael's "Transfiguration" remained one of the most admired of all paintings; Vasari's eloquent description of this painting is the perfect statement of the qualities that to academic critics have always represented greatness in art.

Florence: the City of the Arts

The boy [Perugino] would thus often inquire of such persons as he knew to have seen the world, in what city the best artists were formed? This question he addressed more particularly to his instructor, from whom he constantly received the same reply, namely, that Florence was the place, above all others, wherein men attain to perfection in all the arts, but more especially in painting. And to this, he said, they were impelled by three causes: first, by the censure freely expressed by so many persons and in such various modes, for the air of that city gives a natural quickness and freedom to the perceptions of men, so that they cannot content themselves with mediocrity in the works presented to them, which they always judge with reference to the honour of the good and beautiful in art, rather than with respect to, or consideration for, the man who has produced them: next, that, to obtain the means of life in Florence, a man must be industrious, which is as much as to say that he must keep his skill and judgment in perpetual activity, must be ever ready and rapid in his proceedings; must know, in short, how to gain money, seeing that Florence, not having a rich and abundant domain around her, cannot supply the means of life to those who abide within her walls, at light cost, as can be done in countries where produce abounds largely. The third cause, which is, perhaps, not less effectual than the other two, is the desire for glory and honour, which is powerfully generated by the air of that place, in the men of every profession, and whereby all who possess talent are impelled to struggle, that they may not remain in the same grade with those whom they perceive to be only men like themselves (much less will any consent to remain behind another), even though they may acknowledge such to be indeed Masters; but all labour by every means to be foremost, insomuch that some desire their own exaltation so eagerly as to become thankless for benefits, censorious of their competitors, and, in many ways, evil minded, unless that effect be prevented by natural excellence and sense of justice. It is, however, true that when a man has acquired sufficient for his purposes in Florence, if he wish to effect more than merely to live from day to day, as do the beasts that perish, and desire to become rich, he must depart from her boundaries and seek another market for the excellence of his works and for the reputation conferred by that city; as the learned derive profit from the renown obtained by their studies. For the city of Florence treats her artists as Time treats his works, which, having perfected he destroys, and, by little and little, gradually consumes.

Pater's two best-known essays in art criticism, that on "Leonardo da Vinci," written in 1869 and incorporated in the first edition of the Studies in the History of the Renaissance *in 1873; and that on "The School of Giorgione," first published in 1876 in an influential British periodical, the* Fortnightly Review, *are here given in major part. Both essays are somewhat marred by faulty attribution of paintings (these sections are largely omitted here), but they are remarkable in the accuracy and interest of much of what they say about the two artists and about art itself. Sir Kenneth Clark has written that even with the growth of knowledge since Pater's time and the accessibility since then of Leonardo's* Notebooks, *"we cannot improve on Pater's characterization." The essay on "The School of Giorgione" is particularly important for its expression of Pater's view that there are qualities in one art that cannot be effectively translated into the attributes of another art, and that each art has its own unique order of impressions. Thus, painting cannot be correctly viewed as a form of visible poetry; this amounts to a rejection of Horace's long popular maxim of "ut pictura poesis."*

At the same time, Pater stresses the possibility that one art can pass into the condition of another art, as expressed by his famous statement that "All art constantly aspires towards the condition of music." Again to quote Sir Kenneth Clark, more than other writers on art (such as Ruskin, Gautier, and Baudelaire) Pater realized that "what gave an aesthetic experience its unique value is the sensuous or intuitive perception that matter and form are one . . ."—a synthesis which is most thoroughly achieved in music.

Walter Pater
Leonardo da Vinci

In Vasari's life of Leonardo da Vinci as we now read it there are some variations from the first edition. There, the painter who has fixed the outward type of Christ for succeeding centuries was a bold speculator, holding lightly by other men's beliefs, setting philosophy above Christianity. Words of his, trenchant enough to justify this impression, are not recorded, and would have been out of keeping with a genius of which one characteristic is the tendency to lose itself in a refined and graceful mystery. The suspicion was but the time-honoured mode in which the world stamps its appreciation of one who has thoughts for himself alone, his high indifference, his intolerance of the common forms of things; and in the second edition the image was changed into something fainter and more conventional. But it is still by a certain mystery in his work, and something enigmatical beyond the usual measure of great men, that he fascinates, or perhaps half repels. His life is one of sudden revolts, with intervals in which he works not at all, or apart from the main scope of his work. By a strange fortune the pictures on which his more popular fame rested disappeared early from the world, like the "Battle of the Standard"; or are mixed obscurely with the product of meaner hands, like the "Last Supper." His type of beauty is so exotic that it fascinates a larger number than it delights, and seems more than that of any other artist to reflect ideas and views and some scheme of the world within; so that he seemed to his contemporaries to be the possessor of some unsanctified and secret wisdom; as to Michelet and others to have anticipated modern ideas. He trifles with his genius, and crowds all his chief work into a few tormented years of later life; yet he is so possessed by his genius that he passes unmoved through the most tragic events, overwhelming his country and friends, like one who comes across them by chance on some secret errand.

His *legend,* as the French say, with the anecdotes which everyone remembers, is one of the most brilliant chapters of Vasari. Later writers merely copied it, until, in 1804, Carlo Amoretti applied to it a criticism which left hardly a date fixed, and not one of those anecdotes untouched. The various questions thus raised have since that time become, one after another, subjects of special study, and mere antiquarianism has in this direction little more to do. For others remain the editing of the thirteen books of his manuscripts, and the separation by technical criticism of what in his reputed works is really his, from what is only half his, or the work of his pupils. But a lover of strange souls may still analyse for himself the impression made on him by those works, and try to reach through it a definition of the chief elements of Leonardo's genius. The *legend,* as corrected and enlarged by its critics, may now and then intervene to support the results of this analysis.

His life has three divisions—thirty years at Florence, nearly twenty years at Milan, then nineteen years of wandering, till he sinks to rest under the protection of Francis the First at the *Château de Clou.* The dishonour of illegitimacy hangs over his birth. Piero Antonio, his father, was of a noble Florentine house, of Vinci in the *Val d'Arno,* and Leonardo, brought up delicately among the true children of that house, was the love-child of his youth, with the keen, puissant nature such children often have. We see him in his boyhood fascinating all men by his beauty, improvising music and songs, buying the caged birds and setting them free, as he walked the streets of Florence, fond of odd bright dresses and spirited horses.

From his earliest years, he designed many objects, and constructed models in relief, of which Vasari mentions some of women smiling. His father, pondering over this promise in the child, took him to the workshop of Andrea del Verrocchio, then the most famous artist in Florence. Beautiful objects lay about there—reliquaries, pyxes, silver images for the pope's chapel at Rome, strange fancy-work of the middle age, keeping odd company with fragments of antiquity, then but lately discovered. Another student Leonardo may have seen there—a lad into whose soul the level light and aërial illusions of Italian sunsets had passed, in after days famous as Perugino. Verrocchio was an artist of the earlier Florentine type, carver, painter, and worker in metals, in one; designer, not of pictures only, but of all things for sacred or household use, drinking-vessels, ambries, instruments of music, making them all fair to look upon, filling the common ways of life with the reflexion of some far-off brightness; and years of patience had refined his hand till his work was now sought after from distant places.

It happened that Verrocchio was employed by the brethren of Vallombrosa to paint the "Baptism of Christ," and Leonardo was allowed to finish an angel in the left-hand corner. It was one of those moments in which the progress of a great thing—here, that of the art of Italy— presses hard on the happiness of an individual, through whose discouragement and decrease, humanity, in more fortunate persons, comes a step nearer to its final success.

For beneath the cheerful exterior of the mere well-paid craftsman, chasing brooches for the copes of *Santa Maria Novella,* or twisting metal screens for the tombs of the Medici, lay the ambitious desire to expand the destiny of Italian art by a larger knowledge and insight into things, a purpose in art not unlike Leonardo's still unconscious purpose; and often, in the modelling of drapery, or of a lifted arm, or of hair cast back from the face, there came to him something of the freer manner and richer humanity of a later age. But in this "Baptism" the pupil had surpassed the master; and Verrocchio turned away as one stunned, and as if his sweet earlier work must thereafter be distasteful to him, from the bright animated angel of Leonardo's hand.

The angel may still be seen in Florence, a space of sunlight in the cold, laboured old picture; but the legend is true only in sentiment, for painting had always been the art by which Verrocchio set least store. And as in a sense he anticipates Leonardo, so to the last Leonardo recalls the studio of Verrocchio, in the love of beautiful toys . . . and of bright variegated stones, such as the agates in the "Saint Anne," and in a hieratic preciseness and grace, as of a sanctuary swept and garnished. Amid all the cunning and intricacy of his Lombard manner this never left him. Much of it there must have been in that lost picture of "Paradise," which he prepared as a cartoon for tapestry, to be woven in the looms of Flanders. It was the perfection of the older Florentine style of miniature-painting, with patient putting of each leaf upon the trees and each flower in the grass, where the first man and woman were standing.

And because it was the perfection of that style, it awoke in Leonardo some seed of discontent which lay in the secret places of his nature. For the way to perfection is through a series of disgusts; and this picture— all that he had done so far in his life at Florence—was after all in the old slight manner. His art, if it was to be something in the world, must be weighted with more of the meaning of nature and purpose of humanity. Nature was "the true mistress of higher intelligences." He plunged, then, into the study of nature. And in doing this he followed the manner of the older students; he brooded over the hidden virtues of plants and crystals, the lines traced by the stars as they moved in the sky, over the correspondences which exist between the different orders of living things, through which, to eyes opened, they interpret each other; and for years he seemed to those about him as one listening to a voice, silent for other men.

He learned here the art of going deep, of tracking the sources of expression to their subtlest retreats, the power of an ultimate presence in the things he handled. He did not at once or entirely desert his art; only he was no longer the cheerful, objective painter, through whose soul, as through clear glass, the bright figures of Florentine life, only made a little mellower and more pensive by the transit, passed on to the white wall. He wasted many days in curious tricks of design, seeming to lose himself in the spinning of intricate devices of line and colour. He was smitten with a love of the impossible—the perforation of mountains, changing the course of rivers, raising great buildings, such as the church of *San Giovanni,* in the air; all those feats for the performance of which natural magic professed to have the key. Later writers, indeed, see in these efforts an anticipation of modern mechanics; in him they were rather dreams, thrown off by the overwrought and labouring brain. Two ideas were especially confirmed in him, as reflexes of things that had touched his brain in childhood beyond the depth of other impressions—the smiling of women and the motion of great waters.

And in such studies some interfusion of the extremes of beauty and terror shaped itself, as an image that might be seen and touched, in the mind of this gracious youth, so fixed that for the rest of his life it never left him. As if catching glimpses of it in the strange eyes or hair of chance people, he would follow such about the streets of Florence till the sun went down, of whom many sketches of his remain. Some of these are full of a curious beauty, that remote beauty which may be apprehended only by those who have sought it carefully; who, starting with acknowledged types of beauty, have refined as far upon these, as these refine upon the world of common forms. But mingled inextricably with this there is an element of mockery also; so that, whether in sorrow or scorn, he caricatures Dante even. Legions of grotesques sweep under his hand; for has not nature too her grotesques—the rent rock, the distorting lights of evening on lonely roads, the unveiled structure of man in the embryo, or the skeleton?

. . . The science of that age was all divination, clairvoyance, unsubjected to our exact modern formulas, seeking in an instant of vision to concentrate a thousand experiences. Later writers, thinking only of the well-ordered treatise on painting which a Frenchman, Raffaelle du Fresne, a hundred years afterwards, compiled from Leonardo's bewildered manuscripts, written strangely, as his manner was, from right to left, have imagined a rigid order in his inquiries. But this rigid order would have been little in accordance with the restlessness of his character; and if we think of him as the mere reasoner who subjects design to anatomy, and composition to mathematical rules, we shall hardly have that impression which those around Leonardo received from him. Poring over his crucibles, making experiments with colour, trying, by a strange variation of the alchemist's dream, to discover the secret, not of an elixir to make man's natural life immortal, but of giving immortality to the subtlest and most delicate effects of painting, he seemed to them rather the sorcerer or the magician, possessed of curious secrets and a hidden knowledge, living in a world of which he alone possessed the key. What his philosophy seems to have been most like is that of Paracelsus or Cardan; and much of the spirit of the older alchemy still hangs about it, with its confidence in short cuts and odd byways to knowledge. To him philosophy was to be something giving strange swiftness and double sight, divining the sources of springs beneath the earth or of expression beneath the human countenance, clairvoyant of occult gifts in common or uncommon things, in the reed at the brookside, or the star which draws near to us but once in a century. How, in this way, the clear purpose was overclouded, the fine chaser's hand perplexed, we but dimly see; the mystery which at no point quite lifts from Leonardo's life is deepest here. But it is certain that at one period of his life he had almost ceased to be an artist.

The year 1483—the year of the birth of Raphael and the thirty-first of Leonardo's life—is fixed as the date of his visit to Milan by the letter in which he recommends himself to Ludovico Sforza, and offers to tell him, for a price, strange secrets in the art of war. It was that Sforza who murdered his young nephew by slow poison, yet was so susceptible of religious impressions that he blended mere earthly passion with a sort of religious sentimentalism, and who took for his device the mulberry-tree—symbol, in its long delay and sudden yielding of flowers and fruit together, of a wisdom which economises all forces for an opportunity of sudden and sure effect. The fame of Leonardo had gone before him, and he was to model a colossal statue of Francesco, the first Duke of Milan. As for Leonardo himself, he came not as an artist at all, or careful of the fame of one; but as a player on the harp, a strange harp of silver of his own construction, shaped in some curious likeness to a horse's skull. The capricious spirit of Ludovico was susceptible also to the power of music, and Leonardo's nature had a kind of spell in it. Fascination is always the word descriptive of him. No portrait of his youth remains; but all tends to make us believe that up to this time some charm of voice and aspect, strong enough to balance the disadvantage of his birth, had played about him. His physical strength was great; it was said that he could bend a horseshoe like a coil of lead.

The *Duomo,* work of artists from beyond the Alps, so fantastic to the eye of a Florentine used to the mellow, unbroken surfaces of Giotto and Arnolfo, was then in all its freshness; and below, in the streets of Milan, moved a people as fantastic, changeful, and dreamlike. To Leonardo least of all men could there be anything poisonous in the exotic flowers of sentiment which grew there. It was a life of brilliant sins and exquisite amusements: Leonardo became a celebrated designer of pageants; and it suited the quality of his genius, composed, in almost equal parts, of curiosity and the desire of beauty, to take things as they came.

Curiosity and the desire of beauty—these are the two elementary forces in Leonardo's genius; curiosity often in conflict with the desire of beauty, but generating, in union with it, a type of subtle and curious grace.

The movement of the fifteenth century was two-fold; partly the Renaissance, partly also the coming of what is called the "modern spirit," with its realism, its appeal to experience. It comprehended a return to antiquity, and a return to nature. Raphael represents the return to antiquity, and Leonardo the return to nature. In this return to nature, he was seeking to satisfy a boundless curiosity by her perpetual surprises, a microscopic sense of finish by her *finesse,* or delicacy of operation, that *subtilitas naturae* which Bacon notices. So we find him often in intimate relations with men of science,—with Fra Luca

Paccioli the mathematician, and the anatomist Marc Antonio della Torre. His observations and experiments fill thirteen volumes of manuscript; and those who can judge describe him as anticipating long before, by rapid intuition, the later ideas of science. He explained the obscure light of the unilluminated part of the moon, knew that the sea had once covered the mountains which contain shells, and of the gathering of the equatorial waters above the polar.

He who thus penetrated into the most secret parts of nature preferred always the more to the less remote, what, seeming exceptional, was an instance of law more refined, the construction about things of a peculiar atmosphere and mixed lights. He paints flowers with such curious felicity that different writers have attributed to him a fondness for particular flowers, as Clement the cyclamen, and Rio the jasmin; while, at Venice, there is a stray leaf from his portfolio dotted all over with studies of violets and the wild rose. In him first appears the taste for what is *bizarre* or *recherché* in landscape; hollow places full of the green shadow of bituminous rocks, ridged reefs of trap-rock which cut the water into quaint sheets of light,—their exact antitype is in our own western seas; all the solemn effects of moving water . . . It is the landscape, not of dreams or of fancy, but of places far withdrawn, and hours selected from a thousand with a miracle of *finesse*. Through Leonardo's strange veil of sight things reach him so; in no ordinary night or day, but as in faint light of eclipse, or in some brief interval of falling rain at daybreak, or through deep water.

And not into nature only; but he plunged also into human personality, and became above all a painter of portraits; faces of a modelling more skilful than has been seen before or since, embodied with a reality which almost amounts to illusion, on the dark air. To take a character as it was, and delicately sound its stops, suited one so curious in observation, curious in invention. . . .

Sometimes this curiosity came in conflict with the desire of beauty; it tended to make him go too far below that outside of things in which art really begins and ends. This struggle between the reason and its ideas, and the senses, the desire of beauty, is the key to Leonardo's life at Milan—his restlessness, his endless re-touchings, his odd experiments with colour. How much must he leave unfinished, how much recommence! His problem was the transmutation of ideas into images. What he had attained so far had been the mastery of that earlier Florentine style, with its naïve and limited sensuousness. Now he was to entertain in this narrow medium those divinations of a humanity too wide for it, that larger vision of the opening world, which is only not too much for the great, irregular art of Shakespeare; and everywhere the effort is visible in the work of his hands. This agitation, this perpetual delay, give him an air of weariness and *ennui*. To others he seems to be aiming at an impossible effect, to do something that art, that painting, can never do. Often the expression of physical beauty at this or that point seems strained and marred in the effort, as in those heavy German foreheads—too heavy and German for perfect beauty.

For there was a touch of Germany in that genius which, as Goethe said, had "thought itself weary"—*müde sich gedacht*. What an anticipation of modern Germany, for instance, in that debate on the question whether sculpture or painting is the nobler art! But there is this difference between him and the German, that, with all that curious science, the German would have thought nothing more was needed. The name of Goethe himself reminds one how great for the artist may be the danger of overmuch science; how Goethe, who, in the *Elective Affinities* and the first part of *Faust,* does transmute ideas into images, who wrought many such transmutations, did not invariably find the spellword, and in the second part of *Faust* presents us with a mass of science which has almost no artistic character at all. But Leonardo will never work till the happy moment comes—that movement of *bien-être,* which to imaginative men is a moment of invention. On this he waits with a perfect patience; other moments are but a preparation, or after-taste of it. Few men distinguish between them as jealously as he. Hence so many flaws even in the choicest work. But for Leonardo the distinction is absolute, and, in the moment of *bien-être,* the alchemy complete: the idea is stricken into colour and imagery: a cloudy mysticism is refined to a subdued and graceful mystery, and painting pleases the eye while it satisfies the soul. . . .

About the "Last Supper," its decay and restorations, a whole literature has risen up, Goethe's pensive sketch of its sad fortunes being perhaps the best. The death in childbirth of the Duchess Beatrice was followed in Ludovico by one of those paroxysms of religious feeling which in him were constitutional. The low, gloomy Dominican church of *Saint Mary of the Graces* had been the favourite oratory of Beatrice. She had spent her last days there, full of sinister presentiments; at last it had been almost necessary to remove her from it by force; and now it was here that mass was said a hundred times a day for her repose. On the damp wall of the refectory, oozing with mineral salts, Leonardo painted the "Last Supper." Effective anecdotes were told about it, his retouchings and delays. They show him refusing to work except at the moment of invention, scornful of anyone who supposed that art could be a work of mere industry and rule, often coming the whole length of Milan to give a single touch. He painted it, not in fresco, where all must be *impromptu,* but in oils, the new method which he had been one of the first to welcome, because it allowed of so many afterthoughts, so refined a working out of perfection. It turned out that on a plastered wall no process could have been less durable. Within fifty years it had fallen into decay. And now we have to turn back to Leonardo's own studies, above all to one drawing of the central head at the *Brera,* which, in a union of tenderness and severity in the face-lines, reminds one of the monumental work of Mino da Fiesole, to trace it as it was.

Here was another effort to lift a given subject out of the range of its traditional associations. Strange, after all the mystic developments of the middle age, was the effort to see the Eucharist, not as the pale Host of the altar, but as one taking leave of his friends. Five years afterwards the young Raphael, at Florence, painted it with sweet and solemn effect in the refectory of Saint Onofrio; but still with all the mystical unreality of the school of Perugino. Vasari pretends that the central head was never finished. But finished or unfinished, or owing part of its effect to a mellowing decay, the head of Jesus does but consummate the sentiment of the whole company—ghosts through which you see the wall, faint as the shadows of the leaves upon the wall on autumn afternoons. This figure is but the faintest, the most spectral of them all.

The "Last Supper" was finished in 1497; in 1498 the French entered Milan, and whether or not the Gascon bowmen used it as a mark for their arrows, the model of Francesco Sforza certainly did not survive. What, in that age, such work was capable of being—of what nobility, amid what racy truthfulness to fact—we may judge from the bronze statue of Bartolomeo Colleoni on horseback, modelled by Leonardo's master, Verrocchio (he died of grief, it was said, because, the mould accidentally failing, he was unable to complete it), still standing in the *piazza* of Saint John and Saint Paul at Venice. Some traces of the thing may remain in certain of Leonardo's drawings, and perhaps also, by a singular circumstance, in a far-off town of France. For Ludovico became a prisoner, and ended his days at Loches in Touraine. After many years of captivity in the dungeons below, where all seems sick with barbarous feudal memories, he was allowed at last, it is said, to breathe fresher air for awhile in one of the rooms of the great tower still shown, its walls covered with strange painted arabesques, ascribed by tradition to his hand, amused a little, in this way, through the tedious years. In those vast helmets and human faces and pieces of armour, among which, in great letters, the motto *Infelix Sum* is woven in and out, it is perhaps not too fanciful to see the fruit of a wistful after-dreaming over Leonardo's sundry experiments on the armed figure of the great duke, which had occupied the two so much during the days of their good fortune at Milan.

The remaining years of Leonardo's life are more or less years of wandering. From his brilliant life at court he had saved nothing, and he returned to Florence a poor man. Perhaps necessity kept his spirit excited: the next four years are one prolonged rapture or ecstasy of invention. He painted now the pictures of the Louvre, his most authentic works, which came there straight from the cabinet of Francis the First, at Fontainebleau. One picture of his, the "Saint Anne"—not the "Saint Anne" of the Louvre, but a simple cartoon, now in London— revived for a moment a sort of appreciation more common in an earlier time, when good pictures had still seemed miraculous. For two days a crowd of people of all qualities passed in naïve excitement through the chamber where it hung, and gave Leonardo a taste of the "triumph" of Cimabue. But his work was less with the saints than with the living women of Florence. For he lived still in the polished society that he loved, and in the houses of Florence, left perhaps a little subject to light thoughts by the death of Savonarola . . . he saw Ginevra di Benci, and Lisa, the young third wife of Francesco del Giocondo. As we have seen him using incidents of sacred story, not for their own sake or as mere subjects for pictorial realisation, but as a cryptic language for fancies all his own, so now he found a vent for this thought in taking one of these languid women, and raising her, as Leda or Pomona, as Modesty or Vanity, to the seventh heaven of symbolical expression.

"La Gioconda" is, in the truest sense, Leonardo's masterpiece, the revealing instance of his mode of thought and work. In suggestiveness, only the "Melancholia" of Dürer is comparable to it; and no crude symbolism disturbs the effect of its subdued and graceful mystery. We all know the face and hands of the figure, set in its marble chair, in that circle of fantastic rocks, as in some faint light under sea. Perhaps of all ancient pictures time has chilled it least. As often happens with works in which invention seems to reach its limit, there is an element in it given to, not invented by, the master. In that inestimable folio of drawings, once in the possession of Vasari, were certain designs by Verrocchio, faces of such impressive beauty that Leonardo in his boyhood

copied them many times. It is hard not to connect with these designs of
the elder, by-past master, as with its germinal principal, the unfathomable smile, always with a touch of something sinister in it, which plays
over all Leonardo's work. Besides, the picture is a portrait. From childhood we see this image defining itself on the fabric of his dreams; and
but for express historical testimony, we might fancy that this was but
his ideal lady, embodied and beheld at last. What was the relationship
of a living Florentine to this creature of his thought? By what strange
affinities had the dream and the person grown up thus apart, and yet so
closely together? Present from the first incorporeally in Leonardo's
brain, dimly traced in the designs of Verrocchio, she is found present at
last in *Il Giocondo's* house. That there is much of mere portraiture in
the picture is attested by the legend that by artificial means, the presence of mimes and flute-players, that subtle expression was protracted
on the face. Again, was it in four years and by renewed labour never
really completed, or in four months and as by stroke of magic that the
image was projected?

The presence that rose thus so strangely beside the waters, is expressive of what in the ways of a thousand years men had come to desire.
Hers is the head upon which all "the ends of the world are come," and
the eyelids are a little weary. It is a beauty wrought out from within
upon the flesh, the deposit, little cell by cell, of strange thoughts and
fantastic reveries and exquisite passions. Set it for a moment beside one
of those white Greek goddesses or beautiful women of antiquity, and
how would they be troubled by this beauty, into which the soul with all
its maladies has passed! All the thoughts and experience of the world
have etched and moulded there, in that which they have of power to
refine and make expressive the outward form, the animalism of Greece,
the lust of Rome, the mysticism of the middle age with its spiritual
ambition and imaginative loves, the return of the Pagan world, the sins
of the Borgias. She is older than the rocks among which she sits; like
the vampire, she has been dead many times, and learned the scerets of
the grave; and has been a diver in deep seas, and keeps their fallen day
about her; and trafficked for strange webs with Eastern merchants; and,
as Leda, was the mother of Helen of Troy, and, as Saint Anne, the
mother of Mary; and all this has been to her but as the sound of lyres
and flutes, and lives only in the delicacy with which it has moulded the
changing lineaments, and tinged the eyelids and the hands. The fancy
of a perpetual life, sweeping together ten thousand experiences, is an
old one; and modern philosophy has conceived the idea of humanity as

wrought upon by, and summing up in itself, all modes of thought and life. Certainly Lady Lisa might stand as the embodiment of the old fancy, the symbol of the modern idea.

During these years at Florence Leonardo's history is the history of his art; for himself, he is lost in the bright cloud of it. The outward history begins again in 1502, with a wild journey through central Italy, which he makes as the chief engineer of Cæsar Borgia. The biographer, putting together the stray jottings of his manuscripts, may follow him through every day of it, up the strange tower of Siena, elastic like a bent bow, down to the seashore at Piombino, each place appearing as fitfully as in a fever dream.

One other great work was left for him to do, a work all trace of which soon vanished, "The Battle of the Standard," in which he had Michelangelo for his rival. The citizens of Florence, desiring to decorate the walls of the great council-chamber, had offered the work for competition, and any subject might be chosen from the Florentine wars of the fifteenth century. Michelangelo chose for his cartoon an incident of the war with Pisa, in which the Florentine soldiers, bathing in the Arno, are surprised by the sound of trumpets and run to arms. His design has reached us only in an old engraving, which helps us less perhaps than our remembrance of the background of his "Holy Family" in the Uffizi to imagine in what superhuman form, such as might have beguiled the heart of an earlier world, those figures ascended out of the water. Leonardo chose an incident from the battle of Anghiari, in which two parties of soldiers fight for a standard. Like Michelangelo's, his cartoon is lost, and has come to us only in sketches, and in a fragment of Rubens. Through the accounts given we may discern some lust of terrible things in it, so that even the horses tore each other with their teeth. And yet one fragment of it, in a drawing of his at Florence, is far different—a waving field of lovely armour, the chased edgings running like lines of sunlight from side to side. Michelangelo was twenty-seven years old; Leonardo more than fifty; and Raphael, then nineteen years of age, visiting Florence for the first time, came and watched them as they worked.

We catch a glimpse of Leonardo again, at Rome in 1514, surrounded by his mirrors and vials and furnaces, making strange toys that seemed alive of wax and quicksilver. The hesitation which had haunted him all through life, and made him like one under a spell, was upon him now with double force. No one had ever carried political indifferentism farther; it had always been his philosophy to "fly before the

storm"; he is for the Sforzas, or against them, as the tide of their fortune turns. Yet now, in the political society of Rome, he came to be
suspected of secret French sympathies. It paralysed him to find himself
among enemies; and he turned wholly to France, which had long
courted him.

France was about to become an Italy more Italian than Italy itself.
Francis the First, like Lewis the Twelfth before him, was attracted by
the *finesse* of Leonardo's work; "La Gioconda" was already in his cabinet, and he offered Leonardo the little *Château de Clou,* with its vine-
yards and meadows, in the pleasant valley of the Masse, just outside the
walls of the town of Amboise, where, especially in the hunting season,
the court then frequently resided. *A Monsieur Lyonard, peinteur du
Roy pour Amboyse*—so the letter of Francis the First is headed. It
opens a prospect, one of the most interesting in the history of art,
where, in a peculiarly blent atmosphere, Italian art dies away as a
French exotic.

Two questions remain, after much busy antiquarianism, concerning
Leonardo's death—the question of the exact form of his religion, and
the question whether Francis the First was present at the time. They
are of about equally little importance in the estimate of Leonardo's
genius. The directions in his will concerning the thirty masses and the
great candles for the church of Saint Florentin are things of course, their
real purpose being immediate and practical; and on no theory of religion could these hurried offices be of much consequence. We forget
them in speculating how one who had been always so desirous of beauty,
but desired it always in such precise and definite forms, as hands or
flowers or hair, looked forward now into the vague land, and experienced the last curiosity.

1869

The School of Giorgione

It is the mistake of much popular
criticism to regard poetry, music, and painting—all the various products of art—as but translations into different languages of one and the
same fixed quantity of imaginative thought, supplemented by certain
technical qualities of colour, in painting; of sound, in music; of rhythmical words, in poetry. In this way, the sensuous element in art, and
with it almost everything in art that is essentially artistic, is made a mat-

PASTORAL CONCERT—GIORGIONE   (*Louvre, Paris*)

ter of indifference; and a clear apprehension of the opposite principle—
that the sensuous material of each art brings with it a special phase or
quality of beauty, untranslatable into the forms of any other, an order of
impressions distinct in kind—is the beginning of all true æsthetic criticism. For, as art addresses not pure sense, still less the pure intellect, but
the "imaginative reason" through the senses, there are differences of
kind in æsthetic beauty, corresponding to the differences in kind of the
gifts of sense themselves. Each art, therefore, having its own peculiar
and untranslatable sensuous charm, has its own special mode of reaching the imagination, its own special responsibilities to its material. One
of the functions of æsthetic criticism is to define these limitations; to
estimate the degree in which a given work of art fulfils its responsibilities to its special material; to note in a picture that true pictorial charm,
which is neither a mere poetical thought or sentiment, on the one hand,
nor a mere result of communicable technical skill in colour or design,
on the other; to define in a poem that true poetical quality, which is
neither descriptive nor meditative merely, but comes of an inventive
handling of rhythmical language, the element of song in the singing; to

note in music the musical charm, that essential music, which presents
no words, no matter of sentiment or thought, separable from the special
form in which it is conveyed to us.

To such a philosophy of the variations of the beautiful, Lessing's
analysis of the spheres of sculpture and poetry, in the "Laocoön," was
an important contribution. But a true appreciation of these things is
possible only in the light of a whole system of such art-casuistries. Now
painting is the art in the criticism of which this truth most needs
enforcing, for it is in popular judgments on pictures that the false
generalisation of all art into forms of poetry is most prevalent. To suppose that all is mere technical acquirement in delineation or touch,
working through and addressing itself to the intelligence, on the one
side, or a merely poetical, or what may be called literary interest, addressed also to the pure intelligence, on the other:—this is the way of
most spectators, and of many critics, who have never caught sight all the
time of that true pictorial quality which lies between, unique pledge, as
it is, of the possession of the pictorial gift, that inventive or creative
handling of pure line and colour, which, as almost always in Dutch
painting, as often also in the works of Titian or Veronese, is quite independent of anything definitely poetical in the subject it accompanies.
It is the *drawing*—the design projected from that peculiar pictorial
temperament or constitution, in which, while it may possibly be ignorant of true anatomical proportions, all things whatever, all poetry, all
ideas however abstract or obscure, float up as visible scene or image: it
is the *colouring*—that weaving of light, as of just perceptible gold
threads, through the dress, the flesh, the atmosphere, in Titian's "Lace-
girl," that staining of the whole fabric of the thing with a new, delightful physical quality. This *drawing,* then—the arabesque traced in the air
by Tintoret's flying figures, by Titian's forest branches; this colouring
—the magic conditions of light and hue in the atmosphere of Titian's
"Lace-girl," or Rubens's "Descent from the Cross":—these essential
pictorial qualities must first of all delight the sense, delight it as directly
and sensuously as a fragment of Venetian glass; and though this delight
alone become the vehicle of whatever poetry or science may lie beyond
them in the intention of the composer. In its primary aspect, a great
picture has no more definite message for us than an accidental play of
sunlight and shadow for a few moments on the wall or floor: is itself, in
truth, a space of such fallen light, caught as the colours are in an Eastern
carpet, but refined upon, and dealt with more subtly and exquisitely
than by nature itself. And this primary and essential condition ful-

filled, we may trace the coming of poetry into painting, by fine gradations upwards; from Japanese fan-painting, for instance, where we get,
first, only abstract colour; then, just a little interfused sense of the
poetry of flowers; then, sometimes, perfect flower-painting; and so,
onwards, until in Titian we have, as his poetry in the "Ariadne," so
actually a touch of true childlike humour in the diminutive, quaint
figure with its silk gown, which ascends the temple stairs, in his picture
of the "Presentation of the Virgin," at Venice.

But although each art has thus its own specific order of impressions,
and an untranslatable charm, while a just apprehension of the ultimate
differences of the arts is the beginning of æsthetic criticism; yet it is
noticeable that, in its special mode of handling its given material, each
art may be observed to pass into the condition of some other art, by
what German critics term an *Anders-streben*—a partial alienation from
its own limitations, through which the arts are able, not indeed to supply the place of each other, but reciprocally to lend each other new
forces.

Thus some of the most delightful music seems to be always approaching to figure, to pictorial definition. Architecture, again, though it has
its own laws—laws esoteric enough, as the true architect knows only
too well—yet sometimes aims at fulfilling the conditions of a picture, as
in the *Arena* chapel; or of sculpture, as in the flawless unity of Giotto's
tower at Florence; and often finds a true poetry, as in those strangely
twisted staircases of the *châteaux* of the country of the Loire, as if it were
intended that among their odd turnings the actors in a theatrical mode
of life might pass each other unseen; these being a poetry also of
memory and of the mere effect of time, by which architecture often
profits greatly. Thus, again, sculpture aspires out of the hard limitation
of pure form towards colour, or its equivalent; poetry also, in many
ways, finding guidance from the other arts, the analogy between a
Greek tragedy and a work of Greek sculpture, between a sonnet and a
relief, of French poetry generally with the art of engraving, being more
than mere figures of speech; and all the arts in common aspiring towards the principle of music; music being the typical, or ideally consummate art, the object of the great *Anders-streben* of all art, of all that
is artistic, or partakes of artistic qualities.

All art constantly aspires towards the condition of music. For a while
in all other kinds of art it is possible to distinguish the matter from the
form, and the understanding can always make this distinction, yet it is
the constant effort of art to obliterate it. That the mere matter of a

poem, for instance, its subject, namely, its given incidents or situation—that the mere matter of a picture, the actual circumstances of an event, the actual topography of a landscape—should be nothing without the form, the spirit, of the handling, that this form, this mode of handling, should become an end in itself, should penetrate every part of the matter: this is what all art constantly strives after, and achieves in different degrees.

This abstract language becomes clear enough, if we think of actual examples. In an actual landscape we see a long white road, lost suddenly on the hill-verge. That is the matter of one of the etchings of M. Alphonse Legros: only, in this etching, it is informed by an indwelling solemnity of expression, seen upon it or half-seen, within the limits of an exceptional moment, or caught from his own mood perhaps, but which he maintains as the very essence of the thing, throughout his work. Sometimes a momentary tint of stormy light may invest a homely or too familiar scene with a character which might well have been drawn from the deep places of the imagination. Then we might say that this particular effect of light, this sudden inweaving of gold thread through the texture of the haystack, and the poplars, and the grass, gives the scene artistic qualities, that it is like a picture. And such tricks of circumstance are commonest in landscape which has little salient character of its own; because, in such scenery, all the material details are so easily absorbed by that informing expression of passing light, and elevated, throughout their whole extent, to a new and delightful effect by it. And hence, the superiority, for most conditions of the picturesque, of a river-side in France to a Swiss valley, because, on the French river-side, mere topography, the simple material, counts for so little, and, all being very pure, untouched, and tranquil in itself, mere light and shade have such easy work in modulating it to one dominant tone. The Venetian landscape, on the other hand, has in its material conditions much which is hard, or harshly definite; but the masters of the Venetian school have shown themselves little burdened by them. Of its Alpine background they retain certain abstracted elements only, of cool colour and tranquillising line; and they use its actual details, the brown windy turrets, the straw-coloured fields, the forest arabesques, but as the notes of a music which duly accompanies the presence of their men and women, presenting us with the spirit or essence only of a certain sort of landscape—a country of the pure reason or half-imaginative memory.

Poetry, again, works with words addressed in the first instance to the pure intelligence; and it deals, most often, with a definite subject or situation. Sometimes it may find a noble and quite legitimate function in the conveyance of moral or political aspiration, as often in the poetry of Victor Hugo. In such instances it is easy enough for the understanding to distinguish between the matter and the form, however much the matter, the subject, the element which is addressed to the mere intelligence, has been penetrated by the informing, artistic spirit. But the ideal types of poetry are those in which this distinction is reduced to its *minimum;* so that lyrical poetry, precisely because in it we are least able to detach the matter from the form, without a deduction of something from that matter itself, is, at least artistically, the highest and most complete form of poetry. And the very perfection of such poetry often appears to depend, in part, on a certain suppression or vagueness of mere subject, so that the meaning reaches us through ways not distinctly traceable by the understanding, as in some of the most imaginative compositions of William Blake, and often in Shakespeare's songs, as pre-eminently in that song of Mariana's page in *Measure for Measure,* in which the kindling force and poetry of the whole play seems to pass for a moment into an actual strain of music.

And this principle holds good of all things that partake in any degree of artistic qualities, of the furniture of our houses, and of dress, for instance, of life itself, of gesture and speech, and the details of daily intercourse; these also, for the wise, being susceptible of a suavity and charm, caught from the way in which they are done, which gives them a worth in themselves. Herein, again, lies what is valuable and justly attractive, in what is called the fashion of a time, which elevates the trivialities of speech, and manner, and dress, into "ends in themselves," and gives them a mysterious grace and attractiveness in the doing of them.

Art, then, is thus always striving to be independent of the mere intelligence, to become a matter of pure perception, to get rid of its responsibilities to its subject or material; the ideal examples of poetry and painting being those in which the constituent elements of the composition are so welded together, that the material or subject no longer strikes the intellect only; nor the form, the eye or the ear only; but form and matter, in their union or identity, present one single effect to the "imaginative reason," that complex faculty for which every thought and feeling is twin-born with its sensible analogue or symbol.

It is the art of music which most completely realises this artistic ideal, this perfect identification of matter and form. In its consummate moments, the end is not distinct from the means, the form from the matter, the subject from the expression; they inhere in and completely saturate each other; and to it, therefore, to the condition of its perfect moments, all the arts may be supposed constantly to tend and aspire. In music, then, rather than in poetry, is to be found the true type of measure of perfected art. Therefore, although each art has its incommunicable element, its untranslatable order of impressions, its unique mode of reaching the "imaginative reason," yet the arts may be represented as continually struggling after the law or principle of music, to a condition which music alone completely realises; and one of the chief functions of æsthetic criticism, dealing with the products of art, new or old, is to estimate the degree in which each of those products approaches, in this sense, to musical law.

By no school of painters have the necessary limitations of the art of painting been so unerringly though instinctively apprehended, and the essence of what is pictorial in a picture so justly conceived, as by the school of Venice; and the train of thought suggested in what has been now said is, perhaps, a not unfitting introduction to a few pages about Giorgione, who, though much has been taken by recent criticism from what was reputed to be his work, yet, more entirely than any other painter, sums up, in what we know of himself and his art, the spirit of the Venetian school.

The beginnings of Venetian painting link themselves to the last, stiff, half-barbaric splendours of Byzantine decoration, and are but the introduction into the crust of marble and gold on the walls of the *Duomo* of Murano, or of Saint Mark's, of a little more of human expression. And throughout the course of its later development, always subordinate to architectural effect, the work of the Venetian school never escaped from the influence of its beginnings. Unassisted, and therefore unperplexed, by naturalism, religious mysticism, philosophical theories, it had no Giotto, no Angelico, no Botticelli. Exempt from the stress of thought and sentiment, which taxed so severely the resources of the generations of Florentine artists, those earlier Venetian painters, down to Carpaccio and the Bellini, seem never for a moment to have been so much as tempted to lose sight of the scope of their art in its strictness, or to forget that painting must be before all things decorative, a thing for the eye, a space of colour on the wall, only more dexterously blent than the marking of its precious stone or the chance interchange of sun and shade upon it:—this, to begin and end with; whatever higher matter of thought, or poetry, or religious reverie might play its part therein, between. At last, with final mastery of all the technical secrets of his art, and with somewhat more than "a spark of the divine fire" to his share, comes Giorgione. He is the inventor of *genre,* of those easily movable pictures which serve neither for uses of devotion, nor of allegorical or historic teaching—little groups of real men and women, amid congruous furniture or landscape—morsels of actual life, conversation or music or play, but refined upon or idealised, till they come to seem like glimpses of life from afar. Those spaces of more cunningly blent colour, obediently filling their places, hitherto, in a mere architectural scheme, Giorgione detaches from the wall. He frames them by the hands of some skilful carver, so that people may move them readily and take with them where they go, as one might a poem in manuscript, or a musical instrument, to be used, at will, as a means of self-education, stimulus or solace, coming like an animated presence, into one's cabinet, to enrich the air as with some choice aroma, and, like persons, live with us, for a day or a lifetime. Of all art such as this, art which has played so large a part in men's culture since that time, Giorgione is the initiator. Yet in him too that old Venetian clearness or justice, in the apprehension of the essential limitations of the pictorial art, is still undisturbed. While he interfuses his painted work with a high-strung sort of poetry, caught directly from a singularly rich and high-strung sort of life, yet in his selection of subject, or phase of subject, in the subordination of mere subject to pictorial design, to the main purpose of a picture, he is typical of that aspiration of all the arts towards music, which I have endeavoured to explain,—towards the perfect identification of matter and form.

Born so near to Titian, though a little before him, that these two companion pupils of the aged Giovanni Bellini may almost be called contemporaries, Giorgione stands to Titian in something like the relationship of Sordello to Dante, in Browning's poem. Titian, when he leaves Bellini, becomes, in turn, the pupil of Giorgione. He lives in constant labour more than sixty years after Giorgione is in his grave; and with such fruit, that hardly one of the greater towns of Europe is without some fragment of his work. But the slightly older man, with his so limited actual product (what remains to us of it seeming, when narrowly explained, to reduce itself to almost one picture, like Sordello's one fragment of lovely verse), yet expresses, in elementary motive and principle, that spirit—itself the final acquisition of all the long endeavours of Venetian art—which Titian spreads over his whole life's activity.

And, as we might expect, something fabulous and illusive has always mingled itself in the brilliancy of Giorgione's fame. The exact relationship to him of many works—drawings, portraits, painted idylls—often fascinating enough, which in various collections went by his name, was from the first uncertain. Still, six or eight famous pictures at Dresden, Florence and the Louvre, were with no doubt attributed to him, and in these, if anywhere, something of the splendour of the old Venetian humanity seemed to have been preserved. But of those six or eight famous pictures it is now known that only one is certainly from Giorgione's hand. The accomplished science of the subject has come at last, and, as in other instances, has not made the past more real for us, but assured us only that we possess less of it than we seemed to possess. Much of the work on which Giorgione's immediate fame depended, work done for instantaneous effect, in all probability passed away almost within his own age, like the frescoes on the façade of the *fondaco dei Tedeschi* at Venice, some crimson traces of which, however, still give a strange additional touch of splendour to the scene of the *Rialto*. And then there is a barrier or borderland, a period about the middle of the sixteenth century, in passing through which the tradition miscarries, and the true outlines of Giorgione's work and person are obscured. It became fashionable for wealthy lovers of art, with no critical standard of authenticity, to collect so-called works of Giorgione, and a multitude of imitations came into circulation. And now . . . what remains of the most vivid and stimulating of Venetian masters, a live flame, as it seemed, in those old shadowy times, has been reduced almost to a name by his most recent critics. . . .

. . . Nor has the criticism, which thus so freely diminishes the number of his authentic works, added anything important to the well-known outline of the life and personality of the man: only, it has fixed one or two dates, one or two circumstances, a little more exactly. Giorgione was born before the year 1477, and spent his childhood at Castelfranco, where the last crags of the Venetian Alps break down romantically, with something of park-like grace, to the plain. A natural child of the family of the Barbarelli by a peasant-girl of Vedelago, he finds his way early into the circle of notable persons—people of courtesy. He is initiated into those differences of personal type, manner, and even of dress, which are best understood there . . . Not far from his home lives Catherine of Cornara, formerly Queen of Cyprus; and, up in the towers which still remain, Tuzio Costanzo, the famous *condottiere*—a picturesque remnant of medieval manners, amid a civilisation rapidly changing. Giorgione paints their portraits; and when Tuzio's son, Matteo, dies in early youth, adorns in his memory a chapel in the church of Castelfranco, painting on this occasion, perhaps, the altar-piece, foremost among his authentic works, still to be seen there, with the figure of the warrior-saint, Liberale, of which the original little study in oil, with the delicately gleaming, silver-grey armour, is one of the greater treasures of the National Gallery. In that figure, as in some other knightly personages attributed to him, people have supposed the likeness of the painter's own presumably gracious presence. Thither, at last, he is himself brought home from Venice, early dead, but celebrated. It happened, about his thirty-fourth year, that in one of those parties at which he entertained his friends with music, he met a certain lady of whom he became greatly enamoured, and "they rejoiced greatly," says Vasari, "the one and the other, in their loves." And two quite different legends concerning it agree in this, that it was through this lady he came by his death; Ridolfi relating that, being robbed of her by one of his pupils, he died of grief at the double treason; Vasari, that she being secretly stricken of the plague, and he making his visits to her as usual, Giorgione took the sickness from her mortally, along with her kisses and so briefly departed.

But although the number of Giorgione's extant works has been thus limited by recent criticism, all is not done when the real and the traditional elements in what concerns him have been discriminated; for, in what is connected with a great name, much that is not real is often very stimulating. For the æsthetic philosopher, therefore, over and above the real Giorgione and his authentic extant works, there remains the *Giorgionesque* also—an influence, a spirit or type in art, active in men so different as those to whom many of his supposed works are really assignable. A veritable school, in fact, grew together out of all those fascinating works rightly or wrongly attributed to him; out of many copies from, or variations on him, by unknown or uncertain workmen, whose drawings and designs were, for various reasons, prized as his; out of the immediate impression he made upon his contemporaries, and with which he continued in men's minds; out of many traditions of subject and treatment, which really descend from him to our own time, and by retracing which we fill out the original image. Giorgione thus becomes a sort of impersonation of Venice itself, its projected reflex or ideal, all that was intense or desirable in it crystallising about the memory of this wonderful young man.

And now, finally, let me illustrate some of the characteristics of this *School of Giorgione,* as we may call it, which, for most of us ... will still identify itself with those famous pictures at Florence, at Dresden and Paris. A certain artistic ideal is there defined for us—the conception of a peculiar aim and procedure in art, which we may understand as the *Giorgionesque,* wherever we find it, whether in Venetian work generally, or in work of our own time. . . .

I have spoken of a certain interpenetration of the matter or subject of a work of art with the form of it, a condition realised absolutely only in music, as the condition to which every form of art is perpetually aspiring. In the art of painting, the attainment of this ideal condition, this perfect interpenetration of the subject with the elements of colour and design, depends, of course, in great measure, on dexterous choice of that subject, or phase of subject; and such choice is one of the secrets of Giorgione's school. It is the school of *genre,* and employs itself mainly with "painted idylls," but, in the production of this pictorial poetry, exercises a wonderful tact in the selecting of such matter as lends itself most readily and entirely to pictorial form, to complete expression by drawing and colour. For although its productions are painted poems, they belong to a sort of poetry which tells itself without an articulated story. The master is pre-eminent for the resolution, the ease and quickness, with which he reproduces instantaneous motion— the lacing-on of armour, with the head bent back so stately—the fainting lady—the embrace, rapid as the kiss, caught with death itself from dying lips—some momentary conjunction of mirrors and polished armour and still water, by which all the sides of a solid image are exhibited at once, solving that casuistical question whether painting can present an object as completely as sculpture. The sudden act, the rapid transition of thought, the passing expression—this he arrests with that vivacity which Vasari has attributed to him, *il fuoco Giorgionesco,* as he terms it. Now it is part of the ideality of the highest sort of dramatic poetry, that it presents us with a kind of profoundly significant and animated instants, a mere gesture, a look, a smile, perhaps—some brief and wholly concrete moment—into which, however, all the motives, all the interests and effects of a long history, have condensed themselves, and which seem to absorb past and future in an intense consciousness of the present. Such ideal instants the school of Giorgione selects, with its admirable tact, from that feverish, tumultuously coloured world of the old citizens of Venice—exquisite pauses in time, in which, arrested thus, we seem to be spectators of all the fullness of existence, and which are like some consummate extract or quintessence of life.

It is to the law or condition of music, as I said, that all art like this is really aspiring; and, in the school of Giorgione, the perfect moments of music itself, the making or hearing of music, song or its accompaniment, are themselves prominent as subjects. On that background of the silence of Venice, so impressive to the modern visitor, the world of Italian music was then forming. . . . In sketch or finished picture, in various collections, we may follow it through many intricate variations —men fainting at music; music at the pool-side while people fish, or mingled with the sound of the pitcher in the well, or heard across running water, or among the flocks; the tuning of instruments; people with intense faces, as if listening, like those described by Plato in an ingenious passage of the *Republic,* to detect the smallest interval of musical sound, the smallest undulation in the air, or feeling for music in thought on a stringless instrument, ear and finger refining themselves infinitely, in the appetite for sweet sound; a momentary touch of an instrument in the twilight, as one passes through some unfamiliar room, in a chance company.

In these then, the favourite incidents of Giorgione's school, music or the musical intervals in our existence, life itself is conceived as a sort of listening—listening to music, to the reading of Bandello's novels, to the sound of water, to time as it flies. Often such moments are really our moments of play, and we are surprised at the unexpected blessedness of what may seem our least important part of time; not merely because play is in many instances that to which people really apply their own best powers, but also because at such times, the stress of our servile, everyday attentiveness being relaxed, the happier powers in things without are permitted free passage, and have their way with us. And so, from music, the school of Giorgione passes often to the play which is like music; to those masques in which men avowedly do but play at real life, like children "dressing up," disguised in the strange old Italian dresses, parti-coloured, or fantastic with embroidery and furs, of which the master was so curious a designer, and which, above all the spotless white linen at wrist and throat, he painted so dexterously.

But when people are happy in this thirsty land water will not be far off; and in the school of Giorgione, the presence of water—the well, or marble-rimmed pool, the drawing or pouring of water, as the woman pours it from a pitcher with her jewelled hand in the "Fête Champêtre," listening, perhaps, to the cool sound as it falls, blent with the music of the pipes—is as characteristic, and almost as suggestive, as that of music itself. And the landscape feels, and is glad of it also—a landscape full of clearness, of the effects of water, of fresh rain newly passed through the air, and collected into the grassy channels. The air, more-over, in the school of Giorgione, seems as vivid as the people who breathe it, and literally empyrean, all impurities being burnt out of it, and no taint, no floating particle of anything but its own proper ele-ments allowed to subsist within it.

Its scenery is such as in England we call "park scenery," with some elusive refinement felt about the rustic buildings, the choice grass, the grouped trees, the undulations deftly economised for graceful effect. Only, in Italy all natural things are as it were woven through and through with gold thread, even the cypress revealing it among the folds of its blackness. And it is with gold dust, or gold thread, that these Venetian painters seem to work, spinning its fine filaments, through the solemn human flesh, away into the white plastered walls of the thatched huts. The harsher details of the mountains recede to a harmonious dis-tance, the one peak of rich blue above the horizon remaining but as the sensible warrant of that due coolness which is all we need ask here of the Alps, with their dark rains and streams. Yet what real, airy space, as the eye passes from level to level, through the long-drawn valley in which Jacob embraces Rachel among the flocks![1] Nowhere is there a truer instance of that balance, that modulated unison of landscape and persons—of the human image and its accessories—already noticed as characteristic of the Venetian school, so that, in it, neither personage nor scenery is ever a mere pretext for the other.

Something like this seems to me to be the *vraie vérité* about Gior-gione, if I may adopt a servicable expression, by which the French recognise those more liberal and durable impressions which, in respect of any really considerable person or subject, anything that has at all intricately occupied men's attention, lie beyond, and must supplement, the narrower range of the strictly ascertained facts about it. In this, Giorgione is but an illustration of a valuable general caution we may abide by in all criticism. As regards Giorgione himself, we have indeed to take note of all those negations and exceptions, by which, at first sight, [the new criticism] seems merely to have confused our apprehen-sion of a delightful object, to have explained away in our inheritance from past time what seemed of high value there. Yet it is not with a full understanding even of those exceptions that one can leave off just at this point. Properly qualified, such exceptions are but a salt of genuine-

---

[1] The picture here referred to, *Jacob Meeting Rachel*, in the Dresden Gallery, is now generally attributed to Palma Vecchio.

ness in our knowledge; and beyond all those strictly ascertained facts, we must take note of that indirect influence by which one like Giorgione, for instance, enlarges his permanent efficacy and really makes himself felt in our culture. In a just impression of that, is the essential truth, the *vraie vérité*, concerning him.

1877

This famous chapter from The Florentine Painters of the Renaissance *develops a theme that is central to Berenson's conception of art: the idea that the highest part is that which gives an illusion of three-dimensional reality. It was because he believed this so thoroughly that Berenson was completely out of sympathy with the major developments in twentieth-century art. Berenson's notion of art as heightened reality is one answer to Pascal's statement: "What a vanity is painting, which arouses our admiration by its close imitation of things that we do not admire at all in reality."*

Bernard Berenson
Giotto and the Tactile Imagination[1]

I

Florentine painting between Giotto and Michelangelo contains the names of such artists as Orcagna, Masaccio, Fra Filippo, Pollaiuolo, Verrocchio, Leonardo, and Botticelli. Put beside these the greatest names in Venetian art, the Vivarini, the Bellini, Giorgione, Titian, and Tintoretto. The difference is striking. The significance of the Venetian names is exhausted with their significance as painters. Not so with the Florentines. Forget that they were painters, they remain great sculptors; forget that they were sculptors, and still they remain architects, poets, and even men of science. They left no form of expression untried, and to none could they say, 'This will perfectly convey my meaning.' Painting, therefore, offers but a partial and

1 *The Florentine Painters of the Renaissance,* by Bernard Berenson, 1896.

MADONNA AND CHILD—GIOTTO
(*National Gallery of Art,
Kress Collection, Wash-
ington, D.C.*)

not always the most adequate manifestation of their personality, and we
feel the artist as greater than his work, and the man as soaring above
the artist.

The immense superiority of the artist even to his greatest achievement in any one art form means that his personality was but slightly
determined by the particular art in question, that he tended to mould it
rather than let it shape him. It would be absurd, therefore, to treat the
Florentine painter as a mere link between two points in a necessary
evolution. The history of the art of Florence can never be, as that of
Venice, the study of a placid development. Each man of genius brought
to bear upon his art a great intellect, which, never condescending
merely to please, was tirelessly striving to reincarnate what it comprehended of life in forms that would fitly convey it to others; and in this
endeavour each man of genius was necessarily compelled to create forms
essentially his own. But because Florentine painting was pre-eminently
an art formed by great personalities, it grappled with problems of the
highest interest, and offered solutions that can never lose their value.

What they aimed at, and what they attained, is the subject of the following essay.

II

The first of the great personalities in Florentine painting was Giotto. Although he offers no exception to the rule that the great Florentines exploited all the arts in the endeavour to express themselves, he, Giotto, renowned as architect and sculptor, reputed as wit and versifier, differed from most of his Tuscan successors in having peculiar aptitude for the essential in painting *as an art.*

Before we can appreciate his real value, we must come to an agreement as to what in the art of figure-painting—the craft has its own altogether diverse laws—*is* the essential; for figure-painting we may say at once, was not only the one pre-occupation of Giotto, but the dominant interest of the entire Florentine school.

Psychology has ascertained that sight alone gives us no accurate sense of the third dimension. In our infancy long before we are conscious of the process, the sense of touch, helped on by muscular sensations of movement, teaches us to appreciate depth, the third dimension, both in objects and in space.

In the same unconscious years we learn to make of touch, of the third dimension, the test of reality. The child is still dimly aware of the intimate connexion between touch and the third dimension. He cannot persuade himself of the unreality of Looking-Glass Land until he has touched the back of the mirror. Later, we entirely forget the connexion, although it remains true that every time our eyes recognize reality, we are, as a matter of fact, giving tactile values to retinal impressions.

Now, painting is an art which aims at giving an abiding impression of artistic reality with only two dimensions. The painter must, therefore, do consciously what we all do unconsciously—construct his third dimension. And he can accomplish his task only as we accomplish ours, by giving tactile values to retinal impressions. His first business, therefore, is to rouse the tactile sense, for I must have the illusion of being able to touch a figure, I must have the illusion of varying muscular sensations inside my palm and fingers corresponding to the various projections of this figure, before I shall take it for granted as real, and let it affect me lastingly.

It follows that the essential in the art of painting—as distinguished from the art of colouring, I beg the reader to observe—is somehow to stimulate our consciousness of tactile values, so that the picture shall have at least as much power as the object represented, to appeal to our tactile imagination.

Well, it was of the power to stimulate the tactile consciousness—of the essential, as I have ventured to call it, in the art of painting—that Giotto was supreme master. This is his everlasting claim to greatness, and it is this which will make him a source of highest aesthetic delight for a period at least as long as decipherable traces of his handiwork remain on mouldering panel or crumbling wall. For great though he was as a poet, enthralling as a story-teller, splendid and majestic as a composer, he was in these qualities superior in degree only, to many of the masters who painted in various parts of Europe during the thousand years that intervened between the decline of antique, and the birth, in his own person, of modern painting. But none of these masters had the power to stimulate the tactile imagination, and, consequently, they never painted a figure which has artistic existence. Their works have value, if at all, as highly elaborate, very intelligible symbols, capable, indeed, of communicating something, but losing all higher value the moment the message is delivered.

Giotto's paintings, on the contrary, have not only as much power of appealing to the tactile imagination as is possessed by the objects represented—human figures in particular—but actually more; with the necessary result that to his contemporaries they conveyed a *keener* sense of reality, of life-likeness than the objects themselves! We whose current knowledge of anatomy is greater, who expect more articulation and suppleness in the human figure, who, in short, see much less naïvely now than Giotto's contemporaries, no longer find his paintings more than life-like; but we still feel them to be intensely real in the sense that they powerfully appeal to our tactile imagination, thereby compelling us, as do all things that stimulate our sense of touch while they present themselves to our eyes, to take their existence for granted. And it is only when we can take for granted the existence of the object painted that it can begin to give us pleasure that is genuinely artistic, as separated from the interest we feel in symbols.

At the risk of seeming to wander off into the boundless domain of aesthetics, we must stop at this point for a moment to make sure that we are of one mind regarding the meaning of the phrase 'artistic pleasure', in so far at least as it is used in connexion with painting.

What is the point at which ordinary pleasures pass over into the specific pleasures derived from each one of the arts? Our judgement about the merits of any given work of art depends to a large extent upon our answer to this question. Those who have not yet differentiated the specific pleasures of the art of painting from the pleasures they derive from the art of literature, will be likely to fall into the error of judging a picture by its dramatic presentation of a situation or its rendering of character; will, in short, demand of a painting that it shall be in the first place a good *illustration*. Others who seek in painting what is usually sought in music, the comunication of a pleasurable state of emotion, will prefer pictures which suggest pleasant associations, nice people, refined amusements, agreeable landscapes. In many cases this lack of clearness is of comparatively slight importance, the given picture containing all these pleasure-giving elements in addition to the qualities peculiar to the art of painting. But in the case of the Florentines, the distinction is of vital consequence, for they have been the artists in Europe who have most resolutely set themselves to work upon the specific problems of the art of figure-painting, and have neglected, more than any other school, to call to their aid the secondary pleasures of association. With them the issue is clear. If we wish to appreciate their merit, we are forced to disregard the desire for pretty or agreeable types, dramatically interpreted situations, and, in fact, 'suggestiveness' of any kind. Worse still, we must even forgo our pleasure in colour, often a genuinely artistic pleasure, for they never systematically exploited this element, and in some of their best works the colour is actually harsh and unpleasant. It was in fact upon form, and form alone, that the great Florentine masters concentrated their efforts, and we are consequently forced to the belief that, in their pictures at least, form is the principal source of our aesthetic enjoyment.

Now in what way, we ask, can form in painting give me a sensation of pleasure which differs from the ordinary sensations I receive from form? How is it that an object whose recognition in nature may have given me no pleasure, becomes, when recognized in a picture, a source of aesthetic enjoyment, or that recognition pleasurable in nature becomes an enhanced pleasure the moment it is transferred to art? The answer, I believe, depends upon the fact that art stimulates to an unwonted activity psychical processes which are in themselves the source of most (if not all) of our pleasures, and which here, free from disturbing physical sensations, never tend to pass over into pain. For instance: I am in the habit of realizing a given object with an intensity that we shall value as 2. If I suddenly realize this familiar object with an intensity of 4, I receive the immediate pleasure which accompanies a doubling of my mental activity. But the pleasure rarely stops here. Those who

are capable of receiving direct pleasure from a work of art, are generally led on to the further pleasures of self-consciousness. The fact that
the psychical process of recognition goes forward with the unusual
intensity of 4 to 2 overwhelms them with the sense of having twice the
capacity they had credited themselves with: their whole personality is
enhanced, and, being aware that this enhancement is connected with
the object in question, they for some time after take not only an increased interest in it, but continue to realize it with the new intensity.
Precisely this is what form does in painting: it lends a higher coefficient
of reality to the object represented, with the consequent enjoyment of
accelerated psychical processes, and the exhilarating sense of increased
capacity in the observer. (Hence, by the way, the greater pleasure we
take in the object painted than in itself.)

And it happens thus. We remember that to realize form we must give
tactile values to retinal sensations. Ordinarily we have considerable
difficulty in skimming off these tactile values, and by the time they have
reached our consciousness, they have lost much of their strength. Obviously, the artist who gives us these values more rapidly than the object
itself gives them, gives us the pleasures consequent upon a more vivid
realization of the object, and the further pleasures that come from the
sense of greater psychical capacity.

Furthermore, the stimulation of our tactile imagination awakens our
consciousness of the importance of the tactile sense in our physical and
mental functioning, and thus, again, by making us feel better provided
for life than we were aware of being, gives us a heightened sense of
capacity. And this brings us back once more to the statement that the
chief business of the figure painter, as an artist, is to stimulate the tactile
imagination.

The proportions of this book forbid me to develop further a theme,
the adequate treatment of which would require more than the entire
space at my command. I must be satisfied with the crude and unillu-
mined exposition given already, allowing myself this further word
only, that I do not mean to imply that we get no pleasure from a picture
except the tactile satisfaction. On the contrary, we get much pleasure
from composition, more from colour, and perhaps more still from
movement, to say nothing of all the possible associative pleasures for
which every work of art is the occasion. What I do wish to say is that
unless it satisfies our tactile imagination, a picture will not exert the
fascination of an ever-heightened reality; first we shall exhaust its ideas,

and then its power of appealing to our emotions, and its 'beauty' will not seem more significant at the thousandth look than at the first.

My need of dwelling upon this subject at all, I must repeat, arises from the fact that although this principle is important indeed in other schools, it is all important in the Florentine school. Without its due appreciation it would be impossible to do justice to Florentine painting. We should lose ourselves in admiration of its 'teaching', or perchance of its historical importance—as if historical importance were synonymous with artistic significance!—but we should never realize what artistic idea haunted the minds of its great men, and never understand why at a date so early it became academic.

Let us now turn back to Giotto and see in what way he fulfils the first condition of painting as an art, which condition, as we agreed, is somehow to stimulate our tactile imagination. We shall understand this without difficulty if we cover with the same glance two pictures of nearly the same subject that hang side by side in the Uffizi at Florence, one by "Cimabue," and the other by Giotto. The difference is striking, but it does not consist so much in a difference of pattern and types, as of realization. In the Cimabue we patiently decipher the lines and colours, and we conclude at last that they were intended to represent a woman seated, men and angels standing by or kneeling. To recognize these representations we have had to make many times the effort that the actual objects would have required, and in consequence our feeling of capacity has not only not been confirmed, but actually put in question. With what sense of relief, of rapidly rising vitality, we turn to the Giotto! Our eyes have scarcely had time to light on it before we realize it completely—the throne occupying a real space, the Virgin satisfactorily seated upon it, the angels grouped in rows about it. Our tactile imagination is put to play immediately. Our palms and fingers accompany our eyes much more quickly than in presence of real objects, the sensations varying constantly with the various projections represented, as of face, torso, knees; confirming in every way our feeling of capacity for coping with things—for life, in short, I care little that the picture endowed with the gift of evoking such feelings has faults, that the types represented do not correspond to my ideal of beauty, that the figures are too massive, and almost unarticulated; I forgive them all, because I have much better to do than to dwell upon faults.

But how does Giotto accomplish this miracle? With the simplest means, with almost rudimentary light and shade, and functional line, he contrives to render, out of all the possible outlines, out of all the possible variations of light and shade that a given figure may have, only those that we must isolate for special attention when we are actually realizing it. This determines his types, his schemes of colour, even his compositions. He aims at types which both in face and figure are simple, large-boned, and massive—types, that is to say, which in actual life would furnish the most powerful stimulus to the tactile imagination. Obliged to get the utmost out of his rudimentary light and shade, he makes his scheme of colour of the lightest that his contrasts may be of the strongest. In his compositions he aims at clearness of grouping, so that each important figure may have its desired tactile value. Note in the "Madonna" we have been looking at, how the shadows compel us to realize every concavity, and the lights every convexity, and how, with the play of the two, under the guidance of line, we realize the significant parts of each figure, whether draped or undraped. Nothing here but has its architectonic reason. Above all, every line is functional; that is to say, charged with purpose. Its existence, its direction, is absolutely determined by the need of rendering the tactile values. Follow any line here, say in the figure of the angel kneeling to the left, and see how it outlines and models, how it enables you to realize the head, the torso, the hips, the legs, the feet, and how its direction, its tension, is always determined by the action. There is not a genuine fragment of Giotto in existence but has these qualities, and to such a degree that the worst treatment has not been able to spoil them. Witness the resurrected frescoes in Santa Croce at Florence!

The rendering of tactile values once recognized as the most important specifically artistic quality of Giotto's work, and as his personal contribution to the art of painting, we are all the better fitted to appreciate his more obvious though less peculiar merits—merits, I must add, which would seem far less extraordinary if it were not for the high plane of reality on which Giotto keeps us. Now what is behind this power of raising us to a higher plane of reality but a genius for grasping and communicating real significance? What is it to render the tactile values of an object but to communicate its material significance? A painter who, after generations of mere manufacturers of symbols, illustrations, and allegories, had the power to render the material significance of the objects he painted, must, as a man, have had a profound sense of the significant. No matter, then, what his theme, Giotto feels its real significance and communicates as much of it as the general limitations of his art and of his own skill permit. When the theme is sacred story, it is scarcely necessary to point out with what processional gravity, with what hieratic dignity, with what sacramental intentness he endows it; the eloquence of the greatest critics has here found a darling subject. But let us look a moment at certain of his symbols in the Arena at Padua, at the 'Inconstancy,' the 'Injustice,' the 'Avarice,' for instance. 'What are the significant traits', he seems to have asked himself, 'in the appearance and action of a person under the exclusive domination of One of these vices? Let me paint the person with these traits, and I shall have a figure that perforce must call up the vice in question.' So he paints 'Inconstancy' as a woman with a blank face, her arms held out aimlessly, her torso falling backwards, her feet on the side of a wheel. It makes one giddy to look at her. 'Injustice' is a powerfully-built man in the vigour of his years, dressed in the costume of a judge, with his left hand clenching the hilt of his sword, and his clawed right hand grasping a double-hooked lance. His cruel eye is sternly on the watch, and his attitude is one of alert readiness to spring in all his giant force upon his prey. He sits enthroned on a rock, overtowering the tall waving trees, and below him his underlings are stripping and murdering a wayfarer. 'Avarice' is a horned hag with ears like trumpets. A snake issuing from her mouth curls back and bites her forehead. Her left hand clutches her money bag, as she moves forward stealthily, her right hand ready to shut down on whatever it can grasp. No need to label them: as long as these vices exist, for so long has Giotto extracted and presented their visible significance.

Still another exemplification of his sense for the significant is furnished by his treatment of action and movement. The grouping, the gestures never fail to be just such as will most rapidly convey the meaning. So with the significant line, the significant light and shade, the significant look up or down, and the significant gesture, with means technically of the simplest, and, be it remembered, with no knowledge of anatomy, Giotto conveys a complete sense of motion such as we get in his Paduan frescoes of the "Resurrection of the Blessed," of the "Ascension of our Lord," of the God the Father in the "Baptism," or the angel in "St. Joachim's Dream."

This, then, is Giotto's claim to everlasting appreciation as an artist: that his thorough-going sense for the significant in the visible world enabled him so to represent things that we realize his representations more quickly and more completely than we should realize the things themselves, thus giving us that confirmation of our sense of capacity which is so great a source of pleasure.

Benjamin Robert Haydon
Michelangelo and Gothic Sculpture

I have seen a cast of Michel Angelo's Moses! It disappointed me. It is fierce, awkwardly composed, vulgar in its limbs, & affected & artificial in its attitude, its parts, &c., mannered. In the combinations of Nature there is a harmony of parts. If the arm of a fat man would never join to the body of a spare one, the leg of a Hercules would not suit the body of a Paris. These are palpable. Nature never obtrudes, as it were, one part above another. We are born with our hands of the same size, use makes the right one the largest. The intense use of any part produces a larger devellopement [development] of the parts, but the parts used will never suit the body or legs not used. They will become, in truth, as it were, distorted and unnatural. Therefore to choose models whose avocations are mechanical in one particular pursuit & which has brought into action one particular part, is erroneous. In the Theseus you see activity inherently characteristic, but it is the activity and strength of natural formation & not habitual exercise. No part is obtruded, all is equally able, big arms, body, and limbs.

Style is a result & not a cause. Whatever object is represented, the intentions of Nature in its formation should be ascertained. The means which Nature has bestowed on that object to enable it to execute its own intentions should be investigated, & then the observations produced by time, accident, & other causes, should be clearly known, that he who takes upon him to represent any object should be able to reject accident from essence, and shew the object in all its essential qualities, as Nature first created it. The result will be style. Every thing can then have a style peculiar to itself, that is, it can be represented essentially as Nature made it, while manner is to represent every thing in one way, totally thoughtless of the separate intentions of Nature in each separate thing represented.

There are certain inherent principles of Nature which never can be varied, such as muscles in action can be never so rigid as when in relaxation, that the form of a part in action is different from one in repose, that the opposite contours of a limb or trunk can never be the same in external shape, because they are never so from internal formation, &c., &c. When any of these great inherent principles are broken, it argues that the Artist did not know them, and that if he did not know them, they are so essential that his works can never with safety be held up to the young as examples. No doubt the conception of a character may be so grand, the beauty of an idea may be so beautiful, the pathos of an expression may be so intense, that the errors or inadequacy of the means of representation may be forgiven. Yes, they may be forgiven, but in order to bring Art to the perfection the Ancients brought it, or to the perfection we hourly see in Nature, there must be nothing to forgive. An idea or a conception being the nobler part of the two, we may in our conviction of human imperfection overlook it, but to feel it as requisite to overlook any thing, proves we have a feeling that there is something to be overlooked, and something of which we have an idea that has not been adequately represented. An Art whose mode of conveying intellectual associations is per se capable of exciting beauty of feeling, independently of them, ought surely to have its intellectual feelings engaged in all the truth & purity of which its language is capable; our Brothers the Poets are not born if their grammar is bad or the language obscure, and why should bad grammar or obscurity of language be born in our Art? Of course the languages are different in their essence. The language of Poets is an artificial assemblage of words, agreed on by the respective nations to which they belong to mean the things to which they are applied, altho they have no one natural claim to such associations & altho the neighbouring nation to which they are read will be perfectly ignorant of their reference, while our language is the things themselves, and the most imperfect representation of the thing intended is at once comprehended and the idea meant to be conveyed at once understood. Yet this facility of being comprehended the Greeks never suffered to act as an excuse, and why should the moderns? It is not so much an Ignorance as a misapplication of science that is to be reprobated, tho' this in some degree is ignorance too, a disregard for the laws of Nature, to suit the whims of a disordered fancy, an affectation of idealizing, or giving style without having by the result any clear notions what either mean.

Michel Angelo was a tremendous Genius. This is evident. The vast power of intellect displayed in the conception & arrangement of the Capella Sistina[1] to shew the empire of Theocracy is enough for this [*an illegible word*] of the imagination, but Michel Angelo had not clear notions of the essential qualities of the human form, as the Moses proves, and as the figure of Lazarus in Angerstein's Picture of Piombo had long since proved, 1810. The Torso was his ruin. The inflated,

[1] The Sistine Chapel.

unnatural protrusion of muscular action without regard to the inherent laws of nature which a back must be liable to if its shoulders be
as big as the dome of St. Paul's, sanctioned an equal protrusion in the
other parts, and gave him false ideas of form & grandeur. Michel
Angelo was a grand Genius and he made the human form bend into
his grand notions, but he might have been equally grand in his forms
and less untrue.

Michel Angelo's greatness was in the imagination, motion, & that the
mode of conveying his idea was false & mannered (as by the Moses),
and in his wish to give an air of grand motion by contrast of one limb
with another, the head with the body, he overstepped simplicity, &
gave what man termed a swaggering air of blackguardism. Homer's just
making the head of Jupiter in a simple straight forward nod & making
Olympus shaking as he did it, is to my feeling more truly grand, than
all the swings of head or hoists of limbs of such figures as the Moses.
The Jeremiah is another instance of the real sublimity of simplicity
instead of contrast, because in this immoveable simplicity there is a
look of consciousness that no effort was requisite to create an awe.
What do we admire in the aims & manners of rank? Why, that enviable, easy, self possession & that amiable, conscious unconsciousness
of having no equal present & that consequently the slightest smile, the
gentlest turn, the most inaudible whisper are enough. Struggle & effort
to excite attention are never visible in those whose talents & rank entitle them to it, but in those who having no claim in Society are always
on the stretch to say something ridiculous or make some odd motion
to supply the deficiency of nature or Birth. Many of the old Gothic
monuments with both their hands across their breasts & lying on their
backs are infinitely more sublime than the works of John de Bologna
or a host of Michel Angelo's imitators. There is directly a look in their
immoveable stillness as if they were above the troubles of life, whereas
in the fierce contrasted twists of the other as if the tickling of a fly's
leg was sufficient to put them into a violent passion, and if every thing
in life affected them with the spasms of an electric shock; of course all
this depends on the characters represented, a Prophet, a Lawgiver, & a
Philosopher must not be represented in a way that a hero or a warrior
must. There is in Nature no law to regulate characters in Art. Every
character has a style & a law of its own. Truth must not be made to
bend to system, but system must yield to truth, but yet there are general principles to which all may be referred, from their immutable
influence on human feelings. There ought to be in Art no style in

colour, drapery, form, or expression. The story, the period, the country should regulate every thing. In the finest periods in Art & Poetry, the highest characters have been only Nature grandly rendered, none of her laws & characteristics violated, none of her immutable truths forgotten, while in the periods of decay, tired of Nature and her simple grandeur, the Genius of the Time has always endeavoured to attract by novelty & artifice what their great Predecessors were content to do, by embellishing truth. Nature is thus forgotten, and a system substituted in her stead, which being always easier to imitate from its palpable qualities, is looked on as Nature elevated, when it is only violated & the terms style, system, ideality, and other cant terms are substituted for inherent truth.

Actuated by these feelings, I must own the Moses disappointed me. The arms have muscles marked which could not be in action, the feet have parts which could not belong to nature; in short, it is mannered. The conception & air is grand, but oh, how it shrunk by the majestic Simplicity of the Theseus. His joints seem as if they were oiled balls rolling in sockets of slippery ice, so supple, so active in turn, knowledge, anatomy all subservient to truth, unalterable truth. His broad & grand back in its fleshy beauty made the Moses look like an overgrown bully. It won't do, it won't do. I cannot bear an affected violation of knowledge when Nature does not warrant, and I frankly own I hope in God I may never [come] to that time when I may.

(*Diary,* November 8, 1817)

Here, long before Ruskin, is an acute awareness of the greatness of Gothic sculpture, and a perceptive discussion of Michelangelo's greatness well this side of idolatry.

Matisse on Donatello and Michelangelo. Matisse once pointed to the difference in two plaster casts that I had of heads by Donatello and Michelangelo. In the Donatello, he said, if one cut away the surface modeling nothing would be left, but the Michelangelo could be rolled down a hill till most of the surface elements were knocked off, and the form would still remain.

Leo Stein, *Appreciation*

No one who has not seen the Sistine Chapel can have a clear idea of what a human being can achieve.

Goethe

THE BAROQUE

Fromentin is at his best in his account of his pilgrimage through the museums of Belgium and Holland, Les Maîtres d'autrefois, *written in 1875. This is perhaps the first book of modern art criticism, one that brings an informed sensibility to bear upon accepted masterpieces and reputations. Much has been learned about Rembrandt's life and work since Fromentin wrote the chapter reprinted here. It is still, however, for all its critical lapses, a brilliant summing-up.*

The translation of the Fromentin book used is that by Mrs. Mary C. Robbins, published as The Old Masters of Belgium and Holland.

Eugène Fromentin
Rembrandt[1]

     The life of Rembrandt is, like his painting, full of half-tints and dark corners. Often as he shows himself as he was in the full light of his works, of his public and private life, clear, luminous, and sparkling with wit, good humor, and haughty grace and grandeur,—equally often he secretes himself, and seems always to be hiding something, whether he painted or whether he lived. He had no palace with the conditions of a great lord's house, no train and galleries in the Italian fashion, but a modest abode, the blackened house of a petty merchant, the interior confusion of a collector, a book-hunter, a lover of prints and curiosities. He had no public business to draw him from his studio, and make him enter into the politics of his time; no great favor ever attached him to any prince. He had no

---

[1] *The Old Masters of Belgium and Holland.* Boston: Houghton Mifflin Company, 1882.

official honors, nor orders, nor decorations,—nothing which connects him closely or distantly with such a fact or with such personages as would have kept him from being forgotten; for history in mentioning them might incidentally have spoken of him. Rembrandt belonged to the third estate, and hardly to that, as would have been said in France in 1789. He belonged to those crowds in which individuals are lost, whose manners are on a dead level, their habits without any character to elevate them; and even in Holland, that country of so-called equality in classes, Protestant, republican, without prejudices of nobility, the singularity of his genius did not prevent the social mediocrity of the man from keeping him down in the obscure layers, and drowning him in them.

For a long time nothing was known of him but from the testimony of Sandrart or his pupils,—those at least who have written, Hoogstraaten and Houbraken; and these reports were reduced to a few legends of the studios, to doubtful authorities, to too hasty judgments, and to gossip. What was perceived of himself were his eccentricities, his manias, a few trivialities, and certain faults that were almost vices. He was called interested, grasping, even miserly, rather disposed to bargain; and on the other hand he has been called dissipated, and disorderly in his expenses, witness his bankruptcy. He had many pupils, whom he put into cells in his rooms which were divided into compartments, watched them to see that between them was no contact, no influence, and drew a great revenue from his mistrustful teaching. Some fragments of oral lessons are collected by tradition, which are truths of simple good sense, but they brought about no particular result. He had not seen Italy, did not recommend that journey; which was for his ex-disciples, become doctors in æsthetics, a grievance and an occasion for regretting that their master had not added this necessary culture to his healthy doctrines and his original talent. He was known to have singular tastes, a love for old monkish robes, for Oriental frippery, for helmets, swords, and Asiatic carpets. Before knowing more exactly the detail of his artistic furniture, and all the instructive and useful curiosities with which he had encumbered his house, it seemed to be but a disorder of fantastic things, belonging to natural history and bric-a-brac, savage panoplies, stuffed animals, and dried grasses. It savored of the *capharnäum* and the laboratory, a little of occult science and the cabala; and this oddity, joined to the passion he was supposed to have for money, give to the meditative and crabbed face of this furious worker the indescribable and suspicious air of an alchemist.

He had a passion for sitting in front of a mirror and painting himself, not as Rubens did in his heroic pictures, under a chivalrous exterior, as a warrior amid a confusion of epic figures, but all alone, in a little frame, looking right into his own eyes, for himself alone, and solely for the value of a shimmering light, or a more rare half-tint, playing over the rounded planes of his fat face with its flushed pulp. He turned up his mustache, put air and movement into his curly hair, smiled with a strong and ruddy lip; and his little eye, lost under thick jutting brows, darted a singular glance, in which were ardor, fixity, insolence, and contentment. It was not everybody's eye. The face had strong planes, the mouth was expressive, the chin wilful. Between his two eyebrows labor had traced two vertical furrows, two swellings, and that fold contracted by the habit of frowning, which belongs to concentrated brains which refract received sensations, and make an effort from without in. He adorned himself besides, and travestied himself after the fashion of theatrical people. He borrowed from his store the wherewithal to clothe himself, cover his head, or adorn himself; he put on turbans, velvet caps, felt hats, doublets, mantles, sometimes a cuirass; he hooked jewelry into his headgear, fastened round his neck chains of gold with precious stones: and when you get a little into the secret of his researches, you begin to ask if all this complacency of the painter for the model was not the weakness of the man, to which the artist lent himself. Later, after his mature years, in his days of difficulty, he is seen to appear in graver, more modest, and more truthful garments, without gold or velvet, in sombre raiment, with a handkerchief tied round his head, his countenance saddened, wrinkled, emaciated, the palette in his rough hands. This costume of a man disenchanted was a new form which prevailed with him when he had passed fifty years, but it only complicates the more the true idea that one would like to form of him.

All this together did not make a very harmonious whole, did not sustain itself, accorded ill with the meaning of his works, the high aim of his conceptions, the profound seriousness of his habitual purposes. The outbursts of this character difficult to define, the revealed points of his almost unprecedented habits, were relieved with a certain sharpness upon the background of a dull, neutral existence, smoky with uncertainties and biographically sufficiently confused.

Since then, light has been shed upon almost all of the doubtful parts of this shadowy picture. Rembrandt's history has been written and very well written in Holland, and even in France after the Dutch writers. Thanks to the labors of one of his most fervent admirers, M.

Vosmaert, we know now of Rembrandt, if not all that is necessary to know, at least all that will probably ever be known; and this suffices to make us love, pity, esteem, and I believe comprehend him well. Considering him by the exterior, he was an excellent man, loving his home, his domestic life, his fireside; a family man, with the nature of a husband rather than a libertine; a man of one wife, who could never bear either celibacy or widowhood, whom circumstances not wholly explained forced to marry three times; a retired man of course,—not very economical, for he did not know how to balance his accounts; not avaricious, for he became bankrupt; and if he spent little money for his comfort, he lavished it apparently for the curiosities of his mind; difficult to live with, perhaps suspicious, solitary;—in everything and in his modest sphere a singular being. He lived in no luxury, but he had a kind of concealed opulence,—treasures buried in valuable objects of art, which caused him much joy, but which he lost in the final disaster, and which under his eyes, before the door of an inn, on a truly sinister day, were sold at a low rate. All this personal property was not bric-a-brac, as has been seen from the inventory published at the time of the sale, though posterity occupied itself a long time with it without understanding it. There were marbles, Italian pictures, Dutch pictures, a great number of his own works, and especially engravings of the rarest kind, which he exchanged for his own, or paid dearly for. He cared for all these things, which were beautiful, curiously collected, and choice, as the companions of his solitude, the witnesses of his work, the confidants of his thought, the inspirers of his mind. Perhaps he treasured them as would a dilettante, a man of erudition, a person delicate in his intellectual enjoyments; and such was probably the unaccustomed form of an avarice whose intimate meaning was not understood. As to his debts which crushed him, he already had them at the epoch when, in a correspondence which has been preserved, he called himself rich. He was proud enough, and signed his bills of exchange with the carelessness of a man who does not know the value of money, and does not count with sufficient exactness either what he possesses or what he owes.

He had one charming wife, Saskia, who, like a ray of sunshine in his perpetual chiaroscuro, during those too brief years, in spite of a lack of elegance and very real charm, put into them something of a more lively brilliancy. What is wanting to this gloomy interior, as to this labor, morose with all its profundity, is expansion, a little loving youth, feminine grace, and tenderness. Did Saskia bring him all that?

It cannot be seen directly. He was in love with her, it is said; painted her often, muffled her, as he did himself, in eccentric or magnificent disguises; covered her, as he did himself, with I know not what luxury of the moment; represented her as a Jewess, an Odalisque, a Judith, perhaps as a Susanna, and a Bathsheba, never painted her as she really was, and never left of her one portrait, dressed or not, which was faithful,—that is, we prefer to believe so. This is all that we know of his too soon extinguished domestic joys. Saskia died young, in 1642, the very year when he produced "The Night Watch." The pleasant and laughing faces of his children—for he had several in his three marriages— are not once met with in his pictures. His son Titus died some months before him. The others disappeared in the obscurity which covered his last years and followed his death.

It is known that Rubens, in his grand life which was so exciting and always happy, had, on his return from Italy, when he felt himself out of place in his own country, and again after the death of Isabel Brandt, when he found himself a widower and alone in his house, a moment of great weakness, and something like a sudden failing of power. The proof of it is in his letters. With Rembrandt it is impossible to know what his heart suffered. Saskia died, and his labor continued without stopping a day; this is proved by the date of his pictures, and better still by his etchings. His fortune crumbled, he was dragged into the Insolvent room, everything he loved was taken from him; he took his easel, installed himself elsewhere, and neither his contemporaries nor posterity have heard a cry or a complaint from this strange nature, that might have been believed to be wholly overwhelmed. His productiveness neither weakens nor declines. Favor abandons him with fortune, happiness, and comfort; he replies to the injustice of Fate and the unfaithfulness of opinion by the portrait of Six, and "The Syndics," not to speak of the "Young Man at the Louvre," and ever so many others classed among his most composed, most satisfying and vigorous works. During his mourning, in the midst of humiliating misfortunes, he preserved a strange impassibility, which would be wholly inexplicable if it were not known what is the capability, as a moving spring to produce indifference or prompt forgetfulness, of a soul occupied with profound views.

Had he many friends? It is not thought that he had. It is certain that he did not have all those he deserved to have,—not Vondel, who himself was a familiar friend of the house of Six; nor Rubens, whom he knew well, who came to Holland in 1636, visited all the celebrated

THE NIGHT WATCH—REMBRANDT (*Rijksmuseum, Amsterdam*)

painters, Rembrandt alone excepted, and died in the year preceding "The Night Watch," without the name of Rembrandt figuring either in his letters or his collections. Was he honored, much surrounded, very well known? Not at all. When he is spoken of in the *Apologies*, in the writings, in the little fugitive poems, made for an occasion in his time, it is under orders, rather from a spirit of justice, as if by chance, and without great warmth. The literary men had other preferences, after whom came Rembrandt, the only one of all who was illustrious. In official ceremonies, in the great days of pomp of all kinds, he was forgotten, or, so to speak, he was never seen anywhere in the front ranks or on the platforms.

In spite of his genius, his glory, the prodigious infatuation which attracted painters to him in the beginning, what was called society was, even at Amsterdam, a social circle which perhaps half opened its doors to him, but to which he never belonged. His portraits recommended him no better than his person. Although he had made magnificent ones of people of distinction, they were not those pleasant, natural, lucid works which could give him a position in a certain kind of society, would be appreciated there, and give him admittance to it. I have told you that Captain Kock, who figures in "The Night Watch," consoled himself later with Van der Helst; as to Six,—a young man in relation to Rembrandt, and who, I insist upon believing, only let himself be painted because he could not help it,—when Rembrandt went to the house of this official personage, he went rather to see the Burgomaster and Mecænas than a friend. From habit and preference, he consorted with people of low rank, shopmen, and petty citizens. His associations have been even too much vilified; they were very humble, but not degrading, as has been said. He has even been occasionally reproached with having drunken habits (though he hardly ever frequented drinking-houses, which was rare at that time), because, ten years after the loss of his wife, people thought they perceived that this lonely man had some suspicious relations with his serving-maid.

The servant was reprimanded, and Rembrandt passably condemned. Moreover, at that moment everything went ill, fortune as well as honor; and when he left the Breestraat, homeless, penniless, but at quits with his creditors, neither his talent nor his acquired glory sustained him. His trace was lost, he was forgotten, and for the time he disappeared in the lowly, needy, and obscure life from which, to tell the truth, he had never issued.

In everything, as can be seen, he was a man apart, a dreamer; perhaps a silent man, although his face says the contrary; possibly an angular character, rather rough, unbending, cutting, not pleasant to contradict, still less to convince; vacillating at bottom, stiff in his manner, undoubtedly peculiar. If he was celebrated and cherished and praised at first, in spite of the jealous and short-sighted, the pedants and the fools, they well revenged themselves when he was no longer there.

In his execution he neither painted, drew, nor engraved like any one else. His works were, even in their methods, enigmas. He was admired not without disquietude, he was followed without being very well understood. It was especially at his work that he seemed like an alchemist. Seeing him at his easel, with a palette that must certainly have been daubed, from which came so much heavy paint, and whence escaped so many subtle essences; or leaning over his copperplates, and using his burin contrary to all rules,—one would seek, at the tip of his burin or his brush, secrets which came from much farther off. His manner was so novel that it confounded the strong minds, and filled with enthusiasm the simple spirits. All the young, enterprising, insubordinate, and giddy scholars in painting ran after him. His immediate pupils were mediocre, their followers were detestable. A striking thing resulted from the teaching in cells of which I have spoken; not one kept his independence. They imitated him as no master was ever imitated by servile copyists, and it is evident took from him only the worst of his methods.

Was he learned and cultivated? Was he even a man of any reading? Because he had a taste for theatrical effects, and touched upon history, mythology, and Christian dogmas, people say he was. It is said that he was not, because the examination of his furniture revealed innumerable engravings and almost no books. Was he, in fine, a philosopher, as the word philosopher is understood? What did he gain from the movement of reform? Did he, as has been maintained in our day, contribute his part as an artist towards destroying dogmas, and revealing the purely human sides of the Gospel? Did he pronounce his opinion intentionally upon the political, religious, and social questions which had turned his country upside down for so long, and which very fortunately were finally solved? He painted mendicants, the disinherited and beggars, even more than rich men, Jews oftener than Christians; does it follow that he had for the wretched classes anything but purely picturesque predilections? All this is more than conjectural, and I do not see the necessity of sifting farther a subject already so profound, and adding another to so many hypotheses.

The fact is, that it is difficult to isolate him from the intellectual and moral movement of his country and his time, which he breathed in the seventeenth century in Holland as he did the native air on which he lived. Had he come earlier, he would have been inexplicable; had he been born anywhere else, he would play still more strangely this rôle of a comet outside of the axis of modern art, which has been attributed to him; had he come later, he would have no longer the immense merit of closing a past, and opening one of the great gates of the future. In every relation he has deceived many people. As a man he was lacking in exterior, whence it has been concluded that he was coarse. As a student he has disturbed more than one system, whence it has been concluded that he was wanting in taste. As an artist loving the beautiful, he has given of the things of the earth some very ugly ideas. It has not been remarked that he was looking elsewhere. In short, greatly as he was praised, wickedly as he was vilified, unjustly as he was esteemed, for good or for evil, or contrary to his nature, no one exactly suspected his true grandeur.

Observe that he is the least Dutch of the Dutch painters, and that if he belongs to his time, he does not wholly belong to it. What his compatriots observed he did not see; to that from which they turned aside, he returned. They had bidden farewell to the fable, and he came back to it; to the Bible, and he illustrated it; to the Gospels, and he delighted in them. He clothes them in his own way, but he extracts from them a meaning unique, new, and universally intelligible. He dreams of St. Simeon, of Jacob and Laban, of the Prodigal Son, of Tobias, the Apostles, the Holy Family, King David, Calvary, the Samaritan, Lazarus, and the Evangelists. He wanders around Jerusalem and Emmaus, ever, as one feels, attracted by the synagogue. These consecrated themes he sees appear in nameless surroundings, in meaningless costumes. He conceives them, formulates them, with as little care for tradition as slight regard for local truth. And still, such is his creative force, that this mind, so individual and personal, gives to the subjects it treats a general expression, an intimate and typical meaning, which the grand epic thinkers and draughtsmen do not always attain.

Somewhere in this study I have said that his principle was to extract from things one element among all others, or rather to abstract them all to seize one expressly. He has thus, in all his works, performed the labor of an analyzer, a distiller, or, to speak more nobly, of a metaphysician, rather than a poet. Never did reality seize him as a whole. To see the way in which he treated bodies, one might doubt the interest he took in their envelope. He loved women, and has seen them only deformed; he loved the tissues, and did not imitate them; but in return, in spite of lack of grace, beauty, pure lines, and delicacy of flesh, he expressed the naked body by suppleness, roundness, elasticity, with a love for substances, a feeling for the living being, which are the delight of artist workmen. He decomposed and reduced everything, color as well as light, so that, while eliminating from appearances everything that is manifold, condensing what is scattered, he succeeded in drawing without outlines, in painting a portrait almost without apparent features, in coloring without color, in concentrating the light of the solar system into a ray. It is not possible in a plastic art to push farther the curiosity of a being about itself. For physical beauty he substitutes moral expression; for the imitation of things, their almost entire metamorphosis; for examination, psychological speculations; for clear, learned, or simple observation, the perceptions of a visionary, and apparitions so real that he is the dupe of them himself. By this faculty of second sight, thanks to his somnambulistic intuition, in the super-

natural he sees farther than any one soever. Life he perceives in a
dream, as an accent of the other world which renders real life almost
cold, and makes it seem pale. See at the Louvre his "Portrait of a
Woman," two paces from Titian's "Mistress." Compare the two beings,
interrogate well the two paintings, and you will understand the difference of the two brains. His ideal, as in a dream pursued with closed
eyes, is light; the nimbus around objects, phosphorescence on a black
ground. It is fugitive, uncertain, formed of imperceptible lineaments,
all ready to disappear before they are fixed, ephemeral and dazzling.
To arrest the vision, place it upon canvas, give it its form and relief,
preserve its fragile texture, give it its brillancy, and let the result be
a strong, masculine, and substantial painting, as real as any other,
which would resist contact with Rubens, Titian, Veronese, Giorgione,
Vandyck,—this is what Rembrandt attempted. Did he accomplish it?
Universal testimony is there to say.

One last word. Proceeding as he proceeded himself, by extracting
from this work, so vast and of such manifold character, what represents
him in his principle, reducing it to its natural elements, eliminating
his palette, his brushes, his coloring oils, his glazings, his thick paints,
all the mechanisms of the painter, one might finally come to where he
could seize the primal essence of the artist in the engraver. Rembrandt
is wholly to be found in his etchings. His spirit, tendency, imaginations, reveries, good sense, chimeras, difficulties in rendering the impossible, realities in the nothings, are revealed by twenty of his etchings; they give one a presentiment of the painter, and, better still,
explain him. There is the same workmanship, the same purpose, the
same neglect, the same persistency, the same singularity in execution,
the same tormenting and sudden success by expression. Confronting
them closely, I see no difference between the "Tobias" at the Louvre
and an engraved plate. There is no one who does not set this engraver
above all others. Without going so far, when it is a question of his
painting, it would be well to think often of the Hundred Florin Piece,
when one fails to understand him in his pictures. It would then be
seen that all the dross of this art, one of the most difficult in the world
to purify, alters nothing of the incomparably beautiful flame which
burns within; and I think that finally every name that has been given
to Rembrandt would be altered to give him opposite names.

In truth, his was a brain served by an eye that could see at night, and
by an able hand with no great dexterity. This painful labor came from
an agile and free mind. This man of no account; this ferreter, this

costumer, this erudite being nourished on extravagances; this man of
the lower levels, of so lofty a flight; this moth nature, which flies to
whatever shines; this soul, so sensitive to certain forms of life, so indifferent to others; this ardor without tenderness, this lover without
visible flame; this nature of contrasts, contradictions, and double meanings, moved and eloquent, loving and not very lovable; this disgraced
man so well endowed; this pretended materialist; this *trivial, hideous*
person,—was a pure spiritualist, or, to express it in a single word, an
idealist; I mean, a spirit whose domain is that of ideas, and whose
language is the language of ideas. The key of the mystery is there.

Taken thus, Rembrandt is wholly explained; his life, his work, his
learnings, his conceptions, his poetry, his methods, his way of working,
even to the color of his painting, which is only a bold and studied
spiritualization of the material elements of his art.

*Unlike the great "literary" critics of art, Ruskin and Pater, Stevenson
wrote an art criticism that was primarily concerned with the dignity of
technique, to borrow the title of his magnificent chapter printed below.
He was a critic in the twentieth-century tradition, and no one who has
written on art in our own century has cared more about painting or
written about it with more sensitivity to tactile values. His masterpiece
is his book on Velásquez (published in final form in 1899), from which
two sections are here given.*

Robert Alan Mowbray Stevenson
The Dignity of Technique[1]

It is not the lover of pictures, but
the devotee of his own spiritual emotions who needs to be told that
technique is art; that it is as inseparable from art as features from facial
expression, as body from soul in a world where force and matter seem
inextricably entangled. In fact, the man who has no interest in technical questions has no interest in art; he loves it as those love you who
profess only love for your soul. The concert-goers who disclaim any

[1] From *Velasquez*, by R. A. M. Stevenson. London: George Bele & Sons, 1900.

technical interest in music will be found to like a performance because they forget it in trains of thought about scenery, morals, or poetry. But one may walk on the hills to become healthy or to escape crowds, and yet deserve no suspicion of a fondness for beauty. Under a mistaken conception of culture as the key of all the arts and sciences, intellectual people too often feel obliged to pretend an interest in arts for which they have no natural inclination. They insufficiently distinguish men born to take pleasure in the abstract and speculative from those born to love the concrete and sensuous—the black-and-white from the coloured mind. They cannot believe that the least taught ploughman whose senses are in tune with the pulse of nature may make a better artist than the man of loftiest thought who is encased in nerves insensitive to the quality of musical intervals or the character of shapes and colours. The man of abstract mind apprehends great ideas presented in the abstract medium of literature, but in the concrete of painting he is easily deceived by associations with words into spending his admiration on mean forms, on foolish labour, on purposeless colour. He looks at the merest pretence of modelling, at the coarsest sham of colouring, at the contradiction of the whole by the part, at the burial of beauty in niggling, and his dull eyes accept the imposture on the recommendation of his humbugged hearing.

The "apostles of culture" grant but one gift—intellect—to many-sided man, and accord but one faculty of imagination to the dweller in a house whose various windows look down five separate avenues of sense. Often some of these windows are blocked, and so many men must misunderstand each other's reports of the external world, but the man of culture too often keeps no window clean, and from a dark chamber of the mind would explain to everyone else the true inner meaning of what they see. It is this prophet that despises technique because technique differs as the material of each art differs—differs as marble, pigments, musical notes and words differ. He hates matter; because owing to matter the imagination in each art is a gift whose absence cannot be compensated for either by one of the other imaginations or by the abstract intellect itself. Imagination in words is not imagination in colour or form, as the cases of Turner and Goethe amply prove. Without matter there is no art; without matter there is no stuff in which imagination may create an image. Sentiment is not imagination; spirituality is not artistic feeling. We all cry, laugh, and put on airs; we do not all imagine occasions and fashions of crying, laughing, and striking attitudes. We feel the excitement of a street fight, yet we cannot all come home and image that excitement as Dinet did in "Une Bagarre," with its tempestuous pattern of uplifted hands and swaying bodies quivering in an uncertain flicker of shadows and windy lamplight. It is a sensitiveness to the special qualities of some visible or audible medium of art which distinguishes the species artist from the genus man. We are all spirits; it is not in spirituality that the painter differs from us, but in that sensitive perception of visible character which enables him to imagine a picture all of a piece, all tending to express the same sentiment, all instinct and alive with feeling. Moreover, any difference that may exist between the material bases of the arts, exacts a corresponding difference between the qualities of temperament and imagination in the artists who practise them, also between the aims that are legitimate to the various arts, and between the feelings and laws by which works are to be judged and admired. Arts such as painting and sculpture, that appeal to the eye and display their contents simultaneously, differ vastly from those that unfold their matter to the ear in sequence. Painting and sculpture differ between themselves more slightly, and there is still less difference between pictures, whether realistic or decorative in aim, whether worked in oil or water, tint or line, monochrome or colour.

An art of space scarcely differs more from an art of time than one used purely from one mixed with representation of life, with utility or with symbolism. There is only one quite pure art—namely, symphonic music. Every shade of the complicated emotion in a symphony by Beethoven depends entirely upon technique—that is to say, upon the relations established amongst notes which are by themselves empty of all significance. The materials of other arts are more or less embarrassed in application by some enforced dependence on life. Words, since they serve as fixed counters or symbols, cannot be wholly wrenched from a determined meaning and suggestion; architecture satisfies a need of common life as well as an æsthetic craving, and painting not only weaves a purely decorative pattern, but also pretends to imitate the appearance of the world. None of these arts tranquilly pursue the beauties intrinsic to their medium; none circle in their orbit undisturbed; all upon examination appear to be, as it were, double stars, linked like Algol to a dark companion.

I might sum these statements in one or two principles. *First,* Art is not Life; for life is first-hand passionate emotion, while art deals with emotion second-hand, retrospective and disinterested. Life is variable, and a mixture of all materials—space, time, sound, colour, form, etc.; art is limited, partially controllable by the artist, and comparatively permanent. *Second,* Sentiment is not Imagination; for sentiment precedes art, and is common to all men, while imagination is a special power to arrange the material of some art in harmony with a mood. *Third,* There are as many separate faculties of imagination as there are separate mediums in which to conceive an image—clay, words, paint, notes of music. *Fourth,* The materials of the arts may be used with a double aim, or solely for their own direct and immediate qualities—as notes and intervals in music, which derive their character solely from the relations in which the artist chooses to place them; they have no fixed meaning, and a dominant and a tonic are interchangeable.

Our faith in any art reposes, however, upon the belief that its material, even if unavoidably adulterated with foreign significations, is nevertheless as capable as the sounds of music of expressing character in virtue of artistic arrangement. Otherwise, no medium of expression but the symphony should deserve the name of art. Now, as paint serves both to record impressions of the external world and to decorate a given space and shape, an artist, however partial to either, must give some measure of attention to each of these aims. He must study how the eye takes in nature, and how it takes pleasure in a canvas; and he must learn to reconcile these two ways of seeing when they disagree, as they sometimes may. When you look at nature, nothing remains absolutely fixed in appearance. Size, colour, pattern, and proportion seem to fluctuate as you change your point of view, move your focus, widen or narrow your angle of vision. No object seems big but by relation to a smaller, no mass simple except when viewed as a whole in contrast to another, and no tone so bright that a brighter cannot make it dark. But when you see forms and colours set in the one plane of a picture, confined to its scale of pigment, and permanently bounded in size, proportion, and place by its four obstinate sides, then you see them fixed in unalterable relations, and always bound to express one and the same point of view. The laws by which one pictures an effect on the flat consequently differ from those that regulate ordinary sight. Many collocations of form or colour that please in a sunlit space of three dimensions with fluctuating borders become intensely disagreeable in a flat, framed panel. When he leaves nature for art, a man leaves bright boundless space where he has no dominion for a dark cloistered place where he is master—master of a medium susceptible of arrangement by harmony, contrast, and gradation; master to make his material speak in character, follow a vein of sentiment, express a mood of seeing. But he must learn to obey what, for want of a better word, one may call the laws of decorative effect.

Plainly, then, there are two interests to be reconciled in a picture, the facts and impressions of nature on one hand, and, on the other, the beauties and exigencies of the framed pictorial world. A *modus vivendi* must be established between the imitative and the decorative, and the compact between these two may be called the convention of the art of painting. To object to the conventionality of art is to believe in absolute realism, which, if possible, would be a science and not an art. As things are, when you merely draw a line on an empty canvas you commit yourself to art, for you have given the line a positive character by placing it in some relation to the four sides of the canvas. To show a line quite unconditioned or uncomposed, one would require a canvas without limits—that is to say, nature. Convention, then, there must be, but it need not be rigid; it may vary with the impressions of artists, with the facts of nature, and with the characters of the mediums employed. The introduction of perspective, for instance, was a notable change in the convention of painting, since it implied a limitation in the use of our general knowledge of an object to what can be seen from one point of view. Different readings of the convention by men of genius give rise to various styles of painting, and successively attach a varying importance to the elements of technique as they deal with ideal form or real form, local colour or atmospheric, detail or general aspect.

This description of technique, compressed as it is of necessity, is intended for those who hate "mere technique" and despise "matter." Matter does not level man with the beast or the stone; technique is not hateful, but only the point of view it expresses. There is a silly, unimpassioned mind which looks on nature without choice between things, which seems choked with trifles, which possesses no touchstone in its emotions wherewith to distinguish the important from the foolish. There may be such a thing as mere technique, but it is not what the vituperator of realism would have it. In words, it is nonsense verses; in paint, mere decorative consistency, without the meaning or emotion of truth to nature.

Technique in painting, then, must be understood as the method of using any medium of expression so as to bring out the character of a decorative pattern, or to convey the sentiment with which you regard some appearances of the external world. The two aims become one when the decorative pattern to be enforced is suggested by the mood in which you happen to look at your motif. If this be granted, then technique is as important to an art as the body to man. Both of them appear and act for two hidden questionable partners, sentiment and soul. Through them these silent invisible partners can speak with the outer world and influence the minds of men. When we would infer the soul of another man or the sentiment of a picture, we may do so only through the material senses and their analogies.

Technique, then, is the indivisible organic body of a man's conception, and cannot be rightly apprehended when studied in fragments. Yet, since the exigency of words forces us to present things in sequence, we must separate these living parts, and, as it were, dissect them dead. This necessity we will face, and will look separately at the qualities of Velasquez's technique—such as composition, colour, modelling, and brushwork.

His Modelling and Brushwork

While speaking of colour one has gone some way towards describing the office of modelling; but there remains a little to say about this important subject. Modelling is the basis of the art of painting, the master-trick of the craft, since it is imposed upon the painter by the very convention which compels him to express depths of space and

POPE INNOCENT X—VELASQUEZ
*(National Gallery of Art,
Mellon Collection,
Washington, D.C.)*

inclinations of surface by shades of colour laid on one plane. The shortest if not the best description of the convention of painting is given when you say that it compels you to have nothing to do with anything that cannot be shown at one view in a glass. This implies the single point of sight of perspective and the single focus of impressionism. In fact, the impressionists are the descendants of the perspectivists; they fight the same battle, and are pledged to the same cause, to show, not how things are, but how they seem. Notwithstanding the contrary opinion of certain painters, I cannot but consider modelling the most valuable acquirement of an impressionist, as with it he may render his impression of shapes and yet neither rivet the eye nor detain the attention by defined lines or borders. It seems illogical, and it certainly violates the continuity of light to dispense with lines round large masses, while you carefully draw them with a rigger round eyes, mouths, noses, buttons, and other details. Brushwork then enters into the question, as it is the means used to carry out the logic of modelling, especially in the smaller sub-division of a picture where the minuter forms of detail must often be suggested by texture or a device of handling.

If one must divide the indivisible and name some quality of technique in which Velasquez most patently excelled, one feels inclined to choose his modelling. In expressing form by real light he finally attained to that Greek combination of broad, majestic beauty of effect, with the neatest perfection of finish. Other men, it will be said, have shown a fine command of form before him, and Velasquez himself could surely model well enough in his early works. The back of the blacksmith in "The Forge of Vulcan" and the arm of Bacchus in "The Topers," as well as the heads in that picture, are superb bits of modelling. In what consists the difference between this early rendering of form and the modelling of the later pictures? To some extent perhaps in a growing feeling for comparative strengths of definition, which enabled him to avoid tricky or arbitrary expression, and to pass from piecemeal modelling to impressionistic modelling. A definition may not disappear in nature if you pry closely into it; but, when looked at together with a second one, firmer and yet soft in the *ensemble,* the first must often be made to disappear if due relative force is to be kept. A step in Velasquez's progress in comparative definition may be seen by comparing portraits of the second period, like the "Sculptor Montañés" (Prado, 1091), or the "Admiral Pulido," of the National Gallery, with close tight early work, such as "Philip IV" (Prado, 1070), or even Philip, full length, in the National Gallery. Though the pictures of the second period are certainly freer, broader, and less hard than those of the first, perhaps they have lost something of the intimate rendering of form which was to be regained in final work, such as "Philip IV" (Prado, 1080), and "Philip Old" (National Gallery).

Let us admit then that other men have felt form before Velasquez; it was his merit to have shown it under one effect of light and to have expressed it with the sorcery of truth and not by any kind of arbitrary modelling. The term needs explanation; I have used it for ten years, but the other day some one asked me if it meant the use of idealised forms instead of the actual shape of the model. Here, however, the term "arbitrary" applies to the want of reality in the means used to express them, and not to any lack of actuality in the forms themselves. Idealised form can be rendered with the least possible convention, and with a fully coloured and real treatment of light, whereas actual form can be rendered with the much more conventional and unreal mediums of pure line or black and white monochrome. An extreme but well-known instance of arbitrary modelling may be seen in those maps which express the shape of a country by contour lines drawn at successive heights. The steeper the ground the closer the lines approach, till on a cliff they merge into a deep shade. If used as modelling, this arbitrary principle would assume a spectator in the zenith whose eye is the source of light, so that horizontal planes appear whitest and vertical ones darkest.

It is not necessary to describe all the kinds and degrees of arbitrariness in modelling which have been used both before and after Velasquez; a word or two must suffice. Leonardo da Vinci, when he was writing of modelling, blames the conventionality of previous practitioners as out of correspondence with the truths of real light. He accuses them of modelling by means of a monochromatic tint used in three or four bands of increasing darkness from full light to deep shadow. These gradation tints, something, by the way, like those used now in mechanical drawings, could be mixed with the local hue of a drapery or a flesh tint, or else might be superimposed in glazes. In both cases a sort of obligato accompaniment in monochrome was called upon to produce all the modifications of local colour that we understand by the word "values." Without doubt, succeeding painters have used more subtle methods of modelling, but whether they attain to the beauty and finesse of Raphael, of Rubens, of Titian, of Rembrandt, or only of Sir E. Burne-Jones, their modelling seems arbitrary and their beauties conventional beside the naturalism of Velasquez.

When we see a quite white world after a heavy fall of snow, we do not see a monochrome but the chromatic hues of a coloured atmospheric effect. Sometimes it is a tissue of rose, blue, and yellow all in a high fairy-like key, or again it is a harmony of brown and silver; but, whatever it may be, it goes far to disprove the theory that a shadow is only a darker shade of a light. The shapes of this equally white ground are revealed by the various inclination of their slopes to the light, yet this light is yellow on one slope, blue on another, and by no means merely darker or brighter shades of one tint. The distances of the snow-fields are indicated by their absorption in atmospheric hues, but the foreground is not another shade of the colour that wraps the distance. A red, blue, or yellow world would also model chromatically under light, and so we may be sure that every change of plane in the real compositely-hued world should correspond in the picture to a change of value in true colour.

Velasquez's idea of finish in modelling consisted in making his rendering of light logical, convincing, and beautiful. He taught himself not to over-model every bit of a picture because he saw that the range of available values is graduated according to the inclination of real planes and not according to their size or structural importance. To burden a plane with smaller planes, perhaps steeper or equally steep, means frittering away the values that should not only distinguish, but eloquently proclaim important changes of surface. The constant repetition of sharp accidents tires the eye; it is like the false cry of wolf that forestalls the effect of the really momentous occasion. This appears especially evident in landscape, where it is counted unwise to pretend to fully outline and model objects too small to properly exhibit the effect of shadow and light. The artist who insists on giving such accidents an important treatment generally employs a false kind of definition which really belongs to the convention of outline drawing and not to that of full-toned oil painting. Indeed, the traditions of laborious or gorgeous styles of the past linger incongruously in later art, as buttons and lappets, the relics of former fashions, remain on the coats we wear to-day. In a difficult passage of naturalistic modelling, painters are apt to take refuge in the older conventions of line, which contradict and destroy the consistency and mystery of revelation by true light. If bad tone is often a relic of decorative or monochromatic styles, hard and linear definition often comes from traditions of primitive draughtsmanship.

In the art of outline drawing itself, it is held difficult to perceive the true sweep and sentiment of a long line which contains small indentations often steeper in their slopes than the main inclination of the large contour. In this case, however, experience proves that breadth of treatment can be cultivated by training. It is said that in France drawing can be taught even to a man without a turn for it, but, it may be added, drawing with no merit except that of a proportionate subordination of parts. However this may be, it is certainly more difficult to teach a man to perceive relative values of colour and relative forces of definition. He must not only learn to sweep his eye along one line, but to embrace a whole area with an imaginative grasp of sight. Hence it is easy to observe contiguous values and difficult to note the relation of value between tones separated from each other by a considerable angle at the observer's eye. It requires an impressionist to feel the connection between such values with anything like the sensation of certitude with which one feels the harmony of a chord. That is to say, it requires one whose faculty it is to conceive of all the spots and markings of a scene only in some relation to its whole aspect. The *ensemble* of a scene hypnotises and fascinates an impressionist as if it were a real, personal, and indivisible entity and not a mere sum of small quantities.

Breadth of view was Velasquez's most admirable possession; by it he made composition, modelling, and style, the slaves of his impressions. This breadth of view led him in his later pictures to vary his manner of painting according to the sentiment of his impression, so that you will find in his work no pattern of brushwork, no settled degree of intimacy in the modelling, no constantly equal force of realisation in edges, and, in short, no fixed habits or methods of expression. In the comparison of "The Topers" with "Las Meninas," it was pointed out that three single heads which are just sufficiently broad in treatment to look comfortable, would produce, if composed in one frame, a pattern too crowded and spotty from a decorative point of view. But such a compilation of unmodified studies would sin also from an impressionistic point of view. It would imply three focuses of impression, and therefore whatever character each of the separate impressions might have possessed would be jostled out of existence by the others, and it would be impossible that there could be any agreement of meaning between the aspect of the picture and its technique.

To people who have never painted, such terms as impressions, fields of vision, and angles of sight, may seem fanciful, or at least irrelevant to art. An illustration may help to show them that there is no absolute realism of appearance, but that different eyes and different habits of looking at the world would manifest different qualities and different aspects of truth. When a man reads, he does not focus individual letters but takes in a whole line at a glance; so that in ordinary reading for pleasure he overlooks misspellings, reversed letters, etc. On the other hand, a child reading letter by letter, with a smaller field of impression, cannot avoid seeing such mistakes. The large print used for children is extremely fatiguing to grown people as in order to see at one time the amount of letters required to give them the current impression and meaning of writing, they have to work over an unusually wide field of sight. If they hold these large letters at a distance from the eye, proportionate to their size, they will observe that the eye defines differently, and altogether loses very fine strokes. It is easy to apply this to painting, and it may serve to show that what you look for you will see, let it be a large thing and a continuous meaning, or small things and a jerky interrupted meaning.

Many people must have noticed the occasional effect of a portrait upon a blank canvas—an effect of grand importance, too often speedily impaired as the painter proceeds to fill in the space. This blank space happened to correspond roughly to the degree of attention which the painter had accorded to surroundings when he was painting the head; its emptiness justified the closeness of his modelling and the precision of his definitions. When he began to focus elsewhere and to fill in accessories, the head began to look mean and too tightly modelled. Velasquez's most closely-studied heads are for the most part isolated portraits, painted against utter blackness or against an atmospheric grey or fawn tone of great simplicity. Such are, for instance, "The Crucifixion" (Prado, 1055), and "Philip IV" (1080), in the same gallery. Indeed, the black blankness surrounding "The Crucifixion" alone saves its antique Bellini-like details of lettering and wood-graining from looking commonplace and topographical. As he became an impressionist somewhat slowly, the qualities of modelling which Velasquez always possessed appear to best advantage in those early pictures which are simple busts, as "Philip IV. in Armour" (Prado, 1071), and not in those which are full-lengths, as "Philip IV." (Prado, 1073), or the older full-length of Philip in the National Gallery. In his later art, Velasquez never painted a wide view as he would a narrow one, nor a simple subject as a complicated one. When he painted a wide angle of sight, he either concentrated himself on a point, or steeped his whole canvas equally in a soft envelope of light. Indeed, whatever he painted, he always painted the quality of his attention to the scene, and, in virtue of that principle, his best pictures never look spotty, and never tempt one to cut them up into gem-like bits. His *ensemble* is always equally easy to grasp, whether he paints great groups like "Las Meninas" and "The Spinners," solitary full-lengths like "Moenippus" and "Æsop," costume-portraits like "Maria Teresa" (Prado, 1084), or simple busts like the head of Philip (Prado, 1080).

But if the art of all these pictures is based on the same principles, and perhaps for that very reason, the technique is very different in them all. You may note a wonderful variety in Velasquez's style of modelling a head, not only in different periods of his life, but in pictures of the same period, and, what is more, in heads on the same canvas. Some heads are modelled very broadly and softly, without a sharp mark, a hard edge, or small steep planes. The surfaces slide into each other in a loose, supple manner, that almost makes them look as if they were shaped in jelly or fluid. Some consist of bold, rough-hewn planes which give a face the force and vigour of firm chiselling. Others, again, are completed to show the finest niceties of shape and inclination, with an intimacy of feeling and a delicacy of proportion that no man has ever equalled. The handling is always discreet and inspired by the necessities of the occasion; neither does it follow a determined pattern, which might impart a frozen and artificial look, nor does it seek an effect of *bravura* dexterity which might arrogate an undue share of attention and interest. Although no certain rule can be laid down, generally speaking, Velasquez inclines to brush in the obvious direction of the forms, so as to supplement tone and structure by the sentiment of the execution. In many cases, however, he smudges so subtly as to convey no sense of direct handling. The limb or object treated seems to grow mysteriously out of dusky depths and to be shaped by real light.

In the foregoing account of the art of Velasquez, it has been contended that his impulse to arrange a canvas grew out of the scene before his eyes; that his severe and stately colour is founded on nature, and that his execution becomes quiet and exact, or burly and impetuous, as the occasion demands. More than any other man's, his work convinces us that he knew what he saw and was incapable of self-deception; it is wholly free from haphazard passages, treacly approximations to tone, or clever tricks and processes that evade rather than resolve a difficulty. Above all, his art is interesting without the extravagance which may kindle a momentary excitement, but is apt, like a passionate mania for a woman, to die of satiety from its very violence. The restrained force and dignity of Velasquez inspire one with reverence and lasting respect; one cannot easily fathom the depth of his insight nor weary of his endless variety.

Much has changed since this essay was first written. El Greco is no longer regarded as an eccentric and slightly suspect artist, but is now a universally admired "old master," thanks largely to the championship, by critics like Fry, not only of the work of El Greco himself but of the work of modern artists painting along similar lines. Fry's brilliant discussion of baroque qualities as exemplified by El Greco is in no way invalidated by the fact that El Greco is now generally regarded as the culmination of the mannerist style.

Roger Fry
El Greco[1]

Mr. Holmes has risked a good deal in acquiring for the nation the new El Greco. The foresight and understanding necessary to bring off such a *coup* are not the qualities that we look for from a Director of the National Gallery. Patriotic people may even be inclined to think that the whole proceeding smacks too much of the manner in which Dr. Bode in past ages built up the Kaiser Friedrich Museum, largely at the expense of English collections. Even before the acquisition of the El Greco there were signs that Mr. Holmes did not fully understand the importance of "muddling through." And now with the El Greco he has given the British public an electric shock. People gather in crowds in front of it, they argue and discuss and lose their tempers. This might be intelligible enough if the price were known to be fabulous, but, so far as I am aware, the price has not been made known, so that it is really about the picture that people get excited. And what is more, they talk about it as they might talk about some contemporary picture, a thing with which they have a right to feel delighted or infuriated as the case may be—it is not like most old pictures, a thing classified and museumified, set altogether apart from life, an object for vague and listless reverence, but an actual living thing, expressing something with which one has got either to agree or disagree. Even if it should not be the superb masterpiece which most of us think it is, almost any sum would have been well spent on a picture capable of provoking such fierce æsthetic interest in the crowd.

That the artists are excited—never more so—is no wonder, for here is an old master who is not merely modern, but actually appears a good many steps ahead of us, turning back to show us the way. Immortality

[1] From *Vision and Design*, by Roger Fry. New York: Brentano's, *n.d.* (originally published in 1920).

if you like! But the public—what is it that makes them "sit up" so
surprisingly, one wonders. What makes this El Greco "count" with
them as surely no Old Master ever did within memory? First, I suspect,
the extraordinary completeness of its realisation. Even the most casual
spectator, passing among pictures which retire discreetly behind their
canvases, must be struck by the violent attack of these forms, by a
relief so outstanding that by comparison the actual scene, the gallery
and one's neighbours are reduced to the key of a Whistlerian Nocturne.
Partly, for we must face the fact, the melodramatic apparatus; the "horrid" rocks, the veiled moon, the ecstatic gestures. Not even the cinema
star can push expression further than this. Partly, no doubt, the clarity
and the balanced rhythm of the design, the assurance and grace of the
handling; for, however little people may be conscious of it, formal
qualities do affect their reaction to a picture, though they may pass
from them almost immediately to its other implications. And certainly
here, if anywhere, formal considerations must obtrude themselves even
on the most unobservant. The extraordinary emphasis and amplitude
of the rhythm, which thus gathers up into a few sweeping diagonals
the whole complex of the vision, is directly exciting and stimulating.
It affects one like an irresistible melody, and makes that organisation
of all the parts into a single whole, which is generally so difficult for the
uninitiated, an easy matter for once. El Greco, indeed, puts the problem of form and content in a curious way. The artist, whose concern is
ultimately and, I believe, exclusively with form, will no doubt be so
carried away by the intensity and completeness of the design, that he
will never even notice the melodramatic and sentimental content which
shocks or delights the ordinary man. It is none the less an interesting
question, though it is rather one of artists' psychology than of æsthetics,
to inquire in what way these two things, the melodramatic expression
of a high-pitched religiosity and a peculiarly intense feeling for plastic
unity and rhythmic amplitude, were combined in El Greco's work;
even to ask whether there can have been any casual connection between
them in the workings of El Greco's spirit.

Strange and extravagantly individual as El Greco seems, he was not
really an isolated figure, a miraculous and monstrous apparition thrust
into the even current of artistic movement. He really takes his place
alongside of Bernini as a great exponent of the Baroque idea in figurative art. And the Baroque idea goes back to Michelangelo. Formally, its
essence both in art and architecture was the utmost possible enlargement of the unit of design. One can see this most easily in architecture.

To Bramante the façade of a palace was made up of a series of storeys, each with its pilasters and windows related proportionally to one another, but each a co-ordinate unit of design. To the Baroque architect a façade was a single storey with pilasters going the whole height, and only divided, as it were, by an afterthought into subordinate groups corresponding to the separate storeys. When it came to sculpture and painting the same tendency expressed itself by the discovery of such movements as would make the parts of the body, the head, trunk, limbs, merely so many subordinate divisions of a single unit. Now to do this implied extremely emphatic and marked poses, though not necessarily violent in the sense of displaying great muscular strain. Such poses correspond as expression to marked and excessive mental states, to condition of ecstasy, or agony or intense contemplation. But even more than to any actual poses resulting from such states, they correspond to a certain accepted and partly conventional language of gesture. They are what we may call rhetorical poses, in that they are not so much the result of the emotions as of the desire to express these emotions to the onlooker.

When the figure is draped the Baroque idea becomes particularly evident. The artists seek voluminous and massive garments which under the stress of an emphatic pose take heavy folds passing in a single diagonal sweep from top to bottom of the whole figure. In the figure of Christ in the National Gallery picture El Greco has established such a diagonal, and has so arranged the light and shade that he gets a statement of the same general direction twice over, in the sleeve and in the drapery of the thigh.

Bernini was a consummate master of this method of amplifying the unit, but having once set up the great wave of rhythm which held the figure in a single sweep, he gratified his florid taste by allowing elaborate embroidery in the subordinate divisions, feeling perfectly secure that no amount of exuberance would destroy the firmly established scaffolding of his design.

Though the psychology of both these great rhetoricians is infinitely remote from us, we tolerate more easily the gloomy and terrible extravagance of El Greco's melodrama than the radiant effusiveness and amiability of Bernini's operas.

But there is another cause which accounts for our profound difference of feeling towards these two artists. Bernini undoubtedly had a great sense of design, but he was also a prodigious artistic acrobat, capable of feats of dizzying audacity, and unfortunately he loved popularity and the success which came to him so inevitably. He was not fine enough in grain to distinguish between his great imaginative gifts and the superficial virtuosity which made the crowd, including his Popes, gape with astonishment. Consequently he expressed great inventions in a horribly impure technical language. El Greco, on the other hand, had the good fortune to be almost entirely out of touch with the public— one picture painted for the king was sufficient to put him out of court for the rest of his life. And in any case he was a singularly pure artist, he expressed his idea with perfect sincerity, with complete indifference to what effect the right expression might have on the public. At no point is there the slightest compromise with the world; the only issue for him is between him and his idea. Nowhere is a violent form softened, nowhere is the expressive quality of brushwork blurred in order to give verisimilitude of texture; no harshness of accent is shirked, no crudity of colour opposition avoided, wherever El Greco felt such things to be necessary to the realisation of his idea. It is this magnificent courage and purity, this total indifference to the expectations of the public, that bring him so near to us to-day, when more than ever the artist regards himself as working for ends unguessed at by the mass of his contemporaries. It is this also which accounts for the fact that while nearly every one shudders involuntarily at Bernini's sentimental sugariness, very few artists of to-day have ever realised for a moment how unsympathetic to them is the literary content of an El Greco. They simply fail to notice what his pictures are about in the illustrative sense.

But to return to the nature of Baroque art. The old question here turns up. Did the dog wag his tail because he was pleased, or was he pleased because his tail wagged? Did the Baroque artists choose ecstatic subjects because they were excited about a certain kind of rhythm, or did they elaborate the rhythm to express a feeling for extreme emotional states? There is yet another fact which complicates the matter. Baroque art corresponds well enough in time with the Catholic reaction and the rise of Jesuitism, with a religious movement which tended to dwell particularly on these extreme emotional states, and, in fact, the Baroque artists worked in entire harmony with the religious leaders.

This would look as though religion had inspired the artists with a passion for certain themes, and the need to express these had created Baroque art.

I doubt if it was as simple as that. Some action and reaction between the religious ideas of the time and the artists' conception there may have been, but I think the artists would have elaborated the Baroque idea without this external pressure. For one thing, the idea goes back behind Michelangelo to Signorelli, and in his case, at least, one can see no trace of any preoccupation with those psychological states, but rather a pure passion for a particular kind of rhythmic design. Moreover, the general principle of the continued enlargement of the unit of design was bound to occur the moment artists recovered from the debauch of naturalism of the fifteenth century and became conscious again of the demands of abstract design.

In trying thus to place El Greco's art in perspective, I do not in the least disparage his astonishing individual force. That El Greco had to an extreme degree the quality we call genius is obvious, but he was neither so miraculous nor so isolated as we are often tempted to suppose.

The exuberance and abandonment of Baroque art were natural expressions both of the Italian and Spanish natures, but they were foreign to the intellectual severity of the French genius, and it was from France, and in the person of Poussin, that the counterblast came. He, indeed, could tolerate no such rapid simplification of design. He imposed on himself endless scruples and compunctions, making artistic unity the reward of a long process of selection and discovery. His art became difficult and esoteric. People wonder sometimes at the diversity of modern art, but it is impossible to conceive a sharper opposition than that between Poussin and the Baroque. It is curious, therefore, that modern artists should be able to look back with almost equal reverence to Poussin and to El Greco. In part, this is due to Cézanne's influence, for, from one point of view, his art may be regarded as a synthesis of these two apparently adverse conceptions of design. For Cézanne consciously studied both, taking from Poussin his discretion and the subtlety of his rhythm, and from El Greco his great discovery of the permeation of every part of the design with a uniform and continuous plastic theme. The likeness is indeed sometimes startling. One of the greatest critics of our time, von Tschudi—of Swiss origin, I hasten to add, and an enemy of the Kaiser—was showing me El Greco's "Laocoon," which he had just bought for Munich, when he whispered to me, as being too dangerous a doctrine to be spoken aloud even in his private room, "Do you know why we admire El Greco's handling so much? Because it reminds us of Cézanne."

No wonder, then, that for the artist of to-day the new El Greco is of capital importance. For it shows us the master at the height of his powers, at last perfectly aware of his personal conception and daring to give it the completest, most uncompromising expression. That the picture is in a marvellous state of preservation and has been admirably cleaned adds greatly to its value. Dirty yellow varnish no longer interposes here its hallowing influence between the spectator and the artist's original creation. Since the eye can follow every stroke of the brush, the mind can recover the artist's gesture and almost the movements of his mind. For never was work more perfectly transparent to the idea, never was an artist's intention more deliberately and precisely recorded.

Eugène Delacroix
Rubens and the Power of Painting

What an adoration I have for painting! The mere memory of certain pictures, even when I don't see them, goes through me with a feeling which stirs my whole being like all those rare and interesting memories that one finds at long intervals in one's life, and especially in the very early years of it.

Mme V. was recalling some of the Rubens' that she saw at Windsor. She spoke of a big equestrian portrait, one of those big figures in full armor, with a young man near by. It seemed to me as if I saw it. I know a great deal of what Rubens has done, and think I know everything that he can do. The mere memory of a little woman who certainly did not, when she saw the picture, feel the emotion which I experience when just imagining it, when I have not seen it, awoke in me the great images of the pictures by him that so struck my youth in Paris, at the Musée Napoléon, and in Belgium, on the two trips that I have made there.

Glory to that Homer of painting, to that father of warmth and of enthusiasm in the art where he blots out everything—not, if you like, through the perfection which he has brought to one part or another, but through that secret force and that life of the soul which he has attained everywhere. How strange! the picture which perhaps gave me the strongest sensation, the "Raising of the Cross," is not the one most brilliant through the qualities peculiar to him and in which he is incomparable. It is neither through color nor through the delicacy nor the frankness of the execution that this picture triumphs over the others but, curiously enough, through Italian qualities which, in the work of the Italians, do not delight me to the same degree; I think it is

RAPE OF THE DAUGHTERS OF LEUCIPPUS—PETER PAUL RUBENS
(Alte Pinakothek, Munich)

appropriate for me to take note here of the quite analogous way I have felt before Gros' battle pictures, and before the "Medusa," especially when I saw it half finished. The essential thing about these works is their reaching of the sublime, which comes in part from the size of the figures. The same pictures in small dimension would, I am sure, produce quite a different effect on me. In the effect of Rubens and in that of Géricault there is also an indefinable something of the style of Michelangelo, which adds again to the effect produced by the dimension of the figures and which gives them something terrifying. Proportion counts for very much in the greater or lesser power of a picture. Not only, as I was saying, would these pictures, executed in small size, be ordinary work for the master, but, were they merely life-size, they would not attain the effect of the sublime. The proof is that the engraving after the picture by Rubens does not at all produce that effect on me.

I ought to say that the matter of dimensions is not everything, for several of his pictures in which the figures are very large do not give me that type of emotion which, for me, is the most elevated one; neither can I say that it is something exclusively Italian in style, for Gros' pictures, which do not present a trace of it and which are completely his own, transport me to the same degree into that state of the soul which I regard as the most powerful that painting can inspire. The impressions produced by the arts on sensitive organisms are a curious mystery: confused impressions, if one tries to describe them, clear-cut and full of strength if one feels them again, and if only through memory! I strongly believe that we always mix in something of ourselves with feelings which seem to come from the objects that strike us. It is probable that the only reason why these works please me so much is that they respond to feelings which are my own; and since they give me the same degree of pleasure, different as they are, it must be that I find in myself the source of the effect which they produce.

The type of emotion peculiar to painting is, so to speak, *tangible;* poetry and music cannot give it. You enjoy the actual representation of objects as if you really saw them, and at the same time the meaning which the images have for the mind warms you and transports you. These figures, these objects, which seem the thing itself to a certain part of your intelligent being are like a solid bridge on which imagination supports itself to penetrate to the mysterious and profound sensation for which the forms are, so to speak, the hieroglyph, but a hieroglyph far more eloquent than a cold representation, a thing equivalent to no more than a character in the printer's font of type: it is in this sense that the art is sublime, if we compare it to one wherein thought reaches the mind only with the help of letters arranged in an order that has been agreed upon; it is a far more complicated art, if you will (since the font of type is nothing and thought seems to be everything), but a hundred times more expressive if one consider that, independently of the idea, the visible sign, the speaking hieroglyph, a sign without value for the mind in the work of the writer becomes a source of the liveliest enjoyment in the work of the painter. And so, looking upon the spectacle of created things, we have here the satisfaction given by beauty, proportion, contrast, harmony of color, and everything that the eye looks upon with so much pleasure in the outer world—one of the great needs of our nature.

Many people will consider that it is precisely in this simplification of the means of expression that the superiority of literature resides. Such people have never considered with pleasure an arm, a hand, a torso from the antique or from Puget; they care for sculpture even less than painting, and they are strangely deceived if they think that when they have written: *a foot* or *a hand,* they have given to my mind the same emotion as the one I experience when I see a beautiful foot or a beautiful hand. The arts are not algebra, in which the abbreviation of the figures contributes to the success of the problem; success in the arts is by no means a matter of abridging, but of amplifying, if possible, and prolonging the sensation by all possible means. What is the theater? One of the most certain witnesses to man's need for experiencing the largest possible number of emotions at one time. It gathers together all the arts so that each may make us feel their combined effect more strongly; pantomime, costume, and the beauty of the performer double the effect of the word that is spoken or sung. The representation of the place in which the action occurs adds still further to all these types of impression.

It will now be clearer why I have spoken as I have about the *power of painting.* If it possesses but a single moment, it concentrates the *effect* of that moment; the painter is far more the master of that which he wants to express than is the poet or the musician, who is in the hands of interpreters; in a word, if his memory is directed toward fewer aspects of things, he produces an effect which is absolutely one and which can satisfy completely; in addition, the work of the painter is not subject to the same variations, as regards the manner in which it may be understood at different periods. Changing fashion and the prejudices of the moment may cause its value to be looked upon in different ways; but in the end it is always the same, it remains as the artist wanted it to be, whereas the same is not true of things that must pass through the hands of interpreters, as must the works of the theater. Since the feeling of the artist is no longer there to guide the actors or the singers, the execution can no longer respond to the original intention of the work: the accent disappears, and with it the most delicate part of the impression. Indeed it is a happy author whose work is not mutilated, an affront to which he is exposed even during his lifetime! The mere change of an actor changes the whole physiognomy of a piece.

Journal, October 20, 1853.

That man Rubens is admirable. What an enchanter! I get out of sorts with him at times: I have words with him because of his heavy forms, because of his lack of research and of elegance. How superior he is to all those little qualities which make up the whole baggage of the others! There is a man, anyhow, who has the courage to be himself: he forces you to accept those so-called defects deriving from that force which sweeps along the man himself; they subjugate us despite the precepts which are good for everybody in the world—except him. Beyle professed to esteem the earlier work of Rossini more than the last ones which, however, are regarded as superior by the crowd: he gives as his reason the fact that in his youth Rossini did not try to produce *great music,* and that is true. Rubens does not chasten himself, and he is right. By permitting himself everything, he carries you beyond the limit scarcely attained by the greatest painters; he dominates you, he overpowers you with all his liberty and boldness.

I take note also that his principal quality, if it is possible to make a forced choice, is the prodigious relief of his figures, which is to say their prodigious life. Without this gift, there is no great artist; the solving of the problem of relief and bulk is reached only by the greatest painters. I have said elsewhere, I think, that even in sculpture there were men who possessed the secret of not achieving relief; that will become evident for any man gifted with a certain sentiment who will compare Puget's work with all other sculptures possible, I do not except even the Antique. He attains life through relief as no one else has been able to do; the same applies to Rubens as regards the painters. Titian and Veronese are flat beside him; let us observe in passing that Raphael, despite his small store of color and of aerial perspective, is in general strong on relief in the individual figures. One would not say as much for the modern among his imitators. There are good jokes to be made about the search for the flat, so esteemed by the arts now in fashion, including architecture.

Journal, October 21, 1860

The difference between classicism and romanticism seems to me . . . the difference between the complete and the fragmentary, the adult and the immature, the orderly and the chaotic . . .

T. S. Eliot

The classic is health, the romantic disease.

Goethe

NEOCLASSICISM AND THE GRAND STYLE

The greatest contribution made by Reynolds in his "Discourses," which originally were lectures for students at the Royal Academy of Art, was his discouragement of provincialism in English art. He called upon painters to follow the exalted tradition of European art as developed in Italy after the middle of the fifteenth century. As a theoretician, he stressed the need for painters to seek ideal beauty of form rather than to depend on minute observation, and he saw in the grand style of the High Renaissance, and specifically in the work of Michelangelo and Raphael, the summit of art. Above all, Reynolds, like a true neoclassicist, felt that the correct imitation of the best models was the basis of successful achievement in art. This, of course, was anathema to the romantic artists of the half century after Reynolds' death, and Blake's vehement outbursts against Reynolds and the "Discourses" were a sign of the turn against neoclassicism. In reading Reynolds today, one can appreciate his sound common sense, his freedom from cant, his neat intelligence, and his thorough knowledge of his art. The elegance and assurance of his style embody the personality so brilliantly described by his friend Oliver Goldsmith:

> *Here Reynolds is laid, and to tell you my mind,*
> *He has not left a better or wiser behind;*
> *His pencil was striking, resistless, and grand;*
> *His manners were gentle, complying, and bland;*
> *Still born to improve us in every part,*
> *His pencil our faces, his manners our heart;*
> *To coxcombs averse, yet most civilly steering,*
> *When they judged without skill he was still hard of hearing;*
> *When they talked of their Raphaels, Corregios, and stuff,*
> *He shifted his trumpet,[1] and only took snuff.*

[1] His ear trumpet. Reynolds was deaf.

Sir Joshua Reynolds
The Leading Principles of the Grand Style
(from *Discourse 3*)

It is not easy to speak with propriety to so many Students of different ages and different degrees of advancement. The mind requires nourishment adapted to its growth; and what may have promoted our earlier efforts, might retard us in our nearer approaches to perfection.

The first endeavours of a young Painter, as I have remarked in a former discourse, must be employed in the attainment of mechanical dexterity, and confined to the mere imitation of the object before him. Those who have advanced beyond the rudiments, may, perhaps, find advantage in reflecting on the advice which I have likewise given them, when I recommended the diligent study of the works of our great predecessors; but I at the same time endeavoured to guard them against an implicit submission to the authority of any one master however excellent; or by a strict imitation of his manner, precluding themselves from the abundance and variety of Nature. I will now add that Nature herself is not to be too closely copied. There are excellencies in the art of painting beyond what is commonly called the imitation of nature: and these excellencies I wish to point out. The students who, having passed through the initiatory exercises, are more advanced in the art, and who, sure of their hand, have leisure to exert their understanding, must now be told, that a mere copier of nature can never produce any thing great; can never raise and enlarge the conceptions, or warm the heart of the spectator.

The wish of the genuine painter must be more extensive: instead of endeavouring to amuse mankind with the minute neatness of his imitations, he must endeavour to improve them by the grandeur of his ideas; instead of seeking praise, by deceiving the superficial sense of the spectator, he must strive for fame, by captivating the imagination.

The principle now laid down, that the perfection of this art does not consist in mere imitation, is far from being new or singular. It is, indeed, supported by the general opinion of the enlightened part of mankind. The poets, orators, and rhetoricians of antiquity, are continually enforcing this position; that all the arts receive their perfection from an ideal beauty, superior to what is to be found in individual nature. They are ever referring to the practice of the painters and sculptors of their times, particularly Phidias, (the favourite artist of antiquity), to illustrate their assertions. As if they could not sufficiently express their admiration of his genius by what they knew, they have recourse to poetical enthusiasm. They call it inspiration; a gift from heaven. The artist is supposed to have ascended the celestial regions, to furnish his mind with this perfect idea of beauty. "He," says Proclus[2], "who takes for his model such forms as nature produces, and confines himself to an exact imitation of them, will never attain to what is perfectly beautiful. For the works of nature are full of disproportion, and fall very short of the true standard of beauty. So that Phidias, when he formed his Jupiter, did not copy any object ever presented to his sight; but contemplated only that image which he had conceived in his mind from Homer's description." And thus Cicero, speaking of the same Phidias: "Neither did this artist," says he, "when he carved the image of Jupiter or Minerva, set before him any one human figure, as a pattern, which he was to copy; but having a more perfect idea of beauty fixed in his mind, this he steadily contemplated, and to the imitation of this all his skill and labour were directed."

The Moderns are not less convinced than the Ancients of this superior power existing in the art, nor less sensible of its effects. Every language has adopted terms expressive of this excellence. The *gusto grande* of the Italians, the *beau ideal* of the French, and the *great style, genius,* and *taste* among the English, are but different appellations of the same thing. It is this intellectual dignity, they say, that ennobles the painter's art; that lays the line between him and the mere mechanick; and produces those great effects in an instant, which eloquence and poetry, by slow and repeated efforts, are scarcely able to attain.

Such is the warmth with which both the Ancients and Moderns speak of this divine principle of the art; but, as I have formerly observed, enthusiastick admiration seldom promotes knowledge. Though a student by such praise may have his attention roused, and a desire excited, of running in this great career; yet it is possible that what has been said to excite, may only serve to deter him. He examines his own mind, and perceives there nothing of that divine inspiration, with which, he is told, so many others have been favoured. He never travelled to heaven to gather new ideas; and he finds himself possessed of no other qualifications than what mere common observation and a plain understanding can confer. Thus he becomes gloomy amidst the splendour of figurative declamation, and thinks it hopeless, to pursue an object which he supposes out of the reach of human industry.

[2] Lib. 2, in Timæum Platonis (Plato's *Timaeus*), as cited by Junius *De Pictura Veterum*.

But on this, as upon many other occasions, we ought to distinguish how much is to be given to enthusiasm, and how much to reason. We ought to allow for, and we ought to commend, that strength of vivid expression, which is necessary to convey, in its full force, the highest sense of the most complete effect of art; taking care at the same time, not to lose in terms of vague admiration, that solidity and truth of principle, upon which alone we can reason, and may be enabled to practise.

It is not easy to define in what this great style consists; nor to describe, by words, the proper means of acquiring it, if the mind of the student should be at all capable of such an acquisition. Could we teach taste or genius by rules, they would be no longer taste and genius. But though there neither are, nor can be, any precise invariable rules for the exercise, or the acquisition, of these great qualities, yet we may truly say that they always operate in proportion to our attention in observing the works of nature, to our skill in selecting, and to our care in digesting, methodizing, and comparing our observations. There are many beauties in our art, that seem, at first, to lie without the reach of precept, and yet may easily be reduced to practical principles. Experience is all in all; but it is not every one who profits by experience; and most people err, not so much from want of capacity to find their object, as from not knowing what object to pursue. This great ideal perfection and beauty are not to be sought in the heavens, but upon the earth. They are about us, and upon every side of us. But the power of discovering what is deformed in nature, or in other words, what is particular and uncommon, can be acquired only by experience; and the whole beauty and grandeur of the art consists, in my opinion, in being able to get above all singular forms, local customs, particularities, and details of every kind.

All the objects which are exhibited to our view by nature, upon close examination will be found to have their blemishes and defects. The most beautiful forms have something about them like weakness, minuteness, or imperfection. But it is not every eye that perceives these blemishes. It must be an eye long used to the contemplation and comparison of these forms; and which, by a long habit of observing what any set of objects of the same kind have in common, has acquired the power of discerning what each wants in particular. This long laborious comparison should be the first study of the painter, who aims at the greatest style. By this means, he acquires a just idea of beautiful forms; he corrects nature by herself, her imperfect state by her more perfect. His eye being enabled to distinguish the accidental deficiencies, ex-

crescences, and deformities of things, from their general figures, he
makes out an abstract idea of their forms more perfect than any one
original; and what may seem a paradox, he learns to design naturally
by drawing his figures unlike to any one object. This idea of the perfect
state of nature, which the Artist calls the Ideal Beauty, is the great
leading principle, by which works of genius are conducted. By this
Phidias acquired his fame. He wrought upon a sober principle, what
has so much excited the enthusiasm of the world; and by this method
you, who have courage to tread the same path, may acquire equal
reputation.

This is the idea which has acquired, and which seems to have a
right to the epithet of *divine;* as it may be said to preside, like a supreme judge, over all the productions of nature; appearing to be
possessed of the will and intention of the Creator, as far as they regard
the external form of living beings. When a man once possesses this
idea in its perfection, there is no danger, but that he will be sufficiently
warmed by it himself, and be able to warm and ravish every one else.

Thus it is from a reiterated experience, and a close comparison of
the objects in nature, that an artist becomes possessed of the idea of
that central form, if I may so express it, from which every deviation
is deformity. But the investigation of this form, I grant, is painful, and
I know but of one method of shortening the road; this is, by a careful
study of the works of the ancient sculptors; who, being indefatigable in
the school of nature, have left models of that perfect form behind them,
which an artist would prefer as supremely beautiful, who had spent his
whole life in that single contemplation. But if industry carried them
thus far, may not you also hope for the same reward from the same
labour? We have the same school opened to us, that was opened to
them; for nature denies her instructions to none, who desire to become
her pupils.

This laborious investigation, I am aware, must appear superfluous
to those who think every thing is to be done by felicity, and the powers
of native genius. Even the great Bacon treats with ridicule the idea of
confining proportion to rules, or of producing beauty by selection. "A
man cannot "tell," says he, "whether Apelles or Albert Dürer were the
more trifler; whereof the one would make a personage by geometrical
proportions; the other, by taking the best parts out of divers faces, to
make one excellent. . . . The painter, (he adds,) must do it by a kind
of felicity, . . . and not by rule[3]."

[3] Essays, p. 252, edit. 1625.

It is not safe to question any opinion of so great a writer, and so profound a thinker, as undoubtedly Bacon was. But he studies brevity to excess; and therefore his meaning is sometimes doubtful. If he means that beauty has nothing to do with rule, he is mistaken. There is a rule, obtained out of general nature, to contradict which is to fall into deformity. Whenever any thing is done beyond this rule, it is in virtue of some other rule which is followed along with it, but which does not contradict it. Every thing which is wrought with certainty, is wrought upon some principle. If it is not, it cannot be repeated. If by felicity is meant any thing of chance or hazard, or something born with a man, and not earned, I cannot agree with this great philosopher. Every object which pleases must give us pleasure upon some certain principles; but as the objects of pleasure are almost infinite, so their principles vary without end, and every man finds them out, not by felicity or successful hazard, but by care and sagacity.

To the principle I have laid down, that the idea of beauty in each species of beings is an invariable one, it may be objected, that in every particular species there are various central forms, which are separate and distinct from each other, and yet are undeniably beautiful; that in the human figure, for instance, the beauty of Hercules is one, of the Gladiator another, of the Apollo another; which makes so many different ideas of beauty.

It is true, indeed, that these figures are each perfect in their kind, though of different characters and proportions, but still none of them is the representation of an individual, but of a class. And as there is one general form, which, as I have said, belongs to the human kind at large, so in each of these classes there is one common idea and central form, which is the abstract of the various individual forms belonging to that class. Thus, though the forms of childhood and age differ exceedingly, there is a common form in childhood, and a common form in age, which is the more perfect, as it is more remote from all peculiarities. But I must add further, that though the most perfect forms of each of the general divisions of the human figure are ideal, and superior to any individual form of that class; yet the highest perfection of the human figure is not to be found in any one of them. It is not in the Hercules, nor in the Gladiator, nor in the Apollo; but in that form which is taken from them all, and which partakes equally of the activity of the Gladiator, of the delicacy of the Apollo, and of the muscular strength of the Hercules. For perfect beauty in any species must combine all the characters which are beautiful in that species.

It cannot consist in any one to the exclusion of the rest: no one, therefore, must be predominant, that no one may be deficient.

The knowledge of these different characters, and the power of separating and distinguishing them, is undoubtedly necessary to the painter, who is to vary his compositions with figures of various forms and proportions, though he is never to lose sight of the general idea of perfection in each kind.

There is, likewise, a kind of symmetry, or proportion, which may properly be said to belong to deformity. A figure lean or corpulent, tall or short, though deviating from beauty, may still have a certain union of the various parts, which may contribute to make them on the whole not unpleasing.

When the Artist has by diligent attention acquired a clear and distinct idea of beauty and symmetry; when he has reduced the variety of nature to the abstract idea; his next task will be to become acquainted with the genuine habits of nature, as distinguished from those of fashion. For in the same manner, and on the same principles, as he has acquired the knowledge of the real forms of nature, distinct from accidental deformity, he must endeavour to separate simple chaste nature, from those adventitious, those affected and forced airs or actions, with which she is loaded by modern education.

Perhaps I cannot better explain what I mean, than by reminding you of what was taught us by the Professor of Anatomy, in respect to the natural position and movement of the feet. He observed that the fashion of turning them outwards was contrary to the intent of nature, as might be seen from the structure of the bones, and from the weakness that proceeded from that manner of standing. To this we may add the erect position of the head, the projection of the chest, the walking with straight knees, and many such actions, which we know to be merely the result of fashion, and what nature never warranted, as we are sure that we have been taught them when children.

I have mentioned but a few of those instances, in which vanity or caprice have contrived to distort and disfigure the human form; your own recollection will add to these a thousand more of ill-understood methods, which have been practised to disguise nature, among our dancing-masters, hair-dressers, and tailors, in their various schools of deformity[4].

However the mechanick and ornamental arts may sacrifice to fashion,

[4] "Those," says Quintilian, "who are taken with the outward shew of things, think that there is more beauty in persons, who are trimmed, curled, and painted, than uncorrupt nature can give; as if beauty were merely the effect of the corruption of manners."

she must be entirely excluded from the Art of Painting; the painter must never mistake this capricious changeling for the genuine offspring of nature; he must divest himself of all prejudices in favour of his age or country; he must disregard all local and temporary ornaments, and look only on those general habits which are every where and always the same. He addresses his works to the people of every country and every age; he calls upon posterity to be his spectators, and says with Zeuxis, *in æternitatem pingo* ("I paint for eternity").

The neglect of separating modern fashions from the habits of nature, leads to that ridiculous style which has been practised by some painters, who have given to Grecian Heroes the airs and graces practised in the court of Louis the Fourteenth, an absurdity almost as great as it would have been to have dressed them after the fashion of that court.

To avoid this error, however, and to retain the true simplicity of nature, is a task more difficult than at first sight it may appear. The prejudices in favour of the fashions and customs that we have been used to, and which are justly called a second nature, make it too often difficult to distinguish that which is natural, from that which is the result of education; they frequently even give a predilection in favour of the artificial mode; and almost every one is apt to be guided by those local prejudices, who has not chastised his mind, and regulated the instability of his affections by the eternal invariable idea of nature.

Here then, as before, we must have recourse to the Ancients as instructors. It is from a careful study of their works that you will be enabled to attain to the real simplicity of nature; they will suggest many observations, which would probably escape you, if your study were confined to nature alone. And, indeed, I cannot help suspecting, that in this instance the ancients had an easier task than the moderns. They had, probably, little or nothing to unlearn, as their manners were nearly approaching to this desirable simplicity; while the modern artist, before he can see the truth of things, is obliged to remove a veil, with which the fashion of the times has thought proper to cover her.

Having gone thus far in our investigation of the great stile in painting; if we now should suppose that the artist has formed the true idea of beauty, which enables him to give his works a correct and perfect design; if we should suppose also, that he has acquired a knowledge of the unadulterated habits of nature, which gives him simplicity; the rest of his task is, perhaps, less than is generally imagined. Beauty and simplicity have so great a share in the composition of a great stile, that he who has acquainted them has little else to laern. It must not, indeed, be forgotten, that there is a nobleness of conception, which goes beyond any thing in the mere exhibition even of perfect form; there is an art of animating and dignifying the figures with intellectual grandeur, of impressing the appearance of philosophick wisdom, or heroick virtue. This can only be acquired by him that enlarges the sphere of his understanding by a variety of knowledge, and warms his imagination with the best productions of ancient and modern poetry.

A hand thus exercised, and a mind thus instructed, will bring the art to an higher degree of excellence than, perhaps, it has hitherto attained in this country. Such a student will disdain the humbler walks of painting, which, however profitable, can never assure him a permanent reputation. He will leave the meaner artist servilely to suppose that those are the best pictures, which are most likely to deceive the spectator. He will permit the lower painter, like the florist or collector of shells, to exhibit the minute discriminations, which distinguish one object of the same species from another; while he, like the philosopher, will consider nature in the abstract, and represent in every one of his figures the character of its species.

If deceiving the eye were the only business of the art, there is no doubt, indeed, but the minute painter would be more apt to succeed; but it is not the eye, it is the mind, which the painter of genius desires to address; nor will he waste a moment upon those smaller objects, which only serve to catch the sense, to divide the attention, and to counteract his great design of speaking to the heart.

This is the ambition which I wish to excite in your minds; and the object I have had in my view, throughout this discourse, is that one great idea, which gives to painting its true dignity, which entitles it to the name of a Liberal Art, and ranks it as a sister of poetry.

It may possibly have happened to many young students, whose application was sufficient to overcome all difficulties, and whose minds were capable of embracing the most extensive views, that they have, by a wrong direction originally given, spent their lives in the meaner walks of painting, without ever knowing there was a nobler to pursue. Albert Dürer, as Vasari has justly remarked, would, probably, have been one of the first painters of his age, (and he lived in an era of great artists,) had he been initiated into those great principles of the art, which were so well understood and practised by his contemporaries in Italy. But unluckily having never seen or heard of any other manner, he, without doubt, considered his own as perfect.

As for the various departments of painting, which do not presume to make such high pretensions, they are many. None of them are with-

THE TRAGIC MUSE—JOSHUA
REYNOLDS (*Huntington Li-
brary and Art Gallery, San
Marino, California*)

out their merit, though none enter into competition with this universal presiding idea of the art. The painters who have applied themselves more particularly to low and vulgar characters, and who express with precision the various shades of passion, as they are exhibited by vulgar minds, (such as we see in the works of Hogarth,) deserve great praise; but as their genius has been employed on low and confined subjects, the praise which we give must be as limited as its object. The merry-making, or quarrelling, of the Boors of Teniers, the same sort of productions of Brouwer, or Ostade, are excellent in their kind; and the excellence and its praise will be in proportion, as, in those limited subjects, and peculiar forms, they introduce more or less of the expression of those passions, as they appear in general and more enlarged nature. This principle may be applied to the Battle-pieces of Bourgognone, the French Gallantries of Watteau, and even beyond the exhibition of animal life, to the Landscapes of Claude Lorraine, and the Sea-Views of Vandervelde. All these painters have, in general, the same right, in different degrees, to the name of a painter, which a satirist, an epigrammatist, a sonneteer, a writer of pastorals, or descriptive poetry, has to that of a poet.

In the same rank, and perhaps of not so great merit, is the cold painter of portraits. But his correct and just imitation of his object has its merit. Even the painter of still life, whose highest ambition is to give a minute representation of every part of those low objects which he sets before him, deserves praise in proportion to his attainment; because no part of this excellent art, so much the ornament of polished life, is destitute of value and use. These, however, are by no means the views to which the mind of the student ought to be *primarily* directed. Having begun by aiming at better things, if from particular inclination, or from the taste of the time and place he lives in, or from necessity, or from failure in the highest attempts, he is obliged to descend lower, he will bring into the lower sphere of art a grandeur of composition and character, that will raise and ennoble his works far above their natural rank.

A man is not weak, though he may not be able to wield the club of Hercules; nor does a man always practise that which he esteems the best; but does that which he can best do. In moderate attempts, there are many walks open to the artist. But as the idea of beauty is of necessity but one, so there can be but one great mode of painting; the leading principle of which I have endeavoured to explain.

I should be sorry, if what is here recommended, should be at all understood to countenance a careless or indetermined manner of painting. For though the painter is to overlook the accidental discriminations of nature, he is to exhibit distinctly, and with precision, the general forms of things. A firm and determined outline is one of the characteristics of the great style in painting; and let me add, that he who possesses the knowledge of the exact form which every part of nature ought to have, will be fond of expressing that knowledge with correctness and precision in all his works. . . .

On Imitation
(from *Discourse 6*)

. . . The subject of this discourse will be *Imitation,* as far as a painter is concerned in it. By imitation I do not mean imitation in its largest sense, but simply the following of other masters, and the advantage to be drawn from the study of their works.

Those who have undertaken to write on our art, and have represented it as a kind of *inspiration,* as a *gift* bestowed upon peculiar favourites at their birth, seem to insure a much more favourable disposition from their readers, and have a much more captivating and liberal air, than he who attempts to examine, coldly, whether there are any means by which this art may be acquired; how the mind may be strengthened and expanded, and what guides will shew the way to eminence.

It is very natural for those who are unacquainted with the *cause* of any thing extraordinary, to be astonished at the *effect,* and to consider it as a kind of magick. They, who have never observed the gradation by which art is acquired; who see only what is the full result of long labour and application of an infinite number and infinite variety of acts, are apt to conclude from their entire inability to do the same at once, that it is not only inaccessible to themselves, but can be done by those only, who have some gift of the nature of inspiration bestowed upon them.

The travellers into the East tell us, that when the ignorant inhabitants of those countries are asked concerning the ruins of stately edifices yet remaining amongst them, the melancholy monuments of their former grandeur and long-lost science, they always answer, that they were built by magicians. The untaught mind finds a vast gulph between its own powers, and those works of complicated art, which it is utterly unable to fathom; and it supposes that such a void can be passed only by supernatural powers.

And, as for artists themselves, it is by no means their interest to undeceive such judges, however conscious they may be of the very natural means by which their extraordinary powers were acquired; though our art, being intrinsically imitative, rejects this idea of inspiration, more perhaps than any other.

It is to avoid this plain confession of truth, as it should seem, that this imitation of masters, indeed almost all imitation, which implies a more regular and progressive method of attaining the ends of painting, has ever been particularly inveighed against with great keenness, both by ancient and modern writers.

To derive all from native power, to owe nothing to another, is the praise which men, who do not much think on what they are saying, bestow sometimes upon others, and sometimes on themselves; and their imaginary dignity is naturally heightened by a supercilious censure of the low, the barren, the groveling, the servile imitator. It would be no wonder if a student, frightened by these terrifick and disgraceful epithets, with which the poor imitators are so often loaded, should let fall his pencil in mere despair; (conscious as he must be, how much he has been indebted to the labours of others, how little, how very little of his art was born with him;) and, consider it as hopeless, to set about acquiring by the imitation of any human master, what he is taught to suppose is matter of inspiration from heaven.

Some allowance must be made for what is said in the gaiety or ambition of rhetorick. We cannot suppose that any one can really mean to exclude all imitation of others. A position so wild would scarce deserve a serious answer; for it is apparent, if we were forbid to make use of the advantages which our predecessors afford us, the art would be always to begin, and consequently remain always in its infant state; and it is a common observation, that no art was ever invented and carried to perfection at the same time.

But to bring us entirely to reason and sobriety, let it be observed, that a painter must not only be of necessity an imitator of the works of nature, which alone is sufficient to dispel this phantom of inspiration, but he must be as necessarily an imitator of the works of other painters: this appears more humiliating, but is equally true; and no man can be an artist, whatever he may suppose, upon any other terms.

However, those who appear more moderate and reasonable, allow, that our study is to begin by imitation; but maintain that we should no longer use the thoughts of our predecessors, when we are become able to think for ourselves. They hold that imitation is as hurtful to the more advanced student, as it was advantageous to the beginner.

For my own part, I confess, I am not only very much disposed to maintain the absolute necessity of imitation in the first stages of the art; but am of opinion, that the study of other masters, which I here call imitation, may be extended throughout our whole lives, without any danger of the inconveniences with which it is charged, of enfeebling the mind, or preventing us from giving that original air which every work undoubtedly ought always to have.

I am on the contrary persuaded, that by imitation only, variety, and even originality of invention, is produced. I will go further; even genius, at least what generally is so called, is the child of imitation. But as this appears to be contrary to the general opinion, I must explain my position before I enforce it.

Genius is supposed to be a power of producing excellencies, which are out of the reach of the rules of art; a power which no precepts can teach, and which no industry can acquire.

This opinion of the impossibility of acquiring those beauties, which stamp the work with the character of genius, supposes, that it is something more fixed than in reality it is, and that we always do, and ever did agree in opinion, with respect to what should be considered as the characteristick of genius. But the truth is, that the *degree* of excellence which proclaims *Genius* is different, in different times and different places; and what shews it to be so is, that mankind have often changed their opinion upon this matter.

When the arts were in their infancy, the power of merely drawing the likeness of any object, was considered as one of its greatest efforts. The common people, ignorant of the principles of art, talk the same language, even to this day. But when it was found that every man could be taught to do this, and a great deal more, merely by the observance of certain precepts; the name of Genius then shifted its application, and was given only to him who added the peculiar character of the object he represented; to him who had invention, expression, grace, or dignity; in short, those qualities, or excellencies, the power of producing which, could not *then* be taught by any known and promulgated rules.

We are very sure that the beauty of form, the expression of the passions, the art of composition, even the power of giving a general air of grandeur to a work, is at present very much under the dominion of rules. These excellencies were, heretofore, considered merely as the effects of genius; and justly, if genius is not taken for inspiration, but as the effect of close observation and experience.

He who first made any of these observations, and digested them, so as to form an invariable principle for himself to work by, had that merit, but probably no one went very far at once; and generally, the first who gave the hint, did not know how to pursue it steadily, and methodically; at least not in the beginning. He himself worked on it, and improved it; others worked more, and improved further; until the secret was discovered, and the practice made as general, as refined practice can be made. How many more principles may be fixed and ascertained, we cannot tell; but as criticism is likely to go hand in hand with the art which is its subject, we may venture to say, that as that art shall advance, its powers will be still more and more fixed by rules.

But by whatever strides criticism may gain ground, we need be under no apprehension, that invention will ever be annihilated, or subdued; or intellectual energy be brought entirely within the restraint of written law. Genius will still have room enough to expatiate, and

keep always at the same distance from narrow comprehension and mechanical performance.

What we now call Genius, begins, not where rules, abstractedly
taken, end; but where known vulgar and trite rules have no longer any
place. It must of necessity be, that even works of Genius, like every
other effect, as they must have their cause, must likewise have their
rules; it cannot be by chance, that excellencies are produced with any
constancy or any certainty, for this is not the nature of chance; but the
rules by which men of extraordinary parts, and such as are called men
of Genius work, are either such as they discover by their own peculiar
observations, or of such a nice texture as not easily to admit being
expressed in words; especially as artists are not very frequently skilful
in that mode of communicating ideas. Unsubstantial, however, as these
rules may seem, and difficult as it may be to convey them in writing,
they are still seen and felt in the mind of the artist; and he works from
them with as much certainty, as if they were embodied, as I may say,
upon paper. It is true, these refined principles cannot be always made
palpable, like the more gross rules of art; yet it does not follow, but
that the mind may be put in such a train, that it shall perceive, by a
kind of scientifick sense, that propriety, which words, particularly words
of unpractised writers, such as we are, can but very feebly suggest.

Invention is one of the great marks of genius; but if we consult
experience, we shall find, that it is by being conversant with the inventions of others, that we learn to invent; as by reading the thoughts of
others we learn to think.

Whoever has so far formed his taste, as to be able to relish and feel
the beauties of the great masters, has gone a great way in his study; for,
merely from a consciousness of this relish of the right, the mind swells
with an inward pride, and is almost as powerfully affected, as if it had
itself produced what it admires. Our hearts frequently warmed in this
manner by the contact of those whom we wish to resemble, will undoubtedly catch something of their way of thinking; and we shall
receive in our own bosoms some radiation at least of their fire and
splendour. That disposition, which is so strong in children, still continues with us, of catching involuntarily the general air and manner
of those with whom we are most conversant; with this difference only,
that a young mind is naturally pliable and imitative; but in a more
advanced state it grows rigid, and must be warmed and softened, before
it will receive a deep impression.

From these considerations, which a little of your own reflection will carry a great way further, it appears, of what great consequence it is, that our minds should be habituated to the contemplation of excellence; and that, far from being contented to make such habits the discipline of our youth only, we should, to the last moment of our lives, continue a settled intercourse with all the true examples of grandeur. Their inventions are not only the food of our infancy, but the substance which supplies the fullest maturity of our vigour.

The mind is but a barren soil; a soil which is soon exhausted, and will produce no crop, or only one, unless it be continually fertilized and enriched with foreign matter.

When we have had continually before us the great works of Art to impregnate our minds with kindred ideas, we are then, and not till then, fit to produce something of the same species. We behold all about us with the eyes of those penetrating observers whose works we contemplate; and our minds accustomed to think the thoughts of the noblest and brightest intellects, are prepared for the discovery and selection of all that is great and noble in nature. The greatest natural genius cannot subsist on its own stock; he who resolves never to ransack any mind but his own, will be soon reduced, from mere barrenness, to the poorest of all imitations; he will be obliged to imitate himself, and to repeat what he has before often repeated. When we know the subject designed by such men, it will never be difficult to guess what kind of work is to be produced.

It is vain for painters or poets to endeavour to invent without materials on which the mind may work, and from which invention must originate. Nothing can come of nothing.

Homer is supposed to be possessed of all the learning of his time: and we are certain that Michael Angelo, and Raffaelle, were equally possessed of all the knowledge in the art which had been discovered in the works of their predecessors.

A mind enriched by an assemblage of all the treasures of ancient and modern art, will be more elevated and fruitful in resources in proportion to the number of ideas which have been carefully collected and thoroughly digested. There can be no doubt but that he who has the most materials has the greatest means of inventions; and if he has not the power of using them, it must proceed from a feebleness of intellect; or from the confused manner in which those collections have been laid up in his mind.

The addition of other men's judgment is so far from weakening our own, as is the opinion of many, that it will fashion and consolidate those ideas of excellence which lay in embryo, feeble, ill-shaped, and confused, but which are finished and put in order by the authority and practice of those, whose works may be said to have been consecrated by having stood the test of ages.

The mind, or genius, has been compared to a spark of fire, which is smothered by a heap of fuel, and prevented from blazing into a flame: This simile, which is made use of by the younger Pliny, may be easily mistaken for argument or proof. But there is no danger of the mind's being over-burdened with knowledge, or the genius extinguished by any addition of images; on the contrary, these acquisitions may as well, perhaps better, be compared, if comparisons signified any thing in reasoning, to the supply of living embers, which will contribute to strengthen the spark, that without the association of more fuel would have died away. The truth is, he whose feebleness is such, as to make other men's thoughts as incumbrance to him, can have no very great strength of mind or genius of his own to be destroyed; so that not much harm will be done at worst.

We may oppose to Pliny the greatest authority of Cicero, who is continually enforcing the necessity of this method of study. In his dialogue on Oratory, he makes Crassus say, that one of the first and most important precepts is, to choose a proper model for our imitation. *Hoc sit primum in præceptis meis ut demonstremus quem imitemur.*

When I speak of the habitual imitation and continued study of masters, it is not to be understood, that I advise any endeavour to copy the exact peculiar colour and complexion of another man's mind; the success of such an attempt must always be like his, who imitates exactly the air, manner, and gestures, of him whom he admires. His model may be excellent, but the copy will be ridiculous; this ridicule does not arise from his having imitated, but from his not having chosen the right mode of imitation.

It is a necessary and warrantable pride to disdain to walk servilely behind any individual, however elevated his rank. The true and liberal ground of imitation is an open field; where, though he who precedes has had the advantage of starting before you, you may always propose to overtake him: it is enough however to pursue his course; you need not tread in his footsteps; and you certainly have a right to outstrip him if you can.

Nor whilst I recommend studying the art from artists, can I be supposed to mean, that nature is to be neglected: I take this study in aid, and not in exclusion, of the other. Nature is, and must be the fountain which alone is inexhaustible; and from which all excellencies must originally flow.

The great use of studying our predecessors is, to open the mind, to shorten our labour, and to give us the result of the selection made by those great minds of what is grand or beautiful in nature: her rich stores are all spread out before us; but it is an art, and no easy art, to know how or what to choose, and how to attain and secure the object of our choice. Thus the highest beauty of form must be taken from nature; but it is an art of long deduction, and great experience, to know how to find it. We must not content ourselves with merely admiring and relishing; we must enter into the principles on which the work is wrought: these do not swim on the superficies, and consequently are not open to superficial observers.

Art in its perfection is not ostentatious; it lies hid, and works its effect, itself unseen. It is the proper study and labour of an artist to uncover and find out the latent cause of conspicuous beauties, and from thence form principles for his own conduct: such an examination is a continual exertion of the mind; as great, perhaps, as that of the artist whose works he is thus studying.

The sagacious imitator does not content himself with merely remarking what distinguishes the different manner or genius of each master; he enters into the contrivance in the composition, how the masses of lights are disposed, the means by which the effect is produced, how artfully some parts are lost in the ground, others boldly relieved, and how all these are mutually altered and interchanged according to the reason and scheme of the work. He admires not the harmony of colouring alone, but examines by what artifice one colour is a foil to its neighbour. He looks close into the tints, examines of what colours they are composed, till he has formed clear and distinct ideas, and has learnt to see in what harmony and good colouring consists. What is learned in this manner from the works of others becomes really our own, sinks deep, and is never forgotten, nay, it is by seizing on this clue that we proceed forward, and, get further and further in enlarging the principles and improving the practice of our art.

There can be no doubt, but the art is better learnt from the works themselves than from the precepts which are formed upon those works; but if it is difficult to choose proper models for imitation, it requires no less circumspection to separate and distinguish what in those models we ought to imitate.

I cannot avoid mentioning here, though it is not my intention at present to enter into the art and method of study, an error which students are too apt to fall into. He that is forming himself, must look with great caution and wariness on those peculiarities, or prominent parts, which at first force themselves upon view; and are the marks, or what is commonly called the manner, by which that individual artist is distinguished.

Peculiar marks, I hold to be, generally, if not always, defects; however difficult it may be wholly to escape them.

Peculiarities in the works of art, are like those in the human figure; it is by them that we are cognizable and distinguished one from another, but they are always so many blemishes; which, however, both in real life and in painting, cease to appear deformities, to those who have them continually before their eyes. In the works of art, even the most enlightened mind, when warmed by beauties of the highest kind, will by degrees find a repugnance within him to acknowledge any defects; nay, his enthusiasm will carry him so far, as to transform them into beauties, and objects of imitation.

It must be acknowledged, that a peculiarity of style, either from its novelty, or by seeming to proceed from a peculiar turn of mind, often escapes blame; on the contrary, it is sometimes striking and pleasing; but this it is a vain labour to endeavour to imitate; because novelty and peculiarity being its only merit, when it ceases to be new, it ceases to have value.

A manner therefore being a defect, and every painter, however excellent, having a manner, it seems to follow, that all kinds of faults, as well as beauties, may be learned under the sanction of the greatest authorities. Even the great name of Michael Angelo may be used, to keep in countenance a deficiency or rather neglect of colouring, and every other ornamental part of the art. If the young student is dry and hard, Poussin is the same. If his work has a careless and unfinished air, he has most of the Venetian school to support him. If he makes no selection of objects, but takes individual nature just as he finds it, he is like Rembrandt. If he is incorrect in the proportions of his figures, Correggio was likewise incorrect. If his colours are not blended and united, Rubens was equally crude. In short, there is no defect that may not be excused, if it is a sufficient excuse that it can be imputed to considerable artists; but it must be remembered, that it was not by these defects they acquired their reputation; they have a right to our pardon, but not to our admiration.

However, to imitate peculiarities or mistake defects for beauties, that man will be most liable, who confines his imitation to one favourite master; and even though he chooses the best, and is capable of distinguishing the real excellencies of his model, it is not by such narrow practice, that a genius or mastery in the art is acquired. A man is as little likely to form a true idea of the perfection of the art, by studying a single artist, as he would be to produce a perfectly beautiful figure, by an exact imitation of any individual living model. And as the painter, by bringing together in one piece, those beauties which are dispersed among a great variety of individuals, produces a figure more beautiful than can be found in nature, so that artist who can unite in himself the excellencies of the various great painters, will approach nearer to perfection than any one of his masters. He, who confines himself to the imitation of an individual, as he never proposes to surpass, so he is not likely to equal, the object of his imitation. He professes only to follow; and he that follows must necessarily be behind.

We should imitate the conduct of the great artists in the course of their studies, as well as the works which they produced, when they were perfectly formed. Raffaello began by imitating implicitly the manner of Pietro Perugino, under whom he studied; hence his first works are scarce to be distinguished from his master's; but soon forming higher and more extensive views, he imitated the grand outline of Michael Angelo; he learned the manner of using colours from the works of Leonardo da Vinci, and Fratre Bartolomeo: to all this he added the contemplation of all the remains of antiquity that were within his reach; and employed others to draw for him what was in Greece and distant places. And it is from his having taken so many models, that he became himself a model for all succeeding painters; always imitating, and always original.

If your ambition, therefore, be to equal Raffaelle, you must do as Raffaelle did; take many models, and not even *him* for your guide alone to the exclusion of others[5]. And yet the number is infinite of those who seem, if one may judge by their style, to have seen no other works but those of their master, or of some favourite, whose *manner* is their first wish, and their last. . . .

To find excellencies, however dispersed, to discover beauties, however concealed by the multitude of defects with which they are surrounded, can be the work only of him, who having a mind always alive to his art, has extended his views to all ages and to all schools; and has

[5] Sed non qui maxime imitandus, etiam solus imitandus est. Quintilian.

acquired from that comprehensive mass which he has thus gathered to himself, a well-digested and perfect idea of his art, to which every thing is referred. Like a sovereign judge and arbiter of art, he is possessed of that presiding power which separates and attracts every excellence from every school; selects both from what is great, and what is little; brings home knowledge from the East and from the West; making the universe tributary towards furnishing his mind and enriching his works with originality, and variety of inventions.

Thus I have ventured to give my opinion of what appears to me the true and only method by which an artist makes himself master of his profession; which I hold ought to be one continued course of imitation that is not to cease but with his life.

Those, who either from their own engagements and hurry of business, or from indolence, or from conceit and vanity, have neglected looking out of themselves, as far as my experience and observation reaches, have from that time, not only ceased to advance, and improve in their performances, but have gone backward. They may be compared to men who have lived upon their principal till they are reduced to beggary, and left without resources.

I can recommend nothing better, therefore, than that you endeavour to infuse into your works what you learn from the contemplation of the works of others. To recommend this has the appearance of needless and superfluous advice; but it has fallen within my own knowledge, that artists, though they were not wanting in a sincere love for their art, though they had great pleasure in seeing good pictures, and were well skilled to distinguish what was excellent or defective in them, yet have gone on in their own manner, without any endeavour to give a little of those beauties, which they admired in others, to their own works. It is difficult to conceive how the present Italian painters, who live in the midst of the treasures of art, should be contented with their own style. They proceed in their common-place inventions, and never think it worth while to visit the works of those great artists with which they are surrounded.

I remember, several years ago, to have conversed at Rome with an artist of great fame throughout Europe; he was not without a considerable degree of abilities, but those abilities were by no means equal to his own opinion of them. From the reputation he had acquired, he too fondly concluded that he stood in the same rank, when compared with his predecessors, as he held with regard to his miserable contemporary rivals. In conversation about some particulars of the works of

Raffaelle, he seemed to have, or to affect to have, a very obscure memory of them. He told me that he had not set his foot in the Vatican for fifteen years together; that indeed he had been in treaty to copy a capital picture of Raffaelle, but that the business had gone off; however, if the agreement had held, his copy would have greatly exceeded the original. The merit of this artist, however great we may suppose it, I am sure would have been far greater, and his presumption would have been far less, if he had visited the Vatican, as in reason he ought to have done, at least once every month of his life.

I address myself, Gentlemen, to you who have made some progress in the art, and are to be, for the future, under the guidance of your own judgment and discretion. I consider you as arrived to that period, when you have a right to think for yourselves, and to presume that every man is fallible; to study the masters with a suspicion, that great men are not always exempt from great faults; to criticise, compare, and rank their works in your own estimation, as they approach to, or recede from, that standard of perfection which you have formed in your own minds, but which those masters themselves, it must be remembered, have taught you to make; and which you will cease to make with correctness, when you cease to study them. It is their excellencies which have taught you their defects.

I would wish you to forget where you are, and who it is that speaks to you. I only direct you to higher models and better advisers. We can teach you here but very little; you are henceforth to be your own teachers. Do this justice, however, to the English Academy; to bear in mind, that in this place you contracted no narrow habits, no false ideas, nothing that could lead you to the imitation of any living master, who may be the fashionable darling of the day. As you have not been taught to flatter us, do not learn to flatter yourselves. We have endeavoured to lead you to the admiration of nothing but what is truly admirable. If you choose inferior patterns, or if you make your own *former* works your patterns for your *latter,* it is your own fault.

The purport of this discourse, and, indeed, of most of my other discourses, is to caution you against that false opinion, but too prevalent among artists, of the imaginary power of native genius, and its sufficiency in great works. This opinion, according to the temper of mind it meets with, almost always produces, either a vain confidence, or a sluggish despair, both equally fatal to all proficiency.

Study therefore the great works of the great masters, for ever. Study as nearly as you can, in the order, in the manner, and on the principles, on which they studied. Study nature attentively, but always with those masters in your company; consider them as models which you are to imitate, and at the same time as rivals with whom you are to contend.

Principles of Art and Simplicity
(from *Discourse 8*)

. . . Poetry having a more extensive power than our art, exerts its influence over almost all the passions; among those may be reckoned one of our most prevelant dispositions, anxiety for the future. Poetry operates by raising our curiosity, engaging the mind by degrees to take an interest in the event, keeping that event suspended, and surprising at last with an unexpected catastrophe.

The Painter's art is more confirmed, and has nothing that corresponds with, or perhaps is equivalent to, this power and advanatge of leading the mind on, till attention is totally engaged. What is done by Painting, must be done at one blow; curiosity has received at once all the satisfaction it can ever have. There are, however, other intellectual qualities and dispositions which the Painter can satisfy and affect as powerfully as the Poet; among those we may reckon our love of novelty, variety, and contrast; these qualities, on examination, will be found to refer to a certain activity and restlessness, which has a pleasure and delight in being exercised and put in motion: Art therefore only administers to those wants and desires of the mind.

It requires no long disquisition to shew, that the dispositions which I have stated actually subsist in the human mind. Variety reanimates the attention, which is apt to languish under a continual sameness. Novelty makes a more forcible impression on the mind, than can be made by the representation of what we have often seen before; and contrasts rouse the power of comparison by opposition. All this is obvious; but, on the other hand, it must be remembered, that the mind, though an active principle, has likewise a disposition to indolence; and though it loves exercise, loves it only to a certain degree, beyond which it is very unwilling to be led, or driven; the pursuit therefore of novelty and variety may be carried to excess. When variety entirely destroys the pleasure proceeding from uniformity and repetition, and when novelty counteracts and shuts out the pleasure arising from old habits and customs, they oppose too much the indolence of our disposition:

the mind therefore can bear with pleasure but a small portion of novelty at a time. The main part of the work must be in the mode to which we have been used. An affection to old habits and customs I take to be the predominant disposition of the mind, and novelty comes as an exception: where all is novelty, the attention, the exercise of the mind is too violent. Contrast, in the same manner, when it exceeds certain limits, is as disagreeable as a violent and perpetual opposition; it gives to the senses, in their progress, a more sudden change than they can bear with pleasure.

It is then apparent, that those qualities, however they contribute to the perfection of Art, when kept within certain bounds, if they are carried to excess, become defects, and require correction: a work consequently will not proceed better and better as it is more varied; variety can never be the groundwork and principle of the performance, it must be only employed to recreate and relieve.

To apply these general observations which belong equally to all arts, to ours in patricular. In a composition, when the objects are scattered and divided into many equal parts, the eye is perplexed and fatigued, from not knowing where to rest, where to find the principal action, or which is the principal figure; for where all are making equal pretensions to notice, all are in equal danger of neglect.

The expression which is used very often on these occasions is, the piece wants *repose;* a word which perfectly expresses a relief of the mind from that state of hurry and anxiety which it suffers, when looking at a work of this character.

On the other hand, absolute unity, that is, a large work, consisting of one group or mass of light only, would be as defective as an heroick poem without episode, or any collateral incidents to recreate the mind with that variety which it always requires.

An instance occurs to me of two painters, (Rembrandt and Poussin,) of characters totally opposite to each other in every respect, but in nothing more than in their mode of composition, and management of light and shadow. Rembrandt's manner is absolute unity; he often has but one group, and exhibits little more than one spot of light in the midst of a large quantity of shadow; if he has a second mass, that second bears no proportion to the principal. Poussin, on the contrary, has scarce any principal mass of light at all, and his figures are often too much dispersed, without sufficient attention to place them in groups.

The conduct of these two painters is entirely the reverse of what might be expected from their general style and character; the works of Poussin being as much distinguished for simplicity, as those of Rembrandt for combination. Even this conduct of Poussin might proceed from too great an affection to simplicity of *another kind;* too great a desire to avoid that ostentation of art, with regard to light and shadow, on which Rembrandt so much wished to draw the attention: however, each of them ran into contrary extremes, and it is difficult to determine which is the most reprehensible, both being equally distant from the demands of nature, and the purposes of art.

The same just moderation must be observed in regard to ornaments; nothing will contribute more to destroy repose than profusion, of whatever kind, whether it consists in the multiplicity of objects, or the variety and brightness of colours. On the other hand, a work without ornament, instead of simplicity, to which it makes pretensions, has rather the appearance of poverty, The degree to which ornaments are admissible, must be regulated by the professed style of the work; but we may be sure of this truth,—that the most ornamental style requires repose to set off even its ornaments to advantage. I cannot avoid mentioning here an instance of repose in that faithful and accurate painter

THE BLIND ORION SEARCHING FOR THE RISING SUN—NICOLAS POUSSIN
(*The Metropolitan Museum of Art, Fletcher Fund, 1924*)

of nature, Shakspeare; the short dialogue between Duncan and Banquo, whilst they are approaching the gates of Macbeth's castle. Their conversation very naturally turns upon the beauty of its situation, and the pleasantness of the air; and Banquo observing the martlets' nests in every recess of the cornice, remarks, that where those birds most breed and haunt, the air is delicate. The subject of this quiet and easy conversation gives that repose so necessary to the mind, after the tumultuous bustle of the preceding scenes, and perfectly contrasts the scene of horrour that immediately succeeds. It seems as if Shakspeare asked himself, What is a Prince likely to say to his attendants on such an occasion? The modern writers seem, on the contrary, to be always searching for new thoughts, such as never could occur to men in the situation represented. This is also frequently the practice of Homer, who, from the midst of battles and horrours, relieves and refreshes the mind of the reader, by introducing some quiet rural image, or picture of familiar domestick life. The writers of every age and country, where taste has begun to decline, paint and adorn every object they touch; are always on the stretch; never deviate or sink a moment from the pompous and the brilliant. Lucan, Statius, and Claudian, (as a learned critick has observed,) are examples of this bad taste and want of judgment; they never soften their tones, or condescend to be natural: all is exaggeration and perpetual splendour, without affording repose of any kind.

As we are speaking of excesses, it will not be remote from our purpose to say a few words upon simplicity; which, in one of the senses in which it is used, is considered as the general corrector of excess. We shall at present forbear to consider it as implying that exact conduct which proceeds from an intimate knowledge of simple unadulterated nature, as it is then only another word for perfection, which neither stops short of, nor oversteps, reality and truth.

In our enquiry after simplicity, as in many other enquiries of this nature, we can best explain what is right, by shewing what is wrong; and, indeed, in this case it seems to be absolutely necessary; simplicity, being only a negative virtue, cannot be described or defined. We must therefore explain its nature, and shew the advantage and beauty which is derived from it, by shewing the deformity which proceeds from its neglect.

Though instances of this neglect might be expected to be found in practice, we should not expect to find in the works of criticks, precepts that bid defiance to simplicity and every thing that relates to it. Du

Piles recommends to us portrait-painters, to add Grace and Dignity to the characters of those, whose pictures we draw: so far he is undoubtedly right; but, unluckily, he descends to particulars, and gives his own idea of Grace and Dignity. *If,* says he, *you draw persons of high character and dignity, they ought to be drawn in such an attitude, that the Portrait must seem to speak to us of themselves, and, as it were, to say to us, 'stop, take notice of me, I am that invincible King, surrounded by Majesty.' 'I am that valiant commander, who struck terrour every where.' 'I am that great minister who knew all the springs of politicks.' 'I am that magistrate of consummate wisdom and probity.'* He goes on in this manner, with all the characters he can think on. We may contrast the tumour of this presumptuous loftiness with the natural unaffected air of the portraits of Titian, where dignity seeming to be natural and inherent, draws spontaneous reverence, and instead of being thus vainly assumed, has the appearance of an unalienable adjunct; whereas such pompous and laboured insolence of grandeur is so far from creating respect, that it betrays vulgarity and meanness, and new-acquired consequence.

The painters, many of them at least, have not been backward in adopting the notions contained in these precepts. The portraits of Rigaud are perfect examples of an implicit observance of these rules of Du Piles; so that though he was a painter of great merit in many respects, yet, that merit is entirely overpowered by a total absence of simplicity in every sense.

Not to multiply instances, which might be produced for this purpose, from the works of History-painters, I shall mention only one,— a picture which I have seen, of the SUPREME BEING, by Coypell.

This subject the Roman Catholick painters have taken the liberty to represent, however indecent the attempt, and however obvious the impossibility of any approach to an adequate representation: but here the air and character, which the Painter has given, and he has doubtless given the highest he could conceive, are so degraded by an attempt at such dignity as Du Piles has recommended, that we are enraged at the folly and presumption of the artist, and consider it as little less than profanation.

As we have passed to a neighbouring nation for instances of want of this quality, we must acknowledge at the same time, that they have produced great examples of simplicity in Poussin and Le Sueur. But as we are speaking of the most refined and subtle notion of perfection, may we not enquire, whether a curious eye cannot discern some faults, even in those great men? I can fancy, that even Poussin, by abhorring that affectation and that want of simplicity, which he observed in his countrymen, has, in certain particulars, fallen into the contrary extreme, so far as to approach to a kind of affectation,—to what, in writing, would be called pedantry.

When Simplicity, instead of being a corrector, seems to set up for herself; that is, when an artist seems to value himself solely upon this quality; such an ostentatious display of simplicity becomes then as disagreeable and nauseous as any other kind of affectation. He is, however, in this case, likely enough to sit down contented with his own work; for though he finds the world look at it with indifference or dislike, as being destitute of every quality that can recreate or give pleasure to the mind, yet he consoles himself, that it has simplicity, a beauty of too pure and chaste a nature to be relished by vulgar minds.

It is in art as in morals: no character would inspire us with an enthusiastick admiration of his virtue, if that virtue consisted only in an absence of vice; something more is required; a man must do more than merely his duty, to be a hero.

Those works of the ancients, which are in the highest esteem, have something beside mere simplicity to recommend them. The Apollo, the Venus, the Laocoon, the Gladiator, have a certain Composition of Action, have contrasts sufficient to give grace and energy in a high degree; but it must be confessed of the many thousand antique statues which we have, that their general characteristick is bordering at least on inanimate insipdity.

Simplicity, when so very inartificial as to seem to evade the difficulties of art, is a very suspicious virtue.

I do not, however, wish to degrade simplicity from the high estimation in which it has been ever justly held. It is our barrier against that great enemy to truth and nature. Affectation, which is ever clinging to the pencil, and ready to drop in and poison every thing it touches.

Our love and affection to simplicity proceeds in a great measure from our aversion to every kind of affectation. There is likewise another reason why so much stress is laid upon this virtue; the propensity which artists have to fall into the contrary extreme; we therefore set a guard on that side which is most assailable. When a young artist is first told that his composition and his attitudes must be contrasted, that he must turn the head contrary to the position of the body, in order to produce grace and animation; that his outline must be undulating, and swelling, to give grandeur; and that the eye must be gratified with a variety of colours;—when he is told this, with certain animating words, of Spirit, Dignity, Energy, Grace, greatness of Style, and brilliancy of Tints, he becomes suddenly vain of his newly acquired knowledge, and never thinks he can carry those rules too far. It is then that the aid of simplicity ought to be called in, to correct the exuberance of youthful ardour.

The same may be said in regard to Colouring, which in its pre-eminence is particularly applied to flesh. An artist in his first essay of imitating nature, would make the whole mass of one colour, as the oldest painters did; till he is taught to observe not only the variety of tints, which are in the object itself, but the differences produced by the gradual decline of light to shadow: he then immediately puts his instruction in practice, and introduces a variety of distinct colours. He must then be again corrected, and told, that though there is this variety, yet the effect of the whole upon the eye must have the union and simplicity of the colouring of nature.

And here we may observe, that the progress of an individual Student bears a great resemblance to the progress and advancement of the Art itself. Want of simplicity would probably be not one of the defects of an artist who had studied nature only, as it was not of the old masters, who lived in the time preceding the great Art of Painting; on the contrary, their works are too simple and too inartificial.

The Art in its infancy, like the first work of a Student, was dry, hard, and simple. But this kind of barbarous simplicity, would be better named Penury, as it proceeds from mere want; from want of knowledge, want of resources, want of abilities to be otherwise: their simplicity was the offspring not of choice, but necessity.

In the second stage they were sensible of this poverty, and those who were the most sensible of the want, were the best judges of the measure of the supply. There were painters who emerged from poverty without falling into luxury. Their success induced others, who probably never would of themselves have had strength of mind to discover the original defect, to endeavour at the remedy by an abuse; and they ran into the contrary extreme. But however they may have strayed, we cannot recommend to them to return to that simplicity which they have justly quitted; but to deal out their abundance with a more sparing hand, with that dignity which makes no parade, either of its riches, or of its art. It is not easy to give a rule which may serve to fix this just and correct medium; because, when we may have fixed, or nearly fixed, the middle point, taken as a general principle, circumstances may oblige us to depart from it, either on the side of Simplicity, or on that of Variety and Decoration.

I thought it necessary in a former discourse, speaking of the difference of the sublime and ornamental style of painting,—in order to excite your attention to the more manly, noble, and dignified manner, to leave perhaps an impression too contemptuous of those ornamental parts of our Art, for which many have valued themselves, and many works are much valued and esteemed.

I said then, what I thought it was right at that time to say; I suppose the disposition of young men more inclinable to splendid negligence, than perseverance in laborious application to acquire correctness; and therefore did as we do in making what is crooked straight, by bending it the contrary way, in order that it may remain straight at last.

For this purpose then, and to correct excess or neglect of any kind, we may here add, that it is not enough that a work be learned; it must be pleasing: the painter must add grace to strength, if he desires to secure the first impression in his favour. Our taste has a kind of sensuality about it, as well as a love of the sublime; both these qualities of the mind are to have their proper consequence, as far as they do not counteract each other; for that is the grand error which much care ought to be taken to avoid.

There are some rules, whose absolute authority, like that of our nurses, continues no longer than while we are in a state of childhood. One of the first rules, for instance, that I believe every master would give to a young pupil, respecting his conduct and management of light and shadow, would be what Leonardo da Vinci has actually given; that you must oppose a light ground to the shadowed side of your figure, and a dark ground to the light side. If Leonardo had lived to see the superior splendour and effect which has been since produced by the exactly contrary conduct,—by joining light to light, and shadow to shadow,—though without doubt he would have admired it, yet, as it ought not, so probably it would not be the first rule with which he would have begun his instructions.

Again; in the artificial management of the figures, it is directed that they shall contrast each other according to the rules generally given; that if one figure opposes his front to the spectator, the next figure is to have his back turned, and that the limbs of each individual figure be contrasted; that is, if the right leg be put forward, the right arm is to be drawn back.

It is very proper that those rules should be given in the Academy; it is proper the young students should be informed that some research is to be made, and that they should be habituated to consider every excellence as reduceable to principles. Besides; it is the natural progress of instruction to teach first what is obvious and perceptible to the senses, and from thence proceed gradually to notions large, liberal, and complete, such as comprise the more refined and higher excellencies in Art. But when the students are more advanced, they will find that the greatest beauties of character and expressions are produced without contrast; nay more, that this contrast would ruin and destroy that natural energy of men engaged in real action, unsolicitous of grace. St. Paul preaching at Athens in one of the Cartoons, far from any affected academical contrast of limbs, stands equally on both legs, and both hands are in the same attitude: add contrast, and the whole energy and unaffected grace of the figure is destroyed. Elymas the Sorcerer stretches both hands forward in the same direction, which gives perfectly the expression intended. Indeed you never will find in the works of Raffaelle any of those school-boy affected contrasts. Whatever contrast there is, appears without any seeming agency of art, by the natural chance of things.

What has been said of the evil of excesses of all kinds, whether of simplicity, variety, or contrast, naturally suggests to the painter the necessity of a general enquiry into the true meaning and cause of rules, and how they operate on those faculties to which they are addressed: by knowing their general purpose and meaning, he will often find that he need not confine himself to the literal sense, it will be sufficient if he preserve the spirit, of the law.

Critical remarks are not always understood without examples: it may not be improper therefore to give instances where the rule itself, though generally received, is false, or where a narrow conception of it may lead the artist into great errors.

It is given as a rule by Fresnoy. That *the principal figure of a subject must appear in the midst of the picture, under the principal light, to distinguish it from the rest.* A painter who should think himself obliged strictly to follow this rule, would encumber himself with needless difficulties; he would be confined to great uniformity of composition, and be deprived of many beauties which are incompatible with its observance. The meaning of this rule extends, or ought to extend, no further than this;—That the principal figure should be immediately distinguished at the first glance of the eye; but there is no necessity that the principal light should fall on the principal figure, or that the principal figure should be in the middle of the picture. It is sufficient that it be distinguished by its place, or by the attention of other figures pointing it out to the spectator. So far is this rule from being indispensable, that it is very seldom practised, other considerations of greater consequence often standing in the way. Examples in opposition to this rule, are found in the Cartoons, in Christ's Charge to Peter, the Preaching of St. Paul, and Elymas the Sorcerer, who is undoubtedly the principal object in that picture. In none of those compositions is the principal figure in the midst of the picture. In the very admirable composition of the Tent of Darius, by Le Brun, Alexander is not in the middle of the picture, nor does the principal light fall on him; but the attention of all the other figures immediately distinguishes him, and distinguishes him more properly; the greatest light falls on the daughter of Darius, who is in the middle of the picture, where it is more necessary the principal light should be placed.

It is very extraordinary that Felibien, who has given a very minute description of this picture, but indeed such a description as may be rather called panegyrick than criticism, thinking it necessary (according to the precept of Fresnoy) that Alexander should possess the principal light, has accordingly given it to him; he might with equal truth have said that he was placed in the middle of the picture, as he seemed resolved to give this piece every kind of excellence which he conceived to be necessary to perfection. His generosity is here unluckily misapplied, as it would have destroyed in a great measure the beauty of the composition.

Another instance occurs to me where equal liberty may be taken in regard to the management of light. Though the general practice is to make a large mass about the middle of the picture surrounded by shadow, the reverse may be practised, and the spirit of the rule may still be preserved. Examples of this principle reversed may be found very frequently in the works of the Venetian school. In the great composition of Paul Veronese, the Marriage at Cana, the figures are for the most part in half shadow; the great light is in the sky; and indeed the general effect of this picture which is so striking, is no more than what we often see in landscapes, in small pictures of fairs and country feasts; but those principles of light and shadow being transferred to a large scale, to a space containing near a hundred figures as large as life, and conducted to all appearance with as much facility, and with an attention as steadily fixed upon *the whole together,* as if it were a small picture immediately under the eye, the work justly excites our admiration; the difficulty being encreased as the extent is enlarged.

The various modes of composition are infinite: sometimes it shall consist of one large group in the middle of the picture, and the smaller groups on each side; or a plain space in the middle, and the groups of figures ranged round this vacuity.

Whether this principal broad light be in the middle space of ground, as in the School of Athens; or in the sky, as in the Marriage at Cana, in the Andromeda, and in most of the pictures of Paul Veronese; or whether the light be on the groups; whatever mode of composition is adopted, every variety and license is allowable: this only is indisputably necessary, that to prevent the eye from being distracted and confused by a multiplicity of objects of equal magnitude, those objects, whether they consist of lights, shadows, or figures, must be disposed in large masses and groups properly varied and contrasted; that to a certain quantity of action a proportioned space of plain ground is required; that light is to be supported by sufficient shadow; and, we may add, that a certain quantity of cold colours is necessary to give value and lustre to the warm colours: what those proportions are cannot be so well learnt by precept as by observation on pictures, and in this knowledge bad pictures will instruct as well as good. Our enquiry why pictures have a bad effect, may be as advantageous as the enquiry why they have a good effect; each will corroborate the principles that are suggested by the other.

Though it is not my *business* to enter into the detail of our Art, yet I must take this opportunity of mentioning one of the means of producing that great effect which we observe in the works of the Venetian painters, as I think it is not generally known or observed. It ought, in my opinion, to be indispensably observed, that the masses of light in a picture be always of a warm mellow colour, yellow, red, or a yellowish-white; and that the blue, the grey, or the green colours be kept almost entirely out of these masses, and be used only to support and set off these warm colours; and for this purpose, a small proportion of cold colours will be sufficient.

Let this conduct be reversed; let the light be cold, and the surrounding colours warm, as we often see in the works of the Roman and Florentine painters, and it will be out of the power of art, even in the hands of Rubens or Titian, to make a picture splendid and harmonious.

Le Brun and Carlo Maratti were two painters of great merit, and particularly what may be called Academical Merit, but were both deficient in this management of Colours; the want of observing this rule is one of the causes of that heaviness of effect which is so observable in their works. The principal light in the Picture of Le Brun, which I just now mentioned, falls on Statira, who is dressed very injudiciously in a pale blue drapery; it is true, he has heightened this blue with gold, but that is not enough; the whole picture has a heavy air, and by no means answers the expectation raised by the Print. Poussin often made a spot of blue drapery, when the general hue of the picture was inclinable to brown or yellow; which shews sufficiently, that harmony of colouring was not a part of the art that had much engaged the attention of that great painter.

The conduct of Titian in the picture of Bacchus and Ariadne, has been much celebrated, and justly, for the harmony of colouring. To Ariadne is given (say the criticks) a red scarf, to relieve the figure from the sea which is behind her. It is not for that reason, alone, but for another of much greater consequence; for the sake of the general harmony and effect of the picture. The figure of Ariadne is separated from the great group, and is dressed in blue, which added to the colour of the sea, makes that quantity of cold colour which Titian thought necessary for the support and brilliancy of the great group; which group is composed, with very little exception, entirely of mellow colours. But as the picture in this case would be divided into two distinct parts, one half cold, and the other warm, it was necessary to carry some of the mellow colours of the great group into the cold part of the picture, and a part of the cold into the great group; accordingly Titian gave Ariadne a red scarf, and to one of the Bacchante a little blue drapery.

The light of the picture, as I observed, ought to be of a warm colour; for though white may be used for the principal light, as was the practice of many of the Dutch and Flemish painters, yet it is better to suppose *that white* illumined by the yellow rays of the setting sun, as was the manner of Titian. The superiority of which manner is never more striking, than when in a collection of pictures we chance to see a portrait of Titian's hanging by the side of a Flemish picture, (even though that should be of the hand of Vandyck,) which, however admirable in other respects, becomes cold and grey in the comparison.

The illuminated parts of objects are in nature of a warmer tint than those that are in the shade: what I have recommended therefore is no more, than that the same conduct be observed in the whole, which is acknowledged to be necessary in every individual part. It is presenting to the eye the same effect as that which it has been *accustomed* to feel, which in this case, as in every other, will always produce beauty; no principle therefore in our art can be more certain, or is derived from a higher source.

What I just now mentioned of the supposed reason why Ariadne has part of her drapery red, gives me occasion here to observe, that this favourite quality of giving objects relief, and which De Piles and all the Criticks have considered as a requisite of the utmost importance, was not one of those objects which much engaged the attention of Titian: painters of an inferior rank have far exceeded him in producing this effect. This was a great object of attention when art was in its infant state, as it is at present with the vulgar and ignorant, who feel the highest satisfaction in seeing a figure, which, as they say, looks as if they could walk round it. But however low I may rate this pleasure of deception, I should not oppose it, did it not oppose itself to a quality of a much higher kind, by counteracting entirely that fulness of manner which is so difficult to express in words, but which is found in perfection in the best works of Correggio, and we may add, of Rembrandt. This effect is produced by melting and losing the shadows in a ground still darker than those shadows; whereas that relief is produced by opposing and separating the ground from the figure either by light, or shadow, or colour. This conduct of in-laying, as it may be called, figures on their ground, in order to produce relief, was the practice of the old Painters, such as Andrea Mantegna, Pietro Perugino, and Albert Dürer; and to these we may add, the first manner of Leonardo da Vinci, Giorgione, and even Correggio; but these three were among the first who began to correct themselves in this dryness of style, by no longer considering relief as a principal object. As those two qualities, relief, and fulness of effect, can hardly exist together, it is not very difficult to determine to which we ought to give the preference. An Artist is obliged for ever to hold a balance in his hand, by which he much determine the value of different qualities; that, when *some* fault must be committed, he may choose the least. Those painters who have best understood the art of producing a good effect, have adopted one principle that seems perfectly conformable to reason; that a part may be sacrificed for the good of the whole. Thus, whether the masses consist of light or shadow, it is necessary that they should be compact and of a pleasing shape; to this end, some parts may be made darker and some lighter, and reflexions stronger than nature would warrant. Paul Veronese took great liberties of this kind. It is said, that being once asked, why certain figures were painted in shade, as no cause was seen in the picture itself; he turned off the enquiry by answering, *"una nuevola che passa,"* a cloud is passing which has overshadowed them.

But I cannot give a better instance of this practice than a picture which I have of Rubens: it is a representation of a Moon-light. Rubens has not only diffused more light over the picture than is in nature, but has bestowed on it those warm glowing colours by which his works are so much distinguished. It is so unlike what any other painters have given us of Moon-light, that it might be easily mistaken, if he had not likewise added stars, for a fainter setting sun.—Rubens thought the eye ought to be satisfied in this case, above all other considerations: he might indeed have made it more natural, but it would have been at the expence of what he thought of much greater consequence,—the harmony proceeding from the contrast and variety of colours.

This same picture will furnish us with another instance, where we must depart from nature for a greater advantage. The Moon in this picture does not preserve so great a superiority in regard to its lightness over the object which it illumines, as it does in nature; this is likewise an intended deviation, and for the same reason. If Rubens had preserved the same scale of gradation of light between the Moon and the objects, which is found in nature, the picture must have consisted of one small spot of light only, and at a little distance from the picture nothing but this spot would have been seen. It may be said indeed, that this being the case, it is a subject that ought not to be painted: but then, for the same reason, neither armour, nor any thing shining, ought ever to be painted; for though pure white is used in order to represent the greatest light of shining objects, it will not in the picture preserve the same superiority over flesh, as it has in nature, without keeping that flesh-colour of a very low tint. Rembrandt, who thought it of more consequence to paint light, than the objects that are seen by it, has done this in a picture of Achilles which I have. The head is kept down to a very low tint, in order to preserve this due gradation and distinction between the armour and the face; the consequence of which is, that upon the whole the picture is too black. Surely too much is sacrificed here to this narrow conception of nature: allowing the contrary conduct a fault, yet it must be acknowledged a less fault than making a picture so dark that it cannot be seen without a peculiar light, and then with difficulty. The merit or demerit of the different conduct of Rubens and Rembrandt in those instances which I have given, is not to be determined by the narrow principles of nature, separated from its effect on the human mind. Reason and common sense tell us, that before, and above all other considerations, it is necessary that the work should be seen, not only without difficulty or inconvenience, but with pleasure and satisfaction; and every obstacle which stands in the way of this pleasure and convenience must be removed. . . .

On the Nature of Genius and the Comprehension of the Whole
(from *Discourse 11*)

The highest ambition of every Artist is to be thought a man of Genius. As long as this flattering quality is joined to his name, he can bear with patience the imputation of carelessness, incorrectness, or defects of whatever kind.

So far indeed is the presence of Genius from implying an absence of faults, that they are considered by many as its inseparable companions. Some go such lengths as to take indications from them, and not only excuse faults on account of Genius, but presume Genius from the existence of certain faults.

It is certainly true, that a work may justly claim the character of Genius, though full of errors; and it is equally true, that it may be faultless, and yet not exhibit the least spark of Genius. This naturally suggests an enquiry, a desire at least of enquiring, what qualities of a work and of a workman may justly entitle a Painter to that character.

I have in a former discourse[6] endeavoured to impress you with a fixed opinion, that a comprehensive and critical knowledge of the works of nature is the only source of beauty and grandeur. But when we speak to Painters we must always consider this rule, and all rules, with a reference to the mechanical practice of their own particular Art. It is not properly in the learning, the taste, and the dignity of the ideas, the Genius appears as belonging to a painter. There is a Genius particular and appropriated to his own trade, (as I may call it,) distinguished from all others. For that power, which enables the Artist to conceive his subject with dignity, may be said to belong to general education; and is as much the Genius of a Poet, or the professor of any other liberal Art, or even a good Critick in any of those arts, as of a Painter. Whatever sublime ideas may fill his mind, he is a Painter only as he can put in practice what he knows, and communicate those ideas by visible representation.

If my expression can convey my idea, I wish to distinguish excellence of this kind by calling it the Genius of mechanical performance. This Genius consists, I conceive, in the power of expressing that which employs your pencil, whatever it may be, *as a whole;* so that the general effect and power of the whole may take possession of the mind, and for a while suspend the consideration of the subordinate and particular beauties or defects.

The advantage of this method of considering objects, is what I wish now more particularly to enforce. At the same time I do not forget, that a Painter must have the power of contracting as well as dilating his sight; because, he that does not at all express particulars, expresses nothing; yet it is certain, that a nice discrimination of minute circumstances, and a punctilious delineation of them, whatever excellence it

6 Discourse III.

may have, (and I do not mean to detract from it,) never did confer on the Artist the character of Genius.

Beside those minute differences in things which are frequently not observed at all, and, when they are, make little impression, there are in all considerable objects great characteristick distinctions, which press strongly on the senses, and therefore fix the imagination. These are by no means, as some persons think, an aggregate of all the small discriminating particulars; nor will such an accumulation of particulars ever express them. These answer to what I have heard great lawyers call the leading points in a case, or the leading cases relative to those points.

The detail of particulars, which does not assist the expression of the main characteristick, is worse than useless, it is mischievous, as it dissipates the attention, and draws it from the principal point. It may be remarked, that the impression which is left on our mind, even of things which are familiar to us, is seldom more than their general effect; beyond which we do not look in recognising such objects. To express this in Painting, is to express what is congenial and natural to the mind of man, and what gives him by reflection his own mode of conceiving. The other presupposes *nicety* and *research,* which are only the business of the curious and attentive, and therefore does not speak to the general sense of the whole species; in which common, and, as I may so call it, mother tongue, everything grand and comprehensive may be uttered.

I do not mean to prescribe what degree of attention ought to be paid to the minute parts; this it is hard to settle. We are sure that it is expressing the general effect of the whole which alone can give to objects their true and touching character; and wherever this is observed, whatever else may be neglected, we acknowledge the hand of a Master. We may even go further, and observe, that when the general effect only is presented to us by a skilful hand, it appears to express the object represented in a more lively manner than the minutest resemblance would do.

These observations may lead to very deep questions, which I do not mean here to discuss; among others, it may lead to an enquiry. Why we are not always pleased with the most absolute possible resemblance of an imitation to its original object. Cases may exist in which such a resemblance may be even disagreeable. I shall only observe that the effect of figures in Wax-work, though certainly a more exact representation than can be given by Painting or Sculpture, is a sufficient proof that the pleasure we receive from imitation is not increased merely in proportion as it approaches to minute and detailed reality; we are pleased, on the contrary, by seeing ends accomplished by seemingly inadequate means.

To express protuberance by actual relief, to express the softness of flesh by the softness of wax, seems rude and inartificial, and creates no grateful surprise. But to express distances on a plain surface, softness by hard bodies, and particular colouring by materials which are not singly of that colour, produces that magick which is the prize and triumph of art.

Carry this principle a step further. Suppose the effect of imitation to be fully compassed by means still more inadequate; let the power of a few well-chosen strokes, which supersede labour by judgment and direction, produce a complete impression of all that the mind demands in an object; we are charmed with such an unexpected happiness of execution, and begin to be tired with the superfluous diligence, which in vain solicits an appetite already satiated.

The properties of all objects, as far as a Painter is concerned with them, are, the outline or drawing, the colour, and the light and shade. The drawing gives the form, the colour its visible quality, and the light and shade its solidity.

Excellence in any one of these parts of art will never be acquired by an artist, unless he has the habit of looking upon objects at large, and observing the effect which they have on the eye when it is dilated, and employed upon the whole, without seeing any one of the parts distinctly. It is by this that we obtain the ruling characteristick, and that we learn to imitate it by short and dexterous methods. I do not mean by dexterity a trick or mechanical habit, formed by guess, and established by custom; but that science, which, by a profound knowledge of ends and means, discovers the shortest and surest way to its own purpose.

If we examine with a critical view the manner of those painters whom we consider as patterns, we shall find that their great fame does not proceed from their works being more highly finished than those of other artists, or from a more minute attention to details, but from that enlarged comprehension which sees the whole object at once, and that energy of art which gives its characteristick effect by adequate expression.

Raffaelle and Titian are two names which stand the highest in our art; one for Drawing, the other for Painting. The most considerable and the most esteemed works of Raffaelle are the Cartoons, and his

Fresco works in the Vatican; those, as we all know, are far from being minutely finished: his principal care and attention seems to have been fixed upon the adjustment of the whole, whether it was the general composition, or the composition of each individual figure; for every figure may be said to be a lesser whole, though in regard to the general work to which it belongs, it is but a part; the same may be said of the head, of the hands, and feet. Though he possessed this art of seeing and comprehending the whole, as far as form is concerned, he did not exert the same faculty in regard to the general effect, which is presented to the eye by colour, and light and shade. Of this the deficiency of his oil pictures, where this excellence is more expected than in Fresco, is a sufficient proof.

It is to Titian we must turn our eyes to find excellence with regard to colour, and light and shade, in the highest degree. He was both the first and the greater master of this art. By a few strokes he knew how to mark the general image and character of whatever object he attempted; and produced, by this alone, a truer representation than his master Giovanni Bellino, or any of his predecessors, who finished every hair. His great care was to express the general colour, to preserve the masses of light and shade, and to give by opposition the idea of that solidity which is inseparable from natural objects. When those are preserved, though the work should possess no other merit, it will have in a proper place its complete effect; but where any of these are wanting, however minutely laboured the picture may be in the detail, the whole will have a false and even an unfinished appearance, at whatever distance, or in whatever light, it can be shewn.

It is vain to attend to the variation of tints, if, in that attention, the general hue of flesh is lost; or to finish ever so minutely the parts, if the masses are not observed, or the whole not well put together.

Vasari seems to have had no great disposition to favour the Venetian Painters, yet he every where justly commends *il modo di fare, la maniera, la belle pratica;* that is, the admirable manner and practice of that school. On Titian, in particular he bestows the epithets of *giudicioso, bello, e stupendo.*

This manner was then new to the world, but that unshaken truth on which it is founded, has fixed it as a model to all succeeding Painters; and those who will examine into the artifice, will find it to consist in the power of generalising, and in the shortness and simplicity of the means employed.

Many Artists, as Vasari likewise observes, have ignorantly imagined

GALATEA—RAPHAEL (*Farnesina Gallery, Rome*)

they are imitating the manner of Titian, when they leave their colours rough, and neglect the detail; but, not possessing the principles on which he wrought, they have produced what he calls *goffe pitture*, absurd foolish pictures; for such will always be the consequence of affecting dexterity without science, without selection, and without fixed principles.

Raffaelle and Titian seem to have looked at nature for different purposes; they both had the power of extending their view to the whole; but one looked only for the general effect as produced by form, the other as produced by colour.

We cannot entirely refuse to Titian the merit of attending to the general *form* of his object, as well as colour; but his deficiency lay, a deficiency at least when he is compared with Raffaelle, in not possessing the power, like him, of correcting the form of his model by any general idea of beauty in his own mind. Of this his St. Sebastian is a particular instance. This figure appears to be a most exact representation both of the form and the colour of the model, which he then happened to have before him; it has all the force of nature, and the colouring is flesh itself; but, unluckily, the model was of a bad form, especially the legs. Titian has with as much care preserved these defects, as he has imitated the beauty and brilliancy of the colouring. In his colouring he was large and general, as in his design he was minute and partial; in the one he was a Genius, in the other not much above a copier. I do not, however, speak now of all his pictures; instances enough may be produced in his works, where those observations on his defects could not with any propriety be applied: but it is in the manner, or language, as it may be called, in which Titian and others of that school express themselves, that their chief excellence lies. This manner is in reality, in painting, what language is in poetry; we are all sensible how differently the imagination is affected by the same sentiment expressed in different words, and how mean or how grand the same object appears when presented to us by different Painters. Whether it is the human figure, an animal, or even inanimate objects, there is nothing, however unpromising in appearance, but may be raised into dignity, convey sentiment, and produce emotion, in the hands of a Painter of genius. What was said of Virgil, that he threw even the dung about the ground with an air of dignity, may be applied to Titian: whatever he touched, however naturally mean, and habitually familiar, by a kind of magick he invested with grandeur and importance.

I must here observe, that I am not recommending a neglect of the detail; indeed it would be difficult, if not impossible, to prescribe *certain* bounds, and tell how far, or when it is to be observed or neglected; much must, at last, be left to the taste and judgment of the Artist. I am well aware that a judicious detail will sometimes give the force of truth to the work, and consequently interest the spectator. I only wish to impress on your minds the true distinction between essential and subordinate powers; and to shew what qualities in the art claim your *chief* attention, and what may, with the least injury to your reputation, be neglected. Something, perhaps, always must be neglected; the lesser ought then to give way to the greater; and since

every work can have but a limited time allotted to it, (for even supposing a whole life to be employed about one picture, it is still limited,)
it appears more reasonable to employ that time to the best advantage,
in contriving various methods of composing the work,—in trying different effect of light and shadow,—and employing the labour of correction
in heightening by a judicious adjustment of the parts the effects of the
whole,—than that the time should be taken up in minutely finishing
those parts.

But there is another kind of high finishing which may safely be
condemned, as it seems to counteract its own purpose; that is, when the
artist, to avoid that hardness which proceeds from the outline cutting
against the ground, softens and blends the colours to excess: this is what
the ignorant call high finishing, but which tends to destroy the brilliancy of colour, and the true effect of representation; which consists
very much in preserving the same proportion of sharpness and blunt-
ness that is found in natural objects. This extreme softning, instead of
producing the effect of softness, gives the appearance of ivory, or some
other hard substance, highly polished.

The portraits of Cornelius Jansen appear to have this defect, and
consequently want that suppleness which is the characteristick of flesh;
whereas, in the works of Vandyck we find that true mixture of softness
and hardness perfectly observed. The same defect may be found in the
manner of Vanderwerf, in opposition to that of Teniers, and such also,
we may add, is the manner of Raffaelle in his oil pictures, in comparison
with that of Titian.

The name which Raffaelle has so justly maintained as the first of
Painters,[7] we may venture to say was not acquired by this laborious
attention. His apology may be made by saying that it was the manner
of his country; but if he had expressed his ideas with the facility and
eloquence, as it may be called, of Titian, his works would certainly now
have been less excellent; and that praise, which ages and nations have
poured out upon him, for possessing Genius in the higher attainments
of art, would have been extended to them all.

Those who are not conversant in works of art, are often surprised
at the high value set by connoisseurs on drawings which appear careless,
and in every respect unfinished; but they are truly valuable; and their
value arises from this, that they give the idea of an whole; and this
whole is often expressed by a dexterous facility which indicates the true

---

[7] This lavish estimate of Raphael has been viewed with disfavor since the middle of the
nineteenth century.

power of a Painter, even though roughly exerted: whether it consists in the general composition, or the general form of each figure, or the turn of the attitude which bestows grace and elegance. All this we may see fully exemplified in the very skilful drawings of Parmegiano and Correggio. On whatever account we value these drawings, it is certainly not for high finishing, or a minute attention to particulars.

Excellence in every part, and in every province of our art, from the highest style of history down to the resemblances of still-life, will depend on this power of extending the attention at once to the whole, without which the greatest diligence is vain.

I wish you to bear in mind, that when I speak of an whole, I do not mean simply an *whole* as belonging to composition, but an *whole* with respect to the general style of colouring; an *whole* with regard to the light and shade; an *whole* of every thing which may separately become the main object of a Painter.

I remember a Landscape-Painter in Rome, who was known by the name of STUDIO, from his patience in high finishing, in which he thought the whole excellence of art consisted; so that he once endeavoured, as he said, to represent every individual leaf on a tree. This picture I never saw; but I am very sure that an artist, who looked only at the general character of the species, the order of the branches, and the masses of the foliage, would in a few minutes produce a more true resemblance of trees, than this Painter in as many months.

A Landscape-Painter certainly ought to study anatomically (if I may use the expression) all the objects which he paints; but when he is to turn his studies to use, his skill, as a man of Genius, will be displayed in shewing the general effect, preserving the same degree of hardness and softness which the objects have in nature; for he applies himself to the imagination, not to the curiosity, and works not for the Virtuoso or the Naturalist, but for the common observer of life and nature. When he knows his subject, he will know not only what to describe, but what to omit; and this skill in leaving out, is, in all things, a great part of knowledge and wisdom.

The same excellence of manner which Titian displayed in History or Portrait-painting, is equally conspicuous in his Landscapes, whether they are professedly such, or serve only as backgrounds. One of the most eminent of this latter kind is to be found in the picture of St. Pietro Martire. The large trees, which are here introduced, are plainly distinguished from each other by the different manner with which the branches shoot from their trunks as well as by their different foliage;

and the weeds in the fore-ground are varied in the same manner, just as much as variety requires, and no more. When Algarotti, speaking of this picture, praises it for the minute discriminations of the leaves and plants, even, as he says, to excite the admiration of a Botanist, his intention was undoubtedly to give praise even at the expense of truth; for he must have known, that this is not the character of the picture; but connoisseurs will always find in pictures what they think they ought to find: he was not aware that he was giving a description injurious to the reputation of Titian.

Such accounts may be very hurtful to young artists, who never have had an opportunity of seeing the work described; and they may possibly conclude, that this great Artist acquired the name of the Divine Titian from his eminent attention to such trifling circumstances, which, in reality, would not raise him above the level of the most ordinary painter.

We may extend these observations even to what seems to have but a single, and that an individual, object. The excellence of Portrait-Painting, and we may add even the likeness, the character, and countenance, as I have observed in another place, depend more upon the general effect produced by the painter, than on the exact expression of the peculiarities, or minute discrimination of the parts. The chief attention of the artist is therefore employed in planting the features in their proper places, which so much contributes to giving the effect and true impression of the whole. The very peculiarities may be reduced to classes and general descriptions; and there are therefore large ideas to be found even in this contracted subject. He may afterwards labour single features to what degree he thinks proper, but let him not forget continually to examine, whether in finishing the parts he is not destroying the general effect.

It is certainly a thing to be wished, that all excellence were applied to illustrate subjects that are interesting and worthy of being commemorated; whereas, of half the pictures that are in the world, the subject can be valued only as an occasion which set the artist to work; and yet, in our high estimation of such pictures, without considering or perhaps without knowing the subject, shews how much our attention is engaged by the art alone.

Perhaps nothing that we can say will so clearly shew the advantage and excellence of this faculty, as that it confers the character of Genius on works that pretend to no other merit; in which is neither expression, character, or dignity, and where none are interested in the subject.

We cannot refuse the character of Genius to the marriage[8] of Paul Veronese, without opposing the general sense of mankind, (great authorities have called it the Triumph of Painting), or, to the altar of St. Augustine at Antwerp, by Rubens, which equally deserves that title, and for the same reason. Neither of those pictures have any interesting story to support them. That of Paul Veronese, is only a representation of a great concourse of people at a dinner; and the subject of Rubens, if it may be called a subject where nothing is doing, is an assembly of various Saints that lived in different ages. The whole excellence of those pictures consists in mechanical dexterity, working however under the influence of that comprehensive faculty which I have so often mentioned.

It is by this, and this alone, that the mechanical power is ennobled, and raised much above its natural rank. And it appears to me, that with propriety it acquires this character, as an instance of that superiority with which mind predominates over matter, by contracting into one whole what nature has made multifarious.

The great advantage of this idea of a whole is, that a greater quantity of truth may be said to be contained and expressed in a few lines or touches, than in the most laborious finishing of the parts, where this is not regarded. It is upon this foundation that it stands; and the justness of the observation would be confirmed by the ignorant in art, if it were possible to take their opinions unseduced by some false notion of what they imagine they ought to see in a Picture. As it is an art, they think they ought to be pleased in proportion as they see that art ostentatiously displayed; they will, from this supposition, prefer neatness, high-finishing, and gaudy colouring to the truth, simplicity, and unity of nature. Perhaps too, the totally ignorant beholder, like the ignorant artist, cannot comprehend a whole, nor even what it means. But if false notions do not anticipate their perceptions, they who are capable of observation, and who, pretending to no skill, look only straight forward, will praise and condemn in proportion as the Painter has succeeded in the effect of the whole. Here general satisfaction, or general dislike, though perhaps despised by the Painter, as proceeding from the ignorance of the principles of art, may help to regulate his conduct, and bring back his attention to that which ought to be his principal object, and from which he has deviated for the sake of minuter beauties.

An instance of this right judgment I once saw in a child, in going through a gallery where there were many portraits of the last ages,

8 "The Marriage at Cana."

which though neatly put out of hand, were very ill put together. The child paid no attention to the neat finishing or naturalness of any bit of drapery, but appeared to observe only the ungracefulness of the persons represented, and put herself in the posture of every figure which she saw in a forced and awkward attitude. The censure of nature, uninformed, fastened upon the greatest fault that could be in a picture, because it related to the character and management of the whole.

I should be sorry, if what has been said should be understood to have any tendency to encourage that carelessness which leaves work in an unfinished state. I commend nothing for the want of exactness; I mean to point out that kind of exactness which is the best, and which is alone truly to be so esteemed.

So far is my disquisition from giving countenance to idleness, that there is nothing in our art which enforces such continual exertion and circumspection, as an attention to the general effect of the whole. It requires much study and much practice; it requires the Painter's entire mind; whereas the parts may be finishing by nice touches, while his mind is engaged on other matters; he may even hear a play or a novel read without much disturbance. The artist who flatters his own indolence, will continually find himself evading the active exertion, and applying his thoughts to the ease and laziness of highly finishing the parts; producing at last what Cowley calls "laborious effects of idleness."

No work can be too much finished, provided the diligence employed be directed to its proper object; but I have observed that an excessive labour in the detail has, nine times in ten, been pernicious to the general effect, even when it has been the labour of great masters. It indicates a bad choice, which is an ill setting out in any undertaking.

To give a right direction to your industry has been my principal purpose in this discourse. It is this, which I am confident often makes the difference between two Students of equal capacities, and of equal industry. While the one is employing his labour on minute objects of little consequence, the other is acquiring the art, and perfecting the habit, of seeing nature in an extensive view, in its proper proportions, and its due subordination of parts.

Before I conclude, I must make one observation sufficiently connected with the present subject.

The same extension of mind which gives the excellence of Genius to the theory and mechanical practice of the art, will direct him likewise in the method of study, and give him the superiority over those who narrowly follow a more confined track of partial imitation. Whoever, in order to finish his education, should travel to Italy, and spend his whole time there only in copying pictures, and measuring statues or buildings, (though these things are not to be neglected,) would return with little improvement. He that imitates the Iliad, says Dr. Young, is not imitating Homer. It is not by laying up in the memory the particular details of any of the great works of art, that any man becomes a great artist, if he stops without making himself master of the general principles on which these works are conducted. If he even hopes to rival those whom he admires, he must consider their works as the means of teaching him the true art of seeing nature. When this is acquired, he then may be said to have appropriated their powers, or at least the foundation of their powers, to himself; the rest must depend upon his own industry and application. The great business of study is, to form a *mind,* adapted and adequate to all times and all occasions; to which all nature is then laid open, and which may be said to possess the key of her inexhaustible riches.

On the Merits and the Defects of Gainsborough (from *Discourse 14*)

In the study of our Art, as in the study of all Arts, something is the result of *our own* observation of Nature; something, and that not little, the effect of the example of those who have studied the same nature before us, and who have cultivated before us the same Art, with diligence and success. The less we confine ourselves in the choice of those examples, the more advantage we shall derive from them; and the nearer we shall bring our performances to a correspondence with nature and the great general rules of Art. When we draw our examples from remote and revered antiquity,—with some advantage undoubtedly in that selection, we subject ourselves to some inconveniences. We may suffer ourselves to be too much led away by great names, and to be too much subdued by overbearing authority. Our learning, in that case, is not so much an exercise of our judgment, as a proof of our docility. We find ourselves, perhaps, too much overshadowed; and the character of our pursuits is rather distinguished by the tameness of the follower, than animated by the spirit of emulation. It is sometimes of service, that our examples should be *near* us; and such as raise a reverence, sufficient to induce us carefully to observe them, yet not so great as to prevent us from engaging with them in something like a generous contention.

We have lately lost Mr. Gainsborough, one of the greatest ornaments of our Academy. It is not our business here, to make panegyricks on the living, or even on the dead who were of our body. The praise of the former might bear the appearance of adulation; and the latter, of untimely justice; perhaps of envy to those whom we have still the happiness to enjoy, by an oblique suggestion of invidious comparisons. In discoursing therefore on the talents of the late Mr. Gainsborough, my object is, not so much to praise or to blame him, as to draw from his excellencies and defects, matter of instruction to the Students in our academy. If ever this nation should produce genius sufficient to acquire to use the honourable distinction of an English School, the name of Gainsborough will be transmitted to posterity, in the history of the Art, among the very first of that rising name. That our reputation in the Arts is now only rising, must be acknowledged; and we must expect our advances to be attended with old prejudices, as adversaries, and not as supporters, standing in this respect in a very different situation from the late artists of the Roman School, to whose reputation ancient prejudices have certainly contributed: the way was prepared for them, and they may be said rather to have lived in the reputation of their country, than to have contributed to it; whilst whatever celebrity is obtained by English Artists, can arise only from the operation of a fair and true comparison. And when they communicate to their country a share of their reputation, it is a portion of fame not borrowed from others, but solely acquired by their own labour and talents. As Italy has undoubtedly a prescriptive right to an admiration bordering on prejudice, as a soil peculiarly adapted, congenial, and, we may add, destined to the production of men of great genius in our Art, we may not unreasonably suspect that a portion of the great fame of some of their late artists has been owing to the general readiness and disposition of mankind, to acquiesce in their original prepossessions in favour of the productions of the Roman School.

On this ground, however unsafe, I will venture to prophecy, that two of the last distinguished Painters of that country, I mean Pompeio Battoni, and Raffaelle Mengs, however great their names may at present sound in our ears. will very soon fall into the rank of Imperiale, Sebastian Concha, Placido Constanza, Massuccio, and the rest of their immediate predecessors; whose names, though equally renowned in their lifetime, are now fallen into what is little short of total oblivion.

I do not say that those painters were not superior to the artist I allude to, and whose loss we lament, in a certain routine of practice, which, to the eyes of common observers, has the air of a learned composition, and bears a sort of superficial resemblance to the manner of the great men who went before them. I know this perfectly well; but I know likewise, that a man, looking for real and lasting reputation, must unlearn much of the common-place method so observable in the works of the artists whom I have named. For my own part, I confess, I take more interest in, and am more captivated with, the powerful impression of nature, which Gainsborough exhibited in his portraits and in his landskips, and the interesting simplicity and elegance of his little ordinary beggar-children, than with any of the works of that School, since the time of Andrea Sacchi, or perhaps, we may say Carlo Maratti; two painters who may truly be said to be ULTIMI ROMANORIUM.

I am well aware how much I lay myself open to the censure and ridicule of the academical professors of other nations, in preferring the humble attempts of Gainsborough to the works of those regular graduates in the great historical style. But we have the sanction of all mankind in preferring genius in a lower rank of art, to feebleness and insipidity in the highest.

It would not be to the present purpose, even if I had the means and materials, which I have not, to enter into the private life of Mr. Gainsborough. The history of his gradual advancement, and the means by which he acquired such excellence in his art, would come nearer to our purpose and wishes, if it were by any means attainable; but the slow progress of advancement is in general imperceptible to the man himself who makes it; it is the consequence of an accumulation of various ideas which his mind has received, he does not perhaps know how or when. Sometimes indeed it happens, that he may be able to mark the time when, from the sight of a picture, a passage in an author, or a hint in conversation, he has received, as it were, some new and guiding light, something like inspiration, by which his mind has been expanded; and is morally sure that his whole life and conduct has been affected by that accidental circumstance. Such interesting accounts we may however sometimes obtain from a man who has acquired an uncommon habit of self-examination, and has attended to the progress of his own improvement.

It may not be improper to make mention of some of the customs and habits of this extraordinary man; points which come more within the reach of an observer; I however mean such only as are connected with his art, and indeed were, as I apprehend, the causes of his arriving to that high degree of existence, which we see and acknowledge in his works. Of these causes we must state, as the fundamental, the love which he had to his art; to which, indeed, his whole mind appears to have been devoted, and to which every thing was referred; and this we may fairly conclude from various circumstances of his life, which were known to his intimate friends. Among others he had a habit of continually remarking to those who happened to be about him, whatever peculiarity of countenance, whatever accidental combination of figures, or happy effects of light and shadow, occurred in prospects, in the sky, in walking the streets, or in company. If, in his walks, he found a character that he liked, and whose attendance was to be obtained, he ordered him to his house: and from the fields he brought into his painting-room, stumps of trees, weeds, and animals of various kinds; and designed them, not from memory, but immediately from the objects. He even framed a kind of model of landskips, on his table; composed of broken stones, dried herbs, and pieces of looking glass, which he magnified and improved into rocks, trees, and water. How far this latter practice may be useful in giving hints, the professors of landskip can best determine. Like every other technical practice it seems to me wholly to depend on the general talent of him who uses it. Such methods may be nothing better than contemptible and mischievous trifling; or they may be aids. I think upon the whole, unless we constantly refer to real nature, that practice may be more likely to do harm than good. I mention it only, as it shews the solicitude and extreme activity which he had about every thing that related to his art; that he wished to have his objects embodied as it were, and distinctly before him; that he neglected nothing which could keep his faculties in exercise, and derived hints from every sort of combination.

We must not forget whilst we are on this subject, to make some remarks on his custom of painting by night, which confirms what I have already mentioned, his great affection to his art; since he could not amuse himself in the evenings by any other means so agreeable to himself, I am indeed much inclined to believe that it is a practice very advantageous and improving to an artist; for by this means he will acquire a new and a higher perception of what is great and beautiful in Nature. By candle-light, not only objects appear more beautiful, but from their being in a greater breadth of light and shadow, as well as having a greater breadth and uniformity of colour, nature appears in a higher style; and even the flesh seems to take a higher and richer tone of colour. Judgment is to direct us in the use to be made of this method of study; but the method itself is, I am very sure, advantageous. I have often imagined that the two great colourists, Titian and Correggio, though I do not know that they painted by night, formed their high ideas of colouring from the effects of objects by this artificial light: but I am more assured, that whoever attentively studies the first and best manner of Guercino, will be convinced that he either painted by this light, or formed his manner on this conception.

Another practice Gainsborough had, which is worth mentioning as it is certainly worthy of imitation; I mean his manner of forming all the parts of his picture together; the whole going on at the same time, in the same manner as nature creates her works. Though this method is not uncommon to those who have been regularly educated, yet probably it was suggested to him by his own natural sagacity. That this custom is not universal appears from the practice of a painter whom I have just mentioned, Pompeio Battoni, who finished his historical pictures part after part; and in his portraits completely finished one feature before he proceeded to another. The consequence was, as might be expected; the countenance was never well expressed; and, as the painters say, the whole was not well put together.

The first thing required to excel in our art, or I believe in any art, is, not only a love for it, but even an enthusiastick ambition to excel in it. This never fails of success proportioned to the natural abilities with which the artist has been endowed by Providence. Of Gainsborough, we certainly know, that his passion was not the acquirement of riches, but excellence in his art; and to enjoy that honourable fame which is sure to attend it.—That *he felt this ruling passion strong in death,* I am myself a witness. A few hours before he died, he wrote me a letter, to express his acknowledgements for the good opinion I entertained of his abilities, and the manner in which (he had been informed) I always spoke of him; and desired he might see me, once more, before he died. I am aware how flattering it is to myself to be thus connected with the dying testimony which this excellent painter bore to his art. But I cannot prevail on myself to suppress that I was not connected with him by any habits of familiarity; if any little jealousies had subsisted between us, they were forgotten, in those moments of sincerity; and he turned towards me as one, who was engrossed by the same pursuits, and who deserved his good opinion, by being sensible of his excellence. Without entering into a detail of what passed at this last interview, the impression of it upon my mind was, that his regret at losing life, was principally the regret of leaving his art; and more especially as he now began, he said, to see what his deficiencies were; which, he said, he flattered himself in his last works were in some measure applied.

When such a man as Gainsborough arrives to great fame, without the assistance of an academical education, without travelling to Italy, or any of those preparatory studies which have been so often recommended, he is produced as an instance, how little such studies are necessary; since so great excellence may be acquired without them. This is an inference not warranted by the success of any individual; and I trust it will not be thought that I wish to make this use of it.

It must be remembered that the style and department of art which Gainsborough chose, and in which he so much excelled, did not require that he should go out of his own country for the objects of his study; they were every where about him; he found them in the streets, and in the fields; and from the models thus accidentally found, he selected with great judgment such as suited his purpose. As his studies were directed to the living world principally, he did not pay a general attention to the works of the various masters, though they are, in my opinion, always of great use, even when the character of our subject requires us to depart from some of their principles. It cannot be denied, that excellence in the department of the art which he professed may exist without them; that in such subjects, and in the manner that belongs to them, the want of them is supplied, and more than supplied, by natural sagacity, and a minute observation of particular nature. If Gainsborough did not look at nature with a poet's eye, it must be acknowledged that he saw her with the eye of a painter; and gave a faithful, if not a poetical, representation of what he had before him.

Though he did not much attend to the works of the great historical painters of former ages, yet he was well aware, that the language of the art, the art of imitation, must be learned somewhere; and as he knew that he could not learn it in an equal degree from his contemporaries, he very judiciously applied himself to the Flemish School, who are undoubtedly the greatest masters of one necessary branch of art; and he did not need to go out of his own country for examples of that school: from that he learnt the harmony of colouring, the management and disposition of light and shadow, and every means which the masters of it practised, to ornament and give splendour to their works. And to satisfy himself as well as others, how well he knew the mechanism and artifice which they employed to bring out that tone of colour which we so much admire in their works, he occasionally made copies from Rubens, Teniers, and Vandyck, which it would be no disgrace to the most accurate connoisseur to mistake, at the first sight, for the works of those masters. What he thus learned, he applied to the originals of nature, which he saw with his own eyes; and imitated, not in the manner of those masters, but in his own.

Whether he most excelled in portraits, landscapes, or fancy-pictures, it is difficult to determine: whether his portraits were most admirable for exact truth of resemblance, or his landscapes for portrait-like representation of nature, such as we see in the works of Rubens, Ruysdaal, and others of those Schools. In his fancy-pictures, when he had fixed on his object of imitation, whether it was the mean and vulgar form of a woodcutter, or a child of an interesting character, as he did not attempt to raise the one, so neither did he lose any of the natural grace and elegance of the other; such a grace, and such an elegance, as are more frequently found in cottages than in courts. This excellence was his own, the result of his particular observation and taste; for this he was certainly not indebted to the Flemish School, nor indeed to any School; for his grace was not academical, or antique, but selected by himself from the great school of nature; and there are yet a thousand modes of grace, which are neither theirs, nor his, but lie open in the multiplied scenes and figures of life, to be brought out by skilful and faithful observers.

Upon the whole, we may justly say, that whatever he attempted he carried to a high degree of excellence. It is to the credit of his good sense and judgment that he never did attempt that style of historical painting, for which his previous studies had made no preparation.

And here it naturally occurs to oppose the sensible conduct of Gainsborough in this respect, to that of our late excellent Hogarth, who, with all his extraordinary talents, was not blessed with this knowledge of his own deficiency; or of the bounds which were set to the extent of his own powers. After this admirable artist had spent the greatest part of his life in an active, busy, and we may add, successful attention to the ridicule of life; after he had invented a new species of dramatick painting, in which probably he will never be equalled, and had stored his mind with infinite materials to explain and illustrate the domestick and familiar scenes of common life, which were generally, and ought to have been always, the subject of his pencil; he very imprudently, or rather presumptuously, attempted the great historical style, for which his previous habits had by no means prepared him: he was indeed so entirely unacquainted with the principles of this style, that he was not even aware, that any artificial preparation was at all necessary. It is to be regretted, that any part of the life of such a genius should be fruitlessly employed. Let his failure teach us not to indulge ourselves in the vain imagination, that by a momentary resolution we can give either dexterity to the hand, or a new habit to the mind.

I have, however, little doubt, but that the same sagacity, which enabled those two extraordinary men to discover their true object, and the peculiar excellence of that branch of art which they cultivated, would have been equally effectual in discovering the principles of the higher style; if they had investigated those principles with the same eager industry, which they exerted in their own department. As Gainsborough never attempted the heroick style, so neither did he destroy the character and uniformity of his own style, by the idle affectation of introducing mythological learning in any of his pictures. Of this boyish folly we see instances enough, even in the works of great painters. When the Dutch School attempt this poetry of our art in their landskips, their performances are beneath criticism; they become only an object of laughter. This practice is hardly excusable, even in Claude Lorrain, who had shewn more discretion, if he had never meddled with such subjects.

Our late ingenious academician, Wilson, has, I fear, been guilty, like many of his predecessors, of introducing gods and goddesses, ideal beings, into scenes which were by no means prepared to receive such personages. His landskips were in reality too near common nature to admit supernatural objects. In consequence of this mistake, in a very admirable picture of a storm, which I have seen of his hand, many figures are introduced in the fore-ground, some in apparent distress, and some struck dead, as a spectator would naturally suppose, by the lightning; had not the painter, injudiciously (as I think) rather chosen that their death should be imputed to a little Apollo, who appears in the sky, with his bent bow, and that those figures should be considered as the children of Niobe.

To manage a subject of this kind, a peculiar style of art is required; and it can only be done without impropriety, or even without ridicule, when we adapt the character of the landskip, and that too, in all its parts, to the historical or poetical representation. This is a very difficult adventure, and it requires a mind thrown back two thousand years, and as it were naturalized in antiquity, like that of Nicolo Poussin, to achieve it. In the picture alluded to, the first idea that presents itself, is that of wonder, at seeing a figure in so uncommon a situation as that in which the Apollo is placed; for the clouds on which he kneels, have not the appearance of being able to support him; they have neither the substance nor the form, fit for the receptacle of a human figure; and they do not possess in any respect that romantick character which is appropriated to such a subject, and which alone can harmonize with poetical stories.

It appears to me, that such conduct is no less absurd than if a plain man, giving a relation of a real distress, occasioned by an inundation accompanied with thunder and lightning, should, instead of simply relating the event, take it into his head, in order to give a grace to his narration, to talk of Jupiter Pluvius, or Jupiter and his thunder-bolts, or any other figurative idea; an intermixture which, though in poetry, with its proper preparations and accompaniments, it might be managed with effect, yet in the instance before us would counteract the purpose of the narrator, and instead of being interesting, would be only ridiculous.

The Dutch and Flemish style of landscape, not even excepting those of Rubens, is unfit for poetical subjects; but to explain in what this inaptitude consists, or to point out all the circumstances that give nobleness, grandeur, and the poetick character, to style, in landscape, would require a long discourse of itself; and the end would be then perhaps but imperfectly attained. The painter who is ambitious of this perilous excellence, must catch his inspiration from those who have cultivated with success the poetry, as it may be called, of the art; and they are few indeed.

I cannot quit this subject without mentioning two examples which occur to me at present, in which the poetical style of landscape may be seen happily executed; the one is Jacob's dream by Salvator Rosa, and the other the return of the Arc from captivity, by Sebastian Bourdon. With whatever dignity those histories are presented to us in the language of Scripture, this style of painting possesses the same power of inspiring sentiments of grandeur and sublimity, and is able to communicate them to subjects which appear by no means adapted to receive them. A ladder against the sky has no very promising appearance of possessing a capacity to excite any heroick ideas; and the Arc, in the hands of a second-rate master, would have little more effect than a common waggon on the highway; yet those subjects are so poetically treated throughout, the parts have such a correspondence with each other, and the whole and every part of the scene is so visionary, that it is impossible to look at them, without feeling, in some measure, the enthusiasm which seems to have inspired the painters.

By continual contemplation of such works, a sense of the higher excellencies of art will by degrees dawn on the imagination; at every review that sense will become more and more assured, until we come to enjoy a sober certainty of the real existence (if I may so express myself) of those almost ideal beauties; and the artist will then find no difficulty in fixing in his mind the principles by which the impression is produced; which he will feel, and practice, though they are perhaps too delicate and refined, and too peculiar to the imitative art, to be conveyed to the mind by any other means.

To return to Gainsborough: the peculiarity of his manner, or style, as we may call it—the language in which he expressed his ideas, has been considered by many, as his greatest defect. But without altogether wishing to enter into the discussion whether this peculiarity was a defect or not, intermixed, as it was, with great beauties, of some of which it was probably the cause, it becomes a proper subject of criticism and enquiry to a painter.

A novelty and peculiarity of manner, as it is often a cause of our approbation, so likewise it is often a ground of censure; as being contrary to the practice of other painters, in whose manner we have been initiated, and in whose favour we have perhaps been prepossessed from our infancy; for, fond as we are of novelty, we are upon the whole creatures of habit. However, it is certain, that all those odd scratches and marks, which, on a close examination are so observable in Gainsborough's pictures, and which even to experienced painters appear rather the effect of accident than design; this chaos, this uncouth and shapeless appearance, by a kind of magick, at a certain distance assumes form, and all the parts seem to drop into their proper places; so that we can hardly refuse acknowledging the full effect of diligence, under the appearance of chance and hasty negligence. That Gainsborough himself considered this peculiarity in his manner and the power it possesses of exciting surprise, as a beauty in his works, I think may be inferred from the eager desire which we know he always expressed, that his pictures, at the Exhibition, should be seen near, as well as at a distance.

The slightness which we see in his best works, cannot always be imputed to negligence. However they may appear to superficial observers, painters know very well that a steady attention to the general effect, takes up more time, and is much more laborious to the mind, than any mode of high finishing or smoothness, without such attention.

His *handling, the manner of leaving the colours,* or in other words, the methods he used for producing the effect, had very much the appearance of the work of an artist who had never learned from others the usual and regular practice belonging to the art; but still, like a man of strong intuitive perception of what was required, he found out a way of his own to accomplish his purpose.

It is no disgrace to the genius of Gainsborough, to compare him to such men as we sometimes meet with, whose natural eloquence appears even in speaking a language, which they can scarce be said to understand; and who, without knowing the appropriate expression of almost any one idea, contrive to communicate the lively and forcible impressions of an energetick mind.

I think some apology may reasonably be made for his manner, without violating truth, or running any risk of poisoning the minds of the younger students, by propagating false criticism, for the sake of raising the character of a favourite artist. It must be allowed, that this hatching manner of Gainsborough did very much contribute to the lightness of effect which is so eminent a beauty in his pictures; as on the contrary, much smoothness, and uniting the colours, is apt to produce heaviness. Every artist must have remarked, how often that lightness of hand which was in his dead-colour, or first painting, escaped in the finishing, when he had determined the parts with more precision; and another loss he often experiences, which is of greater consequence; whilst he is employed in the detail, the effect of the whole together is either forgotten or neglected. The likeness of a portrait, as I have formerly observed, consists more in preserving the general effect of the countenance, than in the most minute finishing of the features, or any of the particular parts. Now Gainsborough's portraits were often little more, in regard to finishing, or determining the form of the features, than what generally attends a dead colour; but as he was always attentive to the general effect, or whole together, I have often imagined that this unfinished manner contributed even to that striking resemblance for which his portraits are so remarkable. Though this opinion may be considered as fanciful, yet I think a plausible reason may be given, why such a mode of painting should have such an effect. It is presupposed that in this undetermined manner there is the general effect; enough to remind the spectator of the original; the imagination supplies the rest, and perhaps more satisfactorily to himself, if not more exactly, than the artist, with all his care, could possibly have done. At the same time it must be acknowledged there is one evil attending this mode;

that if the portrait were seen, previous to any knowledge of the original, different persons would form different ideas, and all would be disappointed at not finding the original correspond with their own conceptions; under the great latitude which indistinctness gives of the imagination, to assume almost what character or form it pleases.

Every artist has some favourite part on which he fixes his attention, and which he pursues with such eagerness, that it absorbs every other consideration; and he often falls into the opposite error of that which he would avoid, which is always ready to receive him. Now Gainsborough, having truly a painter's eye for colouring, cultivated those effects of the art which proceed from colours; and sometimes appears to be indifferent to or to neglect other excellencies. Whatever defects are acknowledged, let him still experience from us the same candour that we so freely give upon similar occasions to the ancient masters; let us not encourage that fastidious disposition, which is discontented with every thing short of perfection, and unreasonably require, as we sometimes do, a union of excellencies, not perhaps quite compatible with each other.—We may, on this ground, say even of the divine Raffaelle, that he might have finished his picture as highly and as correctly as was his custom, without heaviness of manner; and that Poussin might have preserved all his precision without hardness or dryness.

To shew the difficulty of uniting solidity with lightness of manner, we may produce a picture of Rubens in the Church of St. Judule, at Brussels, as an example; the subject is, *Christ's charge to Peter*; which, as it is the highest, and smoothest, finished picture I remember to have seen of that master, so it is by far the heaviest; and if I had found it in any other place, I should have suspected it to be a copy; for painters know very well, that it is principally by this air of facility, or the want of it, that originals are distinguished from copies.—A lightness of effect, produced by colour, and that produced by facility of handling, are generally united; a copy may preserve something of the one, it is true, but hardly ever of the other; a connoisseur therefore finds it often necessary to look carefully into the picture before he determines on its originality. Gainsborough possessed this quality of lightness of manner and effect, I think, to an unexampled degree of excellence; but, it must be acknowledged, at the same time, that the sacrifice which he made to this ornament of our art, was too great; it was, in reality, preferring the lesser excellencies to the greater.

To conclude. However, we may apologize for the deficiencies of

Gainsborough, (I mean particularly his want of precision and finishing,) who so ingeniously contrived to cover his defects by his beauties; and who cultivated that department of art, where such defects are more easily excused; You are to remember, that no apology can be made for this deficiency, in that style which this academy teaches, and which ought to be the object of your pursuit. It will be necessary for you, in the first place, never to lose sight of the great rules and principles of the art, as they are collected from the full body of the best general practice, and the most constant and uniform experience; this must be the ground-work of all your studies: afterwards you may profit, as in this case I wish you to profit, by the peculiar experience and personal talents of artists living and dead; you may derive lights, and catch hints from their practice; but the moment you turn them into models, you fall infinitely below them; you may be corrupted by excellencies, not so much belonging to the art as personal and appropriated to the artist; and become bad copies of good painters, instead of excellent imitators of the great universal truth of things.

Benjamin Robert Haydon
False Notions of the Grand Style

I

The effect of these copies of Michel Angelo is enervating. You sit and muse; such a glorious opportunity for size—such a patron—such a combination of genius and opportunity rarely happens on earth; and it is altogether so much out of the reach of ordinary opportunity, that I think it rather overpowers than stimulates.

I can account for feeble minds becoming feebler from going to Italy. The gap between their humbler notions and what they see is so great that the imagination crushes their hopes, their energies, their ambition. They become copyists, imitators, connoisseurs, dealers, or slaves, and the remainder of their days is a nervous chatter about the grand style.

II

Went to the drawings from Michel Angelo . . . What absurdity to pull things from dark recesses sixty feet high—things which were obliged to be painted lighter, drawn fuller, and coloured harder than nature warrants, to look like life at the distance—and to bring them down to the level of the eye in a drawing-room, and adore them as the purest examples of form, colour, expression and character. They were never meant to be seen at that distance, or in that space.

Thus the student is perplexed, and seduced, and corrupted with ridiculous notions of what is truly grand. The works of this wonderful man have ruined a thousand artists to one they have educated and improved.

On Benjamin West

His Venuses looked as if they never had been naked before, and were too cold to be impassioned; his Adonises dolts; his Cupids blocks —unamorous.

> *In this brief comment, as Aldous Huxley says, "the last word on neo-classicism has been uttered."*

John Gibson
Two Statements

Whatever the Greeks did was right.

The human figure concealed under a frock coat and trousers is not a fit subject for sculpture. I would rather avoid contemplating such objects.

> *This is the same Gibson who declared that Phidias would have said of Michelangelo, "Here is a most clever and wonderful sculptor, but a barbarian."*

An infant's head with a pair of duck's wings under its chin, supposed always to be flying about and singing psalms.

William Hogarth (on the *putti*
of Italian religious art)

ROMANTICISM AND REALISM

The central element in Blake's thought and work is his vision of the imagination, not as the enemy of reality, but as the only force capable of achieving a true sense of the meaning of existence. Constantly, in his poetry and art as well as in his criticism, Blake pays tribute to the liberating effect of the imagination. He regarded Reynolds as the enemy of art because Reynolds denied inspiration and encouraged the notion that artistic creation was the end result of the right training and the right rules. The following excerpts from Blake's writings are all passionate outbursts and exclamations rising out of his profound conviction that the wrong kind of artistic theory and practice resulted, not simply in death in art, but in death in life as well.

William Blake[1]

Some Comments on Sir Joshua Reynolds' Discourses

This Man was Hired to Depress Art.

This is the Opinion of Will Blake: my Proofs of this Opinion are given in the following Notes.

Having spent the Vigour of my Youth & Genius under the Oppression of Sr Joshua & his Gang of Cunning Hired Knaves Without Employment & as much as could possibly be Without Bread, The Reader must Expect to Read in all my Remarks on these Books Nothing but Indignation & Resentment. While Sr Joshua was rolling in Riches, Barry was Poor & Unemploy'd except by his own Energy; Mortimer

---

1 Blake excerpts are from *The Complete Writings of William Blake,* ed. by Geoffrey Keynes. New York: Random House, 1957.

was call'd a Madman & only Portrait Painting applauded & rewarded by the Rich & Great. Reynolds and Gainsborough Blotted & Blurred one against the other & Divided all the English World between them. Fuseli, Indignant, almost hid himself. I am hid.

The Arts & Sciences are the Destruction of Tyrannies or Bad Governments. Why should A Good Government endeavour to Depress what is its Chief & only Support?

The Foundation of Empire is Art & Science. Remove them or Degrade them, & the Empire is No More. Empire follows Art & Not Vice Versa as Englishmen suppose.

Invention depends Altogether upon Execution or Organization; as that is right or wrong so is the Invention perfect or imperfect. Whoever is set to Undermine the Execution of Art is set to Destroy Art. Michael Angelo's Art depends on Michael Angelo's Execution Altogether.

I was once looking over the Prints from Rafael & Michael Angelo in the Library of the Royal Academy. Moser came to me & said: "You should not Study these old Hard, Stiff & Dry, Unfinish'd Works of Art —Stay a little & I will shew you what you should Study." He then went & took down Le Brun's & Ruben's Galleries. How I did secretly Rage! I also spoke my Mind . . . [*a line cut away by the binder*] I said to Moser, "These things that you call Finish'd are not Even Begun; how can they then be Finish'd? The Man who does not know The Beginning never can know the End of Art."

To Generalize is to be an Idiot. To Particularize is the Alone Distinction of Merit. General Knowledges are those Knowledges that Idiots possess.

> When Sr Joshua Reynolds died
> All Nature was degraded;
> The King dropped a tear into the Queen's Ear,
> And all his Pictures Faded.

I consider Reynolds's Discourses to the Royal Academy as the Simulations of the Hypocrite who smiles particularly where he means to Betray. His Praise of Rafael is like the Hysteric Smile of Revenge. His Softness & Candour, the hidden trap & the poisoned feast. He praises Michel Angelo for Qualities which Michel Angelo abhorr'd, & He blames Rafael for the only Qualities which Rafael Valued. Whether Reynolds knew what he was doing is nothing to me: the Mischief is just the same whether a Man does it Ignorantly or Knowingly. I always consider'd True Art & True Artists to be particularly Insulted & Degraded by the Reputation of these Discourses, As much as they were Degraded by the Reputation of Reynolds's Paintings, & that Such Artists as Reynolds are at all times Hired by the Satans for the Depression of Art—A Pretence of Art, To destroy Art.

The Rich Men of England form themselves into a Society to Sell & Not to Buy Pictures. The Artist who does not throw his Contempt on such Trading Exhibitions, does not know either his own interest or his Duty.

> When Nations grow Old, the Arts grow Cold
> And Commerce settles on every Tree,
> And the Poor & the Old can live upon Gold,
> For all are Born Poor, Aged Sixty three.

Reynolds's Opinion was that Genius May be Taught & that all Pretence to Inspiration is a Lie & a Deceit, to say the least of it. For if it is a Deceit, the whole Bible is Madness. This Opinion originates in the Greeks' Calling the Muses Daughters of Memory.

The Enquiry in England is not whether a Man has Talents & Genius, But whether he is Passive & Polite & a Virtuous Ass & obedient to Noblemen's Opinions in Art & Science. If he is, he is a Good Man. If Not, he must be Starved.

Minute Discrimination is Not Accidental. All Sublimity is founded on Minute Discrimination.

I do not believe that Rafael taught Mich. Angelo, or that Mich. Angelo taught Rafael, any more than I believe that the Rose teaches the Lilly how to grow, or the Apple tree teaches the Pear tree how to bear Fruit. I do not believe the tales of Anecdote writers when they militate against Individual Character.

Execution is the Chariot of Genius.

The Lives of Painters say that Rafael Died of Dissipation. Idleness is one Thing & Dissipation Another. He who has Nothing to Dissipate Cannot Dissipate; the Weak Man may be Virtuous Enough, but will Never be an Artist. Painters are noted for being Dissipated & Wild.

Every Eye Sees differently. As the Eye, Such the Object.

QUEEN KATHERINE'S DREAM—WILLIAM BLAKE   (*Photograph by courtesy of the National Gallery of Art, Washington, D.C.*)

Discourse [III] is particularly Interesting to Block heads, as it Endeavours to prove That there is No such thing as Inspiration & that any Man of a plain Understanding may by Thieving from Others become a Mich. Angelo.

The Man who on Examining his own Mind finds nothing of Inspiration ought not to dare to be an Artist; he is a Fool & a Cunning Knave suited to the Purposes of Evil Demons.

The Man who never in his Mind & Thoughts travel'd to Heaven Is No Artist.

Gainsborough told a Gentleman of Rank & Fortune that the Worst Painters always chose the Grandest Subjects. I desired the Gentleman to Set Gainsborough about one of Rafael's Grandest Subjects, Namely Christ delivering the Keys to St Peter, & he would find that in Gainsborough's hands it would be a Vulgar Subject of Poor Fishermen & a Journeyman Carpenter.

The Great Style is always Novel or New in all its Operations.

If Art was Progressive We should have had Mich. Angelos & Rafaels to Succeed & to Improve upon each other. But it is not so. Genius dies with its Possessor & comes not again till Another is Born with It.

A World of Imagination and Vision

I feel that a Man may be happy in This World. And I know that This World Is a World of imagination & Vision. I see Every thing I paint In This World, but Every body does not see alike. To the Eyes of a Miser a guinea is more beautiful than the Sun, & a bag worn with the use of Money has more beautiful proportions than a Vine filled with Grapes. The tree which moves some to tears of joy is in the Eyes of others only a Green thing that stands in the way. Some See Nature all Ridicule & Deformity, & by these I shall not regulate my proportions; & Some Scarce see Nature at all. But to the Eyes of the Man of Imagination, Nature is Imagination itself. As a man is, So he Sees. As the Eye is formed, such are its Powers. You certainly Mistake, when you say that the Visions of Fancy are not to be found in This World. To Me This World is all One continued Vision of Fancy or Imagination, & I feel Flattered when I am told so. What is it sets Homer, Virgil & Milton in so high a rank of Art? Why is the Bible more Entertaining & Instructive than any other book? Is it not because they are addressed to the Imagination, which is Spiritual Sensation, & but mediately to the Understanding or Reason? Such is True Painting, and such was also valued by the Greeks & the best modern Artists.

This is from a letter to the Reverend Dr. John Trusler, on August 23, 1799. It is a marvelously eloquent statement of Blake's central belief.

On True Reality

The Last Judgement is an Overwhelming of Bad Art & Science. Mental Things are alone Real; what is called Corporeal, Nobody Knows of its Dwelling Place: it is in Fallacy, & its Existence an Imposture. Where is the Existence Out of Mind or Thought? Where is it but in the Mind of a Fool? Some People flatter themselves that there will be No Last Judgment & that Bad Art will be adopted & mixed with Good Art, That Error or Experiment will make a Part of Truth, & they Boast that it is its Foundation; these People flatter themselves: I will not Flatter them. Error is Created. Truth is Eternal. Error, or Creation, will be Burned up, & then, & not till Then, Truth or Eternity will appear. It is Burnt up the Moment Men cease to behold it. I assert for My Self that I do not behold the outward Creation & that to me it is hindrance & not Action; it is as the Dirt upon my feet, No part of Me. "What," it will be Question'd, "When the Sun rises, do you not see a round disk of fire somewhat like a guinea?" O no, no, I see an Innumerable company of the Heavenly host crying, 'Holy, Holy, Holy is the Lord God Almighty.' I question not my Corporeal or Vegetative Eye any more than I would Question a Window concerning a Sight. I look thro' it & not with it.

This is from Blake's notes on a Vision of the Last Judgment. It is one of the noblest statements of his conviction that the true reality can only be perceived imaginatively.

Leonardo da Vinci
Let The Sea Be Rough And Tempestuous

How to represent a tempest. If you wish to represent a tempest consider and arrange well its effects as seen, when the wind, blowing over the face of the sea and earth, removes and carries with it such things as are not fixed to the general mass. And to represent the storm accurately you must first show the clouds scattered and torn, and flying with the wind, accompanied by clouds of sand blown up from the seashore, and bough and leaves swept along by the strength and fury of the blast and scattered with other light objects through the air. Trees and plants must be bent to the ground, almost as if they would follow the course of the gale, with their branches twisted out of their natural growth and their leaves tossed and turned about. Of the men who are there some must have fallen to the ground and be entangled in their garments, and hardly to be recognized for the dust, while those who remain standing may be behind some tree, with their arms round it that the wind may not tear them away; others with their hands over their eyes for the dust, bending to the ground with their clothes and hair streaming in the wind. Let the sea be rough and tempestuous and full of foam whirled among the lofty waves, while the wind flings the lighter spray through the stormy air, till it resembles a dense and swathing mist. Of the ships that are therein some should be shown with rent sails and the tatters fluttering through the air, with ropes broken and masts split and fallen. And the ship itself lying in the trough of the sea and wrecked by the fury of the waves with the men shrieking and clinging to the fragments of the vessel. Make the clouds driven by the impetuosity of the wind and flung against the lofty mountaintops, and wreathed and torn like waves beating upon rocks; the air itself terrible from the deep darkness caused by the dust and fog and heavy clouds.

This is an amazing description, perfectly visualized almost down to the last detail, of the kind of romantic painting that neither Leonardo nor any of his contemporaries could have created. It remained for Géricault, 300 years after this was written, to paint in "The Raft of the Medusa," the first great statement of the French romantic movement in art, a work which might have been done as a literal carrying out of Leonardo's precepts.

John Constable
A Declaration of Faith

I have never seen any ugly thing.

John Keats

The Excellence of Every Art Is Its Intensity

Death on the Pale Horse . . . is a wonderful picture, when West's age is considered: But there is nothing to be intense upon; no woman one feels mad to kiss, no face swelling into reality—The excellence of every art is its intensity, capable of making all disagreeables evaporate, from their being in close relationship with Beauty and Truth. Examine 'King Lear,' and you will find this exemplified throughout; but in this picture we have unpleasantness without any momentous depth of speculation excited, in which to bury its repulsiveness.

Letter to George & Thomas Keats
December 21, 1817

The following excerpts from Delacroix's Journal, *ranging over a period of more than thirty years, constitute almost an anthology in themselves of romantic attitudes and ideas, some contradicting or canceling out others. What runs through all as a unifying thread, however, is—as with Blake—the exaltation of the imagination, and the emphasis on the individual, the spontaneous, the unexpected.*

Eugène Delacroix
O Smile of the Dying!

My picture [Dante and Virgil in Hades] is acquiring a twist, an energetic movement that I must absolutely complete in it. I need that good black, that blessed dirt, and those limbs that I know how to paint and few even try to get. The mulatto model will serve my purpose. I must get fullness. If my work loses in naturalness, it will be more beautiful and more fruitful. If it only holds together! O smile of the dying! The look of the mother's eye! Embraces of despair, precious domain of painting! Silent power that at first speaks only to the eyes, and which wins and makes its own all the faculties of the soul! There is the spirit, the real beauty that is proper to you, beautiful painting, so insulted, so misunderstood, delivered up to the blockheads who exploit you. But there are hearts who will still receive you devoutly; souls who will not be satisfied with phrases, any more than with fictions and ingenuities. You have only to appear with your manly and simple vigor, and you will please with a pleasure that is pure and absolute. Admit that I have worked with reason. I do not care for reasonable painting at all. I can see that my turbulent mind needs agitation, needs to free itself, to try a hundred different things before reaching the goal whose tyrannous call everywhere torments me. There is an old leaven, a black depth that demands satisfaction. If I am not quivering like a snake in the hands of Pythoness, I am cold; I must recognize it and submit to it, and to do so is happiness. Everything I have done that is worth while, was done this way. No more *Don Quixotes* and things unworthy of you! Concentrate intensely before your painting and think only of Dante. Therein lies what I have always felt in myself.

Journal, May 7, 1824

Make It Simple And Daring

So there will come a time when I will no longer be agitated with thoughts and emotions and desires for poetry and effusions of all sorts. Poor Géricault! I saw you go down into the narrow house, where there are no longer even dreams. And yet I cannot believe it. How I should like to be a poet! But at least, create in painting! Make it simple and daring. How many things there are to do! Make engravings, if painting is too much for you, and big pictures. The life of Napoleon is the epic of our century for all the arts. But I must hurry. Painting—I have said it a thousand times—has its favors that are peculiar to itself alone. The poet is very rich: remember eternally certain passages from Byron to inflame your imagination for all time. They suit me well.

Journal, May 11, 1824

The Real Man Is the Savage

On man's gifts of reflection and imagination. Fatal gifts.

It is evident that nature cares very little whether man has a mind or not. The real man is the savage; he is in accord with nature as she is. As soon as man sharpens his intelligence, increases his ideas and the way of expressing them, and acquires needs, nature runs counter to him in everything. He has to do violence to her continually. She, on her side, is not slow to respond. If for a moment he lets up in the work he has imposed upon himself, she resumes her rights, she invades, she undermines, she destroys or disfigures his work; it seems as if she were impatient at having to tolerate the masterpieces of man's imagination and of his hand. For the march of the seasons, for the course of the stars, of rivers and of winds, what importance is there in the Parthenon, St. Peter's in Rome, and so many other miracles of art? An earthquake, or the lava of a volcano will punish them: the birds will nest in their ruins; the wild beasts will drag out the bones of their founders from their half-open tombs. But man himself, when he gives way to the savage instinct which is the very basis of his nature, does he not conspire with the elements to destroy the works of beauty? Does not barbarism, like the Fury who watches Sisyphus rolling his stone to the top of the mountain, return almost periodically to overthrow and con-

found, to bring forth night after a too brilliant day? And that indefinable thing which has given to man an intelligence higher than that
of the beasts, does it not seem to take pleasure in punishing him for
that very intelligence?

A fatal gift, did I say? Beyond a doubt; amidst this universal con-
spiracy against the fruits of invention, of genius, and of the spirit
which composes, does man have at least the consolation of wondering
greatly at himself for his constancy, or of a rich and continued enjoyment of the various fruits which have issued from him? The contrary
is most often the case. Not only must the man who is greatest through
talent, through audacity, through constancy, be also the most perse-
cuted, as he usually is, but he is himself fatigued and tormented by his
burden of talent and imagination. He is as ingenious in tormenting
himself as in enlightening others. Almost all the great men have had
a life more thwarted, more miserable than that of other men.

Of what use then is that mind and all that effort? Does living according to nature mean that one must live in filth, swim across rivers for
lack of bridges and of boats, live on acorns in the forests, or hunt deer
and buffalo with bow and arrow, in order to preserve a wretched life
a hundred times more useless than that of the oaks, which at least serve
to feed and harbor some animals? Is Rousseau of this mind, when he
proscribes the arts and the sciences, under pretext of their abuse? Is
everything then a trap, a condition of misfortune, or a sign of corruption in what comes from the intelligence of men? Why does he not
reproach the savage for ornamenting and bedecking his rude bow as
best he can, for decorating with the feathers of birds the apron with
which he hides his wretched nudity? And why should he hide it from
the sun and from his fellow men? Is that not again a sentiment too
elevated for that brute, for that machine made for living, for digesting,
and for sleeping?

Journal, May 1, 1850

The New Is Very Ancient

The new is very ancient, one may even say that it is always the most
ancient thing there is.

Journal, June 8, 1850

The Virtues of Spontaneity

I

Got ahead with the picture of the "Little Arab Seated Beside His Horse." Took up the "Clorinde" again, and believe I have brought it to an effect entirely different, one that leads me back to my original idea, which had escaped me little by little. Unfortunately it often happens that the execution, or difficulties, completely secondary considerations, throw one off from one's intention. The original idea, the sketch, which is so to speak the egg or embryo of the idea, is usually far from being complete; it contains everything, if you will, but it is necessary to free this everything, which is simply a mixing together of all parts. Just the thing that makes of this sketch the essential expression of the idea is not the suppression of details, but their complete subordination to the big lines which are, before all else, to create the impression. The greatest difficulty therefore is that of returning in the picture to that effacing of the details which, however, make up the composition, the web and the woof of the picture.

I do not know whether I am mistaken, but I believe that the greatest artists have had great struggles with that difficulty, the most serious one of all. Here one sees more than ever the drawback of giving to the details, through grace or coquetry in execution, so much interest that later on one mortally regrets sacrificing them when they are injurious to the ensemble. It is here that that breed of painters who are prodigal of easy and witty touches, fellows who go in for expressive torsos and heads, run into confusion through the very thing which they considered to be their great success. The picture, composed of *separate pieces,* each finished with care and placed next to its neighbor, one after another, looks like a masterpiece and the climax of cleverness, as long as it is not finished, which is to say as long as the field is not covered: because finishing, for those painters who finish each detail as they put it on the canvas, is to cover that canvas. In the presence of such work, proceeding without a halt, as it does, in the presence of those parts which seem the more interesting since you have nothing but parts to admire, one is involuntarily seized by a somewhat thoughtless astonishment; but when the last touch has been placed, when the architect of that whole heap of separate parts has placed upon them the pinnacle of his motley edifice and said his last word, one sees nothing but breaks and encumberment; one sees that in no place has he attained order. The interest that one gives to each object disappears in the confusion; what seems like precise and proper execution becomes dryness itself through the constant absence of *sacrifices*. From this putting together as if by accident of parts having no necessary connection, will you demand that penetrating and rapid impression, that original sketch giving the impression of an ideal which the artist is supposed to have glimpsed or caught in the first moment of inspiration? With the great artists, this sketch is not a dream, a confused cloud, it is something other than a mixture of barely perceptible lineaments; the great artists alone have a fixed point of departure, and it is to that pure expression that it is so difficult for them to return in either a prolonged or rapid execution of the work. Will the mediocre artist, concerned with his craft alone, arrive at such a result with the help of those extraordinary feats of strength in the matter of details which mislead as to the idea, instead of bringing it to the light? It is incredible to what point there is confusion concerning the first elements of composition in the minds of the majority of artists. How indeed should they be disturbed about returning through their *execution* to the idea, when they never had one?

Journal, April 23, 1854

II

One always has to spoil a picture a little bit, in order to finish it. The last touches, which are given to bring about harmony among the parts, take away from the freshness. In order to appear before the public one has to cut away all the happy negligences which are the passion of the artist.

Journal, April 13, 1853

The Antique Never Surprises

I am at Champrosay since Saturday, I take a solitary walk in the forest while waiting for my room to be arranged so that I can get back to the famous Poussin. Noticing the Antin oak from a distance, I did not recognize it at first, finding it so ordinary, and my mind went back to an observation I had set down in my notebook about two weeks ago, as to the effect of the sketch in its relation to the finished work. I said that the sketch of a picture or a monument—and the same is true of a ruin or, in a word any work of the imagination in which parts are lacking—ought to react on the soul in just the proportion that we have to add to the work, while it is producing its impression on us. I add that perfect works, like those of a Racine or of a Mozart, do not, at the first moment, produce as much effect as those of less correct or even careless geniuses, who give you salient parts standing out in all the stronger relief because others, beside them, are vague or completely bad.

Standing before this fine tree (the Antin oak) which is so well proportioned, I find a new confirmation of these ideas. At the distance necessary for the eye to seize it as a whole, it seems to be of ordinary size; if I place myself under its branches the impression changes completely: perceiving only the trunk which I almost touch and the springing–point of the thick branches which spread out over my head like the immense arms of the giant of the forest, I am astonished at the grandeur of its details; in a word I see it as big, and even terrifying in its bigness.

Can it be that disproportion is one of the conditions which compel admiration? If, on one side, Mozart, Cimarosa, and Racine cause less of astonishment by reason of the admirable proportion in their works, do not Shakespeare, Michelangelo and Beethoven owe a part of their effect to an opposite course? In my own opinion, that is the fact.

The antique never surprises, never gives that gigantic and exaggerated effect. One finds oneself at ease with those admirable creations; reflection alone makes them seem big and places them on their incomparable height. Michelangelo astonishes, and brings into the soul a troubled sentiment which amounts to admiration, but one is not long in perceiving shocking incongruities which are, in his art, the consequence of too hasty work, caused either by the fire with which the artist engaged upon it or else by the fatigue which probably seized him at the end of a labor impossible of completion.

Journal, May 9, 1853.

Novelty Is in the Mind that Creates

Intense sadness and despondency all evening.

This morning, reading the review of Lord Byron at the beginning of the volume, I felt again awakening in me that insatiable desire to create. Can I tell whether that would be happiness for me? At least, it seems so. Happy poet and happier still in having a tongue that submits to his imaginings! Yet, French is sublime. But I should have to give battle many times to this rebellious Proteus before subjugating him.

What torments my soul is its loneliness. The more it expands among friends and the daily habits or pleasures, the more, it seems to me, it flees me and retires into its fortress. The poet who lives in solitude, but who produces much, is the one who enjoys those treasures we bear in our bosom, but which forsake us when we give ourselves to others. When one yields oneself completely to one's soul, it opens itself completely to one, and then it is that the capricious thing allows one the greatest of good fortunes, that of which the account of Lord Byron speaks, that of sympathizing with others, of studying itself, of painting itself constantly in its works, something that Byron and Rousseau have perhaps not noticed. I am not talking about mediocre people: for what is this rage, not only to write, but to be published? Outside of the happiness of being praised, there is that of addressing all souls that can understand yours, and so it comes to pass that all souls meet in your painting. What good is the approbation of friends? It is quite natural that they should understand you; so what importance is there in that? What is intoxicating is to live in the mind of others. What is so devastating! I ask myself. You can add one soul more to the number of those who have seen nature in a way that is their own. What all these souls have painted is new for them, and you will paint them new again! They have painted their soul, in painting things, and your soul asks its turn, also. And why should you resist when it does so? Is its request more absurd than the need for repose that your limbs ask, when they and all your physical being are fatigued? If they have not done enough for you, neither have they done enough for others. Those very ones who believe that everything has been said and done, will greet you as new and yet will close the door behind you. And then they will say again that everything has been said and done. Just as man, in the feebleness of age, believes that nature is degenerating, so men with commonplace minds and who have nothing to say about what has already been said, think that nature has allowed certain ones, and those only in the beginning of time, to say new and striking things. What there was to say in the times of those immortal spirits, attracted the notice of all their contemporaries, just as in our time, but for all that not many tried to seize the new thing, to enter their name hastily, in order to steal for themselves the harvest that posterity that was to reap. Novelty is in the mind that creates, and not in nature, the thing painted.

Journal, May 14, 1824

The Incredible Power of the Imagination

I start out at six o'clock for Brive. In the coupé, *tête-à-tête* with a brigadier in the gendarmerie, a very decent chap; superb head. He leaves me about nine o'clock. I spend a good night, now sleeping, now seeing by the light of the train lamps the curious country that I'm going through—Uzerche, etc.—and that I regret not seeing by daylight.

As I looked out upon really bizarre objects, I was thinking of *that little world* which man bears within him. People who say that man learns everything through education are idiots, and that includes the great philosophers who have maintained that theory. As singular and unexpected as the spectacles offered to our eyes may be, they never surprise us completely; there is within us an echo which replies to all impressions; either we have seen a given thing at some other place, or else all possible combinations of things are prepared in advance within our brain. When we encounter them in this passing world, we do no more than open a compartment of our brain or of our soul. How can one explain otherwise the incredible power of the imagination and as a final proof, the fact that this power is, relatively speaking, incomparably strong during childhood? Not only did I have as much imagination during childhood and youth, but when objects created deeper impressions within me than now, or offered me incomparable delights, my surprise was no greater than any I now experience. Whence could I have derived all those impressions at that earlier time?

Journal, September 11, 1855

Art Lives Through Fictions

Realism should be defined as the antipode of art. It is perhaps more odious in painting and in sculpture than in history and the novel; I do not mention poetry: for, by reason of the mere fact that the instrument of the poet is a pure convention, a measured language, in a word, which immediately places the reader above the earthy quality of everyday life, one sees how grotesque would be the contradiction in terms if anyone spoke of realistic poetry, admitting that such a monster could be conceived. What, in sculpture for example, would a realistic art be? Mere casts from nature would always be superior to the most perfect imitation which the hand of man can produce: for can one conceive a case in which the mind would not guide the hand of the artist and will anyone believe it possible, likewise, that, despite all attempts to imitate, he will not tinge his singular work with the color of his mind, unless one go to the point of supposing that the eye alone and the hand be sufficient to produce—I will not merely say an exact imitation—but even any work whatsoever?

If *realism* is not to be a word devoid of sense, all men would have the same mind, the same fashion of conceiving things. . .

Art, like poetry, lives through fictions. Propose to the professional realist the painting of supernatural objects: a god, a nymph, a monster, a fury, all those things of the imagination which transport the mind!

Journal, February 22, 1860

> *The answer of "the professional realist" to this criticism had already been given by Courbet in a famous statement: "Show me an angel and I'll paint one."*

The Gracelessness of Realism

I went to see the paintings by Courbet. I was astonished at the vigor and the relief in his principal picture; but what a picture! What a subject! The commonness of the forms would do no harm; it is the commonness and the uselessness of the thought which are abominable; and if only his idea, common and useless as it is, were clear! What are those two figures doing? A fat bourgeoise is seen from the back, completely nude save for a carelessly painted bit of cloth, covering the lower part of her buttocks; she comes out of a little strip of water which does not seem deep enough for even a foot-bath. She makes a gesture which expresses nothing, and another woman, whom one may suppose to be her maid, is seated on the ground, taking off her shoes and stockings. One sees stockings that have just been taken off, one of them only halfway, I think. Between these two figures there is an exchange of thoughts which one cannot understand. The landscape is of an extraordinary vigor, but Courbet has done no more than enlarge a study exhibited there, near his large canvas; the conclusion is that the figures were put in afterward and without connection with their surroundings. This brings up the question of harmony between the accessories and the principal object, a thing lacking in the majority of great painters. It is not the biggest defect in Courbet. There is also a "Spinner Asleep," which presents the same qualities, both of vigor and of imitation. The wheel, the distaff—admirable; the dress, the armchair—heavy and without grace. The "Two Wrestlers" show lack of action, and confirm the artist's impotence in the matter of invention. The background kills the figures; it would be necessary to cut off more than three feet all around.

Oh, Rossini! Oh, Mozart! Oh, geniuses inspired in all the arts; who draw from things only such elements of them as are to be shown to the mind! What would you say before these pictures? Oh, *Semiramis!* Oh, entry of the priests to crown Ninias!

Journal, April 15, 1853

It should be pointed out that Delacroix was able to recognize the genius of Courbet, especially in the two great paintings, "The Studio of the Artist" and "The Burial at Ornans."

The Book of Creation

How necessary it is to give oneself a shaking up, to get one's head out, to try to read in the book of creation, which has nothing in common with our cities and with the works of men!

Journal, January 19, 1847

Landscape Without Line

That famous element, the beautiful, which some see in the serpentine line, others see in the straight line, but they are all resolved that it is to be seen only in line. I am at my window, and I see the most beautiful landscape: the idea of a line does not come to my mind. The lark sings, the river sparkles with a thousand diamonds, the foliage murmurs; where are any lines to produce these charming sensations? Those people refuse to see proportion and harmony unless they are between lines: the rest is chaos for them, and the compass alone is the judge.

Journal, July 15, 1849

This is an obvious answer to Ingres, the inheritor and continuator of the neoclassicism of David and the great rival of Delacroix.

On Delacroix's death, Baudelaire wrote the magnificent tribute,[1] here reprinted for the most part, that beautifully captures the quality of the man and his painting.

Charles Baudelaire
To the Editor of L'Opinion Nationale.

Sir:

Once again I should like to pay homage—a supreme homage—to the genius of Eugène Delacroix. So I ask you to publish in your newspaper these few pages in which I shall try to cover, as briefly as possible, the evolution of his talent; the reason for his superiority, which in my opinion has not yet been sufficiently recognized; and finally, a few anecdotes and remarks concerning his life and character.

I had the good fortune to know the illustrious deceased when I was still very young (from 1845 on, if I remember correctly). In our relations, respect on my part and forbearance on his did not prevent mutual confidence and familiarity, and in the course of our friendship, I had ample time to obtain a most accurate idea not only of his method but also of the most intimate qualities of his great soul. . . .

I think, sir, that the important thing here is simply to seek out the characteristic quality of Delacroix's genius and to attempt to define it; to find out wherein he differs from his most renowned predecessors, while remaining their equal; and to show finally, insofar as the written word makes it possible, the magic art thanks to which he was able to translate the *word* into plastic images more vivid and more appropriate than those of any other creator in the same profession—in short, to reveal the *special* faculty with which fate endowed Eugène Delacroix.

I

What is Delacroix? What was his role, his task in this world? That is the first question. I shall be brief. The Lowlands have Rubens; Italy has Raphael and Veronese; France has Lebrun, David, and Delacroix.

The superficial mind may, at first sight, be shocked by the association of these names, representing such different qualities and methods.

---

[1] From *Eugène Delacroix, His Life and Work,* by Charles Baudelaire. New York: Lear Publishers, 1947.

ARAB RIDER ATTACKED BY LION—EUGÈNE DELACROIX   (*Courtesy of The Art Institute of Chicago, Potter Palmer Collection*)

But the more penetrating mind will see at once that all these painters have something in common, a kind of brotherhood or kinship deriving from their love of the great, the national, the vast, and the universal; a love that has always been expressed in so-called decorative painting or in large-scale *compositions*.

Many others, no doubt, have painted large-scale *compositions*, but those I have named did so in a way best fitted to leave an eternal mark in man's memory. Who is the greatest of these men so great and so diverse? Each individual may decide as he pleases, according to whether his temperament leads him to prefer the prolific, radiant, almost jovial abundance of Rubens; the sweet majesty and harmonious order of Raphael; the blissful and as-if-afternoon color of Veronese; the austere and taut severity of David; or the dramatic and almost literary eloquence of Lebrun.

None of the men can be replaced. All aiming at a similar goal, they used different means drawn from their personal endowment. Delacroix, the most recent in time, expressed with admirable vehemence and fervor what the others had not completely translated. Did some other quality perhaps suffer in the process, a quality which the others possessed? Possibly, but that is not the question at issue.

Many others beside myself have made a point of stressing the fatal consequences of an essentially personal genius; and after all, it is quite possible that the highest expressions of genius—not in the azure sky but on this poor earth where perfection itself is imperfect—have been achieved only at the expense of an inevitable sacrifice.

But no doubt, sir, you will ask: what is this mysterious *je ne sais quoi* which Delacroix, to the glory of our century, has translated better than any other artist? It is the invisible, the impalpable; it is the dream, the nerves, the *soul*. And he has done this—mark it well, sir—with no other means save contour and color. He has done it better than anyone else; he has done it with the perfection of a consummate painter, with the discipline of a subtle writer, with the eloquence of a passionate musician. Moreover, it is one of the symptoms of the spiritual temper of our century that the arts strive, if not to supplement one another, at least to lend each other new strength.

Delacroix is the most *suggestive* of all painters. His works, even his secondary and inferior paintings, give one the most to think about. They recall to the memory poetic emotions and ideas already known but which one thought forever buried in the night of the past.

Delacroix's work sometimes seems to me a kind of remembrance of the greatness and native passion of the universal man. This quite new and special merit of Delacroix, which enabled him with a simple contour to express man's gestures however violent, and with color create what might be called the atmosphere of the human drama, this striking originality has always won for him the sympathies of all poets, and if one could draw philosophical conclusions from a purely material phenomenon, I would ask you to observe, sir, that there were many more writers than painters in the throng gathered to pay their last respects to him. The blunt truth is that the painters have never completely understood him.

And after all, what is there really surprising in this? Do we not know that the time of the Michaelangelos, the Raphaels, the Leonardo da Vincis, even of the Joshua Reynoldses, has long since passed, and that the general intellectual level of artists has fallen markedly? It would no doubt be unfair to look among the artists of our time for philosophers, poets, and scholars; but it would be in order to ask them to show a little more interest than they do in religion, poetry, and science.

Outside of their studios what do they know? What do they like? What do they express? Eugène Delacroix was not only an artist in love with his craft. He was also a man of broad general culture, in contrast to other modern artists, most of whom are little more than famous or obscure daubers, sad specialists, and pure craftsmen, some able to paint academic figures, others fruit, and still others animals. Eugène Delacroix loved everything, could paint everything, appreciated all kinds of talents. His mind was open to all ideas and impressions: he enjoyed them in the most eclectic and the most impartial manner.

It goes without saying that he was an avid reader. His reading of poetry left in him grandiose and quickly defined images, ready-made pictures so to speak. However much he differed from his master Guerin in method and color, he inherited from the great republican and imperial school a love of the poets and a kind of fierce spirit of competition with the written word. David, Guerin, and Girodet were inspired by their reading of Homer, Virgil, Racine, and Ossian. Delacroix was the passionate translator of Shakespeare, Dante, Byron, and Ariosto. An important resemblance and a slight difference.

But let us penetrate a little more deeply into what might be called the master's teaching, a teaching which for me comes not only from the successive study of all his works and the simultaneous study of several of them at the Universal Exposition of 1855, but also from many conversations I had with him.

Delacroix was passionately in love with passion, and coldly determined to find ways of expressing passion in the most visible manner. In this dual approach we find, it may be said in passing, the mark of extreme genius which never calculates to please timorous souls who are easily satisfied and who find sufficient enjoyment in weak, soft, and imperfect works. An immense passion, combined with a formidable will—of such was Delacroix the man.

He used to repeat:

"Since I consider the impression transmitted by nature to the artist

the most important thing to be translated, must not he artist be armed
in advance with all the most rapid means of translation?"

It is clear that in his eyes imagination was the most precious gift,
the most important faculty which remained powerless and impotent if
it did not have at its command a rapid skill which could follow its
despotic and impatient whims. Certainly, he did not have to kindle the
fire of his ever-incandescent imagination, but he always found the day
too short to study means of expressing it.

To this ceaseless preoccupation one must attribute his constant researches with respect to color and the quality of colors, his curiosity
about chemistry, and his conversations with manufacturers of colors.
In that he was akin to Leonardo da Vinci who was also obsessed with
the same curiosity.

Eugène Delacroix, despite his admiration for the passionate phenomena of life, will never be found in the company of that crowd of
vulgar artists and writers who, in their limited intelligence, take refuge
behind the vague and obscure word "realism." The first time I saw
Delacroix—in 1845 I think (how the years pass, rapid and consuming!)
—we talked of many commonplaces, that is, of the vastest yet simplest
problems: of nature, for example. Here, sir, I take the liberty of quot-
ing myself, for a paraphrase would not be worth as much as the words I
wrote years ago, almost at the master's dictation:

"Nature is only a dictionary, he often used to say. To understand the
scope of the meaning implied in that sentence, one must recall the
many ordinary uses of the dictionary. In it one looks for the meeting
of words, their origin and etymology, and finally, one gets from it all
the elements that go into a sentence or a story. But no one has ever
considered the dictionary as a *composition,* in the poetic sense of the
term. Painters who obey their imagination look in their dictionary for
elements fitting in with their conception, and, adjusting them with a
certain art, they give them an altogether new face. Those who have
no imagination copy the dictionary. The result is a very great vice,
the vice of banality, which is more particularly suited to those painters
who specialize in what is called inanimate nature; for example, landscape painters, who usually consider it a triumph not to show their
personality. By dint of observing and copying, they forget to feel and
think.

"In this great painter, different people choose different aspects as the
essence of his art. But all the component parts of his art were, or rather
are, but the very humble servants of a unique and superior faculty.

If very clean execution is necessary, it is in order that the dream may be very clearly translated; if the execution is very quick, it is in order not to lose anything of the extraordinary impression accompanying the conception. The fact that the artist even pays attention to the material quality of his tools is also quite understandable, for all precautions have to be taken to make the execution swift and decisive."

Here let me say in passing that I have never seen a palette as minutely and as delicately prepared as that of Delacroix. It was like a skillfully arranged bouquet of flowers.

"In such a method, which is basically logical, all the human figures, their relative disposition, the landscape or interior which serves as their background or horizon, their clothing, in short, everything must serve to illuminate the general idea and bear its original color, its livery, so to speak. Just as a dream is placed in an atmosphere of color suited to it, so a conception, once it becomes a composition, must move about in an environment of color specifically its own. Obviously there is a special shade given to any one part of the picture: this becomes the key color and determines the others. Everyone knows that yellow, orange, and red inspire and represent ideas of joy, wealth, glory, and love; but there are thousands of yellow or red atmospheres, and all the other colors will be logically affected in a proportionate measure by the dominant atmosphere. The colorist's art is obviously related in some respects to mathematics and music.

"Nevertheless his most delicate operations are the result of a feeling to which long practice has given unerring sureness. Clearly, this great law of general harmony rules out many examples of superficial brilliance and many crudities, even in the most famous painters. There are paintings by Rubens which make one think not only of colored fireworks, but of several sets of fireworks shot off from the same place. The larger a picture is, the broader the stroke must be. That goes without saying. But it is well that the strokes are not materially fused. They fuse naturally at a distance required by the sympathetic law that has associated them. Thus color obtains more energy and freshness.

"A good painting, faithful and equal to the dream that has engendered it, must be produced like a world. Just as the creation as we see it, is the result of several creations, with each one always completed by the one following it, so a picture, harmoniously constructed, consists of a series of superimposed pictures, each new layer giving more reality to the dream and causing it to rise a degree higher toward perfection. On the other hand, I recall having seen in the studios of

Paul Delaroche and Horace Vernet vast paintings not sketched but begun—that is, completely finished in certain parts, while certain other parts still consisted of nothing more than a black or white outline. This type of work might be compared with purely manual labor which must cover a specific quantity of space in a definite time, or a long road divided into a large number of sections. When one section is finished, it does not have to be re-done, and when the whole road is travelled the artist is delivered of his painting.

"All these precepts are of course more or less modified by the varying temperaments of individual artists. Nevertheless I am convinced that for rich imaginations it is the surest method. Consequently, too great deviations from this method attest to an abnormal and unfair importance attached to some secondary aspect of art.

"I do not fear that people will say it is absurd to conceive of one and the same method applied by a host of different individuals. For it is clear that rhetoric and prosody are not arbitrarily invented tyrannies but a collection of rules required by the very organization of the spiritual being; nor have prosody and rhetoric ever prevented the appearance of distinct originality. On the contrary, it would be far truer to say that they have aided originality to flower.

"For the sake of brevity I am forced to pass over a great many corollaries flowing from the main formula which contains, so to speak, all the formulas of true esthetics, and which may be expressed as follows: the whole visible universe is only a storehouse of images and signs to which imagination assigns a relative place and value. It is a kind of food which imagination must digest and transform. All the faculties of the human spirit must be subordinated to the imagination which calls upon all of them at once. Just as knowing the dictionary well does not necessarily imply knowing the art of composition, and the art of composition itself does not imply universal imagination, so a *good* painter may be not a *great* painter; but a great painter must be a good painter, because universal imagination includes the knowledge of all means and the desire to acquire them.

"It is obvious that, in accordance with the ideas I have just tried to elucidate to the best my ability, the vast class of artists, that is, of men devoted to the expression of the beautiful, may be divided into two very distinct camps. The artist who calls himself a *realist* (since this word has a double meaning and has not been clearly defined, we prefer to call him a *positivist*, in order better to characterize his error) asserts: 'I wish to present things as they are, or as they would be even if I did not exist.' The other artist, the imaginative one, says: 'I wish to illuminate things with my spirit and project the reflection to other spirits.' Although these two diametrically opposed methods may heighten or diminish all themes, from religious scenes to the most modest landscape, yet the man of imagination has generally been found in religious painting and in fantasy, while so-called *genre* painting and landscapes have seemed to offer vast resources to lazy minds that are not easily aroused. . . .

"Delacroix's imagination! It has never feared to scale the difficult heights of religion. Heaven belongs to it as does hell, as do war, Olympus, and sensuality. He is indeed the type of painter-poet! He is one of the chosen few, and the breadth of his mind includes religion in its domain. His imagination, glowing as a chapel ablaze with light, burns with every flame and every purple passion. All the sorrow there is in passion moves him. All the splendor there is in the Church illumines him. On his inspired canvases he pours in turn blood, light, and shadows. I think that he would like to add his natural splendor to the majesty of the Bible.

"I have seen a small "Annunciation" by Delacroix in which the angel visiting Mary was not alone but ceremoniously accompanied by two other angels. The effect of this heavenly court was charming and powerful. One of his youthful paintings, "Christ in the Garden of Olives" ("Lord, let this cup pass from me") shimmers with feminine tenderness and poetic unction. Sorrow and pomp, so heightened in religion, always find an echo in his spirit."

And more recently I wrote, concerning his last great work in the Chapel of Holy Angels at Saint-Sulpice Church ("Heliodorus Driven from the Temple" and "Jacob Wrestling with the Angel," a project that was so stupidly criticized):

"Never, not even in "Trajan's Mercy," not even in the "Entry of the Crusaders into Constantinople," has Delacroix revealed a more splendid and more skillfull supernatural coloring; never has he shown a more *consciously* epic design. I realize that some people, masons no doubt, or perhaps architects, have uttered the word *decadence* in connection with this last work. Here it is in order to point out that the great masters, poets or painters, Hugo or Delacroix, are always several years ahead of their timid admirers.

"The public, with respect to genius, is like a clock that is slow. Who among the clear-sighted does not realize that the master's first painting contained all the others in embryo? But that he unremittingly perfects

his natural gifts, that he sharpens them with care, that he draws from
them new effects, that he drives his own nature to the limit—that is
inevitable, fatal, and praiseworthy. And it is precisely the chief hall-
mark of Delacroix's genius that it does not know decadence. It only
shows progress. But his initial qualities were so impetuous and so rich,
they were so powerfully striking even to the most vulgar minds, that
the latter are insensible to his daily progress. Only the serious-minded
clearly perceive this.

"I spoke just a while ago of the remarks of a few *masons*. In using that
term I meant the category of coarse and materialistic minds (their
number is legion) who appreciate objects only in contour or, worse
still, in their three dimensions: breadth, length, and depth, just as do
savages and peasants. I have often heard persons of that ilk set up a
hierarchy of qualities which to me is absolutely unintelligible. They
assert, for example, that the faculty which enables one artist to create
an exact contour or another a contour of supernatural beauty, is superior to the faculty which assembles contours in an enchanting manner.
According to such people, color does not dream, it does not think, it
does not speak. It would appear that when I look at the works of one
of those men called colorists, I indulge in a pleasure which is not sublime in character. They are ready to call me a materialist, reserving for
themselves the aristocratic epithet of spiritualists.

"These superficial minds do not realize that the two faculties can
never be completely separated and that both are the result of an original
germ that has been carefully cultivated. External nature only gives the
artist an ever-recurring opportunity to cultivate this germ. It is but an
incoherent mass of materials which the artist is asked to bring together
and put in order, an *incitamentum,* an awakener of flagging faculties.
Speaking accurately, there is in nature neither line nor color. These are
two abstractions deriving their equal nobility from the same origin.

"Imagine a born artist as a child. He observes certain sinuosities in
nature moving or at rest. From it he derives a certain voluptuousness
and he enjoys capturing these impressions by drawing lines on paper,
fondly exaggerating or lessening the curves. Thus he learns how to
create emphasis, elegance, and character in a drawing. Imagine a child
destined to perfect that aspect of art called color. It is from the clash
or pleasing harmony of two colors and from the pleasure he thereby
derives that he will acquire knowledge of the infinite combinations of
color-tones. In both cases, nature has been pure stimulation.

"Line and color both make one think and dream. The pleasures deriving from them are of a different kind, but completely equal and absolutely independent of the theme of the painting.

"A picture by Delacroix, hung at too great a distance for you to judge the harmony of its contours and the more or less dramatic quality of its theme, already fills you with a kind of supernatural voluptuousness. You feel as if a magic atmosphere has walked toward you and enveloped you. Somber yet delightful, luminous yet tranquil, this impression, which remains indelibly engraved in your memory, proves the true, the perfect colorist. And an analysis of the theme, when you draw closer, will neither add nor subtract anything from this initial pleasure, the source of which is elsewhere and far removed from any secret thought.

"I can give an inverse example. A well-drawn figure fills you with a pleasure that is quite alien to the theme. Voluptuous or terrible, this figure owes its charm solely to the arabesque it describes in space. The limbs of a tortured martyr, the body of a swooning nymph, if they are skillfully drawn, connote a type of pleasure in which the theme plays no part, and if you believe otherwise, I shall be forced to think that you are an executioner or a rake.

"But alas! What is the use of eternally repeating these useless truths?"

But perhaps, sir, your readers will appreciate, much more than this rhetoric, the details I am myself eager to give concerning the character and habits of our great departed painter.

IV

This dual nature of which I have spoken appears above all in the writings of Eugène Delacroix. As you know, many persons were amazed at the wisdom of his written opinions and the temperateness of his style, some regretting, other approving. His *Variations on the Beautiful,* his studies of Poussin, Prud'hon, and Charlet, and other pieces published either in *L'Artiste,* then owned by M. Ricourt, or in the *Revue des Deux Mondes,* only confirm this dual character of great artists which drives them as critics to praise and analyze more lovingly the qualities they themselves need most as creators, and which serve as a foil to those they possess in super-abundance. If Eugène Delacroix had praised and glorified what we most admire in them, violence, suddenness of gesture, turbulent composition, and magic of color, then in truth we would have had reason to be amazed. Why look for what one has almost in excess? And how can one fail to praise what seems rarest and most difficult to acquire? We will always see the same phenomenon manifested in creators of genius, every time they apply their faculties to criticism. At the time of the great struggle between the two schools, the classical and the romantic, the simple-minded were dumbfounded to hear Eugène Delacroix ceaselessly laud Racine, La Fontaine, and Boileau. I know a poet of an ever violent and quivering temperament who is transported into a long ecstasy by a symmetrical and musically square line of Malherbe. . . .

V

Eugène Delacroix was a curious mixture of skepticism, politeness, dandyism, violent will, cunning, despotism, and finally a kind of special kindness and quiet tenderness that always goes hand in hand with genius. His father belonged to that breed of strong men, the last of whom we knew in our childhood—some, fervent followers of Jean-Jacques Rousseau, others, resolute disciples of Voltaire. All of them participated with equal obstinacy in the French Revolution, and the survivors, Jacobins or Cordeliers, rallied in perfect good faith (an important point to be noted) to the standard of Bonaparte.

Eugène Delacroix always retained traces of his revolutionary origins. Of him, as of Stendhal, it may be said that he had a great fear of being duped. Skeptical and aristocratic, he knew passion and the supernatural only by forcing himself to frequent the world of dreams. Hating crowds, he looked upon them as little more than statue-breakers, and the wanton damage done to a few of his works in 1848 was not calculated to convert him to the political sentimentalism of our time. There was even something in him—in his style, manners, and opinions—of Victor Jacquemont. I know that the comparison is somewhat insulting, hence I ask that it be interpreted only with the utmost moderation. There is in Jacquemont something of the enlightened bourgeois mind in revolt and a jesting spirit as fond of mystifying the priests of Brahma as those of Jesus Christ. Delacroix, guided by the taste that is always innate in a genius, could never indulge in such vulgarity. So my comparison refers only to the spirit of prudence and sobriety with which the two men were imbued. Similarly, the traits he inherited from the 18th century seemed borrowed above all from the class that was as far removed from the Utopians as it was from the wild-eyed—the class of polite skeptics, the victors and survivors, who in general owed more to Voltaire than to Jean-Jacques Rousseau. Thus, at first sight, Eugène Delacroix appeared to be simply an *enlightened* man, in the honorable sense of the term, a perfect *gentleman* without prejudices and passions. It was only after one came to know him well that one could penetrate the outer layer and divine the secret recesses of his soul. As for his outward bearing and manners, it would be more correct to compare him with M. Prosper Mérimée. He had the same apparent and slightly affected coldness, the same icy cloak covering over a shy sensitivity and an ardent passion for the good and the beautiful. Beneath the same seeming egotism there was the same devotion to secret friends and favorite ideas.

There was much of the *savage* in Eugène Delacroix. That was the most precious part of his soul, the part devoted entirely to painting his dreams and to the cult of his art. There was in him much of the man of the world. This aspect was designed to conceal the other and to obtain forgiveness for it. That, I believe, was one of the great pre-occupations of his life, to hide the anger in his heart and not to look like a man of genius. His spirit of domination, a quite valid and even inevitable spirit, disappeared almost completely beneath his many kindnesses. He was like the crater of a volcano artistically hidden by bouquets of flowers.

Another mark of resemblance with Stendhal was his penchant for simple formulas, brief maxims, as guides to a good life. Like those all the more enamored of method in that their ardent and sensitive temperament seems to keep them further removed from it, Delacroix liked to draw up these little rules of practical morality which muddleheads and parasites, who practice nothing, contemptuously attribute to M. de la Palisse. But genius does not despise them because it is related to simplicity. They are strong, healthy, simple, and severe maxims, serving as shield and armor to one plunged by the fatality of his genius into a never-ending battle.

Need I tell you that the same spirit of firm and disdainful wisdom inspired M. Delacroix's opinions on political matters? He believed that nothing was changing although everything seemed to be changing, and that certain decisive epochs in the history of peoples invariably produced analogous phenomena. His thinking in these matters, especially in its aspects of cold and bleak resignation, was very much akin to that of a historian for whom I have a very special fondness. You yourself, sir, so much at home in these questions, so capable of esteeming a man's talent even when he opposes you, you too, I am sure, have more than once been forced to admire him. I refer to M. Ferrari, the subtle and learned author of the *History of the Reason for the State.*

So the conversationalist who, in front of M. Delacroix, gave vent to childish utopian enthusiasms, soon felt the effect of his bitter laugh tinged with pitying sarcasm. And if one discussed in his presence the great chimera of modern times, the over-inflated notion of continuous perfectibility and perpetual progress, he would sharply ask: "Then where are your Phidiases? Where are your Raphaels?"

But do not think that this blunt common sense stripped M. Delacroix of any grace. His lively skepticism and his refusal to be duped seasoned like a Byronic salt, his highly poetic and colorful conversation. From himself—that is, from his own genius and the consciousness of his genius—rather than from his long experience as a man of the world, he acquired a marvellous sureness and ease of manner. His politeness, like a prism, tolerated all nuances, from the most cordial affability to the most irreproachable impertinence. He had at least twenty different ways of saying: "My dear sir!", and to a trained ear they ran the gamut of sentiment. Here I must add, for I consider it a new motive for praise, that Eugène Delacroix, although—or rather—because he was a complete man of genius, had much of the dandy about him. He himself confessed that in his youth he had indulged with pleasure in the most materialistic vanities of dandyism, and he told with a laugh but not without a certain pride that, together with his friend Bonnington, he had labored diligently to inculcate in the elegant young people a taste for the English cut in shoes and clothes. This detail will not, I hope, be considered insignificant, for when one has to depict the nature of certain men no memories are superfluous.

I have already said that the attentive observer was struck above all by the natural part of Delacroix's soul, despite the deadening veil of a refined civilization that covered it. Everything in him was energy, but energy flowing from the nerves and the will, for physically he was frail and delicate. The tiger poised for its prey has less fire in its eyes and less impatient quiverings in its muscles than our great painter showed when his whole soul had hit upon an idea or sought to capture a dream. Even the physical characteristics of his face, his Peruvian or Malayan skin, his large black eyes narrowed by intense concentration and as if drinking in the light, his thick and shiny hair, his stubborn forehead, his tightly shut lips conveying an expression of cruelty as a result of the constant straining of his will—in fact, his whole being suggested that he was of exotic birth. More than once, as I looked at him, I thought of the ancient kings of Mexico, of Montezuma whose practiced hand could in a single day sacrifice three thousand human creatures on the pyramid-like Altar of the Sun; or of one of those Hindu princes who, amid the splendors of the most lavish festivals, reveals a kind of unsatisfied avidity and an inexplicable nostalgia in the depths of his eyes, something akin to remembrance and regret of things not known. I ask you to observe how the general color in Delacroix's paintings is similar to the color in Oriental landscapes and interiors, how it produces a sensation analogous to that felt in semi-tropical countries where a tremendous diffusion of light gives an almost crepuscular impression to the sensitive eye, despite the intensity of the local color-tones. The moral in his works, if one may be permitted to speak of morality in painting, also bears a visibly Moloch-like stamp. Everything in his work is only desolation, massacres, conflagrations. Everything bears witness to man's eternal and incorrigible barbarism. Cities smoking and in flames, slaughtered victims, raped women, even children hurled under horses' hooves or cringing under the dagger of delirious mothers—all his work, I say, resembles a terrible hymn composed in honor of doom and irremediable sorrow. Certainly, he was not lacking in tenderness, and at times he wielded his brush to express tender and voluptuous sentiments. But here, too, incurable bitterness was spread in heavy doses, and nonchalance and joy (the usual companions of naive volptuousness) were absent. Only once, I believe, did he attempt the droll and the comic, and, as if sensing that that was beyond and below his nature, he never tried again.

VI

. . . Once he said to a young man I know: "If you are not skillful enough to sketch a man jumping out of a window in the time it takes him to fall from the fourth story to the ground, you will never be able to produce great works." Here I find metaphorically expressed the obsession of his whole life, to execute quickly enough and with sufficient sureness so as not to allow any element in the intensity of an act or idea to be lost.

Delacroix was, as many others have observed, a conversationalist. But the amusing thing is that he was afraid of conversation as if it were a debauch, a dissipation in which he risked squandering his energies. When you came to see him, he began by saying:

"We won't talk this morning, will we? Or only very little, very little."

And then he chatted for three solid hours. His conversation was brilliant, subtle, but full of facts, memories, and anecdotes—in short, meaty conversation. . . .

VII

. . . One of the chief preoccupations of our painter in the last years of his life was the judgment of posterity and uncertainty as to the fate of his works. Sometimes his sensitive spirit would glow with the thought of immortal glory. Sometimes he spoke bitterly of the fragility of his canvases and colors. On other occasions he cited with envy the old masters almost all of whom had the good fortune to be reproduced by clever engravers, capable of adapting the style of their engravings to the nature of their originals, and he deeply regretted not having found someone to reproduce his works. The destructibility of a work of painting compared with the solidity of a work of literature was an ever-recurring theme in his conversation.

When this man, so frail and so obstinate, so nervous and so brave, this unique figure in the history of European art, this sickly and delicate artist who constantly dreamed of covering walls with his grandios conceptions, was struck down by a chest inflammation of which he seems to have had a fatal foreboding, we all felt the same kind of depression, the same sensation of heightened loneliness we had already experienced at the death of Chateaubriand and of Balzac. Only recently we again had this sensation at the disappearance of Alfred de Vigny. In a great national bereavement there is a lowering of general vitality, a darkening of the intellect resembling a solar eclipse—a momentary imitation of the end of the world.

Yet I believe that this impression affects especially those solitary figures on the heights whose only family ties can be formed along their intellectual friendships. As for the other citizens, most of them find out only by degrees what the nation has lost in losing a great man, and what a vacuum he has created in leaving them. Even then, they have to be told what they have lost.

I thank you, sir, with all my heart for having been good enough to allow me to draw freely on my memories of one of the rare geniuses of our unhappy century—so poor and rich at the same time, sometimes too exacting, sometimes too indulgent, and too often unjust.

Paris 1863

(Translated from the French by Joseph M. Bernstein)

Aldous Huxley
Variations on Goya[1]

There are anthologies of almost everything—from the best to the worst, from the historically significant to the eccentric, from the childish to the sublime. But there is one anthology, potentially the most interesting of them all, which, to the best of my knowledge, has never yet been compiled; I mean, the Anthology of Later Works.

To qualify for inclusion in such an anthology, the artist would have to pass several tests. First of all, he must have avoided a premature extinction and lived on into artistic and chronological maturity. Thus the last poems of Shelley, the last compositions of Schubert and even of Mozart would find no place in our collection. Consummate artists as they were, these men were still psychologically youthful when they died. For their full development they needed more time than their earthly destiny allowed them. Of a different order are those strange beings whose chronological age is out of all proportion to their maturity, not only as artists, but as human spirits. Thus, some of the letters written by Keats in his early twenties and many of the paintings which Seurat executed before his death at thirty-two might certainly qualify as Later Works. But, as a general rule, a certain minimum of time is needed for the ripening of such fruits. For the most part, our hypothetical anthologist will make his selections from the art of elderly and middle-aged men and women.

But by no means all middle-aged and elderly artists are capable of producing significant Later Works. For the last half century of a long life, Wordsworth preserved an almost unbroken record of dullness. And in this respect he does not stand alone. There are many, many others whose Later Works are their worst. All these must be excluded from our anthology, and I would pass a similar judgment on that other large class of Later Works which, though up to the standard of the earlier, are not significantly different from them. Haydn lived to a ripe old age and his right hand never forgot its cunning; but it also failed to learn a new cunning. Peter-Pan-like, he continued, as an old man, to write the same sort of thing he had written twenty, thirty, and forty years before. Where there is nothing to distinguish the creations of a man's

[1] Foreword to *The Complete Etchings of Goya*. New York: Crown Publishers, 1943.

maturity from those of his youth it is superfluous to include any of them
in a selection of characteristically Later Works.

This leaves us, then, with the Later Works of those artists who have
lived without ever ceasing to learn of life. The field is relatively narrow;
but within it, what astonishing and sometimes what disquieting trea-
ures! One thinks of the ineffable serenity of the slow movement of
Beethoven's A minor Quartet, the peace passing all understanding of
the orchestral prelude to the "Benedictus" of his *Missa Solemnis*. But
this is not the old man's only mood; when he turns from the contemplation of eternal reality to a consideration of the human world, we
are treated to the positively terrifying merriment of the last movement
of his B-flat major Quartet—merriment quite inhuman, peals of violent
and yet somehow abstract laughter echoing down from somewhere
beyond the limits of the world. Of the same nature, but if possible even
more disquieting, is the mirth which reverberates through the last act
of Verdi's *Falstaff,* culminating in that extraordinary final chorus in
which the aged genius makes his maturest comment on the world—not
with bitterness or sarcasm or satire, but in a huge, contrapuntal par-
oxysm of detached and already posthumous laughter.

Turning to the other arts, we find something of the same nonhuman,
posthumous quality in the Later Works of Yeats and, coupled with a
prodigious majesty, in those of Piero della Francesca. And then, of
course there is *The Tempest*—a work charged with something of the
unearthly serenity of Beethoven's "Benedictus" but concluding in the
most disappointing anticlimax, with Prospero giving up his magic for
the sake (heaven help us!) of becoming once again a duke. And the
same sort of all too human anticlimax saddens us at the end of the
second part of *Faust,* with its implication that draining fens is Man's
Final End, and that the achievement of this end automatically qualifies
the drainer for the beatific vision.

And what about the last El Grecos—for example, that unimaginable
"Immaculate Conception" at Toledo with its fantastic harmony of brilliant, ice-cold colors, its ecstatic gesticulations in a heaven with a third
dimension no greater than that of a mine shaft, its deliquescence of
flesh and flowers and drapery into a set of ectoplasmic abstractions?
What about them, indeed? All we know is that, beautiful and supremely
enigmatic, they will certainly take their place in our hypothetical
anthology.

And finally, among these and all other extraordinary Later Works,
we should have to number the paintings, drawings and etchings of
Goya's final twenty-five or thirty years.

The difference between the young Goya and the old may be best studied and appreciated by starting in the basement of the Prado, where his cartoons for the tapestries are hung; climbing thence to the main floor, where there is a room full of his portraits of royal imbeciles, grandees, enchanting duchesses, *majas,* clothed and unclothed; walking thence to the smaller room containing the two great paintings of the "Second of May"—Napoleon's mamelukes cutting down the crowd and, at night, when the revolt has been quelled, the firing squads at work upon their victims by the light of lanterns; and finally mounting to the top floor where hang the etchings and drawings, together with those unutterably mysterious and disturbing "black paintings," with which the deaf and aging Goya elected to adorn the dining room of his house, the Quinta del Sordo. It is a progress from light-hearted eighteenth-

THE BULLFIGHT—GOYA (*The Metropolitan Museum of Art, Wolfe Fund, 1922*)

century art, hardly at all unconventional in subject matter or in handling, through fashionable brilliancy and increasing virtuosity, to something quite timeless both in technique and spirit—the most powerful of commentaries on human crime and madness, made in terms of an artistic convention uniquely fitted to express precisely that extraordinary mingling of hatred and compassion, despair and sardonic humor, realism and fantasy.

"I show you sorrow," said the Buddha, "and the ending of sorrow"— the sorrow of the phenomenal world in which man, "like an angry ape, plays such fantastic tricks before high heaven as make the angels weep," and the ending of sorrow in the beatific vision, the unitive contemplation of transcendental reality. Apart from the fact that he is a great and, one might say, uniquely original artist, Goya is significant as being, in his Later Works, the almost perfect type of the man who knows only sorrow and not the ending of sorrow.

In spite of his virulent anticlericalism, Goya contrived to remain on sufficiently good terms with the Church to receive periodical commissions to paint religious pictures. Some of these, like the frescoes in the cupola of La Florida, are frankly and avowedly secular. But others are serious essays in religious painting. It is worth looking rather closely at what is probably the best of these religious pieces—the fine "Agony in the Garden." With outstretched arms, Christ raises toward the comforting angel a face whose expression is identical with that of the poor creatures whom we see, in a number of unforgettably painful etchings and paintings, kneeling or standing in an excruciating anticipation before the gun barrels of a French firing squad. There is no trace here of that loving confidence which, even in the darkest hours, fills the hearts of men and women who live continuously in the presence of God; not so much as a hint of what François de Sales calls "holy indifference" to suffering and good fortune, of fundamental equanimity, the peace passing all understanding, which belongs to those whose attention is firmly fixed upon a transcendental reality.

For Goya the transcendental reality did not exist. There is no evidence in his biography or his works that he ever had even the most distant personal experience of it. The only reality he knew was that of the world around him; and the longer he lived the more frightful did that world seem—the more frightful, that is to say, in the eyes of his rational self; for his animal high spirits went on bubbling up irrepressibly, whenever his body was free from pain or sickness, to the very end. As a young man in good health, with money and reputation, a fine position and as many women as he wanted, he had found the world a very agreeable place—absurd, of course, and with enough of folly and roguery to furnish subject matter for innumerable satirical drawings, but eminently worth living in. Then all of a sudden came deafness, and, after the joyful dawn of the Revolution, Napoleon and French imperialism and the atrocities of war; and, when Napoleon's hordes were gone, the unspeakable Ferdinand VII and clerical reaction and the spectacle of Spaniards fighting among themselves; and all the time, like the drone of a bagpipe accompanying the louder noises of what is officially called history, the enormous stupidity of average men and women, the chronic squalor of their superstitions, the bestiality of their occasional violences and orgies.

Realistically or in fantastic allegories, with a technical mastery that only increased as he grew older, Goya recorded it all—not only the agonies endured by his people at the hands of the invaders, but also the follies and crimes committed by these same people in their dealings with one another. The great canvases of the Madrid massacres and executions, the incomparable etchings of "War's Disasters," fill us with an indignant compassion. But then we turn to the "Disparates" and the "Pinturas Negras." In these, with a sublimely impartial savagery, Goya sets down exactly what he thinks of the martyrs of the Dos de Mayo when they are not being martyred. Here, for example, are two men— two Spaniards—sinking slowly toward death in an engulfing quicksand, but busily engaged in knocking one another over the head with bludgeons. And here is a rabble coming home from a pilgrimage— scores of low faces, distorted as though by reflection in the back of a spoon, all openmouthed and yelling. And all the blank black eyes stare vacantly and idiotically in different directions.

These creatures who haunt Goya's Later Works are inexpressibly horrible, with the horror of mindlessness and animality and spiritual darkness. And above the lower depths where they obscenely pullulate is a world of bad priests and lustful friars, of fascinating women whose love is a "dream of lies and inconstancy," of fatuous nobles and, at the top of the social pyramid, a royal family of halfwits, sadists, Messalinas, and perjurers. The moral of it all is summed up in the central plate of the "Caprichos," in which we see Goya himself, his head on his arms, sprawled across his desk and fitfully sleeping, while the air above is peopled with the bats and owls of necromancy and just behind his chair lies an enormous witch's cat, malevolent as only Goya's cats can be, staring at the sleeper with baleful eyes. On the side of the desk

are traced the words, "The dream of reason produces monsters." It is
a caption that admits of more than one interpretation. When reason
sleeps, the absurd and loathsome creatures of superstition wake and
are active, goading their victim to an ignoble frenzy. But this is not all.
Reason may also dream without sleeping, may intoxicate itself, as it
did during the French Revolution, with the daydreams of inevitable
progress, of liberty, equality, and fraternity imposed by violence, of
human self-sufficiency and the ending of sorrow, not by the all too
arduous method which alone offers any prospect of success, but by
political rearrangements and a better technology. The "Caprichos"
were published in the last year of the eighteenth century; in 1808 Goya
and all Spain were given the opportunity of discovering the consequences of such daydreaming. Murat marched his troops into Madrid;
the "Desastres de la Guerra" were about to begin.

Goya produced four main sets of etchings—the "Caprichos," the
"Desastres de la Guerra," the "Tauromaquia" and the "Disparates" or
"Proverbios." All of them are Later Works. The "Caprichos" were not
published until he was fifty-three; the plates of the "Desastres" were
etched between the ages of sixty-five and seventy-five; the "Tauromaquia" series first saw the light when he was sixty-nine (and at the age
of almost eighty he learned the brand-new technique of lithography in
order to be able to do justice to his beloved bulls in yet another
medium); the "Disparates" were finished when he was seventy-three.

For the non-Spaniard the plates of the "Tauromaquia" series will
probably seem the least interesting of Goya's etchings. They are brilliant records of the exploits of the bull ring; but unfortunately, or
fortunately, most of us know very little about bullfighting. Consequently, we miss the finer shades of the significance of these little masterpieces of documentary art. Moreover, being documentary, the etchings of the "Tauromaquia" do not lend themselves to being executed
with that splendid audacity, that dramatic breadth of treatment, which
delights us in the later paintings and the etchings of the other three
series. True, we find in this collection a few plates that are as fine as
anything Goya ever produced—for example, that wonderful etching of
the bull which has broken out of the arena and stands triumphant, a
corpse hanging limp across its horns, among the spectators' benches.
But by and large it is not to the "Tauromaquia" that we turn for the
very best specimens of Goya's work in black and white, or for the most
characteristic expressions of his mature personality. The nature of the
subject matter makes it impossible for him, in these plates to reveal
himself fully either as a man or as an artist.

Of the three other sets of etchings two, the "Caprichos" and "Disparates," are fantastic and allegorical in subject matter, while the third, the "Desastres," though for the most part it represents real happenings under the Napoleonic terror, represents them in a way which, being generalized and symbolical rather than directly documentary, permits of, and indeed demands, a treatment no less broad and dramatic than is given to the fantasies of the other collections.

War always weakens and often completely shatters the crust of customary decency which constitutes a civilization. It is a thin crust at the best of times, and beneath it lies—what? Look through Goya's "Desastres" and find out. The abyss of bestiality and diabolism and suffering seems almost bottomless. There is practically nothing of which human beings are not capable when war or revolution or anarchy gives them the necessary opportunity and excuse; and to their pain death alone imposes a limit.

Goya's record of disaster has a number of recurrent themes. There are those shadowy archways, for example, more sinister than those even of Piranesi's "Prisons," where women are violated, captives squat in a hopeless stupor, corpses lie rotting, emaciated children starve to death. Then there are the vague street corners at which the famine-stricken hold out their hands; but the whiskered French hussars and carabiniers look on without pity, and even the rich Spaniards pass by indifferently, as though they were "of another lineage." Of still more frequent occurrence in the series are the crests of those naked hillocks on which lie the dead, like so much garbage. Or else, in dramatic silhouette against the sky above those same hilltops, we see the hideous butchery of Spanish men and women, and the no less hideous vengeance meted out by infuriated Spaniards upon their tormentors. Often the hillock sprouts a single tree, always low, sometimes maimed by gunfire. Upon its branches are impaled, like the beetles and caterpillars in a butcher bird's larder, whole naked torsos, sometimes decapitated, sometimes without arms, or else a pair of amputated legs, or a severed head— warnings, set there by the conquerors, of the fate awaiting those who dare oppose the Emperor. At other times the tree is used as a gallows— a less efficient gallows, indeed, than that majestic oak which, in Callot's "Misères de la Guerre," is fruited with more than a score of swinging corpses, but good enough for a couple of executions *en passant,* except, of course, in the case recorded in one of Goya's most hair-raising plates, in which the tree is too stumpy to permit of a man's hanging clear of the ground. But the rope is fixed, none the less, and to tighten the noose around their victim's neck, two French soldiers tug at the legs, while with his foot a third man thrusts with all his strength against the shoulders.

And so the record proceeds, horror after horror, unalleviated by any of the splendors which other painters have been able to discover in war; for, significantly, Goya never illustrates an engagement, never shows us impressive masses of troops marching in column or deployed in the order of battle. His concern is exclusively with war as it affects the civilian population, with armies disintegrated into individual thieves and ravishers, tormentors and executioners—and occasionally, when the *guerilleros* have won a skirmish, into individual victims tortured in their turn and savagely done to death by the avengers of their own earlier atrocities. All he shows us is war's disasters and squalors, without any of the glory or even picturesqueness.

In the two remaining series of etchings we pass from tragedy to satire and from historical fact to allegory and pictorial metaphor and pure fantasy. Twenty years separate the "Caprichos" from the "Disparates," and the later collection is at once more somber and more enigmatic than the earlier. Much of the satire of the "Caprichos" is merely Goya's sharper version of what may be called standard eighteenth-century humor. A plate such as "Hasta la Muerte," showing the old hag before her mirror, coquettishly trying on a new headdress, is just Rowlandson-with-a-difference. But in certain other etchings a stranger and more disquieting note is struck. Goya's handling of his material is such that standard eighteenth-century humor often undergoes a sea change into something darker and queerer, something that goes below the anecdotal surface of life into what lies beneath—the unplumbed depths of original sin and original stupidity. And in the second half of the series the subject matter reinforces the effect of the powerful and dramatically sinister treatment; for here the theme of almost all the plates is basely supernatural. We are in a world of demons, witches, and familiars, half horrible, half comic, but wholly disquieting inasmuch as it reveals the sort of thing that goes on in the squalid catacombs of the human mind.

In the "Disparates" the satire is on the whole less direct than in the "Caprichos," the allegories are more general and more mysterious. Consider, for example, the technically astonishing plate, which shows a large family of three generations perched like huddling birds along a huge dead branch that projects into the utter vacancy of a dark sky. Obviously, much more is meant than meets the eye. But what? The question is one upon which the commentators have spent a great deal of ingenuity—spent it, one may suspect, in vain. For the satire, it would seem, is not directed against this particular social evil or that political mistake, but rather against unregenerate human nature as such. It is a statement, in the form of an image, about life in general. Literature and the scriptures of all the great religions abound in such brief metaphorical verdicts on human destiny. Man turns the wheel of sorrow, burns in the fire of craving, travels through a vale of tears, leads a life that is no better than a tale told by an idiot signifying nothing.

> Poor man, what Art? A tennis ball of error,
> A ship of glass tossed in a sea of terror:
> Issuing in blood and sorrow from the womb,
> Crawling in tears and mourning to the tomb.
> How slippery are thy paths, how sure thy fall!
> How art thou nothing, when thou art most of all!

And so on. Good, bad, and indifferent the quotations could be multiplied almost indefinitely. In the language of the plastic arts, Goya has added a score of memorable contributions to the stock of humanity's gnomic wisdom.

The "Disparates" of the dead branch is relatively easy to understand. So is the comment on Fear contained in the plate which shows soldiers running in terror from a gigantic cowled figure, spectral against a jet black sky. So is the etching of the ecstatically smiling woman riding a stallion that turns its head and, seizing her skirts between its teeth, tries to drag her from her seat. The allegorical use of the horse, as a symbol of the senses and the passions, and of the rational rider or charioteer who is at liberty to direct or be run away with, is at least as old as Plato.

But there are other plates in which the symbolism is less clear, the allegorical significance far from obvious. That horse on a tightrope, for example, with a woman dancing on its back; the men who fly with artificial wings against a sky of inky menace; the priests and the elephant; the old man wandering among phantoms: what is the meaning of these things? And perhaps the answer to that question is that they have no meaning in any ordinary sense of the word; that they refer to strictly private events taking place on the obscurer levels of their creator's mind. For us who look at them, it may be that their real point and significance consist precisely in the fact that they image forth so vividly, and yet, of necessity, so darkly and incomprehensibly, some at least of the unknown quantities that exist at the heart of every personality.

Goya once drew a picture of an ancient man tottering along under the burden of years, but with the accompanying caption, "I'm still learning." The old man was himself. To the end of a long life, he went on learning. As a very young man he paints like the feeble eclectics who were his masters. The first signs of power and freshness and originality appear in the cartoons for the tapestries, of which the earliest were executed when he was thirty. As a portraitist, however, he achieves nothing of outstanding interest until he is almost forty. But by that time he really knows what he's after, and during the second forty years of his life he moves steadily forward toward the consummate technical achievements, in oils, of the "Pinturas Negras," and, in etching, of the "Desastres" and the "Disparates." Goya's is a stylistic growth away from restraint and into freedom, away from timidity and into expressive boldness.

From the technical point of view the most striking fact about almost all Goya's successful paintings and etchings is that they are composed in terms of one or more clearly delimited masses standing out from the background—often indeed, silhouetted against the sky. When he attempts what may be called an "allover" composition, the essay is rarely successful. For he lacks almost completely the power which Rubens so conspicuously possessed—the power of filling the entire canvas with figures or details of landscape, and upon the *plenum* imposing a clear and yet exquisitely subtle three-dimensional order. The lack of this power is already conspicuous in the tapestry cartoons, of which the best are invariably those in which Goya does his composing in terms of silhouetted masses and the worst those in which he attempts to organize a collection of figures distributed all over the canvas. And compare, from this point of view, the two paintings of the *Dos de Mayo* —the mamelukes cutting down the crowd in the Puerta del Sol, and the firing squads at work in the suburbs, after dark. The first is an attempt to do what Rubens would have done with an almost excessive facility—to impose a formally beautiful and dramatically significant order upon a crowd of human and animal figures covering the greater part of the canvas. The attempt is not successful, and in spite of its power and the beauty of its component parts, the picture as a whole is less satisfying as a composition, and for that reason less moving as a story, than is the companion piece, in which Goya arranges his figures in a series of sharply delimited balancing groups, dramatically contrasted with one another and the background. In this picture the artist is speaking his native language, and he is therefore able to express what he wants to say with the maximum force and clarity. This is not the case with the picture of the mamelukes. Here, the formal language is not truly his own, and consequently his eloquence lacks the moving power is possesses when he lets himself go in the genuine Goyescan idiom.

Fortunately, in the etchings, Goya is very seldom tempted to talk in anything else. Here he composes almost exclusively in terms of bold separate masses, silhouetted in luminous grays and whites against a darkness that ranges from stippled pepper-and-salt to intense black, or in blacks and heavily shaded grays against the whiteness of virgin paper. Sometimes there is only one mass, sometimes several, balanced and contrasted. Hardly ever does he make the, for him, almost fatal mistake of trying to organize his material in an allover composition.

With the "Desastres" and the "Disparates" his mastery of this, his predestined method of composition, becomes, one might say, absolute. It is not, of course, the only method of composition. Indeed, the nature of this particular artistic idiom is such that there are probably certain things that can never be expressed in it—things which Rembrandt, for example, was able to say in his supremely beautiful and subtle illustrations to the Bible. But within the field that he chose to cultivate—that the idiosyncrasies of his temperament and the quality of his artistic sensibilities compelled him to choose—Goya remains incomparable.

Henry James
Honoré Daumier[1]

If we attempt, at the present day, to write the history of everything, it would be strange if we had happened to neglect the annals of caricature; for the very essence of the art of Cruikshank and Gavarni, of Daumier and Leech, is to be historical; and every one knows how addicted is this great science to discoursing about itself. Many industrious seekers, in England and France, have ascended the stream of time to the source of the modern movement of pictorial satire. The stream of time is in this case mainly the stream of journalism; for social and political caricature, as the present century has practised it, is only journalism made doubly vivid.

The subject indeed is a large one, if we reflect upon it, for many people would tell us that journalism is the greatest invention of our

1 *Picture and Text*, by Henry James. New York: Harper and Brothers, 1893.

age. If this rich affluent has shared the great fortune of the general torrent, so, on other sides, it touches the fine arts, touches manners, touches morals. All this helps to account for its inexhaustible life; journalism is the criticism of the moment *at* the moment, and caricature is that criticism at once simplified and intensified by a plastic form. We know the satiric image as periodical, and above all as punctual—the characteristics of the printed sheet with which custom has at last inveterately associated it.

This, by the way, makes us wonder considerably at the failure of caricature to achieve, as yet, a high destiny in America—a failure which might supply an occasion for much explanatory discourse, much searching of the relations of things. The newspaper has been taught to flourish among us as it flourishes nowhere else, and to flourish moreover on a humorous and irreverent basis; yet it has never taken to itself this helpful concomitant of an unscrupulous spirit and a quick periodicity. The explanation is probably that it needs an old society to produce ripe caricature. The newspaper thrives in the United States, but journalism languishes; for the lively propagation of news is one thing and the large interpretation of it is another. A society has to be old before it becomes critical, and it has to become critical before it can take pleasure in the reproduction of its incongruities by an instrument as impertinent as the indefatigable crayon. Irony, scepticism, pessimism are, in any particular soil, plants of gradual growth, and it is in the art of caricature that they flower most aggressively. Furthermore they must be watered by education—I mean by the education of the eye and hand—all of which things take time. The soil must be rich too, the incongruities must swarm. It is open to doubt whether a pure democracy is very liable to make this particular satiric return upon itself; for which it would seem that certain social complications are indispensable. These complications are supplied from the moment a democracy becomes, as we may say, impure from its own point of view; from the moment variations and heresies, deviations or perhaps simple affirmations of taste and temper begin to multiply within it. Such things afford a *point d'appui;* for it is evidently of the essence of caricature to be reactionary. We hasten to add that its satiric force varies immensely in kind and in degree according to the race, or to the individual talent, that takes advantage of it.

I used just now the term pessimism; but that was doubtless in a great measure because I have been turning over a collection of the extraordinarily vivid drawings of Honoré Daumier. The same impression would remain with me, no doubt, if I had been consulting an equal quantity of the work of Gavarni, the wittiest, the most literary and most acutely profane of all chartered mockers with the pencil. The feeling of disrespect abides in all these things, the expression of the spirit for which humanity is definable primarily by its weaknesses. For Daumier these weaknesses are altogether ugly and grotesque, while for Gavarni they are either basely graceful or touchingly miserable; but the vision of them in both cases is close and direct. If, on the other hand, we look through a dozen volumes of the collection of *Punch* we get an equal impression of hilarity, but we by no means get an equal impression of irony. Certainly the pages of *Punch* do not reek with pessimism; their 'criticism of life' is gentle and forbearing. Leech is positively optimistic; there is at any rate nothing infinite in his irreverence; it touches bottom as soon as it approaches the pretty woman or the nice girl. It is such an apparition as this that really, in Gavarni, awakes the scoffer. Du Maurier is as graceful as Gavarni, but his sense of beauty conjures away almost everything save our minor vices. It is in the exploration of our major ones that Gavarni makes his principal discoveries of charm or of absurdity of attitude. None the less, of course, the general inspiration of both artists is the same; the desire to try the innumerable different ways in which the human subject may *not* be taken seriously.

If this view of that subject, in its plastic manifestations, makes history of a sort, it will not in general be of a kind to convert those persons who find history sad reading. The writer of the present lines remains unconverted, lately, on an occasion on which many cheerful influences were mingled with his impression. They were of a nature to which he usually does full justice, even overestimating perhaps their charm of suggestion; but, at the hour I speak of, the old Parisian quay, the belittered print-shop, the pleasant afternoon, the glimpse of the great Louvre on the other side of the Seine, in the interstices of the sallow *estampes* suspended in window and doorway—all these elements of a rich actuality availed only to mitigate, without transmuting, that general vision of a high, cruel pillory which pieced itself together as I drew specimen after specimen from musty portfolios. I had been passing the shop when I noticed in a small *vitrine,* let into the embrasure of the doorway, half a dozen soiled, striking lithographs, which it took no more than a first glance to recognize as the work of Daumier. They were only old pages of the Charivari, torn away from the text and rescued from the injury of time; and they were accompanied with an inscription to the effect that many similar examples of the artist were to be seen within. To become aware of this circumstance was to enter the shop and to find myself promptly surrounded with bulging *cartons* and tattered relics. These relics—crumpled leaves of the old comic journals of the period from 1830 to 1855—are neither rare nor expensive; but I happened to have lighted on a particularly copious collection, and I made the most of my small good-fortune, in order to transmute it, if possible, into a sort of compensation for my having missed unavoidably, a few months before, the curious exhibition 'de la Caricature Moderne' held for several weeks just at hand, in the École des Beaux-Arts. Daumier was said to have appeared there in considerable force; and it was a loss not to have had that particular opportunity of filling one's mind with him.

There was perhaps a perversity in having wished to do so, strange, indigestible stuff of contemplation as he might appear to be; but the perversity had had an honourable growth. Daumier's great days were in the reign of Louis-Philippe; but in the early years of the Second Empire he still plied his coarse and formidable pencil. I recalled, from a juvenile consciousness, the last failing strokes of it. They used to impress me in Paris, as a child, with their abnormal blackness as well as with their grotesque, magnifying movement, and there was something in them that rather scared a very immature admirer. This small personage, however, was able to perceive later, when he was unfortunately deprived of the chance of studying them, that there were various things in them besides the power to excite a vague alarm. Daumier was perhaps a great artist; at all events unsatisfied curiosity increased in proportion to that possibility.

The first complete satisfaction of it was really in the long hours that I spent in the little shop on the quay. There I filled my mind with him, and there too, at no great cost, I could make a big parcel of these cheap reproductions of his work. This work had been shown in the École des Beaux-Arts as it came from his hand; M. Champfleury, his biographer, his cataloguer and devotee, having poured forth the treasures of a precious collection, as I suppose they would be called in the case of an artist of higher flights. It was only as he was seen by the readers of the comic journals of his day that I could now see him; but I tried to make up for my want of privilege by prolonged immersion. I was not able to take home all the portfolios from the shop on the quay, but I took home what I could, and I went again to turn over the superannuated piles. I liked looking at them on the spot; I seemed still surrounded by the artist's vanquished Paris and his extinct Parisians. Indeed no quarter of the delightful city probably shows, on the whole, fewer changes from the aspect it wore during the period of Louis-Philippe, the time when it will ever appear to many of its friends to have been most delightful. The long line of the quay is unaltered, and the rare charm of the river. People came and went in the shop: it is a wonder how many, in the course of an hour, may lift the latch even of an establishment that pretends to no great business. What was all this small, sociable, contentious life but the great Daumier's subject-matter? He was the painter of the Parisian bourgeois, and the voice of the bourgeois was in the air.

M. Champfleury has given a summary of Daumier's career in his smart little *Histoire de la Caricature Moderne,* a record not at all abundant in personal detail. The biographer has told his story better perhaps in his careful catalogue of the artist's productions, the first sketch of which is to be found in *L'Art* for 1878. This copious list is Daumier's real history; his life cannot have been a very different business from his work. I read in the interesting publication of M. Grand-Carteret (*Les Moeurs et la Caricature en France,* 1888) that our artist produced nearly 4,000 lithographs and a thousand drawings on wood, up to the time when failure of eyesight compelled him to rest. This is not the sort of activity that leaves a man much time for independent adventures, and Daumier was essentially of the type, common in France, of the specialist so immersed in his speciality that he can be painted in only one attitude—a general circumstance which perhaps helps to account for the paucity, in that country, of biography, in our English sense of the word, in proportion to the superabundance of criticism.

Honoré Daumier was born at Marseilles February 26th, 1808; he died on the 11th of the same month, 1879. His main activity, however, was confined to the earlier portion of a career of almost exactly seventy-one years, and I find it affirmed in Vapereau's *Dictionnaire des Contemporains* that he became completely blind between 1850 and 1860. He enjoyed a pension from the State of 2,400 francs; but what relief from misery could mitigate a quarter of a century of darkness for a man who had looked out at the world with such vivifying eyes? His father had followed the trade of a glazier, but was otherwise vocal than in the emission of the rich street-cry with which we used all to be familiar, and which has vanished with so many other friendly pedestrian notes. The elder Daumier wrought verses as well as windowpanes, and M. Champfleury has disinterred a small volume published by him in 1823.

The merit of his poetry is not striking; but he was able to transmit the artistic nature to his son, who, becoming promptly conscious of it, made the inevitable journey to Paris in search of fortune.

The young draughtsman appeared to have missed at first the way to this boon; inasmuch as in the year 1832 he found himself condemned to six months' imprisonment for a lithograph disrespectful to Louis-Philippe. This drawing had appeared in the *Caricature*, an organ of pictorial satire founded in those days by one Philipon, with the aid of a band of young mockers to whom he gave ideas and a direction, and several others, of whom Gavarni, Henry Monnier, Decamps, Grandville, were destined to make themselves a place. M. Eugène Montrosier, in a highly appreciative article on Daumier in *L'Art* for 1878, says that this same Philipon was *le journalisme fait homme;* which did not prevent him—rather in fact fostered such a result—from being perpetually in delicate relations with the government. He had had many horses killed under him, and had led a life of attacks, penalties, suppressions and resurrections. He subsequently established the *Charivari* and launched a publication entitled *L'Association Lithographique Mensuelle,* which brought to light much of Daumier's early work. The artist passed rapidly from seeking his way to finding it, and from an ineffectual to a vigorous form.

In this limited compass and in the case of such a quantity of production it is almost impossible to specify—difficult to pick dozens of examples out of thousands. Daumier became more and more the political spirit of the *Charivari,* or at least the political pencil, for M. Philipon, the breath of whose nostrils was opposition—one perceives from here the little bilious, bristling, ingenious, insistent man—is to be credited with a suggestive share in any enterprise in which he had a hand. This pencil played over public life, over the sovereign, the ministers, the deputies, the peers, the judiciary, the men and the measures, the reputations and scandals of the moment, with a strange, ugly, extravagant, but none the less sane and manly vigour. Daumier's sign is strength above all, and in turning over his pages to-day there is no intensity of force that the careful observer will not concede to him. It is perhaps another matter to assent to the proposition, put forth by his greatest admirers among his countrymen, that he is the first of all caricaturists. To the writer of this imperfect sketch he remains considerably less interesting than Gavarni; and for a particular reason, which it is difficult to express otherwise than by saying that he is too simple. Simplicity was not Gavarni's fault, and indeed to a large degree

THE UPRISING—HONORÉ DAUMIER   (*Phillips Collection, Washington, D.C.*)

it was Daumier's merit. The single grossly ridiculous or almost haunt-ingly characteristic thing which his figures represent is largely the reason why they still represent life and an unlucky reality years after the names attached to them have parted with a vivifying power. Such vagueness has overtaken them, for the most part, and to such a thin reverberation have they shrunk, the persons and the affairs which were then so intensely sketchable. Daumier handled them with a want of ceremony which would have been brutal were it not for the element of science in his work, making them immense and unmistakable in their drollery, or at least in their grotesqueness; for the term drollery sug-gests gaiety, and Daumier is anything but gay. *Un rude peintre de moeurs,* M. Champfleury calls him; and the phrase expresses his extreme breadth of treatment.

Of the victims of his 'rudeness' M. Thiers is almost the only one whom the present generation may recognize without a good deal of reminding, and indeed his hand is relatively light in delineating this personage of few inches and many episodes. M. Thiers must have been dear to the caricaturist, for he belonged to the type that was easy to 'do'; it being well known that these gentlemen appreciate public characters in direct proportion to their saliency of feature. When faces are reducible to a few telling strokes their wearers are overwhelmed with the honours of publicity; with which, on the other hand, nothing is more likely to interfere than the possession of a countenance neatly classical. Daumier had only to give M. Thiers the face of a clever owl, and the trick was played. Of course skill was needed to individualize the symbol, but that is what caricaturists propose to themselves. Of how well he succeeded the admirable plate of the lively little minister in a 'new dress'—tricked out in the uniform of a general of the First Republic— is a sufficient illustration. The bird of night is not an acute bird, but how the artist has presented the image of a selected specimen! And with what a life-giving pencil the whole figure is put on its feet, what intelligent drawing, what a rich, free stroke! The allusions conveyed in it are to such forgotten things that it is strange to think the personage was, only the other year, still contemporaneous; that he might have been met, on a fine day, taking a few firm steps in a quiet part of the Champs-Élysées, with his footman carrying a second overcoat and looking doubly tall behind him. In whatever attitude Daumier depicts him, planted as a tiny boxing-master at the feet of the virtuous colossus in a blouse (whose legs are apart, like those of the Rhodian), in whom the artist represents the People, to watch the match that is about to come off between Ratapoil and M. Berryer, or even in the act of lifting the 'parricidal' club of a new repressive law to deal a blow at the Press, an effulgent, diligent, sedentary muse (this picture, by the way, is a perfect specimen of the simple and telling in political caricature)— however, as I say, he takes M. Thiers, there is always a rough indulgence in his crayon, as if he were grateful to him for lending himself so well.

He invented Ratapoil as he appropriated Robert Macaire, and as a caricaturist he never fails to put into circulation, when he can, a character to whom he may attribute as many as possible of the affectations or the vices of the day. Robert Macaire, an imaginative, a romantic rascal, was the hero of a highly successful melodrama written for Frédérick Lemaître; but Daumier made him the type of the swindler at large in an age of feverish speculation—the projector of showy companies, the advertiser of worthless shares. There is a whole series of drawings descriptive of his exploits, a hundred masterly plates which, according to M. Champfleury, consecrated Daumier's reputation. The subject, the legend, was in most cases, still according to M. Champfleury, suggested by Philipon. Sometimes it was very witty; as for instance when Bertrand, the muddled acolyte or scraping second fiddle of the hero, objects, in relation to a brilliant scheme which he has just developed, with the part Bertrand is to play, that there are constables in the country, and he promptly replies, 'Constables? So much the better—they'll take the shares!' Ratapoil was an evocation of the same general character, but with a difference of *nuance*—the ragged political bully, or hand-to-mouth demagogue, with the smashed tall hat, cocked to one side, the absence of linen, the club half-way up his sleeve, the swagger and pose of being gallant for the people. Ratapoil abounds in the promiscuous drawings that I have looked over, and is always very strong and living, with a considerable element of the sinister, so often in Daumier an accompaniment of the comic. There is an admirable page—it brings the idea down to 1851—in which a sordid but astute peasant, twirling his thumbs on his stomach and looking askance, allows his political adviser to urge upon him in a whisper that there is not a minute to lose—to lose for action, of course—if he wishes to keep his wife, his house, his field, his heifer and his calf. The canny scepticism in the ugly, half-averted face of the typical rustic who considerably suspects his counsellor is indicated by a few masterly strokes.

This is what the student of Daumier recognizes as his science, or, if the word has a better grace, his art. It is what has kept life in his work so long after so many of the occasions of it have been swept into darkness. Indeed, there is no such commentary on renown as the 'back numbers' of a comic journal. They show us that at certain moments certain people were eminent, only to make us unsuccessfully try to remember what they were eminent *for*. And the comparative obscurity (comparative, I mean, to the talent of the caricaturist) overtakes even the most justly honoured names. M. Berryer was a splendid speaker and a public servant of real distinction and the highest utility; yet the fact that to-day his name is on few men's lips seems to be emphasized by this other fact that we continue to pore over Daumier, in whose plates we happen to come across him. It reminds one afresh how Art is an embalmer, a magician, whom we can never speak too fair. People duly impressed with this truth are sometimes laughed at for their superstitious tone, which is pronounced, according to the fancy of the critic, mawkish, maudlin or hysterical. But it is really difficult to see how any reiteration of the importance of art can overstate the plain facts. It prolongs, it preserves, it consecrates, it raises from the dead. It conciliates, charms, bribes posterity; and it murmurs to mortals, as the old French poet sang to his mistress, 'You will be fair only so far as I have said so.' When it whispers even to the great, 'You depend upon me, and I can do more for you, in the long-run, than any one else', it is scarcely too proud. It puts method and power and the strange, real, mingled air of things into Daumier's black sketchiness, so full of the technical *gras*, the 'fat' which French critics commend and which we have no word to express. It puts power above all, and the effect which he best achieves, that of a certain simplification of the attitude or the gesture to an almost symbolic generality. His persons represent only one thing, but they insist tremendously on that, and their expression of it abides with us, unaccompanied with timid detail. It may really be said that they represent only one class—the old and ugly; so that there is proof enough of a special faculty in his having played such a concert, lugubrious though it be, on a single chord. It has been made a reproach to him, says M. Grand-Carteret, that 'his work is lacking in two capital elements—*la jeunesse et la femme*'; and this commentator resents his being made to suffer for the deficiency—'as if an artist could be at the same time deep, comic, graceful and pretty; as if all those who have a real value had not created for themselves a form to which they remain confined and a type which they reproduce in all its variations, as soon as they have touched the aesthetic ideal that has been their dream. Assuredly, humanity, as this great painter saw it, could not be beautiful; one asks one's self what a maiden in her teens, a pretty face, would have done in the midst of these good, plain folk, stunted and elderly, with faces like wrinkled apples. A simple accessory most of the time, woman is for him merely a termagant or a blue-stocking who has turned the corner.'

When the eternal feminine, for Daumier, appears in neither of these forms he sees it in Madame Chaboulard or Madame Fribochon, the old snuff-taking, gossiping portress, in a nightcap and shuffling *savates*, relating or drinking in the wonderful and the intimate. One of his masterpieces represents three of these dames, lighted by a guttering candle, holding their heads together to discuss the fearful earthquake at Bordeaux, the consequence of the government's allowing the surface of the globe to be unduly dug out in California. The representation of confidential imbecility could not go further. When a man leaves out so much of life as Daumier—youth and beauty and the charm of woman and the loveliness of childhood and the manners of those social groups of whom it may most be said that they *have* manners—when he exhibits a deficiency on this scale it might seem that the question was not to be so easily disposed of as in the very non-apologetic words I have just quoted. All the same (and I confess it is singular), we may feel what Daumier omitted and yet not be in the least shocked by the claim of predominance made for him. It is impossible to spend a couple of hours over him without assenting to this claim, even though there may be a weariness in such a panorama of ugliness and an inevitable reaction from it. This anomaly, and the challenge to explain it which appears to proceed from him, render him, to my sense, remarkably interesting. The artist whose idiosyncrasies, whose limitations, if you will, make us question and wonder, in the light of his fame, has an element of fascination not attaching to conciliatory talents. If M. Eugène Montrosier may say of him without scandalizing us that such and such of his drawings belong to the very highest art, it is interesting (and Daumier profits by the interest) to put one's finger on the reason we are not scandalized.

I think this reason is that, on the whole, he is so peculiarly serious. This may seem an odd ground of praise for a jocose draughtsman, and of course what I mean is that his comic force is serious—a very different thing from the absence of comedy. This essential sign of the caricaturist may surely be anything it will so long as it is there. Daumier's figures are almost always either foolish, fatuous politicians or frightened, mystified bourgeois; yet they help him to give us a strong sense of the nature of man. They are sometimes so serious that they are almost tragic; the look of the particular pretension, combined with inanity, is carried almost to madness. There is a magnificent drawing of the series of 'Le Public du Salon', old classicists looking up, horrified and scandalized, at the new romantic work of 1830, in which the faces have an appalling gloom of mystification and platitude. We feel that Daumier reproduces admirably the particular life that he sees, because it is the very medium in which he moves. He has no wide horizon; the absolute bourgeois hems him in, and he is a bourgeois himself, without poetic ironies, to whom a big cracked mirror has been given. His thick, strong, manly touch stands, in every way, for so much knowledge. He used to make little images, in clay and in wax (many of them still exist), of the persons he was in the habit of representing, so that they

might constantly seem to be 'sitting' for him. The caricaturist of that
day had not the help of the ubiquitous photograph. Daumier painted
actively, as well, in his habitation, all dedicated to work, on the narrow
island of St. Louis, where the Seine divides and where the monuments
of old Paris stand thick, and the types that were to his purpose pressed
close upon him. He had not far to go to encounter the worthy man,
in the series of 'Les Papas', who is reading the evening paper at the café
with so amiable and placid a credulity, while his unnatural little boy,
opposite to him, finds sufficient entertainment in the much-satirized
Constitutionnel. The bland absorption of the papa, the face of the man
who believes everything he sees in the newspaper, is as near as Daumier
often comes to positive gentleness of humour. Of the same family is
the poor gentleman, in 'Actualités', seen, in profile, under a doorway
where he has taken refuge from a torrent of rain, who looks down at
his neat legs with a sort of speculative contrition and says, 'To think
of my having just ordered two pairs of white trousers.' The *tout petit
bourgeois* palpitates in both these sketches.

I must repeat that it is absurd to pick half a dozen at hazard, out of
five thousand; yet a few selections are the only way to call attention
to his strong drawing. This has a virtuosity of its own, for all its hit-
or-miss appearance. Whatever he touches—the nude, in the swimming-
baths on the Seine, the intimations of landscape, when his *petits rentiers*
go into the suburbs for a Sunday—acquires relief and character. Doc-
teur Véron, a celebrity of the reign of Louis-Philippe, a Maecenas of
the hour, a director of the opera, author of the *Mémoires d'un Bourgeois de Paris*—this temporary 'illustration', who appears to have been
almost indecently ugly, would not be vivid to us to-day had not Daumier, who was often effective at his expense, happened to have represented him, in some crisis of his career, as a sort of naked inconsolable
Vitellius. He renders the human body with a cynical sense of its possible flabbiness and an intimate acquaintance with its structure. 'Une
Promenade Conjugale', in the series of 'Tout ce qu'on voudra', por-
trays a hillside, on a summer afternoon, on which a man has thrown
himself on his back to rest, with his arms locked under his head. His
fat, full-bosomed, middle-aged wife, under her parasol, with a bunch
of field-flowers in her hand, looks down at him patiently and seems to
say, 'Come, my dear, get up.' There is surely no great point in this; the
only point is life, the glimpse of the little snatch of poetry in prose.
It is a matter of a few broad strokes of the crayon; yet the pleasant
laziness of the man, the idleness of the day, the fragment of homely,

familiar dialogue, the stretch of the field with a couple of trees merely suggested, have a communicative truth.

I perhaps exaggerate all this, and in insisting upon the merit of Daumier may appear to make light of the finer accomplishment of several more modern talents, in England and France, who have greater ingenuity and subtlety and have carried qualities of execution so much further. In looking at this complicated younger work, which has profited so by experience and comparison, it is inevitable that we should perceive it to be infinitely more cunning. On the other hand Daumier, moving in his contracted circle, has an impressive depth. It comes back to his strange seriousness. He is a draughtsman by race, and if he has not extracted the same brilliancy from training, or perhaps even from effort and experiment, as some of his successors, does not his richer satiric and sympathetic feeling more than make up the difference?

However this question may be answered, some of his drawings belong to the class of the unforgetable. It may be a perversity of prejudice, but even the little cut of the 'Connoisseurs', the group of gentlemen collected round a picure and critcizing it in various attitudes of sapience and sufficiency, appears to me to have the strength that abides. The criminal in the dock, the flat-headed murderer, bending over to speak to his advocate, who turns a whiskered, professional, anxious head to caution and remind him, tells a large, terrible story and awakes a recurrent shudder. We see the gray court-room, we feel the personal suspense and the immensity of justice. The 'Saltimbanques', reproduced in *L'Art* for 1878, is a page of tragedy, the finest of a cruel series. M. Eugène Montrosier says of it that 'The drawing is masterly, incomparably firm, the composition superb, the general impression quite of the first order'. It exhibits a pair of lean, hungry mountebanks, a clown and a harlequin beating the drum and trying a comic attitude to attract the crowd, at a fair, to a poor booth in front of which a painted canvas, offering to view a simpering fat woman, is suspended. But the crowd doesn't come, and the battered tumblers, with their furrowed cheeks, go through their pranks in the void. The whole thing is symbolic and full of grimness, imagination and pity. It is the sense that we shall find in him, mixed with his homelier extravagances, an element prolific in indications of this order that draws us back to Daumier.

THE MODERN ART MOVEMENT

Sir Herbert Read

The Modern Epoch in Art[1]

The heart that beat for this world has been almost extinguished in me. It is as though my only bond with 'these' things were memory. . . . One relinquishes this world and builds into a region beyond, a region which can be all affirmation. The cool romanticism of this style without pathos is astounding.

PAUL KLEE. *Diary*, 1915

i

In discussing the origins of naturalism in the Middle Ages, Max Dvořák warned us against the folly of trying to fix a specific 'beginning' to anything so underground as the first growth of an artistic style. The modern movement in art, which in general is a reversal of the movement discussed with such brilliance by Dvořák (in his *Idealismus und Naturalismus in der gotischen Skulptur und Malerei*), offers no exception to this rule. Its origins are extremely obscure, and, like roots, proceed from different levels and contradictory directions. One cannot exclude either the revolutionary romanticism of a Blake or the revolutionary classicism of a David; Constable's scientific naturalism is certainly a factor, but so is the historical idealism of Delacroix (to Cézanne always 'le grand Maître'). The realism of Courbet and Manet; the expressionism of Van Gogh and Munch; the symbolism of Emile Bernard and Gauguin—all these pre-

[1] From *The Philosophy of Modern Art*. London: Faber and Faber.

cede and in some degree predetermine the specifically modern movements of fauvism, cubism, constructivism and surrealism. Perhaps we should abandon our biological analogies and think rather of the complex 'movement' of a chronometer; for historical 'time' seems to reduce, on analysis, to such an interlocking of gears and ratchets. It will be said that even the chronometer has a spring at the centre, but this is not necessarily true of the modern chronometer, which may be set and kept in motion by the simple alternation of night and day.

There is, of course, the further explanation offered by the theory of dialectical materialism. For night and day in our metaphor we may substitute rich and poor, bourgeoisie and proletariat, and in the circulation of élites see a sufficient motive power for all the stylistic changes of art. This is not an argument that can be ignored, for art never exists in a vacuum, but is inextricably entangled in the life of society as a whole. If we discover that the modern artist is relatively isolated from society we must not be led to suppose that such isolation is a characteristic of art itself—an island as such is only defined by reference to a neighbouring land-mass.

Nevertheless, economic facts and social movements can only have an indirect relation to the stylistic evolution of art. In the period that concerns us here, there is one broad economic development of the utmost significance—the gradual decline of private patronage due to the severe restrictions imposed on the accumulation of wealth. Private collectors still buy works of art in the open market—to that extent there are still patrons, if only through the medium of the art-dealer. But they no longer *command* the artist like the monastery or the guild, the court or the castle. The position has been so reversed that the contemporary artist must form the taste and recruit the public (through the intermediary of the art critic, in himself a modern phenomenon) on whose patronage he will then depend. The modern artist is miserably dependent on the media of publicity. That is his deepest humiliation.

There is another and a more limited sense in which the course of art is determined by economic factors. Scientific and industrial progress, particularly in the nineteenth century, threw out as by-products certain theories and inventions which had a direct impact on the technique and social significance of art. These have been too often discussed to need more than a passing reference. The formulation of a scientific theory of colour, which at first led to such aberrations as pointillism, has not had any permanent effect on artistic practice—the artist has discovered by now that he must rely on his sensibility and not attempt to particularize from laws of aesthetic effect. But more significant and more permanent in its influence on the development of art has been the invention of photography and of photographic methods of reproduction. The economic consequences of such inventions are serious enough —the public is provided with a cheap substitute for the plastic arts. It may not be aesthetically so satisfying, but it suffices for the low level of sensibility that seems to be a consequence of mass production and mass education. The effect on the artist has been even more profound, for it has relieved him of one of the social functions of art—that of 'visual aid'. It is true that certain subtleties of imaginative literature will still call for creative illustration; but for instruction and clarification it is better to provide an *Orbis sensualium pictus* by means of the camera. What has been effected is a clear distinction between *illustration* and *interpretation*. This may not seem so significant at first, but implied in it is the distinction between *image* and *symbol,* which, as we shall see presently, is fundamental to an understanding of the modern movement in art.

What in general may be admitted in this connection is that economic and social trends determine and give their fluctuating shades to broad movements of thought and opinion in every epoch. The work of art cannot escape the ambience of such intangible effluences (the philosophies and theologies of the period). To the extent that a work of art is romantic or classical, realistic or symbolic, it will certainly be beyond the personal control of the artist. Even the structure of the work of art (the style of composition) may be a matter of taste or fashion determined by social contacts. But there comes a point in the evolution of art at which all these imponderable forces are but external pressures which result, not in a consequential 'line of force', but in a leap into creative originality of a quite incalculable kind. The dialectical materialist may still claim that social factors have determined that anamorphosis, but the quantum in art, as in physics, may be discontinuous. A brief examination of the concept of *originality* will perhaps make my meaning clear.

ii

It has often been observed that if we have regard only for that quality we call 'sensibility', which would throughout history seem to be the essential element in art, that then no progress whatsoever is discernible between the cave drawings of the palaeolithic period and the drawings of Raphael or Picasso. Sensibility is not the only value in art—as successive civilizations develop their cultures they invariably dilute this basic sensibility with other values of a magical or logical nature—they *use* sensibility in social contexts, and it is the variations of context that seem to explain whatever changes occur in the history of art. There is, of course, a degree beyond which the sensibility cannot be forced or prostituted—the result is then the *rigor mortis* of academicism, or the moral rot of sentimentalism. The vitality of art would seem to depend on the maintenance of a delicate balance between sensibility and whatever intellectual or emotional accretions it derives from the social element in which it is embedded.

The process is, it will be seen, a dialectical one, and it is certainly one in which tensions and contradictions inevitably develop. One way in which a tension may be relaxed takes the form of a decline of sensibility, and the tension must be restored if art is to survive. What precisely happens in such a crisis is in dispute. The alternative suggestions are: (1) the artist retraces the historical development of his art and resumes contact with the authentic *tradition*; or (2) the artist resolves the crisis by a leap forward into a new and original state of sensibility —he revolts against the existing conventions in order to create a new convention more in accordance with a contemporary consciousness. We may admit that in doing so he merely recovers, in all its actuality, the original basic quality of art—aesthetic sensibility in all its purity and vitality. But the context is new, and it is the synthesis of an untrammelled sensibility and a new set of social conditions which constitutes, in the evolution of art, an act of originality.

We must guard against interpreting 'social conditions' in a sense narrowly economic or political. The artist's awareness of these conditions rarely assumes a politically conscious form, and certainly there is no correlation to be made between such consciousness in the artist and his degree of originality. Courbet, Pissarro, William Morris—these are the politically conscious artists and they have an important place in the history of modern art. But a more important place is taken by artists like Cézanne, Gauguin and Matisse, whose awareness of the social context of their work was never expressed in a political formula. It is only a primitive mind that can interpret the social context as Daumier's third-class railway carriage. The social context is the totality of our way of life, and its impact on the artist may be through a philosophy or a science, or even through a pair of old boots (Van Gogh) or a heap of rubbish (Schwitters).

From this point of view a renewed contact with tradition may have as much revolutionary significance as any originality in style or technique. The validity of a tradition depends on its retention of the element of sensibility. We agree to find this element in the paintings of Poussin; therefore, said Cézanne, let us go back to Poussin and try to recover, in front of nature, the element that made Poussin a great artist. Cézanne implied, not that the modern artist should imitate Poussin's style (which was personal to Poussin), but that a study of Poussin's art might lead to the recovery of sensibility—to the re-animation of his (Cézanne's) ability to 'realize' his sensations in the presence of nature. 'Nature' meanwhile had changed, because nature is but another word for the social context already mentioned. *To renew one's sensibility towards one's environment*—that is the method of both the traditionalist and of the revolutionary. Nevertheless, there is still a degree of originality which is not necessarily covered by the phrase.

The sense of 'reality' is surely one of those conventions that change from age to age and are determined by the total way of life. Not only does the concept of reality differ as between a mediaeval philosopher like St Thomas Aquinas and a modern philosopher like Bergson, but a similar difference also exists on the average level of apprehension (the difference between animism and theism, between supernaturalism and materialism, and so on). The 'reality' of a citizen of the Soviet Union is certainly different from the 'reality' of a citizen of the United States. We have now reached a stage of relativism in philosophy where it is possible to affirm that reality is in fact subjectivity, which means that the individual has no choice but to construct his own reality, however arbitrary and even 'absurd' that may seem. This is the position reached by the Existentialists, and to it corresponds a position in the world of art that requires a similar decision. The interpretation (or even the 'imitation') of reality was a valid function for the artist so long as it was agreed that a general and basic reality existed and was only waiting for revelation. Once this sense of security is removed (that is to say, is destroyed by scientific analysis) then philosophy and art are public auctions in which the most acceptable reality commands the highest price.

This may be a passing phase in philosophy and the world may return to systems of faith and revelation in which art once more resumes its interpretative function. But Existentialism is but the latest phase of a development of thought that reaches back to Kant and Schelling, and it is difficult (from a point of view inside the stream) to see any other direction which philosophy can take (it already carries along with it the contradictions of Christianity and atheism). It is in this mental climate that contemporary art has shown a tendency to unsurp the positivist rôle of philosophy and to present its own self-sufficient 'reality'. A certain type of modern artist claims to construct new realities ('réalités nouvelles'), and he will go so far as to assert that his construction is in no way determined even by such vague concepts as universal harmony or the collective unconscious, but is an act of creation in the almost divine sense of the word. Naturally such an artist has to use elements of form and colour which are common to all the arts, and the world has not shown any inclination to recognize his work as art unless it possesses some of the sensuous qualities of the traditional work of art.

The conclusion we are driven to is that originality can only be conceptual, thematic, structural—never sensuous. There are new ways of thinking and doing—we call them inventions; there are new ways of stimulating the senses. But sensation itself can only be modified— coarsened or refined. It has the physical limitations of our animal frame; stretched on that frame the nerve breaks if forced beyond its expressive compass.

At the same time we must recognize, with the Marxists, the historic nature of human consciousness; and, with certain psychologists, the ambiguous nature of this evolutionary acquisition. In terms of art it gave us the symbol where hitherto there had been only the image. Man in his first unreflecting unity with nature needed only the image to project his sensations. Man as a self-conscious individual separated from the rest of creation needed a language of symbols to express his self-ness. The elaboration of that need gave rise not only to conceptual symbols like 'God' but also to a myriad of plastic symbols, some of them constant and archetypal, others temporary and even personal. If we could reconstruct the stages in human evolution which led from the eidetic, vitalistic art of the Palaeolithic period to the symbolic, geometric art of the Neolithic period, we should have a clear conception of the rise of not only human self-consciousness, ethical conscience and the idea of a transcendental God, but also of the origins of that polarity in art which has caused a rhythmic alternation of styles throughout the history of art, and which now exists as an unresolved dialectical contradiction. It is the *co*-existence of the image and the symbol, as norms of art, which explain the apparent complexity and disunity of the modern movement.

iii

The true understanding of art depends upon an appreciation of the nature and uses of symbolism. Symbolism is one of the two ways in which the human mind functions, the other being the direct experience of the external world (the 'presentational immediacy' of sense perception). Since language itself is already symbolism, and the complicated forms of thought depend on a system of symbols such as we have in the science of algebra, it is natural to assume that there is something primitive and ineffective about the presentational immediacy of sense perceptions. This is far from being the case. It is much more difficult to be faithful to our direct experience of the external world than to 'jump to conclusions' which are in effect symbolic references. The poet, said Gautier, is a man for whom the visible world exists; he wishes, by this definition, to exclude from art those secondary elaborations of perception involved in the use of symbols. As the poet is condemned to use the symbolism of language, the ideal would seem to be quixotic. (Nevertheless poetry continues to reveal a fundamental strife between imagism and symbolism.)

The special position of the visual artist may be illustrated by a quotation from Whitehead's *Symbolism: its Meaning and Effect* (1928). 'We look up and see a coloured shape in front of us and we say—there is a chair. But what we have seen is the mere coloured shape. *Perhaps an artist might not have jumped to the notion of a chair. He might have stopped at the mere contemplation of a beautiful colour and a beautiful shape.* But those of us who are not artists are very prone, especially if we are tired, to pass straight from the perception of the coloured shape to the enjoyment of the chair, in some way of use, or of emotion, or of thought. We can easily explain this passage by reference to a train of difficult logical inference, whereby, having regard to our previous experiences of various shapes and various colours, we draw the probable conclusion that we are in the presence of a chair.'

This clearly illustrates the difference between a perceptive experience (the immediate perception of an image) and the use of a symbol (the image plus its mental associations). Whitehead adds: 'I am very sceptical as to the high-grade character of the mentality required to get from the coloured shape to the chair. One reason for this scepticism is that my friend the artist, who kept himself to the contemplation of colour, shape and position, was a very highly trained man, and had acquired this facility of ignoring the chair at the cost of great labour.'

With this distinction in mind we can perhaps begin to understand what Cézanne meant by 'realizing his sensations'. We can understand what Van Gogh meant when he said that 'a painter as a man is too much absorbed by what his eyes see, and is not sufficiently master of the rest of his life'. (Letter 620.) Van Gogh's letters are full of descriptions of his intense concentration on what a philosopher like Whitehead would call 'presentational immediacy'. For example: 'I myself am quite absorbed by the immeasurable plain with cornfields against the hills, immense as a sea, delicate yellow, delicate soft green, delicate violet of a ploughed and weeded piece of soil, regularly chequered by the green of flowering potato-plants, everything under a sky with delicate blue, white, pink, violet tones. I am in a mood of *nearly too great calmness,* in the mood to paint this.' (Letter 650, written in Dutch.)

This 'mood of nearly too great calmness' is the mood of direct experience, of instinctual awareness in which the eidetic image is, as it were, preserved from the contamination of symbolism—from the need for further reference to other elements in our experience. It has been claimed that the capacity for realizing and retaining the image in a state of perceptive vividness is the quality that distinguishes the artist from other men, but in fact it is the distinguishing quality of one type of artist—the imagist. It was by his insistence on the strict purity of his perceptive experience that Cézanne restored to art some degree of primal rectitude.

At the other extreme of artistic practice the artist abandons himself freely to a symbolic activity. Whitehead has said that 'the human mind is functioning symbolically when some components of its experience elicit consciousness, beliefs, emotions, and usages, respecting other components of its experience. The former set of components are the 'symbols', and the latter set constitute the 'meaning' of the symbols' (p. 9). An artist of the symbolist type is creating a combination of forms and colours (or of sounds if he is a musician) which will convey a meaning, and in art this meaning always has an aesthetic or emotional tinge. Art of this kind may therefore be defined as 'the symbolic transfer of emotion', and as Whitehead says, this definition is at the base of any theory of the aesthetics of art—'For example, it gives the reason for the importance of a rigid suppression of irrelevant detail. For emotions inhibit each other, or intensify each other. Harmonious emotion means a complex of emotions mutually intensifying; whereas the irrelevant details supply emotions which, because of their irrelevance, inhibit the main effect. Each little emotion directly arising out of some subordinate detail refuses to accept its status as a detached fact in our consciousness. It insists on its symbolic transfer to the unity of the main effect' (p. 101).

This definition of symbolism agrees closely with those definitions of 'synthètisme' which were formulated by Emile Bernard in 1888 and which, through the medium of Gauguin, were to have a revolutionary effect on the whole development of modern art. Bernard wrote:

'Puisque l'idée est la forme des choses recueillies par l'imagination, il fallait peindre non plus devant la chose, mais en la reprenant dans l'imagination, qui l'avait recueillie, qui en conservait l'idée, ainsi l'idée de la chose apportait la forme convenable au sujet du tableau ou plutôt à son idéal (somme des idées) la simplification que l'essentiel des choses percues et par conséquent en rejette le détail. La mémoire ne retient pas tout, mais ce qui frappe l'esprit. Donc formes et couleurs devenaient simples dans une égale unité. En peignant de mémoire, j'avais l'avantage d'abolir l'inutile complication des formes et des tons. Il restait un schéma du spectacle regardé. Toutes les lignes revenaient à leur architecture géométrique, tous les tons aux couleurs types de la palette prismatique. Puisqu'il s'agissait de simplifier, il fallait retrouver l'origine de tout: dans le soleil, les sept couleurs dont se compose la lumiere blanche (chaque couleur pure de la palette y répondant) dans la géométrie, les formes typiques de toutes les formes objectives.'[2]

This distinction between painting 'devant la chose' and 'en la reprenant dans l'imagination' expresses neatly the two ways open to the artist, and the further insistence on 'simplification' (Bernard) or 'unity of the main effect' (Whitehead) points to that characteristic in symbolic art which can involve a progressive modification of the 'schema' in the direction of abstraction. There is nothing in the paintings of Gauguin which would seem to imply or justify the abstractions of a Kandinsky or a Mondrian; nevertheless, there is what Whitehead calls 'a chain of derivations of symbol from symbol' whereby finally the local relations, between the final symbol and the ultimate meaning, are entirely lost. Thus these derivative symbols, obtained as it were by arbitrary association, are really the results of reflex action suppressing the intermediate portions of the chain. By such a chain of derivations we could conceivably establish an association between such apparently disconnected symbols as Gauguin's "Yellow Christ" and Mondrian's "Boogie-Woogie." Mondrian was fond of describing his art as 'a new realism', but it is clear from his writings that he had invented a new symbolism. Mon-

2 Quoted by Maurice Malingue, *Gauguin, le peintre et son oeuvre* (Paris, 1948), p. 35.

drian insists that art is a parallel experience, not to be identified in any way with our experience, of the external world; but in Whitehead's words we would say that such parallelism is an illusion due to the suppression of intermediate links. The creation of a 'new' reality is not within the scope of our human, time-conditioned faculties.

iv

Let us now leave the realm of theory and try to trace what has actually happened in the evolution of art in the modern epoch. We shall not be able to leave ideas entirely out of account, because my main contention is that art has developed in stages that are parallel to the development of thought, and that both developments have intimate connections with social movements. Perhaps a few words will make clear to what extent the formal evolution of modern art has been 'conditioned' by social and economic forces.

I have already drawn attention to the relative isolation of the artist in modern society. The general effect of the industrial revolution on art has been a gradual exclusion of the artist from the basic economic processes of production. This development may be said to begin with the capitalist system itself; that is to say, with the accumulation of individual wealth. The way in which, from the fifteenth century onwards, the 'patron' gradually forces his own personality, even his own person, into the work of art has often been remarked. At first he is the pious donor, humbly kneeling in a obscure corner of the picture; but he gradually grows in size and importance until, in a painting like Holbein's "Virgin and Child with the Burgomaster Mayer and his Family" (1526), he is painted on the same scale as the holy figures. Man is as good as God—as a theme for the artist. This humanism gave rise to the development of schools of portrait painting and historical painting which for three centuries constituted the main substance of the plastic arts. But such a development left the artist in a precarious position—dependent, not on the social organism as such (his position during the Middle Ages), but on the patronage of a limited class within that organism. For most of this time he maintained vitalizing contacts with the general processes of production—in our sense of the word he was still an industrial artist who might on occasion turn his hand to the design of metalwork, furniture or tapestries. But by the time the industrial revolution was complete, the artist was cut off from even these subsidiary activities and had become parasitically dependent on his patron.

In such a situation the artist might react in several ways. He might

become sycophantic, adopting the point of view of his patron, supporting the existing structure of society, supplying works of art designed
to satisfy the tastes and flatter the vanity of his clients. Such, in general,
is the bourgeois art of the eighteenth and nineteenth centuries. But
such, also, is a situation that implies the progressive degradation of art.
No longer drawing any inspiration or force from the organic wholeness of society, the art in such a situation becomes anaemic and sophisticated, and, in any spiritual sense, purposeless. The basis of patronage
may spread more widely, as it did throughout the nineteenth century,
but the result will only be an art measured to the same capacities of
l'homme moyen sensuel. Just as, according to the Marxists, capitalism
contains in itself the seeds of its own inevitable destruction, so (more
certainly, even) such a relation between the artist and society involves
inevitable decadence.

The artist who resists such decadence may react in two distinct ways.
If he is socially conscious, he may revolt against the social situation as
such and become a revolutionary artist—that is to say, an artist who
consciously uses his art to reform the social situation. That type of artist
is rare—it implies a use of art in the service of preconceived *ideas* which
the true artist cannot accept. Even Courbet, in a political sense probably the most revolutionary artist of the nineteenth century, held that
'the art of painting can consist only in the representation of objects
visible and tangible to the painter' and that 'art is completely individual, and that the talent of each artist is but the result of his own
inspiration and his own study of past tradition' (open letter to a group
of prospective students, 1861). But the same social situation produces
in the artist a state of mind in which he turns from what he regards
as the false aesthetic values of the past to seek new aesthetic values
more consonant with the developing social consciousness of his fellow-
citizens. Constable was not politically minded, but when he wrote
(Notes for his lectures at the Royal Institution, May 26, 1836) that art
'is *scientific* as well as *poetic*; that imagination never did, and never
can, produce works that are to stand by a comparison with *realities*',
he was expressing a revolutionary sentiment, a revolt against the art of
Boucher which in its turn had been the expression of another and very
different social situation. This attitude is still more clearly expressed
in a note of June 16, 1836:

'I have endeavoured to draw a line between genuine art and mannerism, but even the greatest painters have never been wholly untainted
by manner. . . . Painting is a science, and should be pursued as an

enquiry into the laws of nature. Why, then, may not landscape be considered as a branch of natural philosophy, of which pictures are but experiments?"

On that 'experimental' note the modern epoch is announced, and never from that moment until comparatively recently has the artist relented in his experimental attitude. Exactly seventy years later we find Cézanne writing in almost the same terms as Constable (letter of September 21, 1906):

'Shall I ever reach the goal so eagerly sought and so long pursued? I hope so, but as long as it has not been attained a vague feeling of discomfort persists which will not disappear until I shall have gained the harbour—that is, until I shall have accomplished something more promising than what has gone before, thereby verifying my theories, which, in themselves, are easy to put forth. The only thing that is really difficult is to prove what one believes. So I am going on with my researches. . . .'[3]

Research, experiment—these words describe the efforts of all the great artists that fall within these seventy years—Millet, Courbet, Manet, Degas, Monet, Pissarro, Renoir, Rodin, Whistler, Seurat, Van Gogh—it is all a persistent attempt to correlate art and reality. It is the research, not of the absolute, but of the concrete, of the *image*, and behind it all is not only the divorce of the artist from the processes of production, but also the concurrent attempt to establish a philosophy of reality, a phenomenalism that owes nothing to divine revelation or universal truths, but brings to the analysis of human existence the same faculties that the artist brings to the analysis of nature. Constable, Cézanne, Picasso—Hegel, Husserl, Heidegger; these names represent parallel movements in the evolution of human experience.

But this movement, in art, was not to remain unchallenged. To the image as representation is opposed, as we have seen, the symbol as interpretation, and there is no doubt that the 'synthètisme' of Bernard and Gauguin was a conscious reaction against the scientific attitude in art. The theoretical basis of this reaction was given in the definition of "synthètisme' by Bernard already quoted, but what that theory involved in practice was first shown by Gauguin. We can best appreciate the antithetical nature of the contradiction by considering what form and colour meant respectively for Cézanne and Gauguin.

[3] Trans. Gerstle Mack, *Paul Cézanne* (London, 1935), p. 390.

DEJEUNER SUR L'HERBE—EDOUARD MANET (*Louvre, Paris*)

Both artists went through an impressionist phase, and their divergence developed as they felt dissatisfaction with the results of their practice of the impressionist technique. Both artists, incidentally, found a meeting-place in Pissarro, who is the chief *point de repère* for the whole revolution. What Cézanne learned from Pissarro was of fundamental importance for his subsequent development, but it did not affect the direction taken by that development. Cézanne felt that the analytical methods of the Impressionist had led to a certain dissolution of reality; they had, as it were, realized the vitality of objects, the vibrancy of light, the vividness of colour, at the cost of the essential nature of these objects—their solidity—indeed, their reality. The analysis of light and colour had led to a separation of colour and form, and this Cézanne felt to be a betrayal of the painter's function. Without

AFTER THE BATH—EDGAR DEGAS (*The Metropolitan Museum of Art, Bequest of Mrs. H. O. Havemeyer, 1929. The H. O. Havemeyer Collection*)

sacrificing the real advances made by the Impressionists, he set himself the task of realizing and presenting the solid structure of objects. He arrived at a method which he called 'modulation' (as distinct from the Impressionists' 'modelling') in which volume was represented by local colour changes. His own words must be quoted:

'For progress towards realization there is nothing but nature, and the eye becomes educated through contact with her. It becomes concentric through observation and work; I mean that in an orange, an apple, a sphere, a head, there is a focal point, and this point is always nearest to our eye, no matter how it is affected by light, shade, sensations of colour. The edges of objects recede towards a centre located on our horizon.'[4]

4 Letter of July 25, 1904. Trans. Gerstle Mack, *op. cit.*, p. 380.

This rather obscure passage is illuminated by a letter of December 23 of the same year:

'This I declare to be indisputable—I am very dogmatic: an optical sensation is produced in our visual organ which causes us to grade the planes represented by sensations of colour into full light, half-tones and quarter-tones (light does not exist for the painter). Necessarily, while we are proceeding from black to white, the first of these abstractions being a sort of point of departure for the eye as well as for the brain, we are floundering, we do not succeed in mastering ourselves, in ruling over ourselves. During this period—we go to the great masterpieces the ages have handed down to us, and we find in them a solace and a support.'[5]

One further quotation, for it is essential for an understanding of the origins of modern art to be quite sure that we first understand what Cézanne was after:

'Now the idea to be insisted on is—no matter what our temperament or power in the presence of nature—to produce the image of what we see, forgetting everything that has been done before. Which, I believe, should enable the artist to express his entire personality, great or small.

'Now that I am old, almost seventy, the sensations of colour which produce light are a source of distraction, which do not permit me to cover my canvas or to define the delimitations of objects when the points of contact are so tenuous, fragile; the result is that my image or picture is incomplete. Then again the planes are superimposed on one another, from which springs the Neo-impressionist system of outlining the contours with a black line, an error which should be opposed with all our strength. Now if we consult nature we shall find a way to solve this problem.'[6]

'I regret my advanced age, on account of my sensations of colour',—such was the recurrent complaint of Cézanne in his last years. He felt a certain opposition between the surface sensuousness of objects and their real nature—his eyes were, as it were, dazzled by the brilliance of light and colour. Light and colour were not the same thing as *lucidity*. ('I am becoming more lucid in the presence of nature, but—the realiza-

5 Trans. Gerstle Mack, *op. cit.*, p. 381.
6 Trans. Gerstle Mack, *op. cit.*, pp. 382-3.

tion of my sensations is always painful. I cannot reach the intensity which appears to my senses . . .')—(September 8, 1906). And then, in his final letter to Bernard, who significantly enough was the *agent pro-vocateur* in this struggle for theoretical expression (significantly, be-cause he played the same rôle for Gauguin), he says: 'I am progressing towards the logical development of what we see and feel by studying nature; a consideration of processes comes later, processes being for us nothing but simple methods for making the public feel what we our-selves feel, and for making ourselves intelligible.'

There were, therefore, in Cézanne's final phase, two stages in the production of a work of art: first, the realization of sensations, by which he meant a 'logical' analysis of percepts, of what the eye actually sees; second, processes by means of which this analysis could be presented to the public.

Cézanne was an extremely intelligent but simple man, and his efforts to explain his intuitive processes are not very clear. What in his stum-bling way he seems to have grasped is the principle of the 'good *Gestalt*'. Without going too far into the theory of perception than would be justified in a general essay of this kind, it is difficult to give a convinc-ing account of this term, but the underlying idea is that visual percep-tion itself only makes sense, only becomes coherent, by virtue of an organizing faculty within the nervous system. We should not be able to cope with the multiplicity of impressions which the eye receives were we not, at the same time, capable of organizing these impressions into a coherent pattern. In the words of a *Gestalt* psychologist: 'Per-ception tends towards balance and symmetry; or differently expressed: balance and symmetry are perceptual characteristics of the visual world which will be realized whenever the external conditions allow it; when they do not, unbalance, lack of symmetry, will be experienced as a characteristic of objects or the whole field, together with a felt urge towards better balance—the stimulations which under ordinary cir-cumstances affect our eyes are perfectly haphazard from the point of view of the visual organizations to which they may give rise. The organ-ism—does the best it can under the prevailing conditions, and these conditions will not, as a rule, allow it to do a very good job (good, from the point of view of aesthetic harmony). A work of art, on the other hand, is made with that very idea; once completed it serves as a source of stimulation specifically selected for its aesthetic effect.'[7]

[7] K. Koffka: 'Problems in the Psychology of Art'. *Art: a Bryn Mawr Symposium*, 1940.

Before Cézanne the principle of composition in painting was architectonic—the picture-space was 'organized' as an architect organizes his
building, and inevitably questions of balance and symmetry were taken
into consideration. Cézanne's paintings are analysed and criticized as
if they conformed to this principle, and such a method does indeed
'work', though it ignores the essential virtue in Cézanne's compositions.
For architectonic composition is *a priori*; it fits the objects of perception into a preconceived pattern, a system of perspective and elevation,
which is not necessarily inherent in perception itself. A landscape by
Claude or Turner is as artificial as a garden, and as much the result of
intellectual preconceptions. But a landscape by Cézanne begins with no
preconceptions—nothing but the direct contact of eye and nature, and
the 'composition' is determined by what happens 'in the eye'—the
automatic selection of a focal point, limitation of boundaries, subordination of details and colours to the law of the whole. The 'whole' is
the *Gestalt,* but the psychologists recognize that the process does not
end there—that there are 'good' and less good *Gestalts.* 'It is characteristic of a good *Gestalt* not only that it produces a hierarchical unity of
its parts, but also that this unity is of a particular kind. A good *Gestalt*
cannot be changed without changing its quality—in a masterpiece of
painting no line, no form, no colour, can anywhere be changed without
detracting from the quality of the picture.' (Koffka, *op. cit.*, 247–8.)

I think there is no doubt whatsoever that Cézanne was trying to
realize the good *Gestalt.* By intuitive processes he had hit upon a
scientific truth which psychology subsequently discovered by experimental research. Cézanne, therefore, still remains within the characteristic development of nineteenth century art—as much as Constable he
is an artist who regards landscape painting as a branch of natural
philosophy. But Cézanne's natural philosophy was not destined to be
understood by many of his followers, and it was largely on a misinter-
pretation of his purpose that cubism came into being (its subsequent
development is another question). But before we discuss the influence
of Cézanne let us return to the challenge to the scientific attitude in
art made by Gauguin.

v

One's first inclination is to treat Gauguin as an artist altogether
inferior to Cézanne. We cannot doubt his integrity or his sincerity,
and the sacrifices he made for his art were certainly as great as Cézanne's.
The contrast between the two artists lies in the field of sensibility, of

technical accomplishment. Certainly some hard things can be said about Gauguin's technique. He despised the whole business of what he called 'counting the hairs on the donkey'. He had been an Impressionist and had sat at the feet of Pissarro; but his reaction was violent. 'The impressionists study colour exclusively, but without freedom, always shackled by the need of probability. For them the ideal landscape, created from many different entities, does not exist. They look and perceive harmoniously, but without aim. Their edifice rests upon no solid base and ignores the nature of the sensation perceived by means of colour. They heed only the eye and neglect the mysterious centres of thought, so falling into merely scientific reasoning.' (*Intimate Journals*, trans. Van Wyck Brooks (New York, 1936), pp. 132–4.) Form was not to be found in nature, but in the imagination. 'It is well for young men to have a model, but let them draw the curtain over it while they are painting. It is better to paint from memory, for thus your work will be your own: your sensation, your intelligence, and your soul will triumph over the eye of the amateur.' (*Ibid.*, p. 71, 1936.) At every point Gauguin contradicts Cézanne, a fact understood better by Cézanne than by Gauguin. 'He never understood me,' said Cézanne. 'I have never desired and I shall never accept the absence of modelling or of gradation; it's nonsense. Gauguin was not a painter, he only made Chinese images.' To which Gauguin would have replied (in words he wrote to Daniel de Monfried): 'The great error is the Greek, however beautiful it may be. . . . Keep the Persians, the Cambodians, and a bit of the Egyptians always in mind.' (October, 1897.) Or: 'It is the eye of ignorance that assigns a fixed and unchangeable colour to every object. . . . Practise painting an object in conjunction with, or shadowed by— that is to say, close to or half behind—other objects of similar or different colours. In this way you will please by your variety and your truthfulness—your own. Go from dark to light, from light to dark. The eye seeks to refresh itself through your work; give it food for enjoyment, not dejection. . . . Let everything about you breathe the calm and peace of the soul. Also avoid motion in a pose. Each of your figures ought to be in a static position. . . . Study the silhouette of every object; distinctness of outline is the attribute of the hand that is not enfeebled by any hesitation of the will. . . . Do not finish your work too much. . . .' One could go on building up the contradictions, but they all amount to this: *the laws of beauty do not reside in the verities of nature.* The work of art is in some sense a suggestive symbol, stirring our emotions rather than stimulating our sensations.

Between these two points of view, these two distinct conceptions of art, there can be no compromise. Most of the contradictions and varieties of modern art spring from their antithetical opposition. No synthesis within the realm of art seems to be possible; it is not obvious why it should be desirable.

vi

The situation as it developed towards the end of the century was not, however, to remain a simple antithesis. If, for the sake of brevity, we describe the aim of Cézanne as the representation of the real, and that of Gauguin as the creation of beauty, there still remained another ideal of which Van Gogh became the leading exponent. Provisionally we might call it the expression of emotion, but the phrase needs a particular definition. The word *express*, however, inevitably recurs in all our attempts at definition, and Expressionism is the name which has been given to this tendency in modern art. 'To *express* the love of two lovers by a marriage of two complementary colours, their mingling and their opposition, the mysterious vibrations of kindred tones. To *express* the thought of a brow by the radiance of a light tone against a sombre background. To *express* hope by some star, the eagerness of a soul by a sunset radiance. Certainly there is nothing in that of stereoscopic realism, but is it not something that actually exists?'—these words of Van Gogh written at Arles in 1888 show the beginnings of a divergence of aim which in the years to follow was to modify profoundly the evolution of modern art.

Such a humanistic ideal in art was, of course, no new thing. It goes back to Rembrandt, if not farther, and in this tradition are such painters as Delacroix, Millet and Israels—all favourites of Van Gogh. Even Courbet and Manet contribute to the tradition, though their main significance lies elsewhere. Another quotation from Van Gogh's letters will serve to define this tradition and separate it from contemporary trends like Impressionism:

'What a mistake Parisians make in not having a palate for crude things, for Monticellis, for clay. But there, one must not lose heart because Utopia is not coming true. It is only that what I learned in Paris is leaving me, and that I am returning to the ideas I had in the country before I knew the impressionists. And I should not be surprised if the impressionists soon find fault with my way of working, for it has been fertilized by the ideas of Delacroix rather than by theirs. Because, *instead of trying to reproduce exactly what I have before my eyes, I use colour more arbitrarily so as to express myself forcibly.* Well, let that be as far as theory goes, but I am going to give you an example of what I mean.

'I should like to paint the portrait of an artist friend, a man who dreams great dreams, who works as the nightingale sings, because it is his nature. He'll be a fair man. I want to put into the picture my appreciation, the love that I have for him. So I paint him as he is, as faithfully as I can, to begin with.

'But the picture is not finished yet. To finish it I am now going to be the arbitrary colourist, I exaggerate the fairness of the hair, I come even to orange tones, chromes and pale lemon yellow.

'Beyond the head, instead of painting the ordinary wall of the mean room, I paint infinity, a plain background of the richest intensest blue that I can contrive, and by this simple combination of the bright head against the rich blue background, I get a mysterious effect, like a star in the depths of an azure sky.

'In the portrait of the peasant again I worked in this way, but without wishing in this case to produce the mysterious brightness of a pale star in the infinite. Instead, I think of the man I have to paint, terrible in the furnace of the full harvest, the full south. Hence the stormy orange shades, vivid as red hot iron, and hence the luminous tones of old gold in the shadows.

'Oh, my dear boy . . . and the nice people will only see the exaggeration as caricature.'[8]

The whole theory of expressionism, in its strength and weakness, is in this letter. Its strength lies in its humanism—in the fact that art cannot be limited to the search for any absolute, whether of reality or beauty, but must ever return to the essential dignity of our common human qualities, our human nature. Its weakness lies in the imprecision of its terminology—in words like mystery and infinity which, when it comes to the point of translation into practice, into terms of form and colour, have no real meaning. There are no 'infinite' shades of blue, and brightness is no mystery—that, at least, would have been Cézanne's opinion. Gauguin would have been more in sympathy with this language, but he was not really interested in painting a postman, for example, 'as I feel him', but rather in using any suitable model for the creation of an independent aesthetic entity—a work of art that creates and contains its own emotional values and is not dependent on the

[8] Letter 520. From: *Further Letters of Vincent van Gogh to his Brother.* 1886-1889 (London & Boston, 1929).

evaluation of a human context. For Gauguin the work of art, as a symbol, must be detached from any particular occasion, just as a crucifix is detached from the Crucifixion.

Van Gogh had no immediate following in France. It was in the far North, in Scandinavia and later in Germany, that expressionism had its widest expansion. Here the dominant figure is the Norwegian Edvard Munch. Munch was born ten years later than Van Gogh (in 1863), and he may to some extent have been inspired by the Dutchman. There is certainly a close affinity of aim, and even of style, between the two artists. But a countryman of Ibsen's had really no need of external inspiration, and though Munch modified his style after his visits to France, he may be said to have been born with the desire to express himself forcibly. His scope, however, is not quite the same as Van Gogh's: it is more objective. It is true that he could write in his diary in 1889 words which are quite reminiscent of those we have quoted from Van Gogh's letter of the previous year: 'No more painting of interiors with men reading and women knitting! They must be living people who breathe, feel, suffer and love. I will paint a series of such pictures, in which people will have to recognize the holy element and bare their heads before it, as though in church.' (Quoted by J. P. Hodin, *Edvard Munch,* Stockholm—Neuer Verlag—1948, p. 28.) But in Munch's subsequent paintings, as in the work of the expressionist school generally, there is an element of despair, leading to remorseless analysis and masochism, which was not characteristic of Van Gogh. This Kierkegaardian morbidity in Expressionism is a sufficient explanation of its failure to appeal more strongly to the Latin races. There is plenty of wonder in Expressionism, but little joy.

vii

By 1900 the three forces I have described—Realism, Symbolism and Expressionism—were ready to radiate into the new century. Their courses, however, were to be intricate and confused; only Expressionism developed with any logical consistency, though its inner despair was to destroy it. But meanwhile, in Kokoschka, Beckmann, Nolde, Heckel, Schmidt-Rottluff, Rohlfs, Soutine, Chagall and Rouault (not all of whom acknowledge the title of Expressionist) it produced artists of great talent and achievement.

The development of Realism has not been so uniform. In his last phase Cézanne, in his desire to emphasize the solidity of objects, had formed a style which is not merely architectonic in a metaphorical sense, but patently geometrical in a structural sense. The framework of the structure, perhaps a pyramid or a diamond, becomes dominant, and a considerable degree of distortion of the natural object is tolerated in order that the subject may conform to the perception of a 'good *Gestalt*'. Between 1907 and 1900 Picasso and Braque gave a further accentuation to this geometrical scaffolding and thereby affected what can only be described as a quantum-like jump into an altogether different type of art. Both Picasso and Braque were to retreat from their discovery, but it was taken up by Juan Gris, who did not, however, live long enough to pursue the new inspiration to its logical limits. This was done first by artists in the immediate vicinity (Marcel Duchamp, Gleizes, Delaunay, etc.), and almost simultaneously in other centres—Munich (Kandinsky, Klee), Moscow (Tatlin, Malevich, Gabo), Amsterdam (Mondrian) and London (Wyndham Lewis). This general tendency to abstraction, as we may call it, bore fruits of very various kinds, and because confused with such irrelevancies as machine-age romanticism. But at its best and purest—in, for example, the work of Mondrian, Gabo and Ben Nicholson—it undoubtedly expresses some profound need of the age. It may be derided as a flight from reality, but there are at least two possible defences:—it flies from a discredited reality to create a 'new reality', a realm of the absolute, of mystical purity; and in doing so it makes use of laws or elements that are fundamental to the structure of the physical universe. Whatever the explanation, the movement has shown vigour and tenacity for forty years, and the contempt of the critics and the neglect of the public have not sufficed to discourage its exponents.

A much more consistent use of Cézanne's discoveries was made by Henri Matisse. Matisse was not particularly interested in Cézanne's search for solidity, but he did take over Cézanne's insistence on a focal point in perception and consequently in composition—he too is an artist of the good *Gestalt*. But other influences were at work—Gauguin, perhaps, and certainly the discovery of Oriental art (more particularly in Matisse's case, of Persian art). This led Matisse to a complete breakaway from Cézanne's binding of colour to form. Colour is released, as in Gauguin's painting, to play its own dynamic and symbolic rôle. The result is a decorative pattern, but a pattern which still takes its organization from nature and the laws of perception. 'An artist must possess Nature. He must identify himself with her rhythm, by efforts that will prepare the mastery which will later enable him to express himself in his own language.' (Letter to Henry Clifford, February 14, 1948.)

'L'exactitude n'est pas la vérité'—this slogan of Matisse's has been the excuse in our time for much painting that is neither exact nor true. The exhaustion of the scientific impulse in art, which had lasted from Constable to Cézanne, put artists under the necessity of discovering a new principle of organization. Such new principles as have been discovered are either conceptual or instinctual. Cubism, the early 'metaphysical' paintings of Chirico, futurism (with some exceptions), constructivism, neo-plasticism, etc.,—these are all attempts to impose a law of harmony on the visual perception of the artist. (A futurist such as Boccioni could anounce the somewhat contradictory intentions of (*a*) 'opposing the liquefaction of objects which is a fatal consequence of impressionistic vision' and (*b*) 'the translating of objects according to the lines of force which characterize them'—thus achieving a new plastic dynamism, a pictorial lyricism. The short life of the futurist movement is probably to be explained by such inner contradictions.) A conceptual art is in effect a classical art, and it is not difficult to find a correspondence between Mondrian and Poussin, Gleizes and Sir Joshua Reynolds.

In general, however, the instinctual principle has prevailed in modern art since about 1910. Picasso has resolutely refused to treat cubism as a canon of art, external to the immediate intuitions of the artist. 'Mathematics, trigonometry, chemistry, psychoanalysis, music, and what not have been related to cubism to give it an easier interpretation. All this has been pure literature, not to say nonsense, which brought bad results, blinding people with theories. Cubism has kept itself within the limits and limitations of painting, never pretending to go beyond it. Drawing, design and colour are understood and practised in cubism in the spirit and manner that they are understood and practised in all other schools. Our subjects might be different, as we have introduced into painting objects and forms that were formerly ignored. We have kept our eyes open to our surroundings, *and also our brains*.' (Statement of 1923; my italics.)

There are one or two further remarks of Picasso's which serve to bring out the essentially instinctual nature of his activity. For example (from the same 'Statement' of 1923): 'Among the several sins that I have been accused of committing, none is more false than the one that I have, as the principle objective in my work, the spirit of research. When I paint, my object is to show what I have found and not what

GUERNICA—PABLO PICASSO   (*On extended loan to The Museum of Modern Art, New York, from the artist, M. Picasso*)

I am looking for.' Again, from his conversation with Christian Zervos, 1935: 'How can you expect an onlooker to live a picture of mine as I have lived it? A picture comes to me from miles away: who is to say from how far away I sensed it, saw it, painted it; and yet the next day I can't see what I've done myself. How can anyone enter into my dreams, my instincts, my thoughts, which have taken a long time to mature and to come out into the daylight, and above all grasp from them what I have been about—perhaps against my own will?' (Quotations from *Picasso* by Alfred Barr. Museum of Modern Art, New York, 1946.) These statements directly contradict everything for which Cézanne stood—his patient research for the form inherent in the object, his laborious efforts to reproduce this form with scientific exactitude. The result of such a new attitude was an explosive liberation of expression, not only in Picasso himself, but throughout the whole civilized world. It is part of my contention that a long process of germination had been taking place in the social consciousness of the same civilized world—Picasso is preceded by Hegel, Marx, Bergson, Freud, by revolutions in science, economics and social organization. But genius is the capacity to focus diversity—the ability to draw into a single burning point of light the discoveries and inventions of a whole generation. Picasso had this gift and his influence accordingly has been universal. It is safe to say that there has never been an artist who in his own lifetime has had so many imitators. Well may Picasso himself exclaim: 'To repeat is to run counter to spiritual laws; essentially escapism.'

viii

The general effect of the revolution in painting established by Matisse, Picasso, Braque and their immediate contemporaries was subjectivist in character, and the same generalization can be made of other arts (Proust, Joyce, D. H. Lawrence). This development in the arts had been supported by the new hypothesis of the unconscious first clearly formulated at the turn of the century by Freud. Again it must be emphasized that the causal connections are not necessarily direct. A writer like D. H. Lawrence may be tempted to justify the nature of his art by a direct appeal to psycho-analysis, but he is the exception rather than the rule. Subjectivism is a mental climate, announced more than a century ago by Kierkegaard and Hegel. It is a climate that has 'prevailed' for the past forty years, and though we may be rather tired of it, there is no sign of an immediate change.

A specific product of this prevailing climate has been the Surrealist movement. The Fauvistes had always imposed limitations on their spontaneity. They disclaimed any plan of campaign, any programme, but they always sought an 'objective correlate' for their sensations. The objectivity of this correlate was always determined by universal qualities which, in their sum, may be called Harmony. 'What I dream of,' Matisse once wrote (*La grande revue,* December 25, 1908), 'is an art of balance, of purity and serenity devoid of troubling or depressing subject-matter, an art which might be for every mental worker, be he business-man or writer, like an appeasing influence, like a mental soother, something like a good armchair in which to rest from physical fatigue'—a naïve confession which nevertheless describes the normal function of art. The Surrealists rejected this 'bourgeois' conception of art in favour of an activity which should be fundamentally disturbing and essentially impure. The first Manifesto of the Surrealists was not published until 1924, but a very necessary preparation had been taking place during the previous ten or fifteen years, years in which the harmonic conception of art was gradually discredited. The chief instigator in this destructive movement was undoubtedly Duchamp, and the surrealists have always honoured him as their forerunner. But the futurists, along with Chirico, Picabia and the sculptor Archipenko also played their parts, and the foundation of the Dada group in 1916 (in Zürich) was the first conscious negation of the aesthetic principle in art. The way was then clear for a new principle, and it was announced by André Breton as *automatism*—'pure psychic automatism, by which it is intended to express, verbally, in writing or by other means, the real process of thought. It is thought's dictation, all exercise of reason and every aesthetic or moral preoccupation being absent.'

Attempts have been made to find precedents for surrealism in the art of the past (Arcimboldo, Bosch, Goya), but they are mistaken, because however fantastic in their conceptions, these artists were always guided by aesthetic preconceptions. Surrealism is a completely revolutionary concept of art, and the only question is whether it is still 'art.' We should deny the term 'science' to an activity that refused to recognize the laws of induction; we have the same right to deny the term 'art' to an activity that rejects the laws of harmony. But the surrealists have not consistently practised what they have preached, and the colour harmonies of Mirò, the balanced compositions of Ernst and Dali, the dynamic rhythm of Masson, constitute objective correlates of an aesthetic nature in spite of the artist's intention to rid himself of such categories. In fact, 'pure psychic automatism' only takes place in the unconscious (and we only become aware of it in emerging from a state of unconsciousness, that is to say, in dreams). As soon as we attempt to translate unconscious phenomena into perceptual images, the instinctive laws of perception intervene—we automatically project the good *Gestalt*, the composition that obeys aesthetic laws.

Nevertheless, an immense liberation of aesthetic activity was achieved by this subjectivist revolution. It is not possible to resist the *play* of artists like Mirò and Klee—their work simply gives pleasure, and needs no theory to defend it. The work of other surrealists (as of certain expressionists), sometimes intentionally, sometimes unintentionally, is 'troubling or depressing subject-matter' and has its proper place in the case-books of the psychiatrists. One should not necessarily exclude from art the tragic aspects of life—it is perhaps Matisse's limitation that he has—but even in the tragic art of the past the intention was always to 'sublimate' the theme, to resolve the conflict, to create an overwhelming atmosphere of serenity.

ix

Und ich wiederhole: naturferne Kunst ist publikumsfremde Kunst. Muss es sein.

Wilhelm Worringer.

It has not been my aim in this essay to mention every artist of importance, or even to produce one of those charts in which every movement
has its appropriate graph. The truth is obscured by such rigid complex-
ities. It is the broad effects that are significant for my present purpose,
and these are complex enough. If I have succeeded, the reader will be
conscious of a stream which runs fairly consistently through a tract of
time measuring about a century, widening as it approaches our present
sea of troubles. But this stream is carrying down with it the sands and
pebbles that have ineffectually opposed its progress. This silt accumu-
lates as the river is about to attain its end, blocks the flow and creates
a delta—the one stream becomes many separate streams. But here the
metaphor breaks down, for the separate streams do not make their way
fanwise to the ultimate sea; some turn inland again and are lost in the
desert.

This diversion in modern art is due to the failure of the scientific
attitude in art. It has not proved possible, or at any rate finally satisfying, to consider art as 'a branch of natural philosophy, of which pictures
are but experiments'. In art, 'l'exactitude n'est pas la vérité.' 'We all
know that art is not truth. Art is a lie that makes us realize truth, at
least the truth that is given us to understand.' (Picasso.) Art is a closed
system, and it is 'true' in the degree that its rhetoric convinces us,
pleases us, comforts us. It has no spiritual mission; it is accused of
having no social function.

The artists themselves have recognized their isolation. 'Uns trägt kein
Volk,' cried Klee—the people are not with us. But it is useless to blame
the artist for that isolation—as well blame the weathercock for not
turning when there is no wind. (It is true, there is a kind of weathercock
that does not turn because its hinges are rusty—the academic artist.)
The climate of the age (*Zeitgeist, usw.*) is the creation of a thousand
forces, and perhaps the Marxists are right in giving priority, among
these forces, to economic trends. But the failure of the Soviet Union,
after more than thirty years of strenuous effort, to produce a new art
on the basis of a new economy, proves that the inspiration of the artist
cannot be forced. We must wait, wait perhaps for a very long time,
before any vital connection can be re-established between art and society. The modern work of art, as I have said, is a symbol. The symbol,
by its nature, is only intelligible to the initiated (though it may still
appeal mysteriously to the uninitiated, so long as they allow it to enter
their unconscious). The people can only understand the image, and
even this they distrust in its eidetic purity, for even their vision is
conventional. It does not seem that the contradiction which exists

between the aristocratic function of art and the democratic structure of modern society can ever be resolved. But both may wear the cloak of humanism, the one for shelter, the other for display. The sensitive artist knows that a bitter wind is blowing.

The emergence of the modern art movement was dramatically signalized in 1863 by the famous Salon des Refusés *(the Exhibition of the Rejected Painters). Year by year, the jury of the official Salon had been growing more arbitrary and more rigidly exclusive in its rejection of the work of the more experimental painters until, in 1863, an open scandal was created by the jury's refusal of over four thousand works. As a result of the outcry of protest by many artists and critics, the Emperor Napoleon III ordered that all the rejected works, except those voluntarily withdrawn, should be exhibited by themselves in the same building, the Palais de l'Industrie, that housed the official Salon. Thus, for the first time on a large scale, the artistic dictatorship of the Academy of Fine Arts and the* École des Beaux Arts *was challenged and the cleavage between official art and independent art was recognized. The* Salon des Refusés *was never repeated, but it was the true ancestor of all the later group exhibitions by which the Impressionists approached the public.*
   Many of the works exhibited in the Salon des Refusés *were, of course, amateurish and incompetent creations. But the anger and ridicule of the philistines were aroused, not by the obvious failures, but by significant works expressing the new tendencies, above all by Manet's "Déjeuner sur l'herbe" and Whistler's "White Girl." The most brilliant and vivid account of the impact of these works and others on the public is to be found in Chapter 5 of Emile Zola's novel* L'Œuvre *(translated into English as* The Masterpiece*), given here complete, except for a few closing pages. Claude Lantier, the chief figure of this chapter, as of the entire novel, is based mainly on Cézanne, but Claude's painting exhibited at the* Salon des Refusés *is obviously modeled on Manet's "Déjeuner sur l'herbe."*

Emile Zola
The Salon des Refusés of 1863[1]

On May 15, Claude, who had returned the evening before from Sandoz's place at three in the morning, was still sleeping at around nine o'clock, when Mme. Joseph took up

1 Chapter 5 from *L'œuvre* by Emile Zola, transl. from the French by David Thomas.

to him a big bouquet of white lilacs that a messenger had just brought him. He understood—Christine was celebrating in advance the success of his painting; for it was a great day for him, the opening of the *Salon des Refusés,* created that year, where his work, rejected by the jury of the official salon, was going to be exhibited.

This tender thought, these fresh and fragrant lilacs that had awakened him, touched him greatly, as if they were the omen of a fine day. In his nightshirt, with his feet bare, he put the flowers into his water jug on the table. Then, eyes swollen with sleep, flurried, he got dressed, rebuking himself for having slept so late. Last evening, he had promised to meet Dubuche and Sandoz at eight, at the latter's place, so all three could go together to the *Palais de l'Industrie,* where they would find the rest of the group. And he was already an hour late!

But, to tell the truth, he couldn't put his hand on anything in his studio, where everything was in disorder since the departure of the great painting. For five minutes, rummaging on his knees among the old frames, he looked for his shoes. Gilt particles flew; for not knowing where to get the money for a frame, he had had a neighboring carpenter put together four boards, and he had gilded them himself, with his sweetheart, who had shown herself to be quite a clumsy gilder. Finally, dressed and with his shoes on, his felt hat sprinkled with yellow sparks, he was about to leave, when a superstitious thought brought him back towards the flowers, which remained alone in the middle of the table. If he did not kiss these lilacs, he would meet with an affront. He kissed them, absorbing the perfume of their strong springlike scent.

Under the archway, he gave his key to the *concierge,* as usual. "Mme. Joseph, I won't be here all day."

In less than twenty minutes, Claude was on the *rue d'Enfer,* at Sandoz's. But the latter, who he had been afraid would no longer be there, was himself equally late because of the illness of his mother. It was nothing—simply a bad night that had upset him and made him anxious. Calmed down for the time being, he told him that Dubuche had written asking them not to wait for him, and telling them he would meet them there. They left; and, as it was nearly eleven, they decided to lunch at the back of a little deserted dairy on the *rue Saint-Honoré,* taking their time, overcome by indolence in their ardent desire to see, tasting a sort of tender sadness in lingering among such old souvenirs of childhood.

It was just one o'clock as they crossed the *Champs-Elysées.* It was a delightful day, with a high clear sky in which a breeze, still cold, seemed to brighten the blue. Under the sun, colored like ripe wheat, the rows of chestnut trees had new leaves of a freshly varnished and tender green, and the water basins with their spouts gushing forth, the well-kept lawns, the long perspective of the walks, and the expanse of open space gave a quality of great elegance to the vast horizon. Some carriages, rare at this time, came up; while a wave of people, lost and moving like an ant-hill, massed under the enormous arcade of the *Palais de l'Industrie*.

When they entered, Claude shivered lightly, from the cellar-like coolness of the giant vestibule, whose damp pavement echoed under his feet like the tiled floor of a church. He observed, to the right and to the left, the two monumental stairways, and scornfully asked:

"Now then, are we going to cross their filthy Salon?"

"Oh! Hang it, no," replied Sandoz. "Let's go by the garden. Over there is the west stairway that leads to the *Refusés*."

And they passed scornfully between the little tables of the catalogue sellers. Framed by immense red velvet curtains, the glassed-over garden appeared, beyond a shadowed porch.

At this time of day, the garden was almost empty, there being nobody there except at the buffet under the clock, where a crowd of people were having lunch. Everybody was on the first floor in the exhibition rooms; and, alone, the white statues bordered the paths of yellow sand, which cut up the green pattern of the grass. It was a collection of static marble, which was bathed in the diffused light descending like dust from the high panes. To the south, cloth window-shades blocked out half of the nave, yellow under the sun, spotted on both sides by the flashing reds and blues of the stained-glass windows. Some visitors, already worn out, were sitting on the new chairs and benches that were still shining with fresh paint; while the flocks of sparrows who inhabited, in the air, the forest of the cast-iron framework, were coming down with little cries of pursuit, as they settled and dug in the sand.

Claude and Sandoz pretended to walk quickly, without glancing around them. A stiff and noble bronze, the "Minerva" by a member of the Institute, had irritated them at the door. But as they hurried along an endless line of busts, they recognized Bongrand, alone, slowly circling a reclining figure, colossal and overwhelming.

"Well! It's you!" he cried, as they shook his hand. "I have just been looking at this figure by our friend Mahoudeau, that they've at least had the intelligence to accept and to place well. . . ."

And, interrupting himself: "Have you come from above?"

"No, we've just got here," said Claude.

Then, very warmly, he spoke to them of the *Salon des Refusés*. He who belonged to the Institute, but was living apart from his colleagues, brightened up at the adventure: the eternal discontent of painters, the campaign led by little newspapers like *Le Tambour,* the protests, the continuous complaints that had finally disturbed the Emperor; and the artistic *coup d'état* of this silent dreamer, for the measure came solely from him; and the fright and uproar of all at this desecration.

"No," he continued, "you have no idea of the indignation among the members of the examining committee. . . . And still I am distrusted, people remain silent when I am there! . . . All the anger is directed against those frightful realists. It was against them that the temple doors were carefully closed; it is because of them that the Emperor has permitted the public to examine the case; it is they who finally triumph. . . . Ah! I hear fine things about it. I wouldn't take much for your skins, young people!"

He let out a great laugh, arms open, as if to embrace all the youth that he felt rising from the ground. "Your pupils are pushing on," said Claude, simply.

With a gesture, Bongrand silenced him, seized with uneasiness. He had exhibited nothing, and all this output, across which they walked, these pictures, these statues, this effort of human creation, filled him with regret. It was not jealousy, for there was no higher or better soul, but a recurring dull fear of slow decay, this unavowed fear that gripped him. "And in the *Refusés,*" Sandoz asked him, "how is it going?"

"Wonderful! You'll see."

Then, turning toward Claude and taking both his hands: "You, my good fellow, you are renowned. . . . Listen! I, who have been called malicious, would give ten years of my life to have painted your great hussy of a woman."

This eulogy, from such a mouth, touched the young painter to tears. At last, he was a success! He could not find a word of gratitude, he spoke hurriedly of something else, wishing to hide his emotion.

"That worthy Mahoudeau! But she's all right, his figure! What a cursed temperament he has, eh?"

Sandoz and he started to walk around the plaster figure. Bongrand replied with a smile: "Yes, yes, too much of a thigh, too much of a throat. But look at the joints of the limbs, they're as slender and pretty as anything. . . . Well, good-bye, I'm leaving you. I'm going to sit down for a while, my legs are broken."

Claude had raised his head and was listening. An enormous noise, which had not struck him at first, resounded in the air, in a continuous burst; it was the clamor of a tempest beating against the coast, the rumbling of a tireless assault, bursting across from infinity. "Well!" he murmured. "What's that?" "That," said Bongrand as he went away, "is the crowd above, in the exhibition room."

And the two young men, after crossing the garden, went up to the *Salon des Refusés*.

Everything was well set up there, the recognized paintings were not more richly arranged: high hangings of old tapestries in the doors, chair-rails adorned with green serge, red velvet benches, white cloth screens, under the glassy bays of the ceilings, and, in the suite of rooms, the first sight was always the same, the same gold in the frames, the same vivid stains of the canvases. But a special gaiety ruled there, a youthful uproar which one did not at first completely grasp the meaning of. The crowd, already dense, grew from minute to minute, for people were deserting the official Salon, running out, stung with curiosity, struck with the desire to judge the judges, finally amused on the threshold by the certainty of seeing some quite ridiculous things. It was rather warm, a fine dust rose from the floor, people would certainly be choking by four o'clock.

"Hang it!" said Sandoz while elbowing his way around, "it's not going to be easy to maneuver inside and to find your work."

He hurried, in a fever of brotherhood. That day, he only lived for the work and the glory of his old friend.

"Nonsense!" cried Claude. "We'll get there all right! My work won't fly away!"

And he, on the contrary, pretended not to hurry, in spite of his irresistible urge to run. He raised his head and looked around. Soon, in the loud noise of the crowd that had stunned him, he distinguished some light laughter, still restrained, which covered the rumbling of feet and the noise of conversations. In front of certain paintings, visitors were joking. That worried him, for he had a woman's credulity and sensitivity, for all of his revolutionary harshness, always expecting martyrdom and always bleeding, always shocked at being rejected and scoffed at. He murmured: "They're gay, here!"

"Well, why not?" remarked Sandoz. "Just take a look at these wild scamps."

But at this moment, as they were lingering in the first room, Fagerolles, without seeing them, fell on them. He gave a start, clearly annoyed at meeting them. Nevertheless, he composed himself at once, very nicely.

"Well! I was thinking of you. . . . I have been here for an hour."

"Where then have they stuffed Claude's painting?" asked Sandoz.

Fagerolles, who had just remained planted in front of this picture for twenty minutes, studying it and studying the reaction of the public, replied without hesitation: "I don't know. . . . Let's look for it together, all right?"

And he joined them. Awful humbug that he was, he no longer affected as much of the behavior of a cad, he was already correctly clothed, still of a mocking tendency to carp at the world, but his lips henceforth stiff in the serious expression of a youngster who wants to succeed. He added, in a convinced manner: "It is I who regret having sent nothing this year. I would be here with the rest of you, I would have my share of success. And there are some astonishing contraptions here, my children. For example, these horses. . ."

He showed, across from them, the vast painting, in front of which the crowd was gathered laughing. It was, it was said, the work of a former veterinarian, life-size horses let loose in a meadow, but fantastic horses, blue, lavender, rose, and with a shocking anatomy that pierced the skin. "Come now, you're not laughing at us," declared Claude, suspicious.

Fagerolles feigned enthusiasm. "What! But it's full of excellences, there! He knows his horse beautifully, the fine fellow! No doubt, he paints like a sloven. But what difference does that make if he's original and if he brings a proof of it?"

His thin, girlish face remained serious. Imperceptibly, at the bottom of his clear eyes, a yellow gleam of mockery was shining. And he added this wicked allusion, which only he could enjoy: "Well! If you let yourselves be influenced by the imbeciles who are laughing, you will see many more of them, before long."

The three friends, who had started to walk again, advanced with infinite pain in the midst of the surge of shoulders. On entering the second room, they surveyed the walls with a glance; but they did not find the desired work. And what they saw, was Irma Bécot in the arms of Gagnière, both crushed against a chair rail, he in the process of examining a little painting, while she, delighted with the jostling, raised her rosy face and laughed at the crowd. "What!" said Sandoz astonished. "She is with Gagnière now?" "Oh! A passing fancy," explained Fagerolles with an air of calmness. "The story is so odd. . . . You know that a very chic apartment was just finished for her; yes, this young idiot of a marquis, the one that the papers speak of, you remember? A chap who will go far, I have always said! . . . But in vain she has been put in emblazoned beds, she has a mania for folding-beds, there are evenings when the garret of a painter best suits her. And that is why, dropping everything, she sank to the Baudequin Café on Sunday, about one in the morning. We had just left, there was no one there but Gagnière, asleep over his mug of beer. . . . Well, she took Gagnière."

Irma had noticed them and made affectionate gestures to them in the distance. They had to approach her. When Gagnière turned around with his pale hair and his little beardless face, looking even more comical than usual, he showed no surprise in finding them at his back. "It's unheard of," he murmured. "What is?" asked Fagerolles. "But this little masterpiece. . . . Honest, and naïve, and sincere."

He pointed out the miniature painting before which he was absorbed, an absolutely childish painting, one that a street urchin of four would have been able to paint, a little house, alongside a little road, with a little tree next to it, the whole thing askew, surrounded by black strokes, not to mention the ringlet of smoke which was leaving the roof.

Claude had made a nervous gesture, while Fagerolles repeated impassively: "Quite fine, quite fine. . . . But your picture, Gagnière, where is it?" "My picture? It's there."

Indeed, the painting sent by him was located precisely near the little masterpiece. It was a landscape of a pearly gray, a bank of the Seine carefully painted, pretty in style, although a little heavy, and of a perfect balance, without any revolutionary brutality. "Aren't they rather stupid to have refused that!" said Claude, who had approached with interest. "But why, why, I ask you?"

Indeed, no reason could explain the refusal of the jury. "Because it is realistic," said Fagerolles, in a voice so sharp that one could not know if he was chaffing the jury or the painting.

However, Irma, with whom no one was occupied, looked fixedly at Claude with the unconscious smile that the clumsy savagery of this big boy had put on her lips. To say that he had not even had the idea of meeting her again! She found him so different, so odd, not at all beautiful today, briefly, his complexion mottled as after a high fever. And troubled by his lack of attention, she touched his arm with an intimate gesture.

"Tell me, isn't that one of your friends who is looking for you, over there?"

It was Dubuche, whom she knew from having met him once at the Baudequin Café. He was breaking painfully through the crowd, with

his eyes vacantly fixed on the wave of heads. But, all of a sudden, at
the moment when Claude was trying to call attention to himself by
gesturing, the other turned his back to him and bowed very low to a
group of three people, the father fat and short, his face heated with
too warm a blood, the mother very thin, wax-colored, eaten with
anemia, the daughter so puny at eighteen that she still had the thin
wretchedness of her infancy. "Good!" murmured the painter, "there's
an affected fellow. . . . That beast certainly has ugly acquaintances.
Where has he fished up these horrors?"

Gagnière calmly said he knew him by name. The father, Margaillan,
was a big building contractor, already five or six times a millionaire,
who was making a fortune in the great construction enterprises of
Paris, building, on his own, entire boulevards. Without doubt Dubuche
found himself in contact with him through one of the architects with
whom he was straightening up the plans.

But Sandoz, moved by the emaciation of the girl, judged her in a
few words. "Ah! the poor little flayed cat! Such sadness!" "Nonsense!"
declared Claude with ferocity, "they have on their faces all the crimes
of the bourgeoisie, they sweat scrofula and stupidity. It's well done. . . .
Well! Our friend who stood us up is going off with them. Isn't it rather
dull to be an architect? Bon voyage, here's hoping he finds us again!"

Dubuche, who had not noticed his friends, had just offered his arm
to the mother and went out, while explaining the pictures, with a
gesture overflowing with an exaggerated self-satisfaction. "Let's keep
going," said Fagerolles.

And, addressing Gagnière: "Do you know where Claude's painting
has been hidden?" "No, I was looking for it. . . . I am going with you."

He accompanied them, he forgot Irma Bécot against the chair rail.
It was she who had had the notion of visiting the *Salon* on his arm, and
he was so little in the habit of walking like that with a woman that he
lost her constantly on the way, shocked to find her again always near
him, no longer knowing how or why they were together. She ran, she
took his arm again, in order to follow Claude, who was already passing
into another room, with Fagerolles and Sandoz.

Then, all five of them wandered, nose in air, parted by a shove, re-
united by another, carried along by the stream. An abomination of
Chaîne's stopped them, a Christ pardoning the adulteress, figures that
seemed carved out of wood, with a bony framework, and painted with
mud. But, next to it, they admired a very beautiful study of a woman
viewed from the back, with loins projecting and head turned. There

was, all along the walls, a blend of the excellent and the execrable, all styles intermingled, the confections of the historical school elbowing the young madmen of realism, the simple fools mingled pell-mell with the boasters of originality, a dead Jezebel who seemed to have decayed at the bottom of the cellars of the *Ecole des Beaux-Arts,* near the Lady in white, a very curious vision from the eye of a great artist; an immense shepherd looking at the sea, a piece of fakery, opposite a small painting of Spaniards playing tennis, an effect of light of brilliant intensity. Nothing was lacking of the horrors of art, neither military pictures with lead soldiers, nor wan antiquity, nor the Middle Ages botched with bitumen. But out of this incoherent collection, from the landscapes especially, nearly all of a sincere and proper note, and from portraits too, the greater part of very interesting workmanship, there issued a fine odor of youth, of courage, and of passion. If there were fewer bad paintings in the official Salon, the average was surely more mediocre and banal. One felt in a battle, and a gay battle, waged with verve at the moment when the dawn breaks, bugles sound, and one marches against the enemy with the certainty of defeating him before the setting of the sun.

Claude, cheered up by this breath of struggle, roused himself and became angry, and listened now with a challenging expression to the laughter of the public rising, as if he had heard the whistling of bullets. Subdued at the entrance, the laughter sounded louder, as he advanced. Already, in the third room, the women no longer choked under their handkerchiefs, the men stretched their bellies, in order to better relieve themselves. There was the contagious exuberance of a crowd there to enjoy itself, getting excited little by little, bursting out at a mere nothing, enlivened as much by the beautiful things as by the detestable. They laughed less before the Christ of Chaîne than before the study of a woman whose projecting rump, as if pulled out of the picture, appeared extraordinarily comical. The Lady in White, she too amused everyone: people elbowed each other, people writhed, a group was always forming there, with gaping mouths. And each painting had its success, men were calling from afar to show a good one, words of wit were continually circulating from mouth to mouth; so many that Claude, on entering the fourth room, nearly boxed the ears of an old woman whose chuckling infuriated him. "Such idiots!" he said, turning towards the others. "What? A person feels like throwing his masterpiece at their heads!"

Sandoz was also inflamed; and Fagerolles continued to praise the worst paintings very highly, which added to the gaiety; while Gagnière, indefinite in the middle of the jostling, drew behind him the delighted Irma, whose skirts twisted around the legs of all the men.

But suddenly, Jory appeared among them. His big red nose, his blond, boyish face shone brightly. He cleaved the crowd violently, gestured, exulted as from a personal triumph. As soon as he noticed Claude, he shouted: "Ah! Finally, it's you! I have been looking for you for an hour. . . . A success, old fellow, oh! a success. . . ."

"What success?"

"The success of your picture! . . . Come, I must show it to you. No, see for yourself, it's wonderful."

Claude grew pale, strangled by a great joy, as he pretended to welcome the news with coolness. The words of Bongrand came back to him, he believed in his genius.

"Well! Hello!" continued Jory, as he shook the hands of the others.

And tranquilly, he, Fagerolles, and Gagnière surrounded Irma, who smiled at them like a good child surrounded by its family, as she herself said.

"Where is it then?" asked Sandoz impatiently. "Take us there."

Jory took the lead, followed by the group. It was necessary to pound on the door of the last room, in order to enter. But Claude, remaining in the rear, heard continuous laughter rising up, an increasing clamor, the rumbling of a wave which was reaching its height. And as he finally penetrated into the room, he saw an enormous swarming confused mass, thrown together in a heap, which was being crushed before his picture. All the laughter swelled out, opened up there. It was his painting that they were laughing at.

"Well," Jory repeated, triumphant, "there's a success!"

Gagnière, scared and ashamed as if someone had slapped his own face, murmured: "Too much success . . . I would prefer something else."

"Are you stupid!" replied Jory in a burst of exalted conviction. "That is the success. . . . What does it matter that they're laughing! Now that we're launched, tomorrow all the papers will be talking about us."

"Blockheads!" Sandoz alone blurted out, his voice strangled with grief.

Fagerolles kept quiet, with a bearing disinterested and worthy of a friend of the family who was following along as escort. And, alone, Irma remained smiling, finding everything droll; then, with a tender gesture, she leaned against the shoulder of the jeered-at painter, she addressed him familiarly and whispered gently in his ear: "Don't get worked up, my little one. It's a mere trifle, people are just amusing themselves."

But Claude remained motionless. A great chill froze him. His heart stopped a moment, so cruel had deception just been. And, eyes widened, attracted and fixed by an invincible force, he looked at his picture, and he was astonished, hardly recognizing it in this room. It was certainly not the same work as in his studio. It had yellowed under the pale light of the cloth screen; it seemed uniformly diminished, both more brutal and more laborious; and, either because of what was going on around it, or because of its new milieu, he saw at the first glance all its defects, after having lived for months blinded before it. In several strokes, he remade it, moved the planes back, straightened up a limb, changed the value of a shade. Decidedly, the gentleman in the velvet vest was worth nothing, fat, badly seated; the hand alone was beautiful; in the rear, the two little wrestlers, the blonde and the brunette, remained too much like a rough draft, lacking solidity, diverting only for the eyes of an artist. But he was satisfied with the trees, with the glade filled with sunshine, and the nude woman, the woman reclining on the grass, appeared to him superior even to his talents, as if another had painted it and that he still had not known it, in this resplendence of life.

He turned towards Sandoz, saying simply: "They are right to laugh, it is incomplete. . . . It doesn't matter, the woman is fine! Bongrand didn't mock me."

His friend exerted himself to lead him away, but he persisted, and on the contrary drew near again. Now that he had judged his work, he listened to and watched the crowd. The explosion continued, increasing in an ascending scale of insane laughter. From the door onward, he saw the jaws of the visitors gaping, their eyes narrowing, their faces widening; and there were the tempestuous breathing of fat men and the rusty grinding of teeth of thin men, dominated by the shrill little fluting of women. Opposite, against the chair rail, young men were bent back, as if their sides had been tickled. A lady had just let herself fall onto a bench, knees pressed together, suffocating, trying to catch her breath in her handkerchief. The talk of such an odd painting must have spread, as people were rushing from the four corners of the *Salon,* whole packs were arriving and were pushing about, wanting to be part of it all. "Where then?—There!—Oh, that farce!" And words of wit rained down more briskly than elsewhere; it was the one subject that especially stimulated gaiety. People did not understand it, people found it crazy with an oddity that made them sick. "Over there, the lady is too warm, while the gentleman has put on his velvet jacket for fear of catching a cold." "But no, she is already blue, the gentleman has snatched her out of a pond, and he is resting at a distance, holding his nose." "Not polite, this man! He could show us his other face." "I tell you that it is a boarding school of girls, taking the air: look at the two who are playing leap-frog." "Well! a laundering! The flesh is blue, the trees are blue, he has surely put his picture in bluing!" Those who were not laughing were entering in a rage: this blue coloring, this new use of light, seemed an insult. Could one let art be desecrated? Old, gentlemen brandished their canes. A dignified person went out vexed, declaring to his wife that he did not like such nasty jokes. But another, a little meticulous man, having searched in the catalogue for the explanation of the picture, for the education of his young lady and reading aloud the title: "Plein Air," there rose around him a formidable chorus of cries and jeers. The word went around, it was repeated, commented on: open air, oh! open air, the stomach in the air, everything in the air, *tra la la laire!* It became a scandal, the crowd still increased, the faces crowded each other in the growing heat, each one with the round and stupid mouth of ignorant poeple who were judging painting, expressing all sorts of inanities about it, preposterous expressions, stupid and nasty sniggering, such as the view of an original work could draw from bourgeois imbecility.

And, at this moment, as a final blow, Claude saw Dubuche reappear, dragging along the Margaillans. From the moment he arrived before the painting, the architect, embarrassed, seized by a cowardly shame, wished to hurry himself along, to take away his group, while pretending never to have noticed either the painting or his friends. But the entrepreneur was already planted on his short legs, opening his eyes widely, asking him very haughtily in his big gruff voice: "Look here, what bungler has perpetrated that?"

This childishly simple brutality, this cry of an upstart millionaire, which summarized the standard opinion, redoubled the mirth; and he, flattered by his success, his sides tickled by the strangeness of this painting, joined in the fun in his turn, but with such a laugh, so excessive, so high-sounding, beneath his fat chest, that he dominated all the others. It was the hallelujah, the final burst of great organs. "Take my daughter away," said the pale Mrs. Margaillan into Dubuche's ear.

He hurried to rescue Régine, who had lowered her eyes; and he flexed his vigorous muscles, as if he had saved this poor being from a danger of death. Then, having left the Margaillans at the door, after handshakes and bows in the style of a man of the world, he returned to his friends and said bluntly to Sandoz, to Fagerolles, and to Gagnière: "What do you want? It's not my fault. . . . I warned him that the public wouldn't understand. It is beastly, yes, you will say in vain, it is beastly!" "They hooted at Delacroix," interrupted Sandoz, white with rage, fists clutched. "They jeered at Courbet. Ah! hostile race, stupidity of executioners!"

Gagnière, who was now sharing this artistic rancor, got angry at the remembrance of his battles of the *Pasdeloup* concerts, each Sunday, for real music.

"And they hiss Wagner, these are the same ones, I recognize them. . . . Look! That big one, down there. . ."

It was necessary for Jory to restrain him. He would have excited the crowd. He repeated that this was excellent, that there was 100,000 francs' worth of publicity there. And Irma, having slipped away again, had just found two friends of hers in the crowd, two young exhibitioners, who were among the fiercest scoffers, and whom she indoctrinated, whom she forced to find the picture very good by giving them raps on the fingers.

But Fagerolles had not unclenched his teeth. He constantly examined the picture, he threw glances at the public. With his Parisian flair and the supple conscience of a clever good fellow, he realized the mistake; and, vaguely, he felt already that which would be necessary for the painting to make a conquest of everybody, some tricks perhaps, some moderations, an adjustment of the subject, a softening of the workmanship. The influence that Claude had had on him persisted; he remained penetrated by it, forever marked. Only, he found it stark mad to exhibit such a thing. Wasn't it stupid to believe in the intelligence of the public? What's the use of this nude woman with this clothed gentleman? What's the meaning of these two little wrestlers in the background? And the qualities of a master, a piece of painting which there weren't two of in the *Salon!* A great scorn came on him for the admirably gifted painter, who made all of Paris laugh like the worst of the daubers.

This scorn became so strong that he could hide it no longer. He said, in an outburst of invincible frankness: "Ah! listen, my dear fellow, you asked for it, it is you who are too stupid."

Claude, in silence, turning his eyes away from the crowd, looked at him. He had not weakened at all, he was only pale under the laughter, his lips shaking with a light nervous tic: no one knew him, his work alone was insulted. Then, for a moment he withdrew his eyes from the picture, and slowly surveyed the other paintings of the room. And, in the disaster of his illusions, in the vivid grief of his pride, a breath of courage, a gust of health and childhood, came to him from all of this painting so gaily brave, mounting the assault on ancient routine, with such an unruly passion. He was consoled and strengthened by it, without remorse, without contrition, driven, on the contrary, to shock the public more. Certainly, there was much clumsiness there, many childish efforts, but what an attractive general tone, what a thrust of light produced, a silvery gray light, fine, diffused, enlivened with all the dancing reflections of the open air! It was like a window suddenly opened in the old kitchen of bitumen, on the recooked juices of tradition; and the sun entered, and the walls laughed in the spring morning! The luminous quality of his picture, this blueness which was mocked, shone out among the others. Was it not the expected dawn, a new day that was rising for art? He noticed a critic who paused without laughing, famous painters, surprised, with a serious expression, father Malgras, very dirty, going from picture to picture with his air of a fine taster, coming to a halt before his, motionless, absorbed. Then he turned again towards Fagerolles, and astonished him by this delayed answer: "One is as stupid as one is able to be, my dear fellow, and it seems that I will remain stupid. . . . So much the better for you, if you are a clever rogue!"

Immediately, Fagerolles slapped him on the shoulder, like a joking friend, and Claude let Sandoz take him by the arm. They led him out at last, the entire group left the *Salon des Refusés,* deciding to go by way of the architectural room; since, a few minutes ago, Dubuche, who had submitted a project for a museum, had shuffled about and begged them with such a humble look that it seemed difficult not to give him this satisfaction. "Ah!" said Jory jokingly on entering the room, "what an ice-house! One can breathe here."

All took off their hats and wiped their foreheads with relief, as if they had arrived under the coolness of great shadows, at the end of a long walk in the hot sun. The room was empty. From the ceiling, beneath which extended a screen of white cloth, fell an even light, gentle and mournful, which was reflected, like the water of a motionless stream, in the mirror of a strongly polished floor. On the four walls, of a faded red, the projects, the large and small cases, bordered with pale blue, displayed designs washed with water-color tints. And alone, absolutely alone in the middle of this desert, a bearded gentleman remained standing in front of an asylum project, plunged in profound contemplation. Three ladies appeared, were startled, passed through fleeing in little hurried steps.

Dubuche was already showing and explaining his work to his friends. It was just one case, a poor little Museum room, that he had sent in ambitious haste, contrary to his habit, and against the will of his patron, who nevertheless had caused it to be accepted, thinking his honor involved. "Is your museum to house the paintings of the open-air school?" asked Fagerolles without laughing.

Gagnière was admiring it, with a shake of the head, while thinking of something else; while Claude and Sandoz, in friendship, were examining and sincerely interesting themselves in it. "Eh! this is not bad, old fellow," said the first. "The ornaments are still of a pretty degenerate tradition. . . . Never mind, it will do!"

Jory, impatient, finally interrupted him.

"Ah! let's sneak away, shall we? As for me, I've been catching a cold."

The group resumed its advance. But the worst of it was that, to go by the shortest way, they had to cross all of the official *Salon;* and they resigned themselves to it, in spite of the oath that they had taken not to set foot in it, by way of protest. Breaking through the crowd, advancing in a rigid procession, they followed the suite of rooms, throwing angered looks to the right and to the left. It was no longer the gay scandal of their own *Salon,* the clear tones, the exaggerated sunlight. Gold frames full of shadow followed one upon another, things formal and black, studio nudities, yellowing after days in cellars, all the classical cast-off clothing, history, genre, landscape, all drenched in the same conventional cart-grease. A uniform mediocrity seeped through the works, a muddy dirtiness of tone characterized them, in this art of proper deportment but with poor and degenerate blood. And they hurried their steps, and they ran on to escape this still-standing reign of bitumen, condemning everything wholesale with their beautiful sectarian injustice, crying that there was nothing there, nothing, nothing!

Finally, they escaped, and they descended to the garden, meeting Mahoudeau and Chaîne again. The former threw himself into the arms of Claude. "Ah! my dear fellow, your painting, what temperament!"

The painter immediately praised the "Wine-Harvester."

"And you, I say, you've given them a little kick in the head!"

But the sight of Chaîne, to whom no one was speaking of his Adulterous Woman, and who was wandering in silence, filled him with pity. He found a profound melancholy in the abominable painting, in the wasted life of this peasant, victim of bourgeois admirations. He always gave him the joy of an eulogy. He shook him in a friendly manner, he cried: "Very good also, your thing. . . . Ah! my good fellow, design does not frighten you!"

"No, sure enough!" declared Chaîne, whose face was purpled with vanity under the black bushes of his beard.

Mahoudeau and he joined the group; and the former asked the others if they had seen Chambouvard's "Sower." It was extraordinary, the only real piece of sculpture in the *Salon*. Everyone followed him into the garden, that the crowd had now overrun. "Well!" replied Mahoudeau, stopping in the middle of the central path, "there's Chambouvard right in front of his 'Sower.'"

Indeed, a fat man was there, fixed firmly on his heavy legs, and admiring himself. His head sunk in his shoulders, he had the thick and beautiful face of a Hindu idol. It was said that he was the son of a veterinarian in the vicinity of Amiens. At the age of forty-five, he was already the author of twenty masterpieces, of simple and animated statues, of the most modern bodily quality, molded by a worker of genius without affectation; and that by sheer accident of production, bringing forth his works as a field brings forth its grass, good one day, bad the next, in absolute ignorance of what he created. He pushed his lack of critical sense to the point of not making any distinction between the most glorious work of his hands and the detestable grotesque figures that he happened to polish off at times. Without nervous excitement, without a doubt, always solid and convinced, he had a godly pride.

"Astonishing, the 'Sower'!" murmured Claude. "What a construction, and what a gesture!"

Fagerolles, who had not looked at the statue, greatly amused himself with the great man and with the line of young gaping disciples, that he was leading as usual in back of him.

"Look at them then, they are in communion, my word! . . . And as for him, well? Such a good brutish head, transfigured in the contemplation of his navel!"

Alone and at ease in the middle of the curiosity of everyone, Chambouvard was staggered, with the dumbfounded air of a man who was astonished at having begotten such a work. He seemed to see it for the first time, he wasn't returning to it at all. Then a rapture drowned his large face, he swayed his head, he burst into a sweet and invincible laughter, repeating ten times: "It's comical . . . it's comical . . ."

All of his queue, behind him, swooned, as he expected, such was his self-adoration.

But there was a little excitement there: Bongrand, who was walking hands behind his back, eyes vacant, had just come upon Chambouvard; and the public was whispering, interesting itself in the handshake exchanged by the two famous artists, the one short and sanguine, the other tall and trembling. Words of good friendship were heard: "Always wonders!" *"Parbleu!* And you, nothing this year?" "No, nothing. I am resting, I am searching." "Nonsense! You're joking, that comes all by itself." "Goodbye!" "Good-bye!" Already, Chambouvard, accompanied by his court, was going slowly out across the crowd, with the look of a monarch happy to be living; while Bongrand, who had recognized Claude and his friends, was approaching them, hands feverish and pointing out the sculptor to them with a nervous movement of his chin, saying: "There is a fellow whom I envy! To always believe that one is creating masterpieces!"

He complimented Mahoudeau on his "Wine-Harvester," showed himself paternal toward all, with his ample good nature, his ease of an old settled-down and decorated romantic. Then, addressing himself to Claude: "Well! What was I saying to you? You have seen, up there. . . . You have here become leader of a school." "Ah! yes," replied Claude, "they are putting me in my place. . . . It is you who are the master of all of us."

Bongrand gave a gesture of vague suffering, and made off, saying: "Be quiet, now! I am not even my own master!"

A moment later, the group wandered into the garden. They turned again to see the "Wine Harvester," when Jory noticed that Gagnière no longer had Irma Bécot at his arm. The latter was shocked: where the devil could he have lost her? But when Fagerolles related to him that she had gone away into the crowd with two gentlemen, he calmed down; and he followed the others, more buoyant, relieved of this good fortune which had dumbfounded him.

Now, people could only circulate with trouble. All the benches were taken by assault, groups barred the paths where the slow walk of the strollers stopped and flowed back without cease around the successful bronzes and marbles. From the congested refreshment room came a strong murmuring, a noise of saucers and of spoons, which was adding to the animated vibration of the immense nave. The sparrows had ascended again into the forest of cast-iron framework, and their little shrill cries were heard, hailing the setting sun with their screeching, under the warm windowpanes. The atmosphere was heavy, a humid greenhouse-like tepidness, a motionless air, unsavory with the smell of freshly turned-up compost. And dominating this tumult of the garden, the commotion from the first-floor rooms, the rumbling of feet on the iron floors, was constantly roaring, with its noise of a tempest beating against the coast.

Claude, who distinctly made out this stormy rumbling, in the end had nothing but it in his ears, raging and roaring. It was the gaiety of the crowd, whose jeers and laughter blew in a hurricane before his painting. He made an irritated gesture, he cried out: "Ah! What are we doing here? As for me, I am taking nothing from the refreshment room, it stinks from the Institute. Let's go drink a mug of beer outside, all right?"

Everybody left, legs broken-down, faces drawn-out and contemptuous. Outside, they breathed noisily, with an air of delight, on returning to good, springlike nature. Four o'clock had just sounded, the slanting sun shone down the *Champs-Elysées;* and everything was aflame, the crowded lines of the carriages, the new foliage of the trees, the spouts of basins, which were gushing out and flying upward in a golden spray. At a sauntering pace, they descended, hesitated, finally ran aground in a little café, the *Pavilion de la Concorde,* to the left, in front of the square. The room was so narrow that they sat down beside the sidewalk, in spite of the cold falling from the archway of leaves, already thick and dark. But after the four rows of chestnut trees, beyond this band of greenish shade, they had before them the sunny roadway of the avenue, they saw Paris passing there across a halo, the carriages radiating like stars, the big yellow buses more golden than triumphal chariots, horsemen whose mounts seemed to throw off flashes, pedestrians who were tranfigured and shone in the light.

And for close to three hours, with his full mug of beer untouched before him, Claude spoke, disputed in a growing fever, his body tired out, his head thick with all the painting that he had just seen. It was, with the group of friends, the usual discussion on leaving the *Salon,* but this year made more impassioned by the liberal measure of the Emperor*: a mounting wave of theories, an intoxication of extreme opinions which made tongues clammy, all the passion of art with which their youth was burning. "Well! what of it?" he cried. "The public laughed, it was necessary to educate the public. . . . After all, it is a victory. Remove two hundred grotesque paintings and our *Salon* gets the better of theirs. We have bravery and boldness, we are of the future. . . . Yes, yes, people will see later, we will kill it, this *Salon* of theirs. We will enter it as conquerors, with masterpieces as blows. . . . Laugh then, laugh then, great beast of Paris, until you fall on your knees!"

And, breaking off, he showed with a prophetic gesture the triumphal avenue where the luxury and joy of the city were rolling in the

* In sanctioning the *Salon des Refusés.*

sun. His gesture widened out, descended to the *Place de la Concorde,* that one observed diagonally, under the trees, with one of its fountains, whose sheets of water were flowing down, one end receding from its railings, and two of its statues, "Rouen" with giant breasts, "Lille" stretching forth the vastness of her bare foot. "The open air, that amuses them!" he resumed. "So be it! Since they wish it, the open air, the school of the open air! . . . Well? It was between us, it did not exist yesterday, outside of a few painters. And the ones who launch the word, these are the ones who are founding the school. . . . Oh! I myself am willing. Forward for the school of the open air!"

Jory smacked his thighs. "I told you so! I was sure, with my articles, of forcing them to bite, these idiots! We're going to annoy them with it, now!"

Mahoudeau was singing of victory, he too, recalling continually his "Wine-Harvester," whose boldness he explained to the silent Chaîne, who alone was listening; while Gagnière, with the harshness of the timid set free through pure theory, was talking of guillotining the Institute; and Sandoz, with the enflamed sympathy of a fellow worker, and Dubuche, yielding to the contagion of his revolutionary friendships, were becoming inflamed, were tapping on the table, were swallowing Paris, in each draught of beer. Very calm, Fagerolles kept his smile. He had followed them for amusement, for the singular pleasure that he found in pushing the friends into practical jokes that turned out badly. While he was whipping up their spirit of revolt, he took at that very moment the firm resolution to work henceforth towards obtaining the *Prix de Rome:* this day decided it, and he judged it foolish to compromise his talent any more.

The sun was getting lower on the horizon, there was no more than a descending wave of carriages, the return from the *Bois,* in the pale gold of the sunset. And the exit from the *Salon* must be ending, a line was unwinding, gentlemen of critical judgment, each one having a catalogue under his arm.

The following passage from Philip Hamerton's Contemporary French Painters, *first published in 1865, is one of the most intriguing documents in the history of art. Here, almost half a century before Kandinsky's "first" nonobjective painting, is a clear statement of the principles of abstract art. Even more striking, however, is the evidence provided by Hamerton that these principles were being discussed and advocated by "the most recent classicists" (what a pity that he doesn't name them!)*

at a moment when the "realism" of Courbet and Manet was the chief target of the academic critics and when impressionism was about to emerge as the most radical art style of the day.

Philip Hamerton[1]
Contemporary French Painters

[The] tendency of the most recent classicists goes so far, that they are beginning to express contempt for all art which in any way depends upon the interest of the subject. Their feeling is that when an artist tries to attract the public to his work by appealing to the general interest in remarkable personages or events, it argues a want of confidence in the powers of art, and is either charlatanism or an unworthy condescension. . . . Painting . . . should, in their view, offer nothing but its own merchandise. And the especial merchandise of painting they hold to be the visible melodies and harmonies,—a kind of visible music,—meaning as much and narrating as much as the music which is heard in the ears, and nothing whatever more. If it represents persons, it should not be for the persons, but for the beauty or power of the forms. Organic form being the most beautiful, these painters select it, and they prefer the nude, of course, as the pure expression of the form; but when they paint a woman they do not take the slightest interest in her personally, she is merely, for them, a certain beautiful and fortunate arrangement of forms, an impersonal harmony and melody, melody in harmony, seen instead of being heard. It may seem impossible to many readers that men should ever arrive at such a state of mind as this, and come to live in the innermost sanctuary of artistic abstraction, seeing the outer world merely as a vision of shapes; but there is no exaggeration in the preceding sentences, they are simply true, and true of men now living.

This section from Cézanne: A Study of His Development *is a magnificent example of Fry's subtle sensibility and gift of critical exposition. It is also an excellent example of the difference between the preoccupations and emphases of twentieth-century art critics and those of the nineteenth century.*

[1] Philip Gilbert Hamerton (1834–94) was an English artist, art critic, and man of letters who spent considerable time in France and had a great appreciation of French art. He founded and for a quarter-century edited the art periodical *The Portfolio.*

Roger Fry
Cézanne's Still-Lifes[1]

One may take as typical works of
the period we are about to consider—a period which extends to beyond
the middle of the 'eighties—a series of still-lifes. Before certain portraits
and landscapes of Cézanne's maturity, before so impressive a masterpiece of genre painting as the "Cardplayers," it would sound blasphemous to speak of our artist as a painter of still-life pictures, but none
the less it is noteworthy that he is distinguished among artists of the
highest rank by the fact that he devoted so large a part of his time to
this class of picture, that he achieved in still-life the expression of the
most exalted feelings and the deepest intuitions of his nature. Rembrandt alone, and that only in the rarest examples, or in accessories,
can be compared to him in this respect. For one cannot deny that
Cézanne gave a new character to his still-lifes. Nothing else but still-
life allowed him sufficient calm and leisure, and admitted all the delays
which were necessary to him for plumbing the depths of his idea. But
there, before the still-life, put together not with too ephemeral flowers,
but with onions, apples, or other robust and long-enduring fruits, he
could pursue till it was exhausted his probing analysis of the chromatic
whole. But through the bewildering labyrinth of this analysis he held
always, like Ariadne's thread, the notion that changes of colour correspond to movements of planes. He sought always to trace this correspondence throughout all the diverse modifications which changes of
local colour introduced into the observed resultant.

No doubt this idea of colour as revealing plasticity was far from new.
Leonardo da Vinci had not only noticed the diverse colouring of the
diversely oriented planes of an object, he had even given the scientific
explanation. The Impressionist picture existed already, if not on canvas, at least in his writings. But for the most part artists gave but casual
attention to these phenomena, and certainly preferred other methods
of suggesting to the eye the plasticity of objects. So that to the majority
even of picture-lovers the truths which the Impressionists stated appeared to be insane paradoxes. By the true Impressionists, by men like
Cézanne's companions at Auvers, Guillaumin and Pissaro, those
changes of colour which correspond to movements of planes were

[1] From *Cézanne: A Study of His Development* by Roger Fry. New York: The Macmillan
Company, 1929.

vigorously expressed, but they were more concerned to seize the full complexity of the coloured mosaic of vision than to isolate and empha- size those indications in the total complex which are evocative of plastic form. They sought to weave across their canvas the unbroken weft of colour which their eyes had learned to perceive in nature. But this aim could not altogether satisfy such a nature as Cézanne's. The intellect is bound to seek for articulations. In order to handle nature's continuity it has to be conceived as discontinuous; without organiza- tion, without articulation the intellect gets no leverage. And with Cézanne the intellect—or, to be more exact, the intellectual part of his sensual reactions—claimed its full rights.

From this point of view we may regard the history of art as a per- petual attempt at reconciling the claims of the understanding with the appearances of nature as revealed to the eye at each successive period. Each new discovery in the world of visual experience tends to invalidate the constructions which had proved adequate theretofore, and the spirit is bound to reconstruct its shelter, taking into account the new data. This was notably the case with the new data supplied by the Impressionist discipline of the eye. Some artists were so en- amoured of these new visual truths that it was sufficient for them merely to state and restate them in all their complexity. Monet's "Haystacks" and "Water-lilies" are there to prove it. But the greater spirits in this group sought from the very first to draw from these experiences the basis for new constructions. With Cézanne this need proclaimed itself as more urgent and imperious than with Renoir and Degas themselves. Scarcely had he grasped the principles of Impressionism before he set himself to utilize them for further ends. And it is perhaps most evi- dently in this series of still-lifes that he arrived at a synthesis based on the new analysis of atmospheric colour.

Those critics who like to speculate and generalize must often regret that the genre of still-life has been so rarely cultivated throughout the course of European art, so much less, in fact, than was the case in China. Because it is in the still-life that we frequently catch the purest self-revelation of the artist. In any other subject humanity intervenes. It is almost impossible that other men should not influence the artist by their prejudices and partizanship. If the artist rebels against these, the act of rebellion is itself a deformation of his idea. If he disregards them and frees himself from all the commonplaces of sentiment, the effort still leaves its traces on his design. But the still-life excludes all these questions and guards the picture itself from the misconstructions of those whose contact with art is confined to its effect as representation. In still-life the ideas and emotions associated with the objects represented are, for the most part, so utterly commonplace and insignificant that neither artist nor spectator need consider them. It is this fact that makes the still-life so valuable to the critic as a gauge of the artist's personality. How many obscure points in Raphael's artistic psychology might be cleared up if we had a series of still-lifes by him. How fascinating to see what Castagno or Piero della Francesca would have accomplished. One can almost guess at the superb revelations of painter's quality which Luca Signorelli would have supplied.

There are, of course, exceptions to this purely plastic significance of still-life. The symbolist, by a careful choice of objects and by arranging for them a special pictorial context, can force them to reveal some entirely non-plastic emotion. There are also rare cases where an artist has so intensely dramatic a manner that by a special emphasis he can give, even to the still-life, a kind of dramatic significance. Goya, for instance, once painted a plucked fowl in such a way as to suggest an atrocious tragedy, to make it a companion piece to one of his "Desastros de la guerra."

Cézanne at one time might well have had similar aims, but by the period which we are considering he had definitely abandoned them. He eagerly accepts the most ordinary situations, the arrangements of objects which result from everyday life. But though he had no dramatic purpose, though it would be absurd to speak of the drama of his fruit dishes, his baskets of vegetables, his apples spilt upon the kitchen table, none the less these scenes in his hands leave upon us the impression of grave events. If the words tragic, menacing, noble or lyrical seem out of place before Cézanne's still-lifes, one feels none the less that the emotions they arouse are curiously analogous to these states of mind. It is not from lack of emotion that these pictures are not dramatic, lyric, etc., but rather by reason of a process of elimination and concentration. They are, so to speak, dramas deprived of all dramatic incident. One may wonder whether painting has ever aroused graver, more powerful, more massive emotions than those to which we are compelled by some of Cézanne's masterpieces in this genre.

We may take as typical of this series and as one of the most completely achieved, the celebrated still-life of the "Compotier." It dates, no doubt, from well on into the period under consideration, from a time when Cézanne had completely established his personal method. The sensual energy which had led him from early days to knead a dense paste into shape upon his canvas persists still. But his method of handling it has become far more circumspect. Instead of those brave swashing strokes of the brush or palette knife, we find him here proceeding by the accumulation of small touches of a full brush. These small touches had become a necessity from the moment he undertook the careful analysis of coloured surfaces. To the immediate and preconceived synthesis which in the past he had imposed upon appearances, there now succeeds a long research for an ultimate synthesis which unveils itself little by little from the contemplation of the things seen. Not that he fumbles: each touch is laid with deliberate frankness, as a challenge to nature, as it were, and, from time to time, he confirms the conviction which he has won by a fierce accent, an almost brutal contour, which as often as not he will overlay later on, under stress of fresh discoveries and yet again reaffirm. These successive attacks on the final position leave their traces in the substance of the pigment, which becomes of an extreme richness and density. The paste under his hands grows to the quality of a sort of lacquer, saturated with colour and of an almost vitreous hardness.

So perfect a correspondence of material quality to the idea as this picture shows is by no means of common occurrence in art. It is not always possible for the artist to find in the material to his hand the perfect embodiment of his feeling. One might almost say that it is only at certain moments in the history of art or in the career of a particular artist that everything concurs to produce it. Often indeed we may have to divine the idea through a material quality which opposes a certain opacity. At other moments the matter itself becomes eloquent. Thus, to take a few random examples, the refined and spiritualized sensuality of a Fra Angelico finds a perfect response in the opalescent washes of egg-tempera, but the same technique refuses to bear out fully the plastic gravity of a Masaccio, and one can see at once how much happier Signorelli would have been had he dared to venture on the generous impasto of modern oil painting.

There is no pictorial issue about which the public is so exacting as that of material quality. It has its strong preferences which it can sometimes impose on the artist. It is thus that the licked and polished surfaces of a Dou and a Van der Werff were created in response to a particularly unenlightened connoisseurship, and, in general, the Dutch painters were constrained to a fictitious appearance of finish and dared not use a more frankly expressive handling. It is this that renders Rembrandt's case so extraordinary. Because it was Rembrandt, in his

STILL LIFE—PAUL CÉZANNE (*The Metropolitan Museum of Art, Bequest of Mrs. H. O. Havemeyer, 1929. The H. O. Havemeyer Collection*)

later years, who revealed the full expressive possibilities of matter. With him nothing is inert, the material is permeated and, as it were, polarized by the idea, so that every particle becomes resonant. Chardin's tenderer, more fragile sensuality finds its expression in a totally different quality, but here again the response is complete, though perhaps less unfailingly so. There are, that is, inequalities in his work; there are places where the activity of the spirit seems to fail and to leave passages relatively inert, acting as mere foils or backgrounds to others.

It is by such considerations and comparisons that we may judge of the rare perfection of this work of Cézanne's. And one must, I think, venture to proclaim boldly that it represents one of the culminating points of material quality in painting. Under the double impulsion of his analysis of coloured surfaces and of his native feeling for large structural unities Cézanne created a new pictorial beauty. And from our comparison of this quality in the work of other painters we may conclude that he shows himself nearer to Rembrandt than to Chardin. If, on the one hand, his voluptuous feeling for colour reminds one of the seductive sweetness of Chardin, on the other hand for him, if possible more than for Rembrandt, there are no parts of the surface more or less expressive than others, for his sensibility is active throughout. There may be parts where the emphasis falls, but those things that one might consider insignificant are analysed with the same care and stated with the same conviction as those which play a leading part in the composition.

This question of material quality depends, of course, to a great extent on the artist's "handwriting," on the habitual curves which his brush strokes describe. In his earlier works, as we have seen, Cézanne affected an almost florid and exuberant curvature modelled upon that of the Baroque painters, but, one has to admit, without ever attaining to their elegant incontinence. It was, one may suspect, the expression rather of his willed ambition than of his fundamental sensibility to form. Under Pissaro's influence he holds himself in. The new conception of external vision which he was practising evidently absorbed his attention, and he became of necessity far less conscious of his handling. He had, as it were, to leave his hand to manage, as best it could, to convey the ideas he was intent upon. His gestures, in consequence, were more restrained. In this still-life the handling has recovered something of its older spirit, but it remains far more restrained and austere. He has adopted what we may regard as his own peculiar and personal method. He has abandoned altogether the sweep of a broad brush, and builds up his masses by a succession of hatched strokes with a small brush. These strokes are strictly parallel, almost entirely rectilinear, and slant from right to left as they descend. And this direction of the brush strokes is carried through without regard to the contours of objects. This is the exact opposite of Baroque handling. In Rubens, for instance, what strikes us is the vertiginous rapidity and dexterity with which his hand adapted itself to the curved contours of his forms. The grave, methodical but never lifeless handling of Cézanne's "Compotier" is the exact antithesis to that.

The public, which is more attracted in a picture by virtuosity and brilliance than by any other quality, was violently repelled by the broken surfaces of the Impressionists. But in those exhibitions in the seventies—notably that of 1877—where Cézanne appeared as one of their group, it was always against Cézanne that the most violent insults were hurled. His handling seemed not only clumsy and ugly to the last degree, but actually to be a calculated outrage of the spectator's feelings. Nor did this prejudice disappear quickly. In the dispute over the legacy of the Caillebotte Collection to the Luxembourg the State, while grudgingly willing to accept the other Impressionist pictures, for a long time insisted on the exclusion of Cézanne's works on the ground that they could never be exposed in a public gallery. An echo of the same violent reaction was heard in England as lately as in 1910, when, at the Grafton Gallery Exhibition, Cézanne was first seen effectively in this country. It was found then that what were regarded as the monstrosities of later artists like Matisse and Picasso, were more easily to be condoned than the classic austerity of Cézanne's handling. "Butcher" and "bungler" were comparatively mild terms in the vocabulary of abuse employed by some well-known critics who have long since recognized how far their first reactions were at fault.

Even those few critics who ventured to champion Cézanne's work towards the end of the last century felt it necessary to adopt an apologetic tone about the so-called clumsiness and awkwardness of his handling. This attitude of the public, strange and unintelligible as it seems to us now, is not in the least to be wondered at. Artists only—and only open-minded and indulgent artists—are capable of seeing at once through the medium of an unusual and therefore antipathetic "handwriting" those qualities of plastic design which may have necessitated it. In no other pictorial quality is it so difficult to discount the effect of custom and fashion. Many pictures repel us at first sight which might charm us at once by their qualities of organization and design were they not obscured for us by an unfamiliar "handwriting." Artists have even been led to believe in a quality of handling good in itself, forgetting that every sensibility has to discover its own appropriate expression in this respect. And by now this influence of fashion works in the other direction. Cézanne's handling is so universally accepted that we are tempted even to admire too much any picture which reminds one of it.

Hitherto we have considered this picture solely from the point of view of the surface it offers to the eye. It is true that this surface has already yielded us certain important facts about Cézanne's emotional reactions at this period. But we must also consider it from the more fundamental point of view of the organization of the forms and the ordering of the volumes. We have already guessed, behind the exuberances of Cézanne's Baroque designs, a constant tendency towards the most simple and logical relations. Here that simplicity becomes fully evident. One has the impression that each of these objects is infallibly in its place, and that its place was ordained for it from the beginning of all things, so majestically and serenely does it repose there. Such phrases are, of course, rather fantastic, but one has to make use of figurative expressions to render at all the extraordinary feeling of gravity and solemnity which the artist has found how to evoke from the presentment of these commonplace objects. One suspects a strange complicity between these objects, as though they insinuated mysterious meanings by the way they are extended on the plane of the table and occupy the imagined picture space. Each form seems to have a surprising amplitude, to permit of our apprehending it with an ease which surprises us, and yet they admit a free circulation in the surrounding space. It is above all the main directions given by the rectilinear lines of the napkin and the knife that make us feel so vividly this horizontal extension. And this horizontal supports the spherical volumes, which enforce, far more than real apples could, the sense of their density and mass.

One notes how few the forms are. How the sphere is repeated again and again in varied quantities. To this is added the rounded oblong shapes which are repeated in two very distinct quantities in the *compotier* and the glass. If we add the continually repeated right lines and the frequently repeated but identical forms of the leaves on the wallpaper, we have exhausted this short catalogue. The variation of quantities of these forms is arranged to give points of clear predominence in the *compotier* itself to the left, and the larger apples to the right centre. One divines, in fact, that the forms are held together by some strict harmonic principle almost like that of the canon in Greek architecture, and that it is this that gives its extraordinary repose and equilibrium to the whole design.

In the shapes by which he has defined the *compotier* and the glass, Cézanne shows to what a point the urge of this harmonic sense controlled even his vision of the object. Apart from these two objects rectangular and spherical volumes predominate. That is to say, the forms are the most elementary possible. But the circles of the *compotier* and glass seen in perspective give us ovals, and the oval is a form that evokes a different kind of sentiment altogether, as one can see by its disturbing effect in Gothic architecture. It harmonizes ill with the circle and the right line. So that one is not astonished to find that Cézanne has deformed them into oblongs with rounded ends. This deformation deprives the oval of its elegance and thinness and gives it the same character of gravity and amplitude that the spheres possess. One may note, by the by, that this deformation occurs constantly in early Chinese art, and doubtless at the dictates of the same instinctive feeling.

It is probable that Cézanne was himself ignorant of these deformations. I doubt if he deliberately calculated them; they came almost as an unconscious response to a need for the most evident formal harmony. We have seen many similar deformations since Cézanne's day, sometimes justified and sometimes mere responses to the demands of fashion, than which nothing more tiresome can be imagined. A deformation which is not an imaginative and harmonic necessity is only a piece of snobbish orthodoxy. The snobbists of the 'eighties were not likely to be tender to the "ill-drawn" "Compotier" of Cézanne.

The critic, I hold, should be loyal enough to his own impressions to confess to what is probably due to his own defects. I must admit therefore that there is one passage in this otherwise consummate design of which the meaning escapes me. I cannot see the necessity of the shadow cast by a half-opened drawer in the kitchen table. This vertical shadow troubles me. It seems to check the horizontal and slightly diagonal movements of the napkin-folds and to lessen their suavity. It is precisely because otherwise this comparison seems to me of so rare a perfection and so rigorous an exactitude that it disturbs me always to feel a temptation to cover this part of the canvas with an indiscreet finger. It is an experiment that the reader can easily try on the reproduction, and at least settle the point for himself.

It is easy to see that with so strong a feeling for volumes and masses, with the desire to state them in shapes of the utmost precision, the contours of objects became almost an obsession to Cézanne. It is evident that for a painter who is mainly occupied in relations of planes those planes which are presented to the eye at a sharp angle, that is to say in strong foreshortening, are the cause of a certain anxiety. The last of this series of planes forms the contour, and is a plane reduced to a line. This poses a terrible question—the plane which has no extension on the surface of the canvas has yet to suggest its full extension in the picture-space. It is upon that that the complete recession, the rotundity and volume of the form depends. The very fact that this edge of the object often appears with exceptional clearness complicates matters by bringing the eye back, as it were, to the surface of the canvas.

For the decorative painter whose main object is the organization of his design upon the surface, this is no difficulty, rather an advantage; but for painters to whom the plastic construction is all-important it becomes serious. For them, the contour becomes at once a fascination and a dread. One can see this for Cézanne in his drawings. He almost always repeats the contour with several parallel strokes as though to avoid any one too definite and arresting statement, to suggest that at this point there is a sequence of more and more foreshortened planes. He has to forego the quality of the linealist. The harmonious sweep of a contour which fascinates a Boticelli or an Ingres is not for him. And here again he shows his affinity with Rembrandt.

For the pure Impressionists this question of the contour was not so insistent. Preoccupied as they were by the continuity of the visual weft, contour had no special meaning for them; it was defined more or less—often vaguely—by the sum of indications of tone. But for Cézanne, with his intellectual vigour, his passion for lucid articulation and solid construction, it became an obsession. We find the traces of this throughout in this still-life. He actually draws the contour with his brush, generally in a bluish grey. Naturally the curvature of this line is sharply contrasted with his parallel hatchings, and arrests the eye too much. He then returns upon it incessantly by repeated hatchings which gradually heap up round the contour to a great thickness. The contour is continually being lost and then recovered again. The pertinacity and anxiety with which he thus seeks to conciliate the firmness of the contour and its recession from the eye is very remarkable. It naturally lends a certain heaviness, almost a clumsiness, to the effect; but it ends by giving to the forms that impressive solidity and weight which we have noticed. And indeed we have to admit that the conciliation is attained. At first sight the volumes and contours declare themselves boldly to the eye. They are of a surprising simplicity, and are clearly apprehended. But the more one looks the more they elude any precise definition. The apparent continuity of the contour is illusory, for it changes in quality throughout each particle of its length. There is no uniformity in the tracing of the smallest curve. By reason of these incessant affirmations and contradictions similar results follow from quite different conditions. We thus get at once the notion of extreme simplicity in the general result and of infinite variety in every part. It is this infinitely changing quality of the very stuff of the painting which communicates so vivid a sense of life. In spite of the austerity of the forms, all is vibration and movement. Nothing is less schematic than these works, even when, as here, the general forms have an almost geometrical appearance.

I hope this tiresome analysis of a single picture may be pardoned on the ground that, if one would understand an artist, one must sooner or later come to grips with the actual material of his paintings, since it is there, and nowhere else, that he leaves the precise imprint of his spirit. Moreover, after so elaborate a study, we can pass some of his other still-lifes in rapid review.

The "Still-life with a Ginger Jar," which is also from the Pellerin Collection, is conceived in a very different vein. The extreme gravity of the "Compotier" is here replaced by a certain gaiety and lightness. The tone is comparatively light, and the colour, with its inter-play of violet-rose and bluish tints, is almost brilliant. The opposition, so constant with Cézanne, of grey blue and coppery grey is seen here in a heightened key throughout the background, and against this, the oranges, greens and reds of the fruit tell with glowing intensity and freshness. And in harmony with this mood the forms are almost agitated, and, what is very unusual with Cézanne, there are a number of small and nearly equal volumes with no very marked dominance at any point.

In the "Still-life with a Soup-tureen and Bottle," we find again an extreme economy in the forms, and great simplicity in the relation of volumes. The picture is painted with the utmost freedom and with less elaborate research for the contours which are here almost casual. But the volumes are splendidly assured, and the carelessness—relatively speaking—of the handling gives great purity to the vivid colours of this composition. The tablecloth is of a dark, rich vermilion, modified by bluish inflections where the light falls on it from the window. The citron yellows of the apples and the vivid black of the bottle stand out forcibly on the roses and pale greens which compose the background. The colours here "sing" with a ravishing intensity and purity.

To give so large a space to the consideration of the still-life paintings of this period may seem to demand apology—but it is hard to exaggerate their importance in the expression of Cézanne's genius or the necessity of studying them for its comprehension, because it is in them that he appears to have established his principles of design and his theory of form. A certain phrase let fall by him in his old age has often been quoted. It is to the effect that natural forms all tend to the sphere, the cone, and the cylinder. Whether Cézanne regarded this as a discovery of objective truth, as something like a law of nature, one may doubt. Its real meaning for us at all events must rather be that in his endeavour to handle the infinite diversity of nature he found these forms convenient as a kind of intellectual scaffolding to which the actual form could be related and referred. At least it is very noticeable that his interpretation of natural form always seems to imply that he is at once thinking in terms of extremely simple geometrical forms, and allowing those to be infinitely and infinitesimally modified at each point by his visual sensations. This was, in fact, his solution of the artistic problems, which is always how to find some method of creating things which are at once amenable to human understanding, and have the concrete reality which, in every other experience, eludes our comprehension.

One notes at all events how constantly spherical forms absorb his attention. There is a whole series of still-lifes—most of which are little known—devoted to studies of skulls, sometimes a single skull, sometimes three or four together. It is needless to say that for Cézanne at this period a skull was merely a complicated variation upon the sphere. By this time he had definitely abjured all suggestion of poetical or dramatic allusion; he had arrived at what was to be his most characteristic conception, namely, that the deepest emotions could only exude, like a perfume—it is his own image—from form considered in its pure essence and without reference to associated ideas. And not only do the still-lifes give us the clearest insight into his methods of interpreting form, they also help us to grasp those principles of composition which are characteristic of his work henceforth.

Thus in the "Still-life with a Cineraria" we find an intensely personal conception of composition and one that is utterly at variance with his earlier practice. It may be expressed by saying that it indicates a return to Poussin, a renunciation of Delacroix and his Baroque antecedents. Poussin pushed his intense feeling for balance so far that he habitually divided his compositions by a marked line or gap—as it were a cœsura in the line. And here we find Cézanne, probably quite unconsciously, doing the same thing, by placing the handle of the drawer, the dish of cherries, and the large pot one above the other on the centre line. We find him, too, accepting the utmost parallelism of the objects to the picture plane. Thus, in direct opposition to all Baroque ideas, with an almost exaggerated return to the most primitive practice, he arranges the table exactly in the middle and so as to be seen at right angles, parallel, that is, to the picture plane. Elsewhere we find strongly accented verticals. This extremely rigid architecture is only broken by the repeated diagonals of the canvas stretcher on the floor and the recession of the room to the left; this is balanced by the sharper diagonal of the ladle in the pot and the edge of the napkin as it falls over the table. This architectural rigour and this primitive simplicity in the angle of approach, reveals the essence of Cézanne's conception. Everything here reinforces the idea of gravity, density and resistance. In relation to this may be considered the phrase, reported by M. Joachim Gasquet: "Everything we see is dispersed and disappears. Nature is always the same, but nothing remains of it, nothing of what we see. Our art should give to nature the thrill of continuance with the appearance of all its changes. It should enable us to feel nature as eternal."

The colour here, as always, is profoundly expressive of the same feeling. For all its purity and brilliance it, too, enforces the same pensive and solemn mood. Here the background is of a heavy grey modulated with coppery reds, against which blazes the intense emerald-green of the pot, the violent yellow-greens of the cineraria leaves, the vivid ochres of the table, and the whites of the napkin modelled with hatchings of blue and blue green. Finally a deep note of intense blue enamel in the milk can seems to culminate and control this deep and vivid harmony.

Leonardo da Vinci
A New Device for Study

A WAY OF DEVELOPING AND AROUSING
THE MIND TO VARIOUS INVENTIONS

I cannot forbear to mention among these precepts a new device for study which, although it may seem but trivial and almost ludicrous, is nevertheless extremely useful in arousing the mind to various inventions. And this is, when you look at a wall spotted with stains, or with a mixture of stones, if you have to devise some scene, you may discover a resemblance to various landscapes, beautified with mountains, rivers, rocks, trees, plains, wide valleys and hills in varied arrangement; or again you may see battles and figures in action; or strange faces and costumes, and an endless variety of objects, which you could reduce to complete and well-drawn forms. And these appear on such walls confusedly, like the sound of bells in whose jangle you may find any name or word you choose to imagine.

This famous passage seems to look forward to the experiments of automatic painting, and to abstract art.

Wassily Kandinsky
On the Spiritual in Art[1]

I: Introduction

Every work of art is the child of its time; often it is the mother of our emotions. It follows that each period of culture produces an art of its own, which cannot be repeated. Efforts to revive the art principles of the past at best produce works of art that resemble a stillborn child. For example, it is impossible for us to live and feel as did the ancient Greeks. For this reason those who follow Greek principles in sculpture reach only a similarity of form, while the work remains for all time without a soul. Such imitation resembles the antics of apes: externally a monkey resembles a human being; he will sit holding a book in front of his nose, turning over the pages with a thoughtful air, but his actions have no real significance.

But among the forms of art there is another kind of external similarity, which is founded on a fundamental necessity. When there is, as sometimes happens, a similarity of inner direction in an entire moral and spiritual milieu, a similarity of ideals, at first closely pursued but later lost to sight, a similarity of "inner mood" between one period and another, the logical consequence will be a revival of the external forms which served to express those insights in the earlier age. This may account partially for our sympathy and affinity with and our comprehension of the work of primitives. Like ourselves, these pure artists sought to express only inner[2] and essential feelings in their works; in this process they ignored as a matter of course the fortuitous.

---

[1] From *Concerning the Spiritual in Art* (revised, from the translation by Michael Sadleir, by Francis Golffing, Michael Harrison, and Ferdinand Ostertag). New York: The Macmillan Company, 1949.

[2] A work of art consists of two elements, the inner and the outer.

The inner is the emotion in the soul of the artist; this emotion has the capacity to evoke a similar emotion in the observer.

Being connected with the body, the soul is affected through the medium of the senses— the felt. Emotions are aroused and stirred by what is sensed. Thus the sensed is the bridge,

This great point of inner contact is, in spite of its considerable importance, only one point. Only just now awakening after years of materialism, our soul is infected with the despair born of unbelief, of lack of purpose and aim. The nightmare of materialism, which turned life into an evil, senseless game, is not yet passed; it still darkens the awakening soul. Only a feeble light glimmers, a tiny point in an immense circle of darkness. This light is but a presentiment; and the mind, seeing it, trembles in doubt over whether the light is a dream and the surrounding darkness indeed reality. This doubt and the oppression of materialism separate us sharply from primitives. Our soul rings cracked when we sound it, like a precious vase, dug out of the earth, which has a flaw. For this reason, the primitive phase through which we are now passing, in its present derivative form, must be short-lived.

The two kinds of resemblance between the forms of art of today and of the past can be easily recognized as diametrically opposed. The first, since it is external, has no future. The second, being internal, contains the seed of the future. After a period of materialist temptation, to which the soul almost succumbed, and which it was able to shake off, the soul is emerging, refined by struggle and suffering. Cruder emotions, like fear, joy and grief, which belonged to this time of trial, will no longer attract the artist. He will attempt to arouse more refined emo-

---

i.e., the physical relation, between the immaterial (which is the artist's emotion) and the material, which results in the production of a work of art. And again, what is sensed is the bridge from the material (the artist and his work) to the immaterial (the emotion in the soul of the observer).

The sequence is: emotion (in the artist) → the sensed → the art-work → the sensed → emotion (in the observer).

The two emotions will be like and equivalent to the extent that the work of art is successful. In this respect painting is in no way different from a song: each is a communication. The successful singer arouses in listeners his emotions: the successful painter should do no less.

The inner element, i.e., emotion, must exist; otherwise the work of art is a sham. The inner element determines the form of the work of art.

In order that the inner element, which at first exists only as an emotion, may develop into a work of art, the second element, i.e., the outer, is used as an embodiment. Emotion is always seeking means of expression, a material form, a form that is able to stir the senses. The determining and vital element is the inner one, which controls the outer form, just as an idea in the mind determines the words we use, and not *vice versa*. The determination of the form of a work of art is therefore determined by the irresistible inner force: this is the only unchanging law in art. A beautiful work is the consequence of an harmonious cooperation of the inner and the outer; i.e., a painting is an intellectual organism which, like every other material organism, consists of many parts. (*This explanation by Kandinsky of the relation between internal and external, or inner and outer, is a slightly revised version of a translation by Arthur Jerome Eddy of part of an article by Kandinsky which appeared in* Der Sturm, Berlin, 1913; *cf.* Cubists and Post-Impressionists, A. C. McClurg, Chicago, 1914, pp. 119–20.).

tions, as yet unnamed. Just as he will live a complicated and subtle life, so his work will give to those observers capable of feeling them emotions subtle beyond words.

The observer of today is seldom capable of feeling such vibrations. He seeks instead an imitation of nature with a practical function (for example, a portrait, in the ordinary sense) or an intuition of nature involving a certain interpretation (e.g., "impressionist" painting) or an inner feeling expressed by nature's forms (as we say, a picture of "mood"[3]). When they are true works of art, such forms fulfil their purposes and nourish the spirit. Though this remark applies to the first case, it applies more strongly to the third, in which the spectator hears an answering chord in himself. Such emotional chords cannot be superficial or without value; the feeling of such a picture can indeed deepen and purify the feeling of the spectator. The spirit at least is preserved from coarseness: such pictures tune it up, as a tuning fork does the strings of a musical instrument. But the subtilization and extension of this chord in time and space remained limited, and the potential power of art is not exhausted by it.

Imagine a building, large or small, divided into rooms; each room is covered with canvases of various sizes, perhaps thousands of them. They represent bits of nature in color—animals in sunlight or shadow, or drinking, standing in water, or lying on grass; close by, a "Crucifixion," by a painter who does not believe in Christ; then flowers, and human figures, sitting, standing, or walking, and often naked; there are many naked women foreshortened from behind; apples and silver dishes; a portrait of Mister So-and-So; sunsets; a lady in pink; a flying duck; a portrait of Lady X; flying geese; a lady in white; some cattle in shadow, flecked by brilliant sunlight; a portrait of Ambassador Y; a lady in green. All this is carefully reproduced in a book with the name of the artist and the name of the picture. Book in hand, people go from wall to wall, turning pages, reading names. Then they depart, neither richer nor poorer, again absorbed by their affairs, which have nothing to do with art. Why did they come? In every painting a whole life is mysteriously enclosed, a whole life of tortures, doubts, of hours of enthusiasm and inspiration.

What is the direction of that life? What is the cry of the artist's

---

[3] Alas, this word, which in the past was used to describe the poetical aspirations of an artist's soul, has been misused and finally ridiculed. Was there ever a great word that the crowd did not try immediately to desecrate?

LIGHT PICTURE NO. 188—WASSILY KANDINSKY (*Guggenheim Museum, New York*)

soul, if the soul was involved in the creation? "To send light into the darkness of men's hearts—such is the obligation of the artist," said Schumann. "A painter is a man who can draw and paint everything," said Tolstoi.

Of these two definitions we must choose the second, if we think of the exhibition just described. With more or less skill, virtuosity and vigor, objects are created on a canvas, "painted" either roughly or smoothly. To bring the whole into harmony on the canvas is what leads to a work of art. With cold eye and indifferent mind the public regards the work. Connoisseurs admire "technique," as one might admire a tight-rope walker, or enjoy the "painting quality," as one might enjoy a cake. But hungry souls go hungry away.

The public ambles through the rooms, saying "nice" or "interesting." Those who could speak have said nothing, those who could hear have heard nothing. This condition is called "art for art's sake." This annihilation of internal vibrations that constitute the life of the colors, this dwindling away of artistic force, is called "art for art's sake."

The artist seeks material rewards for his facility, inventiveness and sensitivity. His purpose becomes the satisfaction of ambition and greediness. In place of intensive cooperation among artists, there is a battle for goods. There is excessive competition, over-production. Hatred, partisanship, cliques, jealousy, intrigues are the natural consequences of an aimless, materialist art.[4]

The public turns away from artists who have higher ideals, who find purpose in an art without purpose.

"Comprehension" is educating the spectator to the point of view of the artist. It has been said that art is the child of its time. But such an art can only repeat artistically what is already clearly realized by the contemporary. Since it is not germinative, but only a child of the age, and unable to become a mother of the future, it is a castrated art. It is transitory; it dies morally the moment the atmosphere that nourished it alters.

There is another art capable of further developments, which also springs from contemporary feeling. Not only is it simultaneously its echo and mirror but it possesses also an awakening prophetic power which can have far-reaching and profound effect.

The spiritual life to which art belongs, and of which it is one of the mightiest agents, is a complex but definite movement above and beyond, which can be translated into simplicity. This movement is that of cognition. Although it may take different forms, it holds basically to the same internal meaning and purpose.

The causes of the necessity to move forward and upward—through sweat, suffering, evil and torments—are obscure. When a stage has been reached at which obstacles have been cleared from the way, a hidden, malevolent hand scatters new obstacles. The path often seems blocked or destroyed. But someone always comes to the rescue—someone like

---

[4] A few exceptions do not affect the truth of this sad and ominous picture; even the exceptions are chiefly believers in the doctrine of art for art's sake. They serve, therefore, a higher ideal, but one which is ultimately a useless waste of their strength. External beauty is one element in a spiritual milieu. But beyond this positive fact (that what is beautiful is good) lies the weakness of a talent not used to the full (*talent* in the biblical sense).

ourselves in everything, but with a secretly implanted power of "vision."

He sees and points out. This high gift (often a heavy burden) at times he would gladly relinquish. But he cannot. Scorned and disliked, he drags the heavy weight of resisting humanity forward and upward.

Sometimes, after his body has vanished from the earth, men try by every means to recreate it in marble, iron, bronze, or stone, and on an enormous scale. As though there were any intrinsic value in the bodily existence of such divine martyrs and servants of humanity, who despised the flesh but wanted only to serve the spirit. But raising marble is evidence that a number of men have reached the point where the one they would now honor formerly stood alone.

II: Movement

The life of the spirit may be graphically represented as a large acute-angled triangle, divided horizontally into unequal parts, with the narrowest segment uppermost. The lower the segment, the greater it is in breadth, depth and area.

The whole triangle moves slowly, almost invisibly forward and upward. Where the apex was today, the second segment will be tomorrow; what today can be understood only by the apex, is tomorrow the thought and feeling of the second segment.[5]

At the apex of the highest segment often stands one man. His joyful vision is the measure of his inner sorrow. Even those who are nearest to him in sympathy do not understand. Angrily they abuse him as a charlatan or madman. So in his lifetime Beethoven stood, solitary and insulted.[6] How long will it be before a larger segment of the triangle reaches the spot where he once stood? Despite memorials, are there really many who have risen to his level?[7]

There are artists in each segment of the triangle. He who can see beyond the limits of his own segment is a prophet and helps the advance. But those who are near-sighted, or who retard the movement for base reasons, are fully understood and acclaimed. The larger the segment (i.e., the lower it lies in the triangle), the greater the number of

---

5 This "today" and "tomorrow" correspond to the biblical "days" of the Creation.

6 Weber, composer of "Der Freischütz," said of Beethoven's Seventh Symphony: "The extravagances of genius have reached the limit; Beethoven is now ripe for an asylum." On the opening phrase, a reiterated "E," the Abbé Stadler said to his neighbor: "That same old 'E' again; he's run out of ideas, the bore." (*Beethoven* by August Göllerich, p. 1 in the series, *Die Musik*, Ed. by R. Strauss.)

7 Many of our monuments are melancholy answers to the question.

people capable of understanding the artist. Every segment hungers, consciously or unconsciously, for adequate spiritual satisfactions. These are offered by artists, and for such satisfactions the segment below will tomorrow stretch out eager hands.

This schematical presentation, however, does not exploit the entire picture of spiritual life. Among other things it does not show the dark side, a great, dead black spot. It happens too often that the spiritual "bread" becomes nourishment for many who live already in a higher segment. This bread becomes poisonous for such eaters: in smaller quantities it has the effect that the soul gradually sinks from a high segment to a lower one. When used in greater quantity, this poison casts the soul into ever lower divisions. In one of his novels, Sienkiewicz compares the spiritual life to swimming; the man who does not strive tirelessly against sinking will go under. In this strait a man's talent (again in the biblical sense) becomes a curse—not only for the artist, but also for those who partake of his poison. The artist uses his strength to flatter base needs; in an ostensibly artistic form he presents what is impure, what draws weaker elements to him, betrays them and helps them to betray themselves, while they convince themselves and others that they are spiritually thirsty, that they can quench their thirst at this spring. Such art does not help the forward movement, but hinders it, dragging back those who are striving to press onward, and spreading pestilence abroad.

During periods when art has no champion, when true spiritual food is wanting, there is retrogression in the spiritual world. Souls fall ceaselessly from the higher to the lower segments of the triangle, and the whole seems motionless, or even to move down and backwards. During these mute and blind times men attribute a special and exclusive value to external success, for they judge them by outward results, thinking of material well-being. They hail some technical advance, which can help nothing but the body. Real spiritual gains are undervalued or ignored.

The love visionaries, the hungry of soul, are ridiculed or considered mentally abnormal. But the rare souls, who cannot be lulled into lethargy and who feel dark longings for spiritual life, knowledge and advancement, sound, amid the vulgar materialistic chorus, lamentful and disconsolate. The spiritual night falls deeper and deeper around such frightened souls; and their bearers, tortured and weakened by doubt and fear, often prefer complete obliteration to this gradual darkening.

In such periods art ministers to lower needs and is used for material ends. It seeks its content in crude substance, because it knows nothing fine. Objects remaining the same, their reproduction is thought to be the aim of art. The question "what?" disappears; only the question "how?" remains. By what method are these material objects reproduced? The method becomes a rationale. Art loses its soul.

The search for the "how" continues. Art becomes specialized, comprehensible only to artists, and they complain of public indifference to their work. For, since the artist in such times has no need to *say* much, but only to be notorious for some small originality among a small group of patrons and connoisseurs (which incidentally is also profitable), many externally gifted and skilful people come forward, so easy does the conquest of art appear. In each "art center" there are thousands of such artists, of whom the majority seek only some new mannerism, producing millions of works of art, without enthusiasm, with cold hearts and souls asleep.

Meanwhile competition grows. The savage battle for success becomes more and more material. Small groups who have fought their way to the top entrench themselves in the territory they have won. The public, left behind, looks on bewildered, loses interest and turns away.

Despite this confusion, this chaos, this wild hunt for notoriety, the spiritual triangle moves ahead, slowly but surely, with irresistible strength moving ever forward and upward.

An invisible Moses descends from the mountain and sees the dancing around the golden calf. But he brings to man fresh stores of wisdom.

His voice, inaudible to the crowd, is first heard by the artist. Almost unwittingly artists follow the voice. In the very question "how" lies a hidden seed of renascence. Sterile though this "how" may be on the whole, there is always a possibility that the "difference" which we still call personal distinction may be able to see, in the objects about it, not only what is purely material, but also something less corporeal than was seen in the period of realism, when the universal aim was to reproduce things "as they really are," without indulging in fancies.[8]

If the emotional power of the artist can overwhelm the "how" and

---

[8] Frequent reference is made to "material" and "non-material," and to the intermediate phrases, "more" and "less material." Is everything material—or is *everything* spiritual? Can the distinctions we make between matter and spirit be nothing but relative modifications of one or the other? Thought, which although a product of the spirit can be defined with exact science, is matter, but of fine and not coarse substance. Is whatever cannot be *touched* spiritual? The discussion lies beyond the scope of this little book; all that matters here is that the boundaries drawn should not be too definite.

give free scope to his feelings, then art has started on the path by which she will not fail to find the "what" she lost, the "what" which forms the spiritual necessity of the nascent awakening. This "what" will no longer be the material, objective "what" of a stagnant period, but an artistic substance, the soul of art, without which the body (i.e., the "how") can never be healthy, whether an individual or a whole people.

This "what" is the substance which only art can comprise, which only art can clearly express by those means of expression that are proper to it.

III: Spiritual Turning-Point

The spiritual triangle moves slowly ahead. Today one of the largest of the lower segments has reached the point of using the first battle-cry of materialism. The inhabitants of this segment call themselves Jews, Catholics, Protestants, etc. Really they are atheists, and this a few of the boldest, or the narrowest, openly avow. "Heaven is empty," "God is dead." In politics they are liberals or progressives. The fear and hatred which yesterday they felt for these political creeds they now direct against anarchism, of which they know nothing but its dread name.

In economics these people are socialists. They sharpen the sword of justice to slay the hydra of capitalism.

Because they have never solved any problem independently, but are dragged in a cart, as it were, by the noblest of their fellow-men, who have sacrificed themselves, they know nothing of toil, which they watch from a distance. Therefore they rate it lightly, putting their trust in unexceptionable precepts and infallible cures.

The men of the segment next below are blindly dragged higher by those just described. But they cling to their old position, full of dread of the unknown and of betrayal.

The higher segments are not only atheists but justify their godlessness with strange words; for example, those of Virchow[9]—so unworthy of a scholar—"I have dissected many corpses, but never yet come upon a soul."

In politics they are generally leftists, with a knowledge of different parliamentary procedures; they read the political articles in the journals. In economics they are socialists of various shades and can support their "principles" with numerous quotations, passing from Schweitzer's *Emma* via Ricardo's *Iron Law of Wages,* to Marx's *Capital,* and still further.

9 Rudolf Virchow, 1821–1902, German physician and pathologist.

In these higher segments other categories of ideas gradually begin to appear—science and art, literature and music.

In science these men are positivists, recognizing only what can be weighed and measured. Everything beyond they consider harmful non-sense, as they did yesterday the theories which are "proven" today.

In art they are realists, which means that they recognize and value the personaliy, individuality and temperament of the artist up to a certain definite point. This point has been fixed by others, and they believe in it without reserve.

Despite their patent and well-ordered security, despite their infallible principles, there lurks among these higher segments a hidden fear, a nervousness, a sense of insecurity like that in the minds of passengers on a large, solid, ocean-going liner on the high seas when, the continent left behind in mist, dark clouds gather, and the winds raise the water into black mountains. This is the result of their upbringing. They know that the philosophers, statesmen and artists whom they revere today were spurned as arrivistes, gangsters and frauds yesterday. The higher the segment in the triangle, the better-defined this fear, this *modern* sense of insecurity. Here and there are people with eyes that see, minds that correlate. They ask: "If the knowledge of day before yesterday was overturned by that of yesterday, and that of yesterday by that of today, is it not possible that what we call knowledge now will be overturned by the knowledge of tomorrow?" And the bravest of them answer: "It's possible."

Then people appear who can discern matters which the science of today has not yet "explained." They ask: "Will science, if it continues on the road it has followed for so long, ever attain the solution of these questions? And if it does, will man be able to rely on its answers?" In these segments are professional men of learning who remember the time when facts now recognized by the academies as firmly established were scorned. There are also aestheticians who write about an art which was condemned yesterday. In these books they remove the barriers over which art has most recently stepped and they set up new ones. They do not notice that they are erecting barriers not in front of art, but behind it. If they do, they write fresh books and hastily set the barriers a little further on. This process will go on until it is realized that the most advanced principle of aesthetics can never be of value to the future, but only to the past. No theory can be laid down for those things that lie in the realm of the immaterial. That which has no material existence cannot be materially crystallized. That which belongs to the spirit of the future can only be realized in feeling, and the talent of the artist is the only road to feeling. Theory is the lamp which sheds light on the crystallized ideas of the past.[10] As we rise higher in the triangle, we find that confusion increases, just as a city built on the most correct architectural plan may be shaken by the uncontrollable force of nature. Humanity is living in such a spiritual city, subject to sudden disturbances for which neither architects nor mathematicians have made allowance. In one place lies a great wall fallen down like a house of cards, in another are the ruins of a huge tower which once stretched to the sky, built on presumably immortal spiritual pillars. The abandoned churchyard quakes, forgotten graves open, and from them rise forgotten ghosts. Spots appear on the sun, and the sun grows dark; and what power is left against the dark? In this city also live men who are dulled by false knowledge, who hear no crash, who are blinded by strange wisdom, so that they say "our sun shines brighter every day, and soon even the last spots will disappear." But even these people shall hear and see.

Still higher, we no longer find bewilderment. There work is going on which boldly criticizes the pillars men have set up. There we find other professional men of learning who test matter again and again, whom tremble before no problem, and who finally cast doubt on that very *matter* which was yesterday the foundation of everything, so that the whole universe rocks. The theory of the electrons, that is, of waves in motion, designed to replace matter completely, finds at this moment bold champions who overstep here and there the limits of caution and perish in the conquest of the new scientific fortress. They are like self-sacrificing soldiers making a desperate attack. But "no fort is unconquerable."

Thus facts are being established which the science of yesterday dubbed frauds. Even newspapers, which are the most obsequious servants of worldly success and of the masses, which trim their sails to every wind, find themselves compelled to modify their ironical judgments on the "marvels" of science, and even to abandon them. Many learned men, among them ultramaterialists, are dedicating their strength to scientific research on obscure problems, which can no longer be lied about or passed over in silence.[11]

10 Cf. Chap. VII.

11 Zöllner, Wagner, Butleroff (Petersburg), Crookes (London), etc.; later on, C. H. Richet, C. Flammarion. The Parisian newspaper *Le Matin* published about two years ago the dis-

Furthermore, the number is increasing of those men who put no trust in the methods of material science when it deals with questions which have to do with "non-matter," or matter that is not accessible to our senses. Just as art is looking for help from the primitives, so these men are turning to half-forgotten times in order to get help from half-forgotten methods. However, these methods are still alive and in use among nations whom we, from the height of our knowledge, have been accustomed to regard with pity and scorn. To such nations belong the people of India, who from time to time confront our scholars with problems which we have either passed without notice or brushed aside.[12] Madame Blavatzky was the first person, after a life of many years in India, to see a connection between these "savages" and our "civilization." In that moment rose one of the most important spiritual movements, one which numbers a great many people today, and has even assumed a material form in the Theosophical Society. This society consists of groups who seek to approach the problem of the spirit by way of *inner* knowledge. Their methods, in opposition to positivism, derive from an ancient wisdom, which has been formulated with relative precision.[13] The theory of Theosophy which serves as the basis of this movement was set forth by Blavatzky in the form of a catechism in which the pupil receives definite answers to his questions from the theosophical point of view.[14] Theosophy, according to Blavatzky, is synonymous with *eternal truth.* "The new torch-bearer of truth will find the minds of men prepared for his message, a language ready for him in which to clothe the new truths he brings, an organization awaiting his arrival, which will remove the merely mechanical, material obstacles and difficulties from his path." And then Blavatzky continues: "The earth will be heaven in the twenty-first century in comparison with what it is now," and with these words ends her book.

Skeptical though we may be regarding the tendency of the theosophists toward theorizing and their excessive anticipation of definite

coveries of the two last-named, under the title "Je la constate, mais je ne l'explique pas." Finally C. Lombroso, the inventor of the anthropological method of diagnosing crime, and Eusapio Palladino have turned to occult sciences and recognized transcendental phenomena. Besides individual scholars who have dedicated themselves to such studies, whole organizations have sprung up in pursuit of similar aims (e.g., Société des Etudes Psychiques, in Paris, which has even instituted committees in France to acquaint the public with the results of its research).

12 Frequently in such cases use is made of the word hypnotism; that same hypnotism which, in its earlier form of mesmerism, was disdainfully put aside by various learned bodies.

13 See Rudolph Steiner's *Theosophy* and his article on methods of cognition in *Lucifer-Gnosis.*

14 H. P. Blavatzky, *The Key of Theosophy,* London, 1889.

answers in lieu of immense question-marks, it remains a fundamentally spiritual movement. This movement represents a strong agent in the general atmosphere, presaging deliverance to oppressed and gloomy hearts.

When religion, science and morality are shaken (the last by the strong hand of Nietzsche) and when outer supports threaten to fall, man withdraws his gaze from externals and turns it inwards. Literature, music and art are the most sensitive spheres in which this spiritual revolution makes itself felt. They reflect the dark picture of the present time and show the importance of what was at first only a little point of light noticed by the few. Perhaps they even grow dark in their turn, but they turn away from the soulless life of the present toward those substances and ideas that give free scope to the non-material strivings of the soul.

Such a poet in the realm of literature is Maeterlinck. He takes us into a world which may be called fantastic, or more justly transcendental. "La Princesse Maleine," "Les Sept Princesses," "Les Aveugles," etc., are not people of past times like the heroes in Shakespeare. They are souls lost in fog, threatened with asphyxiation, eternally menaced by some invisible and somber force.

Spiritual darkness, the insecurity of ignorance and fear pervade the world in which they move. Maeterlinck is perhaps one of the first prophets, one of the first reporters and clairvoyants of the decadence just described. The gloom of the spiritual atmosphere, the terrible but all-guiding hand, the sense of utter fear, the feeling of having strayed from the path, the absence of a guide, all these are clearly felt in his works.[15]

Maeterlinck creates his atmosphere principally by artistic means. His material machinery (gloomy mountains, moonlight, marshes, wind, the cries of owls, etc.) really plays a symbolic role and helps to give the inner note.[16] Maeterlinck's principal technical weapon is words. The

[15] In the front rank of such seers of the decadence belongs also Alfred Kubin. With irresistible force both Kubin's drawings and his novel *Die andere Seite* seem to draw us into the terrible atmosphere of harsh vacuity.

[16] When one of Maeterlinck's plays was produced in St. Petersburg under his own guidance, he himself at one of the rehearsals had a tower represented by a plain piece of hanging linen. It was of no importance to him to have elaborate scenery prepared. He did as children, the greatest imaginers of all time, always do in their games: they use a stick for a horse or create entire regiments of cavalry out of paper birds, by which a fold of the paper changes a knight into a horse (Kügelgen, *Erinnerungen eines alten Mannes*). On similar lines the imagination of the spectator plays an important part in the modern theater, especially in that of Russia. This is a notable element in the transition from the material to the spiritual in the theater of the future.

word is an inner sound. It springs partly, perhaps principally, from the object denoted. But if the object is not seen, but only its name heard, the mind of the hearer receives an abstract impression only of the object dematerialized, and a corresponding vibration is immediately set up in the "heart." Thus a green, yellow, or red tree in a meadow are accidental realizations of the concept tree which we formed upon hearing the word.

The apt use of a word (in its poetical sense), its repetition, twice, three times, or even more frequently, according to the need of the poem, will not only tend to intensify the internal structure but also bring out unsuspected spiritual properties in the word itself. Further, frequent repetition of a word (a favorite game of children, forgotten in later life) deprives the word of its external reference. Similarly, the symbolic reference of a designated object tends to be forgotten and only the sound is retained. We hear this pure sound, unconsciously perhaps, in relation to the concrete or immaterial object. But in the latter case pure sound exercises a direct impression on the soul. The soul attains to an objectless vibration, even more complicated, I might say more transcendent, than the reverberations released by the sound of a bell, a stringed instrument, or a fallen board. In this direction lie great possibilities for the literature of the future. This verbal potency has already been used in an embryonic form in *Serres Chaudes*.[17] An ostensibly neutral word in its felt quality will become somber as Maeterlinck uses it. A familiar word like "hair," used in a certain way, intensifies an atmosphere of sorrow or despair. This is Maeterlinck's method. He makes us realize that thunder, lightning and a moon behind driving clouds are external, material means, which on the stage, even more than in nature, resemble the bogey-man of childhood: imaginings.

Inner forces do not lose their strength and effect so easily.[18] A word which has two meanings, the first direct, the second indirect, is the material of poetry and literature, which these arts alone can manipulate and through which they speak to the soul.

Something similar may be seen in the music of Wagner. His famous *Leitmotiv* is an attempt to give personality to his characters by something more than theatrical paraphernalia, makeup and light effects. His method of using a definite *motiv* is a musical method. It creates a spiritual atmosphere by means of a musical phrase which precedes the

---

17 *Serres Chaudes, suivies de Quinze Chansons*, by Maurice Maeterlinck, Brussels, 1899.

18 A comparison of the work of Poe and Maeterlinck shows the course of artistic transition from the material to the abstract.

hero, which he seems to radiate from any distance.[19] The most modern musicians, like Debussy, create a spiritual impression, often taken from nature, but embodied in purely musical form. For this reason Debussy is often classed with the impressionist painters, on the ground that he resembles these painters in using natural phenomena for the purposes of art. Whatever truth there may be in this comparison merely accentuates the fact that the various arts of today learn from each other and often resemble each other. But it would be rash to say that this proposition is an exhaustive statement of Debussy's significance. Despite a certain similarity to the impressionists, he shows such a strong drive toward essential content that we recognize at once in his work the flawed, vocal soul of the present, with all its harassing anxiety and jangled nerves. Debussy, even in his impressionist tone-pictures, never uses the wholly material note characteristic of program music, but relies on the creation of an abstract impression.

Russian music (Moussorgsky) has had a great influence on Debussy. So it is not surprising that he stands in close relation to the young Russian composers, the chief of whom is Scriabin. There is an internal affinity in the compositions of the two men, and they have identical faults, which disturb the listener. He is often snatched from a series of modern discords into the charm of conventional beauty. He feels himself often insulted, tossed about like a ball between the internal and the external beauty. The internal beauty is achieved through necessity and renunciation of the conventionally beautiful. To those who are not accustomed to it, it appears as ugliness; humanity in general inclines to external beauty and knows nothing of internal beauty. Almost alone in abandoning conventional beauty and in sanctioning *every* means of expression is the Austrian composer, Arnold Schönberg. This "publicity hound," "fraud," and "dilettante" says in his *Harmonielehre:* "Every combination of notes, every advance is possible, but I am beginning to feel that there are definite rules and conditions which incline me to the use of this or that dissonance."[20]

In other words, Schönberg realizes that the greatest freedom of all, the freedom of an unfettered art, can never be absolute. Every age achieves a certain measure of this freedom, but beyond the boundaries of its freedom the mightiest genius can never go. But this measure must

---

[19] Frequent attempts have shown that such a spiritual atmosphere can belong not only to heroes but to any human being. Very sensitive people cannot, for example, abide a room in which there has been a person who is spiritually antagonistic to them, even though they know nothing of his existence.

[20] *Die Musik*, p. 104, from the *Harmonielehre* (Verlag der Universal Edition).

in each instance be exhausted, let the stubborn resist as they may. Schönberg is endeavoring to make complete use of his freedom and has already discovered mines of new beauty in his search for spiritual structure. His music leads us to where musical experience is a matter not of the ear, but of the soul—and from this point begins the music of the future.

A parallel course has been followed by the impressionists in painting. It is seen in its dogmatic and most naturalistic form in the theory of neo-impressionism which at the same time reaches into the abstract. The theory of neo-impressionism is to put on the canvas the whole glitter and brilliance of nature, and not only isolated aspects.[21]

It is interesting to note three nearly contemporary and quite different movements in painting:

1) Rossetti and his pupil Burne-Jones, with their followers;
2) Böcklin with his scion Stuck, and their school;
3) Segantini, and his worthless train of formal imitators.

I have chosen these three groups to illustrate the search for the abstract in art. Rossetti sought to revive the abstract form of the Pre-Raphaelites. Böcklin busied himself with mythological and legendary scenes but, in contrast to Rossetti, gave a strongly corporeal form to his legendary figures. Segantini, outwardly the most material of the three, selected the most ordinary objects (hills, stones, cattle, etc.), often painting them with the minutest realism, but he never failed to create a spiritual as well as a material value, so that he is really the most non-material of the trio.

These men sought for the "inner" by way of the "external."

By another road, and one more painterly, a great seeker after a new sense of form approached the same problem. Cézanne made a living thing out of a teacup, or rather, in a teacup he realized the existence of something alive. He raised still life to the point where it ceased to be inanimate.

He painted things as he painted human beings, because he was endowed with the gift of divining the internal life in everything. He achieved expressive color and a form that harmonizes this color with an almost mathematical abstraction. A man, a tree, an apple, are not *represented,* but used by Cézanne in building up a painterly thing called a "picture." The same intention actuates the work of one of the greatest

21 See, for example, Paul Signac: *D'Eugène Delacroix au Neo-Impressionisme,* Paris, 1899.

of the young Frenchmen, Henri-Matisse. He paints "pictures," and in
these "pictures" endeavors to render the divine. To attain this end he
requires nothing but the subject to be painted (human being or whatever it may be) and means that belong to painting alone, color and form.

By personal inclination, because he is French and because he is specially gifted as a colorist, Henri-Matisse is apt to lay too much stress
on color. Like Debussy, he cannot always refrain from conventional
beauty; impressionism is in his blood. One sees pictures by Matisse
which are full of great internal vitality, produced by internal necessity;
but also pictures which possess only external charm, because of an
external impulse (how often one is reminded of Manet in this). Here
we find typical French subtlety and delicacy, a melodic quality that is
raised from time to time to a summit above the clouds.

But in the work of another great young artist in Paris, the Spaniard
Picasso, there is never any suspicion of conventional beauty. Torn by
the need for self-expression, Picasso hurries from means to means. A
gulf appears between consecutive modes of expression, because Picasso
leaps; he is continually found by his bewildered followers at a point
different from that where they last saw him. No sooner do they think
they have caught him than he has changed once more. In this way
cubism arose, the latest of the French movements, which is treated in
detail in Part II. Here Picasso is trying to arrive at construction by way
of numerical proportion. In his latest works (1911) he reaches through
logic an annihilation of materiality, not, however, by dissolution of it,
but through a kind of fragmentation of its separate parts and a constructive dispersal of these fragments over the canvas. But, strangely
enough, he seems to wish to preserve the appearance of materiality. He
shrinks from no innovation, and when color distracts him he throws it
overboard, painting a picture in ochre and white; these problems co-
stitute his main strength.

Matisse—color. Picasso—form. Two great signposts pointing toward
a great end.

IV: The Pyramid

At different points along the road are the different arts, each saying
what it is best able to say, by methods peculiarly its own. Despite differences, or perhaps even because of them, the various arts have never been
closer to each other than in this recent hour of spiritual crisis.

In each expression is the seed of an effort toward the non-representational, abstract and internal structure. Consciously or unconsciously they are obeying Socrates' advice: "Know thyself." Consciously or unconsciously, artists are studying and investigating their material, weighing the spiritual value of those elements with which it is their privilege to work.

The natural result of this work is a comparison of the elements of one art with those of another. Music is found to be the best teacher. For some centuries, with few exceptions, music has been the art which has devoted itself not to the reproduction of natural phenomena, but to the expression of the artist's soul and to the creation of an autonomous life of musical sound.

A painter who finds no satisfaction in mere representation, however artistic, in his longing to express his internal life, cannot but envy the ease with which music, the least material of the arts today, achieves this end. He naturally seeks to apply the means of music to his own art. And from this results that modern desire for rhythm in painting, for mathematical, abstract construction, for repeated notes of color, for setting color in motion, and so on.

Comparison of means among the arts and the learning of one art from another can only be successful when the application of the lesson is fundamental. One art must learn how another uses its method, so that its own means may then be used according to the same fundamental principles, but in its own medium. The artist must not forget that each means implies its proper application, and that it is for him to discover this application.

In the application of form, music can achieve results which are beyond the reach of painting. But painting is ahead of music in several particulars. Music, for example, has at its disposal duration of time; while painting can present to the spectator the whole content of its message at one moment.[22] Music, which is outwardly unfettered by nature, needs no external form for its expression.[23] Painting is still almost exclusively dependent on natural forms and phenomena. Its

[22] These statements of difference, like everything in the world, are relative; for music can in a certain sense dispense with extension of time, and painting make use of it.

[23] How miserably music fails when attempting to express material appearances is proved by the affected absurdity of program music. Quite lately such experiments have been made. The imitation in sound of croaking frogs, of farmyard noises, of knife-grinding, makes an excellent night-club act and is amusing enough. But in serious music such extravagance is a warning against imitation of nature. Nature has her own language, and a powerful one; this language cannot be imitated. The sound of a farmyard is never successfully reproduced and is unnecessary waste of time. The mood of nature can be imparted by every art, but only by the artistic rendering of its inner spirit.

business is now to test its strength and means, to know itself, as music has done for a long time, and then to use its powers in a truly painterly way, to a creative end.

Self-examination may divide each art from the rest, while their mutual investigation reunites them in their inward effort. Each art has its peculiar force, which cannot be replaced by that of any other. Finally, the peculiar power of the different arts may be coordinated, and this coordination will eventually lead to an art which we may glimpse even now—the truly monumental art.

Everyone who immerses himself in the hidden internal treasures of his art is an enviable co-worker on the spiritual pyramid which will reach to heaven.

Guillaume Apollinaire
The Cubist Painters[1]

1. The plastic virtues and nature.
The plastic virtues: purity, unity, and truth, keep nature in subjection.

The rainbow is bent, the seasons quiver, the crowds push on to death, science undoes and remakes what already exists, whole worlds disappear forever from our understanding, our mobile images repeat themselves, or revive their vagueness, and the colors, the odors, and the sounds to which we are sensitive astonish us, then disappear from nature—all to no purpose.

This monster, beauty, is not eternal.

We know that our breath has had no beginning and will never cease, but our first conceptions are of the creation and the end of the world.

However, too many painters still adore plants, stones, the sea, or men.

We quickly get used to the bondage of the mystericus. And servitude ends by creating real delights.

Workers are allowed to control the universe, yet gardeners have even less respect for nature than have artists.

The time has come for us to be the masters. And good will is not enough to make victory certain.

On this side of eternity dance the mortal form of love, whose accursed discipline is summed up by the name "nature".

---

[1] From *The Cubist Painters* (transl. by Lionel Abel). New York: George Wittenborn, Inc., 1944.

Flame the symbol of painting. Flame is the symbol of painting, and the three plastic virtues burn with radiance.

Flame has a purity which tolerates nothing alien, and cruelly transforms in its image whatever it touches.

Flame has a magical unity; if it is divided, each fork will be like the single flame.

Finally it has the sublime and incontestable truth of its own light.

Purity. Good western painters of this period hold to their purity, without regard to natural forces.

Purity is a forgetting after study. And for a single pure artist to die, it would be necessary for all pure artists of past ages to have never existed.

Painting purifies itself in Europe with the ideal logic which the older painters handed on to the new ones, as if giving them life.

And that is all.

This painter finds pleasure, that one, pain; one squanders his inheritance, another becomes rich, and still others have nothing but life.

And that is all.

You cannot carry around on your back the corpse of your father. You leave him with the other dead. You remember him, miss him, speak of him with admiration. And if you become a father yourself, you cannot expect one of your children to be willing to split in two for the sake of your corpse.

But in vain do our feet relinquish the soil which holds the dead.

To insist on purity is to baptize instinct, to humanize art, and to deify personality.

The root, the stem and the flower of the lily instance the development of purity to its symbolical blossoming.

Unity. All bodies stand equal before light, and their modifications are determined by the dazzling power, which molds them according to its will.

We do not know all the colors. Each of us invents new ones.

But above all, the painter must contemplate his own divinity, and the pictures which he offers to the admiration of men will confer upon them, likewise, the glory of exercising their divinity—if only for a moment. To achieve this, it is necessary to encompass in one glance the past, the present, and the future.

The canvas should present that essential unity which alone can elicit ecstasy.

Then nothing unstable will send us off half-cocked. We will not be suddenly turning back. Free spectators, we will not sacrifice our lives to our curiosity. The smugglers of appearances will not be able to get their contraband past the salt statues before our customs house of reason.

We will not go astray in the unknown future, which, severed from eternity, is but a word fated to tempt man.

We will not waste our strength on the too fugitive present; the fashionable, for the artist, can only be the mask of death.

The picture will exist ineluctably. The vision will be entire, complete, and its infinity, instead of indicating some imperfection, will simply express the relation between a newly created thing and a new creator, nothing more. Otherwise there would be no unity, and the connection which the different points of the canvas have with various dispositions, objects, and lights, would reveal only an assemblage of odds and ends, lacking all harmony.

For while an infinite number of creatures, each testifying to its creator, can exist without any one creation encroaching on the space of the others, yet it is impossible to conceive them all at once, and death results from their juxtapositon, their union, their love.

Each god creates in his own image; and so do painters. Only photographers manufacture duplicates of nature.

Truth. Neither purity nor unity count without truth, which cannot be compared to reality, since it is always the same, subsisting beyond the scope of nature, which strives to imprison us in that fatal order of things limiting us to the merely animal.

Artists are, above all, men who want to become inhuman.

Painfully they search for traces of inhumanity, traces which are to be found nowhere in nature.

These traces are clues to truth, aside from which there is no reality we can know.

But reality will never be discovered once and for all. Truth is always new. Otherwise truth would be a system even more wretched than nature itself.

But such pitiful truth, more distant, less distinct, less real each day, would reduce painting to a sort of plastic writing, intended simply to facilitate communication between people of the same race.

In our times, a machine to reproduce such signs would be quickly invented.

STILL LIFE WITH GRAPES—GEORGES BRAQUE   (*The Phillips Collection, Washington*)

2. *Abandonment of the representational subject.* Many new painters limit themselves to pictures which have no real subjects. And the titles which we find in the catalogues are like proper names, which designate men without characterizing them.

There are men named Stout who are in fact quite thin, and others named White who are very dark; well now, I have seen pictures entitled Solitude containing many human figures.

In the cases in question, the artists even condescend at times to use vaguely explanatory words such as Portrait, Landscape, Still-life; however, many young painters use as a title only the very general term Painting.

These painters, while they still look at nature, no longer imitate it, and carefully avoid any representation of natural scenes which they may have observed, and then reconstructed from preliminary studies.

Real resemblance no longer has any importance, since everything is sacrificed by the artist to truth, to the necessities of a higher nature whose existence he assumes, but does not lay bare. The subject has little or no importance any more.

Generally speaking, modern art repudiates most of the techniques of pleasing devised by the great artists of the past.

While the goal of painting is today, as always, the pleasure of the eye, the art-lover is henceforth asked to expect delights other than those which looking at natural objects can easily provide.

The ideal: pure painting. Thus we are moving towards an entirely new art which will stand, with respect to painting as envisaged heretofore, as music stands to literature.

It will be pure painting, just as music is pure literature.

The music-lover experiences, in listening to a concert, a joy of a different order from the joy given by natural sounds, such as the murmur of the brook, the uproar of a torrent, the whistling of the wind in a forest, or the harmonies of human speech based on reason rather than on aesthetics.

In the same way the new painters will provide their admirers with artistic sensations by concentrating exclusively on the problem of creating harmony with unequal lights.

Apelles and Protogenes. Everybody knows the story told by Pliny about Apelles and Protogenes. It clearly illustrates the aesthetic pleasure resulting solely from the contradictory harmonies referred to above.

Apelles landed, one day, on the Isle of Rhodes, and went to see the work of Protogenes, who lived there. Protogenes was not in the studio when Apelles arrived. An old woman was there, looking after a large canvas which the painter had prepared. Instead of leaving his name, Apelles drew on the canvas a line so subtle that nothing happier could be conceived.

Returning, Protogenes saw the line, recognized the hand of Apelles, and drew on the latter's line another line of another color, one even more subtle, so that it seemed as if there were three lines.

Apelles came back the next day, and again did not find his man; the subtlety of the line which he drew this time caused Protogenes to despair. The sketch aroused for many years the admiration of connoisseurs, who contemplated it with as much pleasure as if it had depicted gods and goddesses, instead of almost invisible lines.

Pure art and past art. The secret aim of the young painters of the extremist schools is to produce pure painting. Theirs is an entirely new plastic art, it is still in its beginnings, and is not yet as abstract as it would like to be. Most of the new painters depend a good deal on mathematics, without knowing it; but they have not yet abandoned nature, which they still question patiently, hoping to learn the right answers to the questions raised by life.

A man like Picasso studies an object as a surgeon dissects a cadaver.

This art of pure painting, if it succeeds in freeing itself from the art of the past, will not necessarily cause the latter to disappear; the development of music has not brought in its train the abandonment of the various genres of literature, nor has the acridity of tobacco replaced the savoriness of food.

3. The new dimension of space. The new artists have been violently attacked for their preoccupation with geometry. Yet geometrical figures are the essence of drawing. Geometry, the science of space, its dimensions and relations, has always determined the norms and rules of painting.

Until now, the three dimensions of Euclid's geometry were sufficient to the restiveness felt by great artists yearning for the infinite.

The new painters do not propose, any more than did their predecessors, to be geometers. But it may be said that geometry is to the plastic arts what grammar is to the art of the writer. Today, scientists no longer limit themselves to the three dimensions of Euclid. The painters have been led quite naturally, one might say by intuition, to preoccupy themselves with the new possibilities of spatial measurement which, in the language of the modern studios, are designated by the term: the fourth dimension.

The criterion of pure painting: abstract space. Regarded from the plastic point of view, the fourth dimension appears to spring from the three known dimensions: it represents the immensity of space eternalizing itself in all directions at any given moment. It is space itself, the dimension of the infinite; the fourth dimension endows objects with plasticity. It gives the object its right proportions on the whole, whereas in Greek art, for instance, a somewhat mechanical rhythm constantly destroys the proportions.

Greek art had a purely human conception of beauty. It took man as the measure of perfection. But the art of the new painters takes the

infinite universe as its ideal, and it is to this ideal that we owe a new
norm of the perfect, one which permits the painter to proportion
objects in accordance with the degree of plasticity he desires them to
have.

Nietzsche divined the possibility of such an art:

"O divine Dionysius, why pull my ears?" Ariadne asks her philosophical lover in one of the celebrated dialogues on the Isle of Naxos.
"I find something pleasant and delightful in your ears, Ariadne; why
are they not even longer?"

Nietzsche, in relating this anecdote, puts in the mouth of Dionysius
an implied condemnation of all Greek art.

Finally, I must point out that the fourth dimension—this utopian
expression should be analyzed and explained, so that nothing more than
historical interest may be attached to it—has come to stand for the
aspirations and premonitions of the many young artists who contemplate Egyptian, Negro, and Oceanic sculptures, meditate on various
scientific works, and live in the anticipation of a sublime art.

4. Modern art as metaphysical. Wishing to attain the proportions of
the ideal, to be no longer limited to the human, the young painters
offer us works which are more cerebral than sensual. They discard more
and more the old art of optical illusion and local proportion, in order
to express the grandeur of metaphysical forms. This is why contemporary art, even if it does not directly stem from specific religious beliefs, nonetheless possesses some of the characteristics of great, that is
to say religious art.

5. The social function of art: to create the form of a historical period.
It is the social function of great poets and artists to continually renew
the appearance nature has for the eyes of men.

Without poets, without artists, men would soon weary of nature's
monotony. The sublime idea men have of the universe would collapse
with dizzying speed. The order which we find in nature, and which is
only an effect of art, would at once vanish. Everything would break up
in chaos. There would be no season, no civilization, no thought, no
humanity; even life would give way, and the impotent void would
reign everywhere.

Poets and artists plot the characteristics of their epoch, and the
future docilely falls in with their desires.

The general form of an Egyptian Mummy is in conformity with the figures drawn by Egyptian artists, and yet the ancient Egyptians were far from being all alike. They simply conformed to the art of their time.

To create the illusion of the typical is the social role and peculiar end of art. God knows how the pictures of Monet and Renoir were abused! Very well! But one has only to glance at some photographs of the period to see how closely people and things conformed to the pictures of them by these great painters.

Since of all the plastic products of an epoch, works of art have the most energy, this illusion seems to me quite natural. The energy of art imposes itself on men, and becomes for them the plastic standard of the period. Thus, those who mock the new painters are actually laughing at their own features, for people in the future will portray the men of today to be as they are represented in the most alive, which is to say, the newest, art of our time. And do not tell me there are today various other schools of painting in whose images humanity will be able to recognize itself. All the art works of an epoch end by resembling the most energetic, the most expressive, and the most typical works of the period. Dolls belong to popular art; yet they always seem to be inspired by the great art of the same epoch. This is a truth which can easily be verified. Yet who would dare to say that the dolls which were sold at bargain counters, around 1880, were shaped by a sentiment akin to what Renoir felt when he painted his portraits? No one perceived the relationship then. But this only means that Renoir's art was sufficiently energetic to take hold of our senses, even though to the general public of the epoch in which he made his debut, his conceptions seemed absurd and foolish.

6. *Modern art not a hoax.* There has been a certain amount of suspicion, notably in the case of the most recent painters, of some collective hoax or error.

But in all the history of art there is not a single instance of such general collaboration in artistic fraud or error. There are, indeed, isolated cases of mystification and blundering. But the conventional elements of which works of art are to a great extent composed guarantee the impossibility of such instances becoming general.

If the new school of painting were indeed an exception to this rule, it would be so extraordinary as to verge on the miraculous. As readily imagine all the children of some country born without heads, legs or arms, an obvious absurdity. There are no collective errors or hoaxes in art; there are only various epochs and dissimilar schools. Even if the aims pursued by these schools are not all equally elevated or equally pure, all are equally respectable, and, according to the ideas one has of beauty, each artistic school is successively admired, despised, and admired once more.

7. Cubism: historical beginnings. The new school of painting is known as cubism, a name first applied to it in the fall of 1908 in a spirit of derision by Henri Matisse, who had just seen a picture of some houses, whose cube-like appearance had greatly struck him.

The new aesthetics was first elaborated in the mind of André Derain, but the most important and audacious works the movement at once produced were those of a great artist, Pablo Picasso, who must also be considered one of the founders: his inventions, corroborated by the good sense of Georges Braque, who exhibited a cubist picture at the Salon des Indépendants as early as 1908, were envisaged in the studies of Jean Metzinger, who exhibited the first cubist portrait (a portrait of myself) at the Salon des Indépendants in 1910, and who in the same year managed to induce the jury of the Salon d'Automne to admit some cubist paintings. It was also in 1910 that pictures by Robert Delaunay, Marie Laurencin, and Le Fauconnier, who all belonged to the same school, were exhibited at the Indépendants.

The first group exhibition of the cubists, who were becoming more numerous, took place in 1911 at the Indépendants; room 41, which was devoted to their works, made a deep impression. There were the knowing and seductive works of Jean Metzinger; some landscapes, "Male Nude" and "Women with Phlox" by Albert Gleizes; "Portrait of Mme. Fernande X" and "Young Girls" by Marie Laurencin; "The Tower" by Robert Delaunay, "Abundance" by Le Fauconnier, and "Landscape with Nudes" by Fernand Léger.

That same year the cubists made their first appearance outside of France, in Brussels; and, in the preface of the catalogue of this exhibition, I accepted on behalf of the exhibitors the appellations: cubism and cubist.

Towards the end of 1911 the exhibition of the cubists at the Salon d'Automne made a considerable stir, and Gleizes ("The Hunt," "Portrait of Jacques Nayral"), Metzinger ("Woman with Spoon"), and Fernand Léger were ridiculed without mercy. A new painter, Marcel Duchamp, had joined the group, as had the sculptor-architect, Duchamp-Villon.

Other group exhibitions were held in November, 1911 (at the Galerie d'Art Contemporain, rue Tronchet, Paris), and in 1912 (at the Salon des Indépendants; this show was marked by the debut of Juan Gris); in May of the same year another cubist exhibition was held in Spain (Barcelona welcomed the young Frenchmen with enthusiasm); finally in June, at Rouen an exhibition was organized by the Société des Artistes Normands (important for presenting Francis Picabia, who had just joined the new school). (Note written in September, 1912.)

Cubism an art of conception. Cubism differs from the old schools of painting in that it aims, not at an art of imitation, but at an **art of** conception, which tends to rise to the height of creation.

In representing conceptualized reality or creative reality, the painter can give the effect of three dimensions. He can to a certain extent cube. But not by simply rendering reality as seen, unless he indulges in trompe-l'oeil, in foreshortening, or in perspective, thus distorting the quality of the forms conceived or created.

I can discriminate four trends in cubism. Of these, two are pure, and along parallel lines.

Scientific cubism. Scientific cubism is one of the pure tendencies. It is the art of painting new structures out of elements borrowed not from the reality of sight, but from the reality of insight. All men have a sense of this interior reality. A man does not have to be cultivated in order to conceive, for example, of a round form.

The geometrical aspect, which made such an impression on those who saw the first canvases of the scientific cubists, came from the fact that the essential reality was rendered with great purity, while visual accidents and anecdotes had been eliminated. The painters who follow this tendency are: Picasso, whose luminous art also belongs to the other pure tendency of cubism, Georges Braque, Albert Gleizes, Marie Laurencin, and Juan Gris.

Physical cubism. Physical cubism is the art of painting new structures with elements borrowed, for the most part, from visual reality. This art, however, belongs in the cubist movement because of its constructive discipline. It has a great future as historical painting. Its social role is very clear, but it is not a pure art. It confuses what is properly the subject with images. The painter-physicist who created this trend is Le Fauconnier.

Orphic cubism. Orphic cubism is the other important trend of the new art school. It is the art of painting new structures out of elements which have not been borrowed from the visual sphere, but have been created entirely by the artist himself, and been endowed by him with fullness of reality. The works of the orphic artist must simultaneously give a pure aesthetic pleasure, a structure which is self-evident, and a sublime meaning, that is, the subject. This is pure art. The light in Picasso's paintings is based on this conception, to which Robert Delaunay's inventions have contributed much, and towards which Fernand Léger, Francis Picabia, and Marcel Duchamp are also addressing themselves.

Instinctive cubism. Instinctive cubism, the art of painting new structures of elements which are not borrowed from visual reality, but are suggested to the artist by instinct and intuition, has long tended towards orphism. The instinctive artist lacks lucidity and an aesthetic doctrine; instinctive cubism includes a large number of artists. Born of French impressionism, this movement has now spread all over Europe.

Derain. Cézanne's last paintings and his water-colors belong to cubism, but Courbet is the father of the new painters; and André Derain, whom I propose to discuss some other time, was the eldest of his beloved sons, for we find him of the beginning of the fauvist movement, which was a kind of introduction to cubism, and also at the beginnings of this great subjective movement; but it would be too difficult today to write discerningly of a man who so willfully stands apart from everyone and everything.

Modern art and the beautiful. The modern school of painting seems to me the most audacious that has ever appeared. It has posed the question of what is beautiful in itself.

It wants to visualize beauty disengaged from whatever charm man has for man, and until now, no European artist has dared attempt this. The new artists demand an ideal beauty, which will be, not merely the proud expression of the species, but the expression of the universe, to the degree that it has been humanized by light.

Welcome to the new art. The new art clothes its creations with a grandiose and monumental appearance which surpasses anything else conceived by the artists of our time. Ardent in its search for beauty, it is noble and energetic, and the reality is brings us is marvelously clear. I love the art of today because above all else I love the light, for man loves light more than anything; it was he who invented fire.

Clive Bell

The Artistic Problem[1]

We all agree now—by "we" I mean
intelligent people under sixty—that a work of art is like a rose. A rose
is not beautiful because it is like something else. Neither is a work of
art. Roses and works of art are beautiful in themselves. Unluckily, the
matter does not end there: a rose is the visible result of an infinitude of
complicated goings on in the bosom of the earth and in the air above,
and similarly a work of art is the product of strange activities in the
human mind. In so far as we are mere spectators and connoisseurs we
need not bother about these; all we are concerned with is the finished
product, the work of art. To produce the best eggs it may be that hens
should be fed on hot meal mash. That is a question for the farmer. For
us what matters is the quality of the eggs, since it is them and not hot
meal mash that we propose to eat for breakfast. Few, however, can take
quite so lordly an attitude towards art. We contemplate the object, we
experience the appropriate emotion, and then we begin asking "Why?"
and "How?" Personally, I am so conscious of these insistent questions
that, at the risk of some misunderstanding, I habitually describe works
of art as "significant" rather than "beautiful" forms. For works of art,
unlike roses, are the creations and expressions of conscious minds. I beg
that no theological red herring may here be drawn across the scent.

A work of art is an object beautiful, or significant, in itself, nowise
dependent for its value on the outside world, capable by itself of provoking in us that emotion which we call æsthetic. Agreed. But men do
not create such things unconsciously and without effort, as they breathe
in their sleep. On the contrary, for their production are required
special energies and a peculiar state of mind. A work of art, like a rose,
is the result of a string of causes: and some of us are so vain as to take
more interest in the operations of the human mind than in fertilizers
and watering-pots.

In the pre-natal history of a work of art I seem to detect at any rate
three factors—a state of peculiar and intense sensibility, the creative
impulse, and the artistic problem. An artist, I imagine, is one who often
and easily is thrown into that state of acute and sympathetic agitation
which most of us, once or twice in our lives, have had the happiness

[1] From *Since Cézanne*. New York: Harcourt, Brace and Company, 1928.

of experiencing. And have you noticed that many men and most boys, when genuinely in love, find themselves, the moment the object of their emotion is withdrawn, driven by their feelings into scribbling verses? An artist, I imagine, is always falling in love with everything. Always he is being thrown into a "state of mind." The sight of a tree or an omnibus, the screaming of whistles or the whistling of birds, the smell of roast pig, a gesture, a look, any trivial event may provoke a crisis, filling him with an intolerable desire to express himself. The artist cannot embrace the object of his emotion. He does not even wish to. Once, perhaps, that was his desire; if so, like the pointer and the setter, he has converted the barbarous pouncing instinct into the civilized pleasure of tremulous contemplation. Be that as it may, the contemplative moment is short. Simultaneously almost with the emotion arises the longing to express, to create a form that shall match the feeling, that shall commemorate the moment of ecstasy.

This moment of passionate apprehenison is, unless I mistake, the source of the creative impulse; indeed, the latter seems to follow so promptly on the former that one is often tempted to regard them as a single movement. The next step is longer. The creative impulse is one thing; creation another. If the artist's form is to be the equivalent of an experience, if it is to be significant in fact, every scrap of it has got to be fused and fashioned in the white heat of his emotion. And how is his emotion to be kept at white heat through the long, cold days of formal construction? Emotions seem to grow cold and set like glue. The intense power and energy called forth by the first thrilling vision grow slack for want of incentive. What engine is to generate the heat and make taut the energies by which alone significant form can be created? That is where the artistic problem comes in.

The artistic problem is the problem of making a match between an emotional experience and a form that has been conceived but not created. Evidently the conception of some sort of form accompanies, or closely follows, the creative impulse. The artist says, or rather feels, to himself: I should like to express that in words, or in lines and colours, or in notes. But to make anything out of his impulse he will need something more than this vague desire to express or to create. He will need a definite, fully conceived form into which his experience can be made to fit. And this fitting, this matching of his experience with his form, will be his problem. It will serve the double purpose of concentrating his energies and stimulating his intellect. It will be at once a canal and a goad. And his energy and intellect between them will have to keep warm his emotion. Shakespeare kept tense the muscle of his mind and boiling and racing his blood by struggling to confine his turbulent spirit within the trim mould of the sonnet. Pindar, the most passionate of poets, drove and pressed his feelings through the convolutions of the ode. Bach wrote fugues. The master of St. Vitale found an equivalent for his disquieting ecstasies in severely stylistic portraits wrought in an intractable medium. Giotto expressed himself through a series of pictured legends. El Greco seems to have achieved his stupendous designs by labouring to make significant the fustian of theatrical piety.

There is apparently nothing that an artist cannot vivify. He can create a work of art out of some riddle in engineering or harmonics, an anecdote, or the frank representation of a natural object. Only, to be satisfactory, the problem must be for him who employs it a goad and a limitation. A goad that calls forth all his energies; a limitation that focuses them on some object far more precise and comprehensible than the expression of a vague sensibility, or, to say the same thing in another way, the creation of indefinite beauty. However much an artist may have felt, he cannot just sit down and express it; he cannot create form in the vague. He must sit down to write a play or a poem, to paint a portrait or a still life.

Almost everyone has had his moment of ecstasy, and the creative impulse is not uncommon; but those only who have a pretty strong sense of art understand the necessity for the artistic problem. What is known of it by the public is not much liked; it has a bad name and is reckoned unsympathetic. For the artistic problem, which limits the artist's freedom, fixes his attention on a point, and drives his emotion through narrow tubes, is what imports the conventional element into art. It seems to come between the spontaneous thrill of the artist and the receptive enthusiasm of his public with an air of artificiality. Thus, a generation brought up on Wordsworth could hardly believe in the genuineness of Racine. Our fathers and grandfathers felt, and felt rightly, that art was something that came from and spoke to the depths of the human soul. But how, said they, should deep call to deep in Alexandrines and a pseudo-classical convention, to say nothing of full-bottomed wigs? They forgot to reckon with the artistic problem, and made the mistake that people make who fancy that nothing looking so unlike a Raphael or a Titian as a Matisse or a Picasso can be a work of art. They thought that because the stuff of art comes from the depths of human nature it can be expressed only in terms of naturalism. They did not realize that the creating of an equivalent for an æsthetic experience out of natural speech or the common forms of nature is only one amongst an infinite number of possible problems. There are still ladies who feel sure that had they been in Laura's shoes Petrarch might have experienced something more vivid than what comes through his mellifluous but elaborate *rime*. To them he would have expressed himself otherwise. Possibly: but whatever he experienced could not have become art—significant form—till it had been withdrawn from the world of experience and converted into poetry by some such exacting problem.

One problem in itself is as good as another, just as one kind of nib is as good as another, since problems are valuable only as means. That problem is best for any particular artist that serves that particular artist best. The ideal problem will be the one that raises his power most while limiting his fancy least. The incessant recourse of European writers to dramatic form suggests that here is a problem which to them is peculiarly favourable. Its conventions, I suppose, are sufficiently strict to compel the artist to exert himself to the utmost, yet not so strict as to present those appalling technical difficulties—the sort presented by a sestina or a chant royal—that make self-expression impossible to any but a consummate master. The novel, on the other hand, as we are just beginning to suspect, affords for most writers an unsatisfactory, because insufficiently rigorous, problem. Each age has its favourites. Indeed, the history of art is very much the history of the problem. The stuff of art is always the same, and always it must be converted into form before it can become art; it is in their choice of converting-machines that the ages differ conspicuously.

Two tasks that painters and writers sometimes set themselves are often mistaken for artistic problems, but are, in fact, nothing of the sort. One is literal representation: the other the supply of genius direct from the cask. To match a realistic form with an æsthetic experience is a problem that has served well many great artists: Chardin and Tolstoi will do as examples. To make a realistic form and match it with nothing is no problem at all. Though to say just what the camera would say is beyond the skill and science of most of us, it is a task that will never raise an artist's temperature above boiling-point. A painter may go into the woods, get his thrill, go home and fetch his panel-box, and proceed to set down in cold blood what he finds before him. No good can come of it, as the gloomy walls of any official exhibition will show. Realistic novels fail for the same reason: with all their gifts, neither Zola, nor Edmond de Goncourt, nor Mr. Arnold Bennett ever produced a work of art. Also, a thorough anarchist will never be an artist, though many artists have believed that they were thorough anarchists. One man cannot pour an æsthetic experience straight into another, leaving out the problem. He cannot exude form: he must set himself to create a particular form. Automatic writing will never be poetry, nor automatic scribbling design. The artist must submit his creative impulse to the conditions of a problem. Often great artists set their own problems; always they are bound by them. That would be a shallow critic who supposed that Mallarmé wrote down what words he chose in what order he pleased, unbound by any sense of a definite form to be created and a most definite conception to be realized. Mallarmé was as severely bound by his problem as was Racine by his. It was as definite—for all that it was unformulated—as absolute, and as necessary. The same may be said of Picasso in his most abstract works: but not of all his followers, nor of all Mallarmé's either.

George Grosz
Dadaism[1]

If we artists were the expression of anything at all, then we were the expression of the ferment of dissatisfaction and unrest. Every new national defeat results in the eruption of a new period, the dawn of a new movement. In another era we might well have been flagellants or existentionalists.

During the war a few poets, painters and musicians established the Cabaret Voltaire in Zürich, Switzerland. Hugo Ball was the director. His collaborators were Richard Hulsenbeck, Hans Arp, Emmy Hennings and a few other international artists. This group was modern-futuristic rather than political in character. In their search for a name, Ball and Hulsenbeck hit upon the idea of selecting a word at random from the French dictionary. It was by chance that they selected the word *dada*, which means hobbyhorse.

Hulsenbeck introduced the Dada movement into Berlin, where I met him. The atmosphere in Berlin differing from that in Zürich, Dada assumed a political hue. Dadaism still retained its aesthetic aspect but this was pushed more and more into the background with the rise of

[1] From *A Little Yes and a Big No*, by George Grosz. New York: The Dial Press, 1946.

anarchistic-nihilistic politics. I was one of the co-founders, but a writer, Franz Jung, became its chief spokesman. He was of a bold, adventurous nature and feared nothing. He was somewhat Rimbauldian in personality. Being a man of force, he influenced the complete movement the moment he became part of it. He was a heavy drinker. His books did not win popularity because they were written in a style and manner difficult to read. He knew fame for a few weeks, however, when he and a sailor, Knuffgen, confiscated a steamer in the middle of the Baltic Sea, sailed it to Leningrad and presented it as a gift to the Russians. This happened at a time when everyone was expecting the victory of the Communists in Germany. Jung rarely did anything himself. He did not have to. He was always surrounded by sycophants who were bound to him through life and death. Whenever he got drunk he would shoot at us with his revolver. He was one of the most intelligent men I have ever known, but also one of the most unhappy. He earned money as a stock-exchange journalist and eventually published his own newspaper, which dealt primarily with economic questions.

As Dadaists, we held meetings and charged a few marks admission but gave in return no more than truisms. By that I mean, we just insulted the people roundly. Our manners were downright arrogant. We would say, "You heap of dung down there, yes, you, with the umbrella, you simple fool." Or, "Hey, you on the right, don't laugh, you ox." If they answered us, as they naturally did, we would say as they do in the army: "Shut your trap or you'll get kicked in the butt."

Our popularity spread quickly, so that our evening gatherings and Sunday afternoons were soon sold out in advance to people who were both amused and irritated by us. By and by we had to have the police at our meetings, as fights were always breaking out. It reached the point where we had to get permission from the police to hold these meetings. We simply mocked everything. That was Dadaism. Nothing was holy to us. Our movement was neither mystical, communistic nor anarchistic. All of these movements had some sort of program, but ours was completely nihilistic. We spat upon everything, including ourselves. Our symbol was nothingness, a vacuum, a void. To what extent we were the expression of a despair that knew no salvation, I cannot say. I am not attempting to make or seek any explanation. I am merely reporting what I experienced.

When we weren't swearing at the public, we were indulging in so-called "art." That is, we deliberately staged our "artistic" acts. For instance, Walter Mehring would pound away at his typewriter, read-

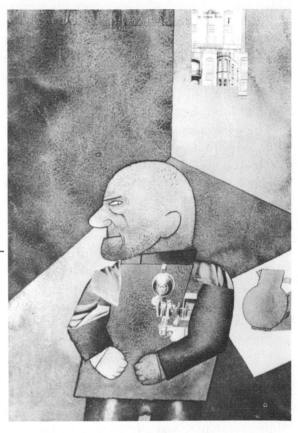

HEARTFIELD THE ENGINEER—
GEORGE GROSZ (*Museum of
Modern Art, New York,
A. C. Goodyear
Collection*)

ing aloud the poem he was composing, and Heartfield or Hausmann or I would come from backstage and shout: "Stop, you aren't going to hand out real art to those dumbbells, are you?"

Sometimes these skits were prepared, but by and large they were improvised. Since we usually did a bit of drinking beforehand, we were always belligerent. The battles that started behind the scenes were merely continued in public, that was all. This was startlingly novel to the people; consequently we were hugely successful. Fads like ours generally lasted for only a few months.

There were a few insane among us. Naturally. There was a certain Baader for example, who was supposed to have been wedded to the earth in some mystic way. He assembled a huge scrap-book that he called "Dadacon" and claimed it was greater than the Bible, including the New Testament. Yes, Baader was indeed a bit cracked—a megalomaniac. To him, his book was the greatest, the most powerful of all times. It consisted of newspaper clippings and photo-montages. He believed that in thumbing through the book as he had arranged it, one was bound to develop a dizzy headache, and that only after the mind was in a complete whirl could one comprehend the "Dadacon." Baader also created a huge statue called "Germany's Greatness and Downfall." By collecting all possible kinds of junk and throwing them together in some fashion, he composed this three-dimensional memorial.

The "Dadacon" had been offered for $35,000 to Ben Hecht, who had come to Germany as war correspondent for the Chicago *Daily News*. His job was to determine whether we Germans were really as vile as Raemakers had depicted us, how the new republic was functioning, and whether it was a real republic and not a ruse of the German general staff. Stories were already circulating that the Kaiser had not gone to Holland at all. It was his double, cleverly chosen by Ludendorff, that Ludendorff, in the role of a simple miner, was plotting counter-revolution in a mine prepared for this purpose. It was said that there had been entire regiments of infantrymen at the outbreak of the revolution that had vanished into the earth and never reappeared. But the story that these regiments had been buried in huge craters by big new shells was not generally believed.

Hecht made his headquarters at the Hotel Adlon, where all the American correspondents lived. It was there that I met him through the good offices of my friend Dr. Dohmann who, like Ben Hecht, loved to spend his leisure time banging out ragtime melodies. "Everybody Shimmies Now" was the great favorite.

He used to come to the affairs arranged by us Dadaists. He even thought of accepting Baader's offer to sell the "Dadacon," but was only willing to pay half the price asked. After much bickering back and forth, the deal fell through and the "Dadacon" was eventually buried in the garden behind Baader's house.

Just as Baader was the "Oberdada," I was the "Propagandada." My job was to invent slogans to promote our cause. Not that any of us knew what Dadaism actually was. It could be almost anything: a void, a new wisdom, a new brand of Mother Sill's pills against seasickness, a sedative, a stimulant. It was everything and yet nothing.

We who followed it were all crazy; even I—a little bit. Of course, back in the army that nice doctor had said that my drawings looked crazy enough to him. He had even put me through a sort of test for idiocy, but I had answered all their idiotic questions satisfactorily.

I was very proud of some of the slogans I invented. There was "Dada today, Dada tomorrow, Dada forever"; the little political parody "Dada, Dada *über alles*"; "come to Dada if you like to be embraced and embarrassed"; "Dada kicks you in the behind and you like it." We had these slogans printed on small stickers which we plastered all over the shop windows, coffee-house tables and shop doors of Berlin. They were alarming little stickers, particularly since the slogans were so mystic and enigmatic. Everyone began to wonder who we were. The popular afternoon paper, *BZ am Mittag*, devoted a whole editorial to the Dada menace. People were aroused against us. They could not understand a movement that made so little sense. But we continued to have wonderfully wild times. We pasted our stickers just everywhere we went. Even the waiter, carrying his tray of drinks and cigars, would have a "Dada kicks me in the behind" sticker on the back of his frock coat and a "Dada forever" on his box of cigars.

If Dada made no sense to the masses, it at least served as an outlet for the rich playboys who financed our movement. One such wealthy admirer had a wine cellar deep down under the basement of his villa in Gruenewald. He had streets and avenues of thousands of bottles of choice wines and liquors. These streets he named after some of his Dada friends. The George Grosz Alley was piled high with kegs of sherry. He even had a map of his wine empire, a region as fantastic as the famous catacombs under the streets of Paris. He had a motor scooter with a tremendous headlight attached, to help him get around. One huge keg he christened "The Dada Barrel" and filled with a wonderful Moselle wine—our particular Dadaist wine.

Every month we would have a party down there. It would be held in the almost ceremonial tradition of a wine-tasters' session, with a huge cheese, a giant salt cellar and as many buns and salt sticks as one desired. Too much smoking was not tolerated since it would spoil the taste of the superbly delicate wines. All this to the accompaniment of special Dada music that Dr. Dohmann would improvise on an upright piano.

Our rich friend had a macabre streak in him. He had a large collection of old drinking cups made out of human skulls. These were mounted in silver, filled with silver, and the domes opened on silver hinges. He claimed that half a dozen of them had once belonged to Attila, the king of the Huns, and had been found on the vast estate of an old Prussian general of the Death's Head Hussars with whom he used to go wild-boar hunting.

We Dadaists had an art peculiarly our own. It was called "garbage-can art" or "garbage-can philosophy." The leader of this school of Dada art was a certain Kurt Schwitters from Hannover. His pockets were always filled with odds and ends. He gathered everything he could find on the streets when he went out for a walk. He would pick up rusty nails, old rags, a toothbrush without bristles, cigar butts, a spoke of a bicycle wheel, a broken umbrella—in short, anything that had been discarded as useless. He would then put them together into a smaller junk heap, which he would proceed to paste on canvas or old boards, fastening them down firmly with wire and cord. The result, called *Merzbilder* ("garbage pictures"), was exhibited and actually sold. Many critics who wanted to keep astride of the times praised this abuse of the public. They assessed this art seriously. Average people, on the contrary, who understood nothing about art, reacted normally and called it "dirt, filth and garbage"—exactly what this sort of art actually was.

Harold Rosenberg
The American Action Painters[1]

"J'ai fait des gestes blancs parmi les solitudes."   APOLLINAIRE

"The American will is easily satisfied in its efforts to realize itself in knowing itself."   WALLACE STEVENS

What makes any definition of a movement in art dubious is that it never fits the deepest artists in the movement—certainly not as well as, if successful, it does the others. Yet without the definition something essential in those best is bound to be missed. The attempt to define is like a game in which you cannot possibly reach the goal from the starting point but can only close in on it by picking up each time from where the last play landed.

Modern Art? Or An Art of the Modern?

Since the War every twentieth-century style in painting has been brought to profusion in the United States: thousands of "abstract" painters—crowded teaching courses in Modern Art—a scattering of new heroes—ambitions stimulated by new galleries, mass exhibitions, reproductions in popular magazines, festivals, appropriations.

[1] From *The Tradition of the New*. New York: Horizon Press, 1959.

AUTUMN RHYTHM—JACKSON POLLOCK (*The Metropolitan Museum of Art, George A. Hearn Fund, 1957*)

Is this the usual catching up of America with European art forms? Or is something new being created? For the question of novelty, a definition would seem indispensable.

Some people deny that there is anything original in the recent American painting. Whatever is being done here now, they claim, was done thirty years ago in Paris. You can trace this painter's boxes of symbols to Kandinsky, that one's moony shapes to Miró or even back to Cézanne.

Quantitatively, it is true that most of the symphonies in blue and red rectangles, the wandering pelvises and bird-bills, the line constructions and plane suspensions, the virginal dissections of flat areas that crowd the art shows are accretions to the "School of Paris" brought into being by the fact that the mode of production of modern masterpieces has now been all too clearly rationalized. There are styles in the present displays which the painter could have acquired by putting a square inch of a Soutine or a Bonnard under a microscope. . . . All this is training based on a new conception of what art is, rather than original work demonstrating what art is about to become.

At the center of this wide practicing of the immediate past, however, the work of some painters has separated itself from the rest by a consciousness of a function for painting different from that of the earlier "abstractionists," both the Europeans themselves and the Americans who joined them in the years of the Great Vanguard.

This new painting does not constitute a School. To form a School in modern times not only is a new painting consciousness needed but a consciousness of that consciousness—and even an insistence on certain formulas. A School is the result of the linkage of practice with terminology—different paintings are affected by the same words. In the American vanguard the words, as we shall see, belong not to the art but to the individual artists. What they think in common is represented only by what they do separately.

Getting Inside the Canvas

At a certain moment the canvas began to appear to one American painter after another as an arena in which to act—rather than as a space on which to reproduce, re-design, analyze or "express" an object, actual or imagined. What was to go on the canvas was not a picture but an event.

The painter no longer approached his easel with an image in his mind; he went up to it with material in his hand to do something to that other piece of material in front of him. The image would be the result of this encounter.

It is pointless to argue that Rembrandt or Michelangelo worked in the same way. You don't get Lucrece with a dagger out of staining a piece of cloth or spontaneously putting forms into motion upon it. She had to exist some place else before she got on the canvas, and paint was Rembrandt's means for bringing her there, though, of course, a means that would change her by the time she arrived. Now, everything must have been in the tubes, in the painter's muscles and in the cream-colored sea into which he dives. If Lucrece should come out she will be among us for the first time—a surprise. To the painter, she *must* be a surprise. In this mood there is no point to an act if you already know what it contains.

"B—is not modern," one of the leaders of this mode said to me. "He works from sketches. That makes him Renaissance."

Here the principle, and the difference from the old painting, is made into a formula. A sketch is the preliminary form of an image the *mind* is trying to grasp. To work from sketches arouses the suspicion that the artist still regards the canvas as a place where the mind records its contents—rather than itself the "mind" through which the painter thinks by changing a surface with paint.

If a painting is an action the sketch is one action, the painting that follows it another. The second cannot be "better" or more complete than the first. There is just as much in what one lacks as in what the other has.

Of course, the painter who spoke had no right to assume that his friend had the old mental conception of a sketch. There is no reason why an act cannot be prolonged from a piece of paper to a canvas. Or repeated on another scale and with more control. A sketch can have the function of a skirmish.

Call this painting "abstract" or "Expressionist" or "Abstract-Expressionist," what counts is its special motive for extinguishing the object, which is not the same as in other abstract or Expressionist phases of modern art.

The new American painting is not "pure" art, since the extrusion of the object was not for the sake of the esthetic. The apples weren't brushed off the table in order to make room for perfect relations of space and color. They had to go so that nothing would get in the way of the act of painting. In this gesturing with materials the esthetic, too, has been subordinated. Form, color, composition, drawing, are auxiliaries, any one of which—or practically all, as has been attempted logically, with unpainted canvases—can be dispensed with. What matters always is the revelation contained in the act. It is to be taken for granted that in the final effect, the image, whatever be or be not in it, will be a *tension*.[2]

2 "With regard to the tensions it is capable of setting up in our bodies the medium of any art is an extension of the physical world; a stroke of pigment, for example, 'works' within us in the same way as a bridge across the Hudson. For the unseen universe that inhabits us an accidental blot or splash of paint may thus assume an equivalence to the profoundest happening. . . .

"If the ultimate subject matter of all art is the artist's psychic state or tension (and this may be the case even in nonindividualistic epochs), that state may be represented either through the image of a thing or through an abstract sign. The innovation of Action Painting was to dispense with the *representation* of the state in favor of *enacting* it in physical movement. The action on the canvas became its own representation. This was possible because an action, being made of both the psychic and the material, is by its nature a sign —it is the trace of a movement whose beginning and character it does not in itself ever altogether reveal (e.g., Freud's point about love-making being mistaken in the imagination for an assault); yet the action also exists as a 'thing' in that it touches other things and affects them. . . .

"In turning to action, abstract art abandons its alliance with architecture, as painting had earlier broken with music and with the novel, and offers its hand to pantomime and dance. One thinks of Rilke's

Dramas Of As If

A painting that is an act is inseparable from the biography of the artist. The painting itself is a "moment" in the adulterated mixture of his life—whether "moment" means the actual minutes taken up with spotting the canvas or the entire duration of a lucid drama conducted in sign language. The act-painting is of the same metaphysical substance as the artist's existence. The new painting has broken down every distinction between art and life.

It follows that anything is relevant to it. Anything that has to do with action—psychology, philosophy, history, mythology, hero worship.[3] Anything but art criticism. The painter gets away from art through his act of painting; the critic can't get away from it. The critic who goes on judging in terms of schools, styles, form—as if the painter were still concerned with producing a certain kind of object (the work of art), instead of living on the canvas—is bound to seem a stranger.

Some painters take advantage of this stranger. Having insisted that their painting is an act, they then claim admiration for the act as art. This turns the act back toward the esthetic in a petty circle. If the picture is an act, it cannot be justified *as an act of genius* in a field whose whole measuring apparatus has been sent to the devil. Its value must be found apart from art. Otherwise the "act" gets to be "making a painting" at sufficient speed to meet an exhibition date.

> Dance the orange. The warmer landscape,
> fling it out of you, that the ripe one be radiant
> in homeland breezes!

"In painting, the primary agency of physical motion (as distinct from illusionary representation of motion, as with the Futurists) is the line, conceived not as the thinnest of planes, nor as edge, contour or connective but as stroke or figure (in the sense of 'figure skating'). In its passage on the canvas each such line can establish the actual movement of the artist's body as an esthetic statement. Line, from wiry calligraphy to footwide flaunts of the house painter's brush, has played the leading part in the technique of Action Painting, though there are other ways besides line of releasing force on canvas."

H. R., from "Hans Hofmann: Nature into action," *Art News,* May, 1957.

[3] "Action cannot be perfected without losing its human subject and being transformed thereby into the mechanics of man-the-machine.

"Action never perfects itself; but it tends toward perfection and away from the personal. This is the best argument for dropping the term 'Abstract Expressionism,' with its associations of ego and personal *Schmerz,* as a name for the current American painting. Action Painting has to do with self-creation or self-definition or self-transcendence; but this dissociates it from self-expression, which assumes the acceptance of the ego as it is, with its wound and its magic. Action Painting is not 'personal,' though its subject matter is the artist's individual possibilities."

H. R., "A dialogue with Thomas B. Hess." *Catalogue of the Exhibition: Action Painting, 1958.* The Dallas Museum For Contemporary Arts.

Art—relation of the painting to the works of the past, rightness of color, texture, balance, etc.—comes back into painting by way of psychology. As Stevens says of poetry, "it is a process of the personality of the poet." But the psychology is the psychology of creation. Not that of the so-called psychological criticism that wants to "read" a painting for clues to the artist's sexual preferences or debilities. The work, the act, translates the psychologically given into the intentional, into a "world"—and thus transcends it.

With traditional esthetic references discarded as irrelevant, what gives the canvas its meaning is not psychological data but *rôle*, the way the artist organizes his emotional and intellectual energy as if he were in a living situation. The interest lies in the kind of act taking place in the four-sided arena, a dramatic interest.

Criticism must begin by recognizing in the painting the assumptions inherent in its mode of creation. Since the painter has become an actor, the spectator has to think in a vocabulary of action: its inception, duration, direction—psychic state, concentration and relaxation of the will, passivity, alert waiting. He must become a connoisseur of the gradations between the automatic, the spontaneous, the evoked.

"It's Not That, It's Not That, It's Not That"

With a few important exceptions, most of the artists of this vanguard found their way to their present work by being cut in two. Their type is not a young painter but a re-born one. The man may be over forty, the painter around seven. The diagonal of a grand crisis separates him from his personal and artistic past.

Many of the painters were "Marxists" (WPA unions, artists' congresses); they had been trying to paint Society. Others had been trying to paint Art (Cubism, Post-Impressionism)—it amounts to the same thing.

The big moment came when it was decided to paint . . . just TO PAINT. The gesture on the canvas was a gesture of liberation, from Value— political, esthetic, moral.

If the war and the decline of radicalism in America had anything to do with this sudden impatience, there is no evidence of it. About the effects of large issues upon their emotions, Americans tend to be either reticent or unconscious. The French artist thinks of himself as a battleground of history; here one hears only of private Dark Nights. Yet it is strange how many segregated individuals came to a dead stop within the past ten years and abandoned, even physically destroyed, the work they had been doing. A far-off watcher unable to realize that these events were taking place in silence might have assumed they were being directed by a single voice.

At its center the movement was away from, rather than toward. The Great Works of the Past and the Good Life of the Future became equally nil.

The refusal of values did not take the form of condemnation or defiance of society, as it did after World War I. It was diffident. The lone artist did not want the world to be different, he wanted his canvas to be a world. Liberation from the object meant liberation from the "nature," society and art already there. It was a movement to leave behind the self that wished to choose his future and to nullify its promissory notes to the past.

With the American, heir of the pioneer and the immigrant, the foundering of Art and Society was not experienced as a loss. On the contrary, the end of Art marked the beginning of an optimism regarding himself as an artist.

The American vanguard painter took to the white expanse of the canvas as Melville's Ishmael took to the sea.

On the one hand, a desperate recognition of moral and intellectual exhaustion; on the other, the exhilaration of an adventure over depths in which he might find reflected the true image of his identity.

Painting could now be reduced to that equipment which the artist needed for an activity that would be an alternative to both utility and idleness. Guided by visual and somatic memories of paintings he had seen or made—memories which he did his best to keep from intruding into his consciousness—he gesticulated upon the canvas and watched for what each novelty would declare him and his art to be.

Based on the phenomenon of conversion the new movement is, with the majority of the painters, essentially a religious movement. In almost every case, however, the conversion has been experienced in secular terms. The result has been the creation of private myths.

The tension of the private myth is the content of every painting of this vanguard. The act on the canvas springs from an attempt to resurrect the saving moment in his "story" when the painter first felt himself released from Value—myth of past self-recognition. Or it attempts to initiate a new moment in which the painter will realize his total personality—myth of future self-recognition.

Some formulate their myth verbally and connect individual works with its episodes. With others, usually deeper, the painting itself is the exclusive formulation, a Sign.

The revolution against the given, in the self and in the world, which since Hegel has provided European vanguard art with theories of a New Reality, has re-entered America in the form of personal revolts. Art as action rests on the enormous assumption that the artist accepts as real only that which he is in the process of creating. "Except the soul has divested itself of the love of created things . . ." The artist works in a condition of open possibility, risking, to follow Kierkegaard, the anguish of the esthetic, which accompanies possibility lacking in reality. To maintain the force to refrain from settling anything, he must exercise in himself a constant No.

Apocalypse and Wallpaper

The most comfortable intercourse with the void is mysticism, especially a mysticism that avoids ritualizing itself.

Philosophy is not popular among American painters. For most, thinking consists of the various arguments that TO PAINT is something different from, say, to write or to criticize: a mystique of the particular activity. Lacking verbal flexibility, the painters speak of what they are doing in a jargon still involved in the metaphysics of *things:* "My painting is not Art; it's an Is." "It's not a picture of a thing; it's the thing itself." "It doesn't reproduce Nature; it is Nature." "The painter doesn't think; he knows." Etc. etc. "Art is not, not not not not. . . ." As against this, a few reply, art today is the same as it always has been.

Language has not accustomed itself to a situation in which the act itself is the "object." Along with the philosophy of TO PAINT appear bits of Vedanta and popular pantheism.

In terms of American tradition, the new painters stand somewhere between Christian Science and Whitman's "gangs of cosmos." That is, between a discipline of vagueness by which one protects oneself from disturbance while keeping one's eyes open for benefits; and the discipline of the Open Road of risk that leads to the farther side of the object and the outer spaces of the consciousness.

What made Whitman's mysticism serious was that he directed his "cosmic 'I' " towards a Pike's-Peak-or-Bust of morality and politics. He wanted the ineffable in *all* behavior—he wanted it *to win the streets.*

The test of any of the new paintings is its seriousness—and the test of its seriousness is the degree to which the act on the canvas is an extension of the artist's total effort to make over his experience.

A good painting in this mode leaves no doubt concerning its reality as an action and its relation to a transforming process in the artist. The canvas has "talked back" to the artist not to quiet him with Sibylline murmurs nor to stun him with Dionysian outcries but to provoke him into a dramatic dialogue. Each stroke had to be a decision and was answered by a new question. By its very nature, action painting is painting in the medium of difficulties.[4]

Weak mysticism, the "Christian Science" side of the new movement, tends in the opposite direction, toward *easy* painting—never so many unearned masterpieces! Works of this sort lack the dialectical tension of a genuine act, associated with risk and will. When a tube of paint is squeezed by the Absolute, the result can only be a Success. The painter need keep himself on hand solely to collect the benefits of an endless series of strokes of luck. His gesture completes itself without arousing either an opposing movement within itself nor the desire in the artist to make the act more fully his own. Satisfied with wonders that remain safely inside the canvas, the artist accepts the permanence of the commonplace and decorates it with his own daily annihilation. The result is an apocalyptic wallpaper.

The cosmic "I" that turns up to paint pictures, but shudders and departs the moment there is a knock on the studio door, brings to the artist a megalomania which is the opposite of revolutionary. The tremors produced by a few expanses of tone or by the juxtaposition of colors and shapes purposely brought to the verge of bad taste in the manner of Park Avenue shop windows are sufficient cataclysms in many of these happy overthrows of Art. The mystical dissociation of painting as an ineffable event has made it common to mistake for an act the mere sensation of having acted—or of having been acted upon. Since there is nothing to be "communicated," a unique signature comes to seem the equivalent of a new plastic language. In a single stroke the painter exists as a Somebody—at least on a wall. That this Somebody is not he seems beside the point.

Once the difficulties that belong to a real act have been evaded by mysticism, the artist's experience of transformation is at an end. In that

---

[4] "As other art movements of our time have extracted from painting the element of structure or the element of tone and elevated it into their essence, Action Painting has extracted the element of decision inherent in all art in that the work is not finished at its beginning but has to be carried forward by an accumulation of 'right' gestures. In a word, Action Painting is the abstraction of the *moral* element in art; its mark is moral tension in detachment from moral or esthetic certainties; and it judges itself morally in declaring that picture to be worthless which is not the incorporation of a genuine struggle, one which could at any point have been lost."

H. R., The Dallas Museum *Catalogue, ibid.*

case what is left? Or to put it differently: What is a painting that is not an object, nor the representation of an object, nor the analysis or impression of it, nor whatever else a painting has ever been—and which has also ceased to be the emblem of a personal struggle? It is the painter himself changed into a ghost inhabiting The Art World. Here the common phrase, "I have bought an O—" (rather than a painting by O—) becomes literally true. The man who started to remake himself has made himself into a commodity with a trademark.

Milieu: The Busy No-Audience

We said that the new painting calls for a new kind of criticism, one that would distinguish the specific qualities of each artist's act.

Unhappily for an art whose value depends on the authenticity of its mysteries, the new movement appeared at the same moment that Modern Art *en masse* "arrived" in America: Modern architecture, not only for sophisticated homes, but for corporations, municipalities, synagogues; Modern furniture and crockery in mail-order catalogues; Modern vacuum cleaners, can openers; beer-ad "mobiles"—along with reproductions and articles on advanced painting in big-circulation magazines. *Enigmas for everybody.* Art in America today is not only nouveau, it's news.

The new painting came into being fastened to Modern Art and without intellectual allies—in literature everything has found its niche.

From this liaison it has derived certain superstitions comparable to those of a wife with a famous husband. Superiorities, supremacies even, are taken for granted. It is boasted that modern painting in America is not only original but an "advance" in world art (at the same time that one says "to hell with world art").

Everyone knows that the label Modern Art no longer has any relation to the words that compose it. To be Modern Art a work need not be either modern nor art; it need not even be a work. A three-thousand-year-old mask from the South Pacific qualifies as Modern and a piece of wood found on a beach becomes Art.

When they find this out, some people grow extremely enthusiastic, even, oddly enough, proud of themselves; others become infuriated.

These reactions suggest what Modern Art actually is. It is not even a Style. It has nothing to do either with the period when a thing was made nor with the intention of the maker. It is something that someone has had the social power to designate as psychologically, esthetically or ideologically relevant to our epoch. The question of the driftwood is: *Who* found it?

Modern Art in America represents a revolution of taste—and serves to identify the caste conducting that revolution. Responses to Modern Art are primarily responses to claims to social leadership. For this reason Modern Art is periodically attacked as snobbish, Red, immoral, etc., by established interests in society, politics, the church. Comedy of a revolution that restricts itself to weapons of taste—and which at the same time addresses itself to the masses: Modern-design fabrics in bargain basements, Modern interiors for office girls living alone, Modern milk bottles.

Modern art is educational, not with regard to art but with regard to life. You cannot explain Mondrian's painting to people who don't know anything about Vermeer, but you can easily explain the social importance of admiring Mondrian and forgetting about Vermeer.

Through Modern Art the expanding caste of professional enlighteners of the masses—designers, architects, decorators, fashion people, exhibition directors—informs the populace that a supreme Value has emerged in our time, the Value of the NEW, and that there are persons and things that embody that Value. This Value is a completely fluid one. As we have seen, Modern Art does not have to be actually new; it only has to be new to *somebody*—to the last lady who found out about the driftwood—and to win neophytes is the chief interest of the caste.

Since the only thing that counts for Modern Art is that a work shall be NEW, and since the question of its newness is determined not by analysis but by social power and pedagogy, the vanguard painter functions in a milieu utterly indifferent to the content of his work.

Unlike the art of nineteenth-century America, advanced paintings today are not bought by the middle class.[5] Nor are they by the populace. Considering the degree to which it is publicized and feted, vanguard painting is hardly bought at all. It is *used* in its totality as material for educational and profit-making enterprises: color reproductions, design adaptations, human-interest stories. Despite the fact that more people see and hear about works of art than ever before, the vanguard artist has an audience of nobody. An interested individual here and there, but no audience. He creates in an environment not of people but of functions. His paintings are employed not wanted. The public for whose edification he is periodically trotted out accepts the choices made for it as phenomena of The Age of Queer Things.

[5] The situation has improved since this essay appeared in 1952. Several younger collectors have appeared who are specializing in the new American painting—and to some degree the work of Americans has entered the world art market.

An action is not a matter of taste.

You don't let taste decide the firing of a pistol or the building of a maze.

As the Marquis de Sade understood, even experiments in sensation, if deliberately repeated, presuppose a morality.

To see in the explosion of shrapnel over No Man's Land only the opening of a flower of flame, Marinetti had to erase the moral premises of the act of destruction—as Molotov did explicitly when he said that Fascism is a matter of taste. Both M's were, of course, speaking the driftwood language of the Modern Art International.

Limited to the esthetic, the taste bureaucracies of Modern Art cannot grasp the human experience involved in the new action paintings. One work is equivalent to another on the basis of resemblances of surface, and the movement as a whole a modish addition to twentieth-century picture making. Examples in every style are packed side by side in annuals and travelling shows and in the heads of newspaper reviewers like canned meats in a chain store—all standard brands.

To counteract the obtuseness, venality and aimlessness of the Art World, American vanguard art needs a genuine audience—not just a market. It needs understanding—not just publicity.

In our form of society, audience and understanding for advanced painting have been produced, both here and abroad, first of all by the tiny circle of poets, musicians, theoreticians, men of letters, who have sensed in their own work the presence of the new creative principle.

So far, the silence of American literature on the new painting all but amounts to a scandal.

Art lies in concealing art. (*Ars est celare artem.*)

Ovid, *Art of Love*

What garlic is to salad, insanity is to art.

Homer Saint-Gaudens

Don't let the hand fall into a smart way of putting the mind to sleep.

John Sloan

The mind and hand of the sculptor must work together—an embracing mind, an active translating hand, a conjunction of the material and the spiritual.

Jacob Epstein

Robert Goldwater
Reflections on the Rothko Exhibition[1]

In Mark Rothko's pictures the apparent end lies close to the apparent beginning—so close in fact, or in apparent fact, that they are almost indistinguishable. If this suggests that the paintings are simple (without complication), so indeed they finally are, or have become; if it implies as well that they are simplist (without subtlety), this is only because here is the unavoidable area of discussion. This is the argument they engender and provoke—whether and why being the first, they are not (as I think they are not) the second. To the extent that this discussion remains unresolved, the works remain enigmas, forcing scrutiny while rejecting inquiry. I believe this is the underlying sense of Rothko's definition of clarity: "The elimination of all obstacles between the painter and the idea, and between the idea and the observer." It is only analysis, desiring to reach a conclusion and thus dismiss observation, that demands a decision. In the painting, no resolution is needed; the two poles—beginning and end, simplist and simple—coexist, and without interruption ask questions of each other. Nor should discursive argument attempt to resolve the riddle by insistence upon any answer of either/or.

The provocation may be stated in another way. Rothko claims that he is "no colorist," and that if we regard him as such we miss the point of his art. Yet it is hardly a secret that color is his sole medium. In painting after painting of this exhibition there are handsome, surprising and disquieting harmonies, and supposedly difficult colors are made to work together with apparent ease. Rothko's concern over the years has been the reduction of his vehicle to the unique colored surface which represents nothing and suggests nothing else. There is no need to enumerate the possibilities that have been refused (every painter must refuse the whole history of painting); what is important is that the colored rectangles remain. They are the obvious object of attention, whether of the naive or the initiated observer. Since they represent nothing and lead nowhere, since gesture is absent and in these soaked surfaces canvas and pigment fuse, the colors confront and arrest us. Yet Rothko says he is "no colorist."

There is a sense in which one is inclined to agree with him, or rather to say that Rothko has been determined to become something other

[1] From *Arts Magazine*, March 1961.

than a colorist. In the late forties, following the grayed harmonies of his symbolist ideographs, in which the muted hues pulled together the sand-toned backgrounds and the fluid shapes that floated in or on them, his color was structural. It established relations of planes and suggested depth, and while there was rarely a wide range within a given canvas, and there was a tendency toward pastel tones, the combinations were gay, harmonious, attractive. But as structural, space–building color was replaced by areas on the single plane of the canvas or floating disembodied in space, Rothko began to employ deliberately difficult combinations. Many of the light–toned warm–hued pictures of the middle fifties juxtapose supposedly clashing bands of the spectrum, and in the increasingly cold and somber works, the murals and the others, of the last several years, browns and reds and blacks are barely separable.

Of course what Rothko means is that the enjoyment of color for its own sake, the heightened realization of its purely sensuous dimension, is not the purpose of his painting. If Matisse was one point of departure, Rothko has since moved far in an opposite direction. Yet over the years he has handled his color so that one must pay ever closer attention to it, examine the unexpectedly joined hues, the slight, and continually slighter, modulations within the large area of any single surface, and the softness and the sequence of the colored shapes. Thus these pictures compel careful scrutiny of their physical existence, of their variations in handling and arrangement, all the while suggesting that these details are means, not ends.

The forcing of this double awareness seems to me a major part of Rothko's achievement. Its existence makes pointless the argument about whether "less is more." Much of the history of modern painting is the history of such "reductions" and "renunciations" that have both broadened and deepened our vision. And this one feels in Rothko's work. There has been a singlemindedness in the pursuit of a vision, an insistence upon one direction, an exploration of the possibilities of one means that is admirable, often overwhelming, and (why not say so?) at times exasperating in its refusal to relax. This has much to do with the size of the pictures, and with Rothko's insistence upon controlling the conditions of his public exhibitions. (One suspects that in the world of the contemporary artist only such braced and tense self-confidence can achieve such concentration. This at least is the face he presents to the world, and who knows what false starts have been made upon canvas or in the mind?) It is related as well to the violence which the artist attributes to his own work, and which to the observer, faced with the horizontal harmonies of these tremendous canvases, seems more closely akin to violent self-control.

Some writers have interpreted Rothko's works in literary terms, likening them to Greek drama, gathering from them the notes of impending doom, or seeing in them the symbolic action of storm clouds gathering on an immense horizon. In his catalogue of the exhibition which he organized, Peter Selz (who has upset the Museum's long-standing tradition of historical objectivity by the accents of eulogy), compares him to a Michelangelo who "has given us the first, not the sixth, day of creation," and whose murals "may be interpreted as celebrating the death of a civilization." (One asks, what civilization?) The reading of such cosmic allegories into these abstract canvases can only arouse the suspicion that the "immediate impingement" of "these silent paintings with their enormous, beautiful, opaque surfaces" (which Selz speaks of elsewhere) is not enough. Such literary fancies are program notes that relax the visual holds of these canvases, filter their immediacy, and push away their enigmatic, gripping presence.

I have tried to suggest something of the character of that presence. If we relate colors to moods in the generally accepted fashion, the emotional tone varies from canvas to canvas, and we may speak of a general impression of gaiety or sadness, aggressiveness or withdrawal. Rothko himself has talked of his expressing basic emotions. Yet one characteristic remains constant: there is always an utter seriousness, even in these pictures where reds and yellows predominate. Partly this stems from the compositional uniformity, partly from the total absence of gesture, a method so all-pervading as to constitute a fundamental point of view. These are motionless pictures, but despite the repetition of the horizontal—line or rectangle—they are not pictures at rest. The floating shapes convey no sense of relaxation. Nor is there a hint of how they came to be, nothing that suggests the action of the artist (*pace* Action Painting), either through gesture or direction or impasta, nothing that defines the imposition of the will, either through an exact edge or a precise measurement. And yet in the unrelenting frontality of these pictures, their constant symmetry, and simplicity, there is the immediate conviction of an enormous will. At close range this will is mitigated. The rectangles terminate softly and irregularly, their sizes and intervals obey no commensurate rhythm, their symmetrical placing is approximate, their uniform surfaces are not quite smooth and even. And lacking all traces of the process of their making, they are divorced from the will that created them. They are thus at once enormously willful and yet unrelated to a formulating will. Apparently unprovoked in the making, they seem removed and indifferent to examination, yet they entice us to discover what is intention, what is chance.

The exhibition as hung at the Museum of Modern Art magnifies the first sixteen of Rothko's thirty-two exhibiting years. Half the canvases in the show have been done during the last six, and many of these belong to the large mural series of 1958-59. Thus even the movement of development has been underplayed, and the insight of origins has been denied the spectator, who is confronted by a vision without sources, posed with a finality that permits no questions and grants no dialogue. It demands acquiescence, and failing that, stimulates rejection.

More than ten years ago, before any public recognition, Rothko stated this imperious attitude: "A picture lives by companionship, expanding and quickening in the eyes of the sensitive observer. It dies by the same token. It is therefore a risky act to send it out into the world. How often it must be impaired by the eyes of the unfeeling and the cruelty of the impotent who would extend their infliction universally."

Yet, in a way not given to most paintings, Rothko's pictures remain sufficient unto themselves. In answer to the old philosophic saw about the noise of the tree that falls in the forest, they exist without the observer—or so one feels. Because of this quality, each one also exists without its fellows, and inevitably an exhibition, even one as little retrospective as this, does some damage to the ideal isolation each canvas properly requires. This is particularly true in the first-floor galleries of the Museum of Modern Art, where the canvases have been hung close together, and where, too often, the vista of another room, another mood, another idea, disturbs the concentrated view. Suddenly we are aware of colors, where we are being asked to commune with presences.

For this reason the most successful arrangement is the small chapel-like room in which have been hung three of the mural series of 1958–59. Partaking of the same somber mood, they reinforce each other, as they were designed to do. It is significant that at the entrance to this room one pauses, hesitating to enter. Its space seems both occupied and empty. One is a distant spectator, examining with a stranger's separateness decorations the center of whose existence has been withdrawn, much as today we look (barred from entering by a chain) at the frescoes of some no longer used ancient chapel in an Italian church. Only there we know that this was once an intimate and active place; here we have become our own admiring strangers. It is thus not surprising that Rothko should have decided against delivering these murals to the "elegant private dining room" for which they had been commissioned.

All the pictures in this exhibition have been hung unframed. Given their soaked, mat colors, their basically rectangular structure, their silent nature, and their growth from large to larger formats, one might suppose (as the mural project suggests) that they might marry the wall, ideally as frescoes, and failing that as totally covering canvas. And yet, despite their size, these are still easel pictures. Their projection from the wall, and the shadow this projection casts, bringing them away from the wall, are essential to their unity. Their floating planes and indeterminate space demand isolation. In order to function they must be kept apart from actual space and tangible architectonic planes as separately existing objects. Otherwise they are in danger of descending gently into the limbo of "decoration"—a threat that, like "emptiness," Rothko employs as a sharpened instrument of their vitality.

Inevitably one asks why these paintings must be so big. There is a critical cliché which holds that small pictures can be just as "monumental" as large ones, and which may even have some validity for certain kinds of pictures (Masaccio, Piero) in which sculptural human forms are cramped into a too confining space, although the implication of size is never the same as its fact. For Rothko's art it manifestly does not apply. The justification of size is simply its effect, and in this it is no different from any other character of the work. Small, these pictures would not be the same; therefore they would have to be other pictures. The human scale counts. Granted Rothko's creative obsession, granted his insistence upon a visionary simplicity, and a subtlety within that simplicity, scale is the means he has employed to make his pictures both distant and demanding. He has imposed his vision upon us. Is not this what art is for?

The great artists are all contemporaries.

Lionel Johnson

A competent portrait knows how to imply the profile in the full face . . .   Aldous Huxley

The average man finds poetry only where it is labeled, but the artist will find it elsewhere and bring it to the notice of all the world.

Leo Stein, *Appreciation*

Samuel Butler

What better comment from a Victorian on post-impressionist art, especially applicable to later "expressionist" and contemporary "non-objective" art:

Accuracy

After having spent years in striving to be accurate, we must spend as many more in discovering when and how to be inaccurate.

The Credulous Eye

Painters may remember that the eye as a general rule is a good simple credulous organ—very ready to take things on trust if it be told them with any confidence of assertion.

Ad Reinhardt[1]
The Last Word
(*A description of a canvas called Abstract Painting*)

A square (neutral, shapeless) canvas, five feet wide, five feet high, as high as a man, as wide as a man's outstretched arms (not large, not small, sizeless), trisected (no composition), one horizontal form negating one vertical form (formless, no top, no bottom, directionless), three (more or less) dark (lightless), non-contrasting (colorless) colors, brushwork brushed out to remove brushwork, a mat, flat, freehand painted surface (glossless, textureless, non-linear, no hard edge, no soft edge) which does not reflect its surroundings—a pure, abstract non–objective, timeless, spaceless, changeless, relationless, disinterested painting—an object that is self–conscious (no unconciousness), ideal, transcendent, aware of no thing but art (absolutely no anti-art).

---

[1] Ad Reinhardt (1913——), painter, author, and educator, has been represented in both national and international shows and has paintings in a number of top-ranking museums and in private collections. With Robert Motherwell and Bernard Karpel, he is the author of *Modern Artists in America* (1950).

... the master stands in no relation to the moment at which he occurs—
a moment of isolation—hinting at sadness—having no part in the progress of his fellowmen. . .

James McNeill Whistler, *Ten O'Clock Lecture,* 1885

Art is limited to the infinite, and beginning there cannot progress.
ibid.

Nature contains the elements, in color and form, of all pictures, as the
keyboard contains the notes of all music. [But] to say to the painter,
that Nature is to be taken as she is, is to say to the player, that he may
sit on the piano.
ibid.

In every artist there is a germ of recklessness without which talent is
inconceivable.

Goethe, *Proverbs in Prose*

(The poet Rilke on Rodin.) This creator lived so completely in his
conceptions, so entirely in the depths of his work, that inspiration or
revelation came to him only through the medium of his art. New life
in the ultimate sense meant to him new surfaces, new gestures. Thus
to him the meaning of life became simple. . .

Rainer Maria Rilke, *Rodin*

His art was not built upon a great idea, but upon a minute, conscientious realization, upon the attainable, upon a craft.
ibid.

... [Rodin] records almost unnoticeable moments, turnings and semi-
turnings of many profiles from many perspectives. . . . The face of a
man is to him like a scene in a drama in which he himself takes part.
He does not urge the model to tell him anything, he does not wish to
know anything except that which he sees; and he sees everything.
ibid.

When Rodin concentrates the surfaces of his works into culminating
points, when he uplifts to greater height the exalted or gives more
depth to a cavity, he creates an effect like that which atmosphere
produces on monuments that have been exposed to it for centuries.
ibid.

(On Rodin's statue of Balzac.) Rodin slowly developed form after form. At last he saw Balzac. He saw a powerful, striding figure that had lost all heaviness in the fall of its voluminous cloak. The hair bristled from the nape of a powerful neck. And backward against the thick locks leaned the face of a visionary in the intoxication of a dream, the face flashing with creative vigor—the face of an element. . . Creation's boastfulness, vanity, ecstasy, and intoxication. . . . There was no sense of weight, but a superb vitality in the free, strong head.

ibid.

The artist has always the masters in his eye.

Ralph Waldo Emerson, *Progress of Culture*

Nothing so resembles a daub as a masterpiece.

Paul Gauguin, *Intimate Journals*

Art for Art's sake. Why not?
Art for Life's sake. Why not?
Art for Pleasure's sake. Why not?
What does it matter, as long as it is art?

ibid.

Art is life seen through a temperament.

Emile Zola

In the old days pictures went forward toward completion by stages. Every day brought something new. A picture used to be a sum of additions. I do a picture—then I destroy it. In the end, though, nothing is lost. . . But there is one very odd thing—to notice that basically a picture doesn't change, that the first "vision" remains almost intact, in spite of appearances.

Picasso

Sculpture is the art of the hole and the lump.

Rodin

". . . artists do not prove things. They do not need to. They know them."

Kneller in Bernard Shaw's *In Good King Charles's Golden Days*

A FAREWELL TO ART

Painting and sculpture, fatigue and faith, have ruined me, and everything is going from bad to worse. It would have been better if from my earliest years I had put myself to making sulphur matches.

                                    Michelangelo

The greatest curse that can befall a father in England is to have a son gifted with a passion and a genius for High Art. Thank God with all my soul and all my nature, my children have witnessed the harassing agonies under which I have ever painted: and the very name of painting, the very name of High Art, the very thought of a picture, gives them a hideous and disgusting taste in their mouths. Thank God, not one of my boys, nor my girl, can draw a straight line, even with a ruler, such less without one. And I pray God, on my knees, with my forehead bent to the earth, and my lips to the dust, that He will, in His mercy, afflict them with every other passion, appetite, or misery, with wretchedness, disease, insanity, or gabbling idiotism, rather than a longing for painting—that scorned, miserable art, that greater imposture than the human species it imitates.

                                    Benjamin Haydon

Painting is a rum thing.

                                    J. M. W. Turner

Damn paint!

                                    Sir Joshua Reynolds

BIOGRAPHIES

HENRY BROOKS ADAMS (1838–1918), scion of one of the most illustrious families in America, had a distinguished career as a teacher and writer of early American history, but he is best remembered today as the author of two remarkable books that have little to do with his specialty. The first, *Mont-Saint-Michel and Chartres,* reflects the great interest of Adams' later life, the study of twelfth-century French culture. The second, the posthumously published *The Education of Henry Adams,* an attempt to come to grips with what he felt to be his failure to cope with the acquisitive age in which he lived, is one of the great autobiographies.

FRANZ ALEXANDER (1891———) was born in Hungary and received his medical degree from the University of Budapest in 1913. He came to the United States in 1930 and was for many years Director of the Chicago Institute for Psychoanalysis. He is one of the best-known and most respected of American psychoanalysts, and has published a number of influential books and articles.

GUILLAUME APOLLINAIRE was the pseudonym of Wilhelm Kostrowitzki (1880–1918), a French poet and critic of Polish descent, who played an important role in the avant-garde movement in Paris before World War I. His poetry and other writings, such as the drama *Les Mamelles de Tirésias* (1917), which has recently been given a musical setting by Poulenc, prepared the way for the dadaism and surrealism of the immediate postwar period; and his criticism, especially his essay on *The Cubist Painters,* was instrumental in publicizing the work of Picasso and others. It was Apollinaire who was perhaps the chief continuator in the twentieth century of the Baudelaire and Zola tradition of the advanced writer as the ally and champion of the advanced painter.

CHARLES BAUDELAIRE (1821–67) was one of the greatest French poets of his century and a key figure in the development of modern literature. Despite the posturings and eccentricities that he indulged in to shock the Philistines and to live up (or down) to the role of *poète maudit,* he was a serious and enormously scrupulous creative artist and critic. Like other French writers of his time, he was passionately interested in painting, and produced a considerable body of informed and sensitive commentary on the painters and artistic issues of his day. Above all, he gave noble and disinterested support to the great Delacroix, particularly in the last part of the painter's career, when he was increasingly lonely and isolated.

CLIVE BELL (1881———) was for many years one of the most effective spokesmen for the modern art movement, and is especially known for his doctrine of *significant form* as the one important element in painting. Most of Bell's writing on art has taken the shape of journalistic essays and reviews, and he achieved his greatest influence during the years when he was writing regularly for periodicals such as the *New Statesman* and *The Nation*. Bell is one of the last surviving members of the so-called Bloomsbury Group, which in its heyday included Virginia Woolf (whose sister Bell married), Bertrand Russell, J. M. Keynes, Lytton Strachey, and others. It was this group that particularly drew the hatred and contempt of D. H. Lawrence, for to him they seemed impotent and ineffectual esthetes and talkers.

BERNARD BERENSON (1865–1959) was born in Lithuania and was brought to the United States as a child by his parents. Even during his undergraduate days at Harvard (where he was a contemporary of Santayana) his extraordinary intellectual gifts were recognized; and when he failed to win a fellowship on graduation in 1887, funds were raised by his friends and admirers to send him to Europe to study. The next few years of travel and discovery revealed Berenson's life work to him. For the remainder of his long career, he devoted himself with unwearying energy and enthusiasm to the great art of the Italian Renaissance, publishing his first work, *The Venetian Painters of the Renaissance,* in 1894, and a whole series of important works in subsequent years. In his later life, his villa I Tatti at Settignano, near Florence, became a mecca not merely for art historians but for many distinguished visitors to Italy.

Berenson formed a bridge between the great "literary" art critics of the nineteenth century, and the highly trained professional art historians of the present day. He helped to bring order out of dilettantish chaos in the study of Renaissance art, and made connoisseurship a rigorous (and highly profitable) discipline. He himself came to feel that he had somewhat misdirected his great gifts by putting them at the service of dealers like Duveen; but nonetheless his achievement was an impressive and lastingly valuable one.

WILLIAM BLAKE (1757–1827), painter, engraver, and poet, is more and more being recognized as the greatest and most original creative artist of his time; indeed, some would go further and consider him, in the words of one of his recent editors, Geoffrey Keynes, "one of the greatest of Englishmen." There has never been any question of his magnificent achievement as a lyric poet, but for more than a hundred years, beginning in his own lifetime, it was customary to regard him either as a hopelessly naïve and muddled visionary or as a man on the dangerous borderline between eccentricity and insanity. His water-colors and engravings were dismissed as amateurish and childlike, not worthy of serious consideration. Not merely has Blake's reputation as a graphic artist soared during the last generation or two, but a large body of careful and perceptive scholarly and critical work has made it possi-ble for us to understand Blake as a thinker of power, coherence, and increasing relevance to our own time.

GEORGE BOAS was born in Providence, R. I., in 1891 and studied at Brown, Columbia, and Harvard universities, as well as at the Uni-versity of California, where he took his Ph.D. in 1912. He became a professor of philosophy at The Johns Hopkins University, specializing in the history of philosophy and in aesthetics. Boas edited *Romanticism in America* in 1940, and wrote *Essays on Primitivism and Related Ideas* and *Wingless Pegasus,* published respectively in 1948 and 1950.

SIR KENNETH CLARK (1903——) is probably the best-known of living English writers on art. He worked for two years with Bernard Berenson in Italy, was Director of the National Gallery in London from 1934 to 1945, and has held two appointments as Slade Professor of Fine Art at Oxford. His first book, *The Gothic Revival,* published in 1929, established his reputation as a scholar and critic of wit, learning, and penetration; and he has since written a number of notable works, among them the standard modern study of Leonardo da Vinci, the wide-ranging and subtle *Landscape into Art,* and *The Nude,* from which one of the selections in this collection is taken.

EUGÈNE DELACROIX (1798–1863) is one of the towering figures in the history of French art. A great romantic painter, who was primarily influenced by the baroque energy and sweep of Rubens, he also, as Baudelaire points out, was a continuator of the revolutionary classicism of David. To the painters who were young when he was growing old, he was a revered idol, and for Cézanne in particular he was always, as

Read reminds us, the great master. At the end of his life he was bitterly conscious of the hostility of most of the ruling figures of French art, but unaware that he was worshipped from afar by the youthful Monet and Bazille, who would watch him at work in his garden from the window of a neighboring apartment.

EUGÈNE FROMENTIN (1820–76) was a man of great talent and sensitivity as a writer and painter who never quite achieved greatness in either role. Attracted, like his older contemporary Delacroix, by North African themes, he became known as the painter of the Sahara; but lacking the genius and energy of Delacroix, he was able to strike only a minor Romantic note.

ROGER FRY (1866–1934) was for many years the most influential art critic in the English-speaking world and a man who did more than anyone else to establish the reputation of the post-impressionists (a term he invented). The Grafton Gallery Exhibition, organized by him in 1910, and devoted to the work of such men as Cézanne, Gauguin, Van Gogh, Matisse, and Picasso, aroused the same kind of fury in England as the Armory Show of 1913 was to do in America. A man with an enormous range of knowledge and enthusiasm in art (only the great Greek achievement of the Periclean age seems to have left him cold), he was from 1905 to 1910 Curator of Paintings at the Metropolitan Museum in New York, and a personal adviser to J. P. Morgan; and throughout his life, his judgment on paintings and art objects of all periods was sought by collectors.

In a career of remarkable achievement as critic, scholar, and lecturer, Fry suffered two continuing disappointments: his painting, which to him was far more important than his criticism, failed to attain distinction; and he never realized his dream of writing a great comprehensive work of art criticism and history. But ephemeral in form as they are, consisting almost entirely of brief magazine articles, reviews, and lecture texts—his magnificent book on Cézanne is a notable exception—his writings on art are still extraordinarily readable and instructive, unsurpassed in their wit, sensitivity, and zest. More than any other one individual, he wrote finis to the nineteenth-century forms of art criticism as essays in morality or literary sensibility.

JOHN GIBSON (1790–1866) was born in England and received his early training as a sculptor there, but spent the last fifty years of his life in Rome. He had a considerable reputation as a sculptor in his own day, but is now best remembered for his passionate admiration for all things Greek and Roman.

ROBERT GOLDWATER (1907——) is a leading American art scholar and critic. He has taught at New York University and Queens College, and is Director of the Museum of Primitive Art in New York. Together with Marco Treves, he edited the collection *Artists on Art,* and he has written extensively on nineteenth- and twentieth-century art.

ERNST H. J. GOMBRICH (1909——) is one of the leading representatives of the group of art scholars for whom, in the phrase of one of their greatest figures, Erwin Panofsky, art history is a humanistic discipline. Now Director of the Warburg Institute in London, he has been Slade Professor of Fine Art at both Oxford and Cambridge. He is the author of numerous articles and several books, one of which, the deceptively simple *Story of Art,* is a classic in its field.

HORATIO GREENOUGH (1805–52) was, like many of the American sculptors of the nineteenth century, heavily influenced by classical models and neoclassical ideas. His most famous work is the seminude heroic statue of George Washington, originally created for the Capitol. In his critical writings, however, Greenough displays an independence and penetration of judgment lacking in his artistic practice.

GEORGE GROSZ (1893–1959) was born in Berlin, and received his training as an artist at the Royal Academy of Art in Dresden, and later in Berlin. Shortly before World War I, he sold his first newspaper caricature, and during the 1920's he became a great satirical and expressionist artist, who dealt mercilessly with the ugliness and banality of German middle-class life. He came to the United States shortly before the Nazi regime took power in Germany, and lived and worked in the United States for the remainder of his life. His autobiography, *A Little Yes and a Big No,* is one of the most vivid personal documents left by any artist.

BENJAMIN ROBERT HAYDON (1756–1846) was a man with a mission: to emancipate English painting from the dominance of the academic portrait-mongers, and to lift it to the status of what he called

"High Art." Unfortunately, for all his soaring ambition, dedicated energy, and intellectual and emotional force, Haydon had little artistic talent, and his grandiose vision of becoming the Napoleon of art ended in bankruptcy and suicide. It was more than lack of talent that defeated Haydon, though. The large-scale "history paintings," the enormous canvases with their literary treatment of biblical or classical themes that Haydon labored at year after year, would have been failures even if he had been a more gifted painter, for at the very moment he was trying to revive the grand style, the real revolution in nineteenth-century painting was being quietly initiated in the landscapes of his countryman, John Constable (1776–1837).

Haydon had a Boswellian flair for vivid detail, a Boswellian delight in the immense variety of human behavior and personality, and a Boswellian unself-conscious wonder at his own qualities. Even at the nadir of his fortunes, just two years before he killed himself, Haydon, describing how a conception of a fresco painting of the Resurrection and Last Judgment entered his head as he stood in attendance at a funeral, could exclaim: "Oh, if I am not let loose before I die, what a pity it will be!"

JOHAN HUIZINGA was born in Holland in 1872 and died there in 1945. He became a professor of history at the University of Leiden in 1915 and remained there until the university was closed under the German Occupation of the Netherlands during World War II. Huizinga wrote many books, and several of these were translated into English and won a high reputation for their author. The best-known are *Homo Ludens, Erasmus of Rotterdam,* and *The Waning of the Middle Ages,* originally published in 1924.

ALDOUS HUXLEY (1894–1963) was best known as a novelist, particularly for such works as *Point Counter Point* (1928) and *Brave New World* (1932). He also wrote, however, a number of brilliant essays on art, which continue into our own day the tradition of the informed and cultivated art critic who is primarily a man of letters.

HENRY JAMES (1843–1916), the great novelist and critic, was fascinated throughout his literary career by the problems of art and artists, and wrote not merely a good many essays and reviews dealing with art, but a number of short stories in which artists play a central role.

WASSILY KANDINSKY (1866–1944) was born in Russia but spent his formative years as a painter in Germany, where expressionism was the dominant aspect of the modern art movement. Together with the German painter Franz Marc (who was killed at Verdun in 1916), he founded the expressionist Blue Rider group in Munich in 1911, a group that was later joined by Paul Klee. During the war years, Kandinsky returned to Russia, but went back to Germany in 1921 and taught at the famous Bauhaus in the 1920's. From 1933 to his death, Kandinsky lived and painted in France.

As early as 1910, Kandinsky created what is generally regarded as the first purely abstract painting, and for the remainder of his career he devoted himself to nonobjective art. His essay *Concerning the Spiritual in Art* is a classic statement of the principles of expressionism in art.

JOHN KEATS (1795–1821) created, during his brief lifetime, some of the greatest poetry in English. His earliest work is lushly romantic, and the intensity, introspection, and haunting melancholy of much of his later poetry embody the romantic style at its best. But in the last year or two of his life, and especially in his unfinished *Hyperion,* his work increasingly took on classical qualities of a noble gravity and seriousness.

D. H. LAWRENCE (1885–1930), novelist, poet, painter, and critic, is now increasingly being seen as one of the significant figures in the culture of our time: indeed, to such admirers as F. R. Leavis, he is the greatest English writer of the century. His entire creative activity, in fact his whole life, constituted a passionate protest against what he regarded as the sterile intellectualism of European civilization. The most famous embodiment of Lawrence's views is, of course, the gamekeeper Mellors in *Lady Chatterley's Lover;* but the same point of view is to be found in virtually all of his writings, and in the selection given in this book it dominates his approach to modern art.

JACQUES MARITAIN (1882——) was for many years a leading Catholic philosopher, and from 1948 to 1952 held the post of Professor of Philosophy at Princeton University. He wrote voluminously on problems of metaphysics, politics, and history, but he always evinced a special interest in art.

WILLIAM MORRIS (1834–96) was, with Ruskin, one of the chief Victorian spokesmen for the view that art is rooted in society, and one of the chief agitators against the ugliness and uniformity of a growing industrialism. A poet, craftsman, and socialist, he worked not only through his writings but through his own furniture factory and printing press to make art a vital factor in everyday life. Though it is commonplace today to stigmatize Morris' furniture as heavy, his typography as ornate, and his poetry as lush, the whole later development of the so-called applied arts owes a great deal to him.

WALTER HORATIO PATER (1839–94) spent most of his mature life as a secluded intellectual at Oxford, where he was a Fellow of Brasenose College; but through his relatively few essays and books he exerted a considerable influence on the young aesthetes of the last decades of the nineteenth century. He was associated with the Pre-Raphaelite movement in English literature and art, and was considered the leading exponent of the "art for art's sake" school in England. Among his works are *Studies in the History of the Renaissance,* a series of essays first collected in 1873 and published in new editions in 1877 and 1888; *Marius the Epicurean* (1885), a novel dealing with the transition from Roman paganism to Christianity; *Imaginary Portraits* (1887); *Plato and Platonism* (1893); and an autobiographical work, *The Child in the House* (1894).

In his own lifetime, Pater was regarded by many as a dangerous opponent of morality and religion and a sinister influence on the young because he advocated, in the famous words of his conclusion to the *Studies in the History of the Renaissance,* "a quickened, multiplied consciousness" as the end of life, and spoke of success in life as the ability "to burn always with [a] hard, gemlike flame." In our own time, however, the reputation of Pater has suffered most from the attacks of those critics who find in his work a mannered, deliberately cultivated preciousness of style and sensibility. It is certainly true that Pater often seems more concerned with literary effect than with meaning, and his celebrated description of the "Mona Lisa" is perhaps more Pater than Leonardo. Yet Pater's art criticism at its best is still worth reading and pondering over, for he anticipated many of the insights of the twentieth century.

SIR HERBERT READ (1893———) has for over two generations been one of the most versatile and stimulating of English men of letters. He has won distinction not only as a writer on art, and especially on the modern art movement, but also as literary critic and historian, as poet and short story writer, and as aesthetic theoretician. His art criticism reflects many influences acting upon an acute sensibility: such diverse intellectual forces as Marxism and gestalt psychology, among others, have helped to mold his thinking.

SIR JOSHUA REYNOLDS was not only one of England's greatest painters in the eighteenth century, but an influential figure in literary and artistic circles in London. Born in Plympton, Devonshire, on July 16, 1723, he remained under the tutelage of his father, the Reverend Samuel Reynolds, rector of Plympton and principal of its grammar school, until his apprenticeship, at seventeen, to a painter in London. Making rapid progress in his profession and having enjoyed the benefits of considerable travel in Italy, he established a studio in the center of London, on Leicester Square, and led the life of an urbane bachelor and social lion, succeeding as a portrait painter so notably that he was appointed official court painter. When the Royal Academy of Art was founded in 1768, he became that august society's first president, and his important lectures or "Discourses on Art" were first intended for students of art at this institution. He gave the first of these on January 2, 1769, and the fifteenth and last on December 10, 1790.

Reynolds, who counted among his friends Dr. Samuel Johnson, Oliver Goldsmith, and Edmund Burke, was respected for his noble style and his dignified view of the nature and possibilities of art. He expressed the classical ideals of his age; and the regard in which he was held won him a knighthood and earned him a state funeral, and burial in St. Paul's Cathedral, when he died on February 23, 1792.

HAROLD ROSENBERG is one of the most influential of American art critics today. He was among the first to publicize the work of the action painters and the abstract expressionists, and his collection of articles *The Tradition of the New* (1959) is outstanding as an important presentation of the avant-garde movement in American painting.

JOHN RUSKIN (1819–1900) was the son of wealthy and doting parents, who carefully cultivated his aesthetic sensibilities and shielded him from the rough-and-tumble of an ordinary boyhood and young manhood. In addition, his mother, an intense Calvinist and a rigorous Sabbatarian, instilled in him a lifelong moralistic fervor.

This sheltered yet demanding upbringing undoubtedly helped to produce the stresses that foredoomed his marriage and punctuated his later years with periods of insanity. It also encouraged him not merely to develop to the full his passion for art, but to see art and morality as closely linked. In the last decades of his life, Ruskin became more and more specifically the critic of Victorian industrialism and *laissez faire* economics; but in his earlier years he produced some of the most influential works of nineteenth-century art history and criticism, among them *Modern Painters* (1843–60), *The Seven Lamps of Architecture* (1849), and *The Stones of Venice* (1851–53).

ROBERT ALAN MOWBRAY STEVENSON (1847–1900), a first cousin and close friend of Robert Louis Stevenson, was born in Edinburgh and given a thorough academic education, culminating in a Cambridge degree. Determined to be an artist, he studied painting first in Edinburgh, then in Antwerp, and finally in Paris at the studio of the well-known portraitist and pedagogue, Carolus Duran. Like Fromentin, however, he had neither the talent nor the boldness to become a painter of the first rank. Recognizing that his abilities lay in criticism rather than in painting, Stevenson more and more devoted himself to writing and lecturing on art. Between 1883 and 1889, he wrote regularly on painting and music for the *Saturday Review*. Between 1889 and 1893, he was Professor of Fine Arts at University College, Liverpool, and then returned to journalism as critic for the *Pall Mall Gazette* until shortly before his death.

GIORGIO VASARI (1511–74) was born in Arezzo and learned his trade as a painter in Florence, where he studied with Andrea del Sarto. The decisive influence on him, however, was that of Michelangelo, whose pupil, follower, and lifelong admirer he became. Like many of Michelangelo's later disciples, Vasari painted in a posed, contrived, insistently dramatic mannerist style. As a painter and an architect (he designed the building that is now the Uffizi Gallery), he was active both in Florence and in Rome on commissions from leading churchmen and political figures. Vasari's writing, however, was much better than his painting. His *Lives*, selections from which are quoted in this collection, is a rich mine of information on Italian artists.

LEONARDO DA VINCI (1452–1519) was a man of incredible intellect and far-ranging interests, whose scientific and inventive genius is justly celebrated—so much so, that it is sometimes forgotten that he was primarily a painter, and that throughout his life the craft of the painter was his basic concern. His *Notebooks* contain not merely his scientific and philosophical speculations but also a rich store of thought and accumulated knowledge on art. In many ways, Leonardo's writings on art look forward to later styles and experiments.

BENJAMIN WEST (1738–1820) was an American Quaker who went to Italy in 1760 to study painting, and there absorbed the neoclassical style. He settled in London in 1763, and lived there for the remainder of his life, achieving the presidency of the Royal Academy in 1792, in succession to Reynolds. West did much to establish the vogue of history painting, so fashionable in both Europe and the United States in the late eighteenth and early nineteenth centuries. In both his painting and his writing, West represents a stolid and unadventurous academicism.

ÉMILE ZOLA (1840–1902), the great French naturalist novelist, was, in the early 1860's, a struggling young journalist in Paris and a passionate and vocal defender of the new painters, many of whom he knew well. Chief among Zola's painter friends was Paul Cézanne, with whom he had grown up in Provence. In numerous articles, Zola championed the cause of the realists, and later the impressionists, making himself almost the official spokesman of their cause. As he grew older, however, and began to achieve fame and material success as a novelist, Zola began to drift somewhat apart from his painter friends, and though still believing in their genius, began to have doubts about the direction they were taking. With the publication of his novel *L'œuvre* in 1886, the break between Zola and Cézanne became complete. The brief acknowledgment which Cézanne made of the receipt of a copy of the novel sent to him by Zola was the last direct communication between the two. There can be no doubt that Cézanne was deeply hurt by the portrayal of himself as Claude Lantier, the painter whose life ends in failure and suicide. It would be wrong, however, to accuse Zola of deliberately wounding his friend: Lantier had some of Cézanne's characteristics, but was not a portrait of him. He was intended simply as a melancholy demonstration of the inevitable workings-out of the strains of heredity transmitted to Claude through his father and above all through his mother, Gervaise. He was not so much Cézanne as he was one more figure in the Rougon-Macquart family history related by Zola in an immense cycle of novels comprising twenty volumes.

ACKNOWLEDGMENTS

The editors and publishers wish to thank the following for their kind permission to use material in this book:

Edward Arnold, Ltd., and St. Martin's Press: "Art and Life" from *The Waning of the Middle Ages* (1949) by Johan Huizinga.

The Bollingen Foundation: "Beauty and Modern Painting" by Jacques Maritain from *Creative Intuition in Art and Poetry* (1953); "The Naked and the Nude" by Kenneth Clark from *The Nude: A Study in Ideal Form* (1956); and "Truth and the Stereotype" by E. H. Gombrich from *Art and Illusion* (1960)—the Mellon Lecture Series, pub. by Pantheon Books.

The Clarendon Press: "Giotto and the Tactile" by Bernard Berenson from *Italian Painters of the Renaissance* (edition of 1959).

Kenneth Clark and *Harper's Magazine:* "Art and Society," pub. August 1961.

Crown Publishers, Inc.: "Variations on Goya" by Aldous Huxley from *The Complete Etchings of Goya* (1943); and excerpts from *The Journal of Eugène Delacroix,* transl. by Walter Pach (1948).

Faber and Faber, Ltd.: "The Modern Epoch in Art" by Herbert Read from *The Philosophy of Modern Art.*

Robert Goldwater and *Arts Magazine:* "Reflections on the Rothko Exhibition," pub. March 1961.

The executors of the estate of George Grosz: "Dadaism" from *A Little Yes and a Big No,* pub. by Dial Press (1946).

Harcourt, Brace & World, Inc., and Chatto and Windus: "The Artistic Problem" by Clive Bell from *Since Cézanne* (1928).

Harvard University Press: excerpts from *The Diary of Benjamin Robert Haydon,* Vol. I and Vol. II, ed. by Willard Bissell Pope, copyright 1960 by the President and Fellows of Harvard College.

Journal of the History of Ideas: "The Mona Lisa in the History of Taste" by George Boas, pub. April 1940.

610

The Macmillan Company: "Cézanne" by Roger Fry from *Cézanne: A Study of His Development,* first published in the U.S. by The Macmillan Company in 1952.

Putnam's & Coward McCann: "Culture and Snobbism" by Roger Fry from *Transformations* (n.d.), and "El Greco" by Roger Fry from *Vision and Design* (n.d.).

Random House: excerpts from *The Complete Writings of William Blake,* ed. by Geoffrey Keynes (1957).

Harold Rosenberg and *Art News:* "The American Action Painters" from *The Tradition of the New,* pub. by Horizon Press (1959).

The Viking Press, Inc.: selection from *Phoenix* by D. H. Lawrence, copyright 1936 by Frieda Lawrence.

George Wittenborn, Inc.: "The Cubist Painters" by Guillaume Apollinaire from *The Cubist Painters* (1944), and "On the Spiritual in Art" by Wassily Kandinsky from *Concerning the Spiritual in Art* (1949).

Special thanks are due Rae Thomas and David Thomas for their help in typing much of the manuscript as well as for their constant encouragement and helpful criticism.

INDEX

SARATOGA SPRINGS PUBLIC LIBRARY

DONATED BY THE

Ex Libris
Society